Environmental Law in Finland

Environmental Law in Finland

Fourth Edition

Pekka Vihervuori

This book was originally published as a monograph in the International Encyclopaedia of Laws/Environmental Law.

Founding Editor: Roger Blanpain
General Editor: Frank Hendrickx
Volume Editor: Kurt Deketelaere

Wolters Kluwer

Published by:
Kluwer Law International B.V.
PO Box 316
2400 AH Alphen aan den Rijn
The Netherlands
E-mail: lrs-sales@wolterskluwer.com
Website: www.wolterskluwer.com/en/solutions/kluwerlawinternational

Sold and distributed by:
Wolters Kluwer Legal & Regulatory U.S.
920 Links Avenue
Landisville, PA 17538
United States of America
E-mail: customer.service@wolterskluwer.com

ISBN 978-94-035-1248-8

e-Book: ISBN 978-94-035-1258-7
web-PDF: ISBN 978-94-035-1268-6

This title is available on www.kluwerlawonline.com

Environmental Law in Finland

Fourth Edition

Pekka Vihervuori

This book was originally published as a monograph in the International Encyclopaedia of Laws/Environmental Law.

Founding Editor: Roger Blanpain
General Editor: Frank Hendrickx
Volume Editor: Kurt Deketelaere

Wolters Kluwer

Published by:
Kluwer Law International B.V.
PO Box 316
2400 AH Alphen aan den Rijn
The Netherlands
E-mail: lrs-sales@wolterskluwer.com
Website: www.wolterskluwer.com/en/solutions/kluwerlawinternational

Sold and distributed by:
Wolters Kluwer Legal & Regulatory U.S.
920 Links Avenue
Landisville, PA 17538
United States of America
E-mail: customer.service@wolterskluwer.com

DISCLAIMER: The material in this volume is in the nature of general comment only. It is not offered as advice on any particular matter and should not be taken as such. The editor and the contributing authors expressly disclaim all liability to any person with regard to anything done or omitted to be done, and with respect to the consequences of anything done or omitted to be done wholly or partly in reliance upon the whole or any part of the contents of this volume. No reader should act or refrain from acting on the basis of any matter contained in this volume without first obtaining professional advice regarding the particular facts and circumstances at issue. Any and all opinions expressed herein are those of the particular author and are not necessarily those of the editor or publisher of this volume.

ISBN 978-94-035-1248-8

e-Book: ISBN 978-94-035-1258-7
web-PDF: ISBN 978-94-035-1268-6

This title is available on www.kluwerlawonline.com

The Author

Pekka Vihervuori, LLD and MSc, is former President of the Supreme Administrative Court (SAC), Finland (2012–2018). Before that, he was Justice of the same court (1998–2012). He is a former Associate Professor of Land and Water Law at the University of Turku, Finland (1985–1989), Legislative Counsellor at the Ministry of Justice of Finland (1989–1995), Professor of Land and Water Law at the University of Helsinki, Finland (1989–1994), Professor of Environmental Law at the University of Turku, Finland (1994–1995) and Professor of Law at Helsinki University of Technology, Finland (1995–1998). He has also lectured at the University of Lapland, Finland. He is the author of four monographs and numerous articles on environmental law, water law and land law. He has also worked for several years as an expert at the National Board of Waters and Environment in Helsinki. From 1989 to 1995 he was engaged in drafting legislation, especially in the field of water law and the law on compensations for environmental damage. As for the latter, he was the Finnish expert on the respective Committee of the Council of Europe. He has also been the chair or member of dozens of State committees in the field of environmental, water, natural resources, land use and administrative and judicial procedure laws, and the chair of a national association of lawyers. He has also been a governmental investigator and rapporteur on the legislative measures necessary for the implementation of International Labour Organization (ILO) Convention (No. 169) concerning Indigenous and Tribal Peoples in Independent Countries, regarding the Saami population's rights to land and water. He was the vice-chair of the High Court of Impeachment from 2012 to 2018. In 2019 he was an investigator on the reform needs of mining legislation, and in 2021–2022 on the administrative litigation regarding climate. He is an honorary member of the Finnish Society for Environmental Law. Since 2019 he has been the chair of the Finnish Advisory Board for Civil Service Ethics.

The Author

Table of Contents

List of Abbreviations

BAT	Best Available Techniques
BEP	Best Environmental Practice
BOD_7	Biological Oxygen Demand
CAP	Common Agricultural Policy
CFC	Chlorofluorocarbon
CFP	Common Fisheries Policy
CITES	Convention on International Trade in Endangered Species of Wild Fauna and Flora
EC	European Community
ECJ	European Court of Justice
EEA	European Economic Area
EIA	Environmental Impact Assessment
EIS	Environmental Impact Statement
EMAS	Eco-Management and Audit Scheme (EC)
ETS	Emission Trading System
EU	European Union
FINAS	The Finnish Accreditation Service
GMO	Genetically Modified Organism
IED	Directive on industrial emissions
IPPC	Integrated Pollution Prevention and Control
LCP	Large Combustion Plant
LULUCF	Land Use, Land-Use Change and Forestry
MARPOL	International Convention for the Prevention of Pollution from Ships
MRCC	Maritime Rescue Coordination Centre
PCB	Polychlorinated Biphenyl
POP	Persistent Organic Pollutant
REACH	European Parliament and Council Regulation Concerning the Registration, Evaluation, Authorization and Restriction of Chemicals

List of Abbreviations

SAC	Supreme Administrative Court
SEEMP	Ship Energy Efficiency Management Plan
SC	Supreme Court
SCI	Sites of Community Importance
SPA	Special (Bird) Protection Area
VOC	Volatile Organic Compound
WEEE	Waste Electrical and Electronic Equipment
YWCA	Young Women's Christian Association

General Introduction

Chapter 1. General Information

§1. Geography

1. Finland is located between the sixtieth and seventieth latitudes, bordering Sweden, Norway, Russia and the Baltic Sea. The total area of the country (excluding the territorial sea, but including inland lakes, etc.) is over 338,000 square kilometres. Thus, Finland is the fifth largest country in Europe – and the land area increases yearly by seven square kilometres due to the gradual rising of the ground (the upheaval), which correspondingly makes the area of the Bothnian Gulf of the Baltic Sea gradually smaller. Geologically, Finnish bedrock belongs to the oldest formations on earth (the Precambrian area known as the Fennoscandian shield), and its ancient mountains have long ago been worn to modest heights, the Halti fjeld in Northwest Lapland (actually a piece of the younger Scandinavian mountains) being the highest peak at 1,328 metres. The mean elevation in Finland is only 152 metres, while that for Europe is 330 metres and that for the whole earth is 840 metres. Still, the topography is very variable. The Ice Age had a great impact on the Finnish soil and landscape. The average thickness of the 'overburden' is about two metres. The southern and western parts of Finland consist of a lowland plain with elongated esker ridges and small hills, locally very varied. The Northern and Eastern parts of the country are more rugged and hilly, and especially the eastern part is dotted with thousands of lakes. Off the southwest coast lies the largest archipelago in Europe.

2. About 76% of the total land area consists of forests. Economically productive forests make up about 59% of the total land area. The proportion of forests has increased due to large-scale (but not always successful) draining of wet peatlands, the proportion of which is the highest in the world (31% of the land area). Half of the earlier marshes (mires) may now be called forests, which makes the distinction between forest and (wet) peatland inaccurate. The trees in forests are largely conifers (spruce and pine), but there are also birch forests and mixed forests in many places. In the south-western corner other leaf trees like oak abound, and in northern Lapland spruce and pine give way to small birch. In the extreme North there are treeless field areas, but true tundra does not exist in Finland. A fifth (20% or 66,000 square kilometres) of the total land area is 'waste land' or unproductive peatland. Finland's peat resources are over 70 million cubic metres, but only a fraction is exploited, mainly as fuel. The proportion of cultivated land is only 8% of the total, representing 26,000 square kilometres. However, in the most densely populated southern and western areas the proportion is significantly higher (over 20%). Built-up areas claim over 13,000 square kilometres or 4% of the total.

3. Finland has 33,522 square kilometres of inland waters, i.e., 9.9% of the total area. Though the definition of a lake is more or less arbitrary, it has been calculated that there are 56,010 lakes with a surface area of over one hectare and 187,890 lakes and ponds with a surface area over 500 square metres. They vary greatly in distribution and size. The mean depth is only seven metres. Due to the very complicated water systems, the total length of shorelines (the Baltic coast included) is as high as 200,000 kilometres. The coastal waters of the Baltic Sea are mostly shallow and the coastline is fragmented. The south-western archipelago is unique in the world. The water in the Gulf of Bothnia and Gulf of Finland is brackish with a salinity of only two to seven per mil, which is much lower than in the southern parts of the Baltic, not to mention the oceans. This is why the flora and fauna of the coastal waters of Finland make a unique mixture of adapted sea and freshwater species.

4. Despite the northern location the climate is milder than that of most areas at the same latitudes, thanks to the west winds warmed by the Gulf Stream. Continental and marine influences make the weather conditions variable and often unpredictable. The Baltic Sea and the nearness of the Atlantic Ocean act as a marine counterbalance to continental eastern and arctic climate factors. During the long winter both may bring cold air, but in summer it is often the hot air from Russian steppes that makes Finland the warmest part of Europe north of the Alps. Helsinki may be the coldest capital in Europe on a day in January, but in July it may be the warmest – or the coldest. During one year the temperature may vary between thirty degrees centigrade above zero and thirty degrees below. The mean temperature is between 5.5 (Southwest) and zero (Central Lapland) degrees centigrade. That is six to ten degrees higher than in other areas with the same latitude. The yearly precipitation (of which 30%–40% falls as snow) varies from 400 millimetres (North) to 700 millimetres (South), most of which occurs between spring and autumn. The period of snow cover varies from year to year, but on an average it is three months in the Southwest and six to seven in the North. Agriculture is possible in this climate, though the growing season (>+5 C) is only 160–180 days in the South and 110–145 days in the North. However, days during the growing season are very long (nearly nineteen hours of sunlight and only slight twilight at midnight). In midwinter there are only a few (slightly) sunny hours, and in the northernmost part of Lapland it is dark twenty-four hours a day during sixty-seven winter days.

§2. POPULATION

5. The population of the country by end of 2021 was 5,548,000, without any major net growth foreseen. Consequently, the population density is as low as seventeen inhabitants per square kilometre. There are, of course, major variations. Life expectancy at birth is 79.0 for males and 84.6 for females. Two-thirds of the population live in the south-western provinces. The population of the Helsinki metropolitan area is about 1.2 million (2022). Good internal traffic connections are of vital necessity. There are about 7 million motor vehicles and 78,000 kilometres of highways. The total length of railway lines is about 5,900 kilometres, and the total length of waterways is about 20,000 kilometres (about half of which coastal and half inland). Annually about 26 million passengers travel by air (2019; but in 2020 only 6.5 million, due to the COVID pandemic). There were about 6.1 million mobile telephones in the country already in 2007, which meant that practically everyone already had a mobile phone. Fixed broadband of at least 100 Mbps is available to 65% of all households and optical fibre to 40% of all households.

6. Finland was populated for the first time shortly after the Ice Age, nearly 10,000 years ago. Since then people have entered the country from various directions. Decades ago, scientists have rejected the old theories of the origin of the Finns, according to which they migrated to the country from what is now Russia at the beginning of the Christian Era. The modern view, based on new archaeological, philological and genetic evidence holds that the Finns are an early mixture of various origins which evidently has come about gradually in what is now Finland. Genetically the Finns are related to their European neighbours, although the Finnish language, which is spoken by 87.3% of the population, is non-Indo-European belonging to the Finno-Ugric group, like its nearest relative Estonian (hardly understandable) and the much more distant Hungarian. The likewise related domestic Saami languages are not understood by Finns, either.

7. The Swedish-speaking minority (6%), which originates from the early Middle Ages, is concentrated on the west and south coasts and the archipelago (including the Åland Islands). The language groups have long been socially, culturally and economically intermingled, and several language shifts have taken place during history. Finnish and Swedish are both official languages protected by the Constitution. In spite of that, the Swedish-speaking population is largely bilingual, especially in the South (the Åland Islands being the main exception), and Swedish is largely mastered also by the Finnish-speaking. In addition, the three Saami languages (2,000 speakers in all) have a constitutional status. From the 1980s, immigration from many distant countries, such as Vietnam, Somalia, the former Yugoslavia and the Middle East, has taken place. Later on, also Russians, partly with a Finnish ancestry, and Estonians, have immigrated, today making up the two biggest native language groups after Finnish and Swedish, but before Arabic, English, Somali, Kurdish, Persian, Chinese, Vietnamese and Thai. Before the collapse of the Soviet Union, the Russian language was practically non-existent. Wealthy Russians have also shown interest on land properties in certain eastern areas. In 2021, about 7,600 applicants gained Finnish citizenship. The number of asylum-seekers peaked in 2015, causing significant stress on the administration and judiciary and also resulting in a change in the political structure. Natural population increase is today negative, while net immigration is positive. In 2021, 8.3% of the total population had a main language other than Finnish, Swedish or Saami.

The small indigenous and genetically distinct Saami/Sami ('Lappish') population lives in the farthest North. Their language is related to Finnish. Their traditional nomadic style of life, based on reindeer herding, has mainly changed to a rather mechanized and more farming-like form of reindeer husbandry, and the majority is not directly involved at all. The status of the Saami (the majority of which live in Scandinavia outside Finland) as an internationally and constitutionally protected indigenous people may have significant effects on land and environmental law in the future (*see* General Introduction, Chapter 2 §1, below). The problems also exist in Sweden and Norway, whereas in Russia they have not yet emerged in practice.

§3. Legal and Political Structure

8. Finland was a part of Sweden in the Middle Ages, the western parts already in the twelfth century. The country was not an occupied colony; from 1,362 the Finns had an equal right to take part in the election of the Swedish King, and the Finnish areas were also equal in regard to parliamentary representation. There were at times significant population migrations between the western and eastern part of Sweden-Finland, as it was also called. In the course of time some economic imbalances emerged. The Swedish wars in Europe especially laid a heavy burden on Finns, who had a key role, e.g., in the Thirty Years' War in Germany. In the eighteenth century some eastern parts and in 1809 the whole country was occupied by Russia, but still not made an integral part of the Russian Empire. Instead, the initially liberal-minded Alexander I allowed Finland to become an autonomous Grand Duchy with the Czar as Grand Duke for more than a century (called the Autonomy Era, 1809–1917). This meant that the Swedish legal system, Parliament (Diet) and a Home Government (the Senate), its own State economy with a customs border towards Russia, later on its own currency, and also several privileges of citizens. The language of administration was during the whole period Swedish and, from 1863, to an ever-increasing extent Finnish (which as a literary language originates from the 1530s).

The Diet, being made up of the four estates, gathered in 1809, but for the next time as late as 1863, at the beginning of a period of liberalism and industrialization. Towards the end of the nineteenth century a new policy of Russification met with strong resistance and strong national feeling, resulting in the independence of Finland in 1917 (which gave rise to a war which was both a civil war and a war of independence). Before that, the weakening of Russia had made it possible to renew the Parliament on the basis of universal and equal suffrage in 1906 (including, for the first time in the world, women). Independence was preserved even during and after World War II, in which the country was first attacked by the Soviet Union (which was for this reason expelled from the League of Nations) and then de facto allied with Germany, but finally had to cede important eastern areas to the Soviets, causing a significant refugee colonization project in the remaining State area, with impacts on ownership rights and land use, particularly for the colonization of the population evacuated from the ceded areas. However, Finland was never occupied by either Germany or the Soviet Union.

9. The legal system of Finland, basic judicial structures included, has preserved its continuity throughout history; a few enactment fragments from the Swedish era and somewhat more from the Autonomy Era are still in force, though largely modernized. Even World War II, despite the political fluctuations, caused no discontinuity. The Constitution Act of 1919 and the Parliament Act of 1928 were in force, as amended later on, until March 2000. The present Constitution Act of Finland (731/1999) replaced both of them but marked no profound changes. Concerning fundamental rights and obligations, the Constitution Act was as far as possible aligned with the requirements of the Council of Europe Convention of Human Rights (Bdg1:23) that being applicable also as such. Especially in respect to the provision on the environment, the Constitution Act exceeded the contents of the Convention.

In 1995, Finland became a member of the European Union (EU). Most of the then European Community (EC) legal system was already in force from the beginning of 1994, due to the agreement on the European Economic Area (EEA) which for Finland remained a one-year arrangement only. (In fact, due to the belated entering into force of the EEA, the legislation was largely harmonized already by 1993.)

10. Finland is a parliamentary republic. In contrast with certain other political systems but in line with that of France, the President, elected for a term of six years directly by the people, has had an amount of real political power, although many of the powers have not been used in practice and there has been a tendency to gradually add to the powers of the prime minister. The latest shift to this direction was made in 2000 by the Constitution Act. The unicameral Parliament (the *Eduskunta/ Riksdagen*, 200 members) is elected every four years. The majority has traditionally been non-socialist. The Cabinet, formally 'the Council of State', must enjoy the confidence of the Parliament. Until the 1970s the cabinets, based on various political coalitions, tended to be rather short-lived, but for almost thirty years Cabinet reshuffling almost only occurs after general elections. Typically, the coalitions have been ideologically mixed, and almost all possible coalitions have been experimented. From 1991 to 1995 the Cabinet was entirely non-socialist, but from 1995 the 'rainbow' Cabinet with a non-socialist majority consisted of the Social Democrats, the Conservatives, the Left Alliance, the (non-socialist) Swedish People's Party and the Green League (which left the Cabinet in 2002, in opposition to the decision in favour of a new nuclear plant), but excluding the non-socialist and rurally based Centre Party. From 2003 to 2007 the main coalition parties were the Social Democrats and the Centre Party, and the Cabinet of 2007–2011 consisted of the Centre Party, the Conservatives, the Greens and the Swedish People's Party. The coalition in 2011–2014 consisted of the Conservatives, the Social Democrats, the Swedish People's Party, the Left Alliance, the Green League and the Christian Democrats, and in 2014–2015 the same coalition continued, but in the end without the Green League. The coalition in 2015–2019[1] consisted of the Centre Party, the Conservatives and (the right-wing populistic) Finns Party (and at the final stage, its

1. The previous Cabinet had to resign due to a vote of no confidence in early 2019, only a short time before the general elections, and acted some time as a caretaker government. All this resulted in the collapse of a huge social and health administration and regional administration reform, including a total reform of environmental administration. In 2021, a much more modest reform on regional social and health arrangements was approved, without any ingredients of environmental or land use ingredients.

opposition group), the one in 2019–2023 of the Social Democrats, the Centre Party, the Green League, the Left Alliance and the Swedish People's Party,[2] and the present one from 2023 consists of the Conservatives, the Finns Party, the Swedish People's Party and the Christian Democrats.

Most of the members of the Cabinet,[3] formally Council of State,[4] are heads of their ministries. In some ministries the substantive competence is split between two ministers, usually from different parties. In such a case one of these ministers is the administrative head of the ministry, but without any right to intervene in the management of the other's sector. It is also possible for a minister to have been allotted tasks of another ministry. In a previous Cabinet, the Ministry of the Environment had two ministers, both of which were (untypically) from the same (Conservative) party. In the Cabinet 1999–2003, the Ministry of the Environment was first headed by a single (Green) minister, although the matters of housing and building in the ministry belonged to one of the Financial Ministers (from the Left League). This Minister of the Environment was, like her predecessor, also in charge of international development in the Foreign Ministry, a sector with important environmental aspects, e.g., in the neighbouring eastern areas. During 2002–2003, the Minister of the Environment was a Social Democrat, but one of the Financial Ministers (from the Left League) was in charge of housing, building and land use planning within the Ministry of the Environment. In 2003–2007 the Minister of the Environment was from the Swedish Party, but the regime of housing (unlike building and land use planning) in the Ministry of Government was headed by another minister (of Municipal Affairs). In 2007–2011, the Minister of the Environment, being in charge of environment and nature, represented the Centre Party, whereas a conservative minister was in charge of land use planning, building and housing. In 2011–2014 the Minister of the Environment was from the Green League, and the Minister of Housing (within the same ministry) was a Social Democrat, while the Minister of Agriculture and Forestry was a Conservative. In 2014–2015, the Green Environmental Minister at the outset continued, but was soon replaced by a Conservative one. In the coalition 2015–2019 one minister from the Centre Party was first in charge for both the Ministry of Agriculture and Forestry and the Ministry of the Environment, and 2017–2019 only for the latter. The same coalition from 2015 was also the first (and for the time being last) where the Ministry of Justice was left without its own minister, while the Labour Minister was also responsible for the Ministry of Justice. This curiosity reflected low respect of legislation and judiciary, and, being ended in 2017, it has largely been regarded as a major failure. During 2019–2023, the Minister of Environment and Climate was from the Green League. The present Minister of Environment and Climate (as of 2023) is a Conservative.

2. In December 2019 a rare change of prime minister took place, due to a short-lived political crisis. Otherwise, almost the same Cabinet with the same programme continued.
3. In this presentation the expression 'Cabinet' is used when also 'government' would be appropriate. This is due to the Constitution, pursuant to which the government consists of President of the Republic and Cabinet. However, the established translation Government decree is used instead of Cabinet decree.
4. This expression is not used in this presentation, due to the fact that Council of State is in many European countries is counterpart of the Finnish SAC. *See also* para. 93.

11. The Constitution guarantees the citizens' civil rights and presupposes a system of independent courts. The system of judiciary is dualistic. On the one hand, there are the courts of general jurisdiction for civil and criminal cases (District Courts, Courts of Appeal and the Supreme Court (SC)), and, on the other hand, there are the administrative courts (in particular, the Regional Administrative Courts and the Supreme Administrative Court (SAC)). The dualism is traditional and based on section 99 in the 1999 Constitution Act, according to which justice in civil, commercial and criminal matters is in the final instance administered by the SC, whereas justice in administrative matters is in the final instance administered by the SAC. The highest courts supervise the administration of justice in their own fields of competence. The two SCs are, dealing with different cases, independent of each other, i.e., the courts of general jurisdiction have no competence to review administrative decisions and vice versa. The system of administrative courts is in many respects similar to those of Germany, France and Sweden. No separate Constitutional Court exists in Finland (*see* General Introduction, Chapter 2, §2, below).

In addition, there are some special courts such as the Market Court and the Social Insurance Court. The previous Land Courts are today a specific bench of certain District Courts, and the previous Water Courts have been transformed first into the Environmental Permit Offices and these further into the environmental permit divisions of the Regional State Administrative Agencies (*see* General Introduction, Chapter 3 and Chapter 4, §1, below).

12. According to section 121 of the Constitution Act of Finland, Finland is divided into municipalities, whose administration shall be based on the self-government of their residents. The country is divided into 309 municipalities (2022), about sixty of which are urban, about sixty semi-urban and less than 200 rural. The municipalities are in charge of a significant part of public services and public administration. They have the right to levy municipal (income) tax, which is not insignificant, but in practice they are dependent on financial arrangements by the State. The municipalities produce, either alone or in cooperation with other municipalities, the basic services regarding social welfare and health, education and technical infrastructure. The area and population of a municipality vary strongly. The total area of the largest municipality is 17,333.62 square kilometres, while that of the smallest is only 6 square kilometres. In terms of population, the biggest (Helsinki) has 664,028 inhabitants and the smallest 692 (in Finland proper) or 111 (in Åland) inhabitants.

Of all municipalities, the half of all consisting of the smaller ones, account for only minor part of all expenditure by municipalities. In comparison, the municipalities in the metropolitan area (in all 1,200,000 inhabitants) are densely populated. In principle, the legal status of each municipality is the same. The system of municipal self-government is guaranteed by the Constitution, whereas there is until now no proper all-round self-government at the intermediate regional level. From 2022, the new Wellbeing Services Counties are the self-governing public entities responsible for organizing publicly funded healthcare and social welfare and rescue services (*see* paragraph 15). Otherwise, the public administration is either governmental (the Regional State Administrative Agencies, the (likewise regional, but somewhat more numerous) Centres for Economic Development, Transport, and the Environment and some additional State district offices) or based on various federations of municipalities, particularly the law-based Regional Councils (*see* below).

13. Pursuant to section 121 of the Constitution Act of Finland, provisions on self-government in administrative areas larger than a municipality are laid down by an Act. In practice, there has been no proper regional self-government. The previous regional federations for general matters on the one hand and for regional land use planning on the other have been unified into the inter-municipal Regional Councils, in order to meet the requirements for regional cooperation in the EU, and in the future the regions (nineteen in all) perhaps constitute the basis for regional autonomy. They do not have any rights of taxation (unlike the State and the municipalities). There are also many other region-level federations of municipalities, for different purposes, e.g., for healthcare maintenance, which do not have any administrative connection to the Regional Councils. It must be emphasized that the word regional (in Regional Council) does not necessarily refer to the same geographical units in other contexts. For example, in the expressions Regional Council, Regional State Administrative Agency and Regional Administrative Court, the geographical meaning of region of each is essentially different.

From the beginning of 1997, the number of the then Provincial Offices, concentrating on matters of general safety, supervision of municipalities, etc., had been reduced from eleven to five (Åland excluded). Apart from the Provincial Offices, several branches of regional State administration had been combined to form the Labour and Business Development Centres, being in administrative charge of general business promotion, agriculture, fisheries and employment. The State environmental administration (Regional Environmental Centres) was also totally outside the Provincial Offices.

From 2010, the State regional administration were totally reformed. The Provincial Offices and several regional authorities were abolished and their tasks divided between two new categories of regional multipurpose authorities, i.e., the Regional State Administrative Agencies and the Centres for Economic Development, Transport and the Environment. The reform also assigned the tasks of the Regional Environmental Centres and the Environmental Permit Offices to these new authorities, and hence ended the existence of separate independent environmental administration.

14. After that, a total reform of public administration on regional and local administration has been on the political agenda and often also dominated the whole parliamentary life. Initially an overwhelming reform of public (and eventually also private) healthcare and social services was at stake, and during the parliamentary period 2015–2019 a huge package of several governmental bills with, *inter alia*, amendments to hundreds of parliamentary acts was introduced in the Parliament. A new level of self-governed regions would have been established (without amending the Constitution Act, however), and the regions would be vested in a vast amount of such public administration tasks which belonged, and today still belonged, to the various branches of State administration. Be health and social sectors aside, a major part of these tasks would have related to the environment, natural resources and land use. As a part of the totality, a new nationwide State authority for several environmental tasks would have established at the same time; however, because, *inter alia,* the Regional State Administrative Agencies and the Centres for Economic Development, Transport, and the Environment would have been abolished anyway. The impacts of the last-mentioned parts were practically not assessed, and a haste characterized the preparation and law drafting at large. The parliamentary majority of the then Cabinet was marginal, and even that was lost in early 2019. Formally the complex wrecked due to the critical conditions set forth by the Constitutional Committee of the Parliament. These related to the health and social service parts. The rest never had time to be examined by the committee.

15. The current Cabinet presented in 2020 its basic model for the reform. Unlike its predecessor, this narrower version only encompassed the health and social services. The reform met much less political resistance, and it was approved already in 2021. Among ample new legislation, the Act on the Division into Wellbeing Services Counties and into Regions (614/2021) and the Act on Wellbeing Services Counties (611/2021) were enacted (in force from 1 July 2021). By the new legislation, twenty-one Wellbeing Services Counties were established (not covering Helsinki municipality and the separately regulated Åland), but the existing eighteen Regional Councils with their previous tasks remained as they were. A Wellbeing Services County is the self-governing public entity responsible for organizing publicly funded healthcare and social welfare and rescue services in its geographical area of operation. The steering County Councils are elected in a new type of public elections, the county elections. No environmental, land use or nature resource tasks or present State powers are vested in the Wellbeing Services Counties, at least not for the time being. Taxation is still a privilege of the State and municipalities only.

16. Parallel to the proper self-government of municipalities, several special, legislatively created municipal board-type authorities have been made responsible for the implementation of national enactments at the local level. Here the steering by the central government has been important, the decisions being substantively controlled by administrative courts, above all for the legal protection of different private parties. The distinction between the two aspects of municipal administration, own self-government and law enforcement, is not always clear and it may also be said that the extent of real municipal self-government varies. In the realm of non-legislated administration, the freedom of municipal authorities is much broader, but this freedom is counterbalanced by the right of every citizen in the municipality to appeal any municipal decision to an administrative court on grounds of illegality. In addition, any person whose rights are concerned can appeal, irrespective of whether he belongs to that municipality.

In 1989–1996 a legislative experiment (the 'Free Municipalities'), following the example of other Scandinavian countries, was carried out. The main aim was to improve the services, to reduce the supervisory influence of central governmental bodies and to let the board administration be arranged more freely than the general legislation provides. During and after the experiment, several parallel legislative measures of permanent nature were taken. The distinction between legislated and non-legislated administration has lost some of its clarity and significance. There has also been disagreement on some of the results of the experiment. For example, the number and influence of elected laymen in various municipal bodies has been strongly reduced in favour of officials, and the total number of municipal bodies is now significantly smaller than before. Especially in the field of environmental decision-making, the enlarged powers of the municipalities have not always been positive, particularly not where separation between promotion of local businesses and protection of environmental interests has been made diffuse.

17. There is a special and far-reaching form of self-government for the Åland in the south-western archipelago. The autonomy and Swedish unilingualism of these islands is constitutionally protected (and the neutrality thereof internationally guaranteed). Most of the Swedish minority, however, lives in continental Finland or in the archipelago outside Åland. In relation to the Finnish membership of the EU, Åland is no exception, notwithstanding certain taxation issues making it possible to maintain the economically important tax-free sales on board Ålandic passenger ferries. In respect to the implementation of EU secondary legislation, Åland has become somewhat of a problem to Finland as a Member State, because the provincial legislative, being independently in charge of several important fields of legislation with a great number of directives, has not always been able to transpose the directives in due time.

§4. Economic Characteristics

18. Of the total labour force 6.9% were unemployed in spring 2023. The rate is now essentially lower than in 2000 or 2010, not to mention the recession years of the early 1990s. Earlier, labour shortages were common in the late 1980s. Also today, labour shortage is real, but depending on the branch at stake. Of the employed labour force (in spring 2023 2,804,000), 75% are employed in the private sector, 19% in the local public sector and 6% in the central public sector. The change from an agrarian society to an industrial and, later, a post-industrial society has been rapid after World War II. The public sector employed at its peak approximately a third of the workforce, but its share has declined significantly. Especially the share of State employees has decreased. The tax rate (tax revenue as % of gross domestic product) was about 43% in 2023. General government deficit relative to gross national product was in 2023 3% and debt 73%.

19. Finland's gross domestic product in 2022 was EUR 269 billion or EUR 48,344/inhabitant. The share of primary production of the gross domestic product in 2022 was 2.6%, industries 22.4%, construction 7.0%, public services 18.3% and private services 49.7%. The (chemical) forest or wood processing industry has traditionally been regarded as the backbone of the Finnish economy, but it has lost the top post to information technology. However, wood processing has, likewise traditionally, been responsible for the most conspicuous domestic environmental problems, but also reduced them more effectively than probably any other sector, with the exception of municipal wastewater treatment.

In terms of agriculture and food production, Finland is largely self-sufficient (albeit dependent on energy imports); in fact, before EU membership there used to be significant overproduction, which the common agricultural policy (CAP) of the EU had only in some respects changed. In the recent years, self-sufficiency of milk products and eggs has been over 100%, of bread grain 70%–200%, of meat 85%–107%, of potatoes 101%, of sugar 37%, of tomatoes 63% and of farmed berries 38%–70% but of apples only 17%.

The value of export of products was in 2022 EUR 88.54 billion and of services 32.96 billion, and the value of import of products 92.4 billion and of services 39.1 billion. Of the exports of products, forest industry products in 2022 made up 17.2% of the total value of exports, 21.6% chemical industry products, 19.6% metal and metal products, 17.9% machinery and equipment, 11.1% electricity and electronic products and 12.7% other products. As for value of imports, 32.4% were in 2022 made up of industrial supplies not elsewhere specified, 19.3% of capital goods (except transport equipment) and parts and accessories, 18.9% of fuels and lubricants, 10.9% of transport equipment and parts and accessories thereof, 8.9% of consumer goods not elsewhere specified, 5.4% of food and beverages and 4.1% of others. The biggest export regions in 2022 were the euro zone (39.9%), other EU countries (18.4%), other Europe (14.4%), Asia (13.1%), North America (8.5%) and others (5.8%) and the biggest import countries Germany, Russia, Sweden, China, the Netherlands, Norway, Poland, Estonia, USA, and Italy.

20. Around 1990, the national economy encountered serious problems. In the late 1990s, the economy regained its stability in most respects. Though politically difficult, significant reductions in public expenditure had anyway taken place. Additionally, efforts to strongly reduce public administration and legal regulation emerged in daily political discussion. They had resulted in significant outsourcing. In the recent years, contrasts between the prospering largest city regions and significant declining parts of eastern and northern Finland have strongly grown, resulting, *inter alia*, in strongly diverging property values. Due to the problems in global economy and the effects of first the COVID pandemic and then the war in Ukraine and declining of connections with Russia, new problems have emerged, especially regarding public economy

European integration and its future is a crucial factor in Finland's economy. Finland joined the Economic and Monetary Union (EMU) from the outset (2002).

21. According to statistics, total energy consumption in Finland in 2022 was 1,296 PJ, 5% less than in 2021. The total energy consumption consisted, by energy source, of fossil oil (264 PJ, 21% of all), coal (83 PJ, 6%), natural gas (39 PJ, 6%), nuclear energy (264 PJ, 19%), net import of electricity (45 PJ, 4%), hydro power (48 PJ, 4%), wind power (42 PJ, 3%), wood fuels (369 PJ, 28%), peat (38 PJ, 3%) and others (104 PJ, 7%). The share of renewable sources in 2022 was 42%. The CO_2 emissions from energy production and consumption in 2022 were 33 million tonnes (of the total 45.8 CO_2 equivalent tonnes, pursuant to preliminary calculation).

22. Prior to 2022, Finland had two nuclear plants with two reactors each, built in the late 1970s by two companies in the coastal municipalities of Eurajoki (*Olkiluoto 1 and Olkiluoto 2*), 250 kilometres northwest of Helsinki, and Loviisa, 80 kilometres east of the capital. A long-lasting public debate on one or even two more nuclear plants ended in 2002, as the Parliament approved (*see* Part I, Chapter 8, §2 below) construction of a fifth nuclear reactor, the first new plant in Western Europe or North America since the Chernobyl disaster in 1986. The new 1,600 MW reactor was planned to be constructed in Eurajoki (*Olkiluoto 3*). In 2005, the Cabinet issued the energy company Teollisuuden Voima Oyj the Construction Permit under the Nuclear Energy Act, after which the constructing was commenced. The plant was originally intended to be in commercial use by 2010. Due to several technical, safety-related, commercial and legal problems and delays in the course of the years, the start was waiting very long, until spring 2022. Commercial production began on 16 April 2023. In May 2010, the Cabinet approved in principle two applications concerning proposed new plant units (a fourth reactor at Olkiluoto, by Teollisuuden Voima Oy and a new plant in northern Finland, Fennovoima Oy), rejected the application concerning one proposed new unit (Fortum Power and Heat Oy), and approved an application concerning an enlarged nuclear fuel waste end disposal plant (Posiva Oy). In July 2010, the Parliament approved the in-principle decisions, but *Olkiluoto 4* has been renounced by the company. The project of Fennovoima Oy, at Pyhäjoki on the coast of the Gulf of Bothnia in northern Finland (*Hanhikivi 1*), is still unfinished and without the final permits. In early 2022, the future of this plant with a Russian co-owner and supplier seemed very uncertain due to the political and economic implications of the Ukraine war, in spite of the finished non-nuclear constructions and infrastructure – and the large-scale changes and impacts in the natural environment. In May 2022, Fennovoima Oy finally terminated the agreement with the Russian supplier and cited significant delays, the supplier's inability to deliver the power plant and Russia's invasion of Ukraine as reasons. There is no future in sight for this plant.

§5. Social and Cultural Characteristics

23. During its history, Finland has been more or less on the borderline of two different cultural spheres. Already before the Middle Ages, the west of the country had close connections to Western Europe, whereas the easternmost parts were in certain respects connected to the East. During the early Middle Ages, Finland was a bone of contention between the Roman Catholic Church and the Greek Orthodox Church (or the political powers behind them). The result was that the country became Roman Catholic and later on Lutheran, with some Russian Orthodox influence in the easternmost parts (having at times belonged to Russia). Though Finland has had full freedom of religion since 1923, about 60% of the population belong to the Lutheran Church. The cultural impacts from these two main influences have also been felt in traditional rural culture and folklore (which is otherwise largely original, though), but the cultural and societal ties to Scandinavia became dominant in most of the country already during the Middle Ages.

The 1809–1917 period as a Grand Duchy under Russia had very little cultural effects. It may be said that Finland is culturally similar to the other Nordic countries. Whether one may call Finland a Scandinavian country or not, depends on the actual definition of the word. Finland is a Scandinavian-style welfare society. From the early 1990s, certain problems in this respect have emerged due to the recession of those years. In addition, the modern trends of privatization have affected the everyday political debate and partly also the services.

In European comparison, the Finnish landowning peasant, as the modern farmer, has always been free and independent, with few minor exceptions. This may be connected to the popular feelings and attitudes on which the legislation is largely based and which may be problematic, e.g., for nature conservation and wildlife protection in the remote countryside.

24. Traditionally, 'the other domestic language', i.e., Swedish for Finnish native speakers and vice versa, has been the first compulsory language to be learned in school. However, from the 1970s English has taken first place. Already before this, English had displaced German as the first foreign language. German or French or in some cases Russian has the position of a second foreign language. Swedish (or Finnish) anyway preserves an important place in the curriculum, although the matter has every now and then been debated, also in the Parliament. In other words, Finnish students have one language more to learn in comparison with most European countries. For the majority, who have Finnish as their mother tongue, this is not always convenient. However, Swedish is also important for Nordic cooperation, and a proficiency in it is still necessary for most public offices.

The travel trade balance of Finland was long negative. Many Finns are accustomed to travelling abroad every summer – even if they have a summer home ('cottage', which may nevertheless be furnished with all modern conveniences) of their own (as is the case for over 500,000 families). In addition, many people like to flee the dark months around Christmas. More than 1 million Finns annually spend one holiday week or more in the Mediterranean area or farther away, while the number of tourists visiting Finland has been significantly smaller. A state of affairs that may even be a benefit from the environmental point of view. The balance has changed, however. Number of overnight stays by foreigners at accommodation establishments in 2019 was about 7,100,000 (but still more by domestic tourists). In 2018, tourism business made up 2.7% of the GDP. The COVID pandemic impacted strongly in 2020 and 2021, but the tourism industry is currently recovering, with the exception of Russian tourists.

25. The Finns traditionally have had a close relationship with nature. During recent years these ties have loosened, though, especially among the urban youth. Fishing and hunting as well as various forms of sports and athletics are popular in Finland, being in fact a part of the way of life. Many of them, like Nordic cross-country skiing, are related to the natural conditions in Finland, though alpine skiing is today more popular (which in turn has also negative environmental impacts). As for competitive sports, ski jumping and rally driving are among the most well-known, not to mention the Finnish Formula one drivers or ice hockey players.

§6. Main Environmental Problems

26. The environment in Finland has traditionally been regarded as clean and unpolluted in comparison with, e.g., Central or Eastern Europe. Even today, this remains largely true. For example, the agricultural products are chemically very clean. Still there are evident problems. Due to the efforts in air pollution prevention, the acidification of the environment is no longer a significant problem, but some other forms of pollution (like local mercury contamination or dioxin residues in the Baltic Sea fish) have been problematic. The sources of pollution are both foreign and domestic. The Finnish natural environment differs in several respects (climate, soil, water) from that in Southern and Central Europe, which makes it difficult to predict the future impacts on, e.g., the forests, which are of vital importance to the national economy of the country. Around 1990, the emissions from the metallurgic industry in the Russian Kola Peninsula seemed to be a serious danger to the nature of Eastern Lapland, but later on it had been concluded that the problem is geographically confined to rather small areas. As for the South, the transboundary sources of pollution have been found in western and southern directions. Here the problems may be, e.g., acidification of small lakes or high ozone levels, caused by transboundary sources, in the lower atmosphere. However domestic emissions to the air have been strongly reduced during the thirty last years, but local problems in cities occur.

The most significant domestic sources of air pollution are still, albeit in a clearly reduced extent, energy production, industry and especially traffic. In 2020 the emissions were approximately 29,900 tonnes (109,000 tonnes in 1996) of SOx as sulphur dioxide, 106,900 tonnes (277,000 tonnes in 1996) of NOx as nitrogen oxide, 59,700 tonnes of non-methane volatile organic compounds (VOCs) (194,000 tonnes in 1996) and particulate matter ($PM_{2.5}$) 17,700 tonnes (27,800 tonnes in 2005). There was also, e.g., a less clearly measurable quantity of particles being emitted into the air. In some urban areas the impurities in the air, especially the dust particles in city air during dry spring days, originating largely from the sand spread on icy sidewalks in the winter, may occasionally be harmful to the health of at least those people who belong to risk groups. Nevertheless, air quality in many urban areas has improved considerably during the past thirty years. Also, the previous smell problems around pulp plants have almost disappeared. One unpredictable environmental change in the future is caused by climate change. Certain changes are already present, such as milder winters and increased storms. There are also indications of the summers turning hotter and drier. Lack of sufficient winter frost in agricultural areas and shortened ice cover periods are disadvantageous to the status of lake and coastal sea waters. Some forestry scientists forecast a radical change in the tree species composition of the forests, in favour of southern deciduous trees.

Finland's total greenhouse gas emissions excluding the land use, land-use change and forestry (LULUCF) in 2022 were, according to preliminary calculations of Statistics Finland, 45.8 million tonnes CO_2 equivalent, which was 2.0 million tonnes less than in 2021. The land use sector (LULUCF) was a net sink of –1.0 million tonnes CO_2 equivalent.

27. Finnish inland waters are as a rule, complicated systems made up of lakes of various shapes and sizes, rivers and brooks. The lakes are generally shallow and, though numerous, their water holding capacity is small in comparison to their surface areas. They can be characterized as oligo or mesotrophic by nature. In addition, high humus infiltration from wet peatlands often makes them strongly coloured and acidic. The annual period of ice cover also makes the natural conditions in lakes different from, e.g., Central European lakes. All this makes that they are not particularly suitable recipients for external waste discharge.

28. Water pollution by industry and municipalities decreased substantially from the early 1980s. Even so, amounts of various pollutants still get into the watercourses, but especially the impacts of phosphorus are now mainly local. For the status of inland surface waters, phosphate load is in general regarded clearly more essential than nitrate load. Of all phosphate load in 2021, 10% came from point sources, 80% from diffuse load and 10% from fallout. Among the diffuse load, more than half originated from agriculture and forestry and less than half from dispersed dwellings. Of the point source phosphorus load 39% originated from municipalities, 41% from industry and 20% from fish farming, and of the nitrogen load 73%, 22% and 5% correspondingly. A different type of water loading and local pollution is caused by peat extraction (mainly through humic substances and particles). Severe regional or local water pollution problems have at previous times been caused by the pulp and paper industry (also called wood processing industry), especially by the effluents from debarking, chemical pulp processing and bleaching plants. They have then accounted for a major part of the total national Biological Oxygen Demand (BOD_7) water load and for the discharge of large quantities of nutrients, as well as numerous processing chemicals and wood-based compounds such as chlorinated organic compounds and resin acids. However, much has been done to minimize the discharges. From 1980 to 2006, the paper and pulp production had grown significantly (before the shutdowns beginning in 2008), whereas the combined BOD_7 load of all industries had decreased to merely 8% of the 1980 levels, having only minor local relevance. The phosphorus and nitrogen discharges from the pulp and paper industry have also decreased substantially (total phosphorus load in 1980 was 590 tonnes, in 1992 450 tonnes, in 2000 250 tonnes, in 2006 183 tonnes, in 2011 156 tonnes, in 2018 121 tonnes and in 2020 100 tonnes; total nitrogen load in 1980 was 3,900 tonnes, in 1992 3,300 tonnes, in 2000 2,500 tonnes, in 2006 2,700 tonnes, in 2011 2,527 tonnes, in 2018 2,166 tonnes and in 2020 1,800 tonnes). During the recent decades, the discharges of chlorinated organic compounds (AOX) have decreased to an insignificant level (reduction of 86% from the early 1990s, being 1,020 tonnes in 2001, 1,222 tonnes in 2006 and 800 tonnes in 2020).

About thirty of the Finnish chemical industry's production plants have been important water polluters, but also here, the discharges have decreased significantly, as well as the separate plants themselves. The foodstuffs industry has been an additional contributor of local wastewater pollution. The municipal sewage waters are nowadays treated effectively in biological-chemical plants (in 2017, 350 plants for at least 100 inhabitants), the efficiency of phosphorus and BOD_7 removal being about 95% (2010, 2017), but nitrogen removal – the usefulness of which in different inland and coastal waters has continuously been debated by experts – is a small problem. The removal rate of nitrogen was 56% in 2010 and 66% in 2017. The diffuse water pollution caused by scattered settlement, agriculture and silviculture is still a real problem. Approximately 15% of the population today live outside population centres and are hence not served by public sewerage systems, and the same holds good for the majority of holiday homes. Sewage treatment facilities are now required by law (*see* Part I, Chapter 4, §1, III). Among local deterioration of waters caused by point sources, mines, fish farming and peat extraction have been perhaps the most often occurring in the recent decades.

The ecological condition of water bodies and the water quality are, however, generally good. Waters in a bad or disturbed condition make up only a small minority of all water bodies. As for chemical water pollution, apparently the most serious and problematic single cases in the past have been the river *Kymijoki* in south-eastern Finland and the small Lake *Kernaalanjärvi* in the heart of a water system in southern Finland. In both cases the bottom sediment still contains significant amounts of Polychlorinated Biphenyls (PCBs), originating from paper industry discharges from previous decades when the hazardous properties of PCBs were not known. However, the PCB seems to be so constantly sedimented that the water itself is free from PCBs and practical problems only arise when the sediment is disturbed (as might happen, e.g., in the case if the *Kymijoki* is channelled for water traffic, as is sometimes proposed).

29. For municipal water supply, both inland lake water and, increasingly (about 65% of total water supply), groundwater is used. For example, the Helsinki region receives its water from the major clear-water Lake *Päijänne* 130 kilometres north of the capital. But there may also be risks involved with surface water. Several inland watercourses, being coloured and humic by nature, are not suitable water sources, because the necessary purification of water may cause reactions between humic acids and chlorine, in which even carcinogens can be produced. And concerning all surface water there is of course the risk of radioactive fallout. Hence, groundwaters are very important sources of water. At the same time also they are often rather vulnerable. One of the main threats is the excavation of esker gravel. Also some wastes and chemicals have appeared to be problematic. In a few cases, municipal water supplies and even public health have been endangered, and in a few cases municipal groundwater intake has been closed because of an unacceptable content of chlorinated phenols used as chemical timber preservatives by wood industries at a time when their hazardous properties were unknown. The chemicals may be preserved long in soil layers. Until the 1970s hundreds of sawmills used chlorinated phenols, and new groundwater pollution problems of old or recent origin may arise.

30. The natural conditions of the Baltic Sea partly depend on oceanographical interaction between the North Sea and the Baltic Sea. In recent years, however, pollution of large areas and also general eutrophication has become a severe environmental problem, in spite of the Helsinki Convention (*see* Part I, Chapter 4, §8, I). All the most acute pollution problems and risks, however, clearly exist outside of the Finnish territorial waters.

31. The wetlands (peatlands) have largely been drained for agricultural or silvicultural purposes. Hence smaller running water ecosystems have been transformed to straight ditches or buried in underground pipes. This has influenced the water runoff conditions and also aggravated water quality problems linked to diffuse discharges. At the same time, natural wetland ecosystems have in many areas become quite rare, causing significant decreases in the biological, geological and hydrological variety of bogs, marshes, swamps, fens, other peatlands, etc. Also, traditional agricultural landscapes with open ditches and bushes have disappeared.

Many large lakes are regulated for hydroelectric purposes, especially in the north of the country. The purpose is to adapt the water flow to the demand of energy, annually, weekly or daily. This may be detrimental especially to nature, coastland use (also recreational use) and fisheries. The quality of the water may also be influenced, especially where large man-made lakes have been constructed. The plan to construct a large man-made lake (the *Vuotos* reservoir) in northern Finland for hydroelectric purposes had long been a matter of debate and environmental concern. In December 2002, the SAC finally dismissed the permit application, on environmental grounds. The exceptionally extensive permit application pursuant to the Water Act had been pending for several years. No new effort has been made.

The main part of potential natural waterpower in Finnish rivers is already brought into use. The construction boom of hydroelectric plants occurred during the war and the first post-war decades, but the environmental problems caused by it emerged in public as late as in the 1970s. The result has been that natural stocks of migratory fish, e.g., Baltic salmon, have practically been lost. The stocks in the Baltic are maintained by fish farming on a large scale. In many large river areas, there is no longer any possibility of fishing migratory fish, once very important for local economies in the North. Obligations on electricity producers to plant fish both in the sea and in the rivers and to compensate damages have been laid down years later, after long, massive and famous trials, but often the ecosystems had already been deeply changed, and restitution thereof is impossible because fish migration is prevented and the natural rapids have been destroyed by plant dams and water regulation. The remaining rivers have been protected against new power plants by legislation (*see* Part II, Chapter 8, §3, I). However, some pressure to rescind the protection has every now and then turned up in connection with the public energy debate. Waterpower, it is true, does not cause any pollution, but its environmental problems are of another kind.

32. As explained before, certain environmental threats are linked to acidification and air pollution, largely being of transboundary origin. But Finland's forests are a matter of environmental concern and a popular topic in public debate also in many other respects. As for the utilization of the wilderness forests in northernmost Lapland, opinions strongly differ as to their natural values and regeneration capacity. Throughout the country, forests have been systematically taken into effective management (largely clear-cutting and subsequent monocultural planting, combined with systematic ditching), which of course implies a threat to the value and variety of nature and has in the course of years given rise to a more or less justified environmental concern in the export countries. However, the forest legislation pays considerable attention to bio and other values of nature. Extensive areas of clear-cutting (which of course only means temporary lack of forestation) are systematically avoided. Methods of environmental certification for Finnish wood have been introduced and at times also debated.

The duties of private forest owners are legislatively linked to economical management and utilization of forests, but there are at the same time owners who prefer 'softer' methods of silviculture, even if these are economically less profitable. An additional factor connected to the changes is that more and more forest properties are owned by people living in towns, due to inheritances. Also, the common rights of access to forests and of gathering berries and mushrooms (*see* General Introduction, Chapter 2, §1, below) are involved. The new values for their part created public pressure to alter the regulations, which was clearly manifested in the 1996 Forestry Act, but of course as a compromise with the important aspects of national economy.

33. Esker and ridge gravel has been used for constructing purposes to such an extent that natural eskers with valuable nature and landscapes have almost disappeared in large areas around population centres in southern Finland. Replacement with materials acquired by stone crushing or dredging of sea bottom gravel poses environmental problems of their own, too.

34. The numerous water bodies notwithstanding, shore areas without private summer homes or other specific uses are becoming more and more rare, especially in the Southwest and around population centres. This has long been an item of public concern, but it had not proved politically possible to create effective restrictions such as those which existed in Sweden and Norway. From January 1997, a major change took place, however, and the 1999 Land Use and Building Act developed the regulation somewhat further (*see* Part III, Chapter 3, §6).

35. As for endangered species, one of the main concerns is the glacial relic ringed seal of Lake *Saimaa*. Another endangered species is the white-backed woodpecker, which has suffered badly from modern forest management methods. However, stocks of many formerly endangered species have been restored, like the whooper swan (a well-known symbol of conservationist concern from the 1950s, thanks to a popular novel writer) and beasts of prey like the wolf, bear and lynx (still a controversial issue). Also, the white-tailed eagle, which once was almost extinct mainly because of reproduction disturbances (certain chemicals in the marine environment caused the breaking of eggs) has recovered, especially thanks to feeding practices.

From 1997, the EC nature conservation network Natura 2000 has been one the main items of general public and political discussion, often in an exceptionally heated way. It has been extremely difficult to keep apart the facts, fiction, prejudices, general opposition feelings against the EU, party politics, real juridical problems, lack of clarity on legal effects and difficulties in the disseminating of appropriate information. Anyway, it has been alleged that environmental attitudes have turned less positive also in general due to this debate.

Today, the main environmental discussion items in Finland refer to the climate and the degradation of biodiversity, especially regarding forests and their use. At the same time, new pressures to weaken environmental legislation have emerged. The condition of the Baltic Sea and its ecosystems and economically important fish stocks is worrying.

Chapter 2. Basic Principles of Environmental Law

§1. Definitions and Notions

36. The notion of 'Environmental Law' is in Finland nowadays rather widely used, but with two, partly different meanings at the same time. First, there is the internationally adopted meaning which covers the legal problems of pollution control and nature conservation and management. But due to certain administrative solutions in the academic world, Environmental Law at times also refers to a wider sphere which also includes the traditional discipline of Land (use) and Water Law. According to this notion, a professor of Environmental Law may also study and teach Water Law or legal problems of land use, registered land surveying, parcelling, planning and building at large. However, in an international context, Finnish professionals mostly recognize the difference and conform to the international usage. This is also true for this volume.

37. In Finland both land and water areas are objects of private ownership. The exchange of real estate is in principle free. Parcelling may be restricted on grounds of planning law. For Åland there are specific and very strict provisions for non-Ålandic purchasers. From 1 January 2020, a piece of real estate may by subjects from outside the EU and the EEA as a main rule only be acquired subject to special permission issued by the Ministry of Defence, as provided in the Act on Transfers of Real Estate Requiring Special Permission (470/2019). Besides private proprietors, the government is for historical reasons a major real estate owner, but the areas concerned are primarily either wildernesses in northern Finland or outer territorial waters in the Baltic Sea (or the middle areas of certain major lakes).

However, claims for the wildernesses of northernmost Lapland have recently been put forward by representatives of the Saami population. These areas belong mostly to the State (administered by the Metsähallitus), but the right to reindeer husbandry is nevertheless guaranteed by the law. Reindeer grazing is allowed, and not only to the Saami population, irrespective of the ownership of the (lichen) grazing lands. Several committee proposals have been presented since 1990, aiming to give (or: to give back) the ownership of State land and waters in the Saami homeland area to the Saami people, e.g., to local 'villages' which perhaps would be established in a legal sense. The proposals have caused a lively debate, even among the Saami minority, many of whom are real property owners, and particularly among the non-Saami local population. The establishing of private ownership would, according to the 1990 committee proposal, also make it possible to take even Natural Parks and National Parks (*see* Part II, Chapter 2, §2, I) as well as the State Wildernesses (*see* Part II, Chapter 2, §4) into private use, e.g., for forestry. The environmentalist organizations were hence against that proposal, which was also controversial in many other respects. The main issue has been the Saami homeland rights in State-owned areas in general, many of which are subjects of forestry and reindeer husbandry as well. A governmental rapporteur on the implementation of International Labour Organization (ILO) Convention (No. 169) concerning 'Indigenous and Tribal Peoples in Independent Countries', made a proposal on the legislative measures necessary regarding the Saami population's rights to land and water (1999). The proposal, as well as several subsequent efforts and proposals, resulted in a very heated debate, with strongly differing opinions. No consensus has been achieved so far. Hence no legislative bill, or ratification of the Convention, seems probable in the near future.

Many privately owned areas in the country belong jointly to groups of private real estate holders, as a result of the history of land parcelling. Especially the water areas are widely in joint possession of this type. The proprietor is here a shareholders' association for a registered village's common areas, which has, however, not always been organized. In fisheries law contexts the association is statutorily called the statutory shareholders' fishery association for the (respective) registered village's common waters (in this book: 'statutory fishery association for a village'). The number of shareholding properties (estates) in a village may vary between two and several thousands. There are also parcelled private water areas, though, most of which are in the southern and western parts of the country. Furthermore, inland and archipelagic water areas are often split by a network of village (and estate) boundaries. Finally, there are the Public Water Areas owned by the State (represented by the Metsähallitus) in the outer territorial waters outside village boundaries at sea, as well as in the middle of the largest inland lakes. The main interest for Public Water Areas has traditionally been fishing. In the recent years, wind power production interests have emerged in several sea areas.

38. The legal position of landowners is traditionally rather strong. This has also influenced the system of Environmental Law, though it should be kept in mind that the interests of the various owners may collide with each other and thus need legal regulation, also in environmental matters. But of course the most essential parts of environmentally relevant legislation are overwhelmingly of a public law nature, especially as far as the most recent decades are concerned. However, rules with both private and public law features have in many cases grown into a coherent system which is often impossible to be placed in either the private law or the public law domains, or divided between them. This holds good for, e.g., Water Law, of which water pollution law in turn was an integral part up to 2000. Finnish Water Law has strong features of both public and private law, but it is usually impractical to try to classify even the individual norms into correspondent sectors.

39. The powers of a land or water owner are often limited and influenced by the general rights of access and related citizens' common rights (usually called everyman's rights, today also everyone's rights), which are traditionally characteristics of the Nordic legal systems. In Finland, and largely also in the other Nordic countries, public access to private land in the countryside is much wider than in most other countries. It is in principle allowed without permission to everyone to roam and temporarily to walk, ski, cycle, or ride in the nature, i.e., in areas owned by someone else, to pick some (non-protected) flowers, to gather wild berries and mushrooms in the forests or to boat and to angle in the water areas. It is also allowed to stop and rest, swim, or to have a picnic in a private area. Tent camping for a short period, e.g., for a weekend is also permitted, provided that no damage or disturbance is caused. For a longer stay and for caravan parking, permission from the landowner is required. Open fires are not allowed without the landowner's permission.[5] The provisions on the protection of nature may result in some restrictions (such as for strict reserves) of everyman's rights. In parts of Lapland, cloudberries may only be gathered by local residents. Unnecessary or excessive nuisance to owners and other disturbance is prohibited, as well as trespassing on croplands or forest plantations, and, where there is no public right of way, in farmyards and areas around private homes. The provisions on littering in the Waste Act also concern everyone.

However, there are not many explicit regulations for this category of rights. It is largely a matter of an unwritten code of practice and of what is not prohibited by Criminal Law. Chapter 28, section 14 of the Penal Code provides that the legal restrictions in this chapter (covering theft, etc.) do not apply to the collection of dry twigs and branches, cones and nuts found on the forest floor, or to the picking of wild berries, mushrooms, flowers or other naturally growing products, with the exception of mosses and lichens, on other people's property. On the contrary, tearing off twigs is punishable.

40. There are explicit provisions for moving in the water areas (in the Water Act and the Water Traffic Act) and for certain common rights of fishing (in the Fisheries Act, *see* Part II, Chapter 6, §3). Everyone has free access to most waterways and also to water areas off waterways, even when they are frozen in winter. Boats may anchor temporarily without permission by the owner, provided that no disturbance is caused. Going ashore under everyman's right is allowed. For environmental reasons, water traffic in a certain area may be forbidden under the Water Traffic Act (*see* Part II, Chapter 8, §3, II).

Use of motor vehicles, motor sledges (snowmobiles) included, on private land off-road is as a rule only possible with the permission of the owner. In addition, the Centre for Economic Development, Transport and the Environment (environmental division) of the region has the competence to prohibit the use of such vehicles in a certain area for environmental reasons (*see* Part II, Chapter 2, §5). However, specific Motor Sledge Trails can be established. The use of snowmobiles is normally permitted on ice of water bodies, without the permission of the owner. Snowmobile drivers must ensure that they cause no damage or disturbance to the environment, nature, local people, or their property. They must drive carefully, and keep off public roads, crossing roads or bridges being the exception.

41. Environmental legislation is closely linked, and even partly based, on internationally established principles of environmental (or natural resources) policies and law. These principles are often given a certain legal status, by listing and defining them in the introductory parts of various legislative acts. Hence, e.g., the principles of prevention of negative impacts and reducing of harm, precaution and care,

5. Section 6 of the Rescue Act applies to all areas, according to which open flames may not be lit during a wildfire warning issued by the Finnish Meteorological Institute or if the conditions due to drought, wind or other reasons are such that there is an obvious risk of wildfire or other fire. Open fire refers to a campfire or other similar use of fire from which it is possible for the fire to escape through the ground or due to sparking.

Best Available Techniques (BAT), Best Environmental Practice (BEP), and polluter pays are defined in the 2000 Environmental Protection Act. However, being principles, they function mainly as general guidelines, not as directly applicable norms.

Similar functions may be achieved by defining the purpose of an act. Hence, e.g., according to the 1996 Forestry Act, the purpose of the act is to promote economically, ecologically and socially sustainable care and use of forests in a way that they offer a continuously good production while their biological diversity is preserved. Concerning the legal relevance of a similar introductory provision in the Fisheries Act (*see* Part II, Chapter 6, §4).

§2. Constitutional Provisions

42. A new act is adopted or an old amended either on the basis of a governmental bill or of a motion submitted by a representative. However, legislation based on the latter is in practice very uncommon. From 2012, there is also a third alternative, the Citizens' Initiative. Such an initiative must be supported by at least 50,000 adult citizens. The legislative bills drafted by the ministries are scrutinized and formally decided upon by the Cabinet prior to their submission to the Parliament. In practice, the basic preparatory work is very often done by ministerial or inter-ministerial committees where different authorities, experts and private interest groups, such as industries, landowners, municipalities and environmentalists, have been represented. This is one of the reasons why there is no significant pressure, e.g., towards arrangements like voluntary agreements in the environmental sector.

After a preliminary debate in plenary session of the Parliament, the introduced bill is referred to a Select Committee, which considers the matter and hears experts. Often the opinion of another Select Committee is acquired (on the Select Committee for Constitutional Law, *see* below). Environmental legislation is normally dealt with by the Environmental Select Committee. The Select Committee in charge drafts a report and the bill – where detailed amendment proposals are very often made – is returned to the plenary session for a first hearing. This hearing comprises a general discussion during which the Parliament may refer the bill to the Grand Committee (the tasks of which mainly concern proposals to EU law), but this seldom takes place. The contents of the bill are decided on in a detailed consideration in plenary session. Then the Parliament either adopts or rejects the bill in a second hearing. An adopted act is submitted to the president for ratification. If the act is not ratified within three months, it is returned to the Parliament. If the Parliament does not change its opinion the act enters into force even without a presidential ratification.

43. The liberty of the legislature to affect private rights is not unlimited. Traditionally, a general protection clause in the Constitution (now section 15 of the 1999 Constitution Act of Finland) guarantees the protection of private ownership. Compulsory acquisition of land (expropriation) is allowed on the basis of a normal parliamentary act if there is a 'public need' and the compensation is sufficient ('full'). Other intrusions on private property rights are in principle not possible (*see* below, however).

The environment in turn had enjoyed no explicit constitutional protection until the 1995 constitutional rights reform of the then Constitution Act, where at least in principle a major change in the substantive constitutional prerequisites concerning the environment took place due to a specific clause, now being section 20 of the 1999 Constitution Act of Finland. Section 20, being an integral part of the provisions on fundamental rights and obligations, reads as follows:

> Responsibility for nature and its diversity, environment and cultural heritage belongs to all.
>
> It is the duty of the government[6] to strive to ensure for everybody a right to a healthy environment and a possibility to have an influence on the decision-making concerning one's environment.

The most relevant functions of this environmental provision seem to be, in addition to being an incentive to environmental legislative efforts, the interpretation effect of the Constitution (*see* below), and, especially in legislative contexts, serving as a more or less effective counterbalance to the other constitutional basic rights, particularly those of section 15. However, the protection of private property may also be parallel to that of the environment, e.g., with respect to pollution prevention. In addition, section 20 is supposed to have also other legal effects. Direct application by courts and authorities is not totally excluded. And according to the preparatory documents, section 20 includes, *inter alia*, a 'constitutional task' for the government in developing the environmental legislation and citizens' participation. This may imply constitutional qualifications with respect to the rules on participation, standing and appeals. But in general, no profound changes in the legislation have resulted, however.

44. The sphere of the constitutional protection is always a matter of legal (and political) interpretation. Many kinds of smaller 'intrusions' have been accepted in regular legislative contexts, e.g., by defining the various duties and obligations connected to ownership in such a way that no breach of a constitutional protection clause is regarded to have been at stake. In addition, an act contrary to section 15, or any provision in the Constitution, may be enacted as a 'constitutional exception', if it is (from 2000) of a strongly limited scope and provided that it is supported by a qualified majority in the Parliament (two-thirds of the members after following elections or, if five-sixths declare the bill urgent and allow immediate voting, two-thirds of the present members). After the reform of 2000, this has nevertheless occurred extremely seldom. The interpretation of the Constitution in legislative contexts, e.g., that of the constitutional basic rights, is primarily a task of the Select Committee for Constitutional Law (*see* below). The limits of governmental involvement by new legislation are tested by the procedure described above. If, e.g., an environmental bill is considered to need a constitutional exception, it is very possible that the bill never passes. If such a result is probable and if there is not a large political support, the bill will in practice not be introduced as such.

6. The Finnish and Swedish expressions translated here as 'government' refer to all bodies vested in public powers, at all levels of administration, municipalities included.

45. The Select Committee for Constitutional Law, in fact acting like a semi-judicial body, has a tradition according to which there is no breach of section 15 (or its predecessor section 12, or the predecessor of this, section 6), if the 'normal, moderate, and reasonable' use of property is not violated. Of course, this interpretation may be discretionary, but the Select Committee often considers itself bound by its own precedents. However, a certain flexibility and a limited tendency to adjust to social progress has at times been visible.

The courts have no power to reconsider the legislative procedure or the constitutionality of a parliamentary act, and there are no plans to establish a separate Constitutional Court. The application of constitutional norms, particularly of those on provisions on fundamental rights and obligations has become and everyday matter in court practice, and the monopolization of them to a single court would be regarded negative. First, provisions of acts (and decrees) are today, where possible, interpreted, in a manner that favours the constitutional fundamental rights and obligations (interpretation effect of the Constitution, interpretation aligned with fundamental rights and obligations). This development is partly related to the parallel applicability of the provisions of the European Convention on Human Rights. Second, there is at present an established practice, based on the constitutional reforms and court practice, to apply the constitutional provisions on fundamental rights and obligations directly, whenever necessary and that being not in breach of explicit legislation (application of constitutional norms).

46. As an *ultima ratio*, section 106 of the 1999 Constitution Act of Finland includes a general clause on the primacy of the Constitution. If, in a matter being tried by a court of law, the application of an Act would be in evident conflict with the Constitution, the court of law shall give primacy to the provision in the Constitution. The provision concerns any court, but in practice its significance is accentuated in the highest courts. The article has been applied a couple of times by both the SC and the SAC. Most often the interpretation effect or direct application of the Constitution Act, where applicable, make the applying of section 106 unnecessary.

As for decrees and other lower level statutes, section 107 is applied. If a provision in a decree or another statute of a lower level than an Act is in conflict with the Constitution or another Act, it shall not be applied by a court of law or by any other public authority.

47. In the course of years several constitutional disputes have emerged in the legislature regarding Environmental Law bills. Many conspicuous bills have become acts through the ordinary procedure with a single majority, even though the Select Committee for Constitutional Law has not always been unanimously in favour. For example, the still valid Soil Excavation Act of 1981 was enacted through the normal procedure, irrespective of the fact that permission for soil or rock excavation causing severe harm to environment or nature may (and must) be denied under its provisions, in most cases without compensation. However, no dispute on the constitutional protection of ownership had emerged during the enactment procedures of, e.g., the Air Pollution Prevention Act of 1982 or the Nuclear Energy Act of 1987, even if it is obvious that they more or less restrict the liberty of the owner to use his property for industrial purposes. The situation may be due to the fact that the protection of ownership has in political life been most strongly connected with agricultural landowner interests. The legislative acts above have been enacted before the mechanism of fundamental rights and obligations included no provision on the environment. Later on, section 20 has played a role in the constitutional considerations. However, it seems that protection of ownership has recently gained new weight in relation to the environment.

Chapter 3. Historical Background

48. The first signs of modern environmental consciousness in Finland appeared in public debate in the late sixties. This resulted in some legislative and administrative measures to protect the environment. That was not, however, the beginning of Finnish environmental law. The numerous water bodies have always been vital for the economic life of Finland, and the main ways of exploitation have traditionally been use of waterpower, floating of timber and discharge of effluents, especially from the wood processing industry. The overall water legislation, which has gradually evolved from medieval Nordic laws, has for a long time protected certain environmental values as well. The primary manifestation of this was a general ban on polluting bodies of water. The prohibition, which was renewed in the laws of the nineteenth century and again in 1902 and 1961, was designed to protect both public interests and the interests of land and water owners, etc., at the same time. There is therefore no way to classify this type of regulation as either private law or public law. The ban was not absolute (except for groundwater), because exemptions were under certain conditions possible in the form of discharge consents. For the purposes of modern environmental protection there has been no need to change the principal idea of the regulation, in which also the compensation rules have been involved. However, through the integrative reform of environmental and Water Law in 2000, the manifestation in statutes has been changed. As for surface waters, the general clause is no longer a ban, but a case-by-case indication on the necessity of an integrated Environmental Permit.

The previous overall reform of Water Law in 1961 was important in many respects, including the environmental aspects of the various forms of water (and water area) management; the formally total reform of 2011 was sooner a codification of the modifications and legal practice after 1961. One of the basic solutions in 1961 was the creation of the then Water Courts, to which competence was concentrated in a wide sphere of judicial and administrative matters. Among these, the court's role as a permit authority was the most prominent. The Water Court model was originally Swedish (although there were some domestic forerunners too), but in Sweden the system was soon afterwards changed and today the Swedish Water Courts do not exist at all. In the 2000 reform of Environmental and Water Law, the Finnish Water Courts were transformed to the then established Environmental Permit Offices (with almost the same tasks). And finally in the general reorganization of the Finnish regional State administration from the beginning of 2010, the Environmental Permit Offices were transformed to Environmental Permit Divisions of the new Regional State Administrative Agencies (with almost identical tasks). In 2019 an effort to totally reorganize the permit authorities, as one of the numerous components of the then pending overall reform of administration, lapsed in the Parliament.

49. The law on the use of adjoining properties has often been environmentally relevant as well. Before 1920, there were practically no explicit regulations to prevent a proprietor from using his property in a way that causes nuisance to his neighbour. The unwritten *libertas dominii* principle clearly favoured the active party, although the legal practice was not uniform. The Neighbourhood Relations Act of

1920 meant a shift of principle in introducing a general ban on private nuisances, with special compensation rules. The structure of the regulation was close to contemporary foreign equivalents. Although a matter of private law regulation, the Act came to include also a kind of permit system and thereby certain traits of public law. A general starting point of the system is the ban on private nuisances ('immissions') (*see* Part I, Chapter 1, §1).

The Act is still in force, with certain amendments, but it has, partly, lost most of its environmental and also judicial importance, mainly in favour of the environmental permit and enforcement systems where also the rights of the would be injured parties are taken into account, or, partly, has become implemented within the environmental permit system. It has anyway turned out that a system based on traditional private law cannot be efficient enough in controlling widespread pollution or preventing public nuisances.

50. In the field of public law, health legislation has been one of the most important from the environmental point of view. The first regulations on hygienic conditions date from 1879. At that stage it was mainly a question of preventing infectious diseases. In the twentieth century, other kinds of health hazards turned to be essential as well. The regulation has been repeatedly renewed, for the last time in 1994, when the present Public Health Act was enacted. A special permit system based on health risks, being already then procedurally included in general environmental permits (1991), was wholly repealed by the 2000 Environmental Protection Act. However, protection of health is clearly one of the aims of the new integrated framework of that Act.

51. The lack of air pollution control legislation was a subject of major concern in the environmental debate of the 1970s. The Public Health Act and the Neighbourhood Relations Act were – from different points of view – in some cases able to meet the needs of air pollution control, but in practice they were not sufficiently effective. This unsatisfactory situation resulted in the enactment of an Air Pollution Prevention Act, but not until 1982. The reasons for the delay were partly administrative and partly political. This was due to the fact that the Ministry of the Environment had not yet been established. Instead, several possible solutions of environmental administration involving air pollution control were put forward. Some of these would have meant the incorporation of air pollution control into the authority system of Water Pollution Law. Later on, the Air Pollution Prevention Act was largely revised and from 2000 air pollution prevention has been wholly integrated into the framework of the then Environmental Protection Act.

52. Waste management was not a subject of special legislation until 1978, when the Waste Management Act, the predecessor of the predecessor (1993) of the present Waste Act (2011), was enacted. Before this, the Public Health Act served as a kind of partial substitute. In 2000, the pollution-related parts of the then Waste Act were transferred into the then Environmental Protection Act. Development of waste law has more and more been influenced by EU waste legislation.

53. As early as towards the end of the nineteenth century, the ideas of nature conservation gained some support especially in certain academic circles. As a starting shot is regarded a speech by A.E. *Nordenskiöld*, the explorer,[7] in 1880. In the beginning, this movement was strong enough to initiate a special field of legislation, and a decision on the first nature reserve was made in 1916. Preparation of nature conservation legislation was started in 1919 and resulted in the Nature Conservation Act of 1923. This Act had apparent connections with contemporary German and Swedish legislations, while some ideas, particularly the notion of National Park, originated in the USA. The Act was formally in force up to the end of 1996, having preserved its original basic structure, but it had been modernized and completed afterwards. The next Nature Conservation Act of 1996 was based on the same grounds, but also essentially influenced by EC conservation law. In the present Nature Protection Act of 2023, new measures of guidance alongside traditional conservation have been inserted.

54. Environmental impact assessment (EIA) was not made subject to specific coherent regulation until 1994, when the reform had become necessary due to EC law. This is not to say that environmental impacts of projects were previously not assessed at all, but the assessments were connected to various permit and plan procedures and hence normally confined to the respective sectors. An integrated approach was only attained through the new regulation.

7. Moved later on to Sweden.

Chapter 4. The Role of Government Institutions in the Shaping and Administration of Environmental Law and Policy

§1. The Governmental Institutions and Their Competences

55. The State administration concerning environmental matters had been rather divided until the 1980s. It was in many respects dualistic. At the central governmental level, nature conservation and water pollution control were vested in the Ministry of Agriculture and Forestry and its subordinates, whereas other largely upcoming means of environmental protection were tasks of the Ministry of the interior. This dualism had certain counterparts in contemporary party politics. According to a common view, the situation also prevented or impeded the progress of environmental legislation, while some competition in the legislative field was to be observed at the same time. The reform efforts finally resulted in the establishing of the Ministry of the Environment in 1983. It had been preceded by an important political dispute. Various models had been presented. The result, still being valid, was a ministry with some important tasks which lay clearly outside the proper protection functions. The main spheres of administration include not only general environmental policies, environmental impacts, (overall) pollution control, waste management and noise abatement, but also land use and building in their various forms, as well as conservation of nature and landscape, and outdoor recreation, building, technical aspects included and housing, especially the public financing thereof. Housing has not much to do with environmental matters, but land use planning and building are more relevant and sometimes also problematic in their relation to environmental protection matters.

The mechanism of land use planning, zoning and town planning included, is a system of general decisions where basic impartiality should be maintained regarding the various needs and interests. Of course, environmental interests represented by the ministry itself may here collide with some other relevant interests. Particular planning (zoning) decisions are, however, for the most part made rather independently outside the ministry, especially by the municipalities. From 2000, the administrative authorities (ministerial or regional) were practically no longer vested with appellate powers regarding land use. Irrespective of the competence in zoning and planning, the outcome of the decisions is often crucial to the future of the environment. As a rule, protection has no principal priority to other needs and interests, but the system of land use planning includes certain decision procedures primarily aiming at environmental protection.

56. The main task of each ministry is the general steering of the respective administration, in addition to law drafting and financial tasks. Administrative decisions in individual matters in turn mainly come under the jurisdiction of other bodies, central, regional or local. In Finland, superior authorities have no general right to intervene in particular matters under consideration by subordinate authorities. This holds true also for the relation between a ministry and its subordinates. Even the power to issue guidelines and instructions, if any, has to be based on the law, and binding norms are not issued by the administration (below the level of decrees) without a specific authorization in law. However, each ministry has, in any case, a key position in shaping the governmental policies. Under the Finnish ministries, there have been several subordinate central agencies with specified tasks, although the recent tendency to assign their duties partly to the ministries and partly to provincial authorities, as explained later on, has strongly reduced their number. In the field of Environmental Law, the most important central Agency was up to 1995 the National Board of Waters and Environment (before 1986 the National Board of Waters), which had district offices of its own, roughly one for each province. There is no such central Agency any more. The previous Environmental Permit Offices have been transformed to Environmental Permit Divisions of the new Regional State Administrative Agencies (or to be exact, of four of them), and the Regional Environmental Centres, respectively, to the divisions for the environment and natural resources of the new thirteen Centres for Economic Development, Transport and the Environment. The administrative structure is very complicated, and the tasks of the divisions are in many cases conflicting or contradictory.

The environmental divisions of the Centres for Economic Development, Transport and the Environment have a wide variety of functions and tasks. First, they have almost all the same fields of competence which are at the national level vested with the Ministry of the Environment. Housing (but not land use planning or building) is the main exception. In addition, there are several tasks under the Ministry of Agriculture and Forestry, most of which are connected to waters and water areas (water body management projects and works, drainage, water supply, etc.). The rest of the water-related tasks (pollution prevention, supervision, recreational and conservation issues, etc.) of the centres come substantively under the Ministry of the Environment. However, the centres have no authority in permit matters under the Environmental Protection Act or the Water Act. Regarding the latter, this was originally due to the overall competence of the three Environmental Permit Offices (2000–2009), formerly the Water Courts (*see* Part I, Chapter 1, §4, and Part II, Chapter 8, §2), which decided, like the present (environmental permit divisions of the) the Regional State Administrative Agencies (2010), independently, e.g., upon water area management and construction permits and respective coercive means. Concerning the Environmental Protection Act and Environmental Permits, the exclusive permit competence of the Regional State Administrative Agencies is of more recent origin, because as late as in 2000 reform also the centres were vested in permit authority, besides the then Environmental Permit Offices.

The competent composition of division of the Regional State Administrative Agencies in Environmental Protection Act and Water Act matters consists ordinarily of members with legal, technical or ecological expertise. Their independent competence in permit matters means that even the Cabinet or the ministries have no legal power to give effect to their policies in individual matters. However, the practical influence of the environmental administration (i.e., the environmental divisions of the Centres for Economic Development, Transport and the Environment, in particular) on the application of the Water Act and, where appropriate, of the Environmental Protection Act, through opinions and accounts should not be underestimated. From the procedural viewpoint, this is based either on the *locus standi* of the (divisions of the) centres or on their status as expert bodies.

57. According to a Nordic tradition, the citizens have in principle access to all official documents. Of course there are some evident restrictions, but the main rule, presently expressed and specified in the Act on the Openness of Government Activities (621/1999), constitutes an important difference in comparison with most European countries. The situation also made it possible that the (then) EC Directive on access to environmental information (90/313/EEC) required practically no legislative measures whatsoever in Finland. The same holds good regarding the current Directive 2003/4/EC. Also the *Århus Convention* (Convention on access to information, public participation in decision-making and access to justice in environmental matters, ECE 1998) had only minor impacts on legislation. The main legislative impact of the same was quite specific, concerning a small group of projects within Annex I to the Convention for which there was no permit system and hence no appeal mechanism, either. On the legislative solution, *see* paragraphs 1376 and 1577–1578.

As far as the Trade Secrets Directive[8] is applicable also in environmental matters, problems may arise, in particular because Finland has not stipulated anything specific regarding environmental information and its relation to business secrets at the implementation stage. Nevertheless, the Environmental Protection Act, irrespective of this, but relevantly still, contained and still contains in section 210(1) a provision, as an exception to the Act, pursuant to which the data and information on the emissions and monitoring of activities under the Environmental Protection Act, as well as data and information on environmental quality are *not* secret. This category of information may in any case be seen as a very important and central part of the totality of environmental information at large. In 2014, the SAC has made an important judgment on this (SAC 2014:58). The activity at stake concerned a quarrying project for which an Environmental Permit had been granted and which contained explosions which in turn caused vibrations in the neighbourhood. Harmful vibrations are one type of environmental pollution pursuant to the Environmental Protection Act. A neighbour had made the Municipal Environmental Protection Authority a request on the times of explosions and the sizes of explosive fields. The Authority regarded these as business secrets and denied, like next the Regional Administrative Court. The SAC in turn applied the (respective) general provision in the (previous) Environmental Protection Act and declared the data not secret.

§2. The Actual Role of the Administrative Institutions

58. Many government institutions have wide powers to shape their policies, of course within the bounds of the law and the budget. The ministries are in charge of their respective fields of administration, and at the same time new legislation is prepared by them. A general trend in administration development work has from the 1980s been to concentrate the politically relevant management tasks to ministries, while the previously strong Central Agencies or National Boards (which are of

8. Directive (EU) 2016/943 of the European Parliament and of the Council of 8 Jun. 2016 on the protection of undisclosed know-how and business information (trade secrets) against their unlawful acquisition, use and disclosure.

course subordinate to the respective ministries) have mainly been transformed into expert bodies with primarily service-orientated tasks (*see also* §1 above). Hence the previous National Board of Waters and Environment has in 1995 been replaced by the Finnish Environment Institute *(Suomen ympäristökeskus/Finlands miljöcentral)* with strongly differing functions.

In the meantime, the practical State administration was being more and more delegated to provincial authorities and municipalities. In the environmental field, the previous Water and Environment District Offices and the divisions for land use and environment of the then Provincial Offices *(lääninhallitus/länsstyrelse)* were merged into the previous Regional Environment Centres. However, the remaining Provincial Offices had from September 1997 been transformed into fewer but regionally larger units (five, except for Åland) with somewhat less tasks than before. At the same time, the regional State units for business development, labour and employment, agriculture and fisheries were concentrated into the new regional Employment and Economic Development Centres of which there were somewhat more than the Provincial Offices. From 2010, both the Employment and Economic Development Centres and the Regional Environmental Centres are, together with, e.g., regional road administration, merged into the thirteen new Centres for Economic Development, Transport and the Environment. The present Regional State Administrative Agencies in turn have been made up of the previous Provincial Offices and Environmental Permit Offices.

59. A general legislative trend has moreover been the strengthening of the self-government of municipalities (*see also* General Introduction, Chapter 1, §3 above). This development has, however, turned out to be problematic from the environmental (like social, health, etc.) point of view, or even contrary to the implementation of Environmental Law, especially if, as was the tendency in the early 1990s (e.g., the 'Free Municipality Experiment'), the principles of substantive self-government were made to refer to all situations where legal powers have been granted to municipal bodies, irrespective of their judicial character which traditionally may also imply mere implementation of law.

Irrespective of this, all law enforcement by politically elected local bodies with various engagements may result in that the environmental provisions of law are in danger of being set aside in favour of local or municipal interests of quite another kind, especially in cases where a municipal body has been given permit authority or supervisory authority by the legislator. It is naturally likewise possible that environmental values are overemphasized. The main counterargument to these doubts is of course the fact that local decision-making as such has benefits from the viewpoint of social legitimacy and justification. However, it is in practice less common that environmental interests are favoured by the local level in the shaping of environmental decision-making.

60. The Municipal Environmental Protection Authorities are compulsory statutory bodies (based on the Act on the Environmental Administration in Municipalities, 64/1986), being headed by a politically elected board, but nevertheless (at least legally) rather independent within the municipal organization. The status of Municipal Environmental Protection Authority may nevertheless be locally vested also in a municipal body with other tasks, the Municipal Executive excluded, or in an inter-municipal body. In general, the Municipal Environmental Protection Authorities have rather far-reaching supervisory duties and powers as well as the competence to decide upon certain minor permits, etc., as specified in the different environmental enactments. This means, at least in principle, that the authorities are free from interference by the respective Municipal Council or Municipal Executive. As regards individual decisions, they are also independent of State interference (although the central government and provincial authorities retain a guiding and supervisory power). The discretion of the Municipal Environmental Protection Authorities is, nevertheless, as a rule very limited and strictly guided by the law (and hence by administrative courts). Typical acts giving implementary competence to the Municipal Environmental Protection Authorities (in addition to that of the relevant State authorities) are the Environmental Protection Act and the Water Act, as well as, e.g., the Soil Excavation Act and (municipal waste management operations excluded) the Waste Act.

61. From the environmental point of view, the status of two other statutory and independent municipal board-led bodies (the Building Supervision Authority and the Public Health Authority) is important as well. They, too, may appear to be problematic in relation to certain trends of administration development. After the 'Free Municipality Experiment', municipalities have largely been given the possibility to arrange their administration. In the experiment, the Environmental Protection Authorities were in several cases the first victims and were merged with other bodies. Today, a Municipal Environmental Protection Authority is compulsory as explained above, but in practice one and the same board may at the same time act as Municipal Environmental Protection Authority and, say, as Building Supervision Authority or Public Health Authority. This combination may function well, although the different legal roles and formalities are not always easily kept apart. But the most unhappy solutions, not very common but sometimes favoured by environmentally ill-informed consultants of administrative development, are such where the same body supervises the activities it is in charge of (promotion of agriculture or business, or responsibility for municipal engineering or constructing).

62. One characteristic of Finnish administrative law – and consequently of environmental law – is the important role of (administrative) courts (eight, from 2014 six Regional Administrative Courts for the mainland and one for Åland and the SAC), both in procedural and substantive matters. In principle, any administrative decision can be reviewed by an administrative court, but never by a court of general jurisdiction. The former Water Courts have been transformed to the Environmental Permit Offices and finally to the (environmental permit divisions of) the Regional State Administrative Agencies, but with respect to the latter, and with respect to the Centres for Economic Development, Transport and the Environment and the Municipal Environmental Protection Authorities, all decisions under, e.g., the Environmental Protection Act and the Water Act, like any other administrative decision in the field of environmental law, are appealable to Regional Administrative Courts. Concerning the Environmental Protection Act and the Water Act, one of the Regional Administrative Courts, that in *Vaasa*, is solely competent (from 2000).

With its permanent technical and ecological expert members, it is in a way the successor of the former Superior Water Court.

One of the central starting points is the basic constitutional relationship between the Cabinet and ministries on the one hand and the SAC on the other. There is a general rule according to which all administrative decisions, including those by the Cabinet and the ministries, except decisions containing general norms, are potential objects of appeal to a Regional Administrative Court (ministries) or to the SAC (Cabinet). In principle, the competence of a court is limited to legal matters only, but in many cases even this notion is extremely wide. Ultimately it is a matter of case-by-case fine-tuning, as in the field of land use. In any case, the central role of administrative courts in Finnish environmental decision-making as a whole is conspicuous in comparison with other Nordic countries. In Finland it is by no means abnormal for, e.g., the individual emission limits for an industrial establishment to be finally set or altered by the administrative courts. This may even be the proper focus of the whole appellate procedure. It is also quite possible that the environmental provisions of a municipal land use plan are substantively reviewed (but never directly altered) by the same courts.

63. One form of policymaking is the drafting of governmental programmes for various purposes. In the field of environmental protection, such programmes as a rule have lacked, at least formally, legal consequences, but they may still have had an influence on the decisions of various authorities. In the legislation, certain national programmes have recognized more or less direct legal consequences, especially where obligations of EU law are concerned (e.g., sections 51 and 204 of the Environmental Protection Act; *see* paragraph 207). Legal consequences of another type are to some extent attached to conservation plans under the Nature Protection Act (*see* Part II, Chapter 2, §2, I).

64. Each authority and other public body shall use the powers vested in it by law independently, without the right of a superior authority to intervene. This is regarded important from the viewpoint of legal certainty. The competent authority most often also has the best expertise and experience. The legality of each decision may be tested by appeals to administrative courts, but the appellate procedures and provisions on standing are often different. Also the competence boundaries of various authorities between each other are fixed by law. Trespassing these limits renders a decision invalid.

65. External influences sometimes set requirements which create pressure on these structures and principles. The main example on such is the cross-sectoral EU regulation on trans-European energy infrastructure, which obliges each Member State to designate one national competent authority which shall be responsible for facilitating and coordinating the total permit granting process for projects of common interest. Due to the fact that the diverse procedures and pieces of law in question belong to sectors that are legally, administratively and functionally distant and often have not much in common, the task has been challenging. For the same reason, the legislation at stake is in this monograph explained already here.

66. The Act on the Permit Procedure of Projects of Common Interest of the EU (684/2014) aims to include the necessary national provisions due to the Regulation on guidelines for trans-European energy infrastructure.[9] The very diverse permits and consents covered by the Act are the following: (1) a project permit for the construction of high-voltage power line pursuant to section 14 of the Electricity Market Act (588/2013) and the consent by a municipality for the course of the line pursuant to section 17 of the said Act; (2) a project permit for the construction of a transmission pipeline crossing the national border pursuant to section 5 of Chapter 6 of the Natural Gas Market Act; (3) a consent for the exploitation or use of the Economic Area pursuant to sections 6 and 7 of the Act on the Economic Zone of Finland, except for consent entirely for research; (4) a permit for a water management project concerning construction according to section 3 of the Water Act; (5) (up to 2025) a Building Permit pursuant to section 125 of the Land Use and Building Act, a Construction Permit pursuant to section 126 of the said Act and an Exceptional Permit pursuant to section 171 of the said Act (as of 1 January 2025) a Building Permit pursuant to section 42 of the Building Act and an Exceptional Permit pursuant to section 57 of the said Act; (6) a permit for extensive handling and storing permit of dangerous chemicals or explosives pursuant to section 23 of the Act on the Safety of the Handling of Dangerous Chemicals and Explosives and a permit for a pipeline system for transfer of dangerous chemicals pursuant to the said Act; and (7) an Expropriation Permit pursuant to section 5 of the Expropriation Act. All these acts have been amended respectively.

The tasks related to the energy projects under the Act shall be performed without delay (section 2). The national competent authority which is responsible for facilitating and coordinating the permit granting process for projects of common interest provided in Article 8(1) of the Regulation is the Energy Agency (section 3). The collaborative scheme in Article 8(3)(c) of the Regulation is applicable (section 4). This means that the comprehensive decision shall be coordinated by the Energy Agency. Pursuant to the Regulation, the Agency shall, in consultation with the other authorities concerned, where applicable in accordance with national law, and without prejudice to time limits set in accordance with Article 10 of the Regulation, establish on a case-by-case basis a reasonable time limit within which the individual decisions shall be issued. It shall monitor compliance with the time limits by the authorities concerned.

The permit applications and the related documents shall be simultaneously be submitted to the Energy Agency and to the competent permit authority (section 5). The Energy Agency shall hear the permit authority on the sufficiency of the application documents before approving them, but it may not approve them against the opinion of the permit authority (section 6).

The combination of the various provisions applicable may appear problematic in practice from the judicial point of view. Each permit depends on its preconditions, and each permit may be appealed against separately. It hence quite possible that, e.g., the national preconditions for an Expropriation Permit have been unduly

9. Regulation (EU) No. 347/2013 of the European Parliament and of the Council of 17 Apr. 2013 on guidelines for trans-European energy infrastructure and repealing Decision No. 1364/2006/EC and amending Regulation (EC) No. 713/2009, (EC) No. 714/2009 and (EC) No. 715/2009.

assessed due to the time limit, and the Regional Administrative Court decides to send the application back to the permit authority. The opinion on the sufficiency of document does not bind the courts, either.

67. A different type of pressure on the specified competences of authorities has been created by the desire of some operators and applicants to deal with one authority only (the so-called one counter model). An example of this is the joint processing of Environmental Permits and Soil Excavation Permits in certain situations (*see* paragraphs 181 and 1034–1036). The substantive provisions remain different, but procedural options have been to make. Regarding the appellate stage, the rights to appeal have due to such options partly been reduced. This necessarily not in line with the provision on environmental fundamental rights and obligations in section 20 of the Constitution Act.

68. Another type of 'one-counter' permit procedure has been created by the Act on Adjusting Certain Environmental Permit Procedures (764/2019), in force from 1 September 2020. In this case, the combining is not obligatory for the parties, but it depends on the option of the applicant. If an Environmental Permit pursuant to the Environmental Protection Act, a permit pursuant to the Water Act or a Soil Excavation Permit pursuant to the Soil Excavation Act is required for the project at stake, the applicant may request that the processing of the application is adjusted with one or more of the following: (1) exceptions pursuant to sections 66 and 83 of the Nature Protection Act; (2) Building Permit, Construction Permit, Demolition Permit and Landscape Measures Permit pursuant to the Land Use and Building Act (or from 1 January 2025 onwards Building Permit, Demolition Permit and Landscape Measures Permit pursuant to the Building Act (751/2023)); (3) Exploration Permit, Mining Permit and Gold Panning Permit pursuant to the Mining Act; and (4) permit for extensive handling and storing permit of dangerous chemicals or explosives pursuant to section 23 of the Act on the Safety of the Handling of Dangerous Chemicals and Explosives and a permit for manufacturing and storing of explosives pursuant to section 58 of the said Act.

The Regional State Administrative Agency is the adjusting authority, if a permit under Water Act or such an Environmental Permit which is in its competence has to be adjusted. Otherwise, the Municipal Environmental Protection Authority at stake is the adjusting authority. The various permit authorities in question act pursuant to their respective provisions, but cooperate in order to achieve adjusted permit provisions. They shall agree with the adjusting authority on a date when their decisions should be issued. In any case, the decisions are issued simultaneously, in a manner specified in the Act. The appellate procedures and appellate courts are determined in each applicable Act.

69. Pretty much in the same manner, the Act on the Permit Procedures of Plants Producing Energy from Renewable Sources and on certain other Administrative Procedures (1145/2020), implementing Directive (EU) 2018/2001 on the promotion of the use of energy from renewable sources, where referring to administrative permit systems, affects permit procedures pursuant to several Acts. The aim of this Act, being in force from 30 June 2021, is to precipitate the procedures at stake and promote the availability of guidance associated with them. The Act is, as specified in it, applicable to several permit procedures pursuant to the Environmental Protection Act, the Water Act, the Nature Protection Act, the Ancient Remains Act, the Act on the Safety of the Handling of Dangerous Chemicals and Explosives, the Fertiliser Act, the Act on Animal By-Products, EU Animal By-Products Regulation,[10] the Aviation Act, the Land Use and Building Act (from 1 January 2025 onwards the Land Use Act and the Building Act), the Expropriation Act, the Act on the Economic Zone of Finland, Electricity Market Act, the Emissions Trading Act, the Act on the Compensation Areas for Wind Power (490/2013), the Territorial Surveillance Act (755/2000), Environmental Impact Assessment Procedures Act (252/2017) and the Pressure Equipment Act (1144/2016). The main rule is that the ordinary provisions in all those enactments are applied.

The Centre for Economic Development, Transport and the Environment of Etelä-Pohjanmaa (Southern Ostrobothnia) has been designated as the Contact Point under the Act for the whole country. The Contact Point shall, in cooperation with the authorities competent under the various acts, take care of procedural guidance and the guidance via the electronic contact point. The guidance also encompasses the procedures concerning the opinions of the Defence Forces regarding wind power plants. A Procedure Handbook, coordinated by the Contact Point, shall be elaborated and published on the internet. All communication for permit procedure purposes shall be possible via the electronic contact point. All relevant documents may be in digital form (which also holds true in ordinary procedures).

70. The administrative procedures for permits to build, repower and operate plants for the production of energy from renewable sources shall not exceed two years for power plants, including other relevant procedures of competent authorities. A procedure for installations with an electrical capacity of less than 150 kW shall not exceed one year. The procedure for updating existing permits shall not exceed one year. The two-year and one-year periods begin when the first relevant application is filed and end when the last relevant decision is notified. The competent authorities shall adjust their schedules, assisted by the Contact Point, where needed. The Contact Point shall keep an eye on the periods and assist in communication between the authorities. The periods are automatically extended with a period as long as that which has elapsed for appellate procedure in administrative court, and with a period as long as that which has elapsed for the exception application procedure pursuant to section 83 of the Nature Protection Act, or for an emissions permit procedure pursuant to section 8 of the Emissions Trading Act (actually section 26 of the current Act). It is required, however, that no other relevant permit procedure is pending at the same time, unless that being dependent on the appellate or permit procedures above. Where duly justified on the grounds of extraordinary circumstances, the Contact Point may extend a two-year or one-year period up to

10. Regulation (EC) No. 1069/2009 of the European Parliament and of the Council of 21 Oct. 2009 laying down health rules as regards animal by-products and derived products not intended for human consumption and repealing Regulation (EC) No. 1774/2002.

one year. The Contact Point may decide that the period does not go on any more if a relevant procedure has been stopped for at least one year, continuously or altogether, due to the applicant.

The decisions of the Contact Point are appealable in the competent Administrative Court.

71. Pursuant to Article 16(7) of Directive 2018/2001, the deadlines above shall apply, without prejudice to obligations under applicable EU environmental law and or, e.g., to judicial appeal. In addition, the regulatory system contains many structural traits that have not been easy to insert into the Finnish administrative and judicial system, and evident problems remain. It seems possible, in spite of the guidance, e.g., that the applicant prioritizes in the beginning of the two-year (or one-year) period those permits the granting of which seems to be self-evident. The period begins to pass anyway. In this case there might be a very short time left for the more complicated ones, e.g., an Environmental Permit or and Expropriation Permit, where also the legal protection and hearing of others is often necessary and time-consuming. This may or may not factually be a benefit for the applicant, because rejecting an application is often a real alternative. If the Regional Administrative Court annuls a relevant administrative decision and sends the case back to the competent authority, there may be a very short time left, especially if the Court has been swift and the pending period there hence short (in which case perhaps only an identical period may be left for the administrative authority). It is hard to say if all this is counterproductive from the applicant's viewpoint or, on the contrary, benefits, e.g., biodiversity or non-applicant property owners' rights. It is not clear, either, what will happen if the competent authority, for one reason or another, exceeds the deadline. In any case, a valid permit or compulsory purchase right cannot be generated as a presumption only.

72. In order to boost investments within green transition the Cabinet had in April 2022 agreed upon the preparation of law amendments according to which certain permit application proceedings pursuant to the Environmental Protection Act or the Water Act would have priority in the proceeding queue in 2022–2025. Accordingly, the Act on the Processing of Environmental Protection and Water Management Matters by Regional State Administrative Agencies (898/2009) has been temporarily amended by Act 1144/2022, in force from 1 January 2023 to 31 December 2026. According to this amendment, the Regional State Administrative Agency shall, when processing it, give priority to an environmental permit application for activities that take into account the principle of no significant harm referred to in Article 17(1) of the Taxonomy Regulation, i.e., Regulation (EU) 2020/852 on a framework facilitating sustainable investment and amending Regulation (EU) 2019/2088 in relation to other pending permit applications under the Environmental Protection Act and the Water Act. The applicant must provide sufficient evidence of the right to priority when applying. Applications for permits to which priority shall be given are those relating to: (1) an energy production installation producing energy from renewable energy and an offshore wind farm and related water management projects; (2) industrial substitution projects based on renewable energy or electrification; (3) the manufacture and exploitation of hydrogen, with the exception of the production of hydrogen from fossil fuels; (4) carbon capture, utilization and storage; or (5) a battery factory and the manufacture, recovery and reuse of battery materials. An application for authorization, which must also be given priority, is an application for a set of activities if the need for authorization is essentially based on the activity referred to above. According to the temporary amendments made at the same time to the Environmental Protection Act and the Water Act, a case concerning such a permit application must be dealt with by the appellate administrative court at stake as a matter of urgency in relation to other permit matters under the same Act. Correspondingly, according to the temporary amendment to the Land Use and Building Act (as of 1 January 2025, the Building Act), an appeal concerning a Detailed Plan considered significant for renewable energy production and an appeal concerning a Master Plan guiding wind power construction provided in section 77a of the Land Use and Building Act (as of 1 January 2025, the Building Act) must be processed as a matter of urgency in relation to other appeals concerning planning matters and permit matters under the same Act. The temporary changes concerning courts are effective from 1 January 2023 to 31 December 2028. The substantive provisions in the Acts remained untouched. The additional resources needed would be safeguarded.

§3. Economic and Market-Based Instruments

73. Legislative and administrative measures are in general regarded as the primary means of environmental protection. There are, of course, often alternatives to legal regulation, especially where the need for individual decision-making and related legal protection of various parties is not of primary importance. In the public discussion of the 1990s, economic means emerged as an alternative, but the real solutions and decisions based on economics long remained few. There were some at least partially environmental fees, like the oil pollution prevention fees collected from oil importers, the waste fee collected from private households and the waste tax collected from waste-producing industries. The idea of 'pollution taxes' has decades ago been introduced into the fiscal legislation, but long in a rather symbolic way so far (such as the previous scaling of fuel prices on environmental grounds, below). However, the overall picture is now different.

74. Without any direct connection to environmental policies, various excise duties had traditionally been levied on energy sources such as traffic fuels and heating oils. Presently, energy taxation in the form of excise duties is a major source of financing for the State. In addition to the fiscal meaning at large, energy taxation is more and more a key instrument of energy, climate and environmental policy. As such, it is used to curb the growth of energy consumption while guiding energy generation and use towards alternatives that cause lower emissions. Finland was the first country in the world to introduce an explicit carbon dioxide tax on certain fuels. Taxation of heating fuels, being based on carbon dioxide and energy content of each fuel, as a complement, applies to facilities covered by the EU emissions trading scheme.

In 1994, an environmentally based excise duty on fuels was introduced by the Act on Excise Duty on Liquid Fuels (1472/1994, several amendments), the Act being at an early stage harmonized with EU law. Presently the Act covers in principle all liquid fuels and certain related products. From 2010, the excise comprises an energy content duty and a carbon dioxide duty. Regarding the assessment of the amount of carbon dioxide duty the equivalent carbon dioxide emissions emerging during the life cycle of the fuel are taken into account. Liquid fuel that is used in the production of electricity is as a rule free, as well as fuel for aircraft and ships in professional use. The duties regarding liquid fuels are enforced and controlled by the Tax Administration and the customs. In addition to excise duty, a strategic stockpile fee is levied on liquid fuels pursuant to the same Act.

75. Energy taxation regarding electricity, coal, peat, natural gas, biogas, pine oil and certain related products is based on the Act on Excise Duty on Electricity and Certain Fuels (1260/1996, several amendments). There are four tax categories: (1) energy content tax on electricity as excise duty, (2) carbon dioxide tax, (3) energy tax, and (4) surtax. Carbon dioxide tax is based on the equivalent carbon dioxide emissions emerging during the life cycle of the fuel. Additionally, a strategic security stockpile fee is levied on the same items except peat. Coal, peat and natural gas used for the production of electricity are exempted from the excise duty, because the duty is levied on the electricity produced by the power plant instead.

The producers and distributors of electricity are the main subjects liable to excise duty on electricity. Excise duty on electricity is divided into two tax brackets. Bracket II implies State aid. Also peat has been strongly subsidized, in spite of being fossil (the latest amendments 1164/2021). Peat extraction, having negative impacts on climate, biodiversity and water quality, but also certain local importance, and hence also the State aid, is one the major bones of content in the energy and environment politics today. Greener energy market and higher peat prices due to emissions trading have recently resulted in a remarkable reduction in the energy use of peat, but the sudden energy supply changes due to the Ukraine war have changed the overall view again.

Also this excise duty is enforced and controlled by the Tax Administration and the customs.

76. Waste tax under the Waste Tax Act (1126/2010, replacing its predecessor with the same title) is at least in principle one of the main fiscal means of environmental economic guidance. The tax on waste is levied in principle on all waste that is delivered and deposited to a public or private landfill, where waste classified as taxable can be deposited. Waste tax applies to waste deposited in landfill sites when the waste cannot be recovered on technical and environmental grounds. All waste specified in the tax schedule appendix to the Waste Tax Act is nevertheless subject to tax. The Waste tax is enforced and supervised by the Tax Administration and the customs.

The tax is charged from the operators of landfill sites, but of course the producer of waste is the ultimate payer in practice. Operators of landfills are obliged to register themselves for this purpose and take care on waste bookkeeping. The notion of waste is the same as in the Waste Act, but it moreover provided that the substance or item is included in the tax array annex to the Waste Tax Act. Anyway, toxic and dangerous waste does not fall within the scope of the Act.

77. The specific notion of landfill in the Waste Tax Act is important, as it does not encompass all different landfills entirely. Landfill is defined (section 3) as a site for waste management where waste is deposited onto or into land and for which an Environmental Permit under the Environmental Protection Act (or corresponding Åland law permit) is needed. As landfill is not regarded an area, being separated from any landfill, where: (1) waste is deposited separated from other waste temporarily for a period of less than three years before end treatment or recovery, or (2) only substances of soil and bedrock are deposited, or (3) separately collected biological waste or sludge from a community wastewater treatment plant is composted or otherwise biologically treated, or (4) the waste is recovered. Consequently, only final disposal of waste is subject to tax, but intermediate storage sites, landfills, compost sites and recovery sites for waste do not fall within the scope of landfill here.

Separately from other waste delivered waste that is reused in the very landfill for such constructions that are necessary for the establishing, use or termination thereof is always exempted from tax, glass waste and concrete waste consisting of pieces with a diameter of 150 millimetres excluded.

78. The tax rate is at present EUR 80 per tonne of waste. Tax is accounted for quarterly on the basis of waste delivered to the landfill site.

79. The application of the Waste Tax Act is normally not particularly problematic. This is not, however, always the case. In, e.g., SAC 2006:72 mixed waste had been placed in landfill A in the 1950s and 1960s. When renovating landfill A after September 1996 this largely decomposed waste was transferred to landfill B. The waste was regarded as taxable waste and not as contaminated soil. The scope problems are also otherwise often caused by industrial activities in particular situations and borderline cases (regarding, e.g., soil substances, construction waste, glass, temporary storing), *see* SAC 2010:76, 2018:185, 2022:16 and 2022:36.

80. The Act on production subsidies for electricity produced by renewable energy sources (1396/2010) has created a State aid mechanism in the shape of feed-in tariffs regarding wind power and renewable source fuels. The purpose of the Act is to promote production of electricity by renewable sources and competitiveness of such energy sources, to make production of electricity more diverse and improve self-sufficiency in electricity production. The Act is very favourable to new wind power industry, and it has been the main reason to a wind power boom in various parts of Finland from 2011 onwards. There is additionally a branch-internal mechanism of wind power promotion in the Act on the Compensation Areas for Wind Power (490/2013).

81. Even the basically American ideas of emission rights trading have already in the 1990s been presented among the economical means of protection of the environment, but it seems that the private ownership of affected land and waters – and also the duty of the government to strive to ensure for everyone an opportunity to influence the decision-making concerning one's environment, provided in section 20 of the Constitution Act – make this alternative unthinkable at least concerning water pollution and other location-relevant forms of pollution. The climate-focused protection of the total atmosphere under the Kyoto Protocol, Paris Agreement and EU law is of course something else. On the whole, administrative and legal means of protection prevail.

82. Certain European trends towards changing the focus of environmental regulation to voluntary or market-based mechanisms have not affected the total legislation to any significant extent. This is partly due to the fact that natural market mechanisms only in part cover the relevant environmental impacts. In terms of environmental economics, there is much left to do in order to internalize the externalities. For example, the compensations for individual damages may only cover part of the total degradation of the environment. Of course many branches of trade and industry have done respectable voluntary work for the environment, especially where the consumers are directly concerned. As for 'voluntary' or 'environmental' or 'negotiated' agreements, the pressure to enter into such agreements has generally been rather small also among the industries. One reason might be that law and decree drafting in Finland is traditionally very open, and the participation of both industry and environmental interests is quite normal at all stages. If, e.g., a decree is passed under a consensus, the difference between it and an agreement is insignificant for the interested parties, but all the annoying unsolved juridical problems which are for the time being inevitably connected to all environmental agreements are avoided.

In practice, there have been some agreements, but it seems that there should sometimes have been more parties to the agreements than there actually were. An agreement on packaging waste was in the early 1990s made between the package-producing industry and the Ministry of the Environment, but it turned out that it was problematic to the package-filling industry and to the municipalities having large powers with respect to domestic waste. Afterwards it became clear that the system had to be based on binding norms due to the then EC Directive on Packaging and Packaging Waste (94/62/EEC). But a system based on producer responsibility was adopted, and several other waste streams followed the same model. These arrangements had clearly something in common with voluntary agreements in that a good deal of practical decisions have been left to the enterprises collectively.

83. As for environmental agreements in general, the essential juridical problems are well-known in Europe. But concerning Finland, there is an additional obstacle to at least some types of agreements. This is due to section 20 of the Constitution Act, where it is provided that it is the duty of the government to strive to ensure that everybody has a possibility to influence the decision-making concerning one's environment. This makes at least those agreements unconstitutional where the environmental impacts are differentiated or located geographically. Also section 15 on the protection of ownership is inevitably problematic in these cases, as the owners of the areas under polluting impacts would not be parties to a typical agreement. It is clear that a mere hearing of the public is far from enough to meet these constitutional preconditions. (There is at least one more constitutional problem with the idea of binding the legislator with respect to a future legislation.) This suggests that agreements in the first place could be possible when concerning nationally coherent environmental requirements.

84. The Eco-Management and Audit Scheme (EC) (EMAS), based on the Regulation 761/2001/EC allowing voluntary participation by organizations in a Community EMAS, is also in use in Finland, although there is, like elsewhere, competition with the related other standards (ISO). The additional domestic provisions (on the competent bodies and accreditors, their tasks, fees, administrative procedures, language to be used, review of decisions of authorities by courts) which are necessary to make the application of the EMAS Regulation possible were initially included in the Act 1412/1994 (being formally linked to the former Regulation 1836/93/EEC). The present EMAS Act (121/2011), based on the Regulation (EC) No. 1221/2009 of 25 November 2009 on the voluntary participation by organizations in a Community EMAS, repealing Regulation (EC) No. 761/2001 and Commission Decisions 2001/681/EC and 2006/193/EC, has replaced that act (and the next one, 914/2002).

85. The competent national body according to Article 11 of the Regulation 1221/2009, being, *inter alia*, responsible for the registration of organizations under EMAS, is the Finnish Environment Institute. EMAS verifiers in Finland are accredited by the Finnish Accreditation Service (FINAS), a branch of the Finnish Safety and Chemicals Agency (Tukes) that is pursuant to the law in general responsible for organizing the various accreditation activities according to the international criteria (*see* the Act 920/2005). There are presently four EMAS registered organizations. However, the idea of environmental management of industries has anyway become very common within major companies, irrespective of any formal qualifications.

The decisions of the Finnish Environment Institute and the FINAS (regarding registration, removal of registration and accreditation) are to be subject to appeal to Regional Administrative Court. A supervisory provision (section 9 of the EMAS Act) imposes on the Finnish Environment Institute the duty to examine such faults in the environmental protection of a registered organization that have come to its knowledge. The institute has the power to request the relevant Centre for Economic Development, Transport and the Environment to examine the activity of a registered organization and give a statement on the matter. The organization is obliged to supply the institute or the centre with information necessary to assess whether the requirements in the Regulation have been fulfilled.

86. As for the Ecolabel, presently based on the Regulation (EC) No. 66/2010 on the EU Ecolabel Regulation, the national provisions are presently contained in the Act on the EU Ecolabel (832/2014), in a similar way than in the previous acts from 1994, 1997 and 2011. The national competent body pursuant to the Regulation is currently the limited company Ympäristömerkintä Suomi Oy (Environmental Labeling Finland). This solution is arranged by the Act 832/2014 through national provisions on competent body, administrative procedures, supervision, fees, reviewability by administrative courts, etc., reflecting the fact that the tasks of the competent body, i.e., of the company, have largely been regarded as belonging to public law. Due to the national provisions, the company hence acts in the Ecolabel tasks as a quasi-authority, the decisions of which are made under the Administration Act and also may be appealed to one of the Regional Administrative Courts. The legal responsibility of the personnel is the same as that of authorities. Market surveillance powers are vested in the Finnish Environment Institute.

There are currently about 40,000 products or services entitled to Ecolabel flower. There is also another environmental product and service label, the common Nordic Environmental Label, called the Swan Label and likewise administered by Ympäristömerkintä Suomi Oy. This practice is not prevented by the Regulation.

87. Within the internal market, the Act on the Requirements for Ecodesign and Energy Label of Products (1005/2008, with amendments), together with the decree 1043/2010, aims to contain the national provisions in respect to the Energy Labelling Regulation.[11]

The Act is applicable to products referred to in Article 1 of the Regulation and to energy-related products on which the EU has laid down product-group specific requirements. The Act is not applicable on means of transport for persons or goods. The Act contains requirements for ecodesign, conformity of energy-related products, requirements for energy labelling of energy-related products, inspection bodies, supervision, administrative enforcement and criminal sanctions, and fees, as well as administrative rectification and appeals. General steering is vested in the Ministry of Economic Affairs and Employment or, regarding construction products, in the Ministry of the Environment. On a practical level, it is the task of the Finnish Safety and Chemicals Agency (Tukes) to supervise the conformity of products. Controls at the Union's external borders pursuant to Regulation (EU) 2019/1020 on market surveillance and compliance of products and amending Directive 2004/42/EC and Regulation (EC) No. 765/2008 and (EU) No. 305/2011 are stipulated in the Act on the Market Surveillance of Certain Products (1137/2016, as amended).

88. Environmental protection enactments with a wide scope are mainly focused on other than market-based regulatory instruments. However, sometimes they also contain certain product-related market surveillance elements. A main example consists of fuels, products containing organic solvents and chemicals or products having an adverse effect on the atmosphere referred to in section 216 of the Environmental Protection Act, concerning which prohibitions and restrictions may be laid down in Government decree by virtue of the said section, as provided therein. The enforcement is in part based on market surveillance, as provided in section 24a and 24b (916/2021) of the Environmental Protection Act, in addition to the general regulations on market surveillance. The same applies to certain EU regulations implemented in and under the Environmental Protection Act. The task of market surveillance authority is vested in the Finnish Safety and Chemicals Agency (Tukes) with regard to products under Government decrees on organic-solvent-containing products, the Finnish Environment Institute with regard to Regulation (EC) No. 1005/2009 on substances that deplete the ozone layer, to Regulation (EU)

11. Regulation (EU) 2017/1369 of the European Parliament and of the Council of 4 Jul. 2017 setting a framework for energy labelling and repealing Directive 2010/30/EU.

No. 517/2014 on fluorinated greenhouse gases and to Government decrees on quality requirements for motor gasoline, diesel and certain other liquid fuels, and the Finnish Transport and Communications Agency Traficom with regard to Regulation (EU) No. 2016/1628 on requirements relating to gaseous and particulate pollutant emission limits and type-approval for internal combustion engines for non-road mobile machinery. Similarly, in the regime of the Waste Act, the Finnish Safety and Chemicals Agency as the market surveillance authority supervises compliance with the requirements concerning packaging, vehicles and their materials and parts, batteries and accumulators, as well as electrical and electronic equipment, as further specified in the Government decrees issued by virtue of section 10 of the Waste Act.

89. There are also environmentally founded enactments in some other market-oriented sectors. A good example is the Act on Environmental and Energy Efficiency Requirements for the Public Procurement of Vehicles and Transport Services (740/2021).

Chapter 5. Sources of Environmental Law

90. In Finland the primary source of law in most fields consists of statutory enactments. This is also the case for environmental law. In comparison with many other Western systems of environmental law, Finnish law in relation to pollution prevention differs in the sense that the role of fixed general emission standards and general standards for the quality of environment has, especially before the influence of EC law, been rather small. Most often, the limits for individual operators are traditionally set on a case-by-case basis by means of conditions (provisions, regulations) in the permit, or similar legal arrangements. In the field of water pollution prevention, case-by-case decision-making has been almost exclusive, whereas for air pollution prevention general standards have partly been used. This situation, however, had to some extent been changed due to European integration, since EC environmental legislation is largely based on general standards. Already the EEA agreement required extensive insertions of Community law from January 1994, and the EU membership from 1995 brought some more. However, it seems still that the basic system has been maintained. While the current EC requirements only were then added to it as supplements, the then new minimum standards usually had no practical effect, because they normally clearly met in the existing system. Today the overall picture is somewhat different.

91. The various enactments are formally divided into a few hierarchical categories. Among these the highest one consists of laws with a constitutional status, today mainly the Constitution Act. Constitutional provisions, fundamental rights and obligations included, have earlier had only indirect significance for environmental law, but also this has changed (not only due section 20 of the Constitution Act). The courts and administrative authorities have traditionally not been in a position to apply directly the rules of the Constitution, but also this situation has essentially changed (*see* General Introduction, Chapter 2, §2, above), although the mainstream of legal reasoning in judicial practice only occasionally operates directly with fundamental rights and obligations. The parliamentary enactments (in Finnish: *laki*; in Swedish *lag*) under the Constitution may be either ordinary acts or, now extremely seldom, 'exceptions to the Constitution' (*see* General Introduction, Chapter 2, §2, above), but as sources of law both groups are equal.

92. In Finland the legislation consists of enactments created during different periods. The earliest are derived from the Swedish era (up to 1809) and the Russian-dominated age of Autonomy (from 1809), but the majority have been enacted since independence (1917). Age is, of course, one of the factors affecting the manner of interpretation. Even repealed old enactments may still have practical relevance in some matters concerning Land law and Water Law (e.g., required water levels may at times be determined according to such a statute, if a hydroelectric plant has been built downstream in the distant past). In the field of environmental law most statutes are, however, relatively new. Because of the busy tempo of legislative work in recent decades the overall image of the environmental statutes is not always wholly consistent, a feature that has strongly been accentuated by the EU-based elements. This naturally has impacts on the interpretation and systematization of environmental law.

93. Several levels of regulation complement the parliamentary acts, within the limits of the Constitution. The governmental level is of course the most important. According to the dualistic system adopted in the Constitution Act of 1999, government level decrees are issued either by the Cabinet-only or by the Cabinet and the President of the Republic. According to the present terminology in force from March 2000, the latter are called Presidential Decrees *or* Decrees of the President of the Republic (in Finnish: *tasavallan presidentin asetus*; in Swedish: *republikens presidents förordning*). They are issued formally by the president upon the Cabinet's suggestion which is practically never altered by the president. Formerly all governmental decrees (except for those called 'decision of the government', *see* below) belonged to this category called plainly Decree (*asetus, förordning*). The main group in practice, however, now consists of Cabinet-only decrees called Government decrees[12] (in Finnish: *valtioneuvoston asetus*; in Swedish: *statsrådets förordning*). In the regime of environmental law, practically all governmental decrees belong to this category. Typically, these decrees usually include detailed explicatory regulation for the application and implementation of the corresponding act, within the powers set out in the Constitution and the respective act. They cannot, of course, alter the act itself. Practically all central environmental acts are followed by a general explicatory Government decree, e.g., the Environmental Protection Act by the Environmental Protection Decree, the Water Act by the Government decree on Water Management Matters, the Nature Protection Act by the Nature Protection Decree, the Land Use and Building Act by the Land Use and Building Decree, the Mining Act by the Government decree on mining and the Waste Act by the Government decree on Waste. Moreover, under all these acts there is also a number of more specific decrees in addition to the general decree.

94. There are also decrees for more specific purposes. If these are of a more technical nature, they are often issued by the competent ministry, where provided by parliamentary act. They are called Ministry Decrees or Decrees of (the relevant) Ministry (in Finnish: *ministeriön asetus*; in Swedish: *ministeriets förordning*).

95. Before March 2000, part of governmental norm decisions were, for historical and even casual reasons, formally not called decrees but 'decision of the government', literally 'Decision of the Council of State' (in Finnish: *valtioneuvoston päätös*; in Swedish: *statsrådets beslut*) or 'Decision of the Ministry' (in Finnish: *ministeriön päätös*; in Swedish: *ministeriets beslut*). These expressions still occur in the names of older decrees, where in force. (To avoid unnecessary questions, the expression Cabinet is used instead of the Council of State in this monograph. Likewise, also the decrees issued by the Cabinet are called Government decrees.) In practice, it was more and more a matter of chance whether a Presidential Decree or a 'decision of the government' was required by the relevant authorization within a

12. *See supra* n. 3.

parliamentary act. In some cases, important substantive environmental requirements were placed in a 'decision of the government', whereas a (Presidential) Decree at the same time paradoxically included mainly procedural rules. Today, all these are mostly covered by the category Government decree. Several of the pre-2000 decrees, although often partly amended, are still in force.

Also authorities below the ministries may according to the Constitution Act be by parliamentary act vested with the power to issue regulations on limited and less significant issues, often of a clearly technical and detailed nature. Even Bylaws issued by municipalities are made possible in certain acts.

96. The courts and the administrative authorities are obliged not to apply a decree (or any other regulation below parliamentary level) which conflicts with a parliamentary act (*see* General Introduction, Chapter 2, §2, above). This has not, however, great practical significance.

97. The enactments (all parliamentary acts, Presidential Decrees and Government decrees, and, in part, Ministerial Decrees and even regulations by lower level authorities) are traditionally published in the official 'Statute Book of Finland' (in Finnish: *Suomen säädöskokoelma*, in Swedish: *Finlands författningssamling*). Of some of the more technical Ministerial Decrees only the title, number and date are, however, published in the Statute Book of Finland; for the full texts of these decrees a ministry shall have a separate Ministerial Regulation Book. The last-mentioned system is largely used for the regulation of agricultural policies, but its significance for environmental law is small. The printed format of the Statute Book does not exist anymore, however, but it is available in electronic form as one of the entries in the freely accessible governmental website FINLEX, http://www.finlex.fi (in Finnish and Swedish).

In the Statute Book of Finland, original enactments, acts and decrees alike, as well as later amendments to them, are numbered annually in chronological order, and they are normally referred to by that number and the respective year, e.g., the Environmental Protection Act is number 527 from 2014, i.e., 527/2014 or, using the issuing date, 27.6.2014/527. Also in this monograph, when an enactment is mentioned for the first time, the Statute Book of Finland reference, e.g., '86/2000', is used. The numbers of later amendments are, following the domestic practice, normally omitted. It is worth noting that the consolidated up-to-date version usually can be found elsewhere, e.g., in commercial legislation books and also on the FINLEX.

98. Åland enjoys a largely autonomous legislative power under the Constitution Act, though some important sectors of national legislation are also valid on Åland. The public administration is largely a matter of Åland only, unlike, e.g., the judiciary. According to the Autonomy of Åland Act (1144/1991), the legislative powers in, among others, the fields of the protection of nature and the environment, of recreational use of nature, of Water Law, of building and land use planning and of neighbourhood relations are vested in the Åland legislature. Previously the scope of autonomy was somewhat smaller. As for compensations for environmental damages, to take an example, the definitions are unclear.

It is not easy to get a general idea of Åland's present environmental law. In this monograph it has not been possible to take the special status of Åland into account in various contexts. Today, the majority of environmental enactments is, anyway, autonomously enacted, which may in practice refer to the reception of national enactments as such or as modified, or, recently more and more, to a totally original Ålandic legislation. The Ålandic legislation is applicable before (State) courts, in practice especially before administrative courts (one for Åland separately, and the SAC). Unlike in the regime of value added taxation, Åland has no exceptional status in respect to the duties pursuant to EC legislation. The huge task of implementing the Community-relevant legislation and updating it in the small Åland has at times been problematic also regarding environmental enactments. The State Government is responsible for the implementation, but has practically no coercive powers. A major part of recorded Finnish non-implementation cases refer to Åland only.

99. Established custom is another recognized source of law in cases where the written statutes are silent. However, in the field of environment law it has, for obvious reasons, no practical relevance. General principles of law may also be regarded as sources of law, but in the field of environmental law the development of legislation has been so rapid that there has not been time enough to establish indisputable principles. True, there are certain well-known principles of environmental protection policy like the polluter pays principle, but they are (if recognized) manifested sooner as the *ratio legis* of certain enactments than as independent natural principles. Some of such principles of environmental law have, however, been included and even defined in environmental legislation, with certain legal relevance (*see also* Part I, Chapter 1, §7). However, the principal rules of civil law, public law and also criminal law may be highly relevant in situations sufficiently analogous to the proper application of those rules. Still, it ought to be borne in mind that Finnish environmental law usually cannot be divided into clearly discernible separate parts, e.g., along the supposed borderline between public law and private law.

100. Finland is not a Common Law country. This means that the role of court precedents is not so central as, e.g., in the Anglo-Saxon world. Nevertheless, the growing importance of judicial practice cannot be denied. Traditionally the most prominent decisions of the SC and the SAC are published annually in the Yearbooks of the two courts. As for the SAC, the number of published environmental decisions has been quite large for decades. The Yearbook today refers to the Internet sites of the courts; no printed version is not produced any more. The Yearbook decisions (and, as regards the SAC, a number more) are also included in the FINLEX, being freely accessible on the Internet http://www.finlex.fi/. The precedents are widely followed in practice. Despite this, they have traditionally not been recognized as having the formal status of a source of law. From the 1980s this has been altered, though. This is due to the process reforms regarding both the SC and, later, the SAC. The SC has long dealt almost only with precedent cases and a leave to appeal is always required. Also in the SAC, leave to appeal is now in an almost overall use, and the need to have a precedent is the main reason for granting a leave. *See also* paragraph 236.

101. Finland is a contracting party to almost all major international and regional European conventions and agreements in the field of environmental protection and nature conservation, although many of them today impact mainly through EU law. In addition, Finland has bilateral treaties with all its neighbours, especially as regards bordering waters. The border water treaties with Sweden and Russia contain specific decision-making systems regarding water management and pollution control.

The Nordic Convention on the Protection of the Environment (between Finland, Norway, Sweden and Denmark) of 1974 (in force from 1976) contains rules on activities with harmful transboundary impacts in cases where no specific agreement (like those for transboundary waters) exists. According to the Convention, the impacts in another country shall be given the same legal effects as the impacts in the own country. As for consents and preventive measures, the *locus standi* of various subjects from the neighbouring country shall be judged as if such a subject were a domestic one in the country where the activities are carried out. This applies both to courts and administrative authorities. The same principle applies for compensations for damages. Compensations have to be dealt with according to the rules of the country where the activities are carried out if those rules are more advantageous to the victim.

102. Environmental law is of course not an isolated sphere of legislation. As for general procedural rules, to take an example, the general provisions are as a starting point generally applicable. The Administration Act *(Hallintolaki/Förvaltningslagen*, 434/2003, later amendments) includes general rules on the procedures in administrative authorities (but not in administrative courts, unless referred to by other provisions). These rules (on hearings, incapacity, notifications, etc.) are, however, complemented and even replaced by the rules in various sectoral enactments. This holds good particularly within environmental law. Hence the permit procedures are largely regulated directly, e.g., by the Environmental Protection Act, the Land Use and Building Act (as of 1 January 2025, the Building Act) or the Water Act, and rules of the Administration Act often only fill possible gaps. As for the appellate stage, the (recently renewed) Administrative Judicial Procedures Act (808/2019) constitutes the generally applicable procedural regulation before the appellate administrative courts, but there are also here several modifications in the specific enactments. Moreover, the Municipality Act (410/2015) includes modifications to both the Administration Act and the Administrative Judicial Procedures Act (such as the municipal appeal (*see* Part V, Chapter 2 below), which however covers only part of the decisions of municipal bodies). Also the provisions of the Municipality Act are often strongly modified by specific enactments. All in all, the procedures for various environmental permits or land use planning are almost – but not totally – autonomous.

103. Concerning the procedures before the courts of general jurisdiction, the Procedural Code (part of the 1734 General Law of Sweden-Finland, being of course almost totally revised on various occasions) is applicable in civil and criminal proceedings (as complemented for criminal proceedings by another Act, 689/1997). In many respects, the Procedural Code and the Administrative Judicial Procedures Act, especially concerning appellate procedures, have gradually, and particularly in the

2019 reform, been made as similar to each other as possible. However, the procedure before administrative courts is in general clearly less expensive and requiring for parties than that before courts of general jurisdiction, especially since the 1993 reform of the Procedural Code. Statistically, administrative judicial procedure is oral in a minority of all cases, especially regarding environmental law. A general effort to take new means of data management and communication with and between parties in administrative courts (called HAIPA) is going on.

Part I. Pollution Control

Chapter 1. General Law

§1. Starting Points in Civil Law and Public Law

104. As already stated in Chapter 3 of the General Introduction, the private law regime of the Neighbourhood Relations Act (26/1920, with later amendments) had not been able to meet the requirements of modern environmental law, where more and more attention was paid to common interests and far-reaching environmental impacts. The main part of the present environmental legislation of Finland is mainly referred to as public law, although some enactments, especially the Water Act, are rather described as combinations of private law and public law. Other environmentally relevant legislation as a rule also includes more or less aspects of legal protection of individuals, and, e.g., the Environmental Protection Act (527/2014), as its predecessor with the same title (86/2000) may, with good reasons, be described also as a protection tool of private impacted interests, in addition to being of course the main instrument of pollution prevention in general. These features have nevertheless been weakened somewhat in the 2014 reform, in order to make the regulation more 'liberal' and 'effective'.

105. The Neighbourhood Relations Act includes (in section 17) a modernized wording a general ban on private nuisances, which means that nobody is allowed to use his property, i.e., land, building or room, in a way that any neighbour, inhabitant of nearby area, or someone in possession of land, building or room in the neighbourhood, is caused unreasonable nuisance through 'substances harmful to the environment, soot, dirt, dust, smell, damp, noise, vibration, radiation, light, heat, or other similar impacts'. When assessing the unreasonableness of the nuisance, attention shall be paid to local conditions, other usualness of the harm, the intensity and duration of the impact, the starting time of the nuisance, and other similar factors. Prior to 2000, the ban was not applied at all, if the neighbour established himself only after the activities began. This exception, called the principle of time priority, was, however, not applied if the nuisance appeared or increased significantly after such establishment. No automatic rule on time priority has been left in the environmental law reform of 2000, but starting time is one of the main factors for the overall assessment of the nuisance. Already before 2000 the principle had been essentially relativized by the Environmental Damages Act (*see* Part IV, Chapter 2, §2), as far as compensations for nuisance were at stake. In addition, no time priority applies to the public law regimes. It is therefore quite possible to order an activity to be stopped if it, e.g., poses a health risk or other forbidden environmental threat to the neighbours who have acquired their estate even after the activity was started. However, a valid permit decision under public law may of course prevent this.

106. Being originally a legal institution of private law, the ban was intended to be primarily applied by courts of general jurisdiction. Through various legislative reforms and decisions of the judiciary, it has, however, become an important piece of the system of general environmental law and is also largely applied by administrative authorities (and administrative courts). This is due to the many links between the Neighbourhood Relations Act and the Environmental Protection Act, in particular to the fact that the necessity of an Environmental Permit under the latter may, among several other things, be based on the possibility that forbidden nuisance will be caused by an activity or installation in its environs. If an Environmental Permit, or prior notification or registration of activity pursuant to the Environmental Protection Act, is needed, the courts of general jurisdiction have no power to order the nuisance to be removed. The injunction competence is instead vested in administrative environmental authorities, but, however, impacted persons have the power to initiate this procedure. Damage caused by nuisance (other than those between two apartments of a same building) is regarded as environmental damage under the Environmental Damages Act, which is normally decided upon by courts of general jurisdiction. However, foreseeable damage due to future (or, occasionally, past) pollution of surface waters caused by the permit applicant is decided upon by the Environmental Permit authority.

§2. The Integration of Control Systems

107. The present coherent system for integrated environmental decision-making under the Environmental Protection Act cannot be fully understood without knowledge on the past stages of the legislation. Previous law, being clearly sectoral and hence less integrated, is still also directly relevant in the sense that a small part of all pollution-related permits cases are still based on it.

108. A characteristic feature of the pollution control system was, until March 2000, that water pollution control was separated from the rest of pollution control. As a rule, the permitting competence and the supervisory competence belonged to the same administrative authorities, but in the system of the then Water Act the implementing authorities were strictly divided into bodies dealing with permit applications on the one hand and supervisory bodies on the other. Independent special courts, the then Water Courts, dealt with the discharge permit applications. Besides permit applications, the Water Courts also dealt with coercive injunction and prohibition matters, criminal actions, water lawsuits and certain appeals against other bodies, but the role as a permit authority was most prominent. The Water Courts were often described virtually as administrative bodies when carrying out their main duty, i.e., dealing with permit applications. On the other hand, the ex officio dealing with compensation issues was an integral part of the permit procedure. This originated actually in expropriation law.

109. All other sectors of pollution control were up to March 2000 based on administrative procedure, which overwhelmingly also meant a permit system. Private damages and compensations were wholly separate of this. A binding link between the two main regimes was the SAC, which was the supreme appellate body both in permit and enforcement cases under the Water Act and in various administrative consent and notification procedures within environmental law.

110. In addition to this dualism, there were several, partly independent permit (or notification) systems for pollution matters outside the then Water Act. The most important of these were the Air Emission Permit system according to the 1982 Air Pollution Prevention Act, the Location Consent system of the Public Health Act, the Location (nuisance law) Consent system of the Neighbourhood Relations Act and the Waste Permit system according to the then Waste Act. The last-mentioned permit now also covered processing of hazardous waste. The Noise Abatement Act in turn had a limited direct applicability, but noise abatement largely functioned through the permit and supervision systems of the Public Health Act and the Neighbourhood Relations Act.

Originally all these permits were separate of each other both procedurally and substantively, a situation that was widely considered unsatisfactory. The multiplicity of procedures meant that the same person, company or authority (as a rule, the bodies of the State and the municipalities are in the same position as private persons) needed several different permits or other decisions from authorities for one plant, etc., at the same time. And from a general point of view, it meant that a uniform consideration of all discharges, effluent and emissions generated in one plant was far from easy to achieve. Waste can in many cases be discharged into air and water interchangeably, and an overall assessment of the various environmental impacts may therefore well be regarded as an essential part of a proper permit procedure. Contradictory consent conditions were also possible and in certain situations even probable.

§3. The Subsequent Reforms Before 2000

111. Until 1991, the efforts to unify the system were not successful. This was partly due to the competition between two rival systems for decision-making in pollution control, i.e., the 'judicial' (competent as to water discharge permits) and the 'administrative' (competent as to other permits). Unification under the former was not politically approved, while landowners and industry (partly for different reasons) regarded the then Water Act system preferable from the legal point of view. In principle, the judicial permit system was far from discretionary, and the landowners were compensated in advance without bringing actions of their own. The latter would perhaps not have been maintained in an administrative permit system. However, the idea of a forensic decision-making system for air pollution control, waste management, etc., was not too realistic, either.

112. In the late 1980s, a governmental committee was set up to consider different solutions to the problem. The committee soon found it nearly impossible, at least in the short-term, to create a uniform decision-making system. The touchstone was again the Water Court system. But for the rest of the pollution control systems an overall consent procedure was proposed. This was to include the then two location systems, plus the then Waste Management Plans and the Hazardous Waste Processing Permit (later together the Waste Permit) as well as the then air pollution prevention notification procedures (later the Air Emission Permit). Only one application would have to be sent in and only one (permit) decision would be made. A government bill was introduced in the autumn of 1990. In 1991, this resulted in a new Environmental Permit Procedure Act (735/1991), which came into force in 1992. The reform included a combined Environmental Permit procedure, which left the then Water Act untouched. The reform was almost entirely of a procedural nature so that the decisions would still be made on the basis of existing substantive laws. Hence, the new permit was rather 'combined' than 'integrated'. This was largely regarded insufficient, and the situation understandably called for further reforms.

113. Due to later sector reforms, a combined Environmental Permit according to the Environmental Permit Procedure Act until February 2000 comprised, where applicable, the Location Consents according to the Neighbourhood Relations Act and the then Public Health Act (later the 1994 Public Health Act), the Waste Permit according to the then Waste Act and the Air Emission Permit according to the then Air Pollution Prevention Act. The combined permit was required when any of the decisions mentioned was necessary for the activities, except for the Location Consent of the Neighbourhood Relations Act, which alone did not make a combined permit necessary.

§4. The 2000 Integration Reform

114. From the mid-1990s, a far more radical reform was looming ahead, mainly due to the then Directive 96/61/EC concerning Integrated Pollution Prevention and Control (IPPC), but also the domestic need to create a uniform permit system for all kinds of emissions, discharges, nuisances and pollution risks became more and more eminent. Nevertheless, many of the obstacles still existed. In the legislative work, the possibility of maintaining a partly sectoral system was considered. It was in fact noticed that Article 7 of the IPPC Directive allowed a system with more than one permit authority for one application, provided that certain procedural and substantive requirements were met. However, the option with separate Water Courts as sectoral permit authorities was rejected, for more reasons than one.[13] However, it was evident from the outset that the new permit system would cover about the same activities and installations as the then existing laws. This naturally resulted in a far more extensive scope of application than that of the IPPC Directive. The legislative alternative where merely IPPC-level permits that would have been integrated but had been rejected at an early stage.

13. On the debate, *see* Yearbook of European Environmental Law 1998, 479.

115. A coherent Environmental Protection Act, the first codification of Finnish pollution prevention law, was proposed by two parallel governmental committees in 1995 and prepared further by the government. After years of law drafting and public debate, the proposal Act, being the core enactment among a totality of twenty-seven new or amended acts, including those of the very large Water Act, was introduced to Parliament in September 1999. The bill was dealt with in a relatively short time – especially in relation to the uncommonly huge scope thereof. Perhaps surprisingly, no serious political obstacles existed any more. Although the parliamentary proceedings were finished in December 1999, the formal approval by the president could not take place until February 2000, for technical reasons. The new legislation entered into force on 1 March 2000. Due to the scope of the new legislation, a special Act on the complicated transitional arrangements was also enacted.

Åland has pollution prevention regulations of its own.

116. The reform of 2000 was profound in many respects. Above all, the new framework integrated the various permit systems into one. Hence the previous Air Pollution Prevention Act, the Noise Abatement Act and the Environmental Permit Procedure Act were totally repealed, and the scopes of applicability of, e.g., the then Water Act, the Public Health Act, the then Waste Act and the Neighbourhood Relations Act were more or less essentially reduced. In general, the pollution-centred and permit-related parts of the latter were upset. Also other important changes of legislative structure were made. The competence borderline between courts and administration was altered. Even one category of special courts, i.e., the three Water Courts, was affected, and independent administrative permit authorities, the three Environmental Permit Offices, were established instead. Also in a few other respects, the organizational solutions were significant. The Environmental Permit Offices started to act as permit authorities in the most important pollution cases under the Environmental Protection Act and in all cases pursuant to the remaining parts of the Water Act (construction, water regulation, water intake, etc.). The Regional Environment Centres (now Centres for Economic Development, Transport and the Environment) and the Municipal Environmental Protection Authorities also became permit (and supervision) authorities according to the Environmental Protection Act, depending on rather complicated competence rules based mainly on the size and significance of the activity at stake.

Due to the general reform of regional administration in 2009, there are today only two levels of permit authorities under the Environmental Protection Act, namely the Regional State Administration Agencies (environmental permit divisions) and the Municipal Environmental Protection Authorities. The main task of the Centres for Economic Development, Transport and the Environment (environmental divisions) under the Environmental Protection Act is supervision and enforcement (but under the Water Act only supervision, but enforcement mainly not). This is the state of affairs also after 2014, pursuant to the updated Environmental Protection Act (527/2014).

117. Following the previous legislation, the provisions from 2000 on, both substantive and procedural, are relevant not only for pollution prevention in general, but also for legal protection of various private rights and interests. This trait was affected and even strengthened in 2000 by the fact that the Constitution Act of Finland, section 20 provides that it is the duty of the government to strive to ensure for everyone the right to a healthy environment and the opportunity to influence the decision-making concerning one's environment. One of the important tools here is made up by environmental permit systems as frames for participation and means of horizontal legal protection of affected individuals and their properties. In the 2014 reform, some of these traits were weakened, however.

The present Environmental Protection Act of 2014 mainly follows the main lines of the 2000 Act, although the number of sections is far higher. A main novelty in the present Environmental Protection Act is that the formerly more overall applicable regulation has been scaled depending on whether an Directive on industrial emissions (IED) installation,[14] i.e., one to which the IED Directive, or the Industrial Emission Directive (2010/75/EU) applies. Where not, a permit may nevertheless be required, depending on the installation or activity, but regarding a smaller group of activities than before. Where no permit is required, a prior notification may be required instead. And where none of these is required, the installation or activity may anyway be subject to a registration duty pursuant to the Act.

§5. The Starting Points of the Environmental Protection Act

118. The proper sections of the Environmental Protection Act of 2014, about 270 in all, and its annexes, supplemented by the Environmental Protection Decree (713/2014), include, of course, all the main requirements of the IED (previously IPPC) Directive and also a remarkable amount of other EU pollution-related directives for stationary activities or installations. Detailed provisions are largely left to topic-specific decrees under the Act (based on the empowering provisions particularly in sections 9–10). Officially the present Environmental Protection Act is declared to implement (which in most cases meant re-implementation) totally or partially altogether about forty various EU directives. A number of others have been implemented by amendments after 2014. In addition, the Act encompasses complementary provisions to EU regulations.

119. Due to the integration approach, the legislative solutions in the Environmental Protection Act of 2000 were, and in the 2014 Act are intended to be as non-sectoral as possible, provided that applicable EU law has left scope for domestic options. However, some sectoral provisions are still more or less visible in the Environmental Protection Act, in particular where the provisions in question for natural reasons only apply to certain ambient sector and respective impacts. For example, the provisions on the obligations of the Environmental Permit holder in respect to

14. The expression in the Act literally translated: 'directive installation'. This is perhaps suitable for the tongue of the less acquainted, but it is far from logical, because the Environmental Protection Act aims to implement dozens of environmental directives in addition to the IED.

fisheries management, being only applicable to wastewater discharge, are practically identical to those in the Water Act (those applicable to various water management and construction projects).

120. The scope of applicability of the Environmental Protection Act is, among other things, for large parts based on the very extensive notions of 'emission' and 'pollution of the environment' defined in section 5 of the Act. As a starting point, all industrial and other activities that cause or may cause pollution of the environment are covered, pursuant to section 2(1).

'Emission' means according to section 5(1)(1) any direct or indirect release, discharge or deposit of substances, energy, noise, vibration, radiation, light, heat or odour caused by human activity from point or diffuse sources into air, water or onto land.

According to the definition in section 5(1)(2), as 'pollution of the environment' (or: 'environmental pollution') is regarded any emission that either alone or together with other emissions:

(a) causes adverse health effect;
(b) is detrimental to the nature and its functions;
(c) prevents or materially hinders the use of natural resources;
(d) causes a loss of general amenity of the environment or of special cultural values;
(e) reduces of suitability of the environment for general recreational use;
(f) causes damage or harm to property or to use of it; or
(g) constitutes other comparable violation of public or private interest.

According to an additional definition, as 'adverse health effect' is regarded 'disease that can be diagnosed in people, other health disorders or the presence of a factor or circumstance that may impair the health of the population or the healthiness of an individual's living environment'.

121. As an 'operator of activity', a notion by which a major part of the various obligations set forth by the Act are specified, is defined by section 5(1)(8) as any natural or juristic person who operates an activity causing risk of pollution or who de facto is in charge thereof.

'An activity that poses a risk of pollution' in turn means such establishment or use of an installation and such an activity which is from technical and operational viewpoint closely connected to it, or such arranging of an activity, that environmental pollution may be caused (section 5(1)(3)).

122. Pursuant to a basic general provision in section 7(1), operators shall organize their activities in such a way that environmental pollution can be prevented in advance. Moreover, where pollution cannot be fully prevented, it shall be limited to the lowest level possible. Emissions from their activities into the environment and to sewerage systems shall be limited to the lowest level possible. These obligations bind all operators and activities under the Act, irrespective of necessity of permit or registration duty (unlike section 8 of the Act, see paragraph 142 below).

123. In addition to the activities that cause or may cause pollution of the environment, the Act is applicable to any activities that generate waste and to waste treatment or disposal (section 7(2)). Those activities are, however, in many other respects covered by the Waste Act, the provisions of which are in turn in many respects directly applicable in the permit system of the Environmental Protection Act.

There are nevertheless certain exceptions of general nature on the scope of application, such as discharges caused by the normal use of vessels for which there is separate legislation. Hence the Environmental Protection Act does not apply to activities under the Act on Environmental Protection in Maritime Transport (*see* Chapter 4, §8, II below). Also the activities outside Finland regulated in the Marine Pollution Prevention Act (1415/1994) are excluded (*see* Chapter 4, §8, II below) Likewise, the Environmental Protection Act is not applicable to the prevention of adverse effects caused by radiation, but merely not as far as the prevention is provided in the Nuclear Energy Act or the Radiation Act (*see* Chapter 7 below). This means that, e.g., such emissions to the environment that include radiating substance are normally covered by the Environmental Protection Act.

The Environmental Protection Act has a scope of application which in general is of course different from, e.g., those of the Nature Protection Act or the Land Use and Building Act. However, there are some important connections and overlapping provisions. It is, e.g., provided that no activity for which Environmental Permit, prior notification or registration is required, may be located against a local Detailed Plan according to the Land Use and Building Act (as of 1 January 2025, the Land Use Act), as provided in section 12 of the Environmental Protection Act. Even more widely, all provisions of the Nature Protection Act and all decisions based on it are directly applicable to applications for Environmental Permits (section 48(3) of the Environmental Protection Act).

124. In any case, the total scope of application of the Environmental Protection Act is very extensive and, e.g., far extends the regime of the IED Directive, particularly insofar as the permit system is concerned. Regulating through permits may for good reasons be described as the most important instrument of the Act. The previous Act of 2000 covered practically all stationary activities with a relevant pollution risk, but in the present 2014 Act the environmentally less preventive and less participatory notification and registration mechanisms gained terrain instead of Environmental Permit.

125. Important exceptions in the general control are made up by activities causing pollution of soil or groundwater. Both forms of pollution, mere relevant risk thereof included, are totally forbidden (sections 16 and 17 of the Environmental Protection Act), those being in line with the previous provisions in the former Waste Act and Water Act. There is also of course a link to permits here, because a project with such probable risks could not be permitted at all. The previously separate regimes of groundwater pollution prevention (Water Act) and soil pollution prevention (Waste Act) have here been merged. This has been made possible by the integrated pollution prevention approach of the Environmental Protection Act (admittedly, though, to the disadvantage of water-centred integration, because groundwater is in other respects still protected and regulated by the Water Act). Chapter 14 of the Environmental Protection Act deals with the permits, notifications and coercive measures with respect to the reinstatement of polluted soils and groundwater. Where soil or groundwater already is polluted, one administrative decision may at the same time flexibly contain both (administrative) injunction-type and permit-type ingredients (*see* Part I, Chapter 6 below).

126. Pollution of seas outside Finnish territorial waters and exclusive economic zone, i.e., pollution of international seas or territorial waters of another country (where caused by an activity within Finland's own territorial waters or in land area), is absolutely forbidden (sections 18(1)) and 211 of the Environmental Protection Act, as well as dumping of waste in the territorial waters or the economic zone (section 18(2)); on dumping in other sea areas *see* Chapter 4, §8 below.

127. If an activity provided in the Environmental Protection Act causes environmental impacts in another country, the impact is, when applying the Act, taken into account like a similar impact in Finland, if not otherwise agreed upon with the State at stake. As said above, the bans in section 18 are applied also to the territorial waters or economic zone of another State (section 211 of the Act).

If the permit by a body specified in the border river agreement with Sweden, an Environmental Permit is not required on the basis of section 27(2)(1) or 27(2)(2) only. What has been decided by such a body has to be taken into account in an Environmental Permit (section 211(2) of the Act).

128. However, also many other instruments have been used for various purposes, mainly targeting other items than installations and stationary activities. In addition to the Environmental Permit, notification and registration systems, the Environmental Protection Act encompasses provisions directly applicable in activities (or authorizations to issue provisions of that kind by decrees), on a variety of environmentally relevant items. The directly applicable provisions also include certain market-oriented and largely EU-based provisions on the environmental requirements of chemicals and machines and products, although mainly laid down in specific decrees under the Act (based on sections 216 and 217 of the Act). Chemicals are in general, but largely only complementary to European Parliament and Council Regulation Concerning the Registration, Evaluation, Authorization and Restriction of Chemicals (REACH) Regulation, regulated in the Chemicals Act (599/2013), and in the Act on the Safety of the Handling of Dangerous Chemicals and Explosives (390/2005), and the safety of consumer products in the Consumer Safety Act (920/2011).

129. The declaration-level purpose of the Environmental Protection Act pursuant to section 1 of the Act is to: (1) prevent pollution of the environment and risk of thereof, prevent and reduce emissions, eliminate adverse impacts caused by pollution and prevent environmental damage; (2) safeguard a healthy, pleasant, ecologically sustainable and biologically diverse environment, support sustainable development and combat climate change; (3) promote sustainable use of natural resources, reduce the amount and harmfulness of waste, and prevent adverse impacts caused by waste; (4) make the assessment of activities causing pollution and the consideration of the impacts as a whole more effective; and (5) improve the opportunities of citizens to affect decision-making concerning the environment.

130. The main authorities in the decision-making pursuant to the Environmental Protection Act are the Regional State Administrative Authorities, the Centres for Economic Development, Transport and the Environment, and the Municipal Environmental Protection Authorities, and for supervision, the two last-mentioned. Among other authorities, the Finnish Environment Institute acts as the competent authority under Regulation (EC) No. 1005/2009 on substances that deplete the ozone layer and Regulation (EU) No. 517/2014 on fluorinated greenhouse gases and repealing Regulation (EC) No. 842/2006, and supervises compliance with these regulations, unless otherwise provided. In addition, the Institute maintains and develops the exchange of information on the BAT, monitors the development of the BAT and communicates about them. Moreover, the Institute is responsible for monitoring and renovating shipwrecks that pose a risk of environmental damage, unless otherwise provided by law, and for arranging the treatment of animals contaminated as a result of oil or other chemical spills.

§6. Authorizations on Issuing Decrees under the Environmental Protection Act

131. The authorizations regarding decrees under the Environmental Protection Act, in sections 9 and 10, but also in several other sections, refer to a wide range of detailed environmental requirements targeting emissions, environmental quality, technical specifications of various activities, diffuse sources of pollution, as well as certain products, substances and machines. Many of the decree provisions are directly applicable in private activities, but only the authorities normally apply others. In many cases a provision is applicable in both ways. As a starting point, the obligations imposed by decrees are only minimum requirements, but in practice they may at times also appear as maximum requirements, particularly so, if there is no procedure where the level needed could be properly assessed.

Sector-specific Government decrees typically contain detailed environmental requirements for a category of activities (sections 9 and 10). The decrees are partly applied, as standardized minimum requirements, by the permit authority when laying down provisions in a permit (where needed), and otherwise, in cases of mere registration duty, where any, primarily by the operator himself. Some decrees have no direct relationship at all to the permit, registration or notification mechanism. In addition to the product-related decrees under the Act, a good example is made up by Government decree on petrol vapour recovery at distribution stations (1085/2011, issued by virtue of the previous Act, but remained in force in 2014, amended in 2016 due to Directive 2014/99/EU amending Directive 2009/126/EC). On the contrary, Government decree on landfills (331/2013, remaining in force under the present Environmental Protection Act) is in practice always applied in Environmental Permit contexts, as Environmental Permit for landfills is comprehensively required (Table 1(13)(g) and Table 2(13)(f) of Annex 1 to the Environmental Protection Act together).

Some of decrees also contain unconditional prohibitions, as Government decree on environmental requirements on installations producing titanium dioxide (712/2014) regarding substances and wastes listed in section 2 of the Act. This decree is also cross-sectoral, as it sets limit values for both discharges to waters and emissions to the air.

132. The Cabinet is entitled to issue by Government decrees necessary provisions in order to prevent and reduce pollution of the environment, in addition to general requirements, as more specifically provided in sections 9–10. In practice, many of the decrees follow more or less closely the respective EU directives.

According to section 9 of the Environmental Protection Act, Government decrees can be issued to specify further the obligations in sections 7 and 8:

(1) on emissions to the environment or to a sewerage system, on the prevention and limitation of emissions and their adverse impacts, and on the prohibition of emissions;
(2) on the monitoring of emissions and emission limit values of activities subject to a permit, notification or registration requirement;
(3) on the obligation of operators of activities subject to a permit, notification or registration requirement to provide information on emissions and their impacts to the authority specified by Government decree;
(4) on the obligation of operators of activities subject to a permit, notification or registration requirement to provide the authority specified by Government decree with information on raw materials, fuels and other chemicals used in the activities, waste generated by the activities and the treatment of waste as part of the activities;
(5) on the expertise required for various activities subject to a permit, notification or registration requirement; and
(6) on the limitation of the release or depositing of sludge in the environment or on the prohibition of the release or depositing of sludge in the environment that poses a risk of environmental pollution.

133. Section 10 includes an authorization to specify by Government decree further environmental pollution prevention provisions on:

(1) environmental protection requirements and conditions for the siting of activities in different areas, and the distance requirements necessary for preventing adverse impacts from the activities;
(2) methods, equipment, buildings and structures used to prevent emissions and the spread thereof, to prevent accidents or the risk thereof, and to ensure energy efficiency;
(3) the extent and operating times of the activities;
(4) waste management; and

(5) measures after the termination of the activities.

The decree provisions here may, however, exclusively apply to one of the following:

(1) energy production plants with a thermal input under 50 megawatts;
(2) asphalt plants;
(3) distribution stations for liquid fuels;
(4) activities in which organic solvents are used;
(5) treatment of waste;
(6) agriculture, livestock farming, fur farming or forestry;
(7) peat production;
(8) fish farming;
(9) rock-crushing plants, stone quarries or other quarry operations;
(10) treatment or discharge of urban wastewater; or
(11) stationary concrete stations or concrete product factories.

134. Presently the necessity to have an Environmental Permit, or a notification duty, is provided in the very Environmental Protection Act, albeit in detail by annexes, not any more by decree under the Act. Due to this, Chapter 4 of the Act contains clearly less empowerments to issue decrees than the respective stipulations in the previous Act.

135. A specific category of Government decrees refers to the quality of the environment (Chapter 15 of the Environmental Protection Act), *see* §18 below.

136. General environmental requirements on the planning, maintenance and use of machines and accessories are laid down in section 217(2) of the Act. More detailed provisions on the same may be issued by Government decree. Government decrees on fuel, chemicals and products may be issued by virtue of section 216.

137. When preparing Government decrees referred to in Chapter 2, 14 or 15 of the Act, or in section 216 or 219, the authorities and others whose activities the item particularly concerns, shall be provided with an opportunity to give an opinion.

§7. General Obligations and Principles of the Environmental Protection Act

138. General obligations and principles are provided in Chapter 2 of the Environmental Protection Act. Regarding environmental quality, the general obligations regarding environmental quality are provided in Chapter 15 of the Act.

139. A general knowledge requirement for operators is provided in section 6. Pursuant to this, an operator shall have knowledge of the environmental impacts and risks of his activities, and of the management of these impacts and risks and ways to reduce adverse impacts.

140. A general obligation for operators to prevent and limit environmental pollution is provided in section 7(1), *see* paragraph 122. In addition to this, activities that pose a risk of environmental pollution shall comply with the general obligations and principles laid down in the Waste Act (646/2011), Chapter 2, and with the general principles regarding the safe use of chemicals and the obligations to prevent environmental pollution and the risk thereof, as provided in the Chemicals Act (599/2013) and EU chemicals legislation.

141. Section 20 of the Environmental Protection Act stipulates the following general principles concerning activities posing a risk of environmental pollution:

(1) proper care and precaution shall be taken to prevent environmental pollution as entailed by the nature of the activity, and the probability of pollution, risk of accidents and possibilities to prevent accidents and limit their impacts shall be taken into account (principle of precaution and care); and
(2) a combination of various measures shall be used in providing appropriate and cost-effective means to prevent pollution (principle of BEP).

142. Further general obligations regarding prevention of pollution (section 8 of the Environmental Protection Act) apply to any environmental pollution caused by an activity subject to a permit requirement (Chapter 4 of the Act), notification requirement (section 115a) or registration requirement (Chapter 11) requirement. Pursuant to section 8, the operator shall ensure and verify the following:

(1) the BAT is used in the activity;
(2) energy use in the activity is efficient;
(3) the emissions caused by the activity and the impacts thereof are monitored, and the authorities are provided with the necessary information about the emissions and impacts, the raw materials, fuels and other chemicals used in the activity, the waste generated by the activity and the waste treated in the activity; and
(4) the operator has access to sufficient expertise in terms of the nature and scope of the activity.

143. General provisions on the location of activities, applicable to all stationary risks of pollution, are set forth in section 11. Pursuant to this, all activities with a pollution risk have, as far as possible, to be located in such a way that pollution or risk thereof does not result and that pollution can be prevented. In the assessment of the suitability of the location attention shall be paid to:

(1) the nature, duration and timing of the activity and the significance of its impacts, the probability of pollution occurring, and the accident risk;
(2) the sensitivity of the impact area to environmental pollution;
(3) the significance of the activity in terms of the health and attractiveness of the human living environment;

(4) the intended use of the site and the impact area, as indicated in a land use Plan with legal effects according to the Land Use and Building Act (as of 1 January 2025, the Land Use Act); and
(5) other possible sites in the area.

144. The provision in section 11 is complemented by section 12 on direct legal effect of a land use plan in the siting. An activity subject to a permit, notification or registration requirement may not be placed in contravention of a valid Detailed Plan according to the Land Use and Building Act (as of 1 January 2025, the Land Use Act). In addition, in areas with a valid Regional Plan or a legally binding Master Plan with legal effects, it shall be ensured that the siting of the activity does not impede the intended use of the area indicated in the plan.

145. A specific siting provision (section 13) refers to peat production only (on peat extraction, *see also* Part II, Chapter 7, §3 below). The provision is not a typical one in the Environmental Protection Act, because it does not refer to pollution prevention, but to values of nature. The explanation is that there is in practice no other decision-making system with overall application to peat projects than the Environmental Permit, in which water pollution has normally the main focus. The environmental problems of peat extraction refer to climate impacts, natural values and water pollution, but the heated political discussion has often resulted in focusing separately one sector only. Section 13 is a good example of this (but it does not mean that siting from, e.g., water protection viewpoint would be irrelevant otherwise, this due to section 11).

Pursuant to section 13, peat production shall not lead to the deterioration of nationally or regionally significant natural values. When assessing the significance of the natural values, the endangeredness of the mire species and mire habitats occurring at the site as well as the importance and extent of the occurrence, and the extent to which the mire is in a natural state shall be taken into account. Correspondingly, the importance of the site to natural values outside of it shall also be taken into account in the assessment of significant natural values. Nevertheless, the activity may be sited in an area if this does not endanger the preservation of the natural values referred to above, or if the application of the main rule above prevents the implementation of activities important to the public interest, and if there are no other obstacles to granting the required permit. Section 13 does not apply if the natural values at stake have already been taken into account in a valid Regional Plan or in a valid Master Plan with legal effects, provided that the peat activity is in the plan located in an area reserved for it. A further exception is possible if the natural state of the mire has been significantly altered due to ditching.

146. The actual judicial relevance of each principle and general duty often eventually depends on other, more specific provisions of the Act. It has been explicitly provided in section 175(4) that administrative enforcement is not available for the direct implementing of section 11 or section 20. However, e.g., the general location provisions of section 11 are directly applicable as permitting requirements. Many of the general provisions have a contextual role as one ingredient in the permit consideration.

147. The case of the BAT requirement is more complicated. According to the definition (section 5), BAT means:

> as effective and advanced as possible, technically and economically feasible methods of production and treatment as well as of planning, constructing, maintenance, use and termination of the activity, by which methods pollution of the environment caused by the activity can be prevented or most effectively reduced, and which are also suitable as the basis for provisions in an Environmental Permit.

According to a complementary definition in section 5, 'techniques are technically and economically feasible when they are generally accessible and can be implemented in the relevant industrial sector for reasonable costs'. Pursuant to section 53, the assessment of the BAT shall take into account the following:

(1) the reduction of the quantity and harmfulness of waste;
(2) the possibility of recovery and reuse of materials used and waste generated in production;
(3) the hazardousness of the materials used and the potential for using less hazardous alternatives;
(4) the quality, quantity and impact of emissions/discharges;
(5) the quality and consumption of raw materials used;
(6) energy efficiency;
(7) the prevention of risks and accident hazards in the activity, and the prevention of adverse impacts in the event of an accident;
(8) the time needed for introducing the BAT and the importance of the starting date for launching operations, and the costs and benefits of preventing and limiting emissions;
(9) impacts in the environment;
(10) the production methods in use on an industrial scale and methods for controlling emissions;
(11) developments in technology and knowledge of the natural sciences;
(12) information on BAT published by the European Commission or international bodies.

148. In Environmental Permit contexts BAT is one, but only one, of the several criteria on issuing a permit and on the contents thereof. It is required here that the regulations laid down in any permit are based on BAT (section 52(3)). However, many parallel requirements have also to be met, and it is quite possible that a permit has to be denied totally or partially irrespective of the fulfilment of BAT, e.g., due to excessive impacts or unsuitable location (*see also* paragraph 206). This holds good particularly in respect to activities other than of typical industries. In such activities technically clear-cut and measurable emissions may lack and a BAT level is not always so comprehensible or environmentally sufficient (peat extraction, fish farming, animal husbandry, etc.). For such activities, the provision in section 52(3) requiring that the permit regulations shall not oblige the operator to apply only one specific technique, are not comprehended in such a literal manner as in the case of industries, especially not, if the setting of the regulation is due to another basis than BAT.

149. Environmental Permits for IED installations (Chapter 7) are, however, a special case also when BAT is concerned. Indeed, BAT is the crucial tool for permitting such installations, due to the IED directive. The additional regulation here is rather multilayered. The following definitions (section 72) make up a starting point here:

(1) reference document means a document prepared in accordance with Article 13 of the IED that describes for the activity in question the applied techniques, emissions and consumption levels, techniques considered for the determination of BAT and the preparation of the relevant conclusions, and emerging techniques;
(2) conclusions means a decision of the European Commission adopted in accordance with Article 13(5) of the IED that contains those parts of the reference document presenting conclusions on the BAT, the descriptions of these techniques and information to assess their applicability, the emission levels, monitoring and consumption levels associated with the techniques and, where appropriate, site remediation measures; and
(3) emission levels mean the range of emission levels obtained under normal operating conditions using a BAT or a combination of techniques, as described in the conclusions, expressed as an average over a given period of time under specified reference conditions.

150. An operator being in charge of an activity subject to permit requirement or notification requirement shall be prepared for measures needed for the prevention of accidents and other exceptional situations and for the limitation of harmful consequences to health and environment. An emergency plan has to be prepared and other precautionary measures taken, as provided in section 20. However, an emergency plan is not required if the supervisory authority considers it unnecessary due to the impacts and risks, or if a corresponding plan has been drawn up under another act, or for farm animal facility (section 19).

§8. The Integrative Approach

151. The provisions on the integrated permit system are applicable irrespective of whether, say, air pollution, water pollution, noise, smell, or a combination of the impact types is at stake. An Environmental Permit is needed for a wide range of various (stationary) activities that being a result of the variety of the relevant environmental impacts and risks. Installations in need of an Environmental Permit range from industries of various types to municipal sewers, landfills, other waste management facilities, animal husbandry, fish farms, fur farms, airports, motor circuits, quarries, harbours, bus depots, shooting ranges, etc., as specified in the Act. Although the same basic provisions, procedural and substantive, are at the same time applicable, e.g., to a large oil refinery and a rather small fur farm, this seems to be no real problem. Naturally there is differentiation in practice depending on the type of emission and on the actual environmental media. The permit system itself seems to be adjustable in many respects, which is also reflected by the three categories of permit authorities. In spite of this, the present Environmental Protection Act has removed several categories of activities from the Environmental Permit regime to the new notification and registration duty categories, at least as a main rule.

152. Prior to 1 March 2000, the need to have a permit depended on the then sectoral legislation, which in turn was based either on positive lists or general descriptions or a combination. Concerning waters, the general notion of 'pollution in a water body' as such was most crucial, as any discharge resulting in a mere risk of pollution needed a permit according to the then Water Act. 'Pollution' here encompassed all kinds of harm to private or public interests. This legislative arrangement was related to the function of the permit system as a safeguard of private property interests of the affected parties, and it has been preserved in the Environmental Protection Acts of 2000 and 2014 (*see* Chapter 4, §1, II below). Also regarding nuisance to neighbours, a general nuisance clause constituted, and still constitutes, necessity of a permit.

153. In the course of different legislative reforms, installation lists or other 'mechanical' ways to express necessity of permit have gained terrain, but the case-by-case assessments for the same purpose have not disappeared, either.

§9. Criteria for the Necessity of an Environmental Permit

154. The current Environmental Protection Act of 2014 differs from its predecessor (2000) in that the regulation on the necessity of a permit is no more divided between the Environmental Protection Act and the Environmental Protection Decree. All the relevant provisions here are now included in the very Act, albeit for detailed parts in an annex (Annex 1) to the Act, instead of the Decree. This structural change was mainly due to constitutional reasons, as delegation of norm issuing competence from the Parliament to the government in a significant matter like this was so avoided.

155. A general permit requirement is laid down in section 27 of the Act, by reference to Annex 1. An Environmental Permit is required for activities, posing a risk of environmental pollution, referred to either in Annex 1, Table 1 (IED installations) or in the 'domestic' Table 2. Provisions on the livestock unit coefficients used to determine the permit requirement of farm animal facilities in certain cases are provided in Annex 3.

156. Table 1 of Annex 1 is equivalent to Annex I to the IED, although the sequence in the Table is somewhat different, in order to facilitate comparison with Table 2 of Annex 1.

157. The 'domestic' list in Table 2 of Annex 1 creates necessity of an Environmental Permit in addition to the IED installations. The technical aim in Table 2 has been that the quantitative upper thresholds ('not exceeds') in it are identical to the corresponding lower thresholds ('exceeds'), where any, in Table 1. The list in Table 2 is as follows:

(1) Forest industry:
  (a) Floating basins for unbarked timber that hold at least 20,000 cubic metres of timber at any one time, but excluding floating basins with a closed water treatment system.
  (b) Installations producing oriented strand board, particleboard or fibreboard, with a production capacity of at least 10,000 cubic metres per year and not exceeding 600 cubic metres per day, or installations producing or surface-treating plywood or other wood-based boards, with an annual production capacity of at least 10,000 cubic metres.
  (c) Wood impregnation plants with a production capacity not exceeding 75 cubic metres per day, or other plants using wood preservatives where the volume of preservatives used per year exceeds 1 tonne.

(2) Metal industry:
  (a) Ironworks or steelworks or metalworks producing iron alloys with a production capacity not exceeding 2.5 tonnes per hour.
  (b) Rolling mills, hammer mills or rod mills for non-ferrous metals, but excluding three specified cold processes.
  (c) Ferrous metal foundries with a production capacity not exceeding 20 tonnes per day, but at least 200 tonnes per year.
  (d) Other foundries or smelting plants with a melting capacity not exceeding 20 tonnes per day, but at least 200 tonnes per year; smelting of a maximum of 4 tonnes of lead or cadmium per day.
  (e) Processing of ferrous metals by the application of protective fused metal coats with an input not exceeding 2 tonnes of crude steel per hour.
  (f) Hot-rolling mill for ferrous metals with a capacity not exceeding 20 tonnes per hour, or hammer mills where the energy of the hammers does not exceed 50 kilojoules per hammer and the calorific power used does not exceed 20 megawatts.
  (g) Surface treatment of metals or plastic materials using an electrolytic or chemical process where the volume of the treatment vats is at least 5 cubic metres and no more than 30 cubic metres.
  (h) Shipyards.
  (i) Loadable battery factories.

(3) Energy production:
  (a) Combustion of fuels in plants where the thermal input of one or more of the energy production units firing solid fuels is at least 20 megawatts and where the total thermal input of all energy production units on the site is less than 50 megawatts; in the assessment of the total thermal input of an energy production installation all the energy production units of at least 1 megawatt but not exceeding 50 megawatts on site are added up.
  (b) Nuclear power plants.

(4) Chemical industry:
   (a) Factories producing detergents with an annual production capacity of at least 50 tonnes.
   (b) Rubber factories with a vulcanization or mastication process.
   (c) Factories producing mineral oil products with an annual production capacity of at least 10,000 tonnes.
   (d) Factories producing starch derivatives.
   (e) Factories producing enzymes.

(5) Manufacture of fuels, or storage or treatment of chemicals or fuels:
   (a) Gasification or liquefaction of fuels other than coal in installations with a thermal input of less than 20 megawatts and an annual fuel production of at least 3,000 tonnes.
   (b) Production plants for solid, liquid or gaseous fuel with an annual production capacity of at least 5,000 tonnes.
   (c) Production plants for charcoal using wood as raw material with an annual production capacity of at least 3,000 tonnes.
   (d) Other storage facilities for liquid fuels or liquid chemicals hazardous to health or to the environment that can store at least 100 cubic metres of such chemicals than those subject to notification, as specified in Annex 4 to the Act, paragraph 2, but excluding storage tanks of energy production plants subject to registration, as specified in Annex 2 to the Act, high-voltage transformer substations, or bulk storage facilities for packaged products not located in an important groundwater area or in another groundwater area suitable for water supply.
   (e) Coal storage facilities.

(6) Activities using organic solvents:
   (a1) Cleaning of surfaces with organic solvents that contain substances and mixtures specified in hazard statements H340, H341, H350, H350i, H351, H360D or H360F when the consumption of the solvents exceeds 1 tonne but does not exceed 200 tonnes per year.
   (a2) Activities where the consumption of organic solvents exceeds 10 tonnes per year but does not exceed 200 tonnes per year: – cleaning of surfaces other than those referred to in paragraph a1 – original coating of vehicles, both within and outside the production facility – coating or painting of metal, plastic, textiles, foil or paper – coating of wooden surfaces – coating of leather – winding wire coating – footwear manufacture – wood and plastic lamination – adhesive coating – the following printing activities: heatset web offset printing, publication rotogravures, other rotogravure, flexography printing, rotary screen printing, including the rotary screen printing of textiles and cardboard, laminating and varnishing units – rubber conversion.
   (a3) Activities where the annual consumption of organic solvents exceeds 25 tonnes but does not exceed 200 tonnes: – continuously functioning tape coating, wood impregnation.

(b) Activities where the annual consumption of organic solvents exceeds 50 tonnes: – vegetable oil and animal fat extraction and vegetable oil refining – manufacture of coatings, varnishes, adhesives and inks – manufacturing of pharmaceutical products.

(c) Installations using organic solvents where the annual consumption of the solvents is at least 10 tonnes, after deducting the amount absorbed by the products, or where the equivalent peak consumption is at least 20 kilograms per hour, including operations during which VOCs are released from the blowing or expansion agents contained within the raw materials.

(7) Mining of ores or minerals, or excavation of soil:

(a) Mining, and mechanized excavation of gold other than subject to notification as specified in Annex 4, paragraph 3.

(b) Ore or mineral processing plants.

(c) Stone quarries or stone quarrying for purposes other than civil engineering work, where stone is processed for at least fifty days.

(d) Peat production and related drainage work.

(e) Stationary crushing plant or limestone grinding mill, or a mobile crushing plant or limestone grinding mill located in a certain area and in operation for at least fifty days in total.

(8) Manufacture of mineral products:

(a) Cement works with a production capacity in rotary kilns not exceeding 500 tonnes per day and in other kilns not exceeding 50 tonnes per day.

(b) Production of lime in kilns with a total production capacity not exceeding 50 tonnes per day.

(c) Mineral wool plants with a melting capacity not exceeding 20 tonnes per day, but exceeding 6,000 tonnes per year.

(d) Plants producing glass or glass fibre with a melting capacity not exceeding 20 tonnes per day, but exceeding 6,000 tonnes per year.

Manufacture of the following ceramic products by firing with a production capacity not exceeding 75 tonnes per day and/ or with a kiln capacity not exceeding 4 cubic metres and with a setting density per kiln not exceeding 300 kilograms per cubic metres.

(e1) Ceramic or porcelain factories with an annual production capacity of at least 200 tonnes.

(e2) Plants producing expanded clay aggregate with an annual production capacity exceeding 3,000 tonnes.

(f) Plants producing plasterboard.

(9) Installations for the production or treatment leather or textiles:

(a) Plants for the pretreatment or dyeing of fibres or textiles with a treatment capacity of at least 1 tonne per day and not exceeding 10 tonnes per day.

(b) Tanneries or fur-dressing shops, but excluding the manufacture of products from pretreated leather.

(c) Non-woven fabric factories.

(d) Wet cleaning facilities for textiles with a capacity of at least 1 tonne per day, the wastewater from which is not discharged to a sewer system subject to Environmental Permit, or chemical cleaning facilities other than subject to registration as specified in Annex 2 to the Act.

(10) Production of food or feed:

(a) Slaughterhouses, other than subject to notification as specified in Annex 4, paragraph 4a, with a carcass production capacity of at least 5 tonnes per day and not exceeding 50 tonnes per day.

(b1) Installations, other than subject to notification as specified in Annex 4 paragraph 4b, for the treatment or processing of meat or meat products that use at least 1,000 tonnes of animal raw materials per year, with the production capacity of finished products not exceeding 75 tonnes per day.

(b2) Installations for the treatment or processing of fish or fish products that use at least 100 tonnes of animal raw materials per year, with the production capacity of finished products not exceeding 75 tonnes per day.

(c1) Installations, other than subject to notification as specified in Annex 4 paragraph 4c, for the treatment of potatoes or root vegetables or the processing of them into products that use at least 2,000 tonnes of vegetable raw materials per year, with the production capacity of finished products not exceeding 300 tonnes per day.

(c2) Installations, other than subject to notification as specified in Annex 4 paragraph 4d, for the treatment of vegetables, oil plants, molasses or malting barley or the processing of them into products that use at least 5,000 tonnes of vegetable raw materials per year, with the production capacity of finished products not exceeding 300 tonnes per day, but excluding production plants for cold-pressed vegetable oil.

(c3) Installations, other than subject to notification as specified in Annex 4 paragraph 4e, for the treatment of vegetable raw materials or the processing of them into products other than those referred to in paragraphs c1 and c2 that use at least 10,000 tonnes of vegetable raw materials per year, with the production capacity of finished products not exceeding 300 tonnes per day, but excluding production plants for cold-pressed vegetable oil or bakeries.

(c4) Breweries, other than subject to notification as specified in Annex 4 paragraph 4f, with a production capacity of at least 250,000 litres per year and not exceeding 300,000 litres per day.

(c5) Production of cider or wine through fermentation, other than subject to notification as specified in Annex 4 paragraph 4g, with a production capacity of at least 750,000 litres per year and not exceeding 300,000 litres per day.

(c6) Installations producing non-alcoholic or alcoholic beverages, other than subject to notification as specified in Annex 4 paragraph 4h, and other than those referred to in paragraphs c4 and c5, where the total production capacity of non-alcoholic and alcoholic beverages is at least 50 million litres per year and does not exceed 300,000 litres per day.

(d1) Installations producing margarine or other vegetable or animal fats or oils with a finished product production capacity of at least 15 tonnes per day but not exceeding 75 tonnes per day, if the portion of animal raw material of the finished product production capacity is at least 10% of weight; in other cases, not exceeding 300–(22.5×A) tonnes per day, where 'A' is the portion of animal raw material of the finished product in per cent of weight.

(d2) Installations, other than those subject to notification as specified in Annex 4 paragraph 4i, producing or mixing feed or high-protein feed with a finished product production capacity of at least 15 tonnes per day but not exceeding 75 tonnes per day, if the portion of animal raw material of the finished product production capacity is at least 10% of weight; in other cases, not exceeding 300–(22.5×A) tonnes per day, where 'A' is the portion of animal raw material of the finished product in per cent of weight.

(d3) Ice cream factories or cheese factories, other than those subject to notification as specified in Annex 4 paragraph 4j, with a finished product production capacity of at least 1,000 tonnes per year but not exceeding 75 tonnes per day, if the portion of animal raw material of the finished product production capacity is at least 10% of weight; in other cases, 300–(22.5×A)tonnes per day, where 'A' is the portion of animal raw material of the finished product in per cent of weight.

(d4) Installations, other than subject to notification as specified in Annex 4 paragraph 4k, producing processed foods with a finished product production capacity of at least 5,000 tonnes per year but not exceeding 75 tonnes per day, if the portion of animal raw material of the finished product production capacity is at least 10% of weight; in other cases, 300–(22.5×A) tonnes per day, where 'A' is the portion of animal raw material of the finished product in per cent of weight.

(e) Collection, treatment and processing facilities, other than those subject to notification as specified in Annex 4 paragraph 4l, for milk only, where the quantity of milk received is at least 100 tonnes per day and not exceeding 200 tonnes per day.

(f) Confectionery factories, other than subject to notification as specified in Annex 4 paragraph 4m, with a production capacity of at least 15 tonnes per day.

(g) Packaging facilities, other than subject to notification as specified in Annex 4 paragraph 4n, for malt liquors, alcoholic or non-alcoholic beverages with an annual production capacity of at least 50 million litres.

(h) Manufacture of gelatine from hides, skins and bones.

(11) Farm animal facilities and fish farming:

(a) Farm animal facilities for at least 300 dairy cows, 500 cattle for fattening or 600 calves, or other farm animal facility the total amount of livestock units, as calculated by the animal unit coefficients in Annex 3, Table 1, is at least 3,000.

(b) Fur farms housing at least 500 breeder female minks or ferrets or at least 250 breeder female foxes or raccoons, or other fur farm the total amount of livestock units, as calculated by the animal unit coefficients in Annex 3, Table 1, is at least 100.

(c) Fish breeding or fish farms where at least 2,000 kilograms of dry food or other feed with equivalent nutritional value is used per year, or where the annual proliferation of fish is at least 2,000 kilograms, or where natural food ponds or groups of ponds are at least 20 hectares in size.

(12) Transport:
   (a) Ports or loading or unloading jetties intended mainly for commercial seafaring and for vessels with a capacity exceeding 1,350 tonnes.
   (b) Aerodromes other than rescue activity heliports.
   (c) Motor racing tracks located outdoors.
   (d) Receiving rail yards or terminals for chemicals where chemicals that are hazardous to health or to the environment are transferred from one transport vehicle to another, from a transport vehicle to storage or from storage to a transport vehicle, but excluding bulk transfers.

(13) Treatment of waste on a professional basis or at an installation and treatment of wastewater:
   (a) Waste incineration plants or waste co-incineration plants firing solid or liquid waste with a capacity not exceeding 3 tonnes per hour for non-hazardous waste and not exceeding 10 tonnes per day for hazardous waste.
   (b) Installations for animal carcasses or animal waste with a treatment capacity not exceeding 10 tonnes per day.
   (c) Separate industrial wastewater treatment plants other than those referred to in (IED) Table 1, paragraph 13c (Separate wastewater treatment plant for wastewater from an IED installation in Table 1 to which Directive 91/271/EEC is not applicable), treating process wastewater from activities referred to in Table 2.
   (d) Treatment and discharge of urban wastewater when the population equivalent of the wastewater being treated is at least 100.
   (e) Waste facilities for extractive waste.
   (f) Treatment of waste falling under the scope of the Waste Act on a professional basis or at an installation other than those referred to in paragraphs 13a, 13b and 13e of Table 2.

(14) Other activities:
   (a) Outdoor shooting ranges other than those referred to in Annex 4, paragraph 7.
   (b) Permanent installations for abrasive blasting outdoors.
   (c) Crematories or pet crematories.
   (d) Fertilizer factories other than those referred to in paragraph 4f of Table 1.
   (e) Oil and gas prospecting and the exploitation of deposits and related activities in Finland's territorial waters and the exclusive economic zone.

158. The notification procedure (Chapter 10a of the Act) and the registration procedure (Chapter 11 of the Act) are lighter alternatives for preventive control than the Environmental Permit (which as such already is adjustable according to various activities and their various scales), especially from the viewpoint of operators. The notification procedures resemble more or less the Environmental Permit procedures, however, and these two end with an administrative decision, whereas registration, applicable to mainly minor scale and individually numerous installations, is the lightest option of preventive control and does not end with any proper decision. Of course, the basic legal preconditions for registration are checked.

159. The activities subject to registration requirement, listed in Annex 2 to the Act, are the following:

(1) Energy production plants where the total thermal input is at least 1 megawatt but under 50 megawatts and where the thermal input of each energy production unit using solid fuels is under 20 megawatts; in the assessment of the total thermal input of an energy production installation all the energy production units of at least 1 megawatt but not exceeding 50 megawatts on site are added up.
(2) Asphalt plants.
(3) Distribution stations for liquid fuel used in motorized vehicles or motor boats with a total fuel tank volume of at least 10 cubic metres.
(4) Dry cleaning facilities if the equipment and systems used in the operations are specifically designed for laundries and do not release emissions into the air or water, and if waste from the operations is delivered for treatment in accordance with section 29 of the Waste Act.
(5) Activities and installations where the consumption of organic solvents does not exceed 10 tonnes per year:
  (a) original coating of vehicles, both within and outside the manufacturing facility;
  (b) cleaning of surfaces other than cleaning with organic solvents that contain substances and mixtures specified in hazard statements H340, H341, H350, H350i, H351, H360D or H360F, when the consumption of the solvents exceeds 2 tonnes per year.
(6) Operations and installations where the consumption of organic solvents exceeds 5 tonnes but does not exceed 10 tonnes per year:
  (a) coating other than the painting of wooden surfaces, including coating or painting of metal, plastic, textiles, foil or paper;
  (b) winding wire coating;
  (c) footwear manufacture;
  (d) wood and plastic lamination;
  (e) adhesive coating.
(7) Operations and installations where the consumption of organic solvents exceeds 10 tonnes but does not exceed 50 tonnes per year:
  (a) coating of wooden surfaces;
  (b) coating of leather;
  (c) the following printing activities: heatset web offset printing, publication rotogravures, other rotogravure, flexography printing, rotary screen printing, including the rotary screen printing of textiles and cardboard, laminating and varnishing units;
  (d) rubber conversion;
  (e) extraction of vegetable oils or animal fats and processing of vegetable oils, extraction of animal fat and vegetable oil manufacturing.
(8) Stationary concrete plants and concrete product factories.

160. The activities subject to notification duty (Annex 4 to the Act) are again the following:

(1) Sawmills with an annual production capacity of at least 20,000 cubic metres of sawn goods.
(2) Storages of chemicals that are hazardous to health or to the environment, where such chemicals can be stored:
 (a) at least 100 cubic metres but under 1,000 cubic metres, excluding fuel tanks of liquid fuel distribution stations or fuel tanks of energy production installations subject to registration as specified in Annex 2, high-voltage transformer substations or bulk storage facilities for packaged products, not located in an important groundwater area or in another groundwater area suitable for water supply, or storages built into rock;
 (b) at least 1,000 cubic metres but under 50,000 cubic metres, excluding fuel tanks of liquid fuel distribution stations or fuel tanks of energy production installations subject to registration as specified in Annex 2, high-voltage transformer substations or bulk storage facilities for packaged products, not located in an important groundwater area or in another groundwater area suitable for water supply, or storages built into rock.
(3) Mechanized gold washing, when the amount of excavated earth masses is under 500 cubic metres per year surface layers included and the working time does not exceed fifty days per year and a permit or right of use according to the Water Act is not required.
(4) The following activities in food and feed production, the wastewaters if which are conveyed to a sewer system subject to Environmental Permit:
 (a) Slaughterhouses with a carcass production capacity of at least 5 tonnes per day and not exceeding 50 tonnes per day.
 (b) Installations for the treatment or processing of meat or meat products that use at least 1,000 tonnes of animal raw materials per year, with the production capacity of finished products not exceeding 75 tonnes per day.
 (c) Installations for the treatment of potatoes or root vegetables or the processing of them into products that use at least 2,000 tonnes of vegetable raw materials per year, with the production capacity of finished products not exceeding 300 tonnes per day.
 (d) Installations for the treatment of vegetables, oil plants, molasses or malting barley or the processing of them into products that use at least 5,000 tonnes of vegetable raw materials per year, with the production capacity of finished products not exceeding 300 tonnes per day, but excluding production plants for cold-pressed vegetable oil.
 (e) Installations, other than those referred to in paragraphs (c) and (d) above, for the treatment of vegetable raw materials or the processing of them into products that use at least 10,000 tonnes of vegetable raw materials per year, with the production capacity of finished products not exceeding 300 tonnes per day, but excluding production plants for cold-pressed vegetable oil or bakeries.
 (f) Breweries with a production capacity of at least 250,000 litres per year and not exceeding 300,000 litres per day.

(g) Production of cider or wine through fermentation with a production capacity of at least 750,000 litres per year and not exceeding 300,000 litres per day.

(h) Installations, other than those referred to in paragraphs (f) and (g) above, producing non-alcoholic or alcoholic beverages where the total production capacity of non-alcoholic and alcoholic beverages is at least 50 million litres per year and does not exceed 300,000 litres per day.

(i) Installations producing or mixing feed or high-protein feed with a finished product production capacity of under 22,500 tonnes per year and at least 15 tonnes per day but not exceeding 75 tonnes per day, if the portion of animal raw material of the finished product production capacity is at least 10% of weight; in other cases, not exceeding 300–(22.5×A) tonnes per day, where 'A' is the portion of animal raw material of the finished product in per cent of weight.

(j) Ice cream factories or cheese factories with a finished product production capacity of at least 1,000 tonnes per year but not exceeding 75 tonnes per day, if the portion of animal raw material of the finished product production capacity is at least 10% of weight; in other cases, 300–(22.5×A) tonnes per day, where 'A' is the portion of animal raw material of the finished product in per cent of weight.

(k) Installations producing processed foods with a finished product production capacity of at least 5,000 tonnes and under 30,000 tonnes per year but not exceeding 75 tonnes per day, if the portion of animal raw material of the finished product production capacity is at least 10% of weight; in other cases, 300–(22.5×A) tonnes per day, where 'A' is the portion of animal raw material of the finished product in per cent of weight.

(l) Collection, treatment and processing facilities for milk only, where the quantity of milk received is at least 100 tonnes per day and not exceeding 200 tonnes per day.

(m) Confectionery factories with a production capacity of at least 15 tonnes per day.

(n) Packaging facilities for malt liquors, alcoholic or non-alcoholic beverages with an annual production capacity of at least 50 million litres.

(5) Farm animal facilities for:

(a) at least 50 and under 300 dairy cows, at least 100 and under 500 cattle for fattening, at least 130 and under 600 calves, at least 60 horses or ponies, at least 250 ewes or goats, at least 100 and not exceeding 750 full-grown sows, at least 250 and not exceeding 2,500 pigs for fattening, at least 4,000 and not exceeding 40,000 laying hens or at least 10,000 and not exceeding 40,000 broilers;

(b) several animal species referred to in paragraph (a) above or in Annex 3 the total livestock unit amount of which, as determined by livestock unit coefficients in Annex 3, Table 1, is at least 250 and under 3,000 and is not subject to notification directly due to the amount of farm animals referred to in a) above.

(6) Depots for more than fifty buses or lorries or machinery depots of equivalent size.

(7) Outdoor shooting ranges intended for no more than 10,000 shots per year and with no range for shotgun shooting.
(8) Permanent zoos or amusement parks.

161. Regarding final necessity of Environmental Permit, the detailed Tables of Annex 1 are far from exhaustiveness, however. Additionally, irrespective of Annex 1, and also irrespective of Annexes 2 and 4 and the notification and registration duties, an Environmental Permit is required (section 27(2) of the Environmental Protection Act) for:

(1) any activity that may cause pollution (on the definition, *see* section 5, above paragraph 120) of a surface water body (territorial sees included), and the project in question is not one requiring a permit under the Water Act;
(2) discharge of wastewater that may lead to the pollution of a ditch or spring, or of a streamlet provided in section 3(1)(6) of Chapter 1 of the Water Act; and
(3) any activity that can cause in the environment unreasonable nuisance to neighbours, as defined in section 17(1) of the Neighbourhood Relations Act.

Unlike the listed activities in Annex 1, these permit requirements depend on the impacts and the harmfulness thereof in each individual case.

162. In groundwater areas the requirements are partly higher than in other areas. Environmental Permit is always required, if one of the following activities is going to be located in an important groundwater area or in another groundwater area suitable for water supply:

- energy production installation listed in Annex 2;
- asphalt plant listed in Annex 2;
- liquid fuel distribution station listed in Annex 2;
- concrete plant and concrete product factory listed in Annex 2;
- any activity listed in Annex 2(5–7), if organic solvents are used at least 10 tonnes; and
- any activity listed in Annex 4.

163. Moreover, Environmental Permit is pursuant to section 28 required, if one of the following activities is going to be located in an important groundwater area or in another groundwater area suitable for water supply and risk of groundwater pollution is posed:

- activity listed in Annex 1, but operating on a smaller scale;
- activity listed in Annex 2(1) or 2(3), but operating on a smaller scale;
- activity listed in Annex 4, but operating on a smaller scale; or
- wet cleaning facility for textiles referred to in Annex 2(4).

It has to be borne in mind, however, that pollution of groundwater by any activity is prohibited anyway (section 17), irrespective of permit, notification or registration.

164. The relation between Environmental Permit requirement and notification requirement is in a summarizing way provided in section 29a of the Act. Environmental Permit is required for an activity listed in Annex 4, if the activity:

(1) is part of the activity of an IED installation;
(2) may cause an impact referred to in section 27(2);
(3) Environmental Permit is required (already) due to section 28; or
(4) EIA is applied to the activity due section 3(2) of the Environmental Impacts Assessment Act.

165. The relationship between Environmental Permit requirement and registration requirement is in a summarizing way provided in section 30 of the Act. Environmental Permit is required for an activity listed in Annex 2, if the activity:

(1) is part of the activity of an IED installation;
(2) may cause an impact referred to in section 27(2); or
(3) Environmental Permit is required (already) due to section 28.

These important restrictions to permit derogations, being generally applicable, mean that the necessity to have a permit due to either pollution risk of surface water body or nuisance, both assessed case by case, always takes priority.

166. An Environmental Permit is not required for a short-term activity undertaken on an experimental basis when the purpose is to test an emerging technique, raw material or fuel, a manufacturing or incineration method or treatment equipment, or to treat waste at an installation or on a professional basis to investigate the impact, feasibility or other corresponding feature of such an activity (section 31). Provisions on the notification required for such an activity are included in section 119. However, an Environmental Permit is anyway required if the activity may cause consequences referred to in section 27(2). This means that the relation between Environmental Permit requirement and notification requirement also here follows the general rule regarding water pollution risks and neighbourhood nuisances.

167. Derogations from the Environmental Permit requirement regarding treatment of waste on a professional basis or at an installation, referred to in Annex 1, Table 2(13) above, are provided in section 32(1). No Environmental Permit is required for such activities in the case of: (1) the use in agriculture and forestry of waste generated therein and comprising natural material harmless to the environment and health; (2) recovery and use of wastewater sludge, septage, or dry closet waste, treated so as to render them harmless, or harmless ash or slag, in accordance with the Fertiliser Act; (3) the recovery of green waste comprising natural material harmless to health, generated in agriculture and forestry, in energy production; (4) the treatment of extractive waste generated in peat production, inert waste generated in some other extractive operation or uncontaminated soil in accordance with an Extractive Waste Management Plan, in connection with the activity in question, in ways other than by depositing the waste at a waste deposit area for extractive waste that poses a risk of major accident; or (5) the recovery of soil excavated in connection with the treatment of contaminated soil at an excavation site in accordance with a decision provided in section 136 of the Environmental Protection Act.

168. Similarly, no Environmental Permit is required on the basis of section 32(2) for other waste recovery referred to in Annex 1, Table 2(13), or for the disposal of waste other than hazardous waste on the site where it is generated, if provisions concerning the environmental protection requirements for these activities are given by Government decree issued under section 10 of the Environmental Protection Act or section 14 of the Waste Act. The registration of such operations is laid down in section 116. If an Environmental Permit is valid for such activity upon the entry into force of an applicable Government decree, the Environmental Permit shall be void.

169. As an example, Government decree on the use of certain wastes in earthworks (843/2017), issued under both the Environmental Protection Act and the Waste Act, lays down such detailed preconditions under which Environmental Permit becomes unnecessary.

170. Also, an already permitted activity is in need of a new Environmental Permit when a change in the activity takes place and the emissions or effects thereof are due to the change increased, or other essential change in the activity is made. No permit is needed for these reasons, however, if the change does not increase the environmental impacts or risks and there is either no need to check the permit due to the change (section 29(1) of the Act). The wording of the provisions is in fact a compromise between certain conflicting needs, i.e., efficient enforcement and pollution prevention on the one hand and flexible practice and the interests of the operator on the other. However, if the earlier permitted activity due to the changes becomes one of an IED installation, a permit is anyway required.

§10. Municipal Environmental Protection Bylaws

171. One of the novelties in the 2000 reform were the Municipal Environmental Protection Bylaws, or Regulations, a complementary (but to a municipality voluntary) instrument of environmental guidance at local level. The provisions are today included in sections 202 and 203 in the 2024 Environmental Protection Act. The Municipal Councils may issue these Bylaws on the basis of local circumstances, pertaining to the entire municipality or part thereof. The regulations may only regard activities for which Environmental Permit, notification or registration is not required. Their contents might in practice be concentrated on the abatement of the diffuse loading of the environment. The regulations may not apply to an activity referred to in section 31, section 120 or section 136(1), or to operations of the Defence Forces or the Border Guard.

172. The Bylaws may apply to:

(1) activities, restrictions and structures that prevent emissions or the harmful effects thereof;
(2) abatement of especially disturbing temporary noise or vibration;
(3) environmental protection requirements regarding the location of activities outside local Detailed Plan areas;
(4) areas where conducting wastewater into the ground, a water body or a ditch, spring, artificial pond, or streamlet is prohibited due to a special pollution risk;
(5) zones and areas where the use of manure and fertilizer and other environmentally harmful substances used in agriculture is restricted;
(6) providing information required for supervision; and
(7) measures concerning the improvement of the state of waters and that of the marine environment and considered necessary under a Water Resources Management Programme or a Marine Environment Management Plan drawn up in accordance with the Act on the Arranging of Water Management and Marine Waters Management.

173. The Municipal Environmental Protection Authority may grant an exception to a Municipal Environmental Protection Bylaw as referred to therein.

174. Before a Bylaw is issued, the Centre for Economic Development, Transport and the Environment (environmental division) of the region shall be provided with an opportunity to state their opinion. Decisions to approve environmental protection Bylaws shall be publicized. A decision is deemed to have been publicized when it has been made available to the public. The same applies to publicizing an environmental protection regulation's entry into force. The Centre for Economic Development, Transport and the Environment must be provided with the Bylaws.

§11. Environmental Permit Procedure

175. The competent Environmental Permit authority is today either the Regional State Administrative Agency or the Municipal Environmental Protection Authority, as (mainly) specified in section 34 of the Environmental Protection Act, and in more detail, in sections 1 and 2 (last amended by 952/2020) of the Environmental Protection Decree. Pursuant to the Act, the Regional State Administrative Agency is always the competent body, if (1) the activity may have significant environmental impacts, or the resolution of the application by the State Agency is otherwise warranted by the type or nature of the activity, as in detail provided in Environmental Protection Decree; (2) the environmental impacts of an activity other than that under (1) above may affect a considerably larger area than that belonging to the municipality in which the activity is located, as in detail provided in Environmental Protection Decree; (3) besides an Environmental Permit, the activity is subject to a permit under Chapter 3 of the Water Act or for the establishment of a right of use according to the Water Act that does not concern an outlet pipe or is referred to in sections 68 and 69 of the Act, and the permit applications have to be processed jointly in accordance with section 47; or (4) a permit is required under section 27(2)(1), i.e., there is a risk of pollution of a (surface) water body (section 34(1)).

176. Applications for activities other than those referred to in section 34(1) belong to the competence of the Municipal Environmental Protection Authorities. Regional State Administrative Agency is nevertheless exclusively competent, if (1) the activity is located in the administrative area of several Municipal Environmental Protection Authorities (which consist of one municipality or several municipalities), (2) the activity in question is for military use; or (3) a matter concerning the treatment of polluted soil or groundwater pursuant to section 136 is decided upon in conjunction with the permit, and the competence in such matters has not been specifically transferred to the Municipal Environmental Protection Authority at stake.

177. Pursuant to the Environmental Protection Decree, section 1, the Regional State Administrative Agency always decides upon the applications for activities listed in Annex I, Table 1 (IED installations). Besides the activities specified in section 34(2–3) of the Act, the competence of the Municipal Environmental Protection Authorities encompasses, without prejudice to section 34 of the Act, those of the activities in Annex 1, Table 2, that are listed in section 2 of the decree, whereas some other activities in Annex 1, Table 2, that are listed in the same section, belong to the Regional State Administrative Agency.

178. As a whole, the rules are hence somewhat complicated, but, in general, it may be said that smaller-scale activities are dealt with by the Municipal Environmental Protection Authorities and larger-scale industries and particularly those with significant environmental impacts by the Regional State Administrative Agencies. Activities causing risk of pollution of surface water bodies, however, never belong to the competence of the Municipal Environmental Protection Authorities, irrespective of the installation lists in the Environmental Protection Decree. If such a risk appears regarding an application submitted to a Municipal Environmental Protection Authority, the application shall be transferred to the Regional State Administrative Agency (section 36.1 of the Act).

179. On application by a municipality and after having consulted the Regional State Administrative Agency and the Centre for Economic Development, Transport and the Environment, the Ministry of the Environment may generally decide that in Environmental Permit decisions specified in Annex 1, Table 2 of the Act the competent authority is the Municipal Environmental Protection Authority instead of the Agency (section 38 of the Act). Such a decision may also be restricted to apply only to some of the above-mentioned activities. However, the competence cannot be transferred in permit decisions regarding peat production, mining, mechanized gold panning, ore or mineral processing plants, airports, harbours, nuclear power plants, waste incineration plants, waste co-incineration plants or the operations of the Defence Forces or the Border Guard. A condition for the transfer of competence is that the Municipal Environmental Protection Authority has sufficient expertise to manage the duties appropriately and that the transfer of competence will improve the efficiency or can achieve a balanced division of responsibilities between the authorities. The competence may also be transferred for a fixed period. The decision may be amended if the conditions for the transfer cease to exist.

180. Moreover, there are specific competence provisions for the so-called mixed projects, i.e., projects for which both an Environmental Permit and a Water Act permit are needed (section 47 of the Environmental Protection Act and section 11 of Chapter 12 of the Water Act). Here only one (joint) permit procedure takes place, however, but the substantive provisions of both acts are applied. The competence in such cases is always vested in the Regional State Administrative Agency (section 34(1)(3) of the Environmental Protection Act), due to its position as the main permit authority under the Water Act.

181. SAC 2022:38 is a fresh ruling on a mixed project of this category. The permit at stake was granted to a new mining project (*Sokli*) in northern Finland, consisting of 59.3 km^2 and fourteen separate open quarries. Two natural-state river beds would be transferred. The permit decision was repealed by the SAC on several various reasons, of which one was the negative impact of polluting discharges on valuable natural salmonid fish stocks and ecosystems (this being materially based on the Environmental Protection Act). Another central reason was that the accounts on the complex water arrangements were considered deficient (this being materially based on the Water Act). The matter in its totality was sent back to the permit authority (Regional State Administrative Agency).

182. Today also another type of joint permit process in provided (section 47a of the Act). If a project including soil excavation is subject to both an Environmental Permit and a permit in accordance with the Soil Excavation Act (*see also* paragraphs 67 and 1143–1146), the permit applications shall be processed and decided upon together unless this is deemed unnecessary for specific reasons. One application may be submitted for a joint permit. The joint competence is vested in the permit authority which is competent pursuant to the Environmental Protection Act, and the procedure is mainly provided in the same Act (sections 85–96 and 96).

183. Additionally, the 'one counter' procedure pursuant to the Act 764/2019 (*see* paragraph 68) may at the request of the operator be applicable; notifications in the adjusted permit processing are provided in sections 44 and 85 of the Environmental Protection Act.

184. In projects provided in the Act on the Permit Procedure of Projects of Common Interest of the EU (684/2014) that Act shall be observed, where applicable (section 40a, *see* paragraph 66).

185. If several activities in the same area of activity (site) have such a technical or functional connection that a need appears to assess their impacts or waste management together, a common permit application or simultaneous separate applications are required (section 41).

186. The Environmental Permit is, among other things, intended to have also the function of development consent in the meaning of the (2014 amended) EIA Directive 2011/92/EU, regarding projects within the scope of application of the Environmental Protection Act. If an EIA is needed, the permit application shall also include the EIA report and the respective reasoned conclusion pursuant to the Environmental Impacts Assessment Act (section 39(2) of the Environmental Protection Act). Similarly, where impacts on a site included in the Natura 2000 network have to be assessed according to the Nature Protection Act, section 35, the assessment has to be included.

187. The provisions on Environmental Permit applications and permit procedures, applicable before all permit authorities, are laid down in Chapter 5 of the Environmental Protection Act and in Chapter 3 of the Environmental Protection Decree. Among other things, the requirements of the contents of a permit application, constituting the basis of the procedure, have been specified.

188. The application shall be filed electronically. A natural person acting as an applicant may, however, file the application and its annexes on paper. An applicant may be required to submit paper copies of his electronic documents, if this is necessary for the due handling of the matter (section 39(1)).

189. The person who prepares the application shall have sufficient expertise. In practice, there are often several persons in charge of different fields of expertise. Where needed, the application shall show the documentation and calculation, research and assessment methods the information and data are based on.

190. If the application documents are inadequate or if specific accounts are needed, an opportunity shall be reserved for the applicant to supplement the application within a deadline set by the permit authority. An application that is not supplemented within the deadline may be dismissed (section 40). If deciding on the matter is relevant in terms of the public interest or if important reasons so require, the applicant may be obliged to supplement the application or obtain the accounts necessary for a decision under notice that this will be obtained at the applicant's expense. If new information from the applicant appears to be necessary later on, the authority shall notify the applicant on the specified points at stake and on the reasons for which they are necessary.

191. In addition to the general obligations of public authorities in the Administration Act, section 39a of the Environmental Protection Act lays down a specific duty on providing the applicant with advice (from 2017). The permit authority shall, at the request, provide the applicant with information, in electronic form, on (1) the information that shall be presented in the application and the accounts that shall be annexed to it, (2) the statements that shall be obtained and the fixed times for issuing them, and (3) the estimated date of issue of the decision. The permit authority may also, at the request of the applicant or at its own initiative, arrange a meeting with the applicant, in order to arrange the advising. Other authorities and other parties may be invited, too. If a Regional State Administrative Agency is the permit authority, the Centre for Economic Development, Transport and the Environment of the region (its environmental division) shall always be invited. Advice, where any, shall be provided free of charge. Of course, the permit authority cannot anticipate its future decisions, and equality between the parties shall be maintained, although the interests of the applicant have been the most relevant reason to these advice provisions.

192. When processing a permit application, the authority shall ensure communication with such other authorities that are simultaneously processing other permit matters and plans for operations. If necessary, the authority shall consult the supervisory authority concerned and hold discussions with the supervisory authority concerned and also with the applicant in order to clarify the permit matter and for the purposes of permit consideration. In addition, a public hearing may be held to clarify the matter, at which objections and opinions may be expressed (section 44b).

193. Before deciding upon an application, the authority shall give all who have an individual interest in the case ('those whose right or interest the matter may concern', defined as 'parties', i.e., parties concerned) a possibility to make objections and remarks (section 43). The scope of the notion of party, other than the applicant, in practice of course varies strongly depending on the type and scale of the activity and the impacted area. The number of parties may, depending on the circumstances, consist of only the nearest neighbours suffering from expected nuisance, or a huge group of property owners and other interested subjects in a large area, as in cases of risk for major air or water pollution. Also, anyone else is allowed to express his opinion.

For these purposes, a notification on the application has to be made public using methods specified in section 44 of the Environmental Protection Act (public notice boards, website, as a rule also newspaper, depending on the matter). Moreover, an individual notification shall always be delivered to those of the 'parties' whom the matter 'particularly concerns' (section 44(2)). This expression normally includes the nearest neighbours and where significant water pollution is at stake all those who possibly would have the right to compensation.

The application documents shall be displayed for public viewing locally, i.e., in the municipalities within the area impact area, for at least the duration of the public notice period. A Regional State Administrative Agency shall also publish a summary of a permit application submitted to it for the public on its website, along with other essential contents of the application, where possible. A Municipal Environmental Protection authority shall provide information on the contents of the documents submitted to it on its website, where possible.

194. Anyone has the right to request to be informed of pending environmental permit matters in a certain area by means of electronic communications insofar as the authority's information system is able to receive such requests and automatically send messages (section 45).

195. Before deciding upon an application, the authority shall also request statements from various authorities and other public bodies (section 42). These are regularly the following: (1) Municipal Environmental Protection authorities of the municipalities where the environmental impacts of the activity at stake may occur; (2) the Public Health Authority of the municipality where the activity is located; (3) the authorities representing specified public interests in the matter; (4) the Saami Parliament if the environmental impacts of the activity may occur in the Saami homeland, and from the Skolt Saami Village Committee if the impacts may occur in the Skolt area pursuant to the Skolt Act (253/1995); and (5) other bodies, if necessary for due consideration of the permit. Moreover, a Regional State Administrative Agency shall request a statement from the Centre for Economic Development, Transport and the Environment of the region (its environmental division), from the municipality where the activity is located and, if necessary, from municipalities in the impact area. The permit authority may also obtain other necessary reports and assessments.

196. If a permit application in respect to which a Regional State Administrative Agency has authority and an EIA regarding the same activity are pending simultaneously, the Agency may, subject to the preconditions in section 22a of the Environmental Impacts Assessment Act, assume the task of arranging the hearing due to the EIA report jointly with that due to the permit application, as provided in section 20 of the EIA Act and section 44a of the Environmental Protection Act.

197. The permit authority shall investigate the conditions for granting the permit and shall take into account the statements issued and the objections and opinions submitted on the matter. The permit authority shall also take into account provisions issued on the safeguarding of public and private interests (section 48(1)). A permit application concerning a substantial change in an activity (section 29) shall be resolved in such a way that the consideration takes into account those parts of the activity that the change may affect and the environmental impacts and risks that may be caused by the change (section 48(4)).

198. In addition to the actual permit and its various conditions (and, where appropriate, the stipulations on compensations), a permit decision shall contain the relevant foundations and legal reasoning. Specified demands in objections, opinions and statements to the permit authority shall be examined and answered (sections 48(1) and 83(1)). Where an EIA has taken place, it has also to be indicated how the assessment has been taken into account. The permit decision shall also indicate how the Water Management Plans and Marine Waters Management Plan prepared in accordance with the Act on the Arranging of Water Management and Marine Waters Management and the Flood Risk Management Plans worked out in accordance with the Flood Risk Management Act have been taken into account (section 83(2)).

199. If the permit covers separate operators that have applied for a permit through a joint permit application, the permit decision shall specify the obligations of each operator (section 83(3)).

200. The permit decision shall be announced publicly in accordance with section 62a of the Administrative Procedure Act. The website of the authority is used. The announcement shall also mention the appeal period concerning the decision. The public notice and the permit decision shall be available for inspection at least for the period during which the decision may be appealed. Notwithstanding section 16(3) of the Act on the Openness of Government Activities, the announcement and permit decision may contain information on the name of the operator and the location of the operations. Personal data published on the authority's website must nevertheless be erased from the authority's website when the permitted activities have ended and the measures referred to in section 94 concerning the cessation of operations have been carried out. Information about the public announcement shall also be published in the affected municipalities. In addition, the announcement shall be published in at least one newspaper widely circulated in the area affected, unless the matter is of minor importance or publication is otherwise unnecessary. The permit decision shall be sent to the applicant and to those who have specifically requested to receive the decision, as well as to the supervisory authorities and to the authorities supervising certain public interests. The decision shall also be sent for information to the authorities consulted on the application. A decision rejecting the permit application for an electricity production plant shall be sent to the Ministry of Economic Affairs and Employment. In addition, the decision has to be notified to those who have submitted an objection or expressed an opinion on the matter or have specifically requested individual notification, as well as to those who have been separately informed of the announcement of the permit application pursuant to section 44(2). If there are several signatories to the objection, only the first signatory of the objection may be notified of the issuing of the decision. A public announcement pursuant to section 62a of the Administrative Procedure Act means that the appeal period begins on the seventh day from the announcement regarding all possible appellants. This is in order to make it unequivocal when the period of thirty days for appeals begins or when the decision enters into force if no appeals are submitted in that time. A similar legislative arrangement applies to permits under the Water Act, the Land Use and Building Act (as of 1 January 2025, the Building Act), etc. On the appellate procedure, *see* Part I, Chapter 1, §15 below.

201. Anyone has the right to request that information about decisions on Environmental Permits that have been issued in a specific area be sent electronically, insofar as the authority's information system is capable of receiving such requests and sending messages automatically (section 86). On the Information Service on Environmental Permit Matters (section 85 a), *see* paragraph 292.

§12. Preconditions for Granting an Environmental Permit

202. According to section 48(2) of the Environmental Protection Act, an Environmental Permit shall be issued if the activity fulfils the requirements of the provisions given in and under the said Act and the Waste Act, as investigated by the permit authority. In fact, the wording gives relevance to a large number of substantive provisions, although the immediate preconditions for a permit are set forth in section 49. The equally important section 48(1) describes the basic duties of the permit authority in providing generally that the authority shall take into account what has been provided on the protection of the public and private interests. The latter obligation implies an ex officio approach that is important both to environmental protection and to the horizontal protection of various private interests. Nevertheless, the scope of permit considerations and assessments is limited by the requirement of relevance to pollution or risk thereof (in the wide meaning of the Act), unless where, e.g., the Waste Act or the Nature Protection Act is directly applicable. This legally evident position was once again clearly stated in the recent ruling SAC 2024:15: The procurement of wood raw material was not to be regarded as technically and functionally closely related to a bioproduct mill subject to an Environmental Permit application. Therefore, the bioproduct mill's Environmental Permit could not assess the indirect effects of the procurement of wood raw material on greenhouse gas emissions and carbon sinks. Correspondingly, no permit provisions for wood procurement could be issued. The Environmental Permit could not assess the indirect effects of wood raw material procurement on biodiversity, either.

203. The considerations of the permit authority are anyway essentially judicial: a permit cannot be denied on other grounds other than those defined by law and a permit cannot be granted if the legal preconditions are lacking. This starting point is not affected by the fact that many of the requirements have been expressed in rather general terms. The considerations of the permit authority are, where appropriate, fully reviewable by the appellate administrative courts, which may also come to another end as a whole, or alter the various permit conditions.

204. For granting an Environmental Permit it is required in section 49 of the Environmental Protection Act that the activity, taking the provisions to be laid down in the same decision and the location of the activity into account, will not, alone or together with other activities, cause:

(1) harm to health;
(2) significant other pollution of the environment or risk thereof (literally: other significant consequences defined as pollution in section 5(1)(2), or the risk of such);
(3) a consequence forbidden in sections 16–18 (i.e., pollution of soil or groundwater or of sea outside Finnish territorial waters);
(4) deterioration of special natural conditions or risk to water supply or other potential use important to the public interest in the activity's area of impact; or
(5) unreasonable nuisance provided in section 17(1) of the Neighbourhood Relations Act; or
(6) substantial deterioration in the conditions under which the Saami people practise their traditional livelihoods in the Saami homeland or otherwise maintain and develop their culture, or substantial deterioration in the living conditions of the Skolts or reduced opportunities to engage in nature-based livelihoods in the Skolt area pursuant to the Skolt Act.

Regarding pollution of waters or risk thereof, as assessed case by case, the provision in section 49(2) (above) is important particularly regarding surface waters (lakes, ponds, rivers, territorial sea waters), because groundwater pollution, risk thereof included, is forbidden anyway (section 17), regardless of permit systems (but of course assessed also in permit contexts, where applicable). Pollution of soil is likewise always prohibited (section 16).

205. Certain exceptions to the conditions for granting a permit concerning the Finnish Defence Forces or the Border Guard are provided in section 50.

206. No activity located in contradiction to a Detailed Plan (*see* Part III, Chapter 3, §4) shall be permitted (section 12). Also the location provisions of section 11 of the Act shall be observed (section 48(2)). The effects of the Nature Protection Act may also prevent the granting of an Environmental Permit (section 48(3)), as well as section 13 of the Environmental Protection Act concerning peat production (*see* paragraph 145).

207. In principle, various pollution control plans and programmes made and adopted by administrative authorities are not binding on the courts or individuals, unless explicitly so provided. However, they may more or less show traits of soft law, as the periodical National Water Protection Target Programmes, approved at times by the Cabinet, which have been to some extent observed in practice, although they have not included any detailed or individual recommendations. The recommendations of the Helsinki Commission (on the Helsinki Convention *see* paragraph 468) have also been taken into account in the permit practice, although they formally lack a binding or guiding effect.

The national plans and programmes on environmental protection provided in various pieces of EU law are approved by the Cabinet, as provided in section 204 of the Environmental Protection Act (hearings, publicity, etc.). Such plans and programmes shall be taken into account in the permit consideration, to the necessary degree (section 51).

The implementation of Government decree on Urban Waste Water Treatment (888/2006) shall be monitored through a programme of enforcement. This programme is regarded as a national plan pursuant to the Environmental Protection Act (section 7 of the Decree).

The National Waste Plan pursuant to section 87 of the Waste Act (*see* paragraph 518) must be taken into account in any Environmental Permit for a waste treatment facility or site requiring a permit (section 51(2)).

208. When assessing the significance of a consequence referred to in section 49(1)(2), which here in practice means the significance of pollution of surface waters, risk thereof included (also those being an obstacle to an Environmental Permit due to section 49(1)(2) of the Environmental Protection Act), the contents of a Water Management Plan according to the Act on the Arranging of Water Management and Marine Waters Management, in respect to the condition and use of waters, shall be taken into account. The same applies to a Marine Waters Management Plan pursuant to the same Act (section 51(1) of the Environmental Protection Act).

When assessing the suitability of a location in accordance with section 11(2), and when issuing permit provisions necessary for preventing accidents, the permit shall take account of what is set out in a Flood Risk Management Plan pursuant to the Flood Risk Management Act (620/2010), concerning the location and area of impact of the activity.

In addition to Environmental Permits, what has been said on programmes and plans above also applies to a decision due to notification.

§13. Provisions (Conditions, Regulations) Included in an Environmental Permit

I. Main Provisions

209. Sections 52–70, of which section 52 is thc most fundamental and most extensive, include provisions on the various conditions (provisions) to be included in a permit. Because most often a permit is, wholly or partially granted in practice, the question of its substantive contents is of utmost importance. As in environmental law in general, the very permit and the imposing of its conditions are in fact two strongly intertwined issues. Due to this relationship, section 52 may only be understood on the basis of interaction with (in particular) section 49.

According to the general rule in section 52(1), an Environmental Permit shall contain necessary provisions on:

(1) emissions, emission limit values, the prevention and limitation of emissions and the location of the site of emissions;
(2) the prevention of soil and groundwater pollution;
(3) wastes and reduction of their quantity and harmfulness;
(4) action to be taken in case of a malfunction or in other exceptional situations;
(5) measures to be taken after cessation of operation, such as remediation of the area and prevention of emissions; and
(6) other measures to prevent or reduce environmental pollution or the risk thereof.

'Emission limit value' is defined by section 5(1)(5) as value of undiluted emissions, which may not be exceeded during one or more periods of time and which is expressed as a total amount, concentration, percentage or in another, similar manner.

210. If provisions based on section 52(1) were, due to the nature of the activity in question, not able to sufficiently prevent or reduce the environmental harm, the permit may, except for industrial activity or energy production, also contain necessary conditions on allowed quantities of production, on fodder being used in production, or on energy produced (section 52(2)). This provision reflects the diversity of the activities covered by the Act. In normal industrial activities, it is not a matter of the authorities to decide upon internal production arrangements. It is normally enough for them to concentrate on the emissions. But there are activities where proper emission regulation would be practically impossible. Due to this, e.g., in animal farming or fish farming, the allowed environment is normally expressed by using the maximum number of animals or quantity of fodder used.

211. In the provisions of section 52 of the Act above nothing explicit has been said so far on assessing the necessity of various permit provisions or their contents, e.g., the required level of reducing emissions. These items are in the first place regulated in section 52(3): In laying down permit provisions, the nature of the activity, the properties of the area where the impact of the activity appears, the impact of the activity on the environment as a whole, the significance of measures intended to prevent pollution of the environment as a whole and the technical and financial feasibility of these measures. These general provisions of the Act are, where applicable, complemented by the detailed provisions in decrees, usually as minimum requirements. There is also a general provision in the same section 52(3) requiring that emission limit values and the conditions on preventing and reducing emissions shall be based on BAT (*see* paragraph 147). The last-mentioned is a minimum requirement that does not say that all activities in line with BAT should be permitted at all, but it is an additional requirement for the level of permit conditions. The use of any specific technology may not be required,[15] *see also* paragraph 148. Moreover, attention shall, as needed, be paid to energy efficiency, and efficiency in the use of materials, as well as to precautions for preventing accidents and limiting their consequences.

212. However, section 52(3) is not exhaustive regarding the necessity of permit provisions the types of which are listed in section 52(1). Any provision by which an obstacle to a permit according to section 48 or 49 is eliminated is allowed to make the permit itself possible, although this would be more stringent than what would result from the normal application of section 52(3). In addition, any such provision shall be imposed irrespective of section 52 the necessity of which is caused by a decree (section 48(2)), as is the case, e.g., regarding the various requirements of the Government decree on Landfills. On the relationship between decree-level standards and provisions set in permits, *see* paragraph 213.

213. A provision in an Environmental Permit may – and perhaps also shall – be more stringent than the respective general minimum standard in specified situations. In the present Environmental Protection Act the respective provisions are in section 70. Pursuant to it, a provision in a permit may be stricter than a specific minimum environmental protection requirement laid down in a government decree issued under the Environmental Protection Act or the Waste Act, but only if it is necessary:

15. This provision, inserted into the previous Act in 2002 in order to safeguard the correct implementation of EC law, seems to be very problematic in less typical, non-industrial cases. In practice, the Supreme Administrative Court has e.g., required from gasoline stations in ground water areas technically specified geological arrangements in the subsoil in order to prevent oil and chemicals from polluting important water intake, in order to make the very permitting possible (instead of refusing it due to an absolute obstacle).

(1) in order to meet the requirements for granting the actual permit, i.e., to eliminate an absolute obstacle to the permit, such as adverse health effect according to section 51, by laying down a more stringent condition;
(2) in order to safeguard that environmental quality requirements issued by Government decree are met; or
(3) for ensuring that BAT is used.

The present wording, unlike the previous one, does not include a provision pursuant to which stricter provisions are possible also for the protection of waters.

From 2018, section 70(1) also applies to decisions due to a notification respectively.

214. If a provision in a new decree happened to be more stringent than that in a valid permit decision, there would be a contradiction. In order to avoid this, it has been provided in section 70(2) that where a new decree under the Environmental Protection Act or the Waste Act includes environmental requirements more stringent than the valid permit, or provisions on the validity period of a permit deviating from the permit, or on the reviewing of the same, the provisions of the decree take priority. When approving the insertion of a similar provision in the previous Environmental Protection Act, the Parliament expressed the wish that each permit decision shall contain information on what is now section 70(2). A provision on this has been laid down in section 15(2) of the Environmental Protection Decree.

From 2018, this provision also applies to decisions due to a notification respectively.

215. It is not necessary to repeat in an Environmental Permit such pollution prevention requirements that have been laid down in an act or in a Government decree. The operator shall nevertheless be informed on these obligations in an appropriate manner, if the permit authority deems it necessary. A permit for an IED installation shall, however, always include a reference to the applicable sectoral Government decree (section 15(3)) of the Environmental Protection Decree.

216. A specific type of permit regulations is provided in section 54. An Environmental Permit may contain a provision requiring the permit holder to provide a specific account of the environmental pollution caused by the activity in question or determine the risk of it, if it has not been possible to provide detailed information on emissions, waste or operational impacts for the permit consideration. The account shall be submitted to the permit authority by the date specified in the permit. Sufficient time shall be provided for preparing the account. The account may make up the basis for an amendment of the permit, as provided in section 90 (*see* paragraph 232).

217. If the activity at stake falls within the Emissions Trading Act, no limit values may be imposed concerning greenhouse gas emissions referred to in section 2 of that Act, unless they are necessary to prevent significant local pollution of the environment (section 55). The provision indicates a possible contradiction between the need to prevent pollution of the environment and the need to reduce climate change.

Pursuant to section 56, an Environmental Permit concerning the capture of carbon dioxide shall give the regulations necessary for complying with the provisions on carbon dioxide flow as specified in sections 5 and 6 of the Act on Carbon Capture and Storage (416/2012).

218. Provisions on more specific types of permit regulations, the applicability of which depends on the type of the activity and the nature of the case at stake, are included in sections 57–70 of the Environmental Protection Act. Section 57 deals with fisheries management obligations (either a direct obligation on management measures or a fish management fee to the State, to be used for similar purposes), for which the respective provisions in the Water Act are applicable (*see* Part II, Chapter 6, §5 and Chapter 8, §2).

219. Section 58 provides that the Waste Act is applicable for laying down provisions on wastes and waste management in Environmental Permits (*see* paragraph 584), and sections 59–61 stipulate the permit provisions on financial guarantee required from waste treatment operations (*see* paragraph 585).

220. Sections 62–65 in turn contain the provisions on monitoring and control of the emissions and their impacts by the permit holder, as laid down in the permit decision, including publicity and the participation of the interested subjects. A separate monitoring plan may be required. The necessary provisions cover the operative monitoring of the activity, and the monitoring of emissions, the impact of the activity and on monitoring the state of the environment following the cessation of the activity, and where applicable, monitoring and supervision of waste management, provided in section 120 of the Waste Act, as well as a plan for the monitoring and supervision of waste treatment, and compliance therewith. To facilitate monitoring and control, the permit must include provisions on measurement methods and frequency of measurements. It must also contain provisions on how the results of monitoring and supervision are assessed and submitted to the supervisory authority. The operator may also be ordered to provide other information necessary for monitoring. Information on the results of the monitoring of the emissions of an IED installation, and other such information on the compliance of the IED installation with the permit that is necessary for supervisory purposes shall be submitted to the supervisory authority at least once a year.

When a provision on monitoring the impacts is laid down, attention shall be given to a Water Management Plan or a Marine Waters Management Plan pursuant to the Act on the Arranging of Water Management and Marine Waters Management. Information gained from such monitoring may be used in the monitoring and planning pursuant to that Act.

221. When needed, the permit authority, or another authority assigned by it, may order several permit holders to jointly monitor the impacts of their activities (joint monitoring) or approve participation in monitoring performed in the relevant larger area. Joint monitoring may relate to supervision based on both the Environmental Protection Act and the Water Act. The operator as a permit holder may be required to provide the authority with a plan on more detailed organization of the monitoring, to be initiated when the activity begins or at some other appropriate time with regard to the impacts of the activity. Notwithstanding the permit's or the plan's validity, monitoring regulations and the approved monitoring plan may be amended as necessary. The authority having approved joint monitoring must amend the decision if a new operator has been ordered to participate in joint monitoring.

A decision on monitoring may be amended ex officio or on demand by the permit holder, supervisory authority, an authority representing a public interest, a municipality or a party suffering harm, or a registered association or foundation referred to in section 186 of the Environmental Protection Act. Section 39 shall apply to the application of the permit holder requesting an amendment. The provisions of section 96 shall be applied in the processing of the matter (*see* paragraph 233).

Monitoring data and other information on emissions or environmental quality are public (section 210 of the Act), *see* paragraph 57.

222. An operator who is in charge of an activity subject to Environmental Permit shall ensure that measures are taken to prevent emissions into soil and groundwater, such as the regular upkeep, maintenance and inspections of structures. The permit shall include the necessary regulations on this. The operator shall also ensure soil and groundwater monitoring at regular intervals, taking into account any such hazardous substances at the installation site that may cause pollution of soil or groundwater (relevant hazardous substances). Based on a systematic assessment of the pollution risk, the permit shall moreover give the necessary regulations on the monitoring and the interval for periodic monitoring (section 66).

223. Provisions on conditions for discharges of industrial wastewater to public sewers are laid down in section 67. Section 68 contains detailed provisions on the rights, granted as a part of an Environmental Permit, to convey wastewater on or through another's property, in a ditch or streamlet or in a sewer pipe. The provisions of the Water Act on preconditions and compensations are partly applicable. On the construction of outlet sewer pipes in water bodies, expropriate rights included, by virtue of an Environmental Permit, a reference is made in section 69 to the respective provisions of the Water Act.

II. Provisions in IED Installation Permits

224. In addition to the general provisions on the preconditions of and provisions in an Environmental Permit in the Act, Chapter 7 (sections 72–82) of the Act lays down complementary provisions which are applicable only to IED installations. However, Chapter 7 is not applicable to research, development or the testing of new products and processes (section 73).

225. Where the operations of an IED installation involve the use, production or storage of relevant hazardous substances referred to in section 66 or otherwise the generation of such, the operator shall prepare a baseline report on soil and groundwater (section 82). The report shall be appended to the permit application. The baseline report shall contain information on soil and groundwater contamination caused by the relevant hazardous substances to enable the determination of the state of soil and groundwater for comparison with their state upon the cessation of operations. The baseline report shall contain: (1) information on the current use and past uses of the site; (2) sufficient information on soil and groundwater measurements that reflect the state at the time the baseline report is drawn up; (3) an assessment of the state of soil and groundwater in the area that is prepared based on the information referred to in (1) and (2).

226. Regarding BAT, the concepts reference document, conclusion and emission level in the Act (section 72 of the Act, *see* paragraph 149) pertain to IED installations.

The emission limit values, monitoring and other regulations in Environmental Permit of an IED installation shall be based on the conclusions for implementing the requirement for BAT. The environmental permit shall set emission limit values so that, under the normal operating conditions, the emission levels in the conclusions are not exceeded. If the conclusions do not specify emission levels, the permit shall lay down the regulations necessary for achieving the level of environmental protection associated with the BAT in the conclusions. In the event that the conclusions do not describe the techniques in use at the installation, the assessment criteria in section 53 of the Act (*see* paragraph 147) shall be applied to the assessment of BAT, when setting the emission limit values. If the conclusions do not describe the type of the activity or production methods according to the permit application or all their environmental impacts, the permit regulations, for the parts that are deemed necessary, shall be issued based on BAT as assessed in accordance with section 53. The operator's views shall be heard if such regulations would substantially differ from that presented in the application on BAT, limitations on emissions and monitoring (section 75).

Conclusions that enter into force after an Environmental Permit matter has been initiated are applicable only if this is reasonable for the applicant, taking into account the contents of the application and the conclusions, and the date of entry into force of the conclusions. If the Commission has not adopted the conclusions for the activity at stake, the corresponding parts of the reference documents, referred to in Article 13(7) of the IED and adopted by the Commission before 7 January 2011, shall be applied in the permit consideration. These parts shall be applied in the same way as the conclusions, with the exception of compliance with the emission levels. The Ministry of the Environment shall provide information on the conclusions on its website immediately after the Commission has adopted the relevant decision (section 76).

227. The emission limit values imposed pursuant to the generally applicable section 75(1) shall regarding IED installations be set for the same period of time or a shorter period, and in accordance with the same reference conditions as the emission levels. However, the limit values, periods of time and reference conditions may be deviated from if this is necessary due to the nature of the emissions or monitoring. In a manner provided in more detail in the Environmental Permit, the operator shall, at least once a year, submit to the supervisory authority (the Centre for Economic Development, Transport and the Environment of the region, environmental division) a summary of the results of the emissions monitoring for the same period and in accordance with the same reference conditions as for the emission levels (section 77).

If the emission limit values imposed under section 75(1) would lead to unreasonably higher costs compared to the environmental benefits due to the geographic location or technical properties or the local environmental conditions of the installation, the permit may set emission limits that are less stringent than those in section (75(1)). However, such less stringent emission limit values may neither exceed the emission limit values laid down in a Government decree issued under section 9, nor cause a consequence categorically forbidden in section 49, or compromise compliance with the environmental quality requirement (section 78). The circumstances for these less stringent emission limit values shall be reassessed when the permit is reviewed based on sections 80 and 81 or when the permit is amended based on section 89(1)(1), 89(1)(3) or 89(1)(6), *see* paragraph 242.

228. Upon application of an IED installation operator, the permit authority may grant a temporary derogation from the emission levels and other requirements for BAT for the testing and use of an emerging technique, for a period of no more than nine months (section 79). The derogation may be granted as part of a pending permit matter or in a decision following the notification of an activity undertaken on an experimental basis pursuant to section 119 (*see* paragraph 258).

229. If necessary, an Environmental Permit of an IED installation shall contain regulations on the energy efficiency of the activity at stake and on improving the efficiency. The regulations shall be feasible in terms of technology, financial and production aspects and they may concern: (1) the specification and management of energy efficiency; (2) the monitoring of energy efficiency based on available key figures; (3) the assurance that, upon the construction of a new installation or the substantial refurbishment of an operational installation, the prevention of environmental pollution will be assessed comprehensively and in accordance with BAT, taking into account energy efficiency in addition to emissions. The permit may specify that the operator shall submit information on the development of energy efficiency to the supervisory authority (section 74). However, the laying down of regulations on energy efficiency is not required if the operator has joined an energy efficiency agreement or other similar voluntary arrangement that involves an energy management system within which the operator specifies the procedures for monitoring energy efficiency and commits to continuously improve energy efficiency.

III. Provisions in the Permit on Its Validity

230. Pursuant to the previous Environmental Protection Act (2000), an Environmental Permit was issued either for an unspecified or limited period of time, and the permit authority had normally the power and duty to review later on a permit where the time of validity has not been limited, and, for particular reasons, also a permit where the time of validity has been limited. The time for such a review had to be fixed in the permit decision. The present Environmental Protection Act originally followed the same model, but soon (2015) the Act was amended and possibilities for later review of permit, as a rule resulting in improved environmental protection, were strongly reduced, for deregulation reasons.

This has understandably reduced the number of permit-related cases before the permit authorities. Not quite surprisingly, it has also contributed to a few total rejections of permit applications in such cases where it has been deemed doubtful whether the legal preconditions will prevail for an unspecified period of time, without a real possibility to check the situation, e.g., in water bodies and review the provisions later on. The most remarkable of such cases so far has been the rejection by the SAC of the permit application of the Finnpulp factory project in Kuopio, eastern Finland, at lake *Kallavesi* (SAC 2019:166). Regarding the assessment of preconditions, the decision of the European Court of Justice (ECJ) in the *Weser* case C-461/13 (*Bund für Umwelt und Naturschutz Deutschland e.V. v. Bundesrepublik Deutschland*) was central.

231. The present main rule on the validity of an Environmental Permit is expressed in section 87 of the Environmental Protection Act. The decision on the granting of a permit is valid without any time limit. No ordinary or general possibility to review is provided, except for IED installations.

Pursuant to the previous Environmental Protection Act, Water Management Plans and Programmes of Measures pursuant to the Act on the Arranging of Water Management and Marine Waters Management had to be taken into account when the validity period or regular future review is decided upon. Such a possibility does not exist anymore.

232. However, a permit can be granted for a limited period only by way of an application submitted by the very operator or if there is an important reason for it as regards the special characteristics of the activity, the novelty of the technique or methods used in it or the difficulty of assessing the harmful impacts of the activity. A permit granted for a fixed period expires when the period ends, unless otherwise provided in the permit decision (section 87). Validity periods for Environmental Permits issued jointly with a Soil Excavation Permit (section 47a) are provided in section 10 of the Soil Excavation Act.

One limited possibility to make review of an Environmental Permit (other than IED) possible later on has remained in the Act, as the permit authority may issue more detailed permit regulations or supplement a valid permit on the basis of a specific account based on a previously set provision pursuant to section 54 (section 90, *see* paragraph 216).

233. The procedural provisions for amending, revoking, etc. are, where applicable, largely the same as those for dealing with permit applications (section 96).

§14. Compensations in a Permit Context

234. The pecuniary compensations for environmental damage are in part directly connected to environmental permits. This is a continuation of the traditional line of the 1961 Water Act, regarding both water management and construction and pollution of surface water bodies (but not of groundwater, because the polluting of groundwater has long been absolutely forbidden and hence not expected in permit procedures). Compensations on (anticipated, and partly also past) lawful, permit-based pollution (i.e., any harmful effect of a permitted discharge) of surface waters (to, e.g., owners of water and shoreline areas) have been decided upon ex officio by the permit authorities (prior to March 2000, by the then Water Courts). The rest of environmental protection legislation in turn has lacked this kind of connection, and damages caused by, e.g., noise or pollution of soil or air have been left to civil procedure and the Environmental Damages Act (*see* Part IV, Chapter 2, §2). This dualistic state of affairs (also linked to the status of the previous Water Courts in other respects) was one of the main problems in creating an integrated permit system (*see* §4 above).

Finally, the dualism was preserved within the integrated general framework of the Environmental Protection Act of 2000, and the same holds good regarding the present Environmental Protection Act. Compensations for lawful damage caused by pollution of surface water bodies are decided upon by the permit authority (the Regional State Administrative Agency), and still ex officio. There is a whole chapter (Chapter 13, sections 124–132) on these compensations in the (present) Environmental Protection Act, mainly with procedural contents. Contrary to before 2000, the substantive stipulation is at present, however, to be found in the Environmental Damages Act instead of the compensation provisions of the Water Act. As for other types of environmental damage (nuisances, pollution of air, soil, or groundwater) Chapter 13 is practically irrelevant, as it only includes an informative reference to the Environmental Damages Act. It may seem surprising that a substantive civil liability system has been inserted in an administrative context. In practice, the changes after 2000 are insignificant. Moreover, the progress of water pollution prevention has significantly reduced the total yearly amounts of compensations.

§15. Appeals Against a Decision on an Environmental Permit

235. A permit decision (like all other administrative decisions under the Environmental Protection Act) can be appealed against in the Regional Administrative Court in Vaasa and further on in the SAC, if leave of appeal is granted. The competence of one single regional court for the whole country is related to the fact that the same holds traditionally true for the Water Act; the previous Superior Water Court (in Vaasa) with its technical and ecological expertise and Vaasa Regional Administrative Court were merged in 1999. From March 2000, there are the so-called mixed projects (*see* paragraphs 180, 1244 and 1298) to which both the Environmental Protection Act and the Water Act are applied substantively at the same time (e.g., fish farming with its water supply and wastewater discharge). In these cases, there is only one permit procedure for the totality, and also the appellate procedure is undivided. The procedures largely follow the Water Act. It was moreover regarded natural in the preparatory stage that all appeals under the Environmental Protection Act shall follow the same appellate line, i.e., the, Regional Administrative Court in Vaasa and the SAC, irrespective of which authority has made the administrative decision. Due to this, the water-related ecological expertise in the Regional Administrative Court in Vaasa was in March 2000 also extended to other sectors of ecology. The expert non-lawyer members of the court, as members of the collegial case-by-case compositions of judges, have the same powers and duties as the legally educated judges.

236. All decisions of the Regional Administrative Court in Vaasa under the Environmental Protection Act can be appealed against in the SAC, from 2020 subject to a leave to appeal. According to the present Administrative Judicial Procedures Act (808/2019), such leave must be granted if: (1) with regard to the application of law, in other similar cases, or because of the uniformity of legal praxis, it is important to bring the matter to the SAC for decision; (2) there is specific reason to bring the matter to the SAC for a decision due to an obvious error in the matter; or (3) there is another important reason for granting leave. This means that need of legal precedent is not the only option. Leave to appeal can also be granted to apply to only a section of the Regional Administrative Court decision against which the appeal is lodged.

Also the bench in the SAC in matters under the Environmental Protection Act (and the Water Act) includes technical and ecological experts (five justices and two expert members). These experts, mainly being recognized scientists, have, unlike the colleagues in Vaasa, merely part-time posts, but still important.[16]

237. Right to appeal against an Environmental Permit or an amendment decision by the permit authority is rather extensive. The entitled subjects are listed in section 191(1) of the Environmental Protection Act. They include:

(1) parties, i.e., all whose right or interest may be concerned;
(2) registered associations and foundations the task of which is protection of environment, health or nature or promotion of amenity of an inhabited area, provided that the project impacts their geographical area of activities;
(3) the municipality where the project of the applicant takes place, and any such other municipality the area of which is impacted by the project;
(4) the Centre for Economic Development, Transport and the Environment (in the capacity of regional environmental authority), the municipal Environmental Protection Authority of the municipality where the project takes place and the municipal Environmental Protection Authority of such other municipality the area of which is impacted by the project;

16. *See also* T.M. Paloniitty & S. Kangasmaa, *Securing Scientific Understanding: Expert Judges in Finnish Environmental Administrative Judicial Review*, 27(4) Eur. Energy & Environ. L. Rev., 125–139 (2018).

(5) any other authority in charge of keeping an eye on specific public interest (e.g., the fisheries authorities);
(6) the Finnish Saami Parliament on the grounds that the activity referred to in the environmental permit impairs the rights of the Saami as indigenous peoples to maintain and develop their own language and culture; and
(7) the Skolt Saami Village Committee on the grounds that the activity referred to in the environmental permit causes deterioration in the living conditions of the Skolts and reduces the possibilities to practise nature-based livelihoods in the Skolt area pursuant to the Skolt Act.

Among those whose right or interest may be concerned, i.e., private parties, the owners and holders of the affected area (or, more properly, of the area which is possibly going to be affected) are the most important. The same category also includes holders of fishing rights or water intakes, etc. Where discharges to waters or emissions to the air are at stake, the geographical area may be considerably large or (as for inland waters) otherwise far-reaching or complicated. As for water bodies and territorial waters, the shareholders' associations for a registered village's common areas have been very common parties and appellants. Regarding public interests, the *locus standi* of the regional environmental authorities (environmental divisions of the Centres for Economic Development, Transport and the Environment), and the Municipal Environmental Protection Authorities (of all affected municipalities) is of course crucial. Among other authorities, the State fisheries authorities (units within the Centres for Economic Development, Transport and the Environment) are the most common appellants.

Regarding the right of appeal against decisions by the Regional Administrative Court the same provisions as described above in paragraph 237 above are applicable, but of course totally new claims are not allowed, unless caused by the amendments made by the court, where any. Where the Regional Administrative Court has repealed or amended the decision of the permit authority, an appeal to the SAC by the Centre for Economic Development, Transport and Environment or Municipal Environmental Protection Authorities is supposed to take place only when motivated by public environmental protection interest or other specified reason (section 191(2)).

238. An activity subject to Environmental Permit requirement shall not be initiated or changed before the permit decision authorizing its implementation has gained legal force (section 198(1) of the Environmental Protection Act.) However, this rule has one important exception. Pursuant to section 199 of the Environmental Protection Act, the permit authority may grant the applicant the right to start, despite that the time of appealing (thirty days from the decision) has not elapsed yet or appeals are already pending. This is only allowed for grounded reasons and provided that possible appeals are not made purposeless. Moreover, a security is required for restoration of the environment in the case that the permit is repealed or amended by appellate court. An order according to section 199 can be appealed against like the very permit, and the appellate courts may forbid the activity for the time of proceedings.

Out of this, an appeal regarding compensation only shall not prevent the initiation of an activity. At the appellate stage before the SAC, the decision of the Regional Administrative Court may be enforceable and implemented (without a decision pursuant to section 199), but only provided that the appeal before the SAC does not turn purposeless (section 122 of the Administrative Judicial Procedures Act). This means that the activity based on the issued permit generally cannot be initiated at this stage. The SAC may also explicitly forbid the enforcement and implementation, i.e., forbid the activity, for the time of proceedings.

§16. The Permanence and Constancy of an Environmental Permit

239. As stated above, there is no more left any general possibility to review a valid Environmental Permit (*see* paragraphs 230–231). Concerning obligations on fish management measures or a fish management fee, the more flexible preconditions set forth in the Water Act are applied, however.

240. IED installations make up an exception, as there are wider possibilities to review an Environmental Permit than in general. Section 80 provides review due to new conclusions. Once the Commission has published its decision on the conclusions concerning the main activity of an installation covered by the directive, the permit of the installation shall be reviewed, if it is not in accordance with the existing conclusions and the provisions laid down in or under the Act or if the permit includes regulations on less stringent emission limit values specified in section 78. The review shall take into account all new and updated conclusions that are applicable and that the Commission has adopted after the permit was granted or last reviewed, or the need for its review was assessed. The operator shall submit an account of the need and justification for permit review to the supervisory authority. The account shall be submitted within six months of the Commission publishing a decision on the conclusions. On request, the supervisory authority (the Centre for Economic Development, Transport and the Environment of the region) may grant more time for preparing the account. The supervisory authority shall assess whether or not a review of the permit is necessitated. If the permit review is unnecessary, the same authority shall provide a corresponding assessment to the operator and the review process is concluded. If the permit review is necessary, the supervisory authority shall order the operator to submit an application for review to the permit authority (Regional State Administrative Agency). The application shall be submitted no later than on the date specified by the supervisory authority, which may be at the earliest six months after the order was issued. Different operators may be ordered to submit their application at the same time or at differing times, depending on the organization of the authority's work, the number of pending matters or differences in the situation of the operators. The order does not need to be issued if a permit matter that takes the requirements into account is already pending. The supervisory authority may issue an order even if the operator has neglected to submit the required account.

Upon application of the operator, the permit authority shall review the permit according to the criteria in section 80(1), and, if necessary, issue regulations on the use of less stringent emission limit values pursuant to section 78 (section 81). If the time needed to introduce BAT requires a longer period than the four years specified in Article 21 of the IED, a longer period may be set in the permit regulations for the introduction of the techniques, in accordance with the justifications in section 78. The permit may oblige the operator to comply with the conclusions concerning the primary activity of the installation no earlier than four years after the publication of the decision on the conclusions by the Commission, unless the applicant has indicated the intent to be in compliance at an earlier date. The provisions in section 39 on the permit application shall apply to the application. The permit review shall be resolved as an urgent matter.

241. The permit authority may decide on the lapse of an IED installation permit if: (1) the activity has been interrupted continuously for at least five years or the operator notifies that the activity will not be started at all or the activity has been permanently ceased; (2) the activity or measures essential to its starting up have not been initiated or taken within five years of the permit becoming legally valid, or within a longer period specified in the permit; or (3) an application to review the permit of the IED installation has not been submitted in accordance with section 80(3). Such a matter may be initiated by the permit authority on its own initiative, a supervisory authority, the operator, a municipality or a party suffering harm.

242. An Environmental Permit in force may under certain qualified preconditions be amended on application to the permit authority (section 89). First, an operator may apply for the amendment of a permit. Additionally, the permit authority shall, on application by the supervisory authority, the relevant authority representing a public interest or a party suffering harm, or a registered association or foundation referred to in section 186, amend the permit, if: (1) the pollution or risk thereof caused by the activity substantially differs from what had been estimated in advance; (2) the activity may have a consequence prohibited by the Act; (3) emissions may be substantially reduced without undue cost due to advances in BAT; (4) the external circumstances of the activity have changed substantially since the granting of the permit, resulting in the need to amend the permit; (5) amending the permit after it has been issued is necessary in order to fulfil a binding specified requirement concerning the prevention of environmental pollution set by law in a Government decree or in a EU regulation. In addition, the permit authority shall, on the initiative of the supervisory authority or an authority representing certain public interest, amend the permit provisions concerning the collateral if the permit authority considers that the amount of the collateral specified in the Environmental Permit for waste management is not sufficient to carry out the measures specified in section 59 of the Act or that the collateral otherwise does not meet the requirements of sections 59 to 61.

243. If the amendment is initiated by other than the operator, the permit authority shall, before deciding on the matter, hear the views of the operator and oblige them to provide the reports required for assessing the need and justification for the amendment within a reasonable period. If the decision on the matter is significant from the point of view of public interest or compelling reasons so require, the operator may be obliged to obtain the information necessary for resolving the initiative, at the risk that it will be obtained at the operator's expense. The permit authority may also hear the operator, the party initiating the procedure and the parties referred to in section 43 of the Act on the initiative and on the draft decision it has prepared if this is necessary to clarify the matter.

244. Even revoking a valid Environmental Permit (section 93) is possible, in certain extreme conditions. A matter of revoking may today only be initiated by the supervisory authority. The permit authority may revoke a valid permit if: (1) the applicant has furnished the permit authority with false information that has essentially influenced the preconditions of granting a permit; (2) the regulations in the permit have been violated repeatedly despite a written reminder from the supervisory authority so that the activity may cause consequences contradictory to the preconditions for granting the permit; or (3) the preconditions for continuing the activity cannot be achieved by amending the Permit.

245. If complying with the terms of an Environmental Permit within the set time limit causes undue difficulty for reasons beyond the control of the permit holder and a delay in compliance with the terms does not pose a risk of significant environmental pollution, the permit authority on application can extend the time limit by a maximum of three years. The permit shall be reviewed as needed because of the extension of the time limit. No extension is allowed if the Environmental Protection Act or the Waste Act, or decrees issued under them, or international obligations binding on Finland would be violated (section 91).

246. At the request of an operator or a supervisory authority, the permit authority may update the information in an environmental permit by issuing a written statement on the matter. The statement may be issued if it provides clarification and if it is not used to modify the actual content of the permit in a way that could result in environmental pollution or risk of such or a change in anyone's rights or interests (section 92).

§17. Procedures Concerning Notification and Registration

I. Ordinary Notifications

247. Provisions on the ordinary notification procedure (Chapter 10a) were inserted into the Environmental Protection Act in 2018, when a significant number of activities (*see* paragraphs 117 and 158) subject to Environmental Permit were in a deregulatory reform transferred to the then created version of notification procedure instead. However, the notification procedure came to contain several traits of the Environmental Permit system, for obvious reasons.

A notification, when needed (*see* paragraphs 157 and 161), has to be submitted to the competent authority at least 120 days prior to the initiation of the activity (section 115a). The same applies to changes of activity, pursuant to the same provisions as regarding necessity of Environmental Permit in section 89 (*see* paragraph 242). The local Municipal Environmental Protection Authority is the competent authority in respect to notifications, with the exception of certain activities for military purposes, where any, for which the Regional State Administrative Agency is competent (section 115a).

248. A notification shall contain the necessary and binding information on the activity, its impacts, concerned parties and other items of significance, for the processing of the notification. The Environmental Protection Decree contains more detailed provisions on notifications and the procedure. The person in charge of the preparing of the activity shall have the expertise needed. Where needed, the notification shall show the documentation and calculation, research and assessment methods the information and data are based on.

If the notification is inadequate, an opportunity shall be reserved for the operator to supplement the notification within a deadline set by the authority. A notification that is not supplemented within the deadline or if the notification still is insufficient, the notification shall be dismissed and the activity cannot be initiated (section 115b).

249. An activity subject to notification duty shall not be initiated before 120 days have elapsed from the notification. The authority may however, in its decision allow an earlier initiation. The activity shall not be initiated, if the notification has been channelled to Environmental Permit procedure by virtue of section 29a (*see* paragraph 164). The activity shall not be initiated, either, if the authority, due to the notification, forbids the notified activity (section 115c).

250. The authority makes an administrative decision regarding the notification (section 115d, as amended by 905/2020). When making the decision the authority shall make sure that the provisions in and under the Act, and in and under the Waste Act, regarding the siting of the activity, emissions and the prevention thereof, waste, and the monitoring of the emissions and their impacts are observed. Also the provisions in and under the Nature Protection Act shall be observed. The received statements, opinions and remarks shall be taken into account, as well as what has been provided for safeguarding private and public interests. The decision shall be observed in spite of a possible appeal to the Regional Administrative Court.

A basic requirement for accepting a notification is that the same absolute preconditions as for an Environmental Permit in section 49 (*see* above 204) are fulfilled (section 115d(2)). To provisions (regulations) included in the decision the same provisions as for Environmental Permits in sections 52 and 62 (above) are applied (section 115d(4)).

As to the procedure and decision-making, the permit procedure provisions in sections 39a, 42, 43, 44, 83(1), 85(1), 85(2) and 85 (above) are applicable, either as such or slightly modified (section 115e). Among other things, this means that the concerned parties shall be heard. Also the permit-related provisions in sections 87, 88, 89, 92, 93, 94(1), 94(2) and 94(3) are applied respectively.

251. For certain categories of activities under notification requirement, substantive provisions are laid down by specific decrees. For example, Government decree on farm animal facilities subject to notification duty (138/2019) is applicable to the construction, enlarging and activity of such facilities. The Decree contains provisions on minimum distances between facility buildings or manure storages and various items potentially disturbed by smell, prevention of smell by technical means, recovery of manure, treatment of certain wastewaters, treatment of feed waste, treatment of dead animals and monitoring and reporting.

II. Registration

252. Registration, as it stands from 2018 (Chapter 11), is the slightest version of operator-specific preventive control in the Environmental Protection Act. The basic idea is that directly applicable detailed provisions in decrees are used as far as possible, while proper administrative decision-making is avoided. The activities subject to registration duty are specified in Annex 2 (*see* paragraph 159). The applicable environmental requirements are provided in decrees under section 10. A notification on registration (section 116) shall for registration include the information on the operator, the activity, its site its impacts. The operator shall be informed on the registration.

253. Notifications for registration shall be submitted to the local Municipal Environmental Protection Authority, to be registered in the Environmental Protection Information System (*see* paragraphs 291–293), at least sixty days prior to the initiation of the activity. The Municipal Environmental Protection Authority has to make the registration within sixty days from the submission. Regarding medium combustion plants, the two time limits are thirty days respectively, however. If the notification for registration is insufficient, the authority shall tell the operator to complement the notification. In such a case, the fixed periods above do not begin before the substantive requirements have been met.

254. As registration is secondary to Environmental Permit, and to notification according to Chapter 10a (*see* paragraphs 159, 160 and 165), no notification for registration is needed, if permit or ordinary notification is necessary (section 116.6).

255. The applicable decrees typically have a twofold scope of application. For example, Government decree on the environmental protection requirements for stations of distribution of liquid fuels (314/2020) is applicable to distribution stations with a total fuel tank volume of at least 10 cubic metres subject to registration requirement, but also, as a minimum requirement, to such distribution stations for which Environmental Permit is needed due to section 30 of the Environmental Protection Act. Similarly, Government decree on the environmental protection requirements for middle scale energy protection units and installations (1065/2017; applicable to units with a thermal input of at least 1 megawatt, but less than 50 megawatts, with certain exceptions) and Government decree on the environmental requirements for concrete plants and concrete product factories (858/2018), have a twofold scope of application.

Likewise, the Government decree on the environmental protection requirements of asphalt stations (846/2012), issued under the 2000 Environmental Protection Act, but remained into force also under the present Act, is applicable as minimum requirements in Environmental Permit considerations, where any, and as such in registration.

III. Specific Notifications

256. A specific modification of notifications (Chapter 12) deals with certain temporary or incidental activities.

257. Measures and activities causing temporary noise or vibration (section 118) is a traditional category of such notifications (*see* Part I, Chapter 7, §5 below). Sections 121 and 122 (below) apply also to these.

258. Another notification category (section 119) here deals with experimental measures for which an Environmental Permit is not needed pursuant to section 31 (*see* paragraph 166).

259. A third category (section 120) is made up of certain exceptional situations. If an accident, an unexpected production malfunction or another comparable surprising reason that does not depend on the activity, or demolishing a structure or device, within an activity not subject to permit, notification or registration requirement, causes emissions or risk of emissions or produces waste in such a manner that immediate and evident risk of pollution, or necessity of exceptional waste treatment measures results, the operator or the holder of waste shall immediately submit a notification to the Municipal Environmental Protection Authority.

260. The procedures for all these notification categories have been stipulated in sections 121–122. For notifications in accordance of sections 118 and 119, information on the pendency of the matter shall be provided and the concerned parties heard pursuant to the Administration Act, if the notified activity may significantly impact public or private interests. For notifications provided in section 120, the same applies respectively, but only if there is grounded specific reason for that.

261. Due to any notification of specific nature, the authority shall make a decision containing orders needed for preventing environmental pollution (noise included) and arranging the waste-related duties pursuant to the Waste Act (section 122). The decision shall include the necessary provisions to prevent environmental pollution and to fulfil the obligations under the Waste Act. In addition, a decision regarding experimental measures shall, if needed, include the necessary provisions on the collateral (section 59) and its furnishing. The decision may also lay down provisions on the monitoring of activities and a provision of information to local inhabitants. The measure or activity may be forbidden, if significant harm to private or public interests cannot be sufficiently reduced by orders laid down in the decision. An order or a ban is possible also when the notification duty has been omitted. Failure to notify is moreover a punishable offence. The authority may also allow temporary deviations from duties pursuant to the Environmental Protection Act or the Waste Act, as provided in section 122(3).

262. While section 120 of the Environmental Protection Act (above) deals with incidents within activities not subject to permit, notification or registration requirement, section 123 refers correspondingly to activities subject to such a requirement. If an accident, an unexpected production malfunction or another comparable surprising reason that does not depend on the activity, or demolishing a structure or device, within an activity not subject to permit, notification or registration requirement, creates a situation where the permit or decision for notification or the applicable decree cannot be observed, or a situation where immediate and evident risk of pollution may be caused or exceptional waste management measures are needed, the operator or the holder of waste shall immediately submit a notification to the Municipal Environmental Protection Authority or the Centre for Economic Development, Transport and the Environment of the region, depending on the category of activity. The operator or the holder of waste shall also submit a plan on reducing emissions, waste and pollution during the exceptional circumstances.

263. Following the notification, the authority shall make a decision and issue the orders needed for returning the activity to a State where it is in compliance with the Act and any provisions issued under it, and for eliminating the harm and risk caused by the situation. A deadline shall be set for the measures. Furthermore, temporary orders shall be issued, if needed, based on the operator's plan and other information in order to prevent environmental pollution. The orders may be issued or the activity prohibited even if the obligation to provide notification has been neglected. The provisions on administrative enforcement in Chapter 18 are applicable with when issuing the orders. Provisions on the treatment of polluted soil or groundwater in Chapter 14 and provisions in section 176 on the remediation on damage to protected species and natural habitats may additionally become applicable.

264. Where the exceptional situation requires, the Municipal Environmental Protection Authority or the Centre for Economic Development, Transport and the Environment of the region shall, on its own initiative, start a procedure to amend the permit regulations pursuant to section 89 or a procedure to revoke the permit pursuant to section 93.

265. As usual, the decisions in accordance to sections 122 and 123 of the Act can be appealed to the Regional Administrative Court (of Vaasa). The authority may, however, decide that the decision given by it is in force immediately notwithstanding an eventual appeal, unless the court decides otherwise (section 200 of the Environmental Protection Act).

§18. ENVIRONMENTAL QUALITY

266. One of the novelties in the present Environmental Protection Act is the coherent stipulation of environmental quality and other state of the environment in Chapter 15 (sections 140–153). The provisions include general principles and requirements regarding the different ambient media, but also concrete duties. Many of the provisions are relevant also in Environmental Permit considerations.

267. Regarding the quality of water in surface water bodies (territorial waters in the sea also here included), the aim for all activities under the Act shall be to achieve a level of surface water quality where substances hazardous and harmful to the aquatic environment do not cause harm to health or other significant consequences referred to in section 5(1)(2), or any risk of such (section 140(1)). For this purpose, provisions on environmental quality requirements safeguarding the quality of surface waters shall be issued by Government decree. The provisions may concern the concentration of substances hazardous and harmful to the aquatic environment in surface water, sediment and fauna. Also derogations from environmental quality requirements may be provided by Government decree, when this is needed for the enforcement of EU legislation. The environmental targets for the chemical and ecological state of aquatic areas, and any derogations from these, are, as referred to in the Environmental Protection Act, provided in and under the Act on the Arranging of Water Management and Marine Waters Management (section 140).

268. Likewise concerning quality of natural waters, Government decree on Substances Dangerous and Harmful to the Aquatic Environment (1022/2006), based on the previous Environmental Protection Act, but remained in force and was amended later on (*see also* paragraphs 400, 419, 425, 441 and 1332), includes the relevant (surface) water quality regulation also under the present Act. Pursuant to section 6 of the Decree, the concentrations of the substances listed in Annex 1 C2 and D in water and organisms shall not exceed the environmental quality standards set in the same Annex. If there is a standard for organisms, this shall be used. The Environmental Permits are also here crucial. Regarding activities other than subject to permit requirement, the Centres for Economic Development, Transport and the Environment shall in the Programmes of Measures provided in sections 12 and 26f of the Act on the Arranging of Water Management and Marine Waters Management present the measures needed in order to prevent the quality standards to be exceeded, taking BEP into account, if the breach is caused by an activity for which no Environmental Permit is needed. As to permit-requiring discharges, the measures are decided upon in the Environmental Permit (section 6 of the Decree). A possibility to deviate is provided in section 6a concerning situations where the exceeding is caused by a source out of Finland and effective national measures are not feasible.

269. Regarding ambient air quality, section 141 of the Environmental Protection Act provides that in all activities under the Act such a level of air quality shall be to achieve where the quantity of hazardous or harmful substances or compounds in ambient air, or in the deposition of these, is not present at a level that would cause harm to health or other significant consequences referred to in section 5(1)(2), or any risk of such. In aiming to this, provisions on environmental quality requirements and objectives that may concern the quantity of hazardous or harmful substances or compounds in ambient air, or in the deposition thereof are issued by Government decree to secure air quality. The possibility for derogations is the same as regarding water quality.

On the provisions on monitoring ambient air quality and related duties, *see* Part I, Chapter 2, §4 below.

270. Quality of sound environment is in turn provided in section 142. The aim for all activities under the Act shall be to achieve a level of quality of sound environment where hazardous or harmful sounds (noise) does not occur to an extent that would cause harm to health or other significant consequences referred to in section 5(1)(2), or any risk of such. In aiming to this, provisions on environmental quality requirements and objectives are issued by Government decree to secure the quality of the sound environment (*see* Part I, Chapter 7, §1 below). As provided in section 150, each municipality shall promote the quality of the sound environment in its geographical area, taking into account the environmental quality requirements and targets pursuant to section 142. Noise accounts and Noise Abatement Action Plans are provided in sections 151–153. *See* Part I, Chapter 7, §2.

271. The obligation of each municipality within its territory to *see* to the necessary monitoring of the state of the environment according to local conditions and using the appropriate methods (section 143), also applies to noise. At the same time, the State supervisory authorities, i.e., the Centres for Economic Development, Transport and the Environment, are responsible for the monitoring within their (larger) areas (section 143). *See also* Part I, Chapter 7, §2.

§19. ADDITIONAL ASPECTS OF THE ENVIRONMENTAL PROTECTION ACT

272. The obligations of an Environmental Permit holder or the of an operator of an activity subject to registration requirement provided in and under the Environmental Protection Act on pollution prevention and monitoring do not end when the activity is decommissioned (section 94). If the permit does not contain the provisions needed, the authority shall issue such provisions. If the operator does not exist or cannot be detected, the owner of the area is responsible for necessary monitoring (section 94). The wider obligations of IED operators depend on whether a baseline account on soil and groundwater has earlier been worked out, as provided in section 95.

273. The regulation of measures against climatic change was one of the issues that caused political difficulties in the preparation of the previous Environmental Protection Act Bill. The debate was also one of legislative basic structures, as the climatic changes do not necessarily come under the notion of the pollution of the environment (that being the main focus of the Environmental Protection Act). Ultimately, no specific provisions on the abatement of climatic change were included. However, according to a statement in that bill, the scope of application of the Act can be extended later on with an inclusion of necessary provisions on the item, as required by future international obligations. It is anyway one of the explicit aims of the Environmental Protection Act (section 1(7)) to abate climate change. Certain parts of the Act are moreover in fact directly connected to climate.

274. Measures for protecting the ozone layer, based on international obligations are within the scope of the Environmental Protection Act (especially in Chapter 17). The deterioration of the ozone layer is hence, although not explicitly, one of the many types of pollution of the environment, as defined by section 5(1)(2) of the Environmental Protection Act.

275. The previous Environmental Protection Act made joint implementation of environmental protection measures, especially those of international air pollution prevention obligations, possible. In the present Act the applicable provisions are in sections 213–215. Systematically, joint implementation is always based on an exception regarding a certain activity from specified requirements laid down by Government decree under section 9, issued by the Ministry of the Environment. It is among other things required that the operator takes protection measures elsewhere in Finland or in another country, in such a way that the total emissions or their impacts are as a whole essentially reduced. In cases where the harmful impacts of the activity vary depending on the location of the impacted areas, it is also required that the emissions to the area of Finland be reduced as well. The provisions of the Environmental Protection Act or any requirements under it are not set aside. Necessary conditions may be included in the decision of the Ministry of the Environment. No arrangement shall be against any international obligation of Finland, and it shall be appropriate taking the technical and economic possibilities of environmental protection measures into account. Reliable monitoring is also required. An application for an exception is made public pursuant to section 214. The application procedure takes place separately from the permit procedures of any of the involved activities.

276. An exception establishing joint implementation may be amended or abolished by a new decision on the grounds specified in section 215. According to the preparatory documents of the amendment of the previous Environmental Protection Act, the necessary implementation of future legislation will take place irrespective of any arrangement on joint implementation, without making the government liable for any economic loss suffered by interested parties.

In practice, joint implementation does not seem to be significant so far. The provisions, or the Environmental Protection Act in general, are not applicable to joint implementation in the climate change regime, such as that pursuant to the Kyoto Protocol, as provided in the Act 109/2007.

§20. Supervision and Enforcement of the Environmental Protection Act

277. The duties and powers of supervision and enforcement of the Environmental Protection Act, like the various decisions made under it, are vested in the Centres for Economic Development, Transport and the Environment and the municipal Environmental Protection Authorities (section 23). The two are obliged to inform each other on observations regarding items vested in the other. On the division on duties regarding certain activities, there are provisions in section 189.

In addition to these two with general supervision tasks, several other authorities participate in the supervision, on specified items (section 24). These are the Finnish Safety and Chemicals Agency (Tukes), consumer protection authorities, occupational safety authorities, the Transport and Communications Agency Traficom, municipal Public Health Authorities, food safety authorities, the customs and the Border Guard.

278. Also the task of supervision regarding the compliance of the statutory management requirements of Regulation (EU) No. 1307/2013 of the European Parliament and of the Council of 17 December 2013 establishing rules for direct payments to farmers under support schemes within the framework of the CAP and repealing Council Regulation (EC) No. 637/2008 and Council Regulation (EC) No. 73/2009 is assigned to the Centres for Economic Development, Transport and the Environment, being at the same time the body for financing rural businesses.

279. The supervision shall be arranged on a high-quality level, in a regular and effective manner, being based on the assessment of environmental risks (section 167 of the Environmental Protection Act). The various tasks may be prioritized, if this is necessary for the appropriate performing of duties.

280. For the arranging of their regular supervisory activities, each Centre for Economic Development, Transport and the Environment and each municipal Environmental Protection Authority shall work out a Supervision Plan for its geographic area pursuant to section 168 of the Environmental Protection Act. A Supervision Plan shall include information on the environmental circumstances of the area, activities posing a risk of environmental pollution and available resources and means of supervision. Also the general supervisory arrangements, foundations of risk assessment and cooperation between supervisory authorities shall be described. The plans shall be reviewed at regular intervals.

281. The Centre for Economic Development, Transport and the Environment and the Municipal Environmental Protection Authority shall supervise all activities subject to environmental permit, notification or registration requirement regularly by means of inspections. The objects and frequency of inspections shall be determined on the basis of assessed environmental risks. The inspections and other regular supervision shall be based on Supervision Programmes. Regarding IED installations, a regular inspection shall be performed according to the risk level of the activity at intervals of a minimum of one year and maximum of three years. An extra inspection shall be performed in six months, if it is observed in the supervision that the applicable provisions and requirements have been significantly infringed (section 168). Detailed provisions on supervision may be laid down by Government decree.

282. If there is, due to accident, notification on adverse item, non-compliance of permit or notification decision or other issue, reason to assume that harm to health or environmental pollution pursuant to section 5(1)(2) of the Act or risk thereof is caused by the activity, the authority shall inspect the activity or find the situation out in another appropriate way (section 169).

283. Supervision is based on information gathered in several ways. One important source is made up by the reports of the obligatory monitoring and surveillance of emissions and their impacts by permit holders under section 62 of the Environmental Protection Act. The authorities also perform research work relevant to supervision and are also entitled to take various (also random) control samples and monitor the environment in private areas, and they also have access to various information sources (sections 171 and 172). Various administrative decisions (permits,[17] notification decisions, etc.) and results of monitoring and surveillance, creating a necessary basis for supervision, are registered in the Environmental Protection Information System provided in sections 222 and 223 of the Environmental Protection Act, *see also* paragraphs 291–293.

284. The permit holders are obliged to inform the competent supervisory authority on permanent or long-lasting interruptions of the activity and on such changes in the activity that are relevant to supervision. Also the change of permit holder (actually change of possession of installations, etc.) shall be reported (section 170). Where obligatory monitoring by a permit holder pursuant to section 62 requires, the Centre for Economic Development, Transport and the Environment may grant him a right to make necessary observations, including the keeping of measuring facilities, on another's area, after having heard the owner or possessor and provided that no significant harm is caused (section 171).

285. From the legal point of view, supervisory measures are based either on observations and considerations of the authority itself or on remarks by interested parties on allegedly unlawful activities or measures. This is especially true for enforcement.

286. The supervisory authorities also deal with injunctions and other administrative coercion. In case of infringement, the supervisory authority shall, depending on the circumstances, advise the subject at stake to end the illegal activity and initiate administrative enforcement procedure pursuant to sections 175 and 176 (section 179). The coercive measures may contain injunctive bans and orders, e.g., on

17. Also the relevant information in the respective decisions of the (Vaasa) Regional Administrative Court and the SAC are saved here.

the activity itself or on reinstatement. The provisions of the Administrative Injunctions (Conditional Fines) Act (1113/1990) are applicable.

287. An injured or otherwise concerned party or an association or foundation, or an authority, as defined in section 186 is entitled to request for a decision on administrative coercion, and receive an appealable decision also in that case that no orders are regarded necessary by the authority. In practice this mechanism, being subject to review by administrative courts, is also very important horizontally, i.e., for the legal protection of affected individuals and properties. The courts of general jurisdiction are not competent here (*see also* paragraph 1551).

288. If serious danger or serious disadvantage to health or environment is caused or there is a threat thereof, the Centre for Economic Development, Transport and the Environment in question is allowed to take such necessary measures to prevent or limit the pollution that are not vested in the Rescue Service. It is moreover required that the ordinary procedure pursuant to section 175 is due to the disability of the responsible subject excluded or the responsible subject cannot be detected (section 182a).

289. A supervisory authority may also be obliged to inform the police of offences. Pursuant to section 188 of the Environmental Protection Act, the main rule is that any offence against the same Act which is punishable pursuant to the Penal Code, Chapter 48, sections 1–4 or to section 225 of the Environmental Protection Act, shall be notified. However, if the act or omission in the relevant circumstances is to be considered minor and public interest does not require prosecution, the supervisory authority is entitled not to inform the police.

The Centre for Economic Development, Transport and the Environment has the procedural position of injured party in criminal proceedings as far as public interest has been violated.

290. Very similar supervisory and enforcement systems are provided by most environmental acts, such as the Land Use and Building Act (as of 1 January 2025, the Building Act), the Public Health Act, the Waste Act, the Chemicals Act, the Act on the Safety of the Handling of Dangerous Chemicals and Explosives and the Soil Excavation Act. *See also* Part V, Chapter 1.

291. The Environmental Protection Information System[18] (section 222 of the Environmental Protection Act) is maintained for the management and processing of information related to environmental protection, the implementation of monitoring of environmental legislation, monitoring the state of the environment, and research and planning related to the environment. The Regional State Administrative Agencies (as State Environmental Permit Authorities) shall record in the Information System the decisions they have issued under the Environmental Protection Act and the related decisions of the Vaasa Regional Administrative Court and the SAC. The

---

18. In some domestic contexts, the translation database may appear, but it is not used here because the whole information system also includes several independent registers and interactive parts.

Centres for Economic Development, Transport and the Environment (as State supervisory authorities) shall record in the information system: (1) decisions issued under the Environmental Protection Act and information on related decisions of the Vaasa Regional Administrative Court and the SAC; (2) information on the activities to be registered based on registration notifications submitted to them; (3) inspection reports and other information concerning supervisory measures; (4) the information on operations and emissions of ICP installations provided in section 105(1) of the Act; (5) noise accounts and Noise Abatement Action Plans provided in section 151; (6) Supervision Plans and Supervision Programmes pursuant to section 168 drawn up by State supervisory authorities; and (7) monitoring and related data on activities subject to an Environmental Permit, notification and registration that fall under the supervisory responsibility of a state supervisory authority and other similar information that operators are obliged to provide to the supervisory authority.

292. All in all, the Environmental Protection Information System consists of information that is stored in data systems, registers and files maintained by the Centres for Economic Development, Transport and the Environment; Regional State Administrative Agencies; the Finnish Meteorological Institute; the Finnish Environment Institute and the Ministry of the Environment. In addition to the various forms on data and information based on the Environmental Protection Act, provisions on the data to be stored in the System are laid down also in the Waste Act, the Water Act, the Act on Environmental Protection in Maritime Transport, the Water Supply and Sewerage Act, the Act on the Arranging of Water Management and Marine Waters Management and, from 1 January 2025, the Act on the Environmental Damage Fund (1262/2022). The storage of data can be done as machine-readable data transfer using a technical user connection.

293. Regarding the Water Act, administrative and court decisions are entered in the Environmental Protection Information System in a similar manner as those based on the Environmental Protection Act (section 1 of Chapter 18 of the Water Act). Also, other decisions, notifications and information under the Water Act may be registered.

294. In order to ensure the availability of environmental information, the websites of the State permit authorities also contain an Information Service on Environmental Permit Matters, which publishes information referred to in section 222 (above). These can be searched as a limited search based on the identification of the matter, the name of the operator, the nature or location of the project or a certain time interval. The Information Service publishes information on pending environmental permit matters, notified environmental permit matters and their public notice documents, as well as decisions issued in Environmental Permit matters. The same applies to matters and decisions pursuant to the Water Act. A decision issued under the previous Environmental Protection Act (86/2000) may be published on the website of the authority issuing the decision or on the joint website of the State environmental administration. The same applies to the previous Water Act.

§21. EIA AT PROJECT LEVEL

295. Environmental impacts have traditionally been assessed in the various permit procedures. This has, however, always been possible within the limits of each sectoral legislation. Especially the procedure for applications under the Water Act has in many respects at an early stage met the international requirements of Environmental Impact Statement (EIS) already before the implementation of the proper EIA legislation. However, the zero option or the effects of alternative projects is not necessarily examined here.

296. A major structural change was caused in 1994 by the then EC Directive 85/337/EEC on the assessment of the effects of certain public and private projects on the environment, and by the ECE Convention on EIA in a Transboundary Context, signed at *Espoo*, Finland, in 1991, which also called for legislative measures.

297. The regulation on EIA is based on a main enactment, the Environmental Impact Assessment Procedures Act (at the outset 468/1994, presently 252/2017), complemented by the respective decree, presently Government decree on Environmental Impact Assessment Procedures (277/2017) and on several related provisions in sectoral legislation. The legislation has been amended several times due to amendments in European EIA directives. The present Act was enacted due the need to implement the amendments caused by Directive 2014/52/EU.[19] At the same time the central project list was transferred from decree-level to the Act, as an annex, in order to be better in line with the constitutional division of tasks between the Parliament and the government. Subsequent minor amendments in the Environmental Impact Assessment Procedures Act and certain other acts in line with the Directive have been made in 2021.

The Act also applies in the Finnish economic zone. Åland has EIA regulations of its own.

298. Originally, there was no definition of 'project' in the Act, although this state of affairs never caused appreciable problems, taken other provisions and the Directive into account. Now the definition of 'project' has been inserted in the Act by amendment 556/2021. 'Project' means (1) the execution of installation, operation or construction works, (2) other interventions in the natural environment, and (3) the extraction of mineral resources (section 2(10)). The expression 'construction' here also refers to civil engineering and earthmoving.

299. 'Environmental impact' in the Act (section 2(1), 556/2021) means the direct and indirect effects of a project in the area of Finland and outside it on (a) population and human health, living conditions and amenity, (b) earth, soil, waters, air, climate, vegetation, organisms and diversity of nature, in particular the species and natural habitats protected by the Natural Habitats Directive 92/43/EEC and the

19. Directive 2014/52/EU amending Directive 2011/92/EU on the assessment of the effects of certain public and private projects on the environment.

Birds Directive 2009/147/EC, (c) community structures, property, landscape, townscape and cultural heritage, (d) utilization of natural resources, and (e) the interaction between the factors referred to in points (a) to (d).

300. According to the Environmental Impact Assessment Procedures Act, the system for screening of projects is dualistic, as provided in section 3 of the Act. First, a project EIA is needed automatically when a project that is going to be initiated or amended is included in a list of categories, included in Annex 1 of the Environmental Impact Assessment Procedures Act, as follows:

(1) Rearing of animals and fish farming:
   (a) poultries with more than 85,000 places for broilers or more than 60,000 places for hens;
   (b) piggeries with more than 3,000 places for production pigs (over thirty kilograms) or 900 places for sows;
   (c) fur farms for at least 16,000 breeder female minks or ferrets with their litter, or at least 16,000 breeder female foxes or raccoons with their litter;
   (d) fish farms in sea areas where the annual proliferation of fish is at least 1,000,000 kg.

(2) Extraction of natural resources and the treating thereof:
   (a) extraction, enriching, and processing of mining minerals where the surface of the site exceeds twenty-five hectares or the annual amount of extracted substance is at least 550,000 tonnes;
   (b) extraction of stone, gravel or sand where the surface of the site exceeds twenty-five hectares or the annual amount of extracted substance is at least 200,000 solid cubic metres;
   (c) extraction of asbestos and processing and transformation of asbestos or products containing asbestos;
   (d) extraction, keeping, enriching and processing of uranium or thorium, except for small-scale processing in laboratory or test enrichment plant;
   (e) peat production where the production area is over 150 hectares in size;
   (f) permanent alteration of natural forest, peatland or other wetland over what can be considered a unified area over 200 hectares in size, by carrying out new ditching projects or by draining peatland or wetland areas not previously ditched, by removing the tree stock permanently or by replanting the area with species of trees not indigenous to Finland;
   (g) production of petroleum or natural gas for commercial purposes.

(3) Water resources management and water level regulation:
   (a) dams and other installations where an amount of water held back or stored or an additional amount of water exceeds 10 million cubic metres;
   (b) reservoirs where a new amount of water held back or stored or an additional amount of water exceeds 10 million cubic metres;
   (c) water level regulation projects, if the mean flow of the water is over 20 cubic metres per second and the flow and water level conditions will change substantively compared with the initial situation;

(d) transfer of water resources between river basins where the amount of water transferred exceeds 3 cubic metres per second, except for transfer of drinking water in pipes;

(e) flood prevention projects with a benefit area of at least 1,000 hectares.

(4) Metal industries:

(a) iron or steel factories;

(b) plants where other than raw iron metals are produced from ore, enrichment or secondary raw materials by metallurgic, chemical or electrolytical methods.

(5) Forest industries:

(a) mills producing pulp from timber or similar fibrous materials;

(b) paper or board mills with a production capacity exceeding 200 tonnes per day.

(6) Chemical industries:

(a) crude oil refineries, except for plants where merely lubrication oils are processed;

(b) installations for the gasification and liquefaction of bituminous shale, coal or peat, of at least 500 tonnes daily;

(c) integrated production plants of chemical industry where substances are manufactured on an industrial scale by chemical conversion processes and where one of the following is produced:

- organic chemicals;
- inorganic chemicals;
- phosphorus, nitrogen or potassium based (with one or several nutrients) fertilizers;
- pesticides or biocides;
- pharmaceutical products with chemical or biological methods;
- explosives.

(7) Production of energy:

(a) boiler or power plants with a gross output in excess of 300 MW;

(b) nuclear power stations and other nuclear reactors including the dismantling or decommissioning of such power stations or reactors (except research installations for the production and conversion of fissionable and fertile materials, whose maximum power does not exceed one kilowatt continuous thermal load); nuclear power stations and other nuclear reactors cease to be such an installation when all nuclear fuel and other radioactively contaminated elements have been removed permanently from the installation site;

(c) installations for the reprocessing of irradiated nuclear fuel;

(d) installations designed:

- for the production or milling of nuclear fuel;
- for the processing of irradiated nuclear fuel or high-level radioactive waste;
- for the final disposal of irradiated nuclear fuel;
- solely for the final disposal of radioactive waste;

- solely for the storage (planned for more than ten years) of irradiated nuclear fuels or radioactive waste at a different site other than the production site.

(e) wind farm projects where the number of individual mills is at least ten or where the total output is at least 45 MW.

(8) Transfer and storing of energy and substances:

(a) pipelines for the transport of oil, chemicals or gas with a diameter of more than 800 millimetres and a length of more than 40 kilometres;

(b) construction of overhead electrical power lines with a voltage of 220 kilovolts or more and a length of more than 15 kilometres;

(c) stores for oil, petrochemical products, and chemical products when the total volume of the storage tanks for these substances is over 50,000 cubic metres;

(d) installations for the capture of carbon dioxide streams for the purposes of geological storage from installations covered by this list, or where the total yearly capture of carbon dioxide is one and half megatonnes or more;

(e) pipelines with a diameter of more than 800 millimetres and a length of more than 40 kilometres for the transport of carbon dioxide (CO_2) streams from capture installations to storage sites, including associated booster stations;

(f) geological storage of carbon dioxide with a total intended storage below 100,000 tonnes, except where undertaken for research, development or testing.

(9) Traffic:

(a) construction of motorways and semi-motorways;

(b) construction of a new road of four or more lanes, where such new road would be 10 km or more in a continuous length;

(c) realignment and/or widening of an existing road as to provide four or more lanes, where such realigned and/or widened section of road would be 10 kilometres or more in a continuous length;

(d) construction of long-distance railways;

(e) construction of airports with a basic runway length of 2,100 metres or more;

(f) mainly for commercial purposes intended sea waterways, ports and piers for loading and unloading vessels of over 1,350 tonnes;

(g) channels, inland waterways and ports for vessels of over 1,350 tonnes;

(h) tunnels between Finland and Estonia.

(10) Water supply and sewerage:

(a) groundwater abstraction or artificial groundwater recharge schemes where the annual volume of water abstracted or recharged is at least 3 million cubic metres;

(b) large raw water or wastewater tunnels;

(c) sewage treatment plants that can process a discharge corresponding to over 100,000 people.

(11) Waste management:

(a) waste treatment plants where hazardous waste is:

- incinerated;
- treated chemically;

   - treated biologically and the plant is planned for the yearly waste amount of 5,000 tonnes;
   - disposed in landfill.
(b) waste treatment plants where other than hazardous waste is:
   - incinerated and the plant is planned for the daily waste amount of 100 tonnes;
   - treated chemically and the plant is planned for the daily waste amount of 100 tonnes;
   - treated biologically and the plant is planned for the yearly waste amount of 35,000 tonnes;
   - disposed in a landfill which is planned for the yearly waste amount of 50,000 tonnes.

(12) Changes of projects where the volume corresponds to the projects in (1)–(11) above.

301. The positive list is largely based on the EIA Directive and on the *Espoo* Convention, but also negative environmental impacts due to the special characteristics of Finnish nature and environment have been included in the criteria for listing.

302. Second, out of the positive list, EIA is on the basis of a case-by-case examination obligatory to any project or installation, or change thereof, if it probably will, given also the cumulative effects of other projects, have in terms of quality and extent, significant environmental impacts comparable to those of the projects and installations listed in Annex 1 (section 3(2) of the Environmental Impact Assessment Procedures Act). In the case-by-case examination shall attention also be paid to the characters and location of the project and to the nature of its impacts (section 3(3)). More detailed criteria are, following the EIA Directive, listed in Annex 2 to the Act (556/2021). Section 3(2) may apply to a wide range of projects. With regard to solar panel fields (e.g., 100 ha), which have become more common in recent years, interpretations of the need for an EIA are not coherent in the administration so far. Among the case law, SAC 2023:106 on fish farming in the marine area can be cited. The project's planned annual production volume of 850,000 kg of fish farming was split over two areas (when the limit for one plant in Annex 1 is 1,000,000 kg). The distance between the units was about 3.5 km. The calculated annual nutrient discharge caused by the operations totalled approximately 34,000 kg of nitrogen and 3,300 kg of phosphorus. The project was located in water bodies whose ecological status had deteriorated from good to satisfactory in the most recent river basin management period. The project was to be considered as one project, not as two separate projects. It was a question of locating a project of significant size in a water area whose ecological status had deteriorated from before. The national aquaculture location management plan was irrelevant here. The project had cumulating impacts with other projects. Thus, the Centre for Economic Development, Transport and the Environment could have concluded that the project was likely to cause significant environmental impacts comparable in quality and scope to those of the projects listed in the EIA Act.

In all, EIA is required in somewhat more cases than necessary according to the EC directive (or the *Espoo* Convention).

303. The assessment procedure is an integrated one, irrespective of the different sectors of the environment. The developer is responsible for the assessment, under the guidance of authorities. In fact, the EIA procedure is based on a legally regulated interaction between the developer (or his consultants), the expertise of which shall be sufficient (section 33) and the 'liaison authority', the public and the permit authorities. Today, one of the Centres for Economic Development, Transport and the Environment (its environmental division) is always the liaison authority, except for the production of nuclear energy for which (as defined for this context in section 10, 556/2021) the Ministry of Economic Affairs and Employment has that status. If the project is located in the areas of several Centres for Economic Development, Transport and the Environment, it is upon the Ministry of the Environment to decide which of them is the liaison authority (section 10). The personnel of the liaison authority involved in EIA shall have sufficient expertise (section 33(3)).

The liaison authority in that capacity has no competence to make formal decisions during the various phases of the procedure. Its tasks are important, however. The developer shall have the possibility to receive all relevant information from authorities. Advance negotiations between the liaison authority, the developer and other authorities may take place. The various authorities have to cooperate for the purposes of coordination.

304. In cases where a project outside the positive list in Annex 1 has to be made subject to EIA, an order of the Centre for Economic Development, Transport and the Environment of the region (or, for nuclear installations, as defined for this context in the Act, of the Ministry of Economic Affairs and Employment) is needed (sections 11–13 of the Environmental Impact Assessment Procedures Act) for purposes of judicial clarity and coherent interpretation of the partly tractable screening rules described above.

The decision has to be made without delay, at the latest after one month from receiving the necessary information on the project. Before decision-making, the authorities involved have to be consulted sufficiently, and the operator has to be heard. The operator also has to provide the centre (or ministry) with a description on the project and its probable significant impacts (section 12). The decision shall be made public. An appeal against the decision may be lodged by the developer to the Regional Administrative Court (section 37). Other direct appeals on a decision pursuant to section 3(2) are not allowed, but all those who have standing in a subsequent plan or permit procedure, may then in the same connection appeal against such decisions by which an EIA has been regarded unnecessary, irrespective of the time elapsed.

From 1994 to 2021, in total 952 EIA procedures have been initiated.

305. The impacts have to be assessed according to the EIA are scheme (section 14) at as early stage of planning as possible, taking the other ways of preparation of the project into account and in any case at a stage where the various options of the project are still open (section 15), or, in any case, before the decision of any relevant permit or plan decision referred to in section 25 (*see* below). However, the ordinary procedure is not required if the impacts of the project (nuclear plants excepted) are able to be assessed in a procedure pursuant to the Land Use and Building Act (as of 1 January 2025, the Land Use Act) or another act in a way that meets the requirements provided in sections 15–21, 23 and 24 of the Environmental Impact Assessment Procedures Act (section 5), as and if provided in the other Act at stake.

306. The developer is obliged to have an assessment programme (on the contents, *see* section 3 of the Environmental Impact Assessment Procedures Decree) elaborated and delivered to the liaison authority. The assessment programme shall by the liaison authority be made public in the area going to be impacted by the project, by means of the Internet and public announcements as specified in the Act. All interested persons shall be furnished with relevant information and a possibility to give statements and opinions on the programme. The liaison authority shall acquire statements on the programme from (1) the municipalities going to be impacted and (2) the authorities probably concerned, the permit authorities at stake included (section 17, 556/2021).

Within one month from the expiry of the time for statements and opinions, the liaison authority gives the developer a reasoned opinion on the delivered assessment programme. The authority shall take a stand on the extent and accuracy of the programme. It shall also tell how the necessary accounts are adjusted with accounts that are required by other acts (section 18). Likewise, the opinion shall include a summary on the statements and opinions by others. The reasoned opinion shall also be submitted to the relevant authorities and made public on the website of the authority.

After that, it is the duty of the developer to have the impacts of the project and its alternatives assessed on the basis of the assessment programme and the reasoned opinion of the liaison authority (section 19). The results are presented in the EIS, the document being submitted to the liaison authority. An EIS shall present the relevant information on the project, a description on the present status of the environment, a description on the significant environmental impacts of the project, mitigation and follow-up thereof, comparison of alternatives, information on the execution of the EIA and a popular summary, as specified in more detail by Government Decree. The EIS shall also, as far as needed and as listed in section 4 of the Environmental Impact Assessment Procedures Decree, contain the data and information necessary for making a reasoned conclusion, taking into account current knowledge and assessing methods. The liaison authority has to make the EIS public in the probably impacted area of the project. Likewise, it is responsible for acquiring the relevant statements and opinions on the statement (section 20). Also other participation may be agreed upon.

307. If ongoing land use planning pursuant to the Land Use and Building Act (as of 1 January 2025, the Land Use Act) concerns a project for which EIA is needed and likewise ongoing, the necessary hearings according the two acts may be adjusted to each other, as provided in section 22.

308. The EIA and the account and assessment needs required in a permit procedure for the same project are adjusted to each other as specified in the assessment programme. The accounts may be prepared in common. Hearings due to EIA and Environmental Permit procedure (if pending in the Regional State Administrative Agency) may be combined as stipulated in section 44a of the Environmental Protection Act and provided that the project, in respect to its location, extent and technical properties, has no feasible alternative than that presented in the permit application (section 22a).

309. Finally, within two months after the end of the time for submitting opinions and statements, the liaison authority gives its reasoned conclusion on the sufficiency and quality of the EIS (section 23 of the Environmental Impact Assessment Procedures Act). The opinion shall include a summary on the statements and opinions by others. The reasoned conclusion and other statements and opinions shall be delivered to the developer. At the same time the reasoned conclusion shall be made public and delivered to the relevant permit or plan authorities, municipalities, Regional Councils and other authorities (section 23).

310. However, if the liaison authority is unable to make the reasoned conclusion due to the deficiency of the EIS, it shall inform the developer on the items that have to be supplemented. In this case the hearings and the reasoned conclusion are postponed until the supplement has been received (section 24).

311. For the cases of transboundary impacts from or into Finland, there are special international procedures and EIA requirements, as provided in Chapter 5 (sections 28–30) of the Environmental Impact Assessment Procedures Act, as last amended by 991/2022. The Finnish Environment Institute is responsible for carrying out the duties under an international agreement binding on Finland if a project implemented in Finland is likely to have significant environmental effects in an area falling within the jurisdiction of a party to an international agreement binding on Finland or a Member State of the EU. The Finnish Environment Institute shall reserve the authorities of another state that is a party to an international agreement binding on Finland and those whose circumstances or interests may be affected by the project, associations and foundations the opportunity to participate in the EIA procedure if the project is likely to have significant environmental effects in the territory of the country at stake. In addition, the Finnish Environment Institute shall reserve the opportunity to participate in the EIA procedure if requested by another EU Member State likely to have a significant environmental impact (section 28). Section 29a of the Act lays down provisions on international consultation related to projects carried out in areas under the jurisdiction of Finland, and section 30 of the provisions on the obligations of a permit authority in projects causing cross-border environmental impacts. The Finnish Environment Institute is responsible for carrying out its duties under an international agreement binding on Finland in the EIA procedure of another state if a project implemented in an area under the jurisdiction of a party to the agreement or an EU Member State is likely to have significant environmental impacts on an area under the jurisdiction of Finland, as specified in section 31 of the Act.

312. The formally relevant points of the EIA procedure are linked to the various permit procedures and permit authorities. The EIS and the reasoned conclusion shall be attached to the permit application (or to the permit applications, where several acts are applicable), at the latest before decision-making on the permit (section 25).

313. No permit according to any act shall be granted unless the EIS and the reasoned conclusion have been submitted to the permit authority (section 25). In case of transboundary impacts, the same applies to the documents pursuant to section 29. The permit authorities have to make sure that the reasoned conclusion is up-to-date. At the request of a permit authority, the liaison authority shall present its view on whether its conclusion is up-to-date and, where appropriate, specify the outdated parts and what supplementary accounts are needed. The developer may make a request on such a view before a permit application is lodged (section 27).

The reasoned conclusion shall be included in the permit(s), and the permit(s) shall take into account the results of the hearings on the EIS. It shall also be expressed in the permit how the EIS and the reasoned conclusion (and, in transboundary cases, the documents pursuant to section 29) have been taken into account (section 26).

314. The most common permits for which an EIA is performed are those according to the Environmental Protection Act, but far from all EIA-level projects that come under it. Hence, e.g., the Land Use and Building Act (as of 1 January 2025, the Land Use Act and the Building Act), the Water Act, the Highways Act, the Soil Excavation Act and several others may come into question as well and also several of them can do so at the same time. In most cases already the permit application documents should include a complete EIS, which is, however, not always possible. All EIA-level permit and project plan decisions have to include a comment on how the EIS and the opinion of the liaison authority have been taken into consideration.

315. Although the need to work out an EIA as such does not make any permit necessary, in most cases a permit or project plan decision is necessary according to various sector acts. If so, the Centre for Economic Development, Transport and the Environment of the region (environmental division) has the power to appeal against any such decision on the ground that EIA has been omitted or that the performed EIA has remained essentially insufficient (section 34(1)). Additionally, anyone who is entitled to appeal to a Regional Administrative Court against a permit or plan decision may also plead on the omission or essential insufficiency of an EIA (section 34(2)).

Where no such a procedure exists, the EIA, where necessary, has to be carried out before the project is physically initiated, failing which the Centre for Economic Development, Transport and the Environment has the power to give the developer an injunctive order to stop the activities, under a conditional fine, against which an appeal to the Regional Administrative Court is allowed (section 35 of the Environmental Impact Assessment Procedures Act).

316. It is admittedly a problem that there are a few EIA-level projects for which no permit is needed (e.g., large-scale forestry), or cases where there is a procedure the rules of which do not always allow the relevance of environmental factors (e.g., power lines). However, there are cases where more than one permit or plan decision is needed for one project (e.g., the Plans according to the Land Use and Building Act (as of 1 January 2025, the Land Use Act) and permits according to both the Water Act and the Environmental Protection Act at the same time for, e.g., harbours, or a (Highway) Engineering Plan and a permit according to the Water Act for a road with embankments or a bridge). Even so, the totality of environmental impacts does not necessarily fall under the scope of any of them.

317. The Environmental Impact Procedures Act deals with the level of concrete environmentally relevant projects, also when the expression plan is used. General programme level was, however, also covered by the original Act, though in general terms. As for various programmes and plans (above concrete project level) by public bodies, there was a general duty to have the impacts focused and assessed, although the obligation was admittedly rather vague. Directive 2001/42/EC on the assessment of the effects of certain plans and programmes on the environment caused the enacting of a separate regulative mechanism for EIA with the strategic plan level, *see* below.

§22. EIA AT STRATEGIC PLANNING LEVEL

318. Directive 2001/42/EC of the European Parliament and of the Council of 27 June 2001 on the assessment of the effects of certain plans and programmes on the environment (the SEA Directive) has been implemented from 1 June 2005 by the Act on the Assessment of the Environmental Impacts of the Plans and Programs of Authorities (200/2005) and the Government decree of the Plans and Programs of Authorities (347/2005).

Section 3 of the Act provides an authority being in charge of the preparation of a plan or a programme a general duty to find out and assess the environmental consequences thereof to a sufficient extent, where any significant environmental consequences may be caused.

Pursuant to section 4 of the Act, a plan of an authority, when based on an act, a decree or an administrative order, shall be assessed, where the purpose of the plan is to serve agriculture, forestry or fisheries, energy supply, industry, transport, waste management, water management, telecommunications, tourism, regional development, land use, environmental protection or nature protection and where the plan sets the framework for future permit or approval decisions of projects. An assessment is also needed if the plan or programme is subject to the assessment obligation provided in section 35 of the Nature Protection Act due to the impacts on a Natura 2000 site. The same obligations also encompass amendments to previous plans and programmes, unless insignificant.

319. Within other sectors than those above, an assessment is required if a plan or programme, or an amendment to it, creating framework for consent or permit decisions, is determined likely to have significant environmental effects through case-by-case examination (section 5). General grounds for this are laid down in the Decree 347/2005. The outcome of the examination, the reasoning included, shall be made public.

The Act and Decree are not applicable to the preparation of the State Budget. Without prejudice to section 3 of the Act (above), the Act is not applicable to other financial plans and programmes, either, or to plans and programmes the sole purpose of which is to serve national defence or civil emergency.

320. The land use Plans according to the Land Use and Building Act (as of 1 January 2025, the Land Use Act) are assessed pursuant to the rules in that Act and hence not pursuant to the Act on the Assessment of the Environmental Impacts of the Plans and Programs of Authorities. Assessment of Plans is specially provided in the Land Use and Building Act (as of 2025, the Land Use Act).

321. In the applying of the Act on the Assessment of the Environmental Impacts of the Plans and Programs of Authorities attention is paid to such accounts on the plan or programme or its impacts that have been made in another context. The different assessments shall be adjusted.

It is the duty of the authority in charge of a plan or a programme to account and assess the probably significant environmental impacts of the plan or programme and of the alternatives envisaged. An environmental report is worked out before the adoption of the plan or programme, as an integral part of other preparation. The contents of an environmental report depend on the character of the plan or programme at stake, as specified in Decree 347/2005. The preparation shall be arranged in such a way that the public is served a possibility to get information on the starting points, goals and preparation of the plan or programme, and give an opinion on the matter.

There are specific provisions in section 10 and 10a of the Act 200/2005 (amendment 912/2022) for plans and programmes with probably significant transboundary environmental impacts. The Finnish Environment Institute is the main national authority.

Chapter 2. Air Pollution

§1. Development of the Present Legal Framework

322. As explained above (*see* General Introduction, Chapter 3) Finland has had proper air pollution legislation since 1982. At the outset, there was also disagreement about the basic structure of the upcoming Air Pollution Prevention Act (consent system versus notification system). The notification system was elected at that time, but the Environmental Permit Procedure Act virtually changed it to a permit system from 1992. Soon afterwards, the profound 1995 reform of the Air Pollution Prevention Act, partly speeded up by the then EC air pollution prevention directives, made a real permit also substantively the heart of the system. The then Air Emission Permit, procedurally of course, became one of the combined sub-permits within the Environmental Permit Procedure Act, as was the permit-turned notification procedure 1992–1995. In 2000, separate legislation on air pollution prevention was repealed due to the then Environmental Protection Act being based on an integrated approach. The general notion of pollution of the environment in the Act came to cover also air pollution (*see* Part I, Chapter 1, §5 above). The same holds true also regarding the present Environmental Pollution Act, but recently a significant part of installations with main environmental concern on air have been removed from the permit regime to the essentially more schematic registration procedure.

323. As for stationary activities, the installation-focused decision-making mechanism of the Environmental Protection Act is of primary importance. As for other sources of air pollution, the situation is more problematic. For example, nitrogen oxides are, in addition to energy production, produced by traffic in its various forms, which are not easily targeted by the mechanisms of the Environmental Protection Act.

324. Already the 1987 restrictions on sulphur compounds, based on decrees under the Air Pollution Prevention Act, e.g., meant that the target of the 1985 international First Sulphur Protocol on sulphur emissions was easily observed. From 1980, sulphur emissions declined steeply. The objective of reducing sulphur emissions by 50% from 1980 to 1993 was attained as early as 1988 and 1989. Also the further restrictions of the 1994 Second Sulphur Protocol for 2000 were by a large margin satisfied early. As for nitrogen oxides, a decree of 1991 limited emissions to the 1987 level. The ECE Sofia Protocol of 1988 was hereby partly implemented. In the 2000 general reform, the previous sectoral decrees, largely based on the respective sectoral EC directives, remained in force so far. Later on they have been replaced by new decrees under the present or the previous Environmental Protection Act.

325. The current national implementation provisions regarding the National Emissions Ceilings (NEC) Directive[20] are contained in section 149–149b of the Environmental Protection Act (included in the Chapter on Environmental quality,

20. Directive (EU) 2016/2284 of the European Parliament and of the Council of 14 Dec. 2016 on the reduction of national emissions of certain atmospheric pollutants, amending Directive 2003/35/EC and repealing Directive 2001/81/EC.

perhaps not in a quite logical way). Pursuant to section 149, anthropogenic emissions of sulphur dioxide, nitrogen oxides, non-methane VOCs, ammonia and fine particulate matter shall be limited from 2020 to 2029 and from 2030 onwards, as laid down in Article 4(1) and Annex II of the Directive. The national commitments do not, however, apply to (1) aircraft emissions beyond the landing and take-off cycle; (2) emissions from international maritime traffic; and (3) emissions of nitrogen oxides and non-methane VOCs from agricultural activities, as specified in Article 4(3)(d) of the Directive. The emissions shall be reduced pursuant to the provisions in Article 4(2) of the Directive on a linear reduction trajectory, a non-linear reduction trajectory and deviations. A non-linear reduction trajectory and the reasons for the use of it shall be described in the National Air Pollution Control Programme pursuant to section 149c (below).

326. The Finnish Environment Institute shall prepare and report the necessary national emission inventories and projections as well as informative inventory reports (section 149a). If the national emission inventory shows that one or several emission reduction commitments are not fulfilled, the flexibilities in Article 5(1–4) of the Directive may be used (section 149b).

The Ministry of the Environment has to prepare a National Air Pollution Control Programme[21] subject to approval by the Cabinet, in order to implement the national emission reduction commitments and to achieve the objectives regarding human health and the environment pursuant to Article 1 of the Directive. Article 6 and Annex III apply substantively. The intervals and situations when updating is needed is specified in section 149c(3).

§2. The Detailed General Provisions on Emissions

327. The relationship between general standards imposed in decrees on the one hand and the case-by-case imposing of permit provisions (emission limits, etc.) on the other hand is, for historical reasons, somewhat different in comparison with water pollution prevention, for which the case-by-case approach has always dominated (provided that the standards following the respective EU directives are met, as they normally are). As to air pollution prevention, the pre-2000 Air Pollution Prevention Act had made general emission (or quality) standards, those being partly binding as such, partly guidelines, as a starting point. Also under the Environmental Protection Act (2000, as well as 2014), case-by-case imposition of air pollution prevention measures plays an important, but only a partial role in the whole, whereas general standards laid down by decrees are intended to be the primary tools in pollution control, albeit largely through decision-making at the individual permit level. The recent shift from permits towards registration has accentuated the role of general requirements, those often being in practice both minimum and maximum requirements.

21. Presently *the National Air Pollution Control Programme 2030*, from 2019, *see* http://urn.fi/URN:ISBN:978-952-361-008-8.

328. According to sections 9 and 10 of the Environmental Protection Act, Government decrees of various contents may be issued also with main relevance to air pollution prevention.

329. Government decree on restrictions on idle running of motor vehicles (1266/2002) has been issued pursuant to the previous Environmental Protection Act, but is still in force. Pursuant to this Decree, idle running of vehicle motors (tractors, terrain vehicles, etc. included) off-road is, as a general rule, allowed for not more than two minutes, unless the temperature of the air is below fifteen degrees centigrade. The main prohibition has been included in the present Environmental Protection Act (section 217(1)). The system of parking tickets by municipal parking wardens is applicable (section 1(2) of the Act on the supervision of vehicle parking, 727/2011). The Traffic Act (729/2018) forbids in a similar way the idle running of vehicle motors in road traffic, as specified in section 55 of that Act.

330. Government decree on the quality requirements of petrol, diesel oil and certain other liquid fuels (presently 883/2022) bans, like its predecessors of 2000 and 2010, the placing of leaded petrol on the market. Marketed diesel oil and unleaded petrol shall meet the detailed environmentally based quality requirements set forth in the decree.

331. Government decree on the sulphur content of heavy fuel oil and light fuel oil (908/2022) is, like its predecessors of 2000, 2006 and 2014, relevant on fossil energy production, both within the market and in permit procedures. The Decree is not applicable, e.g., on air traffic, maritime traffic, or fuels covered by Decree 883/2022 (above). The maximum sulphur content in heavy fuel oil used in Finland is 1.00% by weight, with certain exceptions, and that of light fuel oil 0.10% by weight.

332. If the use of a fuel, a product containing VOCs or a chemical or product impacting adversely in the atmosphere generates emissions that may be reasonably assessed to cause harm to health or environmental pollution pursuant to section 5(1)(2) of the Environmental Protection Act, the manufacturing, placing on the market, export or use thereof may be forbidden or restricted, or conditions or information duties imposed, as specified by Government decree (section 216 of the Environmental Protection Act).

333. Certain product-related provisions are, in order to prevent or reduce air pollution resulting from the contribution of VOCs to the formation of tropospheric ozone, laid down in Government decree on the limitation of emissions of VOC due to the use of organic solvents in certain paints and varnishes and vehicle refinishing products (189/2022).

334. The abatement of air pollution caused by stationary emissions of VOCs poses certain traits of legal structural interest. The obligations of the relevant operators were prior to the IED based on Directive 1999/13/EC. In that directive, it had been made possible that a national plan is used to reduce VOC emissions regarding existing activities and installations. This particular possibility had also been recognized in the preparatory documents to the Environmental Protection Act. Due to the problems connected to the legal consequences of administrative plans in Finnish legal approach, the then Environmental Protection Act had in 2002, for the implementation purposes of two air pollution prevention directives, been complemented with a possibility to use either a specified Cabinet decision or a Government decree, instead of a mere plan. The provisions were extended to cover also the then VOC Directive 1999/13/EC, and was also adopted as an option in the then VOC Decree.

335. The present Government decree on restrictions on emissions to the air from certain activities and installations using organic volatile compounds (64/2015) is applicable to such organic-solvent-using activities and installations, subject to Environmental Permit requirement pursuant to Annex 1, Table 1(6)(a), Table 2(6)(a) or Table 2(6)(b) to the Act, or subject to registration requirement pursuant to Annex 2(4–6) to the Act, where solvents are used exceeding the amount specified in the table of Annex 1 to the Decree.

Instead of the emission limits in section 3 of the Decree, that being mainly applicable in Environmental Permit or registration contexts, an operator may draw up an installation-specific plan on the reduction of emissions pursuant to section 6, meeting the requirements laid down in the Decree.

336. The atmospheric emission from large combustion plants (LCPs) (those whose rated thermal input is equal to or greater than 50 megawatts) have in detail been provided by decrees under the Environmental Protection Act, aligned with the relevant EU legislation. Presently already the very Act contains rather detailed provisions on LCPs (sections 97–106). The present decree is Government decree on the limitation of emissions from LCPs (936/2014). The provisions of sections 97–106 and of the Decree is based on the LCP Directive,[22] and on the IED, where relevant. This also means that the Decree is applicable only in permit contexts.

Middle scale combustion plants (units with a thermal input of at least 1 megawatt, but less than 50 megawatts) in turn are stipulated in section 106a–106e (as specified in section 106b) and the MCP Decree,[23] applicable in a registration or permit context, depending on the case.

337. Pursuant to a model adopted under the previous Environmental Protection Act, the Cabinet may, at the common application by LCP operators, having an Environmental Permit granted before 27 November 2002, certain installations excepted, decide upon a national transitional national on the emissions from LCPs (sections 102 and 103). Such a decision sets, pursuant to the IED, a joint obligation on a linear decrease of emissions during the period from 1 January 2016 to 30 June 2020, provided that the total emissions in 2019 and 2020 are equal to or less than pursuant to a Government decree based on section 9 of the Act. From 1 July 2020 the

22. Directive 2001/80/EC on the limitation of emissions of certain pollutants into the air from LCPs.
23. Government Decree on the environmental protection requirements for middle scale energy production units and installations (1065/2017), based on Directive (EU) 2015/2193 on the limitation of emissions of certain pollutants into the air from medium combustion plants.

provisions in the Environmental Permits, or at least the limit values in the Government decree shall be observed. Government decree 936/2014 contains provisions on the decision, too. The relationship between the provisions in an environmental permit and the Cabinet decision are provided in section 103. In reality, the Government decree has been decisive.

338. Plants incinerating or co-incinerating waste have been in detail regulated by decree, but in the present Environmental Protection Act also this category of installations is unusually thoroughly stipulated in the very Act already (sections 107–110). These sections are, in addition to the general provisions in the Act, are applicable to incineration and co-incineration plants, as defined in section 108, where solid or liquid waste is incinerated, subject to certain exceptions in section 107(2).

The incineration of waste is relevant both to air pollution prevention and to waste management. That is why the current Government decree on Incineration of Waste (151/2013), like its predecessor, has been issued by virtue of both the (previous) Environmental Protection Act and the Waste Act. The Decree aims, together with the provisions of the Act, at implementing the IED Directive in respect to plants incinerating or co-incinerating waste. The decree is mainly applicable in considerations regarding Environmental Permits. The scope of application of the Decree is the same as that of sections 107–110 of the Act.

339. The relationship between the predecessor of this Decree and the previous LCP Decree had caused problems. The then Waste Incineration Directive 2000/76/EC, also as such in relation to the incineration of gaseous waste, had appeared to be particularly problematic, resulting in a SAC reference for a preliminary ruling to the ECJ (*Lahti Energia,* C-317/07, Judgment of the ECR 4 December 2008).

340. A very special case is made up of use of manure as fuel. The rather complicated provisions on this item are in section 221b–221f of the Environmental Protection Act. The provisions are connected to the Act on Animal by-Products (517/2015), the Waste Act, the Animal by-product Regulation,[24] the respective implementation regulation[25] and the IED.

§3. Protection of the Ozone Layer

341. In 1989, the then Air Pollution Prevention Act was complemented by a new provision granting the Cabinet competence to give necessary decrees to protect the (entire) atmosphere. In practice this provision concerned the ozone layer. These guidelines and regulations could, according to the 1995 version of the provision,

24. Regulation (EC) No. 1069/2009 laying down health rules as regards animal by-products and derived products not intended for human consumption and repealing Regulation (EC) No. 1774/2002.
25. Commission Regulation (EU) No. 142/2011 of 25 Feb. 2011 implementing Regulation (EC) No. 1069/2009 laying down health rules as regards animal by-products and derived products not intended for human consumption and implementing Council Directive 97/78/EC as regards certain samples and items exempt from veterinary checks at the border under that Directive.

refer to prohibition or restriction of production, import, export, delivery or use of a substance, preparation or product. The empowerment resulted in several decrees, aiming at implementation of the Montreal Protocol and its amendments ratified by Finland. Pursuant to the decrees, the use of Chlorofluorocarbon (CFC) compounds, halons, tetrachloromethane and 1,1,1-trichloroethane in Finland had ceased totally, except for the minor use of CFC in asthma medicines and the small use of tetrachloromethane in few laboratory analyses. In old refrigerators and fire extinguishers the chemicals were allowed. The import of CFC compounds to Finland had reduced 98% from 1990 to 1997. These decrees, being mainly based on the Montreal Protocol and the relevant EC directives, were subsequently merged into one (Government decree on ozone layer depleting substances, 262/1998). This decree, being in many respects more stringent than the previous ones, also included prohibitions on use and reduction of fully halogenated chlorofluorohydrocarbon compounds according to a schedule which is faster than that required by the EC. Use of halons, carbon tetrachloride; 1,1,1-trichloroethane, methylene bromide and HBFC substances was not allowed and products containing them were not marketable. Use of CFC compounds in industrial production was prohibited and products containing them were not marketable, with minor medical exceptions. Use of HCFC compounds was prohibited.

342. The exhaustive Ozone Regulations, the previous Regulation (EC) No. 2037/2000 of 29 June 2000 on substances that deplete the ozone layer and the present Regulation (EC) No. 1005/2009 of the European Parliament and of the Council of 16 September 2009 on substances that deplete the ozone layer have made national provisions on the protection of the ozone layer largely unnecessary. In the present Environmental Protection Act, there is still a chapter (Chapter 17) on this item, but it merely includes the few remaining necessary provisions for implementing the 2009 Ozone Regulation, and also the respective provisions due to Regulation (EU) No. 517/2014 on fluorinated greenhouse gases and repealing Regulation (EC) No. 842/2006. These provisions concern qualification requirements, reporting, registers and inspections. Government decree on fluorinated greenhouse gases and qualifications for persons dealing with equipment containing ozone-depleting substances (766/2016), repealing Government decrees 262/1998 and 452/2009, contains certain complementary provisions to both the Regulations. The Finnish Environment Institute is the competent authority pursuant to the Regulations and the supervisory authority (section 21.4 of the Environmental Protection Act), as well as the market surveillance authority (section 24a–24b of the Act).

§4. Ambient Air Quality

343. As a deviation from the division of monitoring tasks in section 143 of the Environmental Protection Act regarding environmental quality monitoring, the municipality-level monitoring of air quality in the metropolitan area is the responsibility of the municipalities Espoo, Helsinki, Kauniainen and Vantaa in cooperation. In that area, airborne concentrations of particulate matter smaller than 2.5

micrometres shall be continuously monitored by one permanently fixed urban background station, where the ambient air quality is representative of that in the city. The Centres for Economic Development, Transport and the Environment in cooperation with the Finnish Environment Institute are responsible for the monitoring of negative impacts of air pollution upon surface waters as a part of monitoring under the Act on the Arranging of Water Management and Marine Waters Management. Natural Resources Institute Finland (Luke) is responsible for monitoring forest areas and the Finnish Meteorological Institute for monitoring ozone load. The number of urban background stations used for this purpose in the Helsinki Metropolitan Area and elsewhere in Finland shall be adjusted, if needed, to bring it into line with the minimum population-based number required by Directive 2008/50/EC on ambient air quality and cleaner air for Europe (the Ambient Air Quality Directive) (section 143).

344. Each municipality shall, with all means possible, ensure good air quality within its area, taking into account the environmental quality requirements and objectives pursuant to section 14 (section 144). In the implementation of plans worked out to secure air quality in accordance with sections 145 and 146 (below), a municipality may set regulations on restricting and suspending activities other than subject to permit requirement or registration requirement (section 144 of the Environmental Protection Act). If a limit value specified for air pollution under section 141 is exceeded, or there is a threat thereof, the municipality shall prepare a medium-term or long-term air quality protection plan for keeping air quality below the limit value and shortening the duration during which the limit value is exceeded (section 145). No protection plan is needed concerning the exceedance of limit values specified for particulate matter (PM_{10}) provided in section 148, or risk thereof. Municipalities may, at their own discretion, also draw up air quality protection plans for achieving the target values set for ozone. In the case of an exceedance of the limit value due to significant long-distance transport, section 211a (below) shall apply. An air quality protection plan shall include information on deterioration of air quality and necessary ameliorative measures targeted at traffic and other emission-causing activities. Where necessary, the plan shall also include measures for the protection of especially sensitive population groups.

If more than one air quality limit value under section 141 is exceeded or there is a risk thereof, the municipality shall, where appropriate, draw up a coherent air pollution prevention plan where all limit values at stake are taken into account. In the planning the municipality shall assess the need to apply to medium combustion plants in the municipality more stringent emission limit values than those provided in the Medium Combustion Plant Directive,[26] if applying such limit values would effectively and significantly contribute in improving air quality. The results of the exchange of information organized by the Commission pursuant to Article 6(10) of the Directive.

26. Directive (EU) 2015/2193 on the limitation of emissions of certain pollutants into the air from medium combustion plants.

345. A pollution prevention plan shall include information on the deterioration of air quality and the necessary measures targeted at transport and other activities causing emissions (sections 145 and 146). When needed, the plan shall also include measures for the protection of population groups with special sensitivity to air pollution. In the plan, also the need to apply emission limit values that are stricter than those provided in the Medium Combustion Plant Directive to medium combustion plants within the area of the municipality, if the application of such limit values would effectively and significantly contribute to improving air quality (section 145).

346. Short-term action plans in turn are provided in section 146. If the alert threshold specified under section 141 for sulphur dioxide or nitrogen dioxide is exceeded or there is a risk of this occurring, the municipality at stake shall prepare a short-term action plan to reduce the risk and duration of such an exceedance (section 46). When the alert threshold for ambient ozone is exceeded or there is a risk of this occurring, the municipality is only obliged to prepare a short-term action plan if such a plan would be useful in reducing the risk, duration or severity of such an exceedance. At its own discretion, a municipality may prepare a short-term action plan for keeping pollution below the limit value and shortening the time during which the limit value is exceeded, and for achieving the target values set for ozone. In the case of an exceedance of the limit value due to significant long-distance transport, section 211a shall apply. A short-term action plan shall include the information specified in section 145 and corresponding measures provided in section 145 facilitating the most rapid possible improvement in air quality.

347. An air quality protection plan shall be prepared within eighteen months of the end of the calendar year during which the limit value was exceeded or the risk thereof was first detected. If it is evident that the limit value continues to be exceeded, or there is a risk that it will be exceeded immediately after the end of the validity term of the plan, a new plan shall be drawn up so that it is in force as soon as the previous term ends (section 147). If the previous term already has ended, a new plan shall be drawn up immediately after the limit value is exceeded or is at risk to be exceeded again. A short-term action plan in turn shall be prepared without delay after the alert threshold has been exceeded or a risk of such has been detected. The municipality shall request a statement on a draft plan from the State supervisory authority, i.e., the Centre for Economic Development, Transport and the Environment of the region, and other relevant authorities. All others shall in good time be provided with the opportunity to express their opinion on draft plans. A statement on the draft plans shall be requested from the State supervisory authority. The public shall be informed of approved plans and of how the opinions and statements have been taken into account. Approved plans shall be sent to the State supervisory authority and the Ministry of the Environment for information. Municipalities shall submit information on any measures implemented in accordance with the plan as well as any revision of the plan and separate preparation of a short-term action plan to the State supervisory authority and the Ministry of the Environment by 15 May every year.

348. Section 148 of the Act provides measures for exceedance of limit values due to sanding and salting, measures that are in Finland due to weather conditions in winter commonly used for the maintenance of streets, pavements, roads and house yards, but causing dust and (regarding salt) groundwater problems. In an area, where the limit values specified for particulate matter (PM_{10}) by virtue of section 141 are exceeded due to a particulate load caused by sanding or salting for the winter maintenance of roads and streets, the municipality may, instead of an air quality protection plan, prepare a report on the exceedance of the limit values, the reasons for which the limits were exceeded and the measures required to lower concentrations. Such a report has to be prepared within seven months of the end of the calendar year in which the limit value was exceeded for the first time. The provisions in section 147(3) on public participation and on the statement to be requested from the Centre for Economic Development, Transport and the Environment, are applicable also here. If the limit value is once again exceeded after the report is drawn up, the municipality shall submit an account to the Centre for Economic Development, Transport and the Environment and the Ministry of the Environment on measures already taken to lower concentrations, including an assessment of the impacts of the measures and any additional measures required. However, insignificant additional measures may require an entirely new report.

349. Government decree on ambient air quality (79/2017, as amended by 619/2023) implements the Ambient Air Quality Directive, in addition to the provisions above in the Environmental Protection Act.

The detailed specifications largely correspond to those in the Directive. They include the limit values for the protection of human health in respect to sulphur dioxide, nitrogen dioxide, benzene, carbon monoxide, lead and particulate matter (PM_{10}), the ozone target values and long-term objectives, the critical levels of sulphur dioxide and oxides of nitrogen, and information and alert thresholds, as well as the national exposure reduction targets, target values and limit values for $PM_{2,5}$. Ambient air quality assessment areas are also specified.

350. On the basis of a notification from the municipality at stake, the Ministry of the Environment has to initiate cooperation in accordance with Article 25 of the Ambient Air Quality Directive with the neighbouring Member State from which the transboundary long-range transport originates in order to eliminate the exceedance. The Ministry of the Environment must ensure that the competent authority of the Member State concerned is informed of the exceedance and that the Commission of the EU is invited to participate in the cooperation. In the event of an exceedance of a limit value or alert threshold, the Ministry shall, after consulting the municipality, take action, if necessary, to prepare and implement a plan to be drawn up jointly with the Member State concerned in accordance with Article 23 or 24 of the Ambient Air Quality Directive. The Ministry is the competent authority to cooperate on the basis of an initiative made by another Member State based on Article 25 of the Directive and to ensure that the public is informed of such cooperation in Finland.

Information in Finland must be provided through a public data network. The Ministry must ensure that, where necessary, cooperation with neighbouring countries outside the EU is also sought in communications and in drawing up joint plans (section 211a).

351. Government decree on atmospheric arsenic, cadmium, mercury, nickel and polycyclic aromatic hydrocarbons (113/2017), implementing Directive 2004/107/EC of the European Parliament and of the Council of 15 December 2004 relating to arsenic, cadmium, mercury, nickel and polycyclic aromatic hydrocarbons in ambient air, contains substance-specific target values, monitoring, access to information and duties of authorities. In the monitoring, the metropolitan area is assessed separately from the rest of the country. Concerning activities subject to Environmental Permit requirement BAT and BEP shall be applied and, where target values or assessment thresholds in the Act are exceeded, necessary provisions on monitoring shall be issued in the permit.

Chapter 3. Abatement of Climatic Change

352. The obligations under the 1997 Kyoto Protocol to the United Nations Framework Convention on Climate Change in order to achieve stabilization of greenhouse gas concentrations in the atmosphere at a level that would prevent dangerous anthropogenic interference with the climate system had been approved by an Act in 2002. The Cabinet decided in 2003 on the principles applicable to the administrative arrangements of climate policies required by the 1997 Kyoto Protocol. In the commitment period from 2008 to 2012, the Kyoto obligations meant that the EU Member States had to jointly reduce their greenhouse gas emissions by 8%. For this objective, Directive 2003/87/EC establishing a scheme for greenhouse gas emission allowance trading within the Community and amending Council Directive 96/61/EC had established a scheme for greenhouse gas emission allowance trading between enterprises within the EU.

The EU agreed in December 2008 to adopt an EU-wide Climate and Energy package. The package contained Directive 2009/29/EC amending Directive 2003/87/EC to cover the post-2012 period. A target of 20% reduction by 2020, compared to the 1990 levels, was to be implemented, and it was to be divided between the EU Emissions Trading Sector sources, i.e., participants of the Emission Trading System (ETS), and non-EU ETS sources, i.e., the Non-EU Emission Trading Sector. The EU-wide ETS target was to achieve a 21% reduction by 2020, compared to the 2005 levels.

The Emissions Trading period was extended by eight years, thus covering the period 2013–2020. The scope for the Directive was also extended. Besides carbon dioxide emissions, the scope covers perfluorocarbon emissions resulting from the manufacture of aluminium, and nitrous oxide emissions generated by the chemicals industry. The national allocation plans were not continued. The allocation of emission allowances moved towards harmonized methods between various sectors. The allocation of emission allowances by auction came to be the primary method, used in electricity production. Energy-intensive industries were to receive their emission allowances mainly for free, according to strict harmonized allocation principles.

353. In Finland, the Directive has been implemented, aviation excluded, first through the original Emissions Trading Act of 2004 and next through the previous Emissions Trading Act (311/2011) and related pieces of legislation. Amendment 108/2007 made it possible that emission reductions arising from Kyoto Protocol's project mechanisms are used in the emissions trading, this being based on Directive 2003/87/EC establishing a scheme for greenhouse gas emission allowance trading within the Community, as then amended, in respect of the Kyoto Protocol's project mechanisms. At the same time, the Act on the Use of Kyoto Mechanisms (109/2007) was enacted. The previous Emissions Trading Act was aligned with Directive 2009/29/EC of 23 April 2009 amending Directive 2003/87/EC so as to improve and extend the greenhouse gas emission allowance trading scheme of the Community. Several amendments in the Act had been made later on.

A wholly new Emissions Trading Act (1270/2023) was enacted on 28 December 2023, entering into force on 1 January 2024. The new Act replaces the previous Emissions Trading Act of 2011 and the Act on Emissions Trading in Aviation (34/

2010). The new Act essentially contributes to the implementation of the amended Emissions Trading System Directive with respect to installations, maritime transport and aviation emissions trading. In addition, the Act implements the provisions on carbon offsetting schemes for aviation adopted by the International Civil Aviation Organisation and covered by the Directive, and a new reporting obligation for separate road transport, buildings and other sectors, which applies to fuel distributors regarding emissions in 2024. Compared to the previous Emissions Trading Act and the Act on Emissions Trading in Aviation, the content of several parts remained largely unchanged, but the Act was supplemented as a result of amendments to the Directive, and outdated regulation was removed from it. The general structure of the Act was clarified. In addition, the reform updated the provisions and took into account the necessary changes in administration as a result of the extension of the scope of the Directive. In accordance with the amended Directive, the scope of the new Act was extended to cover also maritime transport. Shipping companies must surrender emission allowances from ship emissions caused by a voyage made for commercial purposes or during the ship's stay in port. The amendments of the Directive concerning the allocation of free allowances were incorporated into the Act. The number of free allowances to be allocated to installations was reduced in sectors covered by the CBAM Regulation (Regulation (EU) 2023/956 of the European Parliament and of the Council of 10 May 2023 establishing a carbon border adjustment mechanism) and the conditions for the allocation of free allowances were tightened from 2026 onwards so that in the future operators would have to demonstrate that they have taken the energy efficiency measures specified in the Directive in order to receive free allowances in full. Free allocation of allowances for aviation would be phased out by the end of 2025, with the exception of the Sustainable Aviation Fuel Incentive Mechanism, which aims to reduce the price differential between sustainable and fossil aviation fuels through free allocation, thereby promoting the use of greener fuels and emission reductions. No free allocation of allowances would be granted to maritime transport. Alongside the Energy Authority, the Finnish Transport and Communications Agency Traficom was vested in competences under the Act. The sanctions remained unchanged, in addition to which sanctions under the Directive were extended to maritime transport. The separate Act on the implementation of the Regulation on the EU's carbon border adjustment mechanism (1288/2033) contains provisions on the implementation of the CBAM Regulation. The Ministry of Economic Affairs and Employment is responsible for steering and developing the national implementation of the Regulation. Customs is the competent authority within the meaning of Article 11(1) of the Regulation. The Act also contains provisions on Customs' right of access to information, penalty fees and appeals.

354. The current Emissions Trading Act, in force as of 1 January 2024, applies to emissions trading for installations, maritime transport and aviation, as well as to the CORSIA system for aviation and to the reporting obligation for new, separate road transport, buildings and other sectors, which applies to fuel distributors regarding emissions in 2024. As for installations, the Act applies to sixteen branches and their carbon dioxide emissions listed in Annex I to the Act, and to four other branches, their carbon dioxide emissions and their certain other greenhouse gas emissions. Additionally, the Act applies to combustion installations with a rated thermal input below 20 MW if connected to the same district heating network in a manner specified in section 5. An incineration plant with a thermal input exceeding 20 MW that complies with the requirements concerning a waste incineration plant in accordance with the provisions laid down in an Environmental Permit pursuant to the Environmental Protection Act is subject only to the requirements for monitoring, reporting and verifying emissions under the Act. If the Emissions Trading Act applies to a certain installation, an Emissions Permit and a monitoring plan pursuant to Chapter 6 of the Act are required. The permitting competence is vested in the Energy Authority. The Act includes detailed provisions on the trading mechanism, such as emission monitoring plans (Chapter 5); Emission Permits (Chapter 6); monitoring, reporting and verification of emissions (Chapter 7); change of the plant operator, shipping company or aircraft operator (Chapter 8); total amount and issue of allowances (Chapter 9); free allocation of allowances to operators during the trading period 2021–2030 (Chapter 10); free allocation of allowances to aircraft operators (Chapter 11); Union register (Chapter 12); holding and surrender of allowances (Chapter 13); verification (Chapter 14); carbon offsetting obligations under CORSIA (Chapter 15); access to information, supervision, enforcement and sanctions (Chapter 16) and appeals and related enforcement (Chapter 17).

355. The originally introduced emission allowance trading created in principle a market for greenhouse gas emissions that were earlier free of charge, and defined a price for the emissions. In Finland, the allowances for the first three-year period (2005–2007) were allocated to the installations free of charge on the basis of the quantities of their earlier emissions. For new activities or extension of activities an allowance for additional greenhouse gas emissions is required. The total quantity of allowances allocated for the period 2005–2007, including a reservation for new entrants, was approximately 3% less than the estimated quantity of emissions during that period.

For the period 2008–2012, the allocations were allocated for free. The allocation was decided upon by the Cabinet in February 2008. The proposal for a national allocation plan had been made in February 2007. The Commission had in June 2007 required amendments on the plan. Finland had to reduce the total amount by 2,042,109 million CO_2 tonnes yearly, which meant that the remaining amount for allocation corresponded to 37,557,891 million CO_2 tonnes yearly. This was also due to the amendments 1468/2007 (in force from 1 January 2008) of the Emissions Trading Act, by which the reduction was allocated rather evenly between the groups. According to the Cabinet decision, the total quantity of allowances for 2008–2012 was 187.8 million tonnes (about 37.6 million tonnes per year), allocated to 566 installations. About 7 million allowances had been reserved to new entrants.

The emission allowances allocated free of charge during the period 2013–2020 were allocated in accordance with harmonized EU-level rules, and national allocation plans were therefore no longer be used. In the fourth trading period 2021–2030, allowances were issued mainly by auctioning. Some allowances were also allocated free of charge, but towards the end of the period the share of free allocation will decrease and the auction share will increase. From 2021, free distribution will be granted at a time for five-year periods, i.e., in the fourth trading period for the periods 2021–2025 and 2026–2030. Industries exposed to the risk of carbon leakage receive a free distribution of 100% of the amount calculated based on the free distribution rules. Other industries eligible for free distribution will initially receive 30% of the calculated amount, but the share will fall steadily to zero after 2026 in 2030. The decrease does not apply to district heating or cooling.

356. The Ministry of Economic Affairs and Employment is generally responsible for steering and developing the national implementation of the Act. The Ministry of Transport and Communications is responsible for steering, monitoring and developing emissions trading in maritime transport and aviation and the CORSIA system. The Energy Authority is, besides its role as permit authority, responsible for supervising compliance with provisions and decisions in and under the Act regarding plants and their verifiers, carrying out the tasks assigned to the competent authority in the Free Allocation Regulation and the Commission's Regulation adjusting free allocation for plants, acting as the Finnish auctioneer pursuant to Article 22 of the Auction Regulation and being responsible for the national functions of the EU register pursuant to Article 19 of the Emissions Trading System Directive and act as the National Focal Point for the coordination of information exchange and cooperation pursuant to Article 70 of the Commission verification regulation. Correspondingly, the Finnish Transport and Communications Agency Traficom has several different tasks in terms of air traffic and maritime transport.

357. The decisions of the Energy Authority and other administrative bodies are appealable to the Regional Administrative Court. A decision regarding free allocation of allowances or amendment thereof was, as a system-level exception, originally appealable directly to the SAC, but this exception was removed from 1 March 2023 onwards. Notwithstanding any appeal, several of the decisions under the present Act must be complied with, unless otherwise ordered by the authority that made the decision or by the court. Also, appeals against decisions of the ministries are today appealable to the Regional Administrative Court. A verifier's statement may not be appealed directly, but a request for rectification must first be submitted to the verifier in accordance with the Administrative Procedure Act, and only the latter decision can be appealed to the Regional Administrative Court.

358. The Cabinet had made decisions on the national allocation proposals for 2005–2007 and 2008–2012, which were delivered to the Commission, and since the Commission's final decision has decided on the emission allowances of individual industries. In 2004, the Cabinet proposal for a national allocation plan pursuant to the then Emissions Trading Act was made public and opinions from operators of installations, authorities and other relevant bodies requested. The operators had provided information on their activities and applied for emission allowances. After the Commission had in October 2004 accepted the Finnish proposal as such, the Cabinet made in December 2004 its decision on the operator-level allocation of the allowances. The decision of the Cabinet was appealable directly to the SAC except for the total quantity of emission allowances or the share reserved for new entrants, on which no appeal can be made. Twelve appeals (of which one was withdrawn) were lodged by operators who requested additional emission allowances. The SAC made its decisions in July 2005; two of them were published in the yearbook (SAC 2005:46 and SAC 2005:47). The two concerned the adjustment of the amount of allowances and the treatment of a district heating network as one entity.

Regarding the period 2013–2020, the Ministry of Economic Affairs and Employment Decree on the continued term for submitting applications (371/2011), the Ministry of Economic Affairs and Employment Decree on the applications for free allowances for 2013–2020 (544/2011) and Government on the methods for the allocation of free allowances for 2013–2020 were applicable.

359. A separate act, the Act on the Use of Kyoto Mechanisms (109/2007) stipulates the use of Kyoto Protocol's project mechanisms in Finland. Detailed additional provisions are laid down in the Ministry of the Environment Decree on Joint Implementation projects (913/2007).

360. Reduction of carbon dioxide emissions in the aviation was until 2024 regulated by the Act on Emissions Trading in Aviation (34/2010, later amendments). The Act is proclaimed to be aimed to implement in a cost-effective and economical way Directive 2008/101/EC amending Directive 2003/87/EC so as to include aviation activities in the scheme for greenhouse gas emission allowance trading within the Community (Directive on Aviation Emissions Trading). As of 1 January 2024, the provisions on aviation are contained by the Emissions Trading Act. With regard to emissions trading in aviation, the Act applies to carbon dioxide emissions from flights between aerodromes located in the EEA and from those aerodromes to an aerodrome located in Switzerland and the United Kingdom between 2024 and 2026. From 2027, the Act will apply to carbon dioxide emissions from and to flights departing from and arriving at an aerodrome located in the EEA. As regards the monitoring, reporting and verification of emissions, the Act will also apply from 2025 onwards to the effects of emissions other than carbon dioxide emissions from aviation (section 9). Certain restrictions on the scope of application of emissions trading in aviation are laid down in section 10, and the scope of application of the aviation CORSIA scheme is provided in section 11. The general obligations concerning aviation are laid down in section 15 of the Act.

361. The first emissions trading period began on 1 January 2012 and ended on 31 December 2012. The total quantity of aviation emission allowances to be allocated to aircraft operators during the first period ha*d* to be 97% of the historical aviation emissions. The second emissions trading period began on 1 January 2013 and ended on 31 December 2020. During the second and subsequent emissions trading periods, the total quantity of aviation emission allowances to be allocated to aircraft operators had to be 95% of the previous emissions multiplied by the number of years in the period. In these periods, 3% of the total quantity of aviation emission allowances had to be set aside in a special reserve. Pursuant to the present Emissions Trading Act (section 64), the calculated share of free allocation of allowances to aircraft operators in the total quantity of allowances for aviation shall be 85% in 2024 and 2025, of which 25% in 2024 and 50% in 2025 will be transferred for auctioning. From 2026, free allowances shall be allocated to aircraft operators only on the basis of the use of sustainable aviation fuels referred to in section 65. In accordance with Article 3c(6) of the Emission Trading System Directive, until the end of 2030, an aircraft operator may apply for annual free allocation of aviation allowances based on the use of sustainable aviation fuels in the preceding year. Free allocation shall be deducted from the quantity of allowances to be auctioned. Each year, the European Commission publishes data on the price differential between fossil jet fuel and sustainable aviation fuels for the previous year and provides more detailed provisions on the calculation of fuel price differentials and the allocation of emission allowances (section 65). Section 66 of the Act lays down provisions on applying for free aviation emission allowances by the end of March 2024, section 67 of the Finnish Transport and Communications Agency's decision on the granting of free aviation emission allowances and section 68 on the recording of free allocation of emission allowances.'

362. The general provisions of the Emissions Trading Act are largely applicable also to aviation (and maritime transport).

363. Energy taxation has an important role in the abatement of climatic change, *see* paragraphs 73–75.

364. The Act on Prohibiting the Energy Use of Coal (416/2019) entered into force 1 April 2019. The use of coal for the production of electricity or heat is prohibited from 1 May 2029 (section 5), state of emergency and a certain power reserve excluded. It is commonly estimated that coal use will decline rapidly even before that. In practice, the prohibition targets power plants presently within the scope of emissions trading.

365. The Act on the Reduction of Greenhouse Gas Emissions Caused by Certain Fuels during their Life Cycle (170/2018) and the Act on Biofuels, Bioliquids and Biomass fuels (393/2013) aim to implement several climate-related directives.[27] The legal and administrative mechanisms follow the directives. The Energy Authority is the main enforcing body. *See also* paragraph 875.

366. On Regulation (EU) No. 517/2014 on fluorinated greenhouse gases and repealing Regulation (EC) No. 842/2006 and Government decree on fluorinated

27. Directive 2009/28/EC on the promotion of the use of energy from renewable sources and amending and subsequently repealing Directives 2001/77/EC and 2003/30/EC.

Directive 2009/30/EC amending Directive 98/70/EC as regards the specification of petrol, diesel and gas oil and introducing a mechanism to monitor and reduce greenhouse gas emissions and amending Council Directive 1999/32/EC as regards the specification of fuel used by inland waterway vessels and repealing Directive 93/12/EEC.

Directive (EU) 2015/1513 amending Directive 98/70/EC relating to the quality of petrol and diesel fuels and amending Directive 2009/28/EC on the promotion of the use of energy from renewable sources.

Council Directive (EU) 2015/652 laying down calculation methods and reporting requirements pursuant to Directive 98/70/EC of the European Parliament and of the Council relating to the quality of petrol and diesel fuels.

greenhouse gases and qualifications for persons dealing with equipment containing ozone-depleting substances (766/2016), *see* paragraph 342.

367. Directive 2009/31/EC on the geological storage of carbon dioxide[28] has been implemented mainly by the Act on the capturing and storage of carbon dioxide (416/2012). The Act is applicable to capture of carbon dioxide for geological storage, transport of carbon dioxide by pipeline, intermediate storage and geological storage of carbon dioxide. Pollution prevention regarding the same and permits pertaining to it are stipulated in the Environmental Protection Act. It is forbidden to storage carbon dioxide geologically or in the water column in Finland or in the economic zone, with the exception of geological storage of an amount of carbon dioxide below 100,000 tonnes, provided that the purpose is research, development and experimenting of new products. In Finland captured carbon dioxide may be transferred for geological storage only in such an underground geological formation which is wholly located in the geographical area of a Member State of the EU or its economic zone or continental shelf. Carbon dioxide stream shall consist merely of carbon dioxide, subject to exceptions in section 5(2). A capturer's obligations are provided in section 6. The construction of the electricity transmission network and interim storage facilities must be based on a valid land use Plan with legal effect. The construction of the transmission network and interim storage facilities are governed by the provisions of the Land Use and Building Act (as of 1 January 2025, the Building Act) on the construction of buildings (section 11).

The Ministry of the Environment is in charge of general steering, and the Centres for Economic Development, Transport and the Environment are the supervisory bodies (or, regarding access rights to storage networks, the Energy Authority).

368. An account on the possibilities of carbon dioxide capturing has to be attached to an Environmental Permit application of a LCP (section 100 of the Environmental Protection Act). Further duties, if any, depend on the account.

369. A framework act of quite new type, called the Climate Act (609/2015), was enacted in 2015. But soon the need to update the Climate Act emerged due to the 2016 Paris Agreement, covering Finland by EU ratification, Regulation (EU) 2018/842 on binding annual greenhouse gas emission reductions by Member States from 2021 to 2030 contributing to climate action to meet commitments under the Paris Agreement and amending Regulation (EU) No. 525/2013 and other European Green Deal legislation. A bill for a wholly new Climate Act, preserving the basic technical structures of the current Act, was introduced in the Parliament in March 2022, and a new Climate Act (423/2022) was enacted, being in force from 1 July 2022. The provisions on administrative law litigation and the duties of municipalities were inserted in the autumn of 2022. The Act lays down the objectives and framework for planning Finland's climate policy and monitoring its implementation. The purpose of the Act is to: (1) enhance and coordinate the design and monitoring of the

28. Directive 2009/31/EC on the geological storage of carbon dioxide and amending Council Directive 85/337/EEC, European Parliament and Council Directives 2000/60/EC, 2001/80/EC, 2004/35/EC, 2006/12/EC, 2008/1/EC and Regulation (EC) No. 1013/2006.

implementation of climate change mitigation and adaptation measures and (2) strengthen the opportunities of the Parliament and the public to participate in and influence the planning of climate policy. The purpose of the Act and the climate policy planning system pursuant to it is to ensure, for its part, that: (1) anthropogenic greenhouse gas emissions are reduced and removals by sinks increase so that greenhouse gas emissions are no more than equal to removals by 2035 at the latest and removals increase and emissions continue to decrease thereafter; (2) the combined anthropogenic emissions of greenhouse gases into the atmosphere from the effort sharing and emissions trading sectors together will be reduced by at least 60% by 2030 and by at least 80% by 2040 compared to 1990; (3) total anthropogenic greenhouse gas emissions into the atmosphere from the effort sharing and emissions trading sectors together will be reduced by at least 90% by 2050, but aiming at a level of 95% compared to 1990; and (4) by national measures Finland is adapting to climate change in the way of promoting climate risk management and climate resilience (section 2(1) of the Act). The purpose of the Act and the climate policy planning system pursuant to it is also to ensure, for their part, the fulfilment of the obligations arising from agreements binding on Finland and EU law concerning the reduction and monitoring of greenhouse gases, strengthening sinks and adaptation. If an international agreement binding on Finland or EU law includes stricter targets for greenhouse gas emissions or removals than those mentioned above, the targets referred to in (1)–(3) above shall be based on them (section 2(2)). In addition, the Act and the climate policy planning system in accordance with it shall aim to: (1) ensure for its part fairness of climate action as well as sustainable development; and (2) safeguard for its part the conditions for the Saami to maintain and develop their own language and culture (section 2(3)). The Act applies to the duties of state authorities in drawing up climate policy plans and ensuring their implementation. It also applies to municipalities when they draw up Municipal Climate Plans and monitor their implementation. The emissions trading sector is regulated separately.

370. The Climate Act contains provisions on the tasks of State authorities in drawing up climate change policy plans and ensuring their implementation, in addition to other existing legislation. The Plans drawn up under the Climate Act shall be taken into account, as provided in other legislation, in the planning and decision-making of measures carried out under other legislation concerning the reduction of greenhouse gas emissions and removals, and concerning adaptation to climate change. In their activities, all State authorities shall promote the achievement of the objectives of the Act and the implementation of the climate policy Plans.

371. The climate policy planning system under the Climate Act consists of the following national climate policy Plans: (1) Long-Term Climate Plan; (2) National Climate Change Adaptation Plan; (3) Medium-Term Climate Plan; and (4) Climate Plan for the Land Use Sector.

372. The climate policy planning system defines the objectives for reducing greenhouse gas emissions, strengthening sinks and adapting to climate change, as well as the measures needed to achieve them in the different branches of administration. In general, climate change mitigation and adaptation objectives and actions shall be set in the climate policy plans on the basis of up-to-date scientific knowledge, taking into account the progress of climate change, its likely positive and negative effects, associated hazards and risks, and the potential to prevent accidents and limit their adverse effects. The plans shall present the obligations arising from international agreements binding on Finland and from EU law, and the plans shall contribute to ensuring that the obligations are fulfilled. In addition, when preparing the plans, the following shall be taken into account: (1) data produced in the national greenhouse gas emissions inventory system and the national policy reporting system; (2) assessments of the development of international and EU climate policy; (3) environmental, economic and social factors in accordance with the principle of sustainable development; (4) cost-effectiveness of climate change mitigation and adaptation measures; (5) the level and development of technologies for the reduction of greenhouse gases, the strengthening of sinks and adaptation to climate change; (6) coordination of plans with energy and transport policy planning, where appropriate; (7) the potential impact of the plans on domestic food security; (8) the potential impact of the plans on biodiversity; and (9) factors relevant to the development of society other than those referred to in (1)–(8) above.

373. A Long-Term Climate Plan shall be approved by the Cabinet at least once every ten years. In order to achieve the objectives referred to in section 2 of the Act, the Plan shall set out the following: (1) scenarios for the evolution of total greenhouse gas emissions and removals from the effort sharing, emissions trading and land use sectors, covering at least the next thirty years, taking into account the reduction of greenhouse gas emissions, the strengthening of sinks and adaptation to climate change; (2) key sector-specific pathways based on the greenhouse gas reduction target referred to in section 2(1)(3), and the objective of increasing removals by sinks referred to in section 2(1)(1); (3) an assessment of the long-term development prospects of methods for reducing greenhouse gas emissions and strengthening sinks; and (4) necessary elements other than those referred to above in (1)–(3). The first Long-Term Climate Plan shall be approved by 2025 at the latest.

374. The Cabinet shall approve a Medium-Term Climate Plan once per parliamentary term. In order to achieve the objectives of the Act, the Plan shall set out the following: (1) a target for the development of greenhouse gas emissions from the effort sharing sector;(2) actions to reduce anthropogenic greenhouse gas emissions from the effort sharing sector; (3) information on the evolution of greenhouse gas emissions and removals; (4) estimates of the development of greenhouse gas emissions and the impact of measures on them; and (5) necessary elements other than those above in (1)–(4). The information and estimates referred to in (3) and (4) above shall include the following: (1) data on the development of total greenhouse gas emissions from the effort sharing and emissions trading sectors since 1990; (2) data on the development of greenhouse gas emissions and removals in the emissions trading sector, effort sharing sector and land use sector since 2005; (3) an estimate of the development of total greenhouse gas emissions from the effort sharing and emissions trading sectors and separately from the effort sharing sector over the ten–fifteen years following the adoption of the Plan, based on current measures; (4) an estimate of the evolution of greenhouse gas emissions from the effort sharing sector over the ten–fifteen years following the adoption of the Plan, based on existing and new measures; and (5) other necessary elements.

375. The Cabinet shall approve a Climate Plan for the Land Use Sector at least every other parliamentary term. In order to achieve the objectives referred to in section 2 of the Act, the Plan shall set out the following: (1) a target on the development of greenhouse gas emissions and removals in the land use sector; (2) actions to reduce greenhouse gas emissions and increase removals in the land use sector; (3) information on the evolution of greenhouse gas emissions and removals; (4) estimates of the development of greenhouse gas emissions and removals from the land use sector and the impact of measures on them; (5) other necessary elements. The information and estimates referred to in (3) and (4) above shall include the following: (1) data on the development of total greenhouse gas emissions from the effort sharing and emissions trading sectors since 1990; (2) data on the development of greenhouse gas emissions and removals in the land use sector since 1990; (3) an estimate of the evolution of greenhouse gas emissions and removals from the land use sector over the ten–fifteen years following the adoption of the plan, based on current measures; (4) an estimate of the evolution of greenhouse gas emissions and removals from the land use sector over the ten–fifteen years following the adoption of the plan, based on existing and new measures; and (5) other necessary elements. However, during parliamentary terms when there is no obligation to draw up Climate Plan for the Land Use Sector, the up-to-date nature of the existing plan and the need for new measures shall be assessed.

376. The Cabinet shall approve a National Climate Change Adaptation Plan at least every other parliamentary term (= four years). In order to achieve the objectives referred to in section 2 of the Act, the Adaptation Plan shall set out the following: (1) up-to-date risk and vulnerability analysis; (2) sectoral, cross-administrative and regional review of adaptation as necessary; (3) measures to achieve the adaptation objectives and an assessment of their effectiveness; and (4) necessary elements other than those referred to in (1)–(3) above. However, during parliamentary terms when there is no obligation to draw up an Adaptation Plan, the up-to-date nature of the existing Plan and the need for new measures shall be assessed.

377. When preparing the Plans, the public must be given the opportunity to familiarize themselves with the draft plan and submit opinions on it. In addition, a statement on a draft Plan shall be requested from the key authorities and communities, as well as from the Climate Panel (below) and the Saami Climate Council (below). A statement must also be requested from the Saami Parliament and the Skolt village assembly.

378. Regarding the assessment of the environmental impacts of the Plans, the Act on the Environmental Impact Assessment of Government Plans and Programmes (200/2005), *see* Part I, Chapter 1, §22, is applicable. In connection with the preparation of the Plans, their economic, social and other impacts shall also be investigated to the extent necessary. In the preparation of the plans, the right of the Saami to maintain and develop their own language and culture shall be taken into account. The authorities at stake must negotiate with the Saami Parliament when preparing the plans. Also, the provisions of the Skolt Act on promoting the living conditions and livelihood opportunities of the Skolt population and region as well as on maintaining and promoting the Skolt culture shall be taken into account.

379. The Cabinet shall submit a report to the Parliament on each approved Long-Term Climate Plan, National Climate Change Adaptation Plan, Medium-Term Climate Change Plan and Climate Plan for the Land Use Sector. The Cabinet shall monitor the implementation of the Plans sufficiently to ascertain whether the objectives set in the plans concerning mitigation and adaptation and the objectives of the Act will be achieved. Based on the monitoring, the Cabinet shall, when necessary, make a decision on the additional measures needed to achieve the objectives (section 16(1)). The adequacy of the targets shall be monitored on the basis of up-to-date scientific information on the progress of climate change and to ensure that the targets fulfil the obligations under international agreements binding on Finland and EU legislation. The realization of the estimates on the development of emissions and removals, as included in the Plans, shall be monitored on the basis of the annual greenhouse gas emissions data produced in the National Greenhouse Gas Inventory System.[29] In addition, the monitoring of the Plans shall take into account the data produced in the National Policy Reporting System.[30] The Cabinet shall inform the public of the results of the monitoring.

380. In accordance with a Cabinet decision on additional measures to be made (section 16(1)), the Cabinet shall amend the Plan at stake. Amendments to plans shall be made in accordance with the procedure to be followed in the preparation of the original Plans. In addition, a Plan may also be amended in the event of shortcomings of minor importance in the information it contains. Such a change may be carried out in a lighter procedure. Each calendar year, the Government shall submit an Annual Climate Report to the Parliament. The annual climate report shall include: (1) information on the development of emissions and removals; (2) an assessment of the adequacy of the current and planned measures presented in the climate policy Plans with regard to achieving the targets set for the next fifteen years

29. The national inventory system provided in Art. 37 of Regulation (EU) 2018/1999 on the Governance of the Energy Union and Climate Action, amending Regulation (EC) No. 663/2009 and (EC) No. 715/2009 of the European Parliament and of the Council, Directives 94/22/EC, 98/70/EC, 2009/31/EC, 2009/73/EC, 2010/31/EU, 2012/27/EU and 2013/30/EU of the European Parliament and of the Council, Council Directives 2009/119/EC and (EU) 2015/652 and repealing Regulation (EU) No. 525/2013 of the European Parliament and of the Council.

30. The integrated reporting on greenhouse gas policies and measures and on projection is provided in Art. 18 of Regulation (EU) 2018/1999.

and an assessment of the need for additional measures to achieve them; (3) information on the achievement of the emission reduction targets included in the Medium-Term Climate Plan; (4) information on the achievement of the emission and removal targets included in the Climate Plan for the Land Use Sector; (5) information on the implementation of the existing and planned measures and the additional measures; and (6) to the extent necessary, an assessment of the adequacy and effectiveness of the adaptation measures included in the Adaptation Plan and, if necessary, an account on the implementation of the planned adaptation measures by administrative branch and region. The Ministry of the Environment shall inform the public about the submission of the Annual Climate Report and its main contents.

381. Each ministry prepares the section of climate policy Plans concerning its administrative branch and submits information concerning its administrative branch for the Annual Climate Report. The Ministry of Economic Affairs and Employment is responsible for coordinating and compiling the plans for the Long-Term Climate Plan, the Ministry of Agriculture and Forestry for the National Climate Change Adaptation Plan, the Ministry of the Environment for the Medium-Term Climate Plan, and the Ministry of Agriculture and Forestry for the Climate Plan for the Land Use Sector. Steering and monitoring the implementation of the Plans is the responsibility of each ministry within its sphere of competence. The Ministry of the Environment is responsible for compiling the Annual Climate Report. The unit responsible for the National Greenhouse Gas Inventory System is Statistics Finland. The emissions data service for municipalities is maintained by the Finnish Environment Institute.

382. The Finnish Climate Panel, which is an independent scientific expert body, is appointed by the Cabinet for a fixed term of four years at a time. The Panel shall include representatives from different fields of science. The task of the Panel is to produce and analyse scientific information and to identify information needs on climate change mitigation and adaptation for the planning, implementation, monitoring and decision-making of climate policy. For these tasks, the Panel issues statements on climate policy documents related to climate change mitigation and adaptation. The Climate Panel may also produce other reports and materials, which it communicates to the public and decision-makers as necessary. More detailed provisions on the tasks, composition and other procedures concerning the activities of the Panel, as well as on the election, term of office and remuneration of its members are laid down in the Government decree in the Finnish Climate Panel (349/2023).

383. To support the preparation of climate policy Plans, the Cabinet shall appoint a Saami Climate Council for a fixed period. The Saami Climate Council shall include representatives of holders of Saami traditional knowledge and representatives from key fields of science. The task of the Council is to issue statements on climate policy Plans for the promotion of Saami culture. The Saami Climate Council may also carry out other tasks related to climate change and the production of knowledge base related to Saami culture and rights. More detailed provisions on the tasks, composition, term of office and other procedures concerning the activities of the Council, as well as on the election, term of office and remuneration of its members, are laid down in the Government decree on the Saami Climate Council (435/2023).

384. Each municipality shall prepare or update a Municipal Climate Plan at least once during its Council term. The Plan shall include: (1) the objective of reducing greenhouse gas emissions in the municipality; (2) measures to reduce greenhouse gas emissions in the municipality; (3) information on the development of greenhouse gas emissions in the municipality; (4) information on monitoring the implementation of the Plan; and (5) other items deemed necessary. When setting the objective in (1) above, the municipality shall take into account the objectives referred to in section 2(1)(1)–(3) of the Act. The objective concerning the increase in removals by sinks shall also be taken into account if the municipality sets removal targets or measures concerning sinks in the Plan. If the municipality sets climate change adaptation targets or measures in the Plan, the objective referred to in section 2(1)(4) of the Act shall be taken into account. A Municipal Climate Plan is approved by the Municipal Council. The municipality shall monitor the implementation of the Plan. The Plan shall be taken into account in the municipal strategy and in the annual report of the municipality. A municipality may also draw up the Plan together with other municipalities in the area. The joint plan must include municipality-specific objectives and actions. The joint plan is approved by the council of each municipality. The Ministry of the Environment may grant discretionary government transfers to municipalities for drawing up or updating the plan. The present Cabinet has expressed its will to quash the provisions of Municipal Climate Plans.

385. The right to appeal to the SAC against a Cabinet decision on a climate policy Plan is stipulated in a special way due to the fact that ordinary administrative litigation rules on standing are not as such suitable for a global phenomenon that more or less impacts anyone. The right is pursuant to the Climate Act vested in: (1) any person whose right, obligation or interest may be particularly affected by the effects of climate change or its mitigation or adaptation thereto; (2) a national registered association representing the interests of the persons referred to in (1) in accordance with its statutes or, where the effects of climate change or mitigation or adaptation thereto may be of particular concern to a specific region or part of a country, a similar local or regional association; (3) a national registered association or foundation whose purpose is to promote the protection of nature, health or the environment; (4) a Regional Council, if the effects of climate change or its mitigation or adaptation to it may affect the region in a particular way; (5) a nation-level State authority whose field of activity has a particular public interest in the effects of climate change or its mitigation or adaptation to it, as well as any other State authority whose field of activity and area of activity are particularly affected by the impacts of climate change or its mitigation or adaptation to it; (6) the Saami Parliament; and (7) the Skolt village assembly. The appellant referred to in (1), (2), (4) and (5) above shall explain in his appeal the special manner on which the right of appeal is based. If the particular manner of impact justifying the subjective right of appeal is not indicated, the SAC may dismiss the appeal as inadmissible without giving the appellant the opportunity to supplement it. The decision of the Cabinet may be enforced notwithstanding any appeal, unless otherwise ordered by the court.

386. An appeal against a decision of the Cabinet (section 16(1) of the Climate Act) which states the need for additional measures may be lodged only in connection with the subsequent decision to amend the existing Plan at stake in accordance with section 17(1) of the Act. Following the general provisions in the Administrative Judicial Procedures Act, the Annual Climate Report to the Parliament and the reports on approved Plans are not indicated to be appealable decisions by the Climate Act.

387. Until now, the only effort to initiate a climate law trial is the case before the SAC (SAC 2023:62) where a nationwide conservation association (*Suomen luonnonsuojeluliitto ry*) ja Greenpeace Norden as appellants demanded that the Annual Climate Report 2022 be overturned and the matter be returned to the Cabinet for further preparation. According to the appeal, the Report had not provided a statutory assessment of the additional measures needed to achieve the targets, even though information on the collapse of carbon sinks in the land use sector prior to the Annual Report had shown the need for such additional measures. According to the appellants, by failing to make a statutory decision, the Cabinet had acted at least passively in such a way that the legal protection of the party concerned and the protection of fundamental rights required the possibility to appeal against the decision, even though no actual administrative decision had been made in the matter.

388. The SAC dismissed the appeal. Voting 3–2, the Court stated that the Cabinet's decision to submit the Annual Climate Report to the Parliament was not an administrative decision that could be appealed. The SAC held, however, that assessing the legality of the Cabinet's decision-making procedure in the manner intended by the appellants could be subject to judicial review in a case where failure to make a decision at that stage would lead to a result contrary to the Climate Act or if the Cabinet's actual actions would demonstrate that it does not intend to make appropriate decisions in order to achieve the objectives and obligations required by law fast enough. The Court stated that, in connection with the Annual Climate Report, the Cabinet had not made a decision on measures to reduce carbon sinks or the necessity of such measures or failed to investigate the matter concerning such measures. Based on the account received in the case, it was also not possible to conclude that the Cabinet's decision at this stage would have meant unlawful failure to comply with the objectives and obligations of the Climate Act.

389. Municipal Appeal is applied to municipal Climate Plan decisions.

390. Anyone undertaking a construction project must ensure that the building is designed and constructed in a low-carbon manner as required by its intended use. The carbon footprint and carbon handprint of a new building or a building subject to extensive renovation requiring a Building Permit shall be reported in the climate account submitted for the Permit. A climate account is not required for a new building that does not need to be designed and constructed as a nearly zero-energy building, or for detached houses to be renovated or for buildings undergoing extensive renovation whose energy efficiency is not required to be improved in connection with the renovation work. The assessment of the carbon footprint and carbon handprint shall cover the life cycle of the building or the stages of renovation and subsequent life cycle of a building undergoing major renovation. According to the main rule, the carbon footprint of a new building may not exceed the limit value laid down by the purpose of use category (section 8 of the Building Act as of 1 January 2025).

391. The Finnish Environment Institute shall maintain a National Emissions Database, which shall contain the general carbon footprint and carbon handprint data required for assessing the low-carbon nature of buildings and construction sites, as specified in section 15 of the Building Act.

Chapter 4. Water Pollution Prevention

§1. The Structure of the System

I. General Aspects

392. Finnish Water Law is in many respects influenced by the fact that the water areas are privately owned (*see* General Introduction, Chapter 2, §1). The pre-2000 system of special Water Courts as (*inter alia*) permit-delivering bodies instead of administrative authorities (*see* Part I, Chapter 1, §2 above) was partly linked to this. The relation was not a logical one, though; land areas are also privately owned, but building permits there have always been delivered by administrative bodies. However, compensations and permits were intermingled in the regime of the Water Act (and still are under the Environmental Protection Act). For historical reasons, water pollution law has been an integral part of Water Law and hence regulated by the Water Act. However, a historical shift around the borderline between the forensic and administrative regimes took place in 2000. From March 2000, the integrated pollution prevention framework of the then Environmental Protection Act was, as the present Environmental Protection Act 2014 is, also to be applied to wastewaters and other polluting discharges into waters (*see* Part I, Chapter 1, §4 above).

II. Basic Provisions Regarding Water Pollution and Discharges

393. The system of the previous Water Act was originally based on three principal bans: bans on closing off, altering and polluting a body of water. The notion 'body of (surface) water', or 'water body', covered, and still covers, lakes and ponds of all sizes, rivers and (major) brooks, as well as systems made up of them, but not ditches, small brooks, fountains or groundwater. The sea (territorial waters) is also regarded as a water body, as well as the economic zone. There were separate bans on altering and polluting groundwater. For the purposes of water protection, the bans on pollution were naturally the most important. Nevertheless, the others, especially the ban on altering water bodies, were also important from the environmental point of view (*see* Part II, Chapter 8). In the reform of 2000, the bans on closing off and altering remained (with certain amendments) in the then Water Act, but the bans on polluting were replaced by the new provisions in the then Environmental Protection Act, in fact preserving rather much of the previous regulatory structures.

Most of the bans of the previous Water Act were not exactly absolute prohibitions. Rather, they may be described as provisions for determining the eventual necessity of a permit case by case. As a matter of fact, the entire permit system was based on the bans. Most of them were (and, where applicable, are) written in a way that the prohibited activities are defined by specifying at large both the activities as such and their negative impacts on private and public interests. For effluent and discharges this meant that there were no fixed standards which as such would imply the need for a permit. In this respect, the reception of the then EC water pollution law entailed a principal change. The directives in question required a permit or consent for several discharge categories irrespective of the individual impacts. In practice, however, the ban on pollution most often led at least to the same result. Hence, the EC-based amendments to the Water Act (1993 and 1995) were mostly of a formal nature. The later reforms have not caused any fundamental change.

394. The restrictions on polluting surface water bodies traditionally include all kinds of emissions (of matter or energy) which immediately or later may cause pollution in a body of water. The term 'pollution' has a wide meaning. It may have been any violation of public or private interest caused by a discharge (effluent) of solid, liquid or gaseous substances or energy into a body of water or the sea. The definition of pollution as any violation of public or private interest (of a certain type) has implied a specific 'legal' notion of pollution, with a wide range of variations. Even a violation of the rights of a single fishing rights holder or professional fisherman, etc., was enough. All this has affected the way in which the general concept of pollution of the environment, also covering pollution of waters, has been formulated in the integrated pollution prevention system of the Environmental Protection Act (in section 5 of the present Act, *see* paragraph 120).

A violation of a public interest is always more or less a matter of judicial discretion. On the basis of this definition any potential polluter has to consider whether his eventual discharge would – or even might – lead to a violation. A mere possibility of pollution is, if well grounded, regarded as sufficient to create a permit obligation. If damages would appear only later on, the permit was nevertheless necessary from the very beginning of the discharge. Commencing discharges as defined by the provision without a permit is punishable and subject to administrative injunctions.

In practice, the previous 'ban' was hence far from being absolute, in the respect that statistically speaking only a minority of all permit applications were totally disallowed. Nevertheless, this was not the whole truth. The crucial point was, and still is, the content of the permit decision or the question of provisions laid down in the permit, i.e., the various restrictions and limitations set by the permit authority, and the final technical realization determined by it. This means that the residual loading of a water body may well be very limited and hardly harmful to the water system. Even then the permit was called 'pollution permit', which was here merely an expression of formal statutory accuracy. Most of the permits dealt in practice with rather modest eutrophication caused by nutrients and/or changes caused by oxygen-demanding organic substances. There were, however, and may of course still be, situations where more or less significant real pollution of water bodies has been allowed.

395. The necessity of a permit in the regime of the Environmental Protection Act is, as a starting point, based on lists of installations and activities. However, these lists are not exhaustive, because there are important situations where the necessity of a permit is established irrespective of them. Perhaps the most significant is the probability of pollution of a body of surface water (territorial waters of the Baltic Sea included), assessed case by case. Not very much was changed when the previous ban on polluting surface water bodies in the then Water Act was replaced by a general clause pursuant to which a permit is always needed where such pollution in a water body would (or even could) be at stake. The same stipulation is remained in the present (2014) Environmental Protection Act (section 27(2)(1) and 27(2)(2) of the present Environmental Protection Act). In the preparatory documents of the 2000 Environmental Protection Act it was stressed that the scope and practical applications of the previous ban would also be relevant further on. The previous system has influenced the water-related parts of the Environmental Protection Act in several other respects as well. For example, the provisions on the obligations in respect to fisheries in the Water Act are applicable.

396. After the necessity of an Environmental Permit has been realized on any of the several possible grounds, the provisions of the Environmental Protection Act applicable to water pollution and its prevention are applied without any difference. Hence, it is, for the purpose of deciding on the necessity of a permit only, unnecessary to assess the possible pollution, if there already is another ground for requiring permit.

The prevention of groundwater pollution (*see also* Part II, Chapter 8, §1) is not, at least not in the first place, based on permits, because the ban on polluting groundwater in section 17 of the Environmental Protection Act is absolute and the necessity of a permit as such cannot be based on it. However, an intended site in important or other, for water supply suitable groundwater area is for certain activities enough to remove the activity at stake from the registration category to the Environmental Permit category (section 28(2) of the Environmental Protection Act), and certain others become subject to Environmental Permit requirement instead of the notification or registration requirement due to such a location combined with a risk of groundwater pollution (section 28(2)), a risk the level of which cannot be too high, whereas already the absolute ban in section 17 is applicable due to a certain risk. Irrespective of what the necessity of an Environmental Permit is based, the compliance to section 17 can and shall anyway be controlled by the permit authority (section 66).

397. In practice almost all relevant sources of surface water pollution, like industries, municipalities, fish farms, etc., as a rule came within the scope of the previous ban and the permit system, with the exception of the so-called diffuse loading caused by cultivation, silviculture, scattered settlements, etc. There is actually no exception provided for the diffuse sources and the pollution that results from them. The same holds true for the Environmental Protection Act. Pollution is pollution even if the causes are more than one. But in practice, e.g., improper use of fertilizers or spreading of manure in the fields is more difficult to control than the point sources, and the legal limits to the rather massive loading of waters caused by forest ditching during decades have been more theoretical than practical.

398. The EC Directive 91/676/EEC concerning the protection of waters caused by nitrates from agricultural sources is also a good example, because the detailed implementing provisions under the then Water Act were delayed for a long time. A basic difficulty lay in the alleged possibility that the EC environmental subsidies for agriculture (being partly more the fruit of agricultural politics than of environmental concern, though) are at risk if environmental requirements are imposed by general enactments, albeit required by a directive of the same EC. One contradiction was (and still) is also made up by the fact that phosphates, not nitrates, are the main concern regarding the quality of Finnish water bodies. The Decree mentioned above has in 2000 been replaced by a new decree, and more recently by Government decree on the reducing of certain discharges originating from agriculture and horticulture (1250/1214).

399. Past EC law created the first cases where a permit for a discharge was necessary irrespective of the impacts of the discharge. First, there were substances on the 'dark list' and the 'grey list', or List I and List II, of the then framework Directive 76/464/EEC. Pursuant to the 1993 and 1995 amendments of the then Water Act, the discharges of all such substances had been made by decree at least subject to a duty to have a prior permit without an individual consideration of a possible 'pollution', in order to meet the requirements of the directive for this part. (In the case of several very dangerous List I substances, all discharges thereof have been totally banned, or made subject to directly applicable restrictions.) The same applied to the discharges of municipal or industrial wastewater regulated by the urban wastewater Directive 91/271/EEC and to the activities under the then titanium dioxide directives. In practice, the effect of these additional provisions was minimal, as the interpretation of the general provisions leads most often to the same result. Pursuant to the Act (113/2000) on the implementation of the 2000 reform, all the decrees mentioned here remained in force.

400. Directive 2000/60/EC establishing a framework for Community action in the field of water policy has changed the legal framework above at least formally. The directives above have been repealed, and the same holds good in respect to the corresponding 1994 decrees. The present detailed provisions are included in Government decree on Substances Dangerous and Harmful to the Aquatic Environment (1022/2006) and Government decree on Urban Waste Water Treatment (888/2006). The former has been issued by virtue of the previous Environmental Protection Act, the Act on the Arranging of Water Management and Marine Waters Management and the Water Supply and Sewerage Act, and the latter by virtue of the Environmental Protection Act and the Water Supply and Sewerage Act.

The objective of Decree 1022/2006, as presently amended, is to protect surface waters (sea waters included) and groundwater and improve their quality by preventing pollution and the danger thereof caused by dangerous and harmful substances. The aim is to eliminate at once, or progressively, emissions and leaching of substances dangerous to the aquatic environment and to progressively reduce emissions and the leaching of harmful substances. For this purpose, emission prohibitions, emission limit values and environmental quality, as well as (from 2009) to prevent and reduce emissions of dangerous substances into groundwater. An additional goal is to prevent emissions and the leaching of substances dangerous or harmful to the aquatic environment from causing harm to the operations of water supply and sewerage plants.

401. A general ban in section 4 of the Decree covers discharges of substances in Annex 1A that are hazardous to aquatic environments into surface waters or into sewer systems. Another group of hazardous substances, listed in Annex 1B, has been made subject to emission limit values laid down in the same Annex. The final individual limit values are laid down in each Environmental Permit (section 5). They may be more stringent than those in the Annex, as provided in section 70(1) of the Environmental Protection Act. Water quality standards are also used (section 6), *see* paragraph 268. The concentration of a hazardous substance specified in Annex 1, C2, or D in surface water may not exceed the quality standard laid down in the same Annex. The decree also imposes requirements for the monitoring of surface waters (sections 7–9b); also these provisions are mainly enforced through the Environmental Permits. Due to the fact that the Annex only contains a number of hazardous chemicals, all the main challenges of water protection are not covered.

402. Government decree on Urban Waste Water Treatment 888/2006 applies to the treatment and conducting of urban wastewaters that require an Environmental Permit. This means sewers into which wastewater corresponding the amount produced by at least 100 inhabitants is discharged (Table 2(13)(d) of Annex 1 to the Environmental Protection Act), or a smaller amount, if pollution of water body results (section 27(2)(1) of the Act).

Pursuant to section 4 of the Decree, wastewaters shall be subject to secondary (biological) or an equivalent treatment and the treatment must comply with the requirements listed in Annex to the decree, Table 1. Phosphorus must be removed from wastewaters and the phosphorus removal process must comply with the requirements listed in Table 2 of the Annex. The need for nitrogen removal shall be determined in the permit application and decided upon in the Environmental Permit. Nitrogen shall be removed whenever the reduction of nitrogen load can improve the status of waters. Denitrification requirements must meet the terms set forth in Table 2 of the Annex. All these requirements are specified in the Environmental Permit. The required nitrogen removal must be implemented within seven years of the day the Environmental Permit gained legal force. This provision of seven years seems to be very problematic, compared to the ordinary appellate periods and the prescribed times for new applications, and also in relation to the basic norms in the Environmental Protection Act. No such postponement rule has existed so far, and its relevance (as a formal maximum time) remains to be seen.

Requirements stricter than those specified in Tables 1 and 2 of the Annex shall be laid down in the Environmental Permit, if provided by the Environmental Protection Act or a decree issued under it.

III. Household Wastewater from Scattered Dwellings

403. The diffuse loading from scattered dwellings, in particular from detached or free time dwellings in shore-near areas, has been a eutrophication problem, locally but to some extent also more generally. The Environmental Protection Act 2000 originally provided a new instrument where general obligations to avoid discharges by such dwellings are complemented by a generally applicable decree with technical specifications. The detailed provisions, impacting a very large number of owners and possessors of detached houses and summer dwellings, were largely debated and criticized, affecting also party politics in general. Amendments were made in 2005, and in 2011 this regulatory subsystem was reformed by inserting a new on treatment of household wastewaters in areas outside sewer networks in the then Environmental Protection Act. The basic idea remained the same, however: domestic wastewaters had to be treated by a treatment system before discharging into soil, water body, ditch, pond or brook, in particular that from water closets, but also others.

The current Environmental Protection Act contains a whole chapter (Chapter 16) on this item, on the previous principal basis. The abundant detailed provisions are issued in Government decree on the treatment of household wastewater in areas outside of sewage networks (157/2017).

404. One of the starting points here is the notion of household wastewater (section 154 of the Act). The notion encompasses wastewater originating in water toilets of dwellings, offices, business premises and installations, or in kitchens, washing premises or similar premises and facilities, as well as by its properties and consistency corresponding wastewater originating in milk premises of cattle farms or other business activities. Other central defined notions here are wastewater treatment system (technically a very diverse notion) and wastewater system, as well as load by untreated wastewater.

405. 'Load by untreated wastewater' means such loading of treatment facility made up by household wastewater that is determined as product of the average number of the inhabitants using the wastewater system and the load value of scattered population (below), or, if the household wastewater originates in other activity than dwelling, as the average daily load, based on research. The 'load value of scattered population' (section 154a) shows the average untreated household wastewater load by one inhabitant, in grams per day as to organic substance, phosphorus and nitrogen. A 'load-type-specified value' is based on the origin of the load of different types. Pursuant to Decree 157/2017, the amount of organic substance in untreated household wastewater by one inhabitant, contained in the load value of scattered population, is 50 grams as BOD_7 per day. The corresponding amounts of total phosphorus and total nitrogen are 2.2 grams and 14 grams per day. An annex to the Decree provides in more detail on the consistency of the load value of scattered population for different types of load by origin (excrement, urine, other).

A 'base-level treatment requirement' (section 154b) means that household wastewater shall be cleaned in such a way that the loading of the environment is reduced at least 80% regarding organic substance, at least 70% regarding total phosphorus and at least 30% regarding total nitrogen, compared with the load by untreated wastewater determined by the load value of scattered population. Specifications may be issued by decree.

406. If a property is not connected to a sewer system and an Environmental Permit is not needed for the activity, the wastewaters from it shall be conveyed and treated in such a manner that no risk of environmental pollution is caused (section

155). In addition to this general rule, household wastewater shall be treated before discharging on or in soil, water body or ditch, artificial pond or natural streamlet. Other wastewater than from water toilet may be discharged untreated on or in soil, if the amount thereof is small and no risk of environmental pollution is caused (section 155). A property owner shall see to that there is an appropriate wastewater treatment system on the property. In the assessment of the appropriateness of the system attention shall be paid to the load by untreated wastewater generated by the use of the property, risk of environmental pollution and properties of other wastewater treatment system, the location of the property near a water body or sea or in a groundwater area in use or suitable for use, and other environmental circumstances (section 156). A wastewater treatment system shall be planned, constructed and maintained so that the base-level treatment requirement is continuously met. More specified provisions may be issued by decree.

407. A property owner in an area at a distance of 100 metres or below or in a groundwater area in water supply use or suitable for that shall also see to that a wastewater treatment system based on treatment requirements of the time of building, that being before 2004, or based on a valid Building Permit, meets the base-level treatment requirement. The distance shall be determined from the coastline according to mean water level to the wall of the nearest such building where wastewater is generated (section 156a), that being often a sauna building in practice. As to other areas, the same obligation is in force if (1) if a water toilet is constructed, or such a repair or amendment measure concerning water and sewage facilities subject to permit requirement where the system is renovated or wholly repaired, is taken; or (2) a repair or amendment measure subject to permit requirement and comparable to the construction of a new building is taken (section 156b). Such a property shall also be maintained so that the base-level treatment requirement is met also after the measures.

408. More stringent treatment requirements may be caused by other legislation (section 156c). Municipal Environmental Bylaws may, in accordance to section 202, contain more stringent requirements if they are necessary due to local environmental conditions (section 156c). An indicatory treatment level concerning household wastewater is provided by Government decree for such situations (section 4 of Decree 157/2017).

409. Deviations from the requirements in areas referred to in section 156a may by a designed municipal authority be granted for a period of no more than five years at a time. For a deviation it is required that the environmental load is, paying attention to the use of the property, considered significantly small in comparison to the load by untreated wastewater, or if the required improvement measures as a whole are unreasonable due to their high costs and demanding technology (section 156d). The following are relevant in considering unreasonableness: (1) the location of the property in an area planned to be contained in a sewer network; (2) the advanced age and other particular issues related to the personal situation of the possessor and permanent inhabitants; or (3) long-time unemployment, illness or other comparable social hindrance of the possessor. A deviation lapses if the use of the property is changed in a load-adding way or if the owner or possessor is changed.

410. The owner shall arrange an account on each wastewater treatment system for assessing the load, as well as instructions on use and maintenance, as provided in section 157, and present these to authorities, if required. More detailed provisions are issued by decree. Such an account is not necessary, if a plan pursuant to section 157a is needed. According to section 157a, the property owner shall *see* to that a plan on a household wastewater treatment system is drawn up when the system is constructed or an existing system is improved. The plan shall be attached to a permit application under the Land Use and Building Act (as of 1 January 2025, the Building Act). Requirements for the contents of such a plan are provided in section 157.

411. If wastewater is channelled to a ditch in alien property, the discharger is entitled and obliged to measures specified in section 158.

412. The provisions in Chapter 16 are supervised partly by Municipal Environmental Protection Authorities, partly by the municipal Building Supervision Authorities in connection with permit procedures under the Land Use and Building Act (as of 1 January 2025, the Building Act).

§2. Environmental Permits and Water Pollution

I. Competence

413. From March 2000, the three Environmental Permit Offices had replaced the previous Water Courts as permit authorities under the Water Act and in part, under the Environmental Protection Act (*see* Part I, Chapter 1, §4 above). Concerning discharges to waters, the competence in permit cases was, however, divided between the then Environmental Permit Offices and the then Regional Environment Centres. Where the receiving surface water body is a ditch or a small brook, and the risk of pollution emerges only within it, the permitting competence is, as a starting point, vested in the Municipal Environmental Protection Authority. This always yielded to a State permit authority when a proper surface water body (or the sea) was concerned. In the reorganization of the Finnish regional State administration from the beginning of 2010, the Environmental Permit Offices were abolished and their tasks were transferred to the Environmental Permit Divisions of the new Regional State Administrative Agencies. In addition, also the permitting competence of the previous Regional Environmental Centres under the Environmental Protection Act was transferred to the Environmental Permit Divisions of the Regional State Administrative Agencies. Hence there are presently two levels of permit authorities, one municipal and one of State, instead of the previous three (one municipal and two of State). The plans to once again fundamentally reorganize the permitting authority, as a part of a very extensive administrative reform, failed in early 2019, following the general reform. A second effort is now (2023) in preparation.

414. As in the pre-2000 pollution prevention regime of the 1961 Water Act, an Environmental Permit includes both a normal administrative permit and the permission to cause nuisances and even damages to others. In a way, public and private interests appear as parallel objects of legal protection; the system is a compound of public law and private law. (This also holds more or less true on the other ingredients of an Environmental Permit, in particular where nuisances to neighbours are concerned.)

II. The Preconditions of an Environmental Permit Containing Discharges

415. Pursuant to the pre-2000 Water Act, the substantive provisions for issuing a permit were in two stages. An application had always to be rejected, when the negative environmental impacts looming ahead were particularly strong and extensive. This provision in the then Water Act was practically never applied. Normally, the main considerations were focused on the weighing of interests according to the pre-2000 Water Act. This meant that the detrimental effects of all kinds had to be relatively small as compared with the benefits, in order for the permit to be issued. Here impacts on public and private interests of several kinds were relevant. It was not necessarily a question of money, because also non-monetary, immaterial interests and environmental impacts were relevant. In practice, the natural and usage-linked properties of the recipient water body and the impacts on it were reflected in the weighing. Of course, it is not easy to compare different incommensurable interests and values, e.g., ecological impacts or threats to health, with the benefits gained by the discharge of an industrial plant or a municipality. Ultimately, it was the task of the SAC to decide upon this not typically judicial issue. In practice, the weighing resulted in practice sometimes in favour of actual environmental interests, sometimes in favour of the applicant.

416. Instead, the relevant provisions of the Environmental Protection Act, the previous or the present Act (in particular sections 48 and 49, *see* Part I, Chapter 1, §12) do not contain any weighing of interests. This does not mean, however, that the traditionally strong relevance of the properties of the recipient water body would not be relevant in a particular case. For example, obstacles to issuing a permit in section 49(1) include deterioration of specific natural conditions or hazard to water supply or another important opportunity of use in the area impacted by the activity. In the laying down of permit conditions, e.g., the nature of the activity, the properties of the impacted area, the total impact of the activity, the importance of the measures to prevent pollution in respect to the totality of the environment and the technical and economical possibilities in carrying out these measures shall be taken into account (section 52(3)). The interests of the applicant in turn are basically safeguarded by the fact that a permit has to be granted, if all the legal preconditions are met.

417. In addition, a permit is always to be disallowed, if the discharge would result in pollution of the sea outside the (exclusive) economic zone of Finland, i.e., in international waters or in the territorial waters or the economic zone of another

State (section 18(1) of the Environmental Protection Act). This ban, creating a legislative linkage to the Marine Pollution Prevention Act (*see* §8 below), is at least in principle very significant and absolute. Finally, the absolute ban on polluting groundwater (section 17 of the Environmental Protection Act, *see* Chapter 1, §5 above) always creates an obstacle to any discharge permit with such impacts.

418. The early EC directives on water protection laid down a variety of fixed emission standards (especially those imposed in the daughter directives of the framework Directive 76/464/EEC) or other requirements for the reducing of emissions (such as those on urban wastewater treatment in the Directive 91/271/EEC). The directives were implemented by specific decrees under the then Water Act. In most cases they chiefly have had only formal importance, because the requirements are normally well met by the previous practice. So they had served only as absolute minimum standards and as a kind of checklist. The main exception has been reducing nitrates from urban wastewaters pursuant to Directive 91/271/EEC, which has caused some difficulties and also scientific debate.

419. The basic case-to-case nature of the decision-making was preserved also after 2000, often with a result far more effective than the minimum then required by the largely obsolete directives. The same cannot be as evidently be said of the present directive-based decrees, in particular Government decree on Substances Dangerous and Harmful to the Aquatic Environment (1022/2006) and Government decree on Urban Waste Water Treatment (888/2006), *see* paragraphs 207, 268, 400, 402, 422, 425, 427, 441, 692 and 1332.

III. Provisions Included in the Permit

420. The categories of regular provisions (or regulations or conditions), in Environmental Permits concerning discharges are emission specifications, effluent treatment obligations, fishery management obligations and obligations to monitor the discharges and their impacts (*see* in general Part I, Chapter 1, §13 above). The public water pollution control policy is largely carried out through the permit conditions, especially through emission specifications and effluent treatment obligations (the difference between which is often unclear), e.g., BOD_7 and nutrients (phosphates and sometimes also nitrates) reduction rate for municipal effluent, or feed and fish quantity requirements for fish farms. For each branch of industry, special forms of emission specifications have been developed in practice. The purpose of the permit conditions referring to emissions and their treatment is always to reduce pollution in the particular case.

421. That is why the provisions may vary according to the properties of the water body and the interests linked to it, even between two technically similar plants or discharges (the so-called recipient principle). The permit decisions, though, in practice show quite a lot of uniformity and efficiency as far as the general level of pollution prevention is concerned. Here the *locus standi* of water protection authorities is of importance as well as the role of the appellate courts in determining the level of allowed contamination. Although compensations for water pollution damage, where any, are decided upon in the same permit decision, the pollution control provisions shall first be imposed irrespective thereof. From a more general point of view, the main purpose of most permit provisions is to reduce the detrimental effects for private and public interests. As regards public interests, this is possible irrespective of the agreements made between the applicant and private parties. For example, the imposing of a fishery management obligation (which may be either an annual fee to the authorities or a direct obligation to plant fish, section 44 of the Environmental Protection Act) is possible even if the applicant himself should happen to own the water area.

422. The protection of private rights and interests is not limited to the permit provisions. The permit authority (regarding water protection, in practice, the Regional State Administrative Agency) shall assess the intensity of the pollution likely to remain in spite of the fulfilled conditions. Where this remaining surface water pollution is considered to cause damage to private parties, compensations for it are determined in the permit decision, i.e., in advance (Chapter 13 of the Environmental Protection Act). There is in principle no need to claim compensation, because the rights of everyone are again protected ex officio. However, because it is not always possible to assess the future damages, the compensations may be separated to a specific procedure, but also then the protection of victims takes place ex officio. These daughter procedures may refer to fixed periods of years, as the compensations are often calculated on an annual basis. Also lump sum compensations occur, especially if the permit itself has been given for the time being.

In practice, the most commonly compensated damages have during the course of years been those suffered by water area owners and shore owners. For the former (who are often represented by statutory fishery associations for registered villages), the reduction of the area's fishery value is compensated, and for the latter the loss of recreational value. Hindrance to water supply may also be at issue. The main ecological reason for compensation of damages has been eutrophication caused by industrial effluent, by municipal sewage (though decreasingly) and by fish farming (increasingly). Among polluters causing other kinds of damages are the pulp industry and the chemical industry. There are cases where compensation is paid to hundreds or even thousands of victims (mainly property owners) at the same time. However, due to the strong proceedings in pollution prevention in the recent decades, the need for any compensation has clearly become less common.

423. The provisions on permit conditions of the Environmental Protection Act are rather largely flexible and make possible different practical applications. Those rules have, however, also resulted in some common basic features in the permitting practice. An Environmental Permit may today vary strongly in scope and amount of detailed provisions, depending on the activity at stake and its effects on different environmental media.

§3. Connected Establishments

424. Traditionally, wastewater discharges from properties, installations, plants, etc. connected into public sewers had been agreement-based, but not subject to a proper permit system. The EC water protection directives required in 1994 a new legal approach to the discharges from the connected establishments. Regarding certain dangerous substances in Directive 76/464/EEC, both an official authorization is needed and standards for the discharges were to be followed. Concerning the dangerous substances, a permit granting system had to be created, because the connection agreements between the operator of the public sewer and the connected party hardly could be regarded as 'authorizations'. As for the pretreatment requirements in Directive 91/271/EEC for certain connected industries, the connection agreement rules (presently in the Water Supply and Sewerage Act, 119/2001) had been supplemented. In addition, the total or partial bans on discharges into surface waters of certain 'black list' substances (the then Government decree 363/1994) also applied to discharges into sewerage systems. And a larger group consisted of industries the discharges from which had to be pretreated according to the then Directive 91/271/EEC on Urban Waste Water Treatment, but where there was no direct need for a permit system (Government decree 365/1994).

425. The Government decree on Substances Hazardous and Harmful to Water Environments (1022/2006), aiming to implement in detail and in part Directives 2000/60/EC and 2006/11/EC, has replaced Government decree 363/1994. Pursuant to section 4 of the present decree, the substances hazardous to the environment that are specified in Annex 1A of the Decree shall not be discharged to surface waters or to a sewerage system. The ban does not apply to a discharge if the operator is able to prove that the concentration of a substance hazardous to the environment is so insignificant that the discharge cannot result in risk of pollution or impede activity of the water supply and sewerage system.

426. Several categories of food and animal food industries are subject to notification duty under the Environmental Protection Act, if the wastewaters are discharged to a community sewerage network (Annex 1(4)).

If any industrial discharges are conveyed to a community sewerage system, the Environmental Permit or the decision due to a notification shall, where needed, contain the provisions on pretreatment in order to prevent environmental pollution and to maintain the functioning of the wastewater treatment plant of the sewerage system (section 67 of the Environmental Protection Act).

In the framework of the present Environmental Act, the discharges to a sewerage network, and particularly regarding IED installations, are an integral item of the permitting.

427. The Government decree on Urban Waste Water Treatment (888/2006), issued under the previous Environmental Protection Act but remaining valid, provides in section 3 that the treatment requirements of wastewater shall be taken into account in the planning, construction and maintenance of sewerage systems, BAT are used and the following are paid particular attention to: (1) amount of municipal wastewater and its properties; (2) prevention of leakages; and (3) restriction of pollution of waters caused by spillover discharges.

§4. Financing and Arranging of Water Services

428. A Wastewater Fee under public law was, pursuant to a specific Act (the Waste Water Fee Act of 1973 repealed in 2001 by the Water Supply and Sewerage Act, 119/2001), up to 2001 collected from all those whose effluent is conducted to a municipal sewer (public sewers owned by private corporations, etc., were excluded). The income was used by the municipality for two purposes: partly for the construction and maintenance of the sewers and partly to cover the cost of treatment (purifying) of wastewaters. The fee consisted of a one-time connecting fee and a recurring fee, the criteria of which are specified in the Act. The Act was the first piece of legislation which had been significantly influenced and sped up by the polluter pays principle. In the 1970s, it was of crucial importance for the financing of the numerous new treatment plants for municipal sewage (besides the State subsidies). The coverage of the fee was not total, however, because the Act only applied to municipal sewer systems. Hence cooperatively or privately owned sewer (often: supply and sewer) system operators came to be able to agree on their fees, this irrespective of that the properties within the approved area of activity of a sewer, being a natural monopole, are by the Water Supply and Sewerage Act largely obliged to be connected. For water supply fees there was never special legislation, but they always belonged to the private law regime.

429. The service payments, regarding wastewater and fresh water supply alike, are hence agreed upon by the concerned parties, observing the provisions on the fees in Chapter 4 of the Water Supply and Sewerage Act. These provisions are largely due to the Water Framework Directive. Pursuant to section 18, the fees have to cover long-term investments and costs, and the return on investment shall not exceed a moderate level. Municipal, State or EU aid, where any, shall be taken into account in respect to the covering. The possibilities to supervise the observing of these provisions are limited, however, with the exception of municipally administrated sewerage operating bodies to which the Municipal Appeal (*see* paragraphs 102 and 1551) is applicable.

430. The obligations on water works and water services are still mainly of a public law character, under the general guidance by municipalities and subject to supervision by authorities (Centres for Economic Development, Transport and the Environment, Municipal Environmental Protection Authorities, municipal Public Health Authorities). The provisions of the Water Act (water intake) and the Environmental Protection Act, supplemented by Government decree on Urban Waste Water Treatment (discharges to natural waters) are applicable. Hence, e.g., the private or public law bodies responsible for water supply and/or sewerage are very often permit holders pursuant to the said acts.

431. Municipalities have to develop water supply and sewerage in their area in accordance with community development in order to achieve the objectives of the Water Supply and Sewerage Act in cooperation with the water service bodies in their area, those supplying water to the plants and treating their wastewater, and other municipalities, as well as participate in the regional general planning of water supply and sewerage. The owner or occupant of a property is responsible for the water supply and sewerage of their property. If the need of a larger population or health or environmental protection reasons so require, the municipality shall ensure that measures are taken to establish a water supply and sewerage body corresponding to the need, to expand the operating area of an existing body or to ensure the availability of other necessary water services. Within the territory of a municipality, the areas of operation of a water supply and sewerage body must cover areas where the connection of properties to the body's water supply or sewerage network (or, usually, both) is necessary due to actual or planned urban development. The area of operation shall be approved by the municipality on the proposal of a (public law or private law) body suitable for managing the water services or, if no such body has made such a proposal, after consulting an existing body. If necessary, the municipality shall amend an approved area. The operating area shall be such that the body is able to provide the services for which it is responsible economically and appropriately, and the water supply fees charged to cover the costs of water supply are reasonable and equitable. Before approving or changing the operating area, sufficient information shall be provided and the supervisory authorities shall be given the opportunity to issue a statement, and the owners and occupants of real estate in the area shall be given an opportunity to be heard. The municipality's decision can be appealed to the Administrative Court. The water supply company is responsible for water supply in its operating area in accordance with the needs of community development in accordance with the decision approving the operating area (sections 5–9 of the Water Supply and Sewerage Act).

432. A property within the operating area of an approved water supply and sewerage body has to be connected to it. However, outside an agglomeration (defined as an area with at least two hundred inhabitants in adjacent buildings), a property need not be connected to the network of the body if: (1) the property's water service equipment was constructed before the approval of the body's area of operation; and (2) the property has access to sufficient drinking water that meets the quality requirements laid down in the Public Health Act. Outside agglomerations, a property does not need to be connected if: (1) the property's water supply equipment was built before the approval of the operating area and the discharge and treatment of wastewater complies with the provisions of the Environmental Protection Act; or (2) the property does not have a water toilet and the management and treatment of its wastewater complies with the provisions of the Environmental Protection Act. However, a body may refuse to join any property whose water consumption or the quality or quantity of wastewater discharged into the sewer would impede the operations of the body or the body's ability to provide satisfactory water services to other properties (section 10). An individual property may be exempted from the obligation to join under the conditions laid down in section 11 of the Water Supply and Sewerage Act.

433. Section 5 (1258/2022) of the Public Health Act applies to all domestic water intended for human consumption that is supplied through the water supply network or from tankers, taken using the water user's own equipment or packaged in bottles or containers. The chapter includes provisions on, among other things, the quality requirements for drinking water and risk management.

434. Pursuant to section 15 (1259/2022) of the Water Supply and Sewerage Act, a water supply body has to be aware of the risks to the quantity or quality of the raw water it uses and the condition of its equipment. To this end, it shall monitor the quantity and quality of raw water it uses, the condition of its equipment and the amount of leakage water in the plant's water supply and sewerage networks. Information on the location of networks shall be made available in electronic form. The water supply body shall select the parameters to be monitored from raw water on the basis of the risk management of the water production chain pursuant to the Public Health Act. The body shall also ensure that the results of raw water monitoring as well as the location and characteristics of the related water intake points and observation points are submitted to the Environmental Protection Information System pursuant to the Environmental Protection Act. The body shall also notify the municipal Environmental Protection Authority, the municipal Public Health Authority and the Centre for Economic Development, Transport and the Environment of any abnormal changes observed in the parameters monitored for raw water. What has been said above about a water supply body also applies to a plant supplying water to a water supply plant or treating wastewater from a water supply plant, as well as a plant supplying drinking water referred to in the Public Health Act that supplies household water for use at least 10 cubic metres per day or for the needs of at least fifty people.

435. The provisions of the Water Supply and Sewerage Act also regulate further channelling of urban run-off. A municipality may under preconditions specified by law decide that a water sewerage body, being approved as network operator in a certain area under the Water Supply and Sewerage Act, also takes care of urban run-off sewerage, in accordance with the needs of community development (section 17a). Such caretaking is part of the management of urban run-off at large, as provided in section 103b of the Land Use and Building Act, as of 1 January 2025, the Land Use Act (below). Also in this case it is obligatory for the properties at stake to be connected, with certain exceptions (section 17b and 17c). As a main rule, no sewage discharges shall be channelled into a run-off sewer (section 17d).

§5. Urban Run-Off Management

436. Urban run-off was until 2014 a largely unregulated item. Changes in climate and raised risks of urban floods have in a new manner stressed the importance of organized run-off management, however. Although urban run-off refers to water amounts, it is also a matter of water quality, and the provisions among other things aim at promoting and securing the ordinary functioning of community wastewater treatment plants. The provisions, although being placed in the Land Use and Building Act (as of 1 January 2025, the Land Use Act), also have connections to the Water Supply and Sewerage Act and to the Flood Risk Management Act.

437. Urban run-off management at large is presently regulated in Chapter 13a of the Land Use and Building Act (as of 1 January 2025, the Land Use Act). The notion of urban run-off here encompasses water that is accumulated on earth surface, roofs and other surfaces in built-up areas. Also drainage waters from building sites are included. The general aim of urban run-off management (section 103c of the Act) is: (1) to develop planned management of urban run-off particularly in areas with a Detailed Plan; (2) infiltrate and delay urban run-off in places where they are accumulated; (3) prevent disadvantages and damages to the environment and to properties caused by urban run-off, also taking long-term climate change into account; and (4) promote the giving up of channelling urban run-off into wastewater sewers

438. The municipality is responsible for the urban run-off management in areas with a Detailed Plan, and it may assume the task also concerning other areas (section 103i of the Land Use and Building Act, as of 1 January 2025, the Land Use Act). A property owner or possessor is responsible for channelling the run-off accumulated in his area to the municipal run-off management system, if the run-off cannot be infiltrated in the property or discharged to the sewer network of an approved water sewerage body, as provided in section 17a of Water Supply and Sewerage Act (above), where any (section 103f of the Land Use and Building Act, as of 1 January 2025, the Land Use Act). The property owner is responsible for the management within the property, as provided in section 103h. The municipal authority assigned for the task may issue detailed provisions on run-off management (section 103j) and also binding orders to property owners and holders in order to remove harm caused by run-off (section 103k). The municipality may draw up and approve a run-off management plan, if needed (section 103l), and implement it pursuant to Detailed Plans, as specified in section 103m. A run-off management fee, to be collected from property owners and possessors, may be assumed by a municipality (section 103n–103o).

439. Pursuant to section 9 of the Flood Risk Management Act, a municipality shall carry out a preliminary assessment of the flood risks caused by urban run-off, designate significant flood risk areas for run-off floods and prepare flood hazard maps and flood risk maps for the areas in accordance with sections 7–9 of the said Act, where applicable. The municipality's decision to designate significant flood risk areas may not be appealed separately. The municipality shall draw up a flood risk management plan for an area designated as a significant flood risk area due to run-off flooding in accordance with sections 10, 11 and 12(1) of the Act, where applicable. When drawing up the plan, the provisions on EIA in section 9 of the Land Use and Building Act (as of January 2025, the Land Use Act) shall also be observed. The municipality approves the run-off flood risk management plan.

§6. Protection of Groundwater

I. The Ban Rules

440. The regulatory framework on groundwater protection is in some essential respects different from that concerning (surface) water bodies. The main difference is the absolute ban on polluting groundwater (now section 17 of the Environmental Protection Act) (*see also* Chapter 1, §5 above). Pursuant to the provision, it is forbidden to leave (dump), discharge or convey substance, energy or microbes on or in such a place or treat them in such a way that: (1) in important or other, for water supply suitable groundwater area a change in groundwater quality may cause danger or harm to health or the environment or otherwise significantly impair the quality of groundwater; or (2) the change of quality of groundwater in another's property may cause danger or harm to health or the environment or make the groundwater unfit for otherwise possible purposes; or (3) the measure by impacting groundwater quality otherwise may violate public interests or another's private interests (section 17(1)). Government decree may issue more specified provisions on substances above that are hazardous to health and the environment and the inputs of which into groundwater, either directly or indirectly, are forbidden (section 17(2)).

This means that no permit for activities causing or probably causing groundwater pollution, as defined in section 17 of the Environmental Protection Act, is possible. The ban is, however, not absolute in the meaning of prohibiting changes in the chemical or microbiological character of groundwater as such. In order to apply the ban, a violation of private or public interest must be probable, but also a sufficient risk thereof will do. Violation refers here at least primarily, except for (3) above, to water supply interests (whereas the provisions on surface water bodies protect a wide sphere of different interests). However, the groundwater need not be in use; aquifers that are of importance to future public water supply ('important or other, for water supply suitable groundwater areas', *see* paragraph 1228) are also protected. Nor do areas owned by the eventual polluter himself have any exceptional status as far as public interest is concerned.

441. There have traditionally neither been any fixed water quality standards for groundwater, nor have any chemicals or substances as such been forbidden in respect to groundwater (except for certain impacts of directives already in the 1990s). Hence the interpretation of the ban is based on expert assessment on a more general basis, but the interpretations have been rather strict, anyway. The implementation of the previous EC Directive on the protection of groundwater against pollution caused by certain dangerous substances (80/68/EEC), resulted (in addition to Government decree 364/1994) in a change in the basic approach of the Water Act (of that time). This was due to the fact that the Directive is based on a prior case-by-case control by authorities, and deliberately allows certain discharges into the groundwater. In Finland, this would have entailed creating a totally new permit system, which would have remained practically useless due to the absolute ban on polluting. Also a wrong message could have been given to the public, as it might have seemed that discharges were now to be made legal. To avoid this, the absolute ban on polluting (at that time in the Water Act) was extended to cover all the discharges for which a permit decision according to the Directive would otherwise be needed (the then section 22a of Chapter 1 of the Water Act, and Government decree 364/1994). The respective provision was from March 2000 in section 8(2) of the Environmental Protection Act. As for the necessary prior inspection required by the Directive, an Environmental Permit was as a rule applicable (on other grounds than the ban itself), as well as the permits in accordance with the Act on the Safety of the Handling of Dangerous Chemicals and Explosives (390/2005). In the present Environmental Protection Act there is no provision on discharges to groundwater subject to permit requirement, either.

The Directive 2006/118/EC on the protection of groundwater against pollution and deterioration, related to Directive 2000/60/EC establishing a framework for Community action in the field of water policy, caused a need to complement the general ban by certain absolute emissions into groundwater. The provision at stake is included in section 4a of Government decree on Substances Dangerous and Harmful to the Aquatic Environment (1022/2006), as amended in 2015. Pursuant to the provision, in addition to what is provided in section 17(1) of the Environmental Protection Act, no hazardous substance listed in Annex 1I or belonging to a category of substances in Annex I(E) shall be released into groundwater, directly or indirectly. This extension to the general ban neither applies to small amounts of substances, if deterioration of groundwater quality or risk thereof is not poised at present or in the future nor does it apply to household sewage pursuant to section 154(1) of the Environmental Protection Act, provided that impacts on important or other, for water supply suitable groundwater areas or on in use being groundwater in another's property are excluded. Operators of activities subject to permit or registration requirement shall, where needed, show the relevant evidence on this to a supervisory authority.

442. One of the effects of the 1980 Groundwater Directive had been that the processing of artificial groundwater and re-infiltration of groundwater were (in the then Water Act) made unconditionally subject to the obligation to obtain a permit under the Water Act. This requirement has been preserved in the 2011 Water Act (section 3(1)(3) of Chapter 3); *see* Part II, Chapter 8, §2 and §3, VIII.

443. Altering of groundwater as one reason for necessity to have a permit (section 2 of Chapter 3 of the 2011 Water Act, *see* Part II, Chapter 8, §2 and §3, VIII) is important for the protection of aquifers. If a water management measure causes physical change concerning the quality or quantity of groundwater, which again is going to violate either public interests or private rights or interests, a prior permit by the Regional State Administrative Agency is needed. This sub-provision covers in practice various kinds of measures, both as regards water intake (which is related to other water supply interests) and earth work projects. Violations of both public and private interests are covered. To be protected, the aquifer need not necessarily be taken into use. Possible future sources of public water supply are also protected. Normally, the need for a permit for groundwater intake is determined by this rule, although when the intake quantity is 250 cubic metres per day or more the permit is always necessary.

444. The same permit requirement and the permit system are also applicable to sand and gravel extraction, which is often hazardous to groundwater. Here the relationship between polluting and altering measures has always been difficult. The present absolute ban on pollution in section 8 of the Environmental Protection Act only applies to emissions and discharges and risks thereof. The Water Act was applicable if the quality of the water in an aquifer is going to be threatened through alteration, e.g., due to soil excavation. Today the relevant permit-necessity provisions are in section 3(2)(5) or 3(1)(2) of Chapter 3 of the 2011 Water Act (Part II, Chapter 8, §2).

II. Protected Areas Around Water Intakes

445. Despite the existence of the permit system and although the ban on polluting groundwater is absolute as such, even more intensive protection rules are provided for important groundwater intake areas. The Regional State Administrative Agency can, on the basis of an application by an intake permit holder or applicant (most often a public or private law body at municipal or inter-municipal level operating under the Water Supply and Sewerage Act), by a supervisory authority or by an interested party, ordain the surroundings of the intake place to be a specially protected area, irrespective of the ownership (sections 11 and 12 of Chapter 4 of the Water Act).

The protected area shall not be larger than necessary. The basic model of regulation originates in German and Swedish laws. The restrictions on land use are specified case by case by the Regional State Administrative Agency. For example, building, storing of oil and chemicals, soil extraction, construction of sewage pipes and use of fertilizers or pesticides may be prohibited or restricted. The restrictions may not be stricter than necessary. The administrative courts decide on the restrictions if appeals have been submitted.

446. In principle, compensations for economic losses due to the establishing of the specially protected area are ordered by the same decision of the Regional State Administrative Agency. But it is usually not easy to determine the scope of the real losses, for several reasons. For one thing, the restriction may well refer to activities which would be very unlikely in reality. For another, the legal practice has fully established the principle that no compensation shall be paid for a restriction which had to be observed even without the decision establishing a protected area, by force of general norms of law. From this point of view, the protected area is given a kind of extra security and damage prevention. The general bans and restrictions on polluting and altering groundwater have been the main examples of norms making a restriction non-compensable. This leads to the problem of defining the scope of those bans in an individual case, which is not always easy, because even the bans and permit requirements as such cover not only self-evident damage, but also probable or even possible damage. The matter of compensations has, in some cases, a direct connection with the effectiveness of groundwater protection and the willingness of the municipalities to submit protection applications. However, the protection decision itself may be less important, depending on the interpretation of the general restrictions. Observing the latter within the general supervision by the Centres for Economic Development, Transport and the Environment, which may apply for injunctions against offenders in the Regional State Administrative Agency, irrespective of a specially protected area, where any. The (Vaasa) Regional Administrative Court and the SAC function also here as appellate bodies, and their court practice has offered an interpretative guide. Criminal proceedings are also available.

447. One of the most problematic questions concerning the specially protected areas is that of the restrictions on gravel and sand extraction, to which the general bans are anyway applicable. If the extraction is not considered totally contrary to the general restrictions (or prohibited pursuant to the Soil Excavation Act), the sand or gravel is often divided juridically into two layers. The lowest, which reaches to, e.g., two metres above the highest groundwater level, is covered by the general bans, and the restriction on extraction is hence not compensable. The prohibition to extract the upper layer, which is farther removed from the groundwater, may be compensated to the owner by the municipality or other intake permit holder who has asked the area to be protected (*see also* Part II, Chapter 7, §1, III below).

A variation of the system of protected areas is also provided for surface water intakes, but in practice it has not been used very often. Also with respect to groundwater, protected areas have been applied for less and less by intake permit applicants or holders in recent years, partly for the (often unjustified) fear of compensations, partly for the (contradictory but evident) fact that general restrictions and the possibility of administrative injunctions based directly on them create a more effective basis for protection. The effect of the 2011 Water Act in this respect still remains to be seen, as it is from January 2011 on possible also to the interested parties, and particularly to the landowners, to initiate an application procedure to establish a protected area.

448. In practice, the system for determining and classifying groundwater areas pursuant to Chapter 2a of the Act on the Arranging of Water Management and Marine Waters Management (1299/2004), in force from 2015, may be more relevant, although no proper legal effects have been provided. *See* Part II, Chapter 8, §5.

§7. Protection of Waters from Oil Pollution

449. The protection of groundwater also concerns oil pollution prevention. In this monograph, the regime is, due to common legislative structures, dealt with in the chapter on soil pollution (*see* below Chapter 6).

The rules for the prevention of oil pollution caused by vessels, both on the sea and on inland waters, are explained right below in §8 (in particular under VI) and Chapter 6, §3.

§8. PROTECTION OF THE SEA AND VESSEL-BASED POLLUTION

I. International Obligations

450. Finland is a party to practically all international conventions with a universal scope in the field of the protection of the marine environment. They include, *inter alia,* the International Convention for the Prevention of Pollution from Ships (MARPOL) agreements of 1978 (1973). At the regional level the most important is the (Helsinki) Convention on the Protection of the Marine Environment of the Baltic Sea Area. This Convention contains detailed provisions on vessel-based pollution, land-based pollution (for which there is no global regulation) and dumping (for which the Convention is complementary to other international conventions). The original Helsinki Convention from 1972 was superseded by the 1992 Helsinki Convention (signed by Finland in 1992) that entered into force on 17 January 2000.

Some watercourses near the northern and north-eastern borders empty ultimately into the Arctic Ocean. For this reason, Finland is also party to the Paris Convention for the Protection of the Marine Environment of the North East Atlantic, signed in 1992. Moreover, Finland is a party to the 1972 Oslo Convention for the Prevention of Marine Pollution from Ships and Aircraft.

II. Main Enactments

451. The international seas protection obligations are implemented mainly in two parliamentary acts, the Act on Environmental Protection in Maritime Transport (1672/2009) and the Marine Pollution Prevention Act (1415/1994). The former, concentrating on use of vessels and ports, replaced the previous the Vessel-based Pollution Control Act. The Marine Pollution Prevention Act replaced from January 1995 the previous 1979 Marine Pollution Prevention Act, by which the 1972 Oslo Convention and the 1972 Helsinki Convention had been enforced already. The total reform was mainly due to the new Helsinki and Paris Conventions. By reforming the Marine Pollution Prevention Act, also the very unclear and complicated relationship between it and the then Water Act was clarified. These provisions of the Water Act were later on partly transferred into the 2000 Environmental Protection Act, but part of them remained in the (then and also the present) Water Act. The result is that the Helsinki, Oslo and Paris Conventions are implemented partly by the Water Act (especially concerning dredging and dredged masses) and partly by the Environmental Protection Act, insofar as the territorial sea, the economic zone and land-based pollution are concerned.

452. The Marine Pollution Prevention Act does not refer to the regular use of vessels, but to dumping and stationary activities. This Act and the pollution prevention norms of the Environmental Protection Act (or the Water Act) are in several respects twins both of which apply to the protection of seas and even include similar provisions. The basic criterion for the division of functions is that the Environmental Protection Act, in particular section 18, or the Water Act, is applicable to measures taken within the economic zone and territorial sea area of Finland, and the Marine Pollution Prevention Act to measures taken in the sea outside that area.

453. Prevention of vessel-based oil and chemical accidents again is from 2019 regulated by the Rescue Act. A detailed regulation of the system of preventive measures and rescue works to be carried out by public authorities, harbours, etc. concerning oil and chemical damages, covering both land areas and vessel-based pollution, is contained in this Act.

454. Several pieces of previous legislation have been gathered into the Act on Environmental Protection in Maritime Transport. Hence this Act aims to prevent environmental pollution resulting from the normal operation of ships, by prohibiting discharges and emissions of noxious substances into water and air, or by setting limits on discharges and emissions into water and air. Moreover, the Act stipulates the reception of waste in ports resulting from the normal operation of ships. The Act also lays down the provisions for the national implementation of international commitments binding on Finland and EU legal instruments in respect to the prevention of environmental pollution resulting from the normal operation of ships, as well as other provisions pertaining to the prevention of pollution resulting from the normal operation of ships.

The Act on Environmental Protection in Maritime Transport applies to ships sailing in Finnish waters or within Finland's exclusive economic zone. Exceptions concerning inland waters and domestic voyages are included. This Act also applies to Finnish ships when sailing outside Finnish waters or outside Finland's exclusive economic zone, and to the reception of waste resulting from the normal operation of ships. The Waste Act in turn becomes applicable to the waste resulting from the normal operation of ships once such waste has been delivered ashore from the ship.

The Act does not apply to the release of noxious substances referred to in Article 2(3)(b)(ii) of the MARPOL 73/78 Convention (i.e., Protocol of 1978 relating to the MARPOL, 1973, as amended), directly arising from the exploration, exploitation and associated offshore processing of seabed mineral resources.

455. Chapter 1 of the Act on Environmental Protection in Maritime Transport, as updated by 669/2021, contains, *inter alia*, the relevant definitions, as many as sixty-four different concepts. The diverse contents of the Act are well described by the titles of the various chapters, as largely updated by 669/2021. They are: General provisions (Chapter 1), Prevention of ship-generated oil discharges and spills (Chapter 2), Conveying of harmful and noxious cargo and delivery of fuel between vessels (Chapter 2a, 669/2021), Oil discharge fee (Chapter 3), Prevention of the discharge of noxious liquid substances from ships (Chapter 4), Prevention of discharges of ship-generated sewage (Chapter 5), Prevention of discharges of ship-generated garbage (Chapter 6), Prevention of air pollution from ships (Chapter 7), Energy efficiency of vessels (Chapter 7a), Other international commitments binding on Finland regarding the prevention of environmental pollution resulting from the normal operation of ships (Chapter 8), Ship recycling (Chapter 8a), Waste reception arrangements at Vessel Ports (Chapter 9), Delivery of waste to port reception facilities (Chapter 10), Obligations of the shipmaster in an incident at sea (Chapter 11), Supervision and administrative enforcement (Chapter 12) and Miscellaneous (Chapter 13).

456. The Act on Environmental Protection in Maritime Transport is in some respects in force also in inland water areas. 'Finnish waters' in the Act means both the territorial waters and inland waters.

III. The Territorial Sea and Economic Zone

457. The territorial sea of Finland had been enlarged in 1995 so that the outer borderline of the territorial sea now is, where possible, twelve nautical miles from the outer borderline of the internal waters. After that, an (exclusive) economic zone was established from 1 February 2005. The legislation on the environment and natural resources applicable to the territorial sea was at the same time largely extended to the economic zone.

458. The provisions on the (exclusive) economic zone are included in several acts regarding i.e., natural resources and the environment, but the fundamental provisions are contained in the Act on the Economic Zone of Finland (1058/2004). In the economic zone the State of Finland is entitled to the research, utilize, preserve and manage biotic and abiotic natural resources and to carry out other activities in order to economically utilize and research the economic zone. Finland has the jurisdiction pursuant to international law in respect to the making and use of artificial islands, equipment and other constructions and to the protection of marine environment and oceanographic research, as well as other rights and obligations according to international law (section 2 of the Act on the Economic Zone of Finland).

459. The Environmental Impact Assessment Procedures Act, the Environmental Protection Act, the Act on the Management of Water Resources, the Marine Environment and Water Act, Chapter 8a on maritime area planning of the Land Use and Building Act (as of 1 January 2025, the Land Use Act), and the Act on the capturing and storage of carbon dioxide as well as the provisions issued by virtue of them, are applicable as usual in the economic zone (section 3). Also, the Act on Environmental Protection in Maritime Transport, with respect to regular operations of vessels, and the Oil Damages Prevention Act (1673/2009) with respect to prevention of oil and vessel chemical accidents, and in part also the Waste Act are applicable (section 3 of the Act on the Economic Zone of Finland).

Regarding fisheries and hunting and the preserving of biotic natural resources, the legislation on fisheries, hunting and nature conservation and the EU provisions on the common fisheries policies, as well as agreements with another State, are applicable (section 4). The Act on the Protection of Certain Underwater Cables and Pipelines (145/1965) is also applicable. To the extraction of bottom substances, the Water Act (and not the Soil Excavation Act) is applicable, whereas the Mining Act is applicable to the prospecting and exploitation of minerals (section 5).

460. The Cabinet may grant exploitation rights (for other economic activities than those referred to in section 4 above), as specified in section 6 of the Act. The Cabinet may also, as specified in section 7, give consent for the building and use of artificial islands, of equipment and constructions relating to exploitation rights and of such other equipment and constructions that may impede the rights of Finland in international law.

If the granting of a right pursuant to section 6 or 7 other than for research only is needed for a project provided in the Act on the Permit Procedure of Projects of Common Interest of the EU (684/2014), that Act shall be applied to the process (section 7a).

The provisions on oceanographic research are laid down in sections 8 and 9 of the Act. The criminal law of Finland, including the penalties for environmental offences, is applied in the economic zone as specified in sections 10–16.

IV. Prevention of Sea Pollution Caused by Measures Outside Finland

461. The Marine Pollution Prevention Act starts with a general ban on sea pollution. Outside the economic zone of Finland all Finnish vessels, offshore installations and aircraft are prohibited to take measures that may result in pollution of the sea (section 1). Finnish citizens and companies are also in other respects prohibited from taking similar measures. There are some rather insignificant exceptions. As pollution is regarded here any activity from which is directly or indirectly introduced into the sea substances or energy which are liable to create hazards to human health, to harm living resources or marine ecosystems, to cause hindrance to legitimate uses of the sea including fishing, to impair the quality of sea water, to lead to a reduction of amenities, or to cause any comparable harm.

In the Act on Environmental Protection in Maritime Transport, 'environmental pollution' again means, with regard to the condition of water areas, any hazards to human health, harm to living resources and to life in water areas, hindrances to fishing or to other legitimate use of water areas, impairment of water quality with respect to the use of said water, reduction of amenities, or any similar inconvenience, or harm related to air quality or to the climate, caused by the normal operation of ships, such as harm caused by nitrogen and sulphur in engine exhaust gases, or harm caused by ozone-depleting substances.

462. The Marine Pollution Prevention Act is only to a small extent based on a permit system. This is due to the fact that dumping is almost totally forbidden, except for dredged masses. The absolute ban covers Finnish vessels, offshore installations and aircraft, as well as all vessels and aircraft loaded in Finland with waste, in all sea areas outside the economic zone of Finland. Moreover, the dumping of waste originating in Finland is also otherwise forbidden. Additionally, it is forbidden to abandon a Finnish vessel, offshore installation or aircraft in a sea area outside the economic zone of Finland. There are exceptions for the territorial waters or economic zones of another State. Incinerating of waste is forbidden on a Finnish vessel or offshore installation outside the economic zone of Finland. The same applies to other vessels if the waste originates in Finland, was transported via Finland or was loaded in Finland.

463. There are closely related bans for measures within the territorial waters and economic zone of Finland in the Environmental Protection Act (section 18, *see* paragraph 469), or, regarding incineration of waste in Finnish waters (and mainly also in the economic zone, and, regarding Finnish vessels, outside it) in the Act on Environmental Protection in Maritime Transport (section 11 of Chapter 7), which however only covers waste generated in regular use of vessels. For the last-mentioned reason, there is a similar ban for particular waste incineration activities in Finnish waters and economic zone in the Waste Act (section 18, *see* paragraph 597).

464. The Marine Pollution Prevention Act is supervised by the Ministry of the Environment and various sector authorities.

465. The only permit mechanism for dumping in the Marine Pollution Prevention Act is that for dredged masses (section 9 of the Act). A permit by the Finnish Environment Institute (this is one of the exceptional situations where the institute has administrative competence) is required if the mass is to be dumped from a Finnish vessel or offshore installation or from any vessel loaded in Finland, provided that the aimed dumping site is in a sea area outside Finnish economic zone. If the dumping or its effects should extend to the territorial waters or the economic zone of Finland, the permitting competence is entirely vested with the Regional State Administrative Agency (that of Southern Finland).

466. Another permit mechanism applies to various constructions in the sea. No Finnish citizen or organization is allowed to make constructions in the sea outside the economic zone of Finland without a permit by the Finnish Environment Institute (section 10 of the Act). If the construction should extend to the territorial waters or the economic zone of Finland, the permitting competence is vested with the Regional State Administrative Agency (that of Southern Finland) only. In this case the procedural provisions of the Water Act are applied. The Marine Pollution Prevention Act contains detailed provisions on the permit and the permit procedure.

467. Also for the exploration and exploitation of the seabed and its subsoil a permit, but now by the Finnish Environment Institute, is as a rule needed. If the activity should extend to the territorial waters or the economic zone of Finland, the Regional State Administrative Agency (of southern Finland) is nevertheless competent for the whole project. Here the procedural provisions of the Environmental Protection Act are applied. The Marine Pollution Prevention Act contains detailed provisions on the permit.

V. Land-Based Pollution of the Sea

468. The 1992 Helsinki Convention is, unlike its predecessor, also applicable to internal waters, a fact that eliminated many difficult problems of application. In addition, the rules on land-based pollution are far more extensive and accurate than previously, extending at least in principle to whole catchment areas. Hence, the Convention regulates also emissions of industry, municipalities and fish farming almost everywhere in the country. A consent of a national authority is required for a lot of various discharges and installations. Also requirements for the various permit conditions have been laid down. In all these respects, the Convention, as far as the territorial area is concerned, has been implemented by the Environmental Protection Act or, regarding dredging and dumping of dredged masses, by the Water Act. Of course also other enactments, such as (presently) the Act on Environmental Protection in Maritime Transport, have been used in the implementation. In the Environmental Protection Act, practically all provisions on inland water bodies also apply on the territorial waters in the Baltic Sea.

469. Section 18 of the Environmental Protection Act contains bans on the dumping of substances other than dredged mass or on the abandoning of vessels, etc., in the territorial waters or the economic zone. These provisions are very similar to those in the Marine Pollution Prevention Act but do not overlap geographically. There is also a permit mechanism for the dumping of dredged masses, but that of the Water Act (section 6 of Chapter 2) is more complicated, due to the fact that the provision is also applicable to inland waters and that the relevant areas are normally privately owned. Anyway, the pollution risks caused by the hazardous substances occurring in dredged masses are taken into account in the decision-making under the Water Act, although the present wordings are less clear than they were in the previous Water Act right before enacting the present one.

VI. Vessel-Based Oil and Chemical Pollution

470. Prevention of the discharge of noxious liquid substances from ships is stipulated in Chapter 4 of the Act on Environmental Protection in Maritime Transport. Pursuant to regulation 6 of Annex II to the MARPOL 73/78 Convention, the Annex is applied to the transport of noxious liquid substances falling into categories X, Y, or Z. If a noxious liquid substance does not fall into one of these categories, the substance shall be assessed in accordance with Annex II in order to determine the applicable carriage procedures. The Finnish Transport and Communications Agency Traficom may grant an exemption regarding the categorization of a noxious liquid substance when such a substance is being carried on domestic voyages, provided that adherence to the categorization provisions would cause unreasonable inconvenience or unreasonable expenses, and would be ill-founded due to the minor hazard presented to the environment.

It is prohibited to discharge noxious substances from ships in Finnish waters or in Finland's economic zone, as well as from Finnish ships outside Finnish waters or the economic zone, as set forth in Annex II to the MARPOL 73/78 Convention, in the Helsinki Convention, or in other international commitments, or in EU legal instruments.

Discharge of noxious liquid substances in exceptional circumstances is stipulated in section 3 of Chapter 4, structural and equipment requirements for chemical tankers in section 4 and shipboard marine pollution emergency plans in section 5. Procedures and arrangements manual are provided in section 6, cargo record book in section 7, other certificates concerning the carriage of noxious liquid substances in section 8 and unloading of cargo and supervising the cleaning of tanks in section 9.

471. Prevention of discharges of ship-generated sewage is stipulated in Chapter 5 of the Act on Environmental Protection in Maritime Transport. It is prohibited to discharge either untreated or treated sewage from ships in Finnish waters or in Finland's economic zone, as well as from Finnish ships outside Finnish waters or the economic zone, as set out in Annex IV to the MARPOL Convention, in the Helsinki Convention, or in other international commitments binding on Finland, or in EU legislation, except for certain situations at open sea (section 1 of Chapter 5). Discharge of sewage in exceptional circumstances is stipulated in section 2. Section 3 provides requirements for sewage systems on board, section 4 requirements for recreational craft, section 5 international sewage pollution prevention certificate (ISPP) Certificate, and section 6 the granting of minor exemptions (by the Finnish Transport and Communications Agency Traficom) from the prohibition on the discharge of sewage.

472. Prevention of discharges of ship-generated garbage is contained in Chapter 6 of the Act on Environmental Protection in Maritime Transport. It is prohibited to dispose of garbage from ships in Finnish waters or in Finland's economic zone, as well as from Finnish ships outside Finnish waters or Finland's economic zone, as set out in Annex V to the MARPOL 73/78 Convention, in the Helsinki Convention, or in other international commitments binding on Finland, or in EU legislation (section 1). It is also prohibited to dispose of garbage from Finnish ships or from fixed or floating platforms used for exploration, exploitation and associated offshore processing of seabed mineral resources, as set out in Annex V to the MARPOL 73/78 Convention, in the Helsinki Convention, or in other international commitments binding on Finland, or in EU legislation. The Finnish Transport and Communications Agency Traficom may issue type approvals for garbage comminutors and grinders. Disposal of garbage in exceptional circumstances is stipulated in section 2, conspicuously placed placards on garbage disposal prohibitions and restrictions in section 3, garbage management plans on ships in section 4, garbage record books of ships in section 5.

473. Chapter 7 of the Act on Environmental Protection in Maritime Transport stipulates prevention of air pollution from ships. Pursuant to section 1, it is prohibited to emit air pollutants from ships in Finnish waters or in Finland's economic zone, as well as from Finnish ships outside Finnish waters or the economic zone, as set out in Annex VI to the MARPOL 73/78 Convention, in the Helsinki Convention, or in other international commitments binding on Finland, or in EU law. Prohibition against and restrictions on emissions of VOCs from oil and chemical tankers is laid down in section 2, restrictions on and prohibition against the use of ozone-depleting substances in section 3, emissions of air pollutants in exceptional circumstances in section 4, requirements for shipboard equipment in section 5, IAPP Certificate in section 6, requirements for fuel oil quality in section 7, methods for determining the compliance of marine fuels in section 8, bunker delivery notes, fuel oil samples and recording of oil-related measures on board in section 9, ship emission reduction technologies in section 9a, testing of new ship emission reduction and control technologies in section 10, incineration of ship-generated waste on board ships sailing in Finnish waters in section 11, obligations in respect to suppliers of marine fuel oil in section 11a, verification of marine fuel oil compliance in section 12, reporting and exchange of information concerning marine fuel oils in section 13 and temporary exemptions from fuel oil quality requirements in section 14.

474. Energy efficiency of ships is regulated in Chapter 7a. An Energy Efficiency Design Index (EEDI) shall be calculated for each ship pursuant to VI to the MARPOL 73/78 Convention (section 1). A Ship Energy Efficiency Management Plan (SEEMP) is obligatory for ships of 400 gross tonnage and above (section 2). Amendments to SEEMP due to the mandatory data collection systems for fuel oil consumption of ships are provided in section 2a, related information duties in section 2b, declarations of conformity in section 2c, International Energy Efficiency (IEE) Certificates in section 3 and deviations from requirements regarding energy efficiency in section 4.

475. Chapter 8 of the Act contains other international commitments binding on Finland concerning the prevention of pollution resulting from the normal operation of ships. Prohibition on harmful antifouling systems on ships is laid down in section 1. Additional provisions regarding the International Convention on the Control of Harmful Anti-fouling Systems on Ships (also called the AFS Convention) are included in sections 2 and 3, and provisions regarding ballast waters and the International Convention for the Control and Management of Ships' Ballast Water and Sediments (also called the BWM Convention), aiming to prevent the spread of harmful aquatic organisms from one region to another, in sections 4–16. As a main rule in section 5, release of untreated ballast water or sediment is, regarding ships under the BWM, forbidden in Finnish territorial waters and the economic zone and from Finnish ships also outside of that area.

476. The national provisions regarding the Ship Recycling Regulation[31] are, besides the provisions in the Waste Act, included in Chapter 8a. The governmental authority pursuant to Article 3(1)(9) of the Regulation, designated by the Member

31. Regulation (EU) No. 1257/2013 on ship recycling and amending Regulation (EC) No. 1013/2006 and Directive 2009/16/EC.

State as being responsible for duties related to ships flying its flag or to ships operating under its authority, is the Finnish Transport and Communications Agency Traficom (section 1).

477. Chapter 9 includes provisions on port reception of waste. Pursuant to section 1, every port operator shall ensure that the port has sufficient facilities for the reception of the following types of waste from ships using the port: (1) oily waste; (2) waste containing noxious liquids; (3) sewage; (4) garbage; (5) exhaust gas cleaning residues, whose emission is prohibited in accordance with Annex VI to the MARPOL Convention; and (6) cargo residues. In addition, oil terminals shall have sufficient equipment to receive oily ballast waters and tank washings from tankers using the terminal. There are specified obligations with respect to the acquisition and use of certain reception, transport and treatment facilities. The obligation of the operator of a harbour mainly serving recreational craft to receive waste, concerns harbours accommodating at least fifty recreational craft, or harbours that can offer winter docking for at least fifty recreational craft, and where a fee or other compensation is charged for the berth. The harbour managing body shall provide its personnel with the necessary training to obtain and maintain up-to-date information relevant to their duties. Particular attention shall be paid to the possible handling of dangerous goods. Section 2 stipulates reception facilities in repair ports, section 3 waste reception and management plans for ports, section 4 approval (as a rule by the Centres for Economic Development, Transport and the Environment) of such plans, section 5 hearing of parties and provision of information concerning such plans, section 6 avoiding unnecessary delays in the reception of ship-generated waste and section 7 reporting.

478. Chapter 10 of the Act deals with delivery of waste to port reception facilities. Section 1 lays down an obligation of the master of a ship to deliver there ship-generated waste and cargo residues. Finnish ships entering a Baltic Sea port or within the EU, as well as foreign ships entering a Finnish port shall, before the ship leaves the port, deliver all ship-generated waste and cargo residues into the waste reception facilities of that port. If no reception facilities are available in a harbour mainly serving recreational craft, waste originating from such craft must be delivered to another adequate reception facility, if the waste cannot, in pursuance of the Act, be retained on board. The waste delivery obligation shall, however, not apply to: (1) insignificant amounts of waste, as specified by Government decree; (2) situations where the delivery causes an unnecessary delay to the ship for reasons not attributable to it and provided that certain further requirements set forth in the Act are observed; or (3) delivery of sewage from ship tanks, if there is capacity in the tanks for the voyage to the next port. Additionally, the Finnish Transport and Communications Agency Traficom may require that ships deliver all waste to the port reception facilities prior to departure, if there is justifiable reason to presume that the waste is to be delivered to a port without adequate reception facilities or it is unknown to which port the waste will be delivered, and there is hence the risk of releasing the waste into water.

479. A fee for ship-generated waste and cargo residues to cover waste reception and management expenses shall be charged by the port operator from every ship that calls at the port, regardless of whether or not the ship delivers any waste there (section 2 of Chapter 10 of the Act). The fee shall cover the expenses of managing the ship-generated oily waste, garbage, excluding cargo residue(s) and sewage. In order to cover waste reception and management expenses, the port operator shall also charge a fee from those ships that call at the port and deliver cargo residues to the reception facilities. The fees may be included in the port charges collected otherwise. The port shall make public the amount of and grounds for the fees. The fees may be varied according to the further provisions in section 2. Fishing vessels and recreational craft entitled to carry no more than twelve passengers are exempted.

Duty of the master of a ship or a person authorized by the master to notify the port prior to the arrival of the ship regarding ship-generated waste and cargo residues is laid down in section 3. Certain exceptions to the obligations to deliver waste and to provide notification are stipulated in section 4.

480. Obligations of the shipmaster in incidents at sea are laid down in Chapter 11 of the Act. If oil has been discharged into water, or if there is a risk of an oil leak due to a ship running aground, engine breakdown, collision, or other disaster at sea, the master must immediately report the spill or risk thereof to the relevant maritime rescue or emergence response centre. Outside Finnish waters or Finland's economic zone, the report shall be made to the authorities of the nearest coastal State. Any immediate measures that can be reasonably expected shall be made. If a master of a ship, in Finland's territorial waters or economic zone observes such an extensive amount of oil in the water that, considering the weather and other conditions, there is a risk of an oil disaster, the observation shall be reported to the relevant maritime rescue or emergence response centre. Outside Finnish waters, such an observation shall be reported to the authorities of the nearest coastal State (section 1).

In a rather similar way, notification duties concerning discharges of other noxious substances than oil, or a risk thereof, and immediate response are provided in section 2.

481. Chapter 12 of the Act stipulates supervision and administrative enforcement. The supervisory authorities are the Finnish Transport and Communications Agency Traficom, the Finnish Environment Institute, Centres for Economic Development, Transport and the Environment, the Border Guard, customs, and the police (section 1). The supervisory duties of each are specified in sections 2–8. The Ministry of Transport and Communications and the Ministry of the Environment in turn are responsible for general guidance, follow-up and development. Supervision regarding the construction, equipment, fittings, functions and arrangements of ships is stipulated in the Ship Safety Control Act (370/1995).

482. In order to investigate discharges, or the use of harmful antifouling systems, the Finnish Transport and Communications Agency Traficom, the Border Guard and the police are entitled to carry out inspections on board Finnish ships and to take samples for determining the origins of oil or other noxious substances detected in water. This also applies to foreign ships when in port or at anchor within

Finnish waters or sailing in Finnish waters (section 11 of Chapter 12 of the Act). Powers of the authorities to carry out inspections, receive information and detain foreign ships in the territorial sea or economic zone are in detail provided in section 12. An obligation of the authorities to avoid unnecessary delay and the principle of lesser harm are laid down in section 13.

483. If it is evident that a violation of the Act or of provisions issued under it that has been committed on board a ship sailing in Finnish waters or within its economic zone causes considerable damage or risk thereof to the country's shoreline or any interests pertaining to it, or to the natural resources of the territorial sea or economic zone, the ship may be permitted to continue its voyage only on the condition that a sufficient cash payment is deposited on behalf of the ship for the fulfilment of any such potential liability (section 14). The Ministry of the Interior shall decide on the depositing and amount of the payment. The decision may be appealed to Helsinki Regional Administrative Court, but the decision must be complied with in spite of appeal. The decision of the Administrative Court is not appealable, this being a rare exception within the administrative judicial procedure in general.

484. The Finnish Transport and Communications Agency Traficom and the Centres for Economic Development, Transport and the Environment may, within their competence: (1) prohibit a party acting in violation of the Act, or provisions issued under it, from continuing or repeating activities that are in violation of the provisions; (2) order a party acting in violation of the Act, or provisions issued under it, to fulfil its obligations otherwise; or (3) order a party acting in violation of the provisions to restore the environment to its original condition or to remove any damage or impairment caused to the environment by the said party's violation (section 15). The provisions of the Administrative Injunctions (Conditional Fines) Act (1113/1990) are applicable as usual (section 16).

485. Penal provisions for a multitude of situations are contained in section 3 of Chapter 13, but if 'impairment of the environment' is at stake, the Penal Code is applied. Criminal jurisdiction regarding foreign ships is stipulated in section 6.

Several environmentally important plans or arrangements on board pursuant to the Act are approved by either Finnish Transport and Communications Agency Traficom or an approved ship classification organization. The employees of the classification organizations are in respect to criminal law regarded as public officials in their administrative tasks under the Act.

For certain decisions, those being specified in section 7, a party may submit a claim to the Finnish Transport and Communications Agency Traficom for a revised decision. Otherwise, the administrative decisions are directly appealable before the Regional Administrative Court. Regarding criminal proceedings within the scope of the Act on Environmental Protection in Maritime Transport, the competent District Court is that one (Maritime Court) specified in the Maritime Act and section 10.

When the offence has been committed outside Finnish territory and economic zone, the criminal case shall be dealt with by the Helsinki District Court.

VII. Oil Discharge Fee

486. As of 2006, a special policy instrument, i.e., the administrative penalty-natured oil discharge fee, payable to the State, was introduced and the provisions technically inserted in the then Vessel-based Pollution Control Act as a new Chapter 2a. From 2010 on, the respective provisions are contained in Chapter 3 of the Act on Environmental Protection in Maritime Transport. The oil discharge fee applies to discharges of oil or oily mixtures in breach of the ban laid down in the section 1 of Chapter 2 of the Act on Environmental Protection in Maritime Transport, where the discharge is not insignificant to its quantity and effects. Regarding foreign vessels in transit traffic and violating the discharge prohibition in Finland's economic zone, it is required that considerable damage or risk thereof is caused to Finnish shoreline or to interests connected to it, or to the natural resources of Finnish territorial sea or economic zone. As a main rule, the shipowner, that being a legal or natural person, is the liable party (section 1 of Chapter 3). The fee cannot be imposed on the owner, if he or she can prove that a manager, operator or bareboat charterer has been operating the ship in the owner's stead.

487. The amount of the fee is based on the quantity of the discharge and the gross tonnage of the vessel, as specified in the annex to the Act (section 2 of Chapter 3). Where manifestly unfair due to an emergency or accident or due to other comparable reason, the fee may be skipped or reduced (section 3). The fee is subsidiary to criminal law. Hence a person who has been imposed a penalty for the same discharge and the verdict has gained legal force cannot be imposed an oil discharge fee (section 4). Measures necessary for the solving of the matter in order to impose the oil discharge fee and the powers of the Border Guard to detain ships and impose conditions to continued voyage are stipulated in section 6.

Prior to a decision on the fee, the shipowner shall be reserved an opportunity the owner or the company shall be given the opportunity and sufficient time, depending on the nature of the matter, to present an explanation. The appeal mechanism provided in sections 10 and 11 of Chapter 3 of the Act is a systematic exception in that appeal against an administrative decision, i.e., that of the Border Guard, shall be made to a District Court (that of Helsinki, specialized in maritime law cases for the whole country) and not to an administrative court. The appeal shall be submitted to the Border Guard within thirty days of the date the decision with attached appeal instructions were given to the liable party. An oil discharge fee is payable within thirty days of date of service, provided that that the decision has gained legal force.

VIII. Compensations for Oil Damage Caused by Vessels

488. The compensations for oil damage caused by vessels are regulated on an international basis. Finland is a party to the international agreements governing compensation for oil pollution: the International Convention on Civil Liability for Oil Pollution Damage of 1969, as amended in 1992, and the International Convention on the Establishment of an International Fund for Compensation for Oil Pollution Damage of 1971 (1992). The Civil Liability Convention has originally been implemented through a separate Act, but after the 1992 amendments of the Convention, the whole liability mechanism is included in the Maritime Act (674/1994). The Maritime Act imposes on the shipowner a strict liability with limitations specified in the Act. The Oil Damages Prevention Act imposes the liability for the costs of fighting actual pollution on the originator. This applies also to the expenses incurred by the authorities.

IX. Oil Pollution Prevention and the Funds

489. There is (until 1 January 2025) also compensation legislation of public law regime, namely the national Oil Pollution Prevention Fund, based on special enactments (the Act on the Oil Pollution Prevention Fund, 1406/2004, and the corresponding Government decree, 1409/2004). The fund is established and maintained by the State, but outside the State budget, and managed by the Oil Pollution Prevention Board under the Ministry of the Environment. From the fund, compensation (of a public law character) for oil damage shall be paid to victims of oil pollution and the costs incurred to the authorities and others who have participated in prevention and limitation of oil pollution and reinstatement of the environment from the fund, provided that the applicant proves that the (private law) damage cannot have been fully recovered by the polluter or other liable party, or a third-party liability insurance of the same, or provided that the liable party cannot be identified (section 10 of the Act on the Oil Pollution Prevention Fund). Compensations for damages are determined pursuant to either the Environmental Damages Act (*see* Part IV, Chapter 2, §2, IV) or Chapter 10 of the Maritime Act. The victim's civil law right (where any) to claim compensation from the polluter or other liable party is passed to the Board (section 16 of the Act on the Oil Pollution Prevention Fund). Possible private law claims may be based on different legal mechanisms, such as the Maritime Act, or, for activities other than carriage, the Environmental Damages Act.

490. The Oil Pollution Prevention Fund, together with the Environmental Insurance Mechanism, has been replaced by a new State fund operating outside State budgets called Environmental Damage Fund. The new legislation will, however, not enter into force until 1 January 2025 (*see* paragraph 1544). Concerning oil spills, the new regulatory framework does not apply to damage covered by the Protocol of 1992, amending the International Convention on the Establishment of an International Fund for Compensation for Oil Pollution Damage, 1971, and the 2003 Protocol thereto.

491. Some of the provisions of the new Environmental Damage Fund concern oil spills in the first place. From the Fund, compensation may, among other items, be paid to the authorities at stake for the costs of combating oil and ship chemical spills as provided in the Rescue Act and for the costs incurred from the aftermath. Within the limits of an appropriation transferred from the state budget, a subsidy may be granted from the fund to cover part of the total costs of acquiring equipment used in rescue operations to prevent environmental damage. Subsidies can be awarded to the Wellbeing Services Counties and the City of Helsinki, as well as to the Government of Åland and the municipalities of Åland. Only an appropriation transferred from the state budget to the Environmental Damage Fund may be used for such grants. In practice, oil spills in particular may be subject to the possibility of setting up an ad hoc inspection board to examine the environmental impact of an event on which an individual claim is based and the amount of damages, prevention and restoration costs, for decision-making on compensation from the Fund. A board may be appointed if the compensation paid from the fund can be estimated to exceed EUR 100,000 and the investigation of the matter so requires.

Chapter 5. Waste

§1. General Provisions and Notions

492. Waste management was up to 30 April 2012 based on the Waste Act (1072/1993) and the complementary Waste Decree (1390/1993), as well as on several topic-specific Government decrees. The Waste Act is from 1 May 2012 replaced by a new act, identically called the Waste Act (646/2011). The Act has been amended several times thereafter. The previous decrees based on the 1993 Waste Act remained valid so far also after 1 May 2012, if not contradictory to the new act or differently provided by it. A new Government decree on Waste (179/2012) entered into force 1 May 2012 and has been amended several times after that. It was replaced by a new, rather similar but updated Government decree (978/2021) from 1 December 2021. The more specific pre-2012 decrees have mainly been replaced by new decrees under the present Act.

The present Waste Act is, as its predecessor, in many respects based on EU waste legislation and aims to implement this, but the Act also includes several largely domestic subsystems and regulatory modifications. The 2008 Waste Framework Directive, i.e., Directive 2008/98/EC on waste and repealing certain directives, was one of the main reasons for this extensive legislative reform. In addition, the aim was to implement (or re-implement) also twelve other waste-related directives and two Commission decisions. Many basic structures of the 1993 Act had been preserved, however. In 2021, numerous amendments (714/2021) were made to meet the requirements of the 2018 and 2019 EU waste legislation,[32] but the main structures and arrangements of the Act were preserved.

493. The Waste Act, being addressed to businesses, households, municipalities and State authorities in several respects, encompasses various provisions related to waste and management of waste. The general aim of the Waste Act is to prevent risk and harm to health and the environment caused by wastes, reduce the amount of waste and the harmful properties thereof, promote sustainable use of natural resources, safeguard a working management of waste and prevent littering (section 1). In addition to the relevant definitions and general provisions (Chapter 1), the act consists of general duties and principles (Chapter 2), authorities and their tasks (Chapter 3), responsibility for waste management (Chapter 4), waste management

32. Directive (EU) 2018/851 of 30 May 2018 amending Directive 2008/98/EC on waste.
Directive (EU) 2018/852 of 30 May 2018 amending Directive 94/62/EC on packaging and packaging waste.
Directive (EU) 2018/850 of 30 May 2018 amending Directive 1999/31/EC on the landfill of waste.
Directive (EU) 2018/849 of 30 May 2018 amending Directives 2000/53/EC on end-of-life vehicles, 2006/66/EC on batteries and accumulators and waste batteries and accumulators, and 2012/19/EU on WEEE.
Directive (EU) 2019/904 of 5 Jun. 2019 on the reduction of the impact of certain plastic products on the environment.
Regulation (EU) 2019/1021 of 20 Jun. 2019 on POPs.

arranged by municipalities (Chapter 5), producer responsibility (Chapter 6), beverage packages (Chapter 7), littering (Chapter 8), waste management fees (Chapter 9), planning and guidance (Chapter 10), registers (Chapter 11), international transfer of waste and vessels to be recycled (Chapter 12), supervision and enforcement (Chapter 13), appeals (Chapter 14), miscellaneous provisions, criminal sanctions included (Chapter 15) and transitional provisions (Chapter 16).

494. The scope of application of the Waste Act is wide, being largely based on the notion of waste. The Act applies generally to waste, waste management and littering as well as to products and activities that generate waste (section 2(1)). On waste generated in normal activities of vessels, provided in the Act on Environmental Protection in Maritime Transport, the Waste Act is applicable after the waste has been landed. On waste generated in oil accident or vessel chemical accident pursuant to the Rescue Act the Waste Act applies when the necessary measures to limit the damage and to collect the oil or other harmful substance have been taken. The Environmental Protection Act and the Public Health Act are additionally applicable on waste. Consequently, pollution control regarding waste management and other waste-related activities is mainly based on the Environmental Protection Act. Already from 2000, the relationship between the then Environmental Protection Act and the 1993 Waste Act had become very close, as there was no longer a separate permit system in the then Waste Act, but the Environmental Permit system of the Environmental Protection Act became applicable, with substantive linkages from the Waste Act, though. Also, the provisions on polluted soils are from 2000 included in the Environmental Protection Act.

495. The provisions on waste in the Waste Act apply respectively to mercury waste pursuant to Article 2(5) of the Mercury Regulation[33] and to mercury and mercury compounds, either as such or mixtures, from large sources pursuant to Article 11 of the said Regulation. Section 221 of the Environmental Protection Act contains specific provisions pertaining to mercury, applicable in permit and notification procedures under the said Act.

496. There are some general exemptions to the general scope of application of the Waste Act (section 3 of the Waste Act). The Act is not applicable on: (1) emissions into the atmosphere; (2) carbon dioxide that has been captured and transferred for geological storage as far as regulated otherwise by an act, or geological storage of carbon dioxide with a total intended storage below 100,000 tonnes, if undertaken for research, development or testing; (3) wastewater as far as regulated by an act; (4) explosives pursuant to the Act on the Safety of the Handling of Dangerous Chemicals and Explosives, nuclear waste pursuant to the Nuclear Waste Act or radioactive waste pursuant to the Radiation Act; (5) unpolluted dredged mass that is dumped by virtue of a general right or a permit according to the Water Act; (6) animal by-products under EC Animal by-products regulation No. 1069/2009, manure and treated products under the regulation included, with the exception of such by-products and derived products that are destined for incineration, land filling or

33. Regulation (EU) 2017/852 on mercury, and repealing Regulation (EC) No. 1102/2008.

use in a biological treatment plant; (7) polluted soil substance which has not been extracted from the bedrock or soil; or (8) substances other than referred to in (6) above that are intended for use as feed material as defined in Regulation (EC) No. 767/2009 of 13 July 2009 on the placing on the market and use of feed, amending European Parliament and Council Regulation (EC) No. 1831/2003 and repealing Council Directive 79/373/EEC, Commission Directive 80/511/EEC, Council Directives 82/471/EEC, 83/228/EEC, 93/74/EEC, 93/113/EC and 96/25/EC and Commission Decision 2004/217/EC.

497. The acceptance and registration provisions regarding the Waste Management Register and the Producer Register (Chapter 11) and the provisions on bookkeeping, notification duty, monitoring and transfer documents in sections 118–121 of the Act are not applicable to such waste made up of natural substances harmless to the environment and health that is used in agriculture or forestry otherwise than for energy production, and not to waste made up of such substances, if derived from plants and generated in agriculture and forestry, and used in energy production. There are also some general derogations applicable to certain defence activities.

498. Each municipality is empowered to set forth Municipal Waste Management Bylaws to complement the nationwide provisions in the municipality or part of it, where founded by local conditions (section 91 of the Act). The provisions in the Bylaws only may refer to a limited scope of items specified in section 91. The municipality shall hear the Centre for Economic Development, Transport and the Environment and, where appropriate, other authorities before the decision-making. Municipal appeal against the decision to the Regional Administrative Court can be made pursuant to the Municipality Act. The Bylaw shall be made public and accessible on the web.

499. 'Waste' in the Waste Act means any substance or object which the holder has discarded or intends or is required to discard (section 5).

500. A substance or an object is regarded as not being waste, but as being a 'by-product' (section 5a), if it is generated in such production process the main purpose of which is not the production of this substance or product, and provided that: (1) further use of the substance or object is certain; (2) the substance can be used directly as such or after it has been processed further at the most according to normal industrial practice; (3) the substance or object is generated as an essential part of a production process; and (4) the substance or object fulfils the relevant product, environmental and health protection requirements for the intended use and the use of it in an overall consideration does not lead to risk or harm to health or the environment. Specifications by waste categories may be issued in Government decree.

501. Waste which has undergone a recycling or other recovery operation is considered to have ceased to be waste if it complies with the following conditions: (1) the substance or object is to be used for specific purposes; (2) a market or demand exists; (3) it fulfils the technical requirements for its purpose and meets the existing legislation applicable to comparable products; and (4) the use of it will not in an overall consideration lead to risk or harm to health or the environment (section 5b.1).

502. The detailed assessment criteria in section 5b.1 of the Act described above, when applied to a given category of waste, may be specified by Government decree. The detailed criteria shall include at least (1) permissible waste input material for the recovery operation; (2) allowed treatment processes and techniques; (3) quality criteria for end-of-waste materials resulting from the recovery operation in line with the applicable product standards, including limit values for pollutants where necessary; (4) requirements for management systems to demonstrate compliance with the end-of-waste criteria, including for quality control and self-monitoring, and accreditation, where appropriate; and (5) a requirement for a statement of conformity (section 5b.2).

503. Where the criteria above regarding given waste have not been set in either EU law or Government decree, the Environmental Permit authority at stake may decide on a case-by-case basis that certain waste has ceased to be waste on the basis of the conditions laid down in section 5b.1. What has been laid down in section 5b.2 shall be complied with in the decision-making, taking also into account limit values for pollutants and any possible adverse environmental and human health impacts. The permit procedure provisions in the Environmental Protection Act are applicable (section 5b.3).

504. Regarding concrete waste, Government decree on the criteria for assessing the end of the classification of crushed concrete as waste (466/2022) is applicable.

505. When a material that has ceased to be waste, the person who places the material on the market shall ensure that the material meets relevant requirements under the applicable chemical and product-related legislation. If the material has not been placed on the market, the first user of the material has the same duty (section 5b.4).

506. The definitions of thirty-four different waste-related notions are included in section 6.

507. 'Hazardous waste' is defined as waste which has a hazardous property. Non-hazardous waste means waste which has no hazardous properties. Classification of waste as either hazardous or non-hazardous may be specified by Government decree (section 6.3), *see* paragraph 515. Also the hazardous properties may be specified by Government decree, following the Waste Directive (section 6.4).

508. 'Reuse of waste' is defined as operation by which products or components are used again for the same purpose for which they were conceived. Further specification may be included in Government decree.

509. 'Recovery of waste' is defined as any operation the primary result of which is the using of waste in a production plant or otherwise in economy, in such a way that substances or objects which would otherwise be used for the same purpose, preparing of waste for such purpose included, are replaced. These operations may be specified further by Government decree.

510. 'Material recovery' means any recovery operation, other than energy recovery and the reprocessing into materials, that are to be used as fuels or other means to generate energy. Further specification may be included in Government decree.

511. 'Recycling' means any operation by which waste is reprocessed into products, materials or substances whether for the original or other purposes; energy recovery and the reprocessing into materials that are to be used as fuels or backfilling substance are not included. Further specification may be included in Government decree.

512. 'Disposal', or literally translated, 'end treatment of waste', is defined as deposit into landfill, incineration without energy recovery, or any similar operation other than recovery of waste, although the operation would have as a secondary consequence the reclamation of substances or energy contained in the waste. Preparation for disposal is included. Also the disposal operations may be specified further by Government decree.

513. Other basic notions are, municipal waste, mixed municipal waste, precipitation well or septic tank sludge waste, construction and demolition waste, biowaste, food waste, persistent organic pollutant (POP) waste, household waste, household electrical and electronic equipment waste, producer of waste, holder of waste, producer, waste management, collection of waste, separate collection of waste, reducing of quantity and harmfulness of waste, preparation of reuse, landfilling, treatment of waste, product distributor, international transfer of waste, plastic, single-use plastic product, waste fishing gear and tobacco product.

514. It is important to notice here that holder of waste, being subject to fundamental obligations in and under the Act, refers, besides a producer of waste or another person possessing waste, as such also to owners and possessors of land properties. It is likewise important to recognize the two essentially different meanings of 'producer' in the Act, i.e., producer of waste and producer of product.

515. As for the various subcategories of the notion of waste, the previous Waste Decree (in force until 1 May 2012) contained very detailed provisions and lists, largely based on the then EU waste law. Moreover, a rather comprehensive and basically indicative list on the most common wastes and hazardous wastes was included in the Ministry of the Environment Decree 1129/2001. Both decrees have from 1 May 2012 on been replaced by the Government decree on Waste (179/2012), and the latter again by the present Government decree on Waste (978/2021), containing, *inter alia*, an updated list on the most common wastes and hazardous wastes (Annex 3).

516. During the previous Waste Act and the previous Waste Framework Directive, the notion of waste has caused well-known references submitted to the ECJ by the SAC, *Palin Granit and Vehmassalon kansanterveystyön kuntayhtymän hallitus* (SAC 1998:81 and SAC 2002:82, ECJ 18.4.2002, C-9/00), and *AvestaPolarit Chrome Oy, formerly Outokumpu Chrome Oy* (SAC 2001:10 and SAC 2004:3, ECJ 11.9.2003 C-114/01). The former case dealt with leftover stone resulting from stone quarrying and the latter leftover rock resulting from the extraction of ore and/or ore-dressing sand resulting from the dressing of ore in industrial mining operations.

There are also other related rulings of interest, such as SAC 2004:60 (quarrying of soapstone (vuolukivi marble) from an opencast quarry on the one hand and of production of fireplaces, building stones and semi-finished products out of soapstone raw material at the adjoining upgrading plant) and SAC 20005:90 (crushed slag and granulated slag, both from a ferrochromium factory, were generated in the metal production at an installation of O Ltd.) In the latter, the SAC ruled:

> Because O Ltd does not discard the ferrochromium slag at any stage of the continuous industrial process, but produces out of them by-products, for which there is, due to their properties, a continuous strong demand, and because the appropriate use of the by-products does not cause danger or harm to health and environment, the ferrochromium slag or the by-products produced from it were not to be regarded as waste pursuant to the Waste Act.
>
> Such high-quality steel refuse that separately accredited steel scrap suppliers have not discarded but, after sorting and handling, as such sold to O Ltd. for use as raw material immediately in steel production, without any preceding sorting or transforming, is acquired from the suppliers to be used as raw material at the steel mill of O Ltd. This steel refuse was not to be regarded as waste pursuant to the Waste Act. The fact that part of the acquired steel refuse had been discarded by its original owners, consequently being waste at that stage, did not imply that such scrap still at delivery to O Ltd. would be regarded as waste, provided that the scrap has been sorted and handled and in itself met the quality requirements for raw material in steel making. Due to the costs placed into the material and due to its value it was regarded indisputable that the material is not discarded, intended to be discarded or required to be discarded, but its reuse as raw material of production at the steel factory was regarded certain. Scrap of other kind was to be classified as waste, instead.

517. SAC 20.9.2005 number 2413 may also be accounted here:

> A Ltd delivered granulated nickel slag from its factory to a refining and storage plant of nickel slag factory of B Ltd, for drying and screening. Otherwise the slag would have been banked in the industrial area of A Ltd. When arriving at the premises of B Ltd, the nickel slag from A Ltd was to be regarded as waste. Instead, after the drying and screening procedures by B Ltd and after the derived screening waste and filter dust had been returned, the nickel slag at B Ltd was not any more to be regarded as waste, because the granulated slag, as a result from the drying and screening procedures, was immediately delivered to customers as packaged product, for use in sandblasting and as a raw

material for roofing felt industries, and there was no risk for its properties to cause mentionable environmental harm or danger in appropriate use. The market was already established. B Ltd took economic advantage of the treatment. Hence the nickel slag could not be regarded as a burden that B Ltd would try to discard, but, on the contrary, a product to be used in sand blasting activity and as raw material in roofing felt industry.

One of the provisions which had been set forth in the environmental permit of B Ltd., subsequently subject to appeal by B Ltd., had been based on the presumption that the nickel slag was to be regarded as waste also after the drying and screening procedure by B Ltd. Hence the provision required the slag to be delivered from B Ltd. only to an installation with appropriate permit for receiving of waste. This provision was repealed, due to the opinion of the SAC that the slag at this stage is not waste any more.

Instead, another permit provision, according to which, on the one hand, the area of B Ltd. for the storage of the granulated nickel slag and screening waste had to be coated by watertight material and, on the other hand, the storm waters were to be collected and funnelled outside the local groundwater area, as well as still another provision requiring monitoring of the quality of surface waters and groundwater and of the level of groundwater according to an accepted plan, were upheld, i.e., on the ground that these permit provisions could be based on the Environmental Protection Act irrespective of whether the granulated nickel slag was to be regarded as waste or not.

All the rulings above have been made within the framework of the previous waste directive.

§2. Waste Plans

518. A National Waste Plan (section 87 of the Waste Act), prepared by the Ministry of the Environment, has to be approved by the Cabinet. The plan shall include an assessment on the present status in the decreasing of the amounts and harmful properties of waste and in waste management otherwise, on the targets regarding these, and on the measures to be taken. From 2021 measures to prevent littering and to clean up of littered areas shall be included. The plan may also set out objectives deriving from regional conditions and measures for the development of waste management. An appraisal on the effectiveness of the plan shall be enclosed.

519. From 2021, instead of the previous Regional Waste plans, Each Centre for Economic Development, Transport and the Environment shall set up a regional Cooperation Group to support the preparation, implementation and monitoring of the National Waste Plan. The Cooperation Group shall represent the municipalities of the domain, the operators whose duties or purposes may be at stake as well such associations and foundations that are empowered to initiate administrative enforcement by virtue of section 134(2) and whose duties or purposes may be at stake.

520. A Cooperation Group shall promote the implementation of the National Waste Plan and monitor it. It shall also compile and provide the Ministry of the Environment with the information necessary for the preparation or revision of the National Waste Plan on the 'region's waste treatment capacity and the arranging and development needs of waste management.

521. The necessity of both original plans was legally based on the Waste Framework Directive, but their practical relevance seemed somewhat unclear. Neither of the plans had any legal effects, with the exception provided in section 50(1) of the Environmental Protection Act. According to this, pursuant its current wording, the National Waste Plan shall be taken into account in any permit for a waste treatment facility or site requiring an environmental permit. However, the Plan probably affects to some extent also other decisions and activities of the relevant authorities and private parties.

522. The present National Waste Plan has been approved by the Cabinet in March 2022, replacing the previous plan of 2017. The current plan is applicable up to the end of 2027 or until replaced by a new plan. The plan presents the goal state for 2030 concerning waste management and prevention of waste generation, the objectives in detail until 2027 and the measures needed for meeting the objectives. The vision for 2030 is the following.

523. (1) Material efficient production and consumption save natural resources and mitigate climate change; (2) the amount of waste has decreased from the current level. Reuse and recycling have reached a new level; (3) high-quality waste management is part of a sustainable circular economy; (4) recycling market works well. New jobs will be created through reuse and recycling; (5) valuable raw materials present at low levels are also recovered from recycled materials; (6) material cycles are innocuous and less and less hazardous substances are used in the production; (7) cooperation between industry actors promotes high-quality material cycles; (8) reliable and comprehensive information supports the circular economy. The information can be utilized digitally; (9) in the waste sector there is high-quality research and experiments and competence in waste issues is at a high level; and the legislation supports innovations and operating conditions in the circular economy. A number of thematic objectives are specified in the plan.

524. Each port shall work out a waste plan for waste originating from vessels, as provided substantively and procedurally in the Act on Environmental Protection in Maritime Transport (Chapter 9, sections 3–5). A final plan approved by the regionally competent Centre for Economic Development, Transport and the Environment, or, in case of harbours for recreational craft only, by the Municipal Environmental Protection Authority, is registered in the Environmental Protection Information System provided in the Environmental Protection Act (*see* paragraph 291). The plan shall be observed after having been approved. When approving a plan, the Centre for Economic Development, Transport and the Environment may, where necessary, decide upon the language in which the important groups of users of the harbour shall be informed on the local reception facilities and fees. Also the general duties of a harbour operator regarding waste to be received from vessels are laid down in Chapter 9 of the Act on Environmental Protection in Maritime Transport. The general duties of vessel carriers to deliver in harbours the waste generated in ordinary maritime activities, as well as the applicable fees, are in turn set forth in Chapter 10 of the same Act. The provisions above are aimed to implement Directive 2000/59/EC on port reception facilities for ship-generated waste and cargo residues.

§3. REGISTERS

525. The Waste Management Register and the Producer Register (Chapter 11 and section 142 of the Waste Act) are the two main administrative information systems under the Waste Act operated by State environmental administration.

526. All professional waste transport operators and waste brokers have to make an application for registration in the Waste Management Register to the Centre for Economic Development, Transport and the Environment of the region (section 94 of the Waste Act). The same applies to essential changes in the activity, as well as to ending of activity. An application of an operator established outside Finland shall be submitted to the Centre for Economic Development, Transport and the Environment of Southeast Finland. Applications have to be submitted in the authority's e-service. The application can also be submitted by e-mail or on paper if it is not possible to prepare the application in the e-service. An operator established outside Finland must submit the application in Finnish, Swedish or English. Certificates in a foreign language must be translated into Finnish, Swedish or English by an authorized translator or another reliable translation.

527. The preconditions for approval are laid down in section 95 of the Waste Act. Operations shall be accepted into the Waste Management Register if: (1) the operations are carried out professionally and the devices and equipment used are technically appropriate; (2) the operator has not shown obvious disregard for the provisions of the Waste Act in its business activities during the current year or the previous three calendar years, and the operations are carried out without causing danger or harm to health or the environment; (3) the broker is domiciled in Finland or in another country belonging to the EEA; (4) the transporter has a freight transport licence or a light goods transport licence pursuant to the Act on Transport Services (320/2017), or, if domiciled outside the EEA, has an International Transport Forum transport licence or a transport licence based on a bilateral agreement between Finland and another state; and (5) an operator whose activities do not require an operating licence or whose domicile is outside the EEA shall also be reliable. An operator referred to in (5) shall not be considered reliable if: (1) during the current year or the three preceding calendar years, it has repeatedly or to a significant extent failed to fulfil its registration, declaration or payment obligations related to taxes, statutory pension, accident or unemployment insurance contributions or fees collected by the customs; or (2) it has debts that are more than minor in relation to its solvency to be recovered in enforcement or debts that have been returned from enforcement with certificates of impediment to bankruptcy; or (3) it has been declared bankrupt. If established outside Finland, such an operator shall submit the information required by means of an extract from the register or an equivalent certificate in accordance with the legislation of the state in which the applicant is established or in another generally acceptable manner.

528. An administrative decision on registration shall be issued for each application without delay, including provisions set forth in order to meet the preconditions, and on bookkeeping and supervision. Alternatively, mutual recognition shall be entered in the Register. Approval or recognition is a necessary requirement for the activity to be commenced. The decision, being subject to appeal to the Regional Administrative Court, is valid either for an indefinite time or for a fixed period (section 96). If a registered activity changes substantially or is discontinued, the Centre for Economic Development, Transport and the Environment of the region shall be notified without delay, and, if necessary, a new application must be submitted or the certificate and other information at stake shall be submitted. The Centre shall enter the changed information in the Register and, if necessary, amend the approval decision accordingly. If operations are discontinued, the operator's data has to be erased. A decision on acceptance into the Register or an entry made on the basis of mutual recognition may be amended at the initiative of the Centre if the circumstances have materially changed or it is later found that the grounds for approval were substantially different from those required when the decision was issued (section 97). The Centre may withdraw acceptance or entry in the Waste Management Register if: (1) the conditions for approval can no longer be fulfilled by amending the decision; (2) the operator is no longer reliable as provided for in section 95(2), and the reason why the operator is not considered reliable is essential and serious in nature and the operator has not rectified the defect despite an order; (3) the operator has provided incorrect information that has materially affected the conditions for approval or registration; or (4) the operator has repeatedly shown obvious disregard for the provisions of the Waste Act in the course of its business or has repeatedly violated the provisions of the decision despite a written reprimand, and the operations cause danger or harm to health or the environment. The Centre shall decide that acceptance or entry in the Register shall lapse if the operator does not respond to the request to review the extract of the Register as provided in section 98. The operator shall be given an opportunity to be heard before the withdrawal or expiry. The Centre shall remove from the Register information on operators whose approval or entry is withdrawn or expires (section 99).

529. On intended professional waste collection activity, a notification for entry in the Waste Management Register shall be submitted to the Environmental Protection Authority of the municipality in whose area the collection is carried out. The notification shall be made well in advance of the start of collection. A notification is not needed if the collection requires an Environmental Permit pursuant to the Environmental Protection Act or is approved as part of other activities subject to an Environmental Permit. The notification shall contain the information necessary for entering the operations in the Register concerning the operator and the activities, such as the waste to be collected, waste containers and the location of reception points, as well as measures to prevent harm to health and the environment. The operator shall immediately notify the Authority if the reported information changes substantially or if operations are discontinued. The Authority shall enter the information in the notification in the Waste Management Register in accordance with section 142 and notify the notifier of the entry. The marking shall be removed if the collection operations are discontinued (section 100).

530. In a similar way, the parties under producer responsibility, i.e., producers of products, producer affiliations and maintainers of return systems for beverage packaging, are subject to a registration duty (sections 101–107 on the Producer Register). Here, the competent authority is the Centre for Economic Development, Transport and the Environment of Pirkanmaa region, having the nationwide tasks and powers specific to producer responsibility. The application must be submitted in good time so that the waste management of end-of-life products can be ensured. Section 101 of the Act contains provisions on the content of the application.

531. Each Municipal Waste Management authority keeps a register of waste transports and biowaste treatment on single properties, concerning information referred to in sections 39(2) and 41a(2) of the Act. Personal data concerning transport entered in the register will be stored for five years after the entry in the register. Personal data entered in the register concerning the treatment of biowaste on a property will be stored for five years after notification of the end treatment (section 143).

532. There is a Data Platform for Waste and Side Streams for the secondary waste management service by municipalities (section 33). It is used to identify deficiencies in other services, that being a prerequisite for a secondary municipal waste management service, to manage and process information about the service, and to monitor and supervise the service. It can also be used for other exchanges of waste and side streams. The private law company Motiva Oy maintains the Platform and, in cooperation with the Ministry of the Environment, is responsible for the content and functional development of the platform. The personnel of the company in the performance of these duties is subject to criminal liability of officials (section 143a).

533. Decisions on international transfers of waste and on transfer documents pursuant to section 121 are registered separately by the Finnish Environment Institute (section 142).

534. Omission of registration duty is subject to an Administrative Fine for Negligence (section 131 of the Act, *see* section 5 below). This fine is also applicable to certain other omissions by producers, brokers, collectors or transporters.

535. Right of access to the registers and data platform by different authorities is stipulated in section 143b.

536. The registers pursuant to the Waste Act are part of the Environmental Protection Information System provided for in section 222 of the Environmental Protection Act.

§4. Administration of Waste Management

537. The general guidance, monitoring and development under the Waste Act are vested in the Ministry of the Environment. However, the administration of international transfers of waste is vested in the Finnish Environment Institute, in cooperation with other authorities, and the administration of producer responsibility to one of the Centres for Economic Development, Transport and the Environment, the Centre of Pirkanmaa region located in the city of Tampere. At the regional level, the general guidance and development are the responsibility of all the Centres for Economic Development, Transport and the Environment (section 22 of the Act).

538. Each municipality designates one of its authorities to act as the Municipal Waste Management Authority to be responsible for those municipality-level waste management tasks of authority character under the Waste Act (section 23). It is also possible to transfer the tasks to a body jointly organized by several municipalities, and to delegate competences of the Municipal Waste Management Authority to officials under it. It is the duty of the municipality to arrange the transportation and disposal of household waste and other comparable waste. A municipality has three basic options to arrange the duties of its Waste Management Authority: It may: (1) act independently, (2) act in cooperation with another municipality, or (3) be member of a common body of several municipalities with similar tasks.

539. Within the municipality, this task is separated from the local supervision and enforcement of waste management regulations, which in turn is a duty of the Municipal Environmental Protection Authorities and the Centres for Economic Development, Transport and the Environment. Hence, at local level, each Municipal Waste Management Authority is, besides the various private subjects, among the targets of supervision by the Municipal Environmental Protection Authority (and by the Centre for Economic Development, Transport and the Environment). Regarding international transfers of waste, the supervision and enforcement are vested in the Finnish Environment institute, and regarding producer responsibility, to the Centre for Economic Development, Transport and the Environment of Pirkanmaa region. The Centre for Economic Development, Transport and the Environment of Southeast Finland is responsible for approving, entering and supervising waste transporters and brokers established outside Finland. The Finnish Safety and Chemicals Agency has certain product-related supervisory tasks, and the customs in turn specified supervisory tasks in relation to beverage packagings and transfers of waste.

540. The municipality may decide to transfer its service tasks of waste management, where applicable, to a limited company particularly established for this purpose and owned by the municipality together with other municipalities (section 43). Such a decision may cover reception, transportation and treatment of waste, invoicing of Municipal Waste Fees, dissemination of information on waste management and such related administrative tasks that do not include use of public powers (section 43). The municipality is in any case responsible for the tasks being taken care of according to the law.

541. An effort to reconcile the interests of the various operators of waste management regarding reuse has been made in section 11a (714/2021). According to the provision, a municipality, a producer or another subject in charge of professional collection of waste shall in connection of waste collection ensure enterprises and associations preparing for reuse an equal possibility to receive waste suitable for preparing for reuse from a collection site assigned by the collector, as far as the collector itself does not arrange preparing for reuse at stake. The reception and collection shall be arranged in such a manner that possibility to preparing for reuse is not weakened. The supplying of waste destined for preparing for reuse shall be agreed upon in writing. The supplier may charge from an enterprise or association preparing for reuse for the costs incurred by the cost-efficient collection and storage. The enterprise or association shall furnish the supplier of waste with information on waste treatment.

542. The right to appeal against the various administrative decisions under the Waste Act is as wide-reaching as in the environmental legislation in general. It covers: (1) those whose right or interest may be at stake; (2) any registered association or foundation the task of which is protection of environment, health or nature or promotion of amenity of an inhabited area, provided that the environmental or health impacts appear in its geographical area of activities; (3) the municipality where the activity takes place, and another municipality where the environmental or health impacts become expressed; and (4) the Centre for Economic Development, Transport and the Environment (environmental division), and the Municipal Environmental Protection Authority of a municipality where the activity takes place or where its impacts become expressed (section 138). The competent Regional Administrative Court in a single appellate case is determined in section 137.

§5. Supervision and Enforcement

543. The Municipal Environmental Protection Authority and the Centres for Economic Development, Transport and the Environment as supervisory authorities, as well as the Ministry of the Environment and the Finnish Environment Institute, or the assigned officials, are entitled to receive the information needed for supervision and enforcement, as specified in section 122 of the Waste Act. They also have access to the sites of activities and the right to inspections, measuring and taking samples, the costs of which shall at certain conditions be covered by the possessor of the site or the holder of the product. Plants and activities where hazardous waste is generated, as well as the operations of transporters and brokers, shall be inspected at regular intervals (section 124). Where an Environmental Permit is needed, the supervision and inspections are provided in the Environmental Protection Act. Where no Environmental Permit is needed, the Municipal Environmental Protection Authority may, on the basis of an inspection, issue individual orders to prevent littering or to arrange appropriate waste management (section 125).

544. Where the applicable waste management provisions have not been observed, the supervisory authority, i.e., the Municipal Environmental Protection

Authority or the Centre for Economic Development, Transport and the Environment may, issue administrative enforcement orders. These may include the forbidding of an unlawful activity, order to fulfil one's duties, and order to reinstate the environment or to eliminate the harm at stake (section 126). Also orders regarding temporary measures in respect to waste are possible. The enforcement orders are normally given under a conditional fine or at the risk that the measures needed will be taken by the supervisory authority at the expense of the responsible subject, or that a relevant activity will be stopped or banned (section 129). The authorities may (and have to) react on their own behalf, but also any of the affected private parties or, a registered environmental or inhabitants' association or foundation, or a municipality, may formally initiate the enforcement procedure (section 134; *see also* Part V). The Regional Administrative Court and further the SAC are here appellate judicial bodies.

545. In certain cases, the waste or another item in respect to which the measures by the supervisory authority are taken may also be sold by the authority as provided in section 130, if the object has pecuniary value.

546. Where the properties of products or the labelling thereof is at stake, the administrative enforcement powers are vested in the Ministry of the Environment, the Finnish Safety and Chemicals Agency, or the customs, as specified in section 127 of the Act.

547. Administrative Fine for Negligence to the State (sections 131–133) was one of the novelties in the 2011 Waste Act. Its main purpose is to be used as a sanction imposed to a producer or a producer affiliation that has omitted its duty to apply for registration. The same sanction applies to several omissions by producers, transporters, brokers, collectors, as listed in section 132. The amount of the fine is dependent mainly on the turnover of the subject at stake, as provided in section 132. The fine is imposed by an administrative decision of the supervisory authority, in a procedure specified in section 133.

548. Where a criminal offence is suspected, the supervisory authority shall as a main rule report it to the police (or the customs) in order to initiate pretrial investigation (section 136). The Centre for Economic Development, Transport and the Environment has the rights of a complainant in a criminal trial, insofar public interest has been violated.

549. The criminal sanctions are provided in section 147 (and regarding 'impairment of the environment' in the Penal Code).

550. The obligations and competences in market surveillance are stipulated in section 24a. As the market surveillance authority, the Finnish Safety and Chemicals Agency (Tukes) supervises compliance with the requirements and restrictions concerning packaging, vehicles and their materials and components, batteries and accumulators, electrical and electronic equipment and other products as further provided for in Government decrees issued pursuant to section 5b or 10 of the Act. Provisions concerning market surveillance, external border control and appeals against decisions of market surveillance authorities concerning these products are laid down in the Act on the Market Surveillance of Certain Products.

§6. General Duties and Principles

551. The following waste hierarchy shall be observed in any activity, as far as possible: primarily, the amount of generated waste and harmfulness thereof shall be reduced. If waste is anyway generated, the holder shall, primarily, prepare the waste for reuse or, secondarily, recycle it. If recycling is not possible, the holder shall recover the waste otherwise. If not even recovery is possible, the waste shall be disposed (section 8). Various waste-related professional operators shall observe this hierarchy as a binding obligation, in such a way that the best result from the viewpoint of the purpose of the Waste Act as a whole is achieved. Some more specific provisions are included in section 8 and may be laid down further by Government decree.

The observance of the waste hierarchy is enhanced by a general duty that binds all public authorities and institutes, as well as public law associations. All these are obliged to use, as far as possible, durable, mendable, reusable, recyclable and from recycled raw materials produced products. A similar obligation applies to services used by the same. As small amounts of waste as possible and as harmless waste as possible shall be generated by such services (section 11).

552. The various general waste-related obligations of product producers, of those who place products on the market and of distributors of products are listed in section 9. Under certain circumstances the production, placing on the market, export or use may be forbidden or limited. Product-related provisions on various items may be laid down by Government decree as provided in section 10.

553. The authorities shall in their guidance and planning of waste management aim at ensuring sufficient and need-meeting possibilities to recovery or disposal of mixed municipal waste collected from private households under the responsibility of the municipalities (*see* section 32 of the Act) or to disposal of other waste (section 19(1); principle of self-sufficiency). The municipalities and private operators shall take this into account (section 19(3)).

554. The costs for waste management as well as for the necessary infrastructure and its operation shall be borne by the original waste producer or by the current or previous waste holder (section 20; causation principle).[34] The costs of and fees for final disposal shall include the costs for the establishing, use, termination, aftercare, collateral pursuant to section 59 of the Environmental Protection Act, and other

34. In most environmental contexts 'polluter pays principle' is the normal translation of the Finnish expression *aiheuttamisperiaate*, but here it would not do.

comparable costs final disposal installations or sites. Fees for landfill disposal shall include the estimated aftercare costs for thirty years (section 21).

555. Each holder of waste shall *see* to it that waste referred to in section 19(1) is delivered for recovery in one of the nearest appropriate installations (section 19(2); principle of proximity). Also this shall be taken into account by the municipalities and private operators (section 19(2)).

556. As a basic rule, the holder of waste is responsible for management of waste (section 28(1)), unless falling within the responsibility of the municipality or producer of product. This responsibility is transferred to the property holder at stake, if the holder of waste is negligent or cannot be reached, provided that the property holder has allowed the waste-generating operation on his property or the delivering of the waste there (section 28(2)).

Within land properties, internal collection (reception) of waste is included in the obligations of the holder of waste (the notion of which also comprises owner or holder of property). When a property belongs to a system for waste transportation from properties (*see* paragraphs 569–574), the individual owners and holders are obliged to arrange waste reception sites at their properties, by each possessor separately or jointly with other possessors (section 40).

557. Waste may only be delivered to a subject that is entitled to receive the waste, by virtue of approval or registration in the Waste Management Register under the Waste Act (*see* paragraphs 525–527), or by virtue of a valid Environmental Permit or registration under the Environmental Protection Act (section 29). In cases where no approval, registration or permit is needed, the assignee shall have the sufficient expertise and the economic and technical qualifications for waste management. The responsibility for waste management by a waste holder ends and is transferred to the new holder at the time of reception (section 30(1)). This does not apply to delivery of waste to one who transports waste on behalf of someone else. If waste has been received by someone who is not entitled to this, both the current holder and the previous holder are responsible for the waste (section 30(2)).

558. The holder of waste shall prepare a transfer document regarding hazardous waste and certain other categories of waste to be assigned to receiver provided in section 29. Before starting the transfer of waste, the holder of the waste must draw up a movement document for hazardous waste, POP waste, sludge from septic tanks and sealed tanks, sludge from sand and grease separation wells, polluted soil and construction and demolition waste other than unpolluted soil that is transferred and handed over to the consignee referred to in section 29. The transfer document shall contain the information necessary for control and monitoring as to the type, nature, quantity, origin, place and date of delivery, method of disposal at the point of delivery and carrier. Where such waste is collected from a household, the transporter shall, instead of the holder, draw up a transfer document and ensure that it is delivered to the consignee and stored. The movement document to be used in international shipments of waste is laid down in the Waste Shipment Regulation (section 121). The transfer document shall be drawn up electronically. Its data shall be in machine-readable format. Changes to the document shall be detectable retrospectively and shall be made in such a way that the original data are not lost. The document shall be legible during the shipment of waste, and the information contained therein shall be accessible to all parties involved in the transfer. The holder of the waste shall confirm the accuracy of the information given in the movement document, the acceptance of the waste by the waste carrier and the receipt of the waste by the consignee by means of an electronic signature, electronic seal or other reliable electronic verification method. The holder and consignee shall keep the information in the transfer document for three years after the completion of the shipment. However, a paper document may do if the conditions for making out the electronic document do not exist. The holder shall ensure that the paper document is included during the shipment of waste and that it is finally given to the consignee. The paper document must be validated by signatures or other arrangements, provided that this does not impair the reliability of the confirmation (section 121a–b).

559. A waste transporter shall deliver the waste at a site assigned by the waste holder or by an authority. If the waste fails to be received, the transporter shall return it (section 31).

560. Waste shall not be abandoned or unrestrainedly treated (section 13). Waste or management of waste shall not cause risk or harm to health or the environment, decrease public safety or result in other corresponding violation of public or private interest. Emissions or discharges posing a pollution risk, noise, smell and loss of amenity included, shall be avoided. The activities, plants and sites shall moreover be adapted to the environment and landscape (section 13). These provisions indicate a wide notion of environmental protection also within the waste management regime. BAT and BEPs are applied as general principles. More specific provisions on the prevention of risk and harm may be laid down by Government decree, based on an indicative list in section 14.

561. An operator who utilizes waste professionally or on plant scale shall before utilization or during it remove hazardous substances, mixtures and components from waste, if necessary for treating the waste pursuant to priority order or to abate risk or harm referred to in section 13. This obligation may be specified by Government decree (section 15b).

562. Waste that are different by category and quality shall, in order to implement waste hierarchy, be subject to separate collection and shall not be mixed with other waste or other materials. Derogations are allowed if at least one of the following conditions is met: (1) collecting different types of waste together does not weaken their quality or reduce their potential to undergo preparing for reuse, recycling or other recovery operations in accordance with the priority order; (2) separate collection does not deliver the best possible outcome when considering the overall environmental impacts of the management of the relevant waste; (3) separate collection is not technically feasible taking into consideration good practices in waste collection; or (4) separate collection costs would be disproportionate taking into account the possibilities to improve cost efficiency in separate collection, revenues from sales of separately collected waste and secondary raw materials as well as the costs incurred by the negative environmental and health impacts of collection and treatment of mixed waste collection (section 15.1).

563. More specified provisions may be issued by Government decree (1) on requirements for keeping wastes apart, preconditions for mixing different wastes and application of derogations in section 15.1 on given waste, and (2) on the duties of municipality, producer, property holder and waste holder to arrange separate collection of waste, the requirements of which may be different for different areas considering population density, amounts and utilization possibilities of waste generated, and environmental impacts and costs caused by separate collection (section 15.2).

564. Waste that has been separately collected for preparing for reuse and recycling shall not be transferred for incineration or landfilled. Waste resulting from subsequent treatment operations of the separately collected waste may however, be incinerated or landfilled, if the best result for waste priority order is so achieved (section 15a).

565. As regards asbestos, the waste holder shall *see* to that all asbestos waste generated in the activities is collected and transported separately and specially packed, without delay (section 32 of the Government decree on Waste). *See also* paragraph 603.

566. Each production operator and producer or importer of products is obliged to be aware of the waste being generated, its environmental and health impacts and waste management, as well as of the possibilities to develop the production or products in such a manner that the amount and harmfulness of the waste are reduced (section 12(1)). Each holder of waste in turn is obliged to be aware of the origin, amount, category, quality and other relevant properties of the waste, and of the environmental and health impacts thereof. Where needed, they also serve other stakeholders of waste management with such information that concerns them (section 12(2)). More specified provisions may by Government decree issued on (1) on the duty of the holder of waste to follow and monitor and the environmental and health impacts of the waste and waste management and follow the composition and origin of the waste; (2) the furnishing of information on waste and waste treatment with a previous holder or processor of the waste, and (3) other comparable measures for the enforcement of section 15.2.

567. Each municipality is obliged to arrange the waste management regarding several categories of municipal waste. As amended in 2019 and 2021, these encompass, hazardous waste excluded: (1) waste generated in permanent dwellings, holiday dwellings, dormitories or workers' quarters or otherwise in dwelling, waste generated in small-scale self-made construction and demolition operations of households included; (2) municipal waste generated in the administrative and service activities of the municipality; (3) such municipal waste generated in business premises that is collected together with waste referred to in (1)–(2) above: and (4) other municipal waste that is collected by local pipe collection mechanism or other similar mechanism together with waste referred to in (1)–(3) above (section 32(1)), These categories may be specified further by Government decree. In addition, the municipality shall arrange (1) the waste management of precipitation well and septic tank sludge generated in activities in section 32(1)(1–3) above and (2) the reception and treatment of hazardous waste generated in dwelling. The same applies to (3) hazardous waste generated in agriculture or forestry, with the exception of unreasonably high quantities (section 32(2)). Any of these obligations of the municipalities does not concern waste that has become covered by waste management arranged by a (product) producer or distributor. However, in the separate collection of packaging waste by properties there is a duty of cooperation between the municipality and the packaging producer as provided in section 49a.

568. Secondary, as amended in 2019, the waste management obligation of a municipality also covers other waste than those provided in section 32. This holds good when the waste holder has so requested due to lack of supply of other service, provided that the waste, considering its quality and quantity, is suitable for transportation or treatment within the municipal waste management (section 33(1)). The request may on behalf of the holder of waste be made by transport enterprise or other actor as a part of waste management services. If the value of the secondary waste management service by a municipality (being not caused by unpredictable urgency) is at least EUR 2,000 per year, such a request is allowed only if the waste holder regarding the service needed has published a call for tenders in the Data Platform for Waste and Side Streams (section 33(2)) and if no corresponding service is available within fourteen days.[35] An agreement between the municipality and the service supplier shall be made for no more than three years, as provided in section 33(3). The accessory Data Platform for Waste and Side Streams is regulated in section 143a (*see* paragraph 532), the obligations of the municipality to provide the Platform with waste-related information in section 33(4), and the access to the Platform data by authorities in section 143b.

569. The municipality shall see to it that transportation from private properties, as far as needed, is available. There shall be a sufficient number of local reception sites for hazardous waste and other waste within the municipality, all these being easily accessible. Also other diverse waste management services, such as a possibility to separate collection pursuant to the proximity principle, shall be provided for. The collection and transportation shall be arranged and dimensioned to come up to the quantity and quality of waste as much as possible. Sufficient and sufficiently frequent information on collection and reception sites shall be provided for by the municipality (section 34). All these obligations may be specified further by Government decree.

35. Pursuant to s. 33.2, (714/2021), this does not apply to contracting entities pursuant to the Act on Public Procurement and Concession Contracts (1397/2016) or the Act on Procurements and Concession Contracts of Entities Operating in the Water and Energy Supply, Transport and Postal Services Sector (1398/2016), if it publishes a contract notice on the website at stake.

570. Also transportation of municipal waste (under section 32.1 of the Act) from reception sites (or, in practice, refuse containers) arranged by each property holder (or by several property holders together) is the responsibility of the municipality (section 35, waste transportation from properties). Within transportation from properties the Municipal Waste Management Bylaws shall be observed. In any case, access to transportation services shall be comprehensive and reliable, and be based on reasonable and non-discriminatory conditions (section 35(2)). The waste shall be delivered to the reception or treatment sites assigned by the municipality (section 35). For areas with difficult traffic connections, a small amount of waste holders or a small amount of waste to be transported, the municipality may, however, decide that transportation of unsorted municipal waste from properties is not arranged, unless necessary for environmental or health reasons (section 35(4)). Public participation in the decision-making on these excepted areas and access to information thereon is stipulated in section 38.

571. Municipalities have two main alternatives to arrange waste transportation from properties as required in section 35 (section 36). First, a municipality may decide to be in charge itself (waste transportation arranged by the municipality). If so, merely the municipality or such a transporter that operates on behalf of the municipality is allowed to receive any waste at stake. When planning the procurement of waste transports, a municipality shall carry out a market survey. In the invitation to tender, the duration of waste transport services shall be determined and procurement scheduled in such a way as to enable undertakings of all sizes to participate. The transport procurement shall be allocated to tender in parts so that more than one undertaking can be selected as the provider. Exceptions are allowed only if the split-up would significantly impair the cost-effectiveness or for other similar, well-founded reasons. A non-division may be appealed against in the Market Court.

572. The other alternative for waste transportation from properties is waste transportation arranged by property holders (section 37), regarding waste referred to in section 32(1) and 32(2)(1) and for the whole municipality or parts of it. Within this option, the transportation shall be based on contracts between single property holders and transportation operators. A decision to opt contractual waste transportation arranged by property holders is only allowed if the specific requirements laid down in section 37 are met. These include the general requirement in section 35(2) according to which access to transportation services shall be comprehensive and reliable, and be based on reasonable and non-discriminatory conditions. The transportation system shall promote a generally functioning waste management within the municipality, support the local development of waste management and not cause risk or harm to health or the environment. Moreover, the impacts of the decision as a whole shall be evaluated positive, when particularly the impacts on private households and on the activities of private operators and public authorities are taken into account. If the municipality decides to move from waste transport arranged by property holders to waste transport arranged by the municipality, the decision shall set the date of cessation of the transport of waste organized by property holders, that being not earlier than three years from the decision. However, the municipality may decide on an earlier date for an area where waste transport service is not available or its availability has deteriorated significantly and this may result in littering or harm or danger to health or the environment. Public participation in the decision-making on opting waste transportation arranged by property holders and access to information is stipulated in section 38. Where the option waste transportation arranged by property holders is currently valid, the municipality shall monitor the implementation and continuously control if the requirements by law are met. If needed, the decision may be reviewed by the municipality. The transportation operators within this scheme are obliged to serve both the property holders and the municipality with information specified in section 39(2). The information shall be registered by the Municipal Waste Management Authority (section 143).

573. Within both the schemes of waste transportation from properties, i.e., either waste transportation arranged by the municipality or waste transportation arranged by property holders, property holders and other holders of waste shall deliver all municipal waste under section 32 either to the waste transportation arranged in the area or to a local reception site arranged by the municipality (section 41). The waste holder may, nevertheless, arrange the transportation of such waste that is unsuitable for ordinary waste transportation due to its exceptional size, large amount or other property, provided that this has been accepted in Municipal Waste Management Bylaw or Municipal Environmental Bylaw. Moreover, where transportation of separately collected packaging waste or biowaste is not arranged, the property holder may independently arrange the transportation of separately collected packaging waste and biowaste and deliver the packaging waste to waste management arranged by the producer and biowaste to municipal waste management.

574. As a derogation, the holder of waste referred to in section 32 (above) may also himself treat the waste in his property or hand over his biowaste, precipitation well or septic tank waste or other comparable waste for treatment on a neighbouring property or other nearby property, provided that the self-handling or joint treatment is small-scale and allowed in the Municipal Waste Management Bylaw or the Environmental Protection Bylaw. More specific provisions may be laid down in Government decree (section 41a).

575. A property owner may by the municipality be exceptionally released from the duty to arrange a waste reception site for municipal waste, if the requirements laid down in section 42 are met. It is required that such a decision is justified by the overall waste management of the property, that better results from the viewpoint of waste hierarchy are achieved, and that no harm to the environment or health is caused. A decision may be valid no more than five years.

§7. Municipal Waste Fee and Other Charges

576. For the waste management arranged by the municipality, a Municipal Waste Fee (sections 78–84 of the Waste Act) shall be collected from holders of waste (most often property owners or possessors) the management of which is the responsibility of the municipality. If the transport of waste is arranged by the property owner as provided in section 37, the municipality may charge the fee concerning waste management from the transportation operator.

577. The provisions on the amount of the Municipal Waste Fee, as last amended in 2019, are somewhat complicated. The fee shall cover the costs for waste management, and regarding final disposal, it shall cover at least the costs referred to in section 21 (*see* paragraph 516). The fee shall correspond to the level of service offered by the municipality, and it shall encourage, according to the possibilities, those concerned to reduce the quantity and harmfulness of waste and to apply the waste hierarchy. The costs for secondarily municipal waste management services provided in section 33 shall not be lower than that caused by the management service for qualitatively and quantitatively similar waste pursuant to section 32. Among other things, also the costs for dissemination of waste information, register-keeping and similar municipal tasks may be covered. A separate basic fee may be opted by the municipality for this purpose. A basic fee, where any, may also cover the costs incurred by the municipality for the establishment and maintenance of local reception sites for hazardous waste and other waste. Only a reasonable return of capital is acceptable.

578. The category, quality and amount of waste and density of pick-up serve as the technical grounds for specifying the amount of the fee. In addition, the collection and transportation conditions at the property and in the pick-up area, possible use of municipality-owned collection premises, and length of route in alleged separate transportation may be taken into account. Where it is difficult to reliably make clear the amount or quality of the waste, or where necessary in order to prevent environmental or health problems or to arrange the waste management, also the number of those inhabiting the property, the purpose of the property or other similar ground may be applied. Regarding the basic fee, the last-mentioned criteria are generally applicable. Basic fees are specified either by property or by household.

579. The detailed grounds for Municipal Waste Fees are laid down by the municipality, in the form of a Fee Fare Bylaw. A possibility to express opinion shall be served to the public. Information on the grounds, fee income and the use thereof, shall be publicly accessible, also on the Internet. An individual fee shall be decided upon by the Municipal Waste Management Authority, on the basis of the Fee Fare Bylaw. In a single case, where the fee appears to be unreasonably high or low, the fee may be determined otherwise than provided in the Fee Fare Bylaw, or left uncharged, given the amount of waste, the level of service in waste management arranged by the municipality, and the self-driven recovery and treatment provided in section 41(2–3) In any case, the grounds shall be equal and reasonable.

580. Technically a fee, pursuant to a detailed invoice, is payable to the municipality or to another body acting on behalf thereof. An objection against the invoice may be made to the Municipal Waste Management authority. The objection results to a reviewed invoice, changed or not. This again may be appealed to the Regional

Administrative Court and, if leave of appeal is granted, further to the SAC. In general, the practice with respect to exceptions has been rather strict.

581. Charges for waste transportation arranged by the property holders are also stipulated by the Waste Act (section 85). Such charges shall be equal and reasonable. In an offer to a property holder the grounds of the charge shall be clearly indicated. The invoices shall be appropriately specified. If the Municipal Waste Management Fee in respect to waste management is charged from the transportation operator, the share thereof shall be specified in an offer and an invoice.

The holder of waste is entitled to reduction of charge in cases of service failures specified in section 86 of the Act. It is not allowed to deviate from these provisions by agreement, as far as waste generated by dwelling is concerned.

582. On the Waste Tax, *see* General Introduction, Chapter 4, §3.

§8. Permits

I. Environmental Permits for Waste Management Operations

583. According to the pre-2000 legislation, a Waste Permit under the then Waste Act, being procedurally within the then Environmental Permit, was required for a number of operations and installations. Pursuant to (the previous and) the present Waste Act, there is no such separate permit any more, but an Environmental Permit under the Environmental Protection Act is required from respective waste management activities instead. Pursuant to paragraph 13 of Table 2 of Annex 1 to the present Environmental Protection Act, such activities encompass, e.g., all treatment of waste on a professional basis falling under the scope of the Waste Act. A few exceptions are listed in section 32 of the Environmental Protection Act.

584. An Environmental Permit shall contain necessary provisions on waste and waste management in pursuance of the Waste Act and of provisions based on it. If appropriate, a provision may be laid down on delivering mixed municipal waste, either recoverable or intended for disposal and for which the municipality is responsible under section 32 of the Waste Act, or other waste intended for disposal, to a treatment facility (section 58(1) of the Environmental Protection Act). A permit for waste treatment may be limited to apply to treatment of a certain type of waste (e.g., hazardous waste) only. A permit concerning the recovery or disposal of mixed municipal waste, for which the municipality is responsible (*see* section 32 of the Waste Act), or concerning the disposal of other waste, may, if necessary, stipulate that only waste originating in a certain area may be treated (section 58(2) of the Environmental Protection Act).

585. The regular preconditions for granting an Environmental Permit also apply to waste-related activities. In addition, the operator may be required to furnish sufficient collateral to secure the appropriate waste management, supervision and measures required for terminating operations, or thereafter (sections 59–61 of the

Environmental Protection Act). Other than waste management operators, when subject to a Permit, are obliged to furnish corresponding security if significant amounts of waste are generated in the operations. The collateral may be skipped where landfill is not at stake, if the costs to be covered by the collateral upon the termination of operations are minor in scale, considering the amount and quality of waste and other aspects. Collateral must be sufficient to facilitate the management of the necessary measures, considering the extent and nature of, and provisions issued regarding, the activity in question. Collateral for landfill shall also cover the costs incurred from monitoring, supervision and other aftercare following the closure of the landfill, for a minimum period of thirty years, unless the operator demonstrates that other measures are sufficient. Collateral for a waste area for extractive waste shall also cover the costs of restoring a land area, located within the area of impact of the waste area, to a satisfactory State, said restoration measures being defined in more detail in the Extractive Waste Management Plan. Acceptable collateral includes a guarantee, insurance or pledged deposit. The Permit may, for justified reasons, specify the form of collateral to be accepted and the other conditions of the collateral. The party posting collateral shall be a credit or insurance institution, or another commercial financial institution, domiciled in an EEA Member State. The collateral shall be furnished in favour of the supervisory authority before the commencement of operations. A collateral for an area for extractive waste shall be lodged before the disposal of extractive waste commences in the area. The Permit may stipulate that the operator shall periodically assess the adequacy of the collateral and inform the supervisory authority thereof. If necessary, the Permit provision concerning the collateral shall be amended. The Permit may also lay down that the supervisory authority may, on its own initiative or on the initiative of the operator, approve a modification of the amount of the collateral linked to an index reflecting the change in price levels.

586. The duration of the collateral shall be at least three months from the date on which the operations covered by the collateral are carried out and notified to the supervisory authority, either continuously or periodically renewed. Where the collateral is extended, renewal shall take place before it expires. The landfill collateral shall remain valid until the end of the monitoring and other aftercare following the closure of the landfill. Upon application, the permit authority shall release the collateral once the operator has fulfilled his obligations. The collateral may also be partially released. A decision on the expiry of a Permit and the ending of operations (or a decision following the notification of experimental activities) may provide that the collateral may be released by the supervisory authority once the operator has fulfilled his obligations. The supervisory authority shall have the right to proceed with the realization of the collateral when the operator has neglected to carry out the measures at stake. Before realizing the collateral, the supervisory authority shall order the operator to fulfil its obligations and shall enforce the order by conditional fine. The collateral may be used to cover the costs of the measures at stake.

587. Provisions on the waste management plans for ports are set out in the Act on Environmental Protection in Maritime Transport. *See* above Chapter 4, §8.

II. Permits and Plans Regarding Extractive Waste

588. A certain part of the waste-related provisions in the Environmental Protection Act (sections 111–115) solely applies to extractive waste, largely under permits for activities that are not waste management as such. On the other hand, an Environmental Permit is always required for Extractive Waste Management areas (Table 2 of Annex 1 to the Environmental Protection Act).

These provisions are intended to implement Directive 2006/21/EC on the management of waste from extractive industries and amending Directive 2004/35/EC (in common with certain provisions in the Soil Excavation Act, which may be applicable either alongside with or instead of the Environmental Protection Act, depending on the substance extracted, *see* Part II, Chapter 7). As extractive waste is regarded waste originating from the extraction of an organic or inorganic substance occurring in the earth's crust or from the storing, concentrating and other treatment in mining or comparable activity, concentrating plant, quarrying, other stone crushing or peat extraction.

589. An Environmental Permit regarding extractive waste shall include necessary provisions on the extractive waste, as well as on an Extractive Waste Management Plan and the enforcement thereof (section 113 of the Environmental Protection Act). An Extractive Waste Management Plan (on certain exceptions and the contents of the plan, *see* section 114 of the Environmental Protection Act) shall be required from the permit applicant and, if appropriate, be approved by the permit authority. The Environmental Permit shall additionally contain necessary provisions on the establishing, maintenance, use, closure and rehabilitation thereof.

590. Where the waste facility, due to its faulty functioning, constructional safety, hazardous waste or a chemical dangerous to the environment or health may pose significant risk to health, property or the environment (extractive waste facility causing risk of major accident), also an internal emergency plan is required (section 115 of the Environmental Protection Act). For such facilities, additional obligations have been laid down in the same section.

§9. Landfills

591. As to landfills (for which an Environmental Permit under the Environmental Protection Act is always needed), the Environmental Protection Act and the Waste Act are complemented by the specific Government decree on landfills (331/2013, repealing the previous Decree 861/1997 and remaining in force under the present Environmental Protection Act). The previous decree was originally based on the then proposal for an EC Directive on landfills, and it was later on aligned with the Directive. The requirements were at the outset rather far-reaching particularly with respect to many of the existing small landfills, although some provisions did not immediately concern the existing landfills. The requirements were why the total number of municipal landfills decreased significantly. Whether pollution of soil has occurred in the areas of landfills no more in use is another question (*see* Chapter 5 below).

592. The present Decree, as amended by 1030/2021, is rather extensive (fifty-three sections, annexes), and is aligned with Directive 1999/31/EC on the landfill of waste, the amendment Directive (EU) 2018/850, included, and other directives concerning waste hierarchy and landfill waste, and directives concerning mercury and POPs.

593. The Decree is not applicable to a site where only unpolluted soil waste or waste covered by the Government decree on Extractive Waste (190/2013) is deposited. Moreover, the Decree shall not apply to the placing of dredging mass classified as non-hazardous waste in water body or sea, or to the bottom of it or in the soil below it, or to the dumping of unpolluted dredging mass on land or on land near the waterway from which it has been removed.

594. In practice, the Decree on landfills is always applicable in Environmental Permit contexts pursuant to the Environmental Protection Act (*see* paragraph 131).

§10. Hazardous Waste

595. Waste is in principle 'hazardous' directly on the basis of the general definition (section 6 of the Act, *see* paragraph 508), but in practice the hazardous properties of waste and the limit values applicable to the interpretation of such properties are both specified in Annex 3 to the Government decree on Waste (*see* paragraph 516).

596. Hazardous waste may not be diluted or otherwise mixed with different waste or other substance (section 17). Derogation is, however, allowed, if mixing is necessary in order to treat the waste and there is a valid Environmental Permit for the operation. Where hazardous waste has been mixed in a manner contrary to the ban, separation shall be carried out where necessary in order to prevent risk or harm to the environment and technically possible. Hazardous waste shall be packed and labelled, and appropriate information thereon shall be provided so that the transfers and properties of the waste from place of origin to recovery or disposal can be followed, as provided in detail by Government decree (section 16). This obligation is not applicable to private households.

597. For treatment of hazardous waste, an Environmental Permit is always required (*see* Chapter 1, §9 above). The incineration of hazardous waste has been specifically stipulated in the Government decree on Incineration of Waste (151/2013, later amendments), through which the IED Directive 2010/75/EU has been implemented in detail regarding incineration of waste. The decree applies, with certain exception, to incineration in co-incineration plants, where solid or fluid waste pursuant to the Waste Act is incinerated, as specified in section 1 of the Decree. The incineration of hazardous waste in Finnish territorial waters and economic zone is forbidden (section 18 of the Waste Act).

598. The possibility to impose product-related regulations, bans or restrictions in a decree based on section 10 of the Waste Act (§12 below) may of course be particularly appropriate for hazardous waste. The Act on the restriction of the use of certain hazardous substances in electrical and electronic equipment (387/2013) and the respective Ministry of the Environment decree (419/2013, numerous amendments), as well as Government decree on batteries and accumulators (520/2014), based on both the Waste Act and the Environmental Protection Act, are also relevant.

§11. Specific Categories of Waste

599. The previous Waste Act entitled the Cabinet to give special decrees on waste management. Many of them have been repealed during the current Waste Act. Government decree 711/1998 on PCB waste remained in force also under the present Waste Act, but was later replaced by Government decree 958/2016 on restrictions on the use of PCB facilities and treatment of PCB waste, that being still in force.

600. The obligations regarding asbestos waste (separate collection and transport, etc.) are provided in section 32 of the Government decree on Waste and the testing and treatment of waste containing asbestos at landfills in several provisions of the Government decree on Landfills.

601. By virtue of the pre-2000 Water Act and the then Waste Act, the Government decree 112/1997 on the amalgam containing waste or wastewater from dental care activities has been issued at the same time. Here the EC Directive 83/189/EEC with its later amendments had been implemented. In 2018, the Mercury Regulation[36] and the Minamata Convention on Mercury[37] caused minor amendments in various acts such as the Chemicals Act, the Waste Act and the Environmental Protection Act, as well as in Government decree on Landfills, and also the Decree was repealed.

602. The specific obligations concerning the reducing of and obligations due to construction and demolition waste, in addition to the provisions in the Waste Act, are included in sections 25, 26 and 27 of the Government decree on Waste. Separate collection shall be arranged concerning at least eleven waste categories listed in section 26. The goal is that at least 70% by weight of construction and demolition waste is recovered otherwise than as energy or fuel, extracted soil and stone substances and hazardous waste excluded. When applying for a Building Permit or

36. Regulation (EU) 2017/852 on mercury, and repealing Regulation (EC) No. 1102/2008.
37. United Nations 2013.

Demolition Permit or submitting a demolition notification, a subject undertaking the project must present a demolition material and construction waste report, including estimates of the amounts of demolition materials generated in the construction or demolition project, as specified in section 16 of the Building Act (as of 1 January 2025).

603. Government decree on the use of certain wastes in earthworks (843/2017) aims to promote the recovery of certain waste categories in earthworks laying down such detailed preconditions under which Environmental Permit pursuant to the Environmental Protection Act becomes unnecessary.

604. Regarding oil waste management, section 30 of the Government decree on Waste lays down the duty of a holder of oil waste to arrange separate collection of different types of oil waste. In the treatment of oil waste, priority shall be given to the renewal or other recycling of waste oil, which leads to at least as good an environmental outcome as renewal. Moreover, provisions on the incineration of oil waste are laid down in the Government decree on the Incineration of Waste (151/2013).

605. Extractive waste (*see also* above 588–590) is stipulated essentially by the Environmental Protection Act, the Soil Excavation Act and the Mining Act, in connection with the permit mechanisms therein. There is moreover a specific Government decree on Extractive Waste (190/2013), aligned with Directive 2006/21/EC on the management of waste from extractive industries and amending Directive 2004/35/EC, and Commission Decisions 2009/335/EC, 2009/337/EC and 2009/358–360. The Decree applies to preparation and enforcement of Extractive Waste Management Plans, establishing, care, closure, and aftercare of sites for extractive waste, use of extractive waste in an empty quarry, and surveillance, monitoring and supervision of extractive waste. In accordance with Article 18(1) of the Directive, the Centre for Economic Development, Transport and the Environment of Kainuu region must report to the Commission every three years on the implementation of the Directive in Finland. In addition, in accordance with Articles 18(2) and 22(1)(a) of the Directive, the Centre shall annually submit to the Commission information on events notified by operators as provided for in the Decree. On the plans and permits, *see* above §8, II.

606. The sectoral decrees on producer responsibility, also referring to specific categories of waste, are envisaged below (§14, V–XI).

§12. Commercial and Industrial Rules

607. Section 9(1) of the Waste Act provides generally that all producers of products shall, in order to achieve the goals of the Act and according to the possibilities, see to it: (1) that raw materials are used sparingly and waste, raw materials made from waste and used product or parts thereof are used; (2) that use of raw materials harmful to the environment or health are avoided and replaced by less harmful raw material; (3) that such production methods are opted that waste is generated in as small quantities as possible and that the waste being generated is as harmless to the health and the environment as possible; (4) that products are not unnecessarily packed; (5) that the product is resource efficient, durable in terms of life cycle and life span, mendable, able to be updated and reusable, and recyclable as waste, and it as such and the use thereof generates waste in as small quantities as possible; (6) that the product as waste does not cause risk or harm to health or the environment, or littering, or significant harm or difficulty to waste management; and (7) products containing critical raw materials shall, where possible, be reused and recycled as waste. Much of this may of course be rather vague in practice. That is why the Cabinet may, in order to implement the duties in section 9(1) above, by a Government decree set forth more detailed provisions, as stipulated in section 10. In any case, those who place on the market or distribute products, shall, as far as possible and in order to achieve the goals of the Waste Act, *see* to it that the product meets the requirements under (4), (5), (6) and (7) above (section 9(3)).

608. Moreover (section 9(2)), the producer shall, where needed, see to it: (1) that the product is equipped with labels containing information on its properties facilitating the use, reuse, sorting, waste management and the directing of producer responsibility, or that similar information is attached to the product; (2) the users are informed on the labelling and the significance thereof, and on the arrangements of sorting, reuse and waste management; and (3) that the operators in waste management are informed on the labelling and the significance thereof, on the dismantling and recycling of the product and on the location of hazardous substances and parts in the product, and (4) that there is access to spare parts, instruction manuals, technical information, or other instruments, equipment or software, enabling high-quality repair and safe reuse of products. The requirements above may be provided further in detail be Government decree, as provided in section 10. In any case, those who place on the market or distribute products, shall, as far as possible and in order to achieve the goals of the Waste Act, see to it that the labelling and information rules in section 9(2) are observed (section 9(3)).

609. If in the production, use or discarding of a product such waste is generated that has been found to pose, or may reasonably be expected to pose, significant harm or difficulty to waste management, or risk or harm to health or to the environment, the production, placing on the market, export or use may be banned or stipulate restrictions or conditions thereon (section 9(4)). The bans, restrictions and conditions may be provided further in detail be Government decree, as provided in section 10.

610. Requirements for packaging and labelling of (any) waste, as well information duties in respect to them are laid down in section 7 of the Government decree on Waste. Specific requirements for packaging of hazardous waste are in section 8, and labelling duties regarding hazardous waste in section 9.

611. An Oil Waste Fee was collected from manufacturers and importers of lubricating oil and oil products of certain types under a special Act (894/1986, as amended later on). The funds were used for purposes of oil waste and other hazardous waste management and as subsidies for the establishment and use of reception facilities of hazardous wastes. The Act has been repealed from 1 January 2020 onwards.

§13. International Transfer of Waste

612. The Waste Shipments Regulation[38] applies to international transfer of waste. By international transfer of waste the Waste Act refers to shipments of waste from Finland to another country, import from another country to Finland and transfer of waste through Finland. There are several complementary provisions in the Waste Act (in particular Chapter 12) and on decree-level.

The Finnish Environment Institute is the competent authority and contact person referred to in the regulation and has the supervisory and cooperation tasks pursuant to the regulation (section 22(3) of the Waste Act). Also, the customs supervise international transfers regarding import and export. The customs shall, when necessary, stop an unlawful transfer and notify the case to the Finnish Environment Institute, which shall decide on further measures without delay (section 117).

613. In addition to the provisions in the regulation and elsewhere in the Waste Act, waste may be transferred for disposal, and mixed municipal waste for recovery, from Finland to another country only, when one of the following five requirements options is met (section 109 of the Waste Act): (1) Finland lacks the technical and economic prerequisites or the necessary treatment plants to treat the waste appropriately. (2) The waste is treated in another country in such a way that is essentially better to the environment than treatment in Finland. (3) The waste is treated in another country in such a way that would be acceptable in regard to environmental protection in Finland and the costs of which are essentially lower. (4) The transfer takes place in order to test a new treatment method or for other experiment purposes. (5) The transfer of waste other than hazardous is based on the regional cooperation between municipalities in Finland and Sweden or in Finland and Norway.

614. In addition to the provisions in the regulation and elsewhere in the Waste Act, waste may be transferred for treatment to Finland only when disposal of waste generated in Finland or recovery of mixed municipal waste there is not prevented or delayed due to the transfer (section 110 of the Waste Act). Regarding transfers of waste for disposal, it is moreover required that one of the following conditions is met: (1) hazardous waste is combusted in a specialized plant; (2) waste is treated biologically or physically or chemically; or (3) the disposal into soil, on earth or in a specially designated landfill or the incineration of waste other than hazardous is based on the regional cooperation between municipalities in Finland and Sweden or in Finland and Norway.

---

38. Regulation (EC) No. 1013/2006 of 14 Jun. 2006 on shipments of waste.

615. Additionally, the Finnish Environment Institute is empowered to forbid an international transfer of waste due to offences specified in section 111 and in exceptional contexts issue an export ban or exclude the general export ban, as provided in section 112. A pre-consent for facility in Finland according to Article 14 of Regulation 1013/2006, where possible, is also decided upon by the Finnish Environment Institute pursuant to provisions in section 114. A consent or pre-consent issued by the institute can be withdrawn or changed by the institute as provided in section 115.

§14. Producer Responsibility

I. Holder Responsibility as a Starting Point

616. A general starting point in the Waste Act is that it is the duty of the holder of waste, who most often also is the producer of the waste, to take care of waste management with respect to the particular waste and to cover the costs caused by the waste (sections 20 and 28 of the Waste Act), *see* §6 above.

II. Shifting to Producer Responsibility

617. However, the duty of the holder of waste may be changed into the duty of the producer of the product in which the waste originates (the producer here is of course not the same as the producer of waste). By means of this producer responsibility the waste management costs caused by the product are finally included in the prices and hence internalized in market mechanisms. It should be noted here that, unlike in the basic structure of the Waste Act, producer here refers to the importer or manufacturer of a product, not to the immediate producer of waste.

This change was initially made possible by force of special decrees under the 1993 Waste Act. Initially in 1994, a whole new Chapter 3a (452/2004 and 277/2008) on producer responsibility was inserted in the 1993 Waste Act, complemented with detailed sectoral decrees. The provisions were in part directly aimed at the implementing of Directive 94/62/EC of 20 December 1994 on packaging and packaging waste, Directive 2000/53/EC of 18 September 2000 on end-of-life vehicles, Directive 2002/96/EC of 27 January 2003 on Waste Electrical and Electronic Equipment (WEEE) and Directive 2006/66/EC of 6 September 2006 on batteries and accumulators and waste batteries and accumulators and repealing Directive 91/157/EEC.

618. In the 2010 Waste Act, the provisions on producer responsibility, transposing the corresponding parts of the Waste Framework Directive, are contained in Chapter 6 (sections 46–71). A separate Chapter 7 stipulates the responsibility on beverage packaging. The Government decrees issued by virtue of the 1993 Waste Act remained valid so far, where not contrary to the 2011 Waste Act (section 148 of the Waste Act). Some of the previous product-specific decrees on producer responsibility are hence still partly applicable, but some have in turn been replaced by new ones, taking also the Waste Framework Directive 2008/98/EC and other directives into account. In the reform of 2021 several new and updated provisions on producer liability were enacted and especially provisions on packaging waste (section 49a–d, 714/2021), engaging also the municipalities, were inserted in the very Waste Act.

III. Contents of Responsibility

619. In the producer-based legislative approach, the original right of other stakeholders, municipalities included, to arrange the management of waste has under producer responsibility been somewhat reduced in favour of the (duty and right of the) producer. Within producer responsibility, a producer has, as a main rule, to take care of the waste management and the costs incurred thereof, regarding discarded products that are delivered to the appropriate reception sites or transportation (section 46(1)). The responsibility of the producer applies to products that have been placed on the market in Finland by the producer himself, to products sold directly to users by distance and to a reasonable (in proportion to their amount or respective share of the market) share of corresponding products placed on the market, irrespective of the time thereof (section 46(2)). The producer of the product takes priority to arrange the waste management of the discarded products within his responsibility. Other operators in turn are allowed to establish collection or reception systems for discarded products or provide connected only in cooperation with the producer (section 47(1)). However, services associated with reuse of products or preparation thereof, are free to all operators (section 47(2)). Moreover, a municipality is allowed, within the waste management arranged by it under Chapter 5, complement the transportation and reception of discarded products insofar this has not been arranged by the producer. The discarded products shall hereby be delivered for waste management arranged by the producer (section 47(3)). The joint obligation of a municipality and the packaging producer affiliation to organize the collection of packaging waste by property is provided in section 49a–d (*see* paragraphs 637, 641 and 644).

620. Producer responsibility covers the following products and professional producers who place them on the market or sell directly to users by distance (section 48 of the Waste Act):

(1) the tyres of motor vehicles and other vehicles and devices; as producers thereof are regarded manufacturers, importers and retreaders of tyres or importers of vehicles or pieces of equipment equipped with a tyre;
(2) passenger cars, delivery cars and other comparable vehicles; as producers are regarded and professional importers of cars, as well as brokers who bring into the country in the name of a domestic user;
(3) electricity or electronic devices and the producers thereof; as producers are regarded manufacturers and such importers of electricity or electronic devices and such vendors who offer such devices using own product brand;[39]

39. On responsibility regarding electricity or electronic devices used outside households and placed on the market before 14 Aug. 2005, *see* s. 53(1), (410/2014).

(4) batteries and accumulators and the producers thereof; those contained by electricity or electronic devices, vehicles and other products included; as producers are regarded those who place on the market batteries or accumulators;[40]
(5) newspapers, magazines, office paper products and comparable paper products; as producers are regarded manufacturers and importers of printing paper or paper used in the manufacturing of printed paper products;
(6) packaging; as a producer thereof is regarded a packer of the product or the importer of the packaged product; however, packaging used for packaging food and other products at the point of sale directly to consumers (*service packaging*) and packaging used for packaging unprocessed agricultural and horticultural products (*'farmer's packaging'*) shall be deemed to be produced by the manufacturer or importer;
(7) single-use plastic products include beverage cups sold empty to end-users and their caps and lids which are considered to have been produced by the manufacturer or importer of the product;
(8) single-use plastic products include wet wipes for personal care and consumer use, the producer of which is considered to be the manufacturer or importer of the product;
(9) single-use plastic products include consumer balloons, the producer of which is considered to be the manufacturer or importer of the product;
(10) single-use plastic products include tobacco products with filters and tobacco filters for which the manufacturer or importer of the product is considered to be the producer; and
(11) fishing gear containing plastic, the producer of which is considered to be the manufacturer or importer of the product.

However, producer responsibility does not apply to producers of bale feed packaging material.

The products and producers at stake may be specified by Government decree.

The following producers shall nevertheless only be responsible for the costs of waste management and cleaning operations carried out by municipalities in accordance with section 48b: (1) producers of personal care and consumer wet wipes belonging to single-use plastic products; (2) producers of consumer balloons belonging to single-use plastic products; (3) producers of tobacco products with filters and tobacco filters belonging to single-use plastic products. The cost liability of the producers here applies to products placed on the Finnish market by the producer and products sold directly to users by distance selling, as well as to a share of other similar products considered reasonable in relation to the producer's market share, regardless of the time the products were placed on the market.

The producers of single-use plastic products referred to in section 48(1)(6–10) shall bear the costs of waste management and cleaning operations carried out by municipalities in the areas defined in section 48c annually and by product group, as provided for in section 48b. Section 48c refers to street and square areas where the municipality is responsible for clean-up and to certain other areas possessed or

40. On derogations based on agreement between the holder (other than in household) and the producer, *see* s. 53(2).

arranged by the municipality. Determination of the producer's responsibility for costs is determined in section 48d and reporting and reimbursement of municipal waste management and cleaning costs in section 48e. In order to be entitled to compensation paid by the producer, the municipality must notify the Centre for Economic Development, Transport and the Environment of Pirkanmaa region annually by the end of May of its waste management and cleaning costs for the previous year. The Centre for Economic Development, Transport and the Environment of Pirkanmaa makes the decisions on the compensation to be paid to the municipalities. The decision shall specify the compensation of each producer affiliation and producer by product group, and the decision shall indicate the total amount of compensation paid to each municipality. The producer affiliation and producer must pay the compensation to the Centre, which will then pay them to the municipalities. The producer shall pay the costs of collecting and remitting the compensation to the authorities. The producers shall jointly carry out a survey of the composition of waste collected by the municipality from the areas referred to in section 48c and the litter cleaned up (composition study) at least every three years. Municipalities must provide producers with the information required for the survey and otherwise assist in the implementation of the survey. The report must be submitted to the Ministry of the Environment (section 48f). The municipality must organize the collection of waste caused by tobacco products at stake in the areas referred to in section 48c, as well as advice and information related to the said products and waste in accordance with section 51 of the Act. A Government decree may lay down more detailed provisions on the minimum number and placement of waste containers intended for tobacco waste and on the content of information and advice, excluding information on reusable alternatives.

621. Producer responsibility, as modified in Chapter 7, also applies to the packaging return system and the taxpayers according to the Act on the Excise Duty on Certain Beverage Packaging (1037/2004), as explained in VII below.

622. Pursuant to Chapter 6, a producer shall arrange such a network of sites for the receiving of discarded products within producer responsibility that the products may be freely and easily delivered. In determining the sufficient number of sites within different areas the category, quality and anticipated quantity of the discarded products at stake, as well as the environmental impacts and costs incurred by reception and transportation, shall be taken into account (section 49(1)). The quantities may be different for different product categories and areas. The number of sufficient sites may be stipulated further by Government decree. The dissemination of information regarding sites for the receiving of discarded products is stipulated in section 51 and by decree.

As to paper products, the producer shall nevertheless arrange free transportation from the delivery site of a property, provided that the property is not located within scattered settlement or an area with detached houses (section 49(2)). The property owners at stake in turn shall arrange delivery sites for discarded paper products (section 50).

623. The reuse of discarded products shall in connection to the receiving by the producer be enhanced (section 52). Undamaged and mendable products or parts thereof shall, where appropriate, be kept apart or separated. In order to promote reuse, the producer shall, as far as possible, see to it that holders of products and operators who arrange the waste management of discarded products are furnished with necessary information the possibilities to dismantle and reuse of the product and its parts and on the location of hazardous substances and parts in the product.

624. The producer shall regularly and systematically monitor the fulfilment of the obligations on producer responsibility and develop the reliability of the relevant information (*self-monitoring*). If necessary, self-monitoring shall be supported by regular inspections by an independent and professional person. The producer shall draw up a written self-monitoring plan and attach it to the application for admission to the Producer Register (section 53a). The self-monitoring plan shall contain at least the information specified in section 53a.

625. The obligations of the producer on bookkeeping and notifications to the national[41] supervisory body (the Centre for Economic Development, Transport and the Environment of Pirkanmaa region) are defined in section 54 of the Waste Act. The provisions may be specified further by Government decree. After having been registered in the Producer Register (section 142), the producer, when delivering a product to a distributor, shall inform the latter on being registered (section 55).

626. A holder of waste is entitled to deliver any of the following products aimed to be discarded to a retail site of the distributor or other easily accessible site, without charge:

> (1) portable batteries and accumulators, without an obligation to buy a new product; (2) in households originated and comparable electricity or electronic devices, if a new one is bought instead; and (3) tyres of motor vehicles and other vehicles and devices, if they correspond in quality and quantity the new tyres being bought (section 56). Where discarded batteries and accumulators from vehicles in private use are received by a retailer of corresponding batteries and accumulators, no charge or obligation to buy is allowed. The customers shall be informed on their rights (section 57). The producer is obliged to arrange and finance the transportation of the discarded products collected by the distributor (section 49(3)).

627. A holder of an end-of-life vehicle shall deliver the vehicle to a collector or a pretreatment operator that operates in the name of the producer (section 58). The operator shall serve the holder a certificate of destruction, after having checked the right of the holder to deliver the vehicle. The Finnish Transport and Communications Agency Traficom shall be notified (section 59). Certain extra devices in the vehicle may entitle the collector or a pretreatment operator to require fee for the costs of corresponding extra waste management (section 60).

41. With the exception of Åland.

628. Provisions on the collateral required from producers of electrical and electronic equipment are included in section 61 of the Waste Act.

629. To implement the EU provisions on producer responsibility, the following may be provided by Government decree under section 67: (1) serving of information on the waste management costs in the price of a product; (2) derogation from the obligation of a producer or a distributor to receive a discarded product, and exceptional arrangements of waste management in respect to this, if the product is contaminated and hence poses a health or safety risk to the personnel; and (3) obligation of a producer or a producer affiliation to favour such providers of services that have certified environmental management systems in place.

630. In addition to the general provisions on administrative enforcement in sections 126 and 129 of the Waste Act, specific provisions on rectification concerning producer responsibility are contained in section 128. If a producer or producer affiliation or the operator of a beverage packaging return system has not arranged reuse, recycling, other recovery or other waste management based on producer responsibility, or if it has not complied with the obligation to pay compensation or to carry out a composition study, the Centre for Economic Development, Transport and the Environment of Pirkanmaa region may: (1) oblige the producer, producer affiliation or operator of the return system for beverage packaging to comply with the Act and the rules or regulations issued thereunder and to prove that the changes have been made; and (2) prohibit the producer from placing the product on the market until the producer has been approved or entered in the Producer Register of producers or until the producer has fulfilled his payment obligation or the obligation to carry out a composition study.

IV. Producer Affiliations

631. The obligations of single producers under the Waste Act shall be transferred to non-profit producer affiliations, established and made up of producers, and producers only, and registered in the Producer Register (sections 62, 101–107 and 142). As to packaging producers, all packaging materials shall from 2021 onwards be covered by the producer affiliation at stake. The sector of a packaging producer affiliation shall cover all packaging materials and beverage cups sold empty. Also an individual producer may by the Centre for Economic Development, Transport and the Environment of Pirkanmaa region be accepted directly in the Producer Register, but only if accession to the producer affiliation would be manifestly unnecessary, given the nature and extent of the activity,

632. A new registered producer in the branch is entitled to join, subject to equal and conditions, in order to fulfil his obligations by the affiliation at stake. A producer of beverage packaging may, however, fulfil his obligations under producer responsibility also by joining the return system for beverage packaging (*see* VII below). Within a producer affiliation, the obligations shall be shared between the producers in a balanced way, paying attention to the quality and quantity of the activity, and avoiding barriers to trade and distortion of competition. A producer affiliation shall keep a publicly accessible, up-to-date list of producers the responsibility of whom has been transferred to the affiliation (section 63).

633. Several provisions in the Waste Act, as amended and partly inserted in 2021, refer to the activities of producer affiliations (section 63), contributions by the producers and their adjustment (section 63a), safeguarding the operations of the producers and producer affiliations (section 64), cooperation between producers and producer affiliations (section 65), service procurement by producer affiliations (section 66), authorized representative of producer or other operator (section 66a), serving as an authorized representative in Finland (section 66b), and cooperation task force of producer responsibility systems (section 66c).

634. The producers of different categories of products and the corresponding producer affiliations shall, in appropriate cooperation, see to it that the implementation of producer responsibility does not result in double charges, when different wastes are taken care of in cooperation. Compulsory cooperation may be provided by Government decree under section 65.

V. Discarded Tyres

635. Government decree (1246/1995, amendment 583/2004) on the recycling and treatment of discarded tyres, issued by virtue of the previous Waste Act, has from 8 July 2013 on been replaced by the Government decree on Separate Collection and Recycling of Discarded Tyres (527/2013), this being fully applicable instead of the previous decree from 2015. Amendments have been made in 2021.

Each producer of tyres shall arrange the separate collection and recycling so that yearly the amount corresponding to 95% mass of the tyres placed on the market are prepared for reuse, recovered or otherwise utilized (section 2). To fulfil the obligation in section 49(1) of the Waste Act, the producer shall arrange a priceless and convenient reception of discarded tyres in the whole country. The number of sites of reception shall be at least 350, and there shall as a rule be at least one site of reception, in each municipality (section 3). The tyre distributors must accept end-of-life tyres in their sales facilities free of charge, if they correspond to the ones the customer purchases in terms of type and quantity (section 56(1)(3) of the Waste Act). The stores must also inform consumers of the opportunity to hand over their tyres. Other provisions of the decree stipulate dissemination of information, information and notification duties, economic preconditions and applications. Provisions on self-monitoring (section 4b) have been inserted in 2021. Other new or updated provisions include information on the reception of discarded tyres (section 4), obligation of the authorized representative to inform (section 4a), contributions from producers (section 4c), report on financial arrangements and action plan for organizing reuse and waste management (section 5), producer's application for approval to the Producer Register (section 6), application by the producer affiliation for approval to the Producer Register (section 7), notification of changes in operations (section 8) and reporting of monitoring data (section 9).

VI. Packaging and Packaging Waste

636. The EC Directive on packaging and packaging waste (94/62/EC) was implemented through a decree under the previous Waste Act, i.e., Government decree on packaging and packaging waste (962/1997; amendments), in force from 1 December 1997. The Decree remained in force also under the present Waste Act, but was replaced by a new, identically titled one (518/2014), in order to implement the current EU legislation on packaging and packaging waste. In connection to the 2021 amendments of the Waste Act, a new Government decree on packaging and packaging waste (1029/2021) replaced the previous one from 1 December 2021 on. The obligations of a producer are mainly not applied to producers the turnover of which is less than EUR 1,000,000 (section 48(2) of the Waste Act).

637. Producer responsibility applies to companies that pack their products or import packed products. The responsibility is not total, however. The original Decree (1997) was based on a general acceptance among different interested parties, although this was not easy in all respects, because the decree was not only a matter between the government and the packaging industries. For example, the municipalities, having a general responsibility of waste management in their respective areas, had also to be taken into account. The difficulty to reconcile the interests and roles of the municipalities and the packaging producers has remained, and a totally new approach was approved in the 2021 amendments of the Waste Act (section 49a–d).

638. From 2021, the municipalities and the packaging producer affiliation shall agree by agreement covering at least two-thirds of the inhabitants of Finland to organize separate packaging waste collection concerning waste resulting from the activities under Article 32(1) of the Waste Act, in cooperation and in such a way that (1) the collection by property organized by municipalities and the regional reception organized by the producer affiliation constitute a geographically comprehensive collection network, taking into account population density, which serves the property holders well; (2) packaging waste is recovered efficiently and its quality is suitable for recycling; (3) packaging waste is collected together with other wastes of the same material as far as possible; and (4) the collection and transport of waste is arranged in a cost-effective manner and in such a way that emissions to the environment and the damage to the comfort and safety of the living environment are minimized (section 49a of the Waste Act, 704/2021).

639. Moreover, the municipalities and the packaging producer affiliation shall cooperate in (1) providing adequate advice and information and otherwise improving the sorting of packaging waste on buildings and (2) monitoring the effectiveness and efficiency of separate collection and assessing the need for further measures to increase the amount of packaging waste collected or to improve the quality of packaging waste (section 49a). The producer affiliation shall annually submit the Centre for Economic Development, Transport and the Environment of Pirkanmaa region a summary of the agreement and its implementation in the previous year, as provided in section 49d.

640. In the case of non-agreement, the producer affiliation may initiate mediation by notifying the Ministry of the Environment. The Ministry shall immediately consult both parties and make a proposal for reconciliation (section 49d of the Act). For the case that no contract is reached within six months after the notification, the duties of the producers and the municipalities are laid down in section 49d(2). If an individual municipality does not accede to the contract, the applicable sanctions are provided in section 49d(3).

641. Compensation to municipalities and cost responsibility of packaging producers is provided in section 49d of the Act. In the contract pursuant to Article 49a (above) the parties shall, by packaging materials, agree upon the compensation to be paid by the producer affiliation to the municipalities for the separate collection and transport of packaging waste from residential properties to waste management organized by the producer. Compensation shall be paid to municipalities on the basis of the most equitable criteria possible, taking into account the amount of packaging waste collected and the circumstances by areas affecting the efficiency of the collection. Municipalities shall ensure that the compensation is fully taken into account and by material when setting waste fees for separately collected packaging waste (section 49b(1) of the Act). As a result, the producers shall bear at least 80% of the total cost of packaging waste management, calculated on a packing materials basis, as specified in section 49b(2).

642. The following general annual targets (section 7 of the 2021 Government decree on packaging and packaging waste) are in force: (1) used packaging in total at least 90% by weight of packaging placed on the market and delivered to reuse are reused or recycled; (2) at least 65% by weight of the amount of packaging waste which corresponds to the amount of packaging placed on the market by January 2025 are reused or recycled; and (3) at least 70% by weight of the amount of packaging waste which corresponds to the amount of packaging placed on the market by January 2030 are reused or recycled. In assessing the achievement of (2) and (3), the level of the targets may be adjusted by a maximum of five percentage points by deducting the average share of reusable sales packages placed on the market for the first time in the previous three years in all sales packages placed on the market. The maintainer of the beverage packaging return system pursuant to section 68 of the Waste Act is deemed to meet the objectives set out in (1), (2) and (3) if it fulfils the recycling obligations laid down in the Government decree on the Return System of Beverage Packaging (526/2013). Producers of packaging not covered by the return system for beverage containers shall contribute to ensuring that the recycling targets are met.

The producer (and the maintainer of the beverage packaging return system) shall arrange the separate collecting and recycling by materials so that from 1 January 2025 by weight at least 50% (plastic), 25% (wood), 70% (iron metal), 70% (aluminium metal), 70% (glass) or 75% (paper and board) and from 1 January 2030 by weight at least 55% (plastic), 30% (wood), 80% (iron metal), 80% (aluminium metal), 75% (glass) or 85% (paper and board) of the mass of all packaging waste of the respective material placed in the market is recycled (section 8 of the Decree). In assessing the achievement of the objectives above, the level of the targets may be adjusted by a maximum of five percentage points by deducting the share of reusable sales packages placed on the market for the first time during the previous three years in all sales packages containing the material concerned. The maintainer of a beverage packaging return system pursuant to section 68 of the Waste Act shall be deemed to fulfil the objectives above if it fulfils the recycling obligations laid down in the Government decree on the Return System of Beverage Packaging. Producers of packaging not covered by the return system for beverage containers shall contribute to ensuring that the recycling targets are met.

643. When assessing the achievement of the targets in sections 7 and 8, the weight of recycled packaging waste may only take into account packaging discarded in Finland that is actually recycled and processed as new products, materials or substances in Finland or another country and for which non-recyclable waste materials have been removed by the necessary pretreatment measures. However, the weight of wood packaging repaired for reuse and the weight of metals separated and recycled after incineration may be taken into account, depending on the proportion of packaging waste in the incinerated waste (section 9). Packages of composite materials and other packages of more than one material shall be calculated and indicated according to each material contained in the package. Certain exceptions are allowed. Packaging waste exported outside the EU for preparation or recycling may be taken into account as provided in section 9. The calculation of the recycling rate shall comply with the accounting rules laid down in Article 6a of Directive 94/62/EC and in accordance with Commission decision 2005/270/EC on database tables.

644. Regarding the collection network for household packaging waste arranged by the producer (section 49(1) of the Waste Act), the producer shall see to that the following minimum requirements concerning level of service and accessibility are met (section 10): (1) the network of bring points covers the whole country, including bring points outside the areas where collection and waste management are most profitable; (2) the bring points are placed equally, taking into account population density and the separate collection of packaging waste from buildings organized pursuant to section 49a of the Waste Act; (3) the bring stations are placed at groceries or other customarily used services or on commonly used traffic routes; (4) for separate collecting of glass, metal plastic, paper and board packaging waste at least 1,000 bring points are provided so that they serve as well as possible properties that are excluded from the separate collection from properties. Moreover, the producer shall, as provided in section 49 of the Waste Act, arrange a sufficient amount of reception facilities all over the country for the separate collection of packaging waste not generated in housing and for the reception of packaging waste collected separately from residential properties. The reception facilities must be located equally by areas so that they serve well the reception of packaging waste collected from properties. The joint obligation of municipalities and a packaging producer affiliation to organize separate collection of packaging waste by property is laid down in section 49a of the Waste Act (*see also* paragraphs 637 and 641).

Separate collecting shall be arranged in a way that the packaging is emptied and, when needed, cleaned so that no amounts of residues of food or other substances, if not insignificant, are contained. Other waste may be mixed only if the receiving producer has allowed reception of such used packaging (section 11).

645. The decree also contains essential requirements of a packaging. Pursuant to section 4, any packaging placed on the market shall meet the essential requirements laid down in Annex 2 to the Decree concerning production, composition, reusability and recoverability. Where packaging complies with a harmonized standard or a standard notified to the Commission in compliance with the Package and Packaging Directive, the reference number of which has been published in the Official Journal of the EU, the packaging is considered to meet the essential requirements.

646. Pursuant to section 5 of the Decree, any packaging or part of it placed on the market shall not contain lead, cadmium, mercury or hexavalent chromium in packaging or its components more than 100 parts per million by weight, as, subject to certain exceptions and supervision thereof, is specified in section 5. Markings on packaging are provided in section 6.

647. In the communication of information, it has to be ensured that users of packaging and consumers receive the necessary information, among other things, on the obligations on separate collection and instructions on collecting, as well as on available systems (section 13).

648. Due to the 2021 amendments of the Waste Act, the previous sectoral packaging waste producer affiliations have ceased and a new common producer affiliation, the limited company *Suomen Pakkaustuottajat Oy (SPT)* has started.

649. An affiliation shall, by 30 September each year, provide the Centre for Economic Development, Transport and the Environment of Pirkanmaa region an account on and a plan on further management (section 15).

650. The Centre for Economic Development, Transport and the Environment of Pirkanmaa region shall annually collect the data received pursuant to section 19, as well as assess the amount of packaging used and the gained grades of reuse, recycling and recovery (section 22). An annual report to the Commission shall be submitted in eighteen months from the end of the calendar year at stake. Self-monitoring is provided in section 20 and market surveillance in section 23.

VII. Beverage Packaging

651. As to the return system for deposit beverage packaging (glass, metal or plastic) based on bottle and can recycling, a deviating producer responsibility scheme is applicable (Chapter 7 of the Waste Act comprising sections 68–71, as amended by 724/2021). Here a return system may be established and maintained by a beverage packaging producer within producer responsibility under section 48 or a taxpayer according to the Act on the Excise Duty on Certain Beverage Packaging

(1037/2004), alone or jointly with other producers or taxpayers. A producer or taxpayer may also join such an existing return system where new members are accepted. The provisions in Chapter 7 if the Waste Act on producers and producer affiliations are partly applied, as specified in section 69 of the Waste Act. Within a return system, the obligations shall be shared between the producers and taxpayers in a balanced way, paying attention to the quality and quantity of the activity, and avoiding barriers to trade and distortion of competition. Balanced and equal conditions shall be applied to new members. Requirements to a functioning return system are laid down in section 69. The provisions on producer affiliations are here applicable in several respects. The provisions on the labelling of beverage packaging are contained in section 70. A retailer of beverages in recyclable bottles and cans as referred to in the Act on the Excise Duty on Certain Beverage Packaging is obliged to receive from customers such an amount of empty packaging that is reasonable in respect to the retailed beverages of similar return category, and pay the customer a return reward (section 71).

652. In addition to sections 68–71 of the Waste Act, the Government decree on the Return System of Certain Beverage Packaging (180/2005) continued to stipulate on detailed level the packaging return system also under the current Waste Act. From July 2013 on it was replaced by a new Government decree on the Return System of Beverage Packaging (526/2013), that being still valid. The deposit for a metal beverage shall be (section 2) in the minimum EUR 0.15, for plastic beverage packaging of more than 0.35 litres and less than 1.0 litre in the minimum EUR 0.20, for plastic beverage packaging of more than 1.0 litre in the minimum EUR 0.40, and for other beverage packaging in the minimum EUR 0.10.

The maintainer of the return system shall arrange the reception, reuse and recycling of packaging within the system so that of the amount of packaging corresponding to the amount placed on the market by the members of the system is yearly returned as follows (section 3): of reusable beverage packaging at least 90% mass is returned to use, and of one filling beverage packaging at least 90% mass (of other than metal packaging 80% until 2015) is returned to be used as material. The requirements are applied to a maintainer of a new return system only after the third full calendar year following the outset. Other provisions of the Decree deal with economic preconditions, applications and notifications.

VIII. Disused Paper

653. From the 1980s, collecting and sorting of discarded paper and board at households and municipalities has been promoted by the Municipal Waste Management Bylaws. From 1 January 1999, formal producer responsibility was established by the Government decree on the Recovery of Disused Paper (883/1998). Under the present Waste Act, the Decree initially continued to be in force, but was from 8 July 2013 on replaced by a new Government decree on Separate Collection and Recycling of Disused Paper (528/2013), being fully applicable from 2015 and still in force. From 15 March onwards it is replaced by a new decree (528/2023).

654. The present Decree encompasses all newspapers, magazines, direct marketing publications, telephone catalogues, post order catalogues, envelopes, office paper and other similar paper products (but not books, and not package board). Pursuant to section 3, the producers shall arrange that yearly an amount corresponding at least 85 mass per cent of such items placed on the market is recovered.

655. In order to comply with the obligation laid down in section 49(1) of the Waste Act, the producer must arrange a free and, for the paper holder, effortless reception of disused paper throughout the country for the separate collection of disused paper generated on properties located in detached households or dispersed settlement. In the reception it organizes, the producer shall ensure that the following minimum requirements concerning the level of service and accessibility are met: (1) the network of reception points covers the whole country so that there are reception points also outside areas where collection and waste management are most profitable; (2) the reception points are equal by area, taking into account population density and the transport of recovered paper from properties arranged in the area in accordance with section 49(2) of the Waste Act; and (3) reception points are located in connection with normally used services, along commonly used access routes or otherwise so that they serve properties located in detached house areas and sparsely populated areas as well as possible. Section 49(2) of the Waste Act lays down provisions concerning the producer's obligation to arrange the transport of recovered paper from properties located elsewhere than in detached houses and sparsely populated areas. The related duties on dissemination of information are provided in section 5.

656. According to Article 4 of the Decree, the adjustment of fees referred to in Article 63a(2) of the Waste Act does not apply when determining contributions by producers. The contributions may be waived from section 63a(1) of the Waste Act. In such cases, the fees must be determined so that their share is not unreasonably high compared to the amount of paper products placed on the market by the producer and the fees arising from their waste management and other producer responsibility obligations.

657. The obligations of the authorized representative of an operator established in another country to provide information are laid down in section 6, reports by producer affiliation or producer on the financial arrangements and an action plan for arranging waste management in section 7, on a producer's application for acceptance into the producer register in section 8, on a producer affiliation's application for acceptance into the Producer Register in section 9, on notifications of changes in operations in section 10, on notification of monitoring data in section 11, on the compilation of monitoring data in section 12 and on self-monitoring in section 13.

IX. Waste Electrical and Electronic Equipment

658. In addition to the specific provisions of the Waste Act concerning the waste management of WEEE based on the principle of producer responsibility, the provisions of the present Government decree on WEEE (519/2014) are applicable with respect to reducing the quantity and harmfulness of WEEE, promoting preparation of reuse, recycling and other forms of recovery of WEEE and improving the standard in treatment of WEEE. The provisions aim to implement in detail Directive 2012/19/EU of 4 July 2012 on WEEE. The decree applies (from 15 August 2018) to electrical and electronic equipment that falls within the categories set out in Annex 2, but not to certain equipment specified in the Decree. Several amendments have been made in 2021 (1026/2021).

659. The relevant notions are defined in section 2 of the Decree. The obligations of producers correspondingly apply to producer affiliations. The detailed contents of and registration applications of producers and producer affiliations are provided in sections 15 and 16 of the Decree and the notifications by producer affiliations in section 19.

660. The producers of electrical and electronic equipment and those who place such equipment on the market shall, in addition to section 9 of the Waste Act, see to that no such methods are used in design and production which intentionally hamper the repair, update or reuse of used electrical and electronic equipment or the dismantling or recycling of WEEE, unless overriding advantages with regard to the protection of the environment and safety requirements are presented. In design and production care shall also be taken to that a user or an independent expert easily can remove the battery or accumulator in the equipment. The equipment shall contain information on safe removal, as a main rule, and, where needed, the type of the battery or accumulator (section 3 of the Decree).

661. The minimum collection rates for the producers of WEEE have been laid down in section 4. A collection rate of 65% by weight, as specified in section 4 (1026/2021), is in force from 1 January 2019.

662. WEEE shall be collected separately (section 5 of the Decree). Prior to any further transfer from the collection points other than those at distributors, care shall be taken of that reuse companies and organizations are reserved the possibility to assess and acquire such appliances and components thereof which are prepared for reuse. These possibilities shall be promoted also otherwise. In the collection and transfer, as good preconditions for reuse and recycling as possible shall be secured. The same holds good of the removal of hazardous substances, mixtures and components (section 5).

Producers shall organize the collection network in such a manner that the following minimum requirements are met (section 6(1) of the Decree): (1) the delivery of WEEE to a collection point is free of charge, as provided in section 49(1) of the Waste Act and as easy as possible to holders of waste and other deliverers; (2) the collection stations are placed equally in the whole country, taking the population density into account; (3) all delivered separately collected WEEE is received; (4) the collection network consists of at least 400 collection points arranged by the producers; and (5) there is, as a main rule at least one stationary collection point in every municipality. The collection of trade and industry WEEE is somewhat differently provided in section 6(2).

663. Storage and treatment of separately collected WEEE shall be arranged in the following way (section 7(1) of the Decree): (1) liquids are removed from WEEE other than prepared for reuse, and also in other respects the waste is treated pursuant to Annex 3 of the Decree; (2) the storage and treatment premises meet the requirements laid down in Annex 4; (3) BAT is used; (4) the recovery rate pursuant to section 8 is fulfilled; (5) as far as possible, EMAS (*see* paragraphs 84–85) shall be observed; and (6) the developing and assuming of new treatment methods in order to attain the objectives regarding reuse of appliances and components thereof and recovering of WEEE. Separately collected WEEE shall not be delivered to disposal if not treated in accordance with (1)–(3) above. The prohibition on incineration or landfilling waste collected separately for the preparation or recycling of reuse is provided in section 15a of the Waste Act.

664. The recovery of separately collected WEEE shall be arranged in such a way that the minimum targets for preparation of reuse, recycling and other recovery in Annex 5 are met (section 8(1) of the Decree). The implementation shall be assessed as specified in section 8(2).

665. An Environmental Permit for the storage and other treatment of WEEE pursuant to the Environmental Protection Act shall include the provisions needed for observing the provisions in section 7 regarding storage and other treatment (section 9).

666. International transfer of WEEE is regulated in section 10. The markings on WEEE are provided in section 11 of the Decree, producers' contributions pursuant to section 63a of the Waste Act in section 11a, dissemination of information to users by producers in section 12, information to treatment personnel by producers in section 13, information duties of authorized representatives pursuant to section 66a of the Waste Act in section 14, self-monitoring in section 14a, applications by producers for registering in section 15, applications by producer affiliations for registering in section 16, notifications on amendments in section 16a, returning of groundless fees in section 17 and orders issued to producers and affiliations in registration decisions to promote recovery in section 18.

667. A producer, or an affiliation on behalf of the respective producers, shall, by 30 April each year, provide the Centre for Economic Development, Transport and the Environment of Pirkanmaa region with follow-up data on the preceding year (section 19).

668. The Centre for Economic Development, Transport and the Environment of Pirkanmaa region shall annually collect the data received pursuant to section 19, as well as collect other necessary data and assessments for the purposes of monitoring and supervision (section 20).

669. Cooperation and exchange of information with the other Member States of the EU is specified in section 21 and market surveillance in section 22.

X. Waste Batteries and Accumulators

670. The present Decree on Batteries and Accumulators (520/2014), aiming to implement Directives 2006/66/EY and 2013/56/EU is, as amended by 1027/2021, applicable irrespective of the form, volume, weight, composition and purpose of the battery or accumulator, with limited exceptions in respect to defence and space (section 1 of the Decree). Section 2 contains the relevant definitions. Certain batteries and accumulators may not at all be placed on the market due to their mercury or cadmium content (section 3). A general obligation of the producers to enhance the environmental properties of batteries and accumulators on a life-cycle basis, aiming to avoid hazardous substances, is also laid down (section 4). The producers shall see to that the annual collection rate of separately collected portable batteries and accumulators is annually at least 45% by weight (section 5). This grade shall be monitored by the Centre for Economic Development, Transport and the Environment of Pirkanmaa region.

671. The receiving, treatment and other waste management regarding discarded batteries and accumulators shall, taking environmental impacts of transports into account, in such a way that: (1) separate collection of batteries and accumulators is maximized; (2) all separately collected recognizable batteries and accumulators are recycled or treated in some other way; (3) high recycling efficiency in treatment is gained; and (4) disposal of batteries and accumulators as mixed waste is minimized (section 6).

The producer shall, taking into account the environmental impacts of transports, arrange the collection and receiving of discarded batteries and accumulators in such a manner that the following minimum requirements regarding level of service and accessibility: (1) the delivery of batteries and accumulators to a collection point is free of charge, as provided in section 49(1) of the Waste Act, and as easy as possible to holders of waste and other deliverers; (2) the collection points are placed equally in the whole country, taking the population density into account; (3) the collection points for batteries and accumulators of a certain type receive all batteries and accumulators of that type, irrespective of their composition or origin; (4) the network of stationary collecting points is, where needed, supplemented with transportable collecting points, fetching services or other arrangement; and (5) the collection is, where needed, coordinated with the collection and waste management systems regarding WEEE and, as provided in section 48(1)(2), motor vehicles (section 7).

In addition, producers of vehicle batteries and accumulators shall arrange the collection in such a manner that in the whole country there are, as a main rule, at least 400 stationary collection points and at least one such point in each municipality (section 8).

672. Storage, recycling and other treatment of separately collected batteries and accumulators shall be arranged in the following way (section 9(1)): (1) batteries and accumulators are removed separately collected WEEE and vehicles, if collected together; (2) liquids and acids are removed from the batteries and accumulators; (3) temporary or other storage is arranged in premises with impermeable surface layers and appropriate weatherproof covering; (4) BAT is used; (5) the recycling efficiency requirements in section 10 are met: and (6) EMAS is applied, where possible.

673. The following requirement of recycling efficiency shall be met (section 10): (1) of lead batteries and accumulators at least 65% by weight, as efficient recycling of lead contents as possible included, are recycled; (2) of nickel and cadmium batteries and accumulators at least 65% by weight, as efficient recycling of cadmium contents as possible included, are recycled; and (3) at least 50% by weight of other discarded batteries and accumulators are recycled.

674. The disposal of discarded vehicle batteries and accumulators in landfills is forbidden, as well as disposal by incineration, subject to a minor exception (section 11).

675. An Environmental Permit for the storage, recycling and other treatment of batteries and accumulators pursuant to the Environmental Protection Act shall include the provisions needed for observing the provisions in section 12 regarding storage and other treatment (section 12).

676. International transfers of discarded batteries and accumulators are provided in the Waste Act and the Waste Shipments Regulation.[42] Transfers to other than EU Member States are regarded as fulfilling the requirements set in section 10 only when there is reliable evidence on that the recycling and other treatment thereof is also otherwise arranged in a way that meets the requirements of the Decree (section 13).

677. Markings in batteries and accumulators are provided in section 14, dissemination of information to users in section 15, obligation of authorized representative to inform in section 15a, self-monitoring in section 15b, producers' contributions in section 15c, applications by producers for registering in section 17, applications by producer affiliations for registering in section 18 and changes of operations on section 20.

678. A producer, or an affiliation on behalf of the respective producers, shall, by 30 April each year, provide the Centre for Economic Development, Transport and the Environment of Pirkanmaa region with follow-up data on the preceding year (section 21).

679. The Centre for Economic Development, Transport and the Environment of Pirkanmaa region shall annually collect the data received pursuant to section 21, as well as collect other necessary data and assessments for the purposes of monitoring and supervision (section 22).

42. Regulation (EC) No. 1013/2006 on shipments of waste.

680. Cooperation and exchange of information with other Member States of the EU are specified in section 23 and market surveillance in section 24.

XI. End-of-Life Vehicles

681. In addition to the specific provisions of the Waste Act concerning the waste management of end-of-life vehicles based on the principle of producer responsibility, the provisions of the Government decree on End-of-Life Vehicles and on Restrictions on the Use of Hazardous Substances in Vehicles (123/2015), issued by virtue of the Waste Act and the Environmental Protection Act, are applicable. The provisions aimed to implement in detail Directives 2000/53/EC and 2008/112/EC. The Decree has been updated and amended several times, mainly due to the amendments in the relevant Directives.

As to waste management, the Decree aims to reduce generation of waste from motor vehicles, prepare to reuse, recycle or otherwise recover end-of-life vehicles and their components. Also the level of environmental protection in the treatment of end-of-life vehicles is promoted.

682. The producer shall see to that the collection of components of vehicles from repair of vehicles and end-of-life vehicles is arranged in such a way that the following minimum requirements are met: (1) the delivery of the discarded vehicle components to a collection point is free of charge and as easy as possible, as provided in section 49(1) of the Waste Act; (2) the collection stations are placed equally in the whole country, taking the population density into account; (3) the collection network consists of at least stationary 200 collection points arranged by the producers; (4) the network of stationary collection points is, where needed, supplemented by fetching service or other corresponding arrangements; and (5) that the collection is extended to every municipality (section 5).

A producer shall see to that end-of-life vehicles annually at least 95% in total are prepared for reuse or are otherwise recovered and at least 85% in total are prepared for reuse or recycled (section 6).

683. The storage and pretreatment of end-of-life vehicles shall be arranged in the following way (section 7): (1) danger and harm to the environment is prevented; (2) for reuse suitable components are removed and stored so that they may be prepared for reuse; (3) for reuse unsuitable components are, where possible, transferred for recycling or other recovery; (4) the components which contain the forbidden substances specified in section 4, i.e., lead, cadmium and hexavalent chromium, which have been marked or otherwise made recognizable, where any, shall be removed; and (5) hazardous components and materials are removed and sorted so that they do not spoil the waste generated in the crushing of end-of-life vehicles. The technical minimum requirements in Annex 2 shall be observed.

An Environmental Permit for the professional pretreatment or storage and other treatment of end-of-life vehicles is required pursuant to the Environmental Protection Act. The permit shall include the provisions needed for observing the provisions in section 7 (section 8).

684. The producers shall in their procurement give priority to such pretreatment and other treatment services and collectors which apply certified environmental management schemes.

The obligations regarding encoding standards (Annex 3) and dismantling information are provided in section 9, the contents of Certificate of destruction pursuant to section 59 of the Waste Act in section 10, dissemination of information and guidance in section 11, obligation of authorized representative to inform in section 11a, self-monitoring in section 11b, producers' contributions in section 11c, the data to be included in the sales promotion information of new vehicles in section 12, the financial solidity and management plans of producer affiliation in section 13, applications by producers for registering in section 14, applications by producer affiliations for registering in section 15 and notifications on changes in activity in section 16.

685. A producer, or an affiliation on behalf of the respective producers, shall, by 30 April each year, provide the Centre for Economic Development, Transport and the Environment of Pirkanmaa region with follow-up data on the preceding year (section 17).

686. The Centre for Economic Development, Transport and the Environment of Pirkanmaa region shall annually check and collect the data received pursuant to section 17, as well as collect other necessary data and assessments for the purposes of monitoring and supervision (section 18).

687. Cooperation and exchange of information with other Member States of the EU is specified in section 19.

§15. Sludge Produced at Wastewater Treatment Plants

688. The sludge which is produced at municipal sewerage systems and wastewater treatment plants is also covered by the notion of waste according to the Waste Act. In practice, sludge management is partly connected with the sewers' discharge permits under the Environmental Protection Act. As for using sludge in agriculture, a Government decree (282/1994) had been set forth under the previous Waste Act, aligned with the respective EC Directive (86/278/EEC). Next the Decree was repealed and replaced by Government decree on Waste (179/2012), and this again by the new Government decree on Waste (978/2021). Pursuant to section 31 of the latter, a producer of municipal wastewater treatment sludge (that being defined in section 1(3) of the same Decree) is responsible for testing the quality of the sludge according to Annex 4 to the Decree.

689. The rather comprehensive new Decree of the Ministry of Agriculture and Forestry on Fertiliser Products (964/2023), issued under the Fertilisers Act (and partly, but only partly, connected to EU CAP provisions), lays down, among other things, provisions on the use of fertilizer products and manure as well as on permitted deviations from the properties of fertilizer products. The provisions on the use of sewage sludge in agriculture and horticulture are laid down in section 7 of the Decree. Sewage sludge must be treated before being used to destroy pathogens in accordance with the requirements of the Decree. The maximum permitted application rate of treated sewage sludge is 6,000 kg per year or 30,000 kg dry matter per hectare over a period of five years. The maximum application rate is calculated on the basis of the mass fraction of sewage sludge. If the labelling of a fertilizer product does not contain information on the proportion of sewage sludge, the product shall be considered to be entirely sewage sludge. The mass fraction of sewage sludge in a mixture is the mass of sewage sludge divided by the mass of the entire mixture. Fertilizing products containing sewage sludge may only be applied to arable land where the concentrations of harmful metals do not exceed the maximum permitted concentrations set out in Annex 5 to the Decree. In agriculture and horticulture, a withdrawal period of one year must be observed for feedingstuffs and two years for foodstuffs on agricultural and pasture land on which fertilizer products in accordance with section 7 have been applied (or treated sludge from septic tanks and sealed tanks, as well as other sludge from property-specific or farm-shared wastewater treatment systems and dry toilet waste from farms). During the withdrawal period, plants which can be eaten fresh and the edible parts thereof may not be grown for human consumption or feed in direct contact with the ground or plants, the underground part of which is intended to be eaten. The Decree also encompasses use of phosphorus in landscaping and environmental construction (sections 10 and 11), but in force only as of 1 January 2027.

690. In small-scale treatment of biowaste and precipitation well or septic tank sludge by properties the conditions in section 12 of the Decree on Waste shall be observed. The use of precipitation well and septic tank sludge and outhouse waste in agriculture is regulated in the Decree 964/2023 (above).

691. In addition to the provisions of the decrees above, also other legislation may be applicable to sludge from wastewater treatment plants. Under the Public Health Act, the Public Health Authorities may prohibit the use of sludge in cultivated lands, if a threat to health exists. Where pollution of surface waters or groundwater appears, the Environmental Protection Act is applicable in the ordinary way. In addition, provisions by Government decree under the Environmental Protection Act may be issued on restrictions on discharges of sludge (of any origin) to the environment or on prohibitions on the discharging or locating of sludge that poses a pollution risk (section 9(6) of the Environmental Protection Act).

692. Treated or untreated sludge from municipal wastewater treatment plants shall never be discharged to waters (section 5 of Government decree on Urban Waste Water Treatment, 888/2006).

§16. Littering

693. Section 72 of the Waste Act provides a general ban on littering the environment, as a continuation to the similar provisions in the preceding Waste Acts.

Pursuant to the ban, it is prohibited to place in the environment any waste or any discarded machine, device, vehicle, vessel or other item, in such a manner that untidiness, deterioration of the landscape, a loss of amenity, risk of accident to humans or animals, or other comparable danger or nuisance is caused.

694. The person by whom the littering has been caused is primarily responsible for taking away the item and cleaning up the littered area. If the identity of the responsible person remains unclear or is not reached, or if the litterer has failed to fulfil his obligations, the following are regarded as responsible for the cleaning up:

(1) the keeper of a public road, private road, railway or harbour, for an area littered by the use of the road, railway or harbour at stake;
(2) the possessor of an area that is intended for public recreational use or the keeper of a Recreational Trail or a Motor Sledge Trail, for an area littered by the use of the area or the trail;
(3) the arranger of a public event, for the event area or an adjacent area littered by the event, or the possessor of the event area, if he has agreed to the event and the arranger does not take care of the cleaning up;
(4) within a Detailed Plan according to the Land Use and Building Act (as of 1 January 2025, the Land Use Act), the possessor of an area other than in (1)–(3) above;
(5) the possessor of an area other than in (1)–(4) above, if he knew or should have known about the littering activity or event at stake, and cleaning up by him is otherwise not to be regarded as unreasonable.

If the possessor in (5) above omits his cleaning obligation or is not responsible under (5), the municipality is, as a last resort, responsible for the cleaning up.

695. The obligations above are enforced through an order by the Municipal Environmental Protection Authority, or, where the responsibility lies upon the municipality, by the Centre for Economic Development, Transport and the Environment (section 75 of the Waste Act).

696. The orders by the Municipal Environmental Protection Authority or the Centre for Economic Development, Transport and the Environment are normally given under a conditional fine or at the risk that the measures needed will be taken by the authority at the expense of the responsible subject, or that a relevant activity will be stopped or banned (*see* above section 5).

697. The outdoor tidiness of built-up area properties may also be controlled by the supervision and enforcement means of the Land Use and Building Act (as of 1 January 2025, the Building Act).

The obligations to keep clean the roads, streets, parks, squares, etc., in areas with a Detailed Plan according to the Land Use and Building Act (as of 1 January 2025, the Land Use Act) are provided in the Act on the maintenance and keeping clean of streets and certain public areas (669/1978). The obligations are divided between the municipalities and the adjacent property owners, partly depending on the local choices by the municipality. The detailed rules also cover the extraction of snow and ice and treatment of slippery surfaces.

§17. Vehicle Junks

698. The Act on Vehicle Removes (1508/2019) stipulates the obligations on the owners, possessors and drivers of vehicles and on the rights and duties of municipal and State authorities in respect to wrongly parked or abandoned vehicles. The provisions are partly linked to ordinary control of parking. Specific rules apply to abandoned vehicles and junk vehicles. According to this Act, a vehicle shall be removed by municipal authorities or a Centre for Economic Development, Transport and the Environment in several specified circumstances. The transportation and eventual storage are executed at the expense of the owner or driver.

699. Where a vehicle is to be regarded as waste according to the definition of waste in the Waste Act, it is also regarded as junk vehicle under the Act on Vehicle Removes. Independently of this, it is the duty of the authorities to transport a vehicle for storage, if it is evident in respect to the value, condition and outward appearance of the vehicle other than junk that it has been abandoned (section 7 of the said Act). As to private roads and areas, the owner of the road or an area may ask for transportation for storage. Also the police may make a similar request.

700. It is the duty of the holder of a junk vehicle under the Waste Act to deliver it to an appropriate receiving site or directly to an end-of life vehicle collector or a pretreatment operator pursuant to section 58 of the Waste Act (paragraph 627). The general ban on abandoning waste, sanctioned with penal responsibility, is also applicable. For cases where these duties have been omitted, the municipalities are obliged to take care of the transportation (section 8). The obligation of the municipality encompasses junk vehicles in private courtyards, private storage areas and other similar areas, however, only on a reasoned request by the possessor of the area. Before transportation, the last known holder of the vehicle shall be informed, except when the vehicle is burnt or its condition otherwise poses a risk to the environment or humans. The ownership of a junk vehicle is transferred to the municipality from the moment of seizure, as provided in section 13.

701. On the provisions on end-of-life vehicles and producer responsibility in the Waste Act *see* §14, XI above.

Chapter 6. Soil Pollution

§1. Applicable Provisions

702. Soil pollution (or contamination) prevention and management of polluted soils was previously regulated by the Waste Act of 1993 (in force from 1 January 1994), as it stood until 1 March 2000. Before 1994, the original rules on littering in the Waste Management Act of 1978, were gradually developed towards the provisions of the 1993 Waste Act, both through the precedents of the SAC and through explicit amendments of the provisions on littering (*see* above Part I, Chapter 5, §16). In the 1993 Waste Act, independent provisions on pollution of soils had been inserted, and the provisions on littering had been returned to their original function. In the large environmental law reform of 2000, the relevant provisions of the then Waste Act were removed, developed further and integrated with the previous provisions on groundwater pollution of the Water Act making up Chapter 12 and some other provisions in the Environmental Protection Act of 2000, and respectively Chapter 14 of the present Environment Protection Act.

703. The local soil pollution problems hitherto have mainly dealt with industrial properties with surroundings where, e.g., timber impregnate has been used perhaps decades ago, but the pollution has emerged only recently. The provisions on polluted soils cover all kinds of soil contamination, irrespective of whether it has been caused by waste or not. As for 'historical' pollution originating in the pre-1994 time of the then Waste Management Act, the previous provisions and/or the 1993 Waste Act are still applicable as a starting point, although the difference is not necessarily significant. These situations of historical pollution were first dealt with by specific transitional provisions (section 22 of Act 113/2000 regarding the implementation of the 2000 overall environmental law reform). There are several examples on realized polluter responsibility based on the previous provisions, but the outcome in the present Environmental Protection Act is somewhat more unclear.

704. According to section 16 of the Environmental Protection Act it is forbidden to leave (dump, place), discharge or convey substance, energy or microbes on the ground or in the soil so as to result in such deterioration of soil quality as may endanger or cause harm to health or the environment, substantially impair the amenity of the site or cause comparable violation of the public or private interest (ban on polluting the soil). This ban on soil pollution is absolute and no Environmental Permit can be granted in contradiction to it. The same holds true for the ban on groundwater pollution in section 16 of the same Act.

Without prejudice to the ban, the sludge from wastewater treatment plant, used in agriculture, is controlled pursuant to the Government decree on Waste (*see also* Chapter 5, §15 above).

705. In the assessment of the clean-up need of polluted soil and groundwater the following shall be taken into account: the present and future use of the polluted area, its environment and groundwater and the hazard or disadvantage to health or environment possibly caused by the pollution (section 135(3) of the Environmental Protection Act). More detailed provisions on the maximum allowed concentrations on harmful substances in the soil for assessing the rate of pollution and clean-up need, taking the various purposes of lad use into account (section 135(4)).

706. By virtue of section 14 of the 2000 Environmental Protection Act, Government decree on the Assessment of Soil Pollution and Need of Cleanup (214/2007) has been issued, applicable from 1 June 2007 and remaining in force also under the present Environmental Protection Act.

Pursuant to the Decree, the assessment of soil pollution and clean-up needs shall be based on an assessment of the hazard or harm to health or the environment represented by the harmful substances in the soil. The following shall be taken into account in the assessment: (1) the concentration, overall amounts, properties, location and background concentration of the hazardous substances in the soil; background concentration refers to naturally occurring normal concentrations of hazardous substances in the soil or raised concentrations that are found in topsoil in a wide area in the environment of an area that is suspected to be contaminated; (2) the soil and groundwater conditions of an area suspected to be polluted and factors that have an impact on the spreading of harmful substances inside and outside the area; (3) the current and planned purpose of use for the area suspected to be polluted and its environment or groundwater; (4) the possibility of exposure to harmful substances in the short or long-term; (5) the severity and likelihood of the health and environmental hazard from exposure and possible combined effects of the harmful substances; and (6) the elements of uncertainty in the research data and other source information and assessment methods used. As the conditions change, the pollution and needs of clean-up shall be reassessed, where necessary (section 2).

707. The pollution and needs of clean-up must be assessed if the concentration of one or several harmful substances in the soil exceeds the threshold value prescribed in the appendix to the Decree. The background concentration is regarded as the assessment threshold in areas with a background concentration higher than the threshold value (section 3 of the Decree). The guideline values for harmful substances in soil, prescribed in the appendix to the Decree, shall be used as a tool in the assessment of pollution and needs of clean-up. Soil is regarded as polluted unless otherwise arisen in the assessment pursuant to section 2: (1) in an area used as an industrial, storage or transport area or as other corresponding area if the concentration of one substance or several substances exceeds the prescribed upper guideline value; or (2) in other area, if the concentration of one substance or several substances exceeds the prescribed lower guideline value (section 4). The samples shall be taken with a good representation of the area under examination and its soil and groundwater. The assessment of harmful substances shall be based on standardized methods or other correspondingly reliable methods (section 5).

§2. Enforcement of Clean-Up

708. Where the soil or groundwater has been contaminated, the responsible person shall immediately inform the supervisory authorities of the situation (section 134 of the Environmental Pollution Act). If it is likely that soil or groundwater has been polluted, the Centre for Economic Development, Transport and the Environment of the region is entitled to give the responsible person an order to assess the polluted area and the need for clean-up (section 135(1)). Provisions of Chapter 18 of the Environmental Protection Act on administrative enforcement are applicable.

Where it turns out that the soil or groundwater is polluted, the polluter has to clean up the soil and groundwater to such an extent that a status where no harm to health or danger to the environment exists is achieved (section 133 of the Environmental Protection Act). If the polluter cannot be identified or fails in his obligations, also the holder of the area may be held liable if he had allowed the polluting activity. Similarly, if the area has been transferred to the present holder later on, he may be held liable if he knew or should have known the condition of the area at the time of transferring. Where it is evidently unreasonable to oblige the holder, he will be free, however. As for groundwater pollution, the obliging of the holder requires moreover that the pollution of groundwater has resulted from the pollution of the soil of the same area.

Insofar the holder cannot be made responsible for clean-up, it is ultimately the duty of the municipality to assess the need for measures and to clean up the soil (section 133(3)).

709. If the person who is responsible for clean-up pursuant to section 133 does not act voluntarily, an enforcement order shall be issued (section 137). In voluntary cases an Environmental Permit for the clean-up may be necessary, but if not, a notification shall be made to the Centre for Economic Development, Transport and the Environment forty-five days before the first essential stage of works. The centre shall make a decision due to the notification, including orders to be observed (section 136).

710. To support the effectivity of the rules on responsibility, there is a general obligation on all who sell or otherwise transfer or lease land property to present the new possessor with all available information on the previous activities in the area and on the wastes or substances within it by which a risk for soil or groundwater pollution is created (section 139 of the Environmental Protection Act).

711. Due to the evident parallels, there are cases where both the Environmental Protection Act, Chapter 14, and the Environmental Damages Act, section 7 (*see* Part IV, Chapter 2, §2), as applied to costs of reinstatement, could be used as alternative bases of responsibility. Of course, the former is part of a civil liability system and the latter belongs to the category of administrative enforcement (*see* Part V, Chapter 1).

712. The power to give the necessary orders according to sections 135 and 137 of the Environmental Protection Act is vested in the Centres for Economic Development, Transport and the Environment. Provisions of Chapter 18 of the Environmental Protection Act on administrative enforcement are applicable. The orders are regularly given under a conditional fine or at the risk that the measures needed will be taken by the Authority at the expense of the responsible subject, or that a relevant activity will be stopped or banned. The Centre may (and has to) react on its own behalf, but also any of the affected private parties, a registered environmental or local people's association or a municipal authority may initiate the enforcement procedure (section 92 of the Environmental Protection Act, *see* Part V, Chapters 1 and 2). The Regional Administrative Court and further the SAC are also here the appellate bodies.

713. From 1 January on, the State may support assessments of pollution grade and clean-up regarding areas where the responsible party is unknown, either by State aid or by arranging the assessment and clean-up by State funds.

§3. Rules on the Prevention of Oil Accidents in Land Areas and of Vessel-Based Oil and Chemical Accidents

714. There is one sector of oil-related legislation which mainly refers to soil pollution, and that is legislation concerning oil and accidents and oil damages in land areas. From 2019, the regulation of this sector is, instead a specific Oil Damages Prevention Act, included in the Rescue Act, like the regulation on vessel-based oil and chemical damages, partly by common provisions. For practical reasons, both aspects of the Act are described in the following.

715. Hence the general prevention and dealing with oil pollution in land areas, as well as prevention of oil and chemical damages caused by vessels is regulated by the Rescue Act, today as a part of rescue activities at large.

716. 'Oil damage' is in the Rescue Act defined as either 'oil damage in land area' or 'vessel-based oil damage' (section 2). 'Oil damage in land area' again is defined as 'such damage or harm occurring in a land area that oil, when entered on or into soil or water, causes to humans or the environment by contaminating, deteriorating or polluting soil, waters. vegetation, fauna, devices or constructions', and 'vessel-based oil damage' as 'a vessel-based incident, or a series of incidents with the same origin, which results or may result in an oil discharge and which endangers or may endanger the condition of a water body, marine environment or coast, or related interests, and which requires urgent measures'. And 'vessel-based chemical damage' is respectively defined as 'a vessel-based incident in the sea area, or a series of incidents with the same origin, which results or may result in a discharge of other harmful substance than oil and which endangers or may endanger the condition of a water body, marine environment or coast, or related interests, and which requires urgent measures'. All this means that the notion of oil damage is far wider than in the field of private law only. In fact, the Finnish language and Swedish language expressions for 'damage' here could also, and indeed more accurately, be translated as 'accident', or 'spill', particularly as regards the definition of vessel-based damage.

717. General leadership, guidance and supervision of rescue activities is vested in the Ministry of the Interior. The Regional Rescue Services are responsible for practical rescue activities at large. The Border Guard is responsible for activities due to vessel-based oil and chemical damages in Finnish territorial waters and in the economic zone, and coordinates the precautions (section 27a). The Finnish Environment Institute, the Finnish Transport and Communications Agency Traficom and the Defence Forces participate in the prevention of vessel-based oil and chemical accidents. The Maritime Rescue Coordination Centre (MRCC, a designated Coast Guard District coordination centre within the Border Guard, pursuant to the Maritime Search and Rescue Act (1145/2001)) acts as the point of contact according to international conventions on the prevention of maritime environmental damages and has the responsibility for notifications to other states of vessel-based oil and chemical damages pursuant to international conventions (section 27a). In addition, the MRCC is the contact point pursuant to Article 32(1) of the Offshore Operations Safety Directive.[43]

718. The Regional Rescue Services are responsible for rescue planning in general. Plans in respect to rescue activities at sea due to vessel-based oil damages and vessel-based chemical damages shall be drawn under the leadership by the Border Guard, however (section 34). Where several authorities participate in the rescue activities, a group of leaders may be set. In case of oil or chemical damages, an expert of environmental protection shall be a member or at have the possibility to be heard (section 35).

The various rescue measures under the Rescue Act are ordinarily led by Regional Rescue Services. Regarding vessel-based oil damages in the open sea parts of the territorial waters or in the economic zone, the leader is designated by the Border Guard, however (section 34). The rescue authority in charge of an oil or chemical damage situation shall urgently take all measures needed for preventing or reducing damages, the costs of or the damages caused by which are not evidently disproportionate in relation to the economic and other values that are endangered. The measures shall not unnecessarily hamper restoration of nature and the environment to a pre-incident status (section 32).

719. After-incident measures pursuant to the Act mean such oil pollution prevention measures that are taken in order to clean and restore the soil, groundwater and coast after the necessary measures to confine damages and collect oil have been taken (section 2a(2)(8) of the Rescue Act). The general guidance, monitoring and

43. Directive 2013/30/EU of the European Parliament and of the Council of 12 Jun. 2013 on safety of offshore oil and gas operations and amending Directive 2004/35/EC.

development of such after-incident measures are vested in the Ministry of the Environment (section 111a). Each municipality is responsible for after-incident measures within its area, led by an authority designated by the municipality. If measures are needed in the areas of several municipalities, the Centre for Economic Development, Labour and the Environment shall guide and coordinate.

720. Also the duties of oil storers and port operators are provided in the Rescue Act. First, an obligation to maintain basic preparedness for prevention, specified in detail in section 22a, covers all tanks and tank areas with a capacity of at least 100,000 litres but under 1 million litres. The preparedness required for gasoline stations is provided in the Act on the Safety of the Handling of Dangerous Chemicals and Explosives. If the amount of oil stored elsewhere than on the coast exceeds 1 million, the more ambitious preparedness for a large oil tank area, provided in section 22b, is needed.

721. Also an operator-specific emergency plan for abatement of possible oil and chemical damages may be required (section 22c of the Rescue Act). This obligation covers: (1) operators of ports for (mainly) commercial navigation, and (2) other plant or installation on the coast where at least 1 million litres of oil or other harmful substances are stored.

722. The Regional Rescue Services are moreover, in cooperation with the operator at stake, obliged to draw up an external rescue plan for the sites of one of the following: (1) a nuclear plant pursuant to the Nuclear Act; (2) a production plant for which the operator is obliged to draw up a security account pursuant to section 30(1) or 62(1) of the Act on the Safety of the Handling of Dangerous Chemicals and Explosives; (3) extractive waste area causing risk of major accident, pursuant to section 112(1)(5) of the Environmental Protection Act; (4) certain marshalling yards; and (5) certain harbour areas (section 48).

723. If a vessel accident in Finnish territorial waters or the economic zone poses an evident risk of leakage of oil or other harmful substance, the Border Guard (or the rescue leader in inland waters) may issue orders on necessary measures to prevent or confine pollution. Before that, the Finnish Transport and Communications Agency Traficom and an environmental authority at stake shall be consulted, if possible (section 36b).

The duties of a shipmaster due to a vessel-based oil or chemical damage are laid down in Chapter 11 of the Act on Environmental Protection in Maritime Transport. These include a notification duty and a duty to take such first-hand prevention measures that can be reasonably required.

724. If necessary to prevent oil damage or vessel-based chemical damage and to confine the consequences, the ad hoc leader of abatement may: (1) take private devices, premises and places for temporary use, (2) disembark and move on private land, (3) give orders on construction and water body management measures in private areas, (4) order restrictions on water traffic, and (5) take other necessary measures (section 36a). Orders on measures concerning a vessel in a critical situation and its freight are stipulated in section 36b. Rules on international assistance, requested by the Ministry of the Interior, are provided in section 38.

725. If an oil damage or a vessel-based chemical damage, the risk thereof, or the possibility of extension of damage is so significant that the staff or devices accessible to the abatement authority is insufficient to efficient abatement or prevention, the authority is entitled to order a port operator, a possessor of a plant or an installation, an oil tank holder or anyone else with access to abatement devices or expert staff to render these to the authority for use, if this can take place without unreasonable inconvenience (section 36a).

726. As regards administrative enforcement, the Regional Rescue Services may impose a conditional fine or a threat of taking the neglected action at his or her expense (section 105). The provisions of the Administrative Injunctions (Conditional Fines) Act (1113/1990) are applicable.

The rights of the authorities to obtain necessary information, certain classified information included, from several authorities and private subjects are stipulated in section 89a and 89b.

727. An authority which has been in charge of preventive measures regarding oil damage or vessel-based chemical damage, and a body which has cooperated or contributed, is entitled to compensation for the abatement costs, from the liable party or his insurance company, as provided in the Environmental Damages Act, the Maritime Act, the Act on Motor Liability Insurance, the Rail Traffic Insurance Act or other act (section 99a). Temporarily the necessary costs are paid to the authority at stake.

728. The right of the authority responsible for responding to oil and ship chemical spills and the authorities that participated in or provided executive assistance to them to receive compensation for damage prevention costs from the Environmental Damage Fund is laid down in the Act on the Environmental Damage Fund (1262/2022). The same applies to a municipality's right to receive compensation for the costs of aftermath. The right of the authorities to receive compensation from the International Oil Pollution Compensation Fund is governed by what has been agreed on it that is binding on Finland. On the Fund, *see* Part I, Chapter 4, §8, IX above.

729. Criminal sanctions are provided in section 106.

730. The Ministry of the Interior is entitled to exceptionally allow the use of oil-containing substance (referred to in section 2(1)(3) of Chapter 2 of the Act on Environmental Protection in Maritime Transport) or noxious liquid substance (referred to in section 3(1)(3) of Chapter 4 of the said Act) in the abatement of vessel-based oil or chemical damage. Before decision-making the ministry has to hear the Finnish Environment Institute and make sure that the abatement chemical in question is significantly better than other methods to abate the damage at stake and that no evident risk of pollution of waters or other harm to human health or the environment is caused (section 36c).

§4. Other Regulations Relevant to Soil Pollution Prevention

731. The Act on the Safety of the Handling of Dangerous Chemicals and Explosives and the corresponding Decree are relevant also with regard to oil pollution prevention. The obligation on periodical inspections of underground oil tanks is based on section 54 of the said Act. The system covers even the oil tanks of individual dwellings. Tanks imposing a pollution risk shall be repaired or removed, in cases of immediate risk instantly. The competent (private) inspection bodies are approved and supervised pursuant to Government decree 558/2012.

732. As for the largest (at least more than 100 cubic metres) oil tanks (and those containing dangerous chemicals), an Environmental Permit is required according to the Environmental Protection Decree, section 1(5)(a) (*see* Chapter 1, §9 above).

733. The pollution of soil is not totally unregulated outside the Environmental Protection Act and the field of oil pollution, either. For example, some parts of the Water Act may be quite relevant, in particular those referring to sand or gravel extraction (*see* paragraph 444). Also, the provisions on the quality of sludge from wastewater treatment plants that are spread on agricultural lands are significant (*see* Part I, Chapter 5, §15).

734. It is also possible to apply the Public Health Act for preventive measures and administrative injunctions. But here also the result may depend on water supply interests, because the provisions in the Public Health Act presuppose damage or threat to human health. Of course, a threat to health may also be constituted in other ways, e.g., chemical contamination of edible plants, etc.

735. The rules on the handling and storing of chemicals in the Chemicals Act and the Act on the Safety of the Handling of Dangerous Chemicals and Explosives are, *inter alia,* intended to prevent soil pollution at large. In some cases, the latter is also applicable to dealing with actual soil pollution. This is the case especially when chemicals are treated or stored contrary to the Act in a way that contamination of the environment, e.g., of soil, is caused. Here the operator or other polluter is obliged to carry out clean-up measures so that danger to health or to the environment is eliminated. Supervisory authorities are empowered to impose a conditional fine.

736. In a larger context of soil resources protection, the Soil Excavation Act has to be taken into account. This Act primarily aims to protect the values of landscape and nature in connection with soil (esker gravel, rock) excavation projects, but also the protection of groundwater is taken into account. It also regulates some aspects of soil pollution control. For example, the duties of the excavator in order to prevent soil and groundwater pollution are usually conditions for the granting of Soil Excavation Permits; *see* Part II, Chapter 7, §1 below.

Chapter 7. Noise Pollution

§1. The Enactments

737. Before March 2000, the overall picture of noise abatement legislation in Finland was somewhat heterogeneous. There was, true, a Noise Abatement Act (382/1987), but many major noise polluters and noise situations have in practice been left outside the direct application of it. One of the main items in the Noise Abatement Act consisted of the organization of public authorities (especially local) and their activities in general. The noise abatement provisions for each individual establishment or activity were for the most part treated on the basis of other legislation with differently specified goals, mainly under the Neighbourhood Relations Act and the Public Health Act. Only for temporary noise polluters was there a specific notification procedure in the Noise Abatement Act.

738. Today, noise abatement is mainly covered by the Environmental Protection Act and Environmental Protection Decree aiming at a coherent and integrated environmental protection covering all aspects of the environment, including noise abatement. Noise is by definition one form of pollution of the environment (*see* paragraph 120). Hence, noise is taken into account in all Environmental and notification procedures, and there is a special notification procedure for activities causing temporary noise (§5 below).

When the previous Noise Abatement Act (and the Noise Abatement Decree) from March 2000 was repealed by the Environmental Protection Act, all the other decrees on noise abatement based on the Noise Abatement Act remained valid. The product-related decrees have been repealed later on, but some others are still in force (below).

Also, many other laws are relevant to the abatement of noise pollution, such as the Terrain Traffic Act (1710/1995), the Water Traffic Act (782/2019) and the Road Traffic Act, as well as the Public Health Act (insofar the permit mechanism or other provisions of the Environmental Protection Act are not applicable).

§2. Noise Mapping and Action Plans

739. The provisions on Strategic Noise Mapping and Noise Abatement Action Plans, implementing Directive 2002/49/EC of 25 June 2002 relating to the assessment and management of environmental noise and Commission Directive (EU) 2015/996 of 19 May 2015 establishing common noise assessment methods according to Directive 2002/49/EC of the European Parliament and of the Council, are in the present Environmental Protection Act included in sections 150–153. Detailed provisions have been laid down in the Government decree on Noise Maps and Noise Abatement Action Plans (823/2018).

740. A noise map (noise account) and an Action Plan shall be worked out for all agglomerations with more than 100,000 inhabitants, provided that they due to their population density may be regarded as town-like, and for all highways which have more than 3 million vehicle passages a year, for railways which have more than 30,000 train passages per year and for civil airports which have more than 50,000 movements per year (a movement being a take-off or a landing), excluding those purely for training purposes on light aircraft (section 151 of the Environmental Protection Act).

In a noise map an existing and a future noise situation of the area, quiet areas included, shall be presented in terms of noise indicators. Also the estimated number of people located in the area exposed to noise and the number of residential houses are accounted. An action plan is designed to abate noise and its impacts and prevent the increasing of noise in quiet areas.

741. A noise map and an Action Plan shall be worked out by the Finnish Transport Infrastructure Agency regarding railways, by the airport operators regarding airports, by the holder of another traffic area regarding such areas and by the respective municipality regarding population conglomerates in other than the previous items. The Agency, the airport operators and the holder of another traffic area submit their respective Maps and Plans to the municipality, which pays attention to them while drafting the Map and Plan for (a) population conglomerate(s).

In the drafting of an action plan, those who's dwelling, working or other conditions the plan may impact, as well as registered environmental associations and foundations, shall be offered an opportunity to give an opinion. Various authorities shall be heard. An action plan shall be made public as provided in the Environmental Protection Act.

A Noise Abatement Action Plan shall be reviewed at least at the intervals of five years. It may also be amended and complemented separately, where needed.

742. Pursuant to the Government decree 823/2018, an Action Plan regarding items in section 151 of the Act shall be worked out and saved to Environmental Protection Information System every five years by 18 July. The following plans shall be worked out and saved in 2023.

743. According to the same Decree, an Action Plan may, *inter alia*, contain measures in relation to traffic planning, land use planning, technical measures at noise source, choosing of more quiet noise sources, restrictions on temporal or spatial spreading of noise, and other abatement measures such as economical guidance. It is, however, unclear so far what the legal effects of the plans will be. No explicit legal consequences have been enacted, e.g., regarding environmental permits, land use Plans according to the Land Use and Building Act (as of 1 January 2025, the Land Use Act), or the Engineering Plans pursuant to the Highways Act or the Railways Act. As sources of soft law or case-by-case information the Maps and Plans may probably function, anyway, where applicable and appropriate. The possible status of an Action Plan as an appealable administrative decision is not clear, either.

§3. Other Decrees on Noise

744. Under the Noise Abatement Act of 1987, the Government or the Ministry of the Environment had the power to give general guidelines or general regulations in the form of decrees. Those given by the Cabinet were the most important. They could refer:

(1) to noise levels outdoors and indoors;
(2) to noise emissions by devices and vehicles manufactured, imported, sold or used;
(3) to prevention of spreading of noise and to measures aimed to protect exposed objects; as well as;
(4) to bans or restrictions for noisy activities or devices, given for fixed times.

Pursuant to section 142(2) of the present Environmental Protection Act, the environmental quality requirements and objectives safeguarding the quality of sound environment shall, in order to specify further the general obligations in section 142(1), be issued by Government decree. The requirements and objectives may be different for different categories of noise sources and different areas, and they may focus on specified periods of time only (section 142(2) of the Environmental Protection Act).

745. The pre-2000 decrees still in force are:

- Government decree on Noise Level Guidelines (993/1992). This decree is applicable to the planning of land use, traffic and building, as well as to the permits for building. Both ambient and indoor noise is covered. In practice, the guidelines are also applied as non-binding starting points in the Environmental Permits pursuant to the Environmental Protection Act.
- Government decree (53/1997) on Guideline Levels for Noise Caused by Shooting Ranges. It is in practice applied as guidance in Environmental Permit procedures and in land use planning.

746. Government decree on the guideline values for outdoor noise by wind power plants (1107/2015), is applicable in decisions and supervision pursuant to the Land Use and Building Act (as of 1 January 2025, the Building Act) and the Environmental Protection Act.

Government decree on the noise levels of heavy weapons and explosives (903/2017) contains guideline values and action limit values for areas where heavy weapons and explosives are used, to be applied in the very activities, in land use planning under the Land Use and Building Act (as of 2025 the Building Act) and in permit procedures and supervision under the Environmental Protection Act.

Also the more integrated decrees under the Environmental Protection Act may contain detailed environmental requirements, such as section 8 of Government decree on the environmental protection requirements for middle scale energy production units and installations (1065/2017),

§4. Noise Abatement Through Environmental Permits

747. Before 1 March 2000, individual noise abatement measures concerning installations and stationary activities were largely based on the previous permit and supervision systems of the Public Health Act and on the previous permit system of the Neighbourhood Relations Act, but the problem was that the latter included no reference to the Noise Abatement Act. It was even highly controversial whether the guidelines and regulations were as such to be taken into account when a permit application under either of the two acts was being decided upon. This was especially the case with the Public Health Act, which was clearly limited to health protection but could however presuppose even stricter protection of public health. Moreover, the national health authority had issued specific guidelines on acceptable noise levels and monitoring, wholly apart from the Noise Abatement Act. From March 2000, these problems do not exist anymore.

748. Noise may be relevant to the permit system of the Environmental Protection Act in several ways. First, irrespective of whether the activity or installation at stake is included in Annex I to the Environmental Protection Act, an Environmental Permit is always required for any activity that can cause in the environment unreasonable nuisance to neighbours, as defined in section 17(1) of the Neighbourhood Relations Act and assessed on a case-by-case basis (section 27(2)(3) of the Environmental Protection Act). Second, no Environmental Permit can be granted at all, if unreasonable nuisance provided in section 17(1) of the Neighbourhood Relations Act or adverse health effect would result (section 49(5) of the Environmental Protection Act). Limits for allowed noise levels and the allowed times of a day or a week for causing noise are typical items of permit provisions pursuant to section 52 of the Environmental Protection Act.

§5. The Notification on Temporary Noise or Vibration

749. The Environmental Protection Act also includes a specific notification procedure for noise (or vibration) abatement, applying to temporary activities causing particularly disturbing noise (or vibration). Pursuant to section 118 of the Environmental Protection Act, a prior written notification to the Municipal Environmental Protection Authority has to be made regarding a measure or occasion, such as construction work or public occasion, that causes temporary noise (or vibration) which is supposedly of a particularly disturbing nature. The activities in question may be, e.g., constructing or repair work, motor races, sports meetings, entertainment or rock concerts.

If the measure or occasion takes place in several municipalities, the notification is made to the Centre for Economic Development, Transport and the Environment (environmental division) in the area of which the noise or vibration mainly appears. No notification is needed if an Environmental Permit is required for the same activity. The same holds true for activities in private households, defence activities and such temporary activities for which the municipality has included regulations in

Bylaws pursuant to section 22 of the Environmental Protection Act and provided in the Bylaw that there will be no notification duty for the same situations.

The notification has to be made in good time before the measure shall be taken or the activity is going to be commenced, and in any case not later than thirty days before. The Municipal Environmental Bylaws may provide a shorter period regarding activities without impacts outside of the municipality. Notifications shall be submitted electronically, except for natural persons, who may opt for paper also.

750. The measure shall not be taken or the activity commenced earlier than thirty days (or a shorter period, where applicable) from the notification have elapsed. After having received a notification, the competent authority shall always make a decision in which necessary orders may be included on the prevention of pollution (in this case, i.e., of noise), on monitoring and on the information to the population. On the processing of notifications and decisions due to them, *see* Part I, Chapter 1, §17 above.

§6. Other Regulations

I. Road Traffic Noise

751. The EU product requirements for motor vehicles are applied. On road planning regarding noise *see* paragraph 1366 and on noise mapping and Action Plans *see* §2 above.

II. Noise at and in the Vicinity of Airports

752. A motor-driven aircraft shall be so planned, manufactured, equipped and maintained that noise and other emissions thereof do not cause damage or significant harm to the environment (section 44 of the Aviation Act, 864/2014). The Transport and Communications Agency Traficom issues, where needed more detailed provisions based on the standards referred to in the Chicago Convention on International Civil Aviation.

The Balanced Approach Regulation[44] is applicable. Based on the balanced approach, noise may be managed and restricted pursuant to Article 2(6) of the regulation only after other measures based on balanced approach have been considered and assessed by the Transport and Communications Agency Traficom (section 129 of the Aviation Act). The Agency sets a noise abatement objective for each airport. The Agency shall hear the airport operator, land use planning authorities, the Centres for Economic Development, Transport and the Environment of the region, the Municipal Environmental Protection Authorities, aviation companies, the Defence Forces and others concerned.

44. Regulation (EU) No. 598/2014 on the establishment of rules and procedures with regard to the introduction of noise-related operating restrictions at union airports within a Balanced Approach and repealing Directive 2002/30/EC.

The Transport and Communications Agency Traficom may issue orders and make decisions on aviation and maintenance, if needed for the reducing or preventing of aircraft noise or other adverse environmental impact or in order to allow deviations accepted in international practice, as provided in section 157.

753. The Transport and Communications Agency Traficom is empowered to grant an Aircraft Noise Certificate for an aircraft registered in Finland, provided that reliable account on the noise level of the aircraft is presented, as provided in section 44a of the Aviation Act. A new application is required after amendment works affecting the noise level. The Ministry of Transport and Communications may issue related specific provisions based on standards and recommendations referred to in the Chicago Convention.

754. As a main rule, only aerodromes may be used for take-off and landing of aircraft (section 76 of the Aviation Act). An aircraft may temporarily use an open water area or other land or water area for take-off and landing with the consent of its owner or possessor, even if the area has not been specifically arranged for that purpose. Where necessary for aviation safety, the Transport and Communications Agency Traficom lays down provisions on temporary use of a land or water area, dimensions and surface conditions of an area to be used by aircraft, obstacle limitations and other factors affecting the safety of take-off and landing (section 76). Where necessary for reasons of flight safety, smooth flow of traffic, national defence, engagement in trade or prevention of adverse environmental effects, the Transport and Communications Agency may prohibit the use of an area other than an aerodrome or restrict the use of an area in temporary use for aircraft take-offs and landings. If the prohibition or restriction is imposed for reasons other than flight safety or smooth flow of traffic, the Transport and Communications Agency shall hear the Centre for Economic Development, Transport and the Environment and other authorities as necessary.

755. Construction of an aerodrome or other area serving aviation requires a permit (section 79 of the Aviation Act). A permit is also required for any changes to an aerodrome or other area serving aviation that might affect flight safety or have a significant effect on the landscape. The Construction Permit is issued by the Transport and Communications Agency Traficom. The Cabinet may reserve the right to decide on an individual case. As a main rule, any requirements with respect to planning, environmental law permits, EIA, construction and compulsory purchase pursuant to other legislation shall be complied with in the construction and modification of an aerodrome or other area serving aviation. An EIS and the respective reasoned conclusions shall be attached to the permit application, and the conclusions shall be included in the permit decision, as provided in the Environmental Impacts Assessment Act. Where an EIS already includes such information on environmental impacts as is needed for the application of the Aviation Act, the same enquiry need not be repeated. The permit decision shall indicate how the assessment in accordance with the said Act has been taken into account. For certain facilities and measures, the permits according to the Land Use and Building Act (as of 1 January 2025, the Building Act) are not needed.

756. When EIA is needed, the Construction Permit shall be publicly notified (section 79a). In any case, before a permit to construct an aerodrome is granted, the municipality and, depending on the matter, the Ministry of Defence, the Ministry of the Environment, the Centre for Economic Development, Transport and the Environment and the Regional Council shall be provided with an opportunity to state their opinions (section 80). Where the application for a Construction Permit concerns the construction or modification of an area serving aviation other than an aerodrome or its structures and facilities, the municipality concerned and, depending on the case, other relevant authorities and neighbours shall be provided an opportunity to state their opinions.

757. A Construction Permit shall be granted if the aerodrome or other area at stake, and its buildings, structures and facilities meet the requirements necessary for flight safety and a smooth flow of traffic, and an Environmental Permit under the Environmental Protection Act has been granted (section 81 of the Aviation Act). The Construction Permit may include provisions to ensure flight safety and a smooth flow of traffic. A Construction Permit may be denied for national defence reasons. The Transport and Communications Agency Traficom shall, based on the standards and recommendations of the Chicago Convention, issue more detailed regulations on the preconditions for granting a Construction Permit as necessary to ensure safe and smooth flight operations. A Construction Permit shall be issued for a period of at least five years.

When EIA has been needed, the Construction Permit decision shall explain the statements, opinions and remarks received and how they have impacted the decision. Also, the measures to be taken in order to abate significant harmful environmental impacts shall be explained and a description of the surveillance measures by the Transport and Communications Agency Traficom shall be included (section 81a).

758. From 31 December 2021, a Construction Permit decision, if EIA has been needed, can be appealed against also by registered environmental, conservation and public health associations and foundations, as well as by the affected municipalities, the Centres for Economic Development, Transport and the Environment and the Regional Councils (section 181a of the Aviation Act).

The permit may be revoked if the conditions attached to it are not complied with or the requirements for granting the permit are no longer met, and the permit holder has not corrected the deficiencies within a reasonable time determined by the Transport and Communications Agency Traficom.

759. As a main rule, an airport is required to have an approval certificate issued by the Transport and Communications Agency Traficom, except as otherwise provided below. The airport certificate specifies for which type of traffic or other aviation operations the airport may be used (section 82). An aerodrome which is not required to have an approval certificate in accordance shall, as a main rule, have an aerodrome operating permit granted by the Transport and Communications Agency, unless otherwise provided below (section 84). The aerodrome operating permit specifies the aerodrome operator and manager and determines for which type of traffic or other aviation operations the aerodrome may be used.

760. Construction Permit or operating permit shall not be required for light aviation aerodromes. However, the aerodrome operator shall notify the Transport and Communications Agency and serve it with necessary information ninety days before the construction of a light aviation aerodrome is started, and thirty days before the aerodrome is brought into use (section 86). The Agency may, for reasons of flight safety, prevention of harmful environmental effects or national defence, prohibit the construction or opening of a light aviation aerodrome or impose such conditions on its construction and use as deemed necessary for flight safety, environmental protection or national defence.

761. The imposition of permit conditions on noise abatement for the aviation activities is independently possible through the Environmental Protection Act. Even rejection of an Environmental Permit application (in case of applied enlargement) has occurred in the legal practice (pursuant to legislation prior to that of 2000).

762. The land use planning regulations may also be of relevance here. First, the probable noise pollution caused by an eventual airfield is one of the relevant premises when considering the contents of a potential plan (e.g., Local Master Plan). In other words, there are certainly sites in the country where land reservation for an airport would be contrary to the planning rules in the Land Use and Building Act (as of 1 January 2025, the Land Use Act).

But there is also another link between land use planning and aviation noise. In areas with significant noise levels new settlements may be undesirable. This may imply a legal hindrance to a Detailed Plan and subsequently to building in an area with planning need (*see* Part III, Chapter 3, §4 and §5). The SAC has issued a few precedent judgments on the problem (concerning areas in the neighbourhood of Helsinki-Vantaa airport). Here various premises in addition to the noise aspect were taken into account, such as the number of dwellings previously existing in the respective area and the impacts of land traffic. For some parts of the total Plan area it was decided that the Plan could not be confirmed. During the procedure, a noise level calculation model was drawn up by a foreign expert.

On a related environmental damages case, *see* paragraph 1536.

763. It is questionable whether a municipality might be liable for aviation noise, if a Detailed Plan has been approved in an area where the noise level is above the acceptable level or likely to rise above it. In any case, the Environmental Damages Act (*see* Part IV, Chapter 2, §2) is not applicable to the municipality in this situation.

Chapter 8. Radiation and Vibrations

§1. General Radiation Prevention

764. The Radiation Act (859/2018) contains precautionary regulations on exposure to radiation of various kinds, both man-made and natural, nuclear and non-nuclear. The Act covers use of radiation and other activities which cause or may cause exposure to radiation harmful to health. The provisions in the Nuclear Energy Act (*see* §2 below) on the use of nuclear energy are mainly unaffected, though. In section 2a of the Nuclear Energy Act the provisions of the Radiation Act that are applicable to the use of nuclear energy are specified.

The general principles of radiation control are laid down in Chapter 2 of the Act. According to the principle of justification in section 5, use of radiation and protection measures are justified if the total benefit outweighs the detriments. The optimization principle in section 6 in turn means that in order to optimize protection of individuals occupational and public exposure shall be kept as low as achievable by practical measures and that medical exposure shall be limited to the inevitable in achieving the intended results of examinations and treatments or in taking measures. And the principle of protection of individuals in section 7 regarding occupational and public exposure in radiation activities provides that the magnitude of individual doses shall not exceed the applicable dose limits.

The Radiation and Nuclear Safety Authority may under strict conditions grant an exceptional permit for an individual dose exceeding the dose limit (section 8). Dose limits and limitations on potential exposure are set taking into account the characteristics of the activity in such a manner that the exposure is expected to remain lower than the limitation as a result of the optimizing of radiation protection (section 9), Moreover, occupational and public dose limits are set in such a manner that total radiation dose from activities for which a security permit is needed is expected to be lower than the dose limit.

The taking into account of risks in supervision by authorities is provided in section 11, and safety culture and safety management by managements of organizations in section 12. The various duties of operators are set in Chapter 5 and the individual qualifications for the various experts in Chapter 6. Safety permits are largely required for use of radiation, as provided in Chapter 7. The Radiation and Nuclear Safety Authority is the permit authority. Radiation safety of products is provided in Chapter 8 and safety measurements in Chapter 9. Use of sources of radiation and limitations on use by operators are stipulated on Chapter 10.

765. The Radiation Act also contains rules for radioactive wastes (section 78) except those regulated by the Nuclear Act. An activity shall be arranged in such a manner that radioactive waste is produced as little as by practical measures possible and without jeopardizing the activity being in line with the principles of justification, optimization and the protection of individuals. The responsibility for the wastes lies primarily with the operator (section 79) and secondarily with the State (section 80). Bans and restrictions on import, export, transfer and transit are provided in section 82. Waste and other materials arising from radiation activity may be reused, recycled, recovered and disposed of in accordance with the Waste Act without hindrance to their radioactivity, if the amount of radioactive substance contained therein does not exceed the activity concentration value for exemption or clearance of certain materials by default laid down by virtue of section 85. The same applies to waste that is not radioactive waste in accordance of the Radiation Act, but for which radiation safety must be taken into account in waste management (section 84, 1165/2022).

766. As for natural radiation, reduction of radiation caused especially by naturally occurring radon in soil and bedrock, and indirectly also in construction concrete, is regulated by provisions in Chapter 18. Prior to initiating the following activities the Radiation and Nuclear Safety shall Authority shall be notified on them: (1) mining activities pursuant to the Mining Act; (2) quarrying and other work in underground space depending on the working periods; (3) treatment, use, storage and recycling of such substances and wastes the activity concentration values of U-238 or Th-232 or their decay products exceeds 1 Becquerel per gram: and (4) certain aviation activities.

Building constructors are obliged to minimize radon concentrations indoors in planning and constructing (section 157). A similar obligation regards owners and holders of dwellings (section 158). General reference values for radon in indoor air are set by Ministry of Social Affairs and Health decree. A national radon action plan shall be drawn up (section 159). As for construction in areas with high radon contents in the soil, the rules of the Land Use and Building Act (as of 1 January 2025, the Land Use and the Building Act) are applicable. This means, in extreme situations, that a land use plan or a permit may even be disallowed, or its contents may be affected, if the level of natural radiation is abnormally high.

767. The Radiation and Nuclear Safety Authority (STUK), subordinate to the Ministry of Social Affairs and Health, is the national authority responsible for the supervision of radiation protection and the Radiation Act. The Ministry of Economic Affairs and Employment has the responsibility in matters that concern nuclear energy. The Radiation and Nuclear Safety Authority has various supervisory powers pursuant to Chapter 20, among others, the power to give necessary orders to operators under Conditional Fines or under the risk that the measures needed will be taken by the Authority at the expense of the offender (section 184). Criminal sanctions are available.

§2. Nuclear Safety

I. Establishment and Operation of Nuclear Plants

768. The nuclear sector is regulated by the Nuclear Energy Act (990/1987; several amendments), complemented by the Nuclear Energy Decree (161/1988, several amendments).

769. The Nuclear Energy Act applies (section 2) to: (1) the construction, operation and decommissioning of a nuclear facility; (2) mining and milling operations aimed at producing uranium or thorium; (3) the possession, manufacture, production, transfer, handling, use, storage, transport and import of nuclear material; (4) the possession, manufacture, production, transfer, handling, use, storage, transport, export and import of nuclear waste; (4a) disposal of nuclear waste that is of a lesser extent than large-scale disposal of nuclear waste; (5) as specified by Government decree, the possession, manufacture, assembly, transfer and import of certain material, devices, equipment, or information, should they prove pertinent to the proliferation of nuclear weapons or should the obligations under international treaties in the field of nuclear energy have a bearing on them; and (6) export and import of ores containing uranium or thorium, as specified by Government decree. There are several additional specifications on the scope of application relating to international and EU law.

The objective of the Act (section 1) is to stipulate on general principles for the use of nuclear energy, on the implementation of nuclear waste management, on the licensing and control of the use of nuclear energy, and on the competent authorities, in order to keep the use of nuclear energy in line with the overall good of society, and in particular to ensure that the use of nuclear energy is safe for man and the environment and does not promote the proliferation of nuclear weapons.

770. The general principles are provided in Chapter 2 (sections 4–7). Import of nuclear explosives as well as their manufacture, possession and detonation in Finland are prohibited (section 5). The use of nuclear energy, taking into account its various effects, shall be in line with the overall good of society (section 6). The use of nuclear energy must be safe; it shall not cause injury to people, or damage to the environment or property (section 6). Nuclear waste generated in connection with or as a result of use of nuclear energy in Finland shall be handled, stored and permanently disposed of in Finland (section 6a). This obligation does not, however, apply in less relevant cases (small amounts of nuclear waste which will be, or have been, delivered abroad for research purposes;[45] nuclear waste containing minor quantities of radioactive material and which is delivered to another country for treatment in the appropriate manner; or nuclear waste that has been generated in connection with or as a result of the operation of a research reactor in Finland). Nuclear waste generated in connection with or as a result of the use of nuclear energy elsewhere than in Finland, shall not be handled, stored or permanently disposed of in Finland (section 6b). This obligation does not apply to small amounts of nuclear waste which will be or have been delivered to Finland for research purposes; or to nuclear waste of unknown origin pursuant to section 80(1).

771. Sufficient physical protection and emergency planning as well as other arrangements for limiting nuclear damage and for protecting nuclear energy against illegal activities is a general prerequisite for the use of nuclear energy (section 7). The safety of nuclear energy use shall be maintained at as high a level as practically possible (section (7a)). For the further development of safety, measures shall be

45. From 21 Dec. 2020, nuclear waste at stake may be disposed of in the country of destination (another Member State or a third country), on condition that at the time of shipment an agreement referred to in Art. 4 of Directive 2011/70/Euratom is in force at the time of shipment, as provided in s. 6a(3).

implemented that can be considered justified considering operating experience and safety research and advances in science and technology. The safety of a nuclear facility shall be ensured by means of successive levels of protection independent of each other (safety principle of defence-in-depth; section 7b). This principle has to be extended to the operational and structural safety of the plant.

772. Releases of radioactive materials caused by the use of nuclear energy shall be limited in accordance to the principle laid down in section 2(2) of the Radiation Act (section 7c). The maximum values of radiation exposure caused by a nuclear facility or any other use of nuclear energy on any member of the public will be provided for by Government decree.

Limits on releases of radioactive materials from a nuclear facility, in order that they do not exceed the maximum values for radiation exposure provided by Government decree, shall be confirmed by the Radiation and Nuclear Safety Authority. Supervision of releases of radioactive materials shall be arranged so that compliance with limits as referred to in this section can be reliably established.

773. The design of a nuclear facility shall provide for the possibility of operational occurrences and accidents (section 7d). The probability of an accident must be lower, the more severe the consequences of such an accident would prove for people, the environment or property. The prevention of accidents is the primary objective. Any practical measures required shall be taken to manage accidents and mitigate the consequences thereof. Maximum values for radiation exposure, to be used as a basis for safety design in case of operational occurrences and accidents, shall be provided by decree.

774. Compliance with requirements concerning the safety of a nuclear facility shall be proven reliably. The overall safety of a nuclear facility shall be assessed at least at ten-year intervals. The overall safety of a facility performing large-scale disposal of nuclear waste shall, however, be assessed at least at fifteen-year intervals (section 7e). Safety shall take priority during the construction and operation of a nuclear facility (section 7f). The holder of a Construction Permit (below), shall be responsible for the nuclear facility's construction in accordance with safety requirements. The holder of an operating permit is responsible for the nuclear facility's operation in accordance with safety requirements. In addition, the condition and operating experiences of any nuclear facility shall be systematically monitored and assessed.

775. The design of a nuclear facility shall provide for the facility's decommissioning, the related decommissioning plan being kept up-to-date on a regular basis, at least at six-year intervals (section 7g). When the operation of a nuclear facility has been terminated, the facility shall be decommissioned in accordance with a plan approved by the Radiation and Nuclear Safety Authority. Dismantling the facility and other measures taken for the decommissioning of the facility may not be postponed without due cause.

The nuclear facility shall have the facilities, equipment and other arrangements required to ensure the safe handling and storage of nuclear material required by the plant and any nuclear waste generated during operation (section 7h). Nuclear waste shall be managed so that after disposal of the waste no such radiation exposure is caused that would exceed the level considered acceptable at the time the final disposal is implemented. The disposal of nuclear waste in a manner intended as permanent shall be planned giving priority to safety and so that ensuring long-term safety does not require the surveillance of the final disposal site. Nuclear waste management plans shall be updated.

776. The holder of a permit that enables the use of nuclear energy shall have a sufficient number of qualified staff suitable for the related tasks (section 7i). There are additional provisions on the personnel, as well as on the management system (section 7j), responsible manager appointed by the permit holder (section 7k), arrangements for security being based on threat scenarios involved and on analyses of the need for protection (section 7l), security staff (section 7m–n), plant security regulation (section 7o), emergency response arrangements (section 7p), general security regulations (section 7q), detailed security requirements (section 7r), security inspections and intoxication tests (section 7s), use of forcible means and notification on incident (section 7t), means of force and use of firearms (section 7u), interference with the course of unmanned aircraft (section 7v), personnel health inspections (section 7w), and use-of-force training of security staff (section 7x).

777. The use of nuclear energy without a permit under the Act is prohibited (section 8), with certain minor exceptions regarding research and development. On request, the Ministry of Economic Affairs and Employment must give a binding advance ruling as to whether the intended activity requires that a permit be applied for.

778. It is the permit holder's obligation to assure safe use of nuclear energy (section 9). This obligation cannot be assigned to another. The permit holder shall also assure ensure that the products and services of contractors and subcontractors which affect the nuclear safety of the nuclear facility meet the requirements of the Act. The permit holder shall also carry out such security and emergency arrangements and other arrangements necessary for the limitation of nuclear damage which do not rest with the authorities. A permit holder whose operations generate or have generated nuclear waste (permit holder under a waste management obligation) shall be responsible for all nuclear waste management measures and their appropriate preparation, as well as for their costs (waste management obligation).

779. Cancellation of a permit or expiration of its validity shall not exempt the holder, or one who has had a permit, from compliance with the provisions of section 9, Chapter 6 on nuclear waste management and Chapter 7 on financial provision for the cost of nuclear waste management, or the provisions laid down by virtue of them, or provisions laid down the permit (section 10).

780. Construction of a nuclear facility of considerable general significance shall require a Cabinet decision-in-principle on that the construction project is in line with the overall good of society (section 11). Of the nuclear facilities are deemed to be of considerable general significance are the following: (1) plants operated for the generation of nuclear energy having a thermal power higher than 50 MW; (2) facilities serving as repositories for nuclear waste; and (3) facilities operated for purposes other than the generation of nuclear energy and the possession at any given time, of an amount of nuclear material or waste or involving a radiation risk, as defined by Government decree, that shall be deemed comparable with nuclear facilities under (1) above.

781. Before the decision-in-principle can be made by the Cabinet, *a* recommendation of the municipality is required. The fulfilment of the legal preconditions concerning safety and environmental risks is at the same time checked. A decision-in-principle is applied for by submitting an application to the Cabinet (section 12), on which the Ministry of Economic Affairs and Employment must obtain a preliminary safety assessment from the Radiation and Nuclear Safety Authority and a statement from the Ministry of the Environment as well as from the Municipal Council of the municipality intended to be the site of the facility, and from the neighbouring municipalities. Before the decision-in-principle is made, a public hearing is required (section 13). This means that first the applicant shall publish an overall report, drawn up in accordance with the instructions of the Ministry of Economic Affairs and Employment and checked by it, of the facility project, the assessed environmental impacts of the facility and its safety so that the report is available to the public. The ministry shall provide inhabitants and municipalities in the immediate vicinity of the facility as well as the relevant authorities and the public an opportunity to present their opinions in writing before the decision-in-principle is made. Furthermore, the ministry shall arrange a public hearing in the municipality where the planned site of the facility is located and during this hearing the public shall have the opportunity to give their opinions either orally or in writing. All opinions shall be made known to the Cabinet.

Before making the decision-in-principle, the Cabinet shall ascertain that the municipality where the nuclear facility is planned to be located in its statement is in favour of the facility and that no facts indicating a lack of sufficient prerequisites for constructing a nuclear facility (in section 6), have arisen (section 14). Provided that no such obstacle is found, the Cabinet shall, in its decision-in-principle, consider the issue from the viewpoint of the overall good of society, and take the advantages and disadvantages arising from the nuclear facility into consideration. Particular attention shall here be paid to: (1) the need for the nuclear plant project from the viewpoint of national energy supply; (2) the suitability of the intended location of the facility and its environmental impacts; and (3) arrangements for the nuclear fuel supply and nuclear waste management.

782. If the decision-in-principle is positive to the applicant, i.e., the construction of the nuclear facility is considered to be in line with the overall good of society, the decision shall include the conditions necessary to implement the general principles of Chapter 2 and the safety requirements in accordance with the Act (section 14a). The Cabinet shall take into consideration the proposals presented in the preliminary safety assessment by the Radiation and Nuclear Safety Authority referred to in section 12. The decision-in-principle shall be forwarded, without delay, to the

Parliament (section 15). The Parliament may either reverse the decision-in-principle as such or decide that it remains in force as such. Before the decision of the Parliament, the applicant is not allowed to engage in any measures (specified by Government decree) which, due to their economic significance, might impede the Parliament's, and the Cabinet's, possibilities to determine the issue at their own discretion. A decision-in-principle cannot be appealed against (section 75).

783. The role of the Parliament here is quite exceptional, because according to the Constitution it has no part in single administrative decisions, regardless of the importance of the matter. This is why the Nuclear Energy Act had to be enacted as a constitutional exception, i.e., by the majority then needed for amendment of the Constitution.

784. The Cabinet decides upon the permits to construct and operate a nuclear facility, as well as for mining and ore milling operations aimed at producing uranium or thorium (section 16).

Permits for certain minor operations are decided upon by the Ministry of Economic Affairs and Employment or the Radiation and Nuclear Safety Authority. A permit to use nuclear energy may be granted only to natural persons, corporations or authorities under the jurisdiction of an EU Member State (section 17). There are some exemptions regarding transport, import and export and temporary operations and international organizations.

785. A permit to construct a nuclear facility to which section 11 applies may be granted (section 18), if: (1) a decision-in-principle has deemed the construction of the nuclear facility to be in line with the overall good of society, and the Parliament has decided that the decision-in-principle remains in force and (2) the construction of the facility also meets the prerequisites for granting a Construction Permit for a nuclear facility as provided in section 19 (in the following).

786. A permit for the construction of a nuclear facility other than above can be granted (section 19) provided that: (1) the facility plans meet the safety requirements, and appropriate account has been taken of the safety of workers and the population when planning the operations in question; (2) the location of the nuclear facility is appropriate in respect to the safety of the planned operations and environmental protection has been taken into account appropriately in the planning; (3) physical protection has been taken into account appropriately in the planning; (4) the site has been reserved for the construction of a facility in a Detailed Plan pursuant to the Land Use and Building Act (as of 1 January 2025, the Land Use Act), and the applicant is in possession of the site required for the facility; (5) the methods available to the applicant for arranging nuclear waste management, including the final disposal of nuclear waste and the decommissioning of the facility, are sufficient and appropriate; (6) the applicant's plans for arranging nuclear fuel management are sufficient and appropriate; (7) the applicant's arrangements for the implementation of control by the Radiation and Nuclear Safety Authority in Finland and abroad, and for the implementation of control are sufficient; (8) the applicant has the necessary expertise available; (9) the applicant has sufficient financial prerequisites to implement the project and carry on operations; and (10) the applicant is otherwise considered to have the prerequisites to engage in operations safely and in accordance with Finland's international contractual obligations. Moreover, the planned nuclear facility shall also otherwise fulfil the principles stipulated in sections 5–7.

787. A permit to operate a nuclear facility may be granted (section 20), if a permit has been granted for its construction and if: (1) the nuclear facility and its operation meet the safety requirements, and appropriate account has been taken of the safety of workers and the population, and environmental protection; (2) the methods available to the applicant for arranging nuclear waste management, final disposal of nuclear waste and decommissioning of the facility included, are sufficient and appropriate; (3) the applicant has sufficient expertise available and, in particular, the competence of the operating staff and the operating organization of the nuclear facility are appropriate; (4) the applicant is otherwise considered to have the financial and other prerequisites to engage in operations safely and in accordance with international contractual obligations; and the planned nuclear facility and the operation thereof otherwise fulfils the principles laid down in sections 5–7. Operation of the nuclear facility shall not be started on the basis of a permit granted: (1) until the Radiation and Nuclear Safety Authority has ascertained that the facility meets the safety requirements set, that the physical protection and emergency planning are sufficient, that the necessary control to prevent the proliferation of nuclear weapons has been arranged appropriately, and that the permit holder of the nuclear facility has, as provided, arranged indemnification regarding liability in case of nuclear damage; and (2) until the Ministry of Economic Affairs and Employment has ascertained that provision for the cost of nuclear waste management has been arranged in accordance with the provisions of the Act.

788. After terminating the operation of a nuclear facility, the permit holder shall undertake measures to decommission the nuclear facility in accordance with the plan for and the requirements set on decommissioning pursuant to section 7g as well as apply for a permit for decommissioning of the nuclear facility. The permit shall be applied for well in advance so that the authorities have adequate time to assess the application before the termination of the operating permit. A permit for decommissioning may be granted if: (1) the nuclear facility and its decommissioning meet the requirements relating to safety in accordance with the Act and if the safety of the employees and the population as well as environmental protection have been duly taken into account; (2) the methods available to the applicant for the decommissioning of the nuclear facility as well as other nuclear waste management are adequate and appropriate; (3) the applicant has the necessary expertise available, and especially if the competence of the nuclear facility personnel and the organization of the nuclear facility are appropriate and suitable for decommissioning; (4) the applicant has the financial and other necessary requirements for carrying out the decommissioning safely and in accordance with Finland's international contractual obligations; and (5) the nuclear facility and its decommissioning fulfil the principles provided in sections 5, 6, 6a, 6b and 7.

The decommissioning may not be started before the granting of the permit unless otherwise provided in the other permits of the permit holder. The decommissioning may not be started on the basis of the permit granted for it until: (1) the Radiation and Nuclear Safety Authority has ascertained that the nuclear facility meets the safety requirements for decommissioning, that the security and emergency arrangements are sufficient, that the control necessary to prevent the proliferation of nuclear weapons has been arranged appropriately, and that the nuclear facility operator has arranged, in accordance with the related provisions, indemnification regarding liability in the event of nuclear damage; and (2) the Ministry of Economic Affairs and Employment has ascertained that provision for the costs of nuclear waste management has been arranged in accordance with the provisions of Chapter 7 (section 20a).

789. A permit for the operations regarding other use of nuclear energy than operating a nuclear facility may be granted (section 21), when required by operations, if: (1) the use of nuclear energy meets the safety requirements, and appropriate account has been taken of the safety of workers and the population, and environmental protection; (2) the applicant has possession of the site needed for the use of nuclear energy; (3) nuclear waste management has been arranged appropriately and provision for the cost of nuclear waste management has been made in accordance with the provisions of the Act; (4) the arrangements for the implementation of control by the Radiation and Nuclear Safety Authority, in Finland and abroad, and for the implementation of control are sufficient; (5) the applicant has sufficient expertise available and the operating organization and competence of the operating staff are appropriate; (6) the applicant is considered to have the financial and other prerequisites to engage in operations safely and in accordance with Finland's international contractual obligations; (7) the authorizations required under the Directive on the supervision and control of shipments of radioactive waste and spent fuel (2006/117/Euratom) have been obtained from foreign States, and if said provisions can also be observed otherwise, and if the use of nuclear energy otherwise meets the principles laid down in sections 5–7, and is not in conflict with the obligations under the Euratom Treaty.

790. No use of nuclear energy other than operating a nuclear facility shall be initiated on the basis of a granted permit until the Radiation and Nuclear Safety Authority has ascertained, when so required by the operations, that the use of nuclear energy is in accordance with the safety requirements set, that the physical protection and emergency planning are sufficient, that the control necessary to prevent the proliferation of nuclear weapons is appropriate and that indemnification regarding liability in case of nuclear damage in connection with the operations has been arranged in compliance with the relevant provisions (section 21). When considering the granting of a permit for mining and milling operations aimed at producing uranium or thorium, the requirements are different. In this case (1) and (3–5) above shall be applied so that the prerequisites for a permit therein are regarded to be met if the plans presented by the applicant are sufficient. Additionally, the site of the mining activity or the milling plant shall be appropriate with respect to the safety of the operations intended. In addition, the Radiation and Nuclear Safety Authority shall ascertain that the mining and milling operations meet the prerequisites laid down in (1) and (3–5). In any case, it is required that the municipality of the location of the mining and milling operations aimed at producing uranium or thorium, has explicitly been in favour of the granting of the permit.

791. The Cabinet shall request a statement from the Radiation and Nuclear Safety Authority and from the Ministry of the Environment on a permit application unless this is clearly unnecessary with a view to the nature of the operations. The Radiation and Nuclear Safety Authority shall include in its statement a proposal for permit provisions which are necessary in order to implement the safety requirements in accordance with Chapter 2a (section 23).

On the obligation to enclose to a permit application an EIA report and a reasoned conclusion of a competent authority, when needed, the Environmental Impact Assessment Procedures Act is applied. In such cases, a public notice shall be given of the lodging of the permit application, which shall be published on the websites of the permit authority and the municipalities. The Centre for Economic Development, Transport and the Environment shall also be reserved the possibility to issue a statement on the application. A registered association or foundation, the purpose of which is to promote environmental, health or nature protection or the attractiveness of the living environment and within the operating area of which the said environmental impact will emerge, may express an opinion on the application.

Before a permit for mining and milling operations aimed at producing uranium or thorium is decided upon, the applicant shall submit an (environmental) account to which section 13 is applicable respectively (section 23). Such an application and a possible parallel Mining Permit application under the Mining Act (*see* paragraph 1088) of the same activity shall be decided upon simultaneously by the Cabinet. This means that also all detailed provisions and detailed claims by various parties under the Mining Act, also when they have no connection to the nuclear aspects, shall be dealt with directly by the Cabinet instead of the ordinary administrative procedure and that the SAC will be the first and only appellate court instance (without need to have leave to appeal, though). This is very exceptional.

792. Particular provisions apply to implementation of the Common Market (section 21a) and nuclear facilities built for operation in a vehicle (section 22).

793. Before granting a Construction Permit or an operating permit, or a permit for decommissioning, the Ministry of Economic Affairs and Employment shall reserve the public an opportunity to express their opinions in writing. An adequate time limit shall be set for this. The applicant shall be reserved an opportunity to submit an explanation on the opinions as well as on the statements requested in accordance with the Act (section 23a).

A permit, excluding a Construction Permit, shall be granted for a fixed period of time (section 24). When considering the length of the period, particular attention shall be paid to estimated duration of the operations and ensuring safety. The permit may include a provision that it shall expire if the operations are not started within a fixed period from the granting thereof (section 25).

The permit shall include the terms (provisions) necessary for implementing the general principles in Chapter 2 (section 25). The permit authority shall also observe the proposals relating to safety presented in the statement by the Radiation and Nuclear Safety Authority. The permit shall also include the measures presented by the applicant for preventing or reducing significant detrimental environmental impacts in the case of a project to which the Environmental Impact Assessment Procedures Act applies.

A decision on a Construction Permit shall be notified in public. The decision shall also be delivered to those interested parties that have separately requested for the decision (section 25a).

794. The terms in a valid permit may be later on amended in order to maintain the general principles for the use of nuclear energy and the preconditions for granting of a permit, especially when this is necessary in order to ensure the safe use of nuclear energy, to secure nuclear waste management, to implement security or emergency arrangements, to fulfil the international agreements in the nuclear energy sector to which Finland is a contracting party or to prevent the proliferation of nuclear weapons.(section 25). When amending the permit terms, the same procedure shall be complied with, where applicable, as when granting a permit.

795. The permit authority at stake shall cancel a permit wholly or partly (section 26), if implementation of the general principles for the use of nuclear energy is essentially endangered, e.g., as a consequence of: (1) the permit holder violating the permit conditions or regulations issued by an authority by virtue of the Act; (2) the permit holder neglecting the financial provision obligation referred to in Chapter 7 of the Act, or violating the Nuclear Liability Act (484/1972) in a manner referred to in section 41 of that Act; or (3) the permit holder dying or losing legal capacity or the corporation or foundation holding the permit being dissolved, otherwise discontinuing operations or going into bankruptcy. Cancellation of a permit requires that a reasonable period of time has been allowed to correct the deficiency, where possible by means of the permit holder's actions. When cancelling a permit, the same procedure shall be followed, as appropriate, as when the permit was granted.

796. If a permit to construct or operate a nuclear facility is cancelled or a permit to operate a nuclear facility is denied, the holder of the cancelled permit or the applicant whose permit to operate the nuclear facility has been denied, is entitled to a reasonable amount of compensation from the State for the direct expenses incurred in the construction of the facility (section 27). Compensation shall not be paid, however, if the reason for cancellation is that section 6 or 7 can no longer be observed in the operating, or that the permit holder has acted contrary to the Act or the regulations under it, or for reasons referred to in (2) or (3) of section 26 (above). Nor shall compensation be paid if the permit to operate the facility has been denied because the facility and its operation do not meet the principles laid down in sections 6 and 7 or the prerequisites provided in (4) of section 20 (above). The Ministry of Economic Affairs and Employment and whoever is entitled to compensation shall try to reach an agreement on the amount of the compensation. The text of the agreement shall be sent to the Cabinet for ratification. Should an agreement not be reached, a suit for compensation must be filed before the Regional Administrative Court, within two years following the decision on which the suit for compensation is based has become legally valid.

II. Nuclear Waste Management

797. The provisions on nuclear waste management in the Nuclear Energy Act have been reformed in 2017. The leading principle of nuclear waste management is that the amount of nuclear waste generated in the use of nuclear energy shall be kept as small as reasonably achievable with practical measures with regard both to the activity and the amount without endangering the implementation of the general principles in accordance with sections 5, 6 and 7 of the Nuclear Energy Act (section 27a).

A national nuclear waste management programme shall be drawn up of the national nuclear waste management policy and the management of spent nuclear fuel, presenting the general goals and principles of nuclear waste management, the amounts of nuclear waste, their sites as well as an estimate of the costs and schedule of nuclear waste management. The programme shall be drawn up by the Ministry of Economic Affairs and Employment together with the Radiation and Nuclear Safety Authority. When drafting the programme, the public shall be reserved an opportunity to express their opinions. The programme shall be updated on the basis of the self-assessments and international peer reviews pursuant to section 54a (section 27b).

798. Nuclear waste other than spent nuclear fuel may, regardless of its radioactive nature, be reused, recycled, recovered and disposed of in accordance with the Waste Act, i.e., be released from regulatory control under the Nuclear Energy Act, if the amount of radioactive substances within it does not exceed the clearance level for implementing EU legislation as provided under the Nuclear Energy Act. If the amount of radioactive substances within the waste is greater than the clearance level, the operations require the approval of the Radiation and Nuclear Safety Authority. Approval may be issued if: (1) the exposure and potential exposure caused by the operation are so minor that they would not be detrimental to health; (2) the operation has determined to be justified; and (3) the operation is inherently safe. The approval may be withdrawn if the prerequisites for release from regulatory control are not met or the conditions for release from regulatory control have not been complied with and the deficiencies have not been rectified within the specified time despite a request to do so (section 27c). Clearance levels shall be set in such a way that the exposure caused to members of the public is of minor significance. Clearance levels may apply to facility site, building or waste (section 27d). Nuclear waste shall not be deliberately diluted to release it from regulatory control under the Act.

799. The Ministry of Economic Affairs and Employment or the Radiation and Nuclear Safety Authority, having granted a permit for operations generating nuclear waste, shall, having consulted the Ministry of the Environment on the matter if necessary, determine the principles on the basis of which the waste management obligation pursuant to section 9 is to be implemented (section 28 of the Nuclear Energy Act). For this purpose, a permit holder under the waste management obligation shall present, for assessment by the body granting the permit, a plan for carrying out nuclear waste management.

800. For the duration of the operations subject to a permit, the plan for carrying out nuclear waste management shall be presented regularly at three-year intervals, unless otherwise provided in the permit. The plan shall also include a general plan for the following six years. Unless otherwise provided in the permit, a plan for the decommissioning of the nuclear facility shall be presented regularly, at six-year intervals, for the duration of the operations subject to a permit.

801. The Ministry of Economic Affairs and Employment may order permit holders under the waste management obligation to undertake waste management measures jointly, if by doing so safety can be increased or costs can be substantially reduced or if any other weighty reason so requires. At the same time, provisions shall be laid down, if needed, on the distribution of the costs incurred due to the measures to be carried out jointly (section 29).

802. When the possession of a nuclear facility, a mine intended for the production of uranium or thorium, a milling factory or nuclear waste is assigned to another subject, the Ministry of Economic Affairs and Employment may, on request, completely or partially transfer the waste management obligation to the assignee, if the transfer of the obligation does not endanger the carrying out of nuclear waste management (section 30).

803. If the Ministry of Economic Affairs and Employment considers that a permit holder under a waste management obligation has substantially failed to observe the confirmed time schedules for nuclear waste management of the nuclear waste he has generated or has otherwise violated the provisions on the implementation of nuclear waste management, the Cabinet shall decide whether the permit holder's actions, judged on the whole, give good reason to conclude that nuclear waste management, as a whole or in part, cannot be carried out by the permit holder. If the answer is negative, the Cabinet shall order that such nuclear waste be assigned to the State, or to a domestic corporation under the control of the State, for the implementation of the nuclear waste management measures still required (section 31). The same is possible when, despite an order made under section 65(2), the permit holder under a waste management obligation has not fulfilled the financial provision obligation. However, the Cabinet may not order the transfer of the nuclear waste insofar as making such an order would place the State in a disadvantageous financial position with respect to meeting the purpose of financial provision measures.

804. The Ministry of Economic Affairs and Employment, or the Radiation and Nuclear Safety Authority, having issued a permit for operations that generate nuclear waste, shall order that the waste management obligation has expired (section 32) when: (1) it has been transferred to another subject pursuant to section 30; or (2) the nuclear waste has been transferred outside Finland in the approved permanent manner according to section 6a; or (3) the final disposal of nuclear waste and the decommissioning of a nuclear facility have been carried out in accordance with section 33, and the permit holder under a waste management obligation has paid a lump sum to the State for the monitoring and control of the nuclear waste. Should the Cabinet have issued an order under section 31, the State shall be responsible thereafter for the nuclear waste management measures not yet carried out for the waste at stake, and for the costs to be incurred in carrying out these measures by the permit holder under a waste management obligation.

805. Final disposal of nuclear waste is considered implemented when the Radiation and Nuclear Safety Authority has confirmed the waste to be permanently disposed of in a manner it has approved (section 33). A nuclear facility is considered decommissioned when the same authority has confirmed that the quantity of radioactive materials remaining in the buildings and soil of the facility site complies with the requirements specified under the Act.

806. When the permit holder's waste management obligation has ceased pursuant to (3) of section 32 (above), the ownership of the nuclear waste is transferred to the State, which shall be responsible thereafter for the nuclear waste (section 34). Should it become necessary after the final disposal, the State has the right, at the disposal site, to take all measures required for the monitoring and control of the nuclear waste and for ensuring the safety of the repository.

III. Financial Preparedness for Future Costs of Nuclear Waste Management

807. The permit holder under a waste management obligation shall make financial provision for the future costs referred to in section 9 (section 35 of the Nuclear Energy Act), as provided in the Act. Here nuclear waste is considered to include also such materials, objects and structures which, having become radioactive in connection with or as a result of the use of nuclear energy, require special measures because of the danger arising from their radioactivity, even if they have not yet been taken out of use. The costs of nuclear waste management may also be considered to include the charges incurred in nuclear waste management pursuant to section 77.

808. A permit holder under a waste management obligation shall fulfil the financial obligation by payment for each calendar year of the charges into the National Nuclear Waste Management Fund, and shall furnish the State with the securities pursuant to the Act as a precaution against insolvency (section 36). For purposes of implementing the financial provision, there is the National Nuclear Waste Management Fund, independent of the State budget but controlled and administered by the Ministry of Economic Affairs and Employment (section 38). The permit holder under a waste management obligation shall pay a fund contribution to the fund so that the fund holding on the last day of March is equal to the fund target for the current calendar year (section 42). At the end of each calendar year, the Ministry of Economic Affairs and Employment shall confirm the liability of each party with a waste management obligation for the current calendar year and make a decision on the liability for the following two years. At the same time, the ministry shall confirm the fund target for the following year. The ministry may derogate from the schedule referred to above on reasonable grounds (section 43). The permit holder under a waste management obligation shall supply the State with collateral securities fulfilling the conditions provided in section 45, before the commencement of the waste-generating operation and, otherwise, in any case by the end of June, so that the total guarantees held at that time by the State are equal to the difference between the assessed liability at the end of the calendar year and the fund target (section 44).

809. Detailed provisions on the fund and the securities are included in sections 37–53.

IV. Ensuring of Expertise

810. To meet the general principle in section 5 of the Nuclear Energy Act, any operator who: (1) has a valid permit to operate a nuclear facility of considerable general significance; (2) has a valid permit to construct such a nuclear facility, but not yet a permit to operate it; or (3) has submitted an application on the basis of which the Cabinet has made a decision-in-principle on such a nuclear facility, which is in force, but no permit based on it for construction has not been granted, have to participate in financing of research aimed at ensuring that, should such new factors concerning safe operation of nuclear facilities emerge that could not be foreseen, the authorities have such sufficient and comprehensive nuclear engineering expertise and other facilities at their disposal that can be used, when needed, to analyse without delay the significance of such factors (section 53a).

The obligation shall be fulfilled by annual fees into the National Nuclear Waste Management Fund, collected from nuclear facility operators, amounting to EUR 570 in 2016–2020 and EUR 390 in 2021–2025 for each rated thermal output MW given in the permit or for the highest thermal output MW set forth in the decision-in-principle, or if a Construction Permit has been applied for by virtue of the decision-in-principle, for the rated thermal output MW given in the permit application. A lower amount may be provided for by Government decree.

These fees shall be kept apart from the other funds of the National Nuclear Waste Management Fund.

811. Similarly, to meet the general principle laid down in section 5, any operator for whom an assessed liability has been fixed subject to section 43(2) shall be obliged to participate in financing research aimed at ensuring that the authorities have such sufficient and comprehensive nuclear engineering expertise and other facilities at their disposal that are needed for comparisons of the various ways and methods of carrying out nuclear waste management (section 53b). The obligation shall be fulfilled by paying annually a fee into the National Nuclear Waste Management Fund, amounting to 0.08% of the assessed liability fixed subject to section 43(2). This amount may also be fixed to be lower by Government decree.

Also these assets shall be kept apart from the other funds of the National Nuclear Waste Management Fund.

812. Further provisions in these separate funds are included in section 53c. Financing of research projects, research infrastructure and further training projects is provided in section 53d and applying for, granting and collecting of research funding in section 53e.

V. Nuclear Energy Authorities, Supervision and Enforcement

813. The Ministry of Economic Affairs and Employment is vested in the supreme command and supervision of the nuclear energy sector. Unless otherwise provided, it is also the competent Finnish authority referred to in the Euratom Treaty. The Radiation and Nuclear Safety Authority (STUK), operating under the Ministry of Social Affairs and Health, again is responsible for the supervision of safe use of nuclear energy. In addition, it is responsible for the supervision of physical protection and emergency planning, and for the necessary control of the use of nuclear energy to prevent proliferation of nuclear weapons.

Self-assessments and international peer reviews of the national framework and system are provided in section 54 and 54a.

814. The Radiation and Nuclear Safety Authority participates in the processing of permit applications pursuant to the Act. The Authority, being also a regulatory body, has the right to issue detailed safety regulations and other regulations, as specified in section 55. Separate provisions, partly of reference character only, apply to safety at work (section 59), pressure equipment (section 60), supervision and inspection of pressure equipment, structures and mechanical devices (section 60a), radiation protection, transport of nuclear material and liability for nuclear damage (section 61) and cooperation among authorities (section 62).

815. The supervisory and inspection powers of the Radiation and Nuclear Safety Authority are specified in section 63.

816. If the Radiation and Nuclear Safety Authority finds that, in order to secure the safe use of nuclear energy, it is necessary to make changes in the construction of a nuclear facility or in the operation relating to its construction or use to maintain appropriate physical protection or emergency planning or to fulfil obligations under international contractual obligations in the field of nuclear energy, the Authority shall, having consulted the permit holder, oblige him to carry out the necessary changes within the time specified (section 64).

817. If the provisions, those in permits included, concerning safety, physical protection or emergency planning have not been observed in the use of nuclear energy, the Radiation and Nuclear Safety Authority shall, having consulted the permit holder, issue instructions to remove the defects or faults, and at the same time oblige the permit holder to take the required measures within the time specified (section 65). The same applies to defects or faults that follow from a failure to comply with other provisions in or under the Act, or other permit conditions. In these cases the competence may lie also upon another authority specified by decree.

818. The authority may impose a conditional fine or a threat of interrupting or limiting the operation or taking the neglected action at neglecting party's expense (section 66). Having consulted the permit holder, the Radiation and Nuclear Safety Authority may also interrupt the operation or limit it, if a defect or fault should cause immediate danger, or if there is otherwise justified cause for suspecting that the operation presents such a danger (section 67). Operations may be interrupted or limited until the reason for the issuance of the provision no longer exists. The same applies, if supervision hereunder cannot be implemented otherwise, or if the permit holder has failed to comply with provisions issued by the Authority, or if the permit holder has failed to comply with his obligations under the Nuclear Liability Act.

Criminal sanctions are provided in section 69 and in the Penal Code.

VI. Appeals

819. As a main rule, decisions by the Cabinet (the decision-in-principle excluded), the Ministry of Economic Affairs and Employment and the Radiation and Nuclear Safety Authority can be appealed against pursuant to the Administrative Judicial Procedures Act, regarding Cabinet decisions directly in the SAC and otherwise in a Regional Administrative Court. In some cases, a decision can be enforced in spite of an appeal. In case of the Cabinet permits to construct (sections 18 and 19 of the Nuclear Energy Act), also any registered association and foundation whose purpose is to promote protection of environment, health or nature, or the amenities of living environs and within the geographical area of which the relevant environmental impacts appear, is entitled to appeal (section 75a).

VII. Other Legislation

820. A permit granted under the Nuclear Energy Act does not exempt the permit holder from observing the requirements and provisions laid down for the operations in other legislation (section 57). An Environmental Permit under the Environmental Protection Act is always required (Table 2 of Annex 1 to the Environmental Protection Act). The Water Act is also applied to nuclear plants, for quite different reasons, as the intake of water (also) to a nuclear plant normally requires a permit of the Regional State Administrative Agency (*see* Part II, Chapter 8, §3, VIII). For discharges of condensation water to surface waters, the Environmental Protection Act is applied (due to the thermal energy which tends to entail polluting effects).

821. The provisions of the Land Use and Building Act (as of 1 January 2025, the Land Use Act) on planning and building apply also in an area intended for the site of a nuclear facility. Nevertheless, before a Detailed Plan may be drawn up for the area intended site of a nuclear facility, and prior to the approval of such a plan, a statement shall be obtained from the Radiation and Nuclear Safety Authority (section 58). In practice, already the Regional Plans may include reserved locations for future nuclear plants.

§3. Liability for Nuclear Damage

822. Liability for nuclear damage is based on international agreements. The Paris and Brussels Conventions are implemented by the Nuclear Liability Act (484/1972 with later amendments). The system is based on the strict liability of the nuclear plant operator, who in turn is obliged to have an appropriate insurance or, under certain conditions, give other acceptable security. The strict liability is however limited to certain maximum compensation amounts based on the conventions. Certain exceptional conditions may also imply limitation of liability. Besides civil liability, the Act contains supplementary rules on State liability and State insurance guarantee for nuclear liability insurance. The applicable administrative powers are vested in the Financial Supervisory Authority.

§4. Vibrations

823. Vibration is one of the emission categories mentioned in the definition of pollution of environment in the Environmental Protection Act (section 5(1)1), *see* paragraph 120. Similarly, it is one of the possible physical reasons for nuisance pursuant to section 17 of the Neighbourhood Relations Act. This in turn makes vibration, like noise, highly relevant for the legal preconditions and contents of an Environmental Permit under the Environmental Protection Act (in particular, pursuant to sections 49 and 52 of the said act), e.g., regarding quarrying and stone crushing (*see* below Part II, Chapter 7, §2). Moreover, the notification procedure pursuant to section 118 of the Environmental Protection Act applies to temporary activities causing particularly disturbing vibration (*see* above Part I, Chapter 8, §4). Also the Public Health Act may be applied to vibrations creating a health risk.

As for civil liability for damage caused by vibrations, the Environmental Damages Act is explicitly applicable.

Chapter 9. Other Sectors

§1. CONTROL OF CHEMICALS

I. The Chemicals Act

824. The Chemicals Act (599/2013) aims to protect health and the environment from the hazards and harm caused by chemicals. Unlike its predecessor originally, the Act does not contain a rather comprehensive overall stipulation on chemicals. Instead, the Act lays down provisions on the enforcement of the EU chemicals legislation as listed in section 6, in particular the REACH Regulation and the CLP Regulation, and certain national obligations regarding chemicals. The Act also, for its part, implements Regulation (EC) No. 765/2008 of the European Parliament and of the Council setting out the requirements for accreditation and market surveillance relating to the marketing of products. The Act is additionally applied to biocidal products, the efficacy of which is based on a microorganism. Certain exceptions to the general scope of applicability are provided in sections 3 and 4 of the Act.[46] Market surveillance and related supervisory authorities as well as controls at the Union's external borders pursuant to Regulation (EU) 2019/1020 on market surveillance and compliance of products and amending Directive 2004/42/EC and Regulation (EC) No. 765/2008 and (EU) No. 305/2011 are stipulated in the Act on the Market Surveillance of Certain Products (1137/2016, as amended). The notion of chemical is determined pursuant to the REACH and CLP Regulations (section 6). An operator is anyone who manufactures, imports, places on the market, exports, stores, packs, delivers, has in his possession, keeps or uses a chemical in a manner referred to in the Chemicals Act or the EU chemicals legislation.

825. On the contrary, the Chemicals Act is not exhaustive regarding chemicals. Provisions on the prevention and abatement of harm and danger caused by chemicals to human health and the environment and of the physical harm and danger caused by chemicals are also laid down in fourteen other acts (section 5), such as the Environmental Protection Act, the Act on Environmental Protection in Maritime Transport and the Waste Act, the Safety of the Handling of Dangerous Chemicals and Explosives, the Public Health Act, the Radiation Act and the Tobacco Act (549/2016).

826. A separate act, the Act on the Safety of the Handling of Dangerous Chemicals and Explosives (390/2005) is applicable to the manufacturing, use, transfer, storing, preserving and other handling of hazardous chemicals.

827. Transport of hazardous chemicals and other substances, be is by road, rail, air or vessel, is regulated by the Act on the Transport of Dangerous Substances (540/2023) and the respective Government decree (925/2023). In the Act, a dangerous substance refers to a substance, mixture, solution, object, instrument or article that,

46. Regarding defence activities, *see* Government decree on derogations concerning national defence from the application of chemicals legislation (217/2022).

due to its explosion, fire, infectious, radiological or environmental hazard, flammability, reactivity, toxicity, corrosivity, production of potentially dangerous reactions or other such properties, may cause damage to people, the environment or property during transport. The Act shall be applied unless otherwise provided by EU legislation or an international obligation binding on Finland. According to section 147 of the Act, sections 137 and 176(2) of the Environmental Protection Act apply to the remediation of significant pollution of groundwater or surface water bodies caused by the transport of dangerous goods or damage to nature referred to in section 5a of the Nature Protection Act.

828. In addition to the provisions of EU chemical legislation, the following general principles are applied to activities involving the use of chemicals: (1) the operators are in their activities sufficiently aware of the effects of the chemical on human health and the environment and of the requirements related to the sales of the chemical; (2) sufficient diligence and care is applied to the prevention of harm to human health and the environment, while taking into account the amount and hazardousness of the chemical; and (3) when reasonably possible, the choice between the existing chemicals or methods to use in the prevention of the harm caused by chemicals is made based on the one that is the least hazardous (section 19 of the Chemicals Act).

In addition to the provisions on marketing, labelling and packaging in the chemical legislation of the EU, the marketing of chemicals may not refer to a chemical in a manner that is misleading or untruthful as concerns the risks posed by the chemical to human health or the environment. Article 72 of the Biocidal Products Regulation[47] is applicable to the marketing of the biocidal products referred to in Chapter 5 of the Chemicals Act.

829. An operator who is responsible for placing a hazardous chemical on the market or in use in Finland must provide information on the chemical to the Finnish Safety and Chemicals Agency (Tukes). Such an operator and an operator who has been issued an authorization decision under section 30 of the Act must also provide information to the Agency on the amounts of biocidal products and hazardous chemicals it has placed on the market or in use. Further provisions on submitting information referred to in subsections 1 and 2 above shall be given by a decree of the Ministry of Social Affairs and Health.

830. Anyone who exports a chemical from the EEA shall submit a notification and otherwise follow the procedure laid down in the PIC Regulation[48] (section 23). Placing restrictions on the retail trade of chemicals and the obligation to provide information are provided in section 25.

831. The authorization of biocidal products is stipulated in Chapter 5 of the Chemicals Act. The following biocide categories are covered: a biocidal product

47. Regulation (EU) No. 528/2012 concerning the making available on the market and use of biocidal products.
48. Regulation (EU) No. 649/2012 concerning the export and import of hazardous chemicals.

means: (1) a protective chemical intended for the treatment of timber to protect it from degradation or destruction caused by harmful organisms (wood preservative), or to prevent the growth of slime and blocking caused by the growth of harmful microorganisms in cooling or water circulation systems, or to protect cellulose pulp and wood-containing pulp from degradation and destruction caused by harmful organisms (slimicide); (2) an antifouling product that is intended to prevent the growth of microbes and more developed plant and animal species from attaching themselves to vessels, the equipment in fish farms and other structures used in water (antifouling product); and (3) a biocidal product intended for use as a fly control product or insecticide, for pest control of species occurring in human dwellings, cowsheds, warehouses and other indoor facilities, or for some other purpose equivalent to these.

832. A biocidal product may not be placed on the market or used without due authorization for the product, unless otherwise provided later in the Act or in the Biocidal Products Regulation.[49] Decisions concerning the authorization are made by the Finnish Safety and Chemicals Agency (Tukes) (section 27). The authorization applications are stipulated on sections 29–33. Biocidal products shall be used as intended following the instructions for use. Also other provisions laid down by law are also applicable to the use of biocidal products (section 35).

Chapter 6 contains certain additional provisions on biocides, such as qualification on the use of biocidal products intended for pest control.

833. Where a chemical is not restricted in the REACH Regulation, the Cabinet may decide to restrict or ban, for a specified period of time or until further notice, the manufacture, import, placing on the market and other supply, export or use of the chemical or article containing the chemical or other handing of the chemical equivalent to these, and give orders concerning restrictions and conditions for operations, if the use of the chemical or article containing the chemical is found or justifiably assessed to cause serious harm or a hazard to human health or the environment. The decision above can also be taken to invoke a safeguard clause in the EU chemicals legislation. If preventing the harm or hazard requires rapid measures, the Safety and Chemicals Agency (Tukes) may issue temporary order necessary bans and restrictions. In this case, the matter must be brought to the Cabinet without delay (section 45b).

834. An operator that does not comply with the provisions of the Act or EU chemicals legislation, the supervisory authority at stake may ban the operator from continuing operations or repeating procedures in violation of the provisions or it may order the operator to otherwise fulfil the obligations laid down by law. Particularly, the Finnish Environment Institute may ban a chemical or article containing a chemical from being placed on the market or from being made available on the market, or give orders on the return procedure or notification of the hazard inflicted, or

49. Regulation (EU) No. 528/2012 concerning the making available on the market and use of biocidal products.

order that the chemical be made harmless by taking appropriate measures in compliance of the PIC Regulation or section 23(1) or section 23(2) of the Act, the order or ban is issued by the Finnish Environment Institute. The Administrative Injunctions (Conditional Fines) Act is applicable.

835. Rights of supervisory authorities to receive information and carry out inspections are provided in section 48, rights to obtain samples and conduct research in section 49, the using of an expert in section 50, international exchange of information in section 51, and rights to receive information from other authorities and disclosing confidential information in section 52.

The Administrative Judicial Procedures Act is applicable as usual, subject to a couple of modifications (section 55).

Claims to protect business and professional secrets are stipulated in section 56 of the Chemicals Act. Restrictions on trade and professional secrets concerning chemicals are listed in section 57, and those regarding biocidal products in section 58. A very detailed stipulation on criminal sanctions is included in Chapter 9.

836. The general responsibility of implementation of the Chemicals Act is divided between two ministries and subordinate authorities respectively. This fact reflects the various objectives of the legislation – and at the same time the administrative difficulties in creating the system; initially the ministries were two. The Ministry of Social Affairs and Health is responsible for matters concerning prevention and control of health hazards and physical hazards and harms, and the Ministry of the Environment for matters concerning the prevention and control of the environmental disadvantages caused by chemicals (section 7).

837. The Chemicals Act is supervised by several authorities, within the respective sectors of competence of each, as specified in sections 8–13: the Finnish Safety and Chemicals Agency (Tukes), the Finnish Environment Institute, the occupational safety authorities, Centres for Economic Development, Transport and the Environment, the Municipal Environmental Protection Authorities, Finnish Medicines Agency Fimea and the customs. Regarding defence activities, the Defence Forces are vested in specified duties (section 14; on the general exceptions applicable to Defence Forces *see* section 3).

The Finnish Safety and Chemicals Agency acts as the competent authority pursuant to Article 121 of the REACH Regulation, Article 43 of the CLP Regulation, Article 81 of the Biocidal Products Regulation and Article 8 of the Detergents Regulation[50] as well as the appointed body pursuant to Article 45 of the CLP regulation and the competent authority pursuant to the Mercury Regulation[51] (section 15).

The Finnish Environment Institute acts as the competent authority pursuant to Article 15 of the POP Regulation[52] and as the designated national authority under

50. Regulation (EC) No. 648/2004 on detergents.
51. Regulation (EU) 2017/852 on mercury, and repealing Regulation (EC) No. 1102/2008.
52. Regulation (EC) No. 850/2004 on POPs and Amending Directive 79/117/EEC.

Article 4 of the PIC Regulation.[53] The Finnish Environment Institute also acts as the designated national authority pursuant to the Rotterdam Convention, unless otherwise provided in the PIC Regulation (section 15).

The Finnish Safety and Chemicals Agency organizes a national helpdesk to provide an advisory service under Article 124 of the REACH Regulation, Article 44 of the CLP Regulation and Article 81 of the Biocidal Products Regulation for manufacturers, importers, downstream users, distributors and any other interested parties (section 16).

Registries of the Finnish Safety and Chemicals Agency are provided in section 17, and the national Advisory Committee on Chemicals in section 18.

II. Industrial Handling and Storage of Chemicals

838. From the environmental point of view, an important subsystem in the original Chemicals Act was made up of the provisions for the control needed for the industrial handling and storage of chemicals, especially of substances dangerous to health and the environment. This subsystem, being totally reformed in 1999, had been strongly influenced by the COMAH or *Seveso II* Directive 96/82/EC. Today, the provisions have been removed from the Chemicals Act, and the Act on the Safety of the Handling of Dangerous Chemicals and Explosives (390/2005, amendments) is applicable instead.

839. The purpose of the Act on the Safety of the Handling of Dangerous Chemicals and Explosives is to prevent and control personal, environmental and property damages caused by the manufacturing, use, transfer, storing, preserving and other handling of hazardous chemicals and explosives. Moreover, the Act aims at promoting general safety.

The Act is, with certain exceptions, also applicable to defence activities. It is not applicable to transport outside the production premises, that being provided in the Act on Transport of Dangerous Substances, or to temporary storing closely connected to transport, to the preparation, use and storing of explosives in mines, as far as provided in the Mining Act, to the use and storing of hazardous chemicals in vessels, to radioactive substances or to products containing radioactive substances.

840. The requirements of the Council Directive 96/82/EC on the control of major accident hazards involving dangerous substances, also known as the COMAH or the *Seveso II* Directive, including the subsequent amendment Directive 2003/105/EC, have been taken into account by the Act on the Safety of the Handling of Dangerous Chemicals and Explosives, but also by the Government decree on the Supervision of Handling and Storage of Dangerous Chemicals (685/2015), the Government decree on Safety Requirements for Liquid Petroleum Gas Facilities (858/2012), the Government decree on Safety in Dealing with Natural Gas (551/2009),

53. Regulation (EC) No. 689/2008 concerning the export and import of dangerous chemicals, and of Rotterdam Convention on the prior informed consent procedure for certain hazardous chemicals and pesticides in international trade.

the Government decree on the Supervision of Manufacturing and Storage of Explosives (819/2015). All these have been issued by virtue of the Act on the Safety of the Handling of Dangerous Chemicals and Explosives. The Land Use and Building Act (as of 1 January 2025, the Land Use Act and the Building Act), the Environmental Protection Act, the Rescue Act (379/2011), the Ministry of the Interior Decree on outer rescue plans for items posing a particular danger (406/ 2011) and the Government decree on the control of major accident hazards liable to affect workers (922/1999) are likewise relevant.

841. Council Directive 75/324/EEC of 20 May 1975 on the approximation of the laws of the Member States relating to aerosol dispensers, as amended numerous times, is from 1 December 2020 implemented separately, mainly by the Act on the Conformity of Aerosols (794/2020) and the respective decree (834/2020).

842. The operators are obliged to be aware of the properties of the chemicals produced, handled or stored by them (section 7 of the Act on the Safety of the Handling of Dangerous Chemicals and Explosives). To prevent and control damages of chemicals and explosives, the operator shall, where reasonably possible, opt for such chemical, explosive or method among several possible that poses the least hazard (section 8). Sufficient care to avoid personal, environmental and property damages shall be taken. Where a careless handling of hazardous chemical or explosive has caused pollution of the environment or of constructions, the operator or other polluter is responsible for clean-up so that danger to health or the environment is eliminated (section 9). The operator shall take all necessary means to prevent accidents and to restrict the impacts thereof on man, the environment and property, as specified in section 10. Sections 11–16 contain obligations of the operator in respect to organization and personnel, on operating and maintenance, on equipment and devices, on the planning of the industrial area, on buildings and constructions and on the prevention of access of those not concerned.

843. Industrial installations where hazardous chemicals or explosives are produced, handled or stored, shall be sited at such distance from dwelling areas, buildings and areas in public use, schools, hospitals and care institutions, industrial installations, storages, transport areas and other outside activities that explosions, fires or chemical discharges do not cause any beforehand assessable risk of personal, environmental or property damages in these premises (section 17). Also, the distance from particularly important and particularly sensitive areas from the viewpoint of the nature, from other items important to environmental protection and recreational areas shall be such that explosions, fires or chemical discharges do not cause any beforehand assessable risk of personal, environmental or property damages in these items (section 18). Without a specific, reasoned ground, an industrial installation may not be sited in important or other, for water supply suitable groundwater area, if it cannot be proved on the basis of the characteristics of the chemical that no risk to groundwater is caused. In any case, the risk of groundwater pollution shall be eliminated by construction planning and maintenance (section 18). The site shall also be such that an outside activity or natural conditions do not create risk of accident (section 19). The present and future land use assigned in a land use plan (pursuant to the Land Use and Building Act, as of 1 January 2025, the Land Use Act) with legal consequences, and the provisions in the plan, where any, shall be taken into account (section 20).

844. The handling and storing of hazardous chemicals is regarded as either extensive or small-scale, depending on the quantities and dangerousness, and paying attention also to all chemicals handled or stored by the same operator in the same installation (section 22; *see also* sections 4 and 5 of Decree 685/2015). For extensive handling and storing permit of the Finnish Safety and Chemicals Agency (Tukes) is needed, as specified in section 23. For small-scale handling and storing, a notification to the local rescue authority is required, instead (section 24). When an area contains both extensive and small-scale activities, the notification is submitted to the Finnish Safety and Chemicals Agency (Tukes). Provisions based on the safety requirements may be included in a permit. Where an EIA is needed for the installation, it is the duty of the operator to submit an EIS. The permit decisions have to include a comment on how the EIS and the opinion of the liaison authority have been taken into consideration. Because often an Environmental Permit pursuant to the Environmental Protection Act is also needed, the EIA may be relevant in both procedures. Supervision and inspections on extensive industrial handling and storing are provided in section 26a.

In a permit procedure pursuant to section 23, a neighbour within the risk area has been regarded to have sufficient individual interest for appeal (SAC 2008:51).

The Act on the Permit Procedure of Projects of Common Interest of the EU (684/2014; *see* paragraph 66) may be applicable to permits pursuant to section 23 (and section 27).

845. The Act also contains provisions on systematic inspections of industrial facilities (section 27), supervision and inspections on small-scale handling and storing (section 27a), internal rescue plans (section 28), on assigned responsible persons for handling and storing hazardous chemicals (section 29) and on specified measures to prevent major accidents and the publicity of the accounts (sections 30–32).

846. In addition to the permit provided in section 23 (above), an area with extensive storing of hazardous chemicals by two or more operators shall be approved by the Finnish Safety and Chemicals Agency if the conditions specified in section 33 are met. As the safety preconditions of such a permit, the general obligations of the Act are applicable. Specified conditions may be imposed in the permit (section 34).

847. Moreover, the Act contains obligations regarding storing of hazardous chemicals (sections 35–36), transfer of hazardous chemicals (sections 37–40). A subsystem of its own is provided for the prevention and protection regarding explosions (sections 41–45), as well as for products that are connected to hazardous chemicals (sections 48–52) and for installation and maintenance of equipment (sections 53–57). Pursuant to section 54, the owner or possessor is responsible for inspections of underground oil tanks at fixed intervals, where located in important or other, for water supply suitable groundwater areas. The inspector shall be approved by the Finnish Safety and Chemicals Agency.

Storages of chemicals hazardous to health or environment largely need registration pursuant to the Environmental Protection Act (Annex 4(2) to the said Act).

848. The manufacturing and storing of explosives (permits, inspections, etc.) are stipulated in sections 58–66 of the Chemicals Ac, the approval, import and transfer of explosives in sections 67–77, the use, delivery and storing of explosives in sections 78–90 and fireworks in sections 91–97. The obligations regarding accidents caused by hazardous chemicals or explosives (notification duties, inspections) are laid down in sections 98–99. The inspection bodies are stipulated in sections in sections 100–104, specified bans, restrictions and enforcement measures (i.e., cancelling of a permit) in sections 105–113, and supervision by authorities in sections 114–122 and conditional fine, etc. in section 123 and penalties (largely referring to the Penal Code) in section 124.

III. Biocidal Products

849. The Biocidal Products Regulation, complemented by the Chemicals Act (*see* above, in particular 828–832) has made the previous special legislation on biocides mainly unnecessary. The present Government decree on Biocidal Products (418/2014), issued by virtue of the Chemicals Act, contains only a few complementary provisions on authorization decisions and qualifications.

IV. Agricultural Chemicals

850. The implementation of the legislation on agricultural chemicals, such as plant protection products and fertilizers, is largely the responsibility of the Ministry of Agriculture and Forestry and subordinate authorities, in cooperation with other branches of administration. The Finnish Food Safety Authority is largely responsible for the supervision of the use of both plant protection products and fertilizers (*see* below).

851. The Fertiliser Act (711/2022) applies to production, placing on the market, use, transport, import and export of fertilizer products and their ingredients, and additionally also on the use of manure. The Act also contains the provisions on the supervision and other enforcement of the Fertiliser Products Regulation (Regulation (EU) 2019/1009 laying down rules on the making available on the market of EU fertilizing products and amending Regulation (EC) No. 1069/2009 and (EC) No. 1107/2009 and repealing Regulation (EC) No. 2003/2003). A fertilizer product shall not, among other things, contain such amounts of harmful substances, products or organisms that its use, pursuant to the directions of use, may cause danger to the health or safety of humans or animals, plant health or the environment (*see* section 5 of the Fertiliser Act).

852. The Finnish Food Authority is responsible for the implementation of the Fertiliser Products Regulation and the Fertilisers Act, as well as for supervising and arranging compliance with them. In addition to the Finnish Food Authority, the Centres for Economic Development, Transport and the Environment supervise fertilizer products in their regions, and the import of fertilizer products is supervised by the customs. Provisions on the market surveillance of fertilizer products are laid down in the Act on the Market Surveillance of Certain Products.

853. An operator who uses fertilizer products or manure in agriculture, horticulture or landscaping and environmental construction in connection with business activity shall keep a record file of the fertilization and, upon request, provide the information with the supervisory authority. The file shall include the places where fertilizing products or manure have been applied, the quantities of phosphorus contained in the fertilizing products and manure and the date on which the fertilizing products or manure were applied. The file shall be kept for five years from the end of the year in which the fertilizing product or manure was applied. A Government decree lays down more detailed provisions on the use of fertilizer products and phosphorus contained in manure, as well as on the content and organization of files (section 6 of the Fertilisers Act). Government decree on the Use of Phosphorus-containing Fertiliser Products and Manure (64/2023) contains more detailed provisions.

854. Under a previous Fertilisers Act, the Ministry of Agriculture and Forestry has enacted by Decree (45/1994, that being in force to the entering into force of the present Act in July 2022) that the maximum amount of cadmium in fertilizers containing phosphorus was more stringent than that of the then EC law. A temporary exception concerning the highest permissible cadmium concentration for Finland was, due to the natural conditions, allowed already by the agreement on the EEA, and a temporary exemption was also agreed upon when Finland became a member country of the EU. The Fertiliser Products Regulation lays down maximum permitted limit values for harmful substances, such as heavy metals, by product category. The maximum limit value for cadmium there is now 60 mg Cd/kg P2O5 for inorganic fertilizers and organo-mineral fertilizers containing 5% or more phosphate (P2O5). This does not affect the situation in Finland, as Finland may retain the derogation last granted in 2006 by Commission Decision 2006/348/EC to limit the maximum cadmium content in fertilizers to 22 mg Cd/kg P2O5 until this maximum limit value is equal to or lower than that laid down in the Fertilising Products Regulation. The present national modifications are included in the Decree of the Ministry of Agriculture and Forestry on Fertilising Products (964/2023).

855. The Act on Plant Protection Products (1563/2011) contains the provisions on general requirements, studies and examination, devices for spreading and testing thereof, operations, authorities, supervision, enforcement and criminal sanctions concerning plant production products. The Act also applies to the supervision and enforcement of Regulation (EC) No. 1107/2009 concerning the placing of plant protection products on the market and repealing Council Directives 79/117/EEC and 91/414/EEC, as well as to the implementation, Chapter V excluded, of Regulation

(EC) No. 396/2005 of the European Parliament and of the Council on maximum residue levels of pesticides in or on food and feed of plant and animal origin and amending Council Directive 91/414/EEC. From November 2020, the provisions also contain the implementation provisions for Commission Directive (EU) 2019/782 amending Directive 2009/128/EC of the European Parliament and of the Council as regards the establishment of harmonized risk indicators.

The general aim of the Act is to safeguard proper and sustainable use of plant protection products and reducing of risks arising from the use thereof.

The general steering and supervision is the task of the Ministry of Agriculture and Forestry. The main responsibility for supervision and enforcement of the Act is divided between the Finnish Safety and Chemicals Agency (Tukes) and the Food Authority, and also the customs participate. The two main authorities may be assisted by authorized inspectors, and the Food Authority also by the Centres for Economic Development, Transport and the Environment.

856. Spraying from aircraft is forbidden, with two exceptions (section 20). First, the Food Authority may allow it in the connection of measures against herbivores pursuant to the Plant Health Act (1110/2019), if there is an imminent threat to plant health and other effective means of prevention may not be reasonably used. Second, the Ministry of Agriculture and Forestry may, at the proposal of a regional unit of the Finnish Forest Centre, in connection of measures pursuant to the Act on the Abatement of Forest Damage (1087/2013, *see* Part II, Chapter 5, §2), allow spraying of plant protection substance from aircraft in order to prevent extensive damage of forest trees by insects or fungi, and the damage may not be by other effective means reasonably prevented. Additional provisions on aircraft spraying have been laid down in section 21. Among other things, the impacts on the health of humans and the environment shall be smaller than by spraying from earth level. The product in use shall be approved for aircraft spraying, the person in charge shall have a valid certificate, and the device in use shall be tested pursuant to the Act. Particular care shall be taken so that no danger to the health of man or animals or unreasonable harm to the environment is caused. Several local authorities shall be informed in advance, and the very operation shall take place under the supervision of the Centre for Economic Development, Transport and the Environment.

§2. Genetically Modified Organisms

857. Gene technology with respect to Genetically Modified Organisms (GMOs) and products containing such organisms has been regulated by the Gene Technology Act (377/1995, several amendments) and the Government decree on Gene Technology (928/2004). The aim of the Gene Technology Act, which is largely based on the EC GMO Directives, at present Directive 90/219/EEC on the contained use of genetically modified microorganisms and Directive 2001/18/EC on the deliberate release into the environment of GMOs and repealing Council Directive 90/220/EEC, is to promote the safe use and development of gene technology in accordance with the precautionary principle and in a way that is ethically acceptable, and to protect human and animal health and the environment when carrying out the contained use or deliberate release into the environment of GMOs.

858. The general guidance and supervision of the Act is divided between the Ministry of Social Affairs and Health (general guidance and particularly human health), the Ministry of the Environment (prevention and control of adverse environmental impacts) and the Ministry of Agriculture and Forestry (agriculture, forestry, fisheries and game). The main official functions under the Gene Technology Act are carried out by the Board for Gene Technology, appointed by the Cabinet for five years at a time. Among other tasks, the Board is the competent authority pursuant to Directives 90/219/EEC and 2001/18/EY, and also the competent authority pursuant to Regulation (EC) No. 1946/2003 on transboundary movements of GMOs and to the Cartagena Protocol on Biosafety.

859. A risk assessment is required from the operator when transgenic organisms are containedly used or deliberately released to the environment. It shall be safeguarded that possible adverse effects on the health of man or animals and on the environment through gene transfer directly or indirectly from GMOs to other organisms are assessed (section 8). The use of antibiotic resistance marker genes which are harmful to human or animal health or the environment is prohibited when deliberately releasing GMOs into the environment. When using GMOs the carefulness and caution required by the organism or organisms in question shall be observed (section 8a). Duties to obtain information, update documents, keep a record and monitor are provided in sections 9–11.

860. Contained use of modified microorganisms is classified into four classes and the corresponding isolation levels on the basis of risk assessment in order to protect the health of man and animals and the environment, as provided in section 13. If there is doubt as to which class is appropriate for the intended contained use, more stringent containment and protective measures shall be used until the Board for Gene Technology has, based on sufficient evidence, approved the application of less stringent measures.

861. Premises for contained use shall be notified to the Board for Gene Technology (section 14), as well as the first use of genetically modified microorganisms and plants in class 2 (section 14a). Intended first contained use of modified microorganisms and plants in classes 3 and 4 and of animals in class 2 requires application to the Board for Gene Technology, as provided in section 14b. The right to commence contained use depends on the class and the stage of the required administrative proceedings, as provided in section 15, or, for previously notified premises, in section 16. On the basis of an application submitted to it, the Board for Gene Technology shall grant a permit for contained use, if the use does not, according to the outcome of the risk assessment, cause harm to the health of man or animals or the environment, taken the required isolation and protection measures. Provisions may be imposed in the permit (section 16a). The operator is obliged to submit to the Board essential new information related to the risk assessment. The permit may be amended on the basis of the information (section 16b). Notification shall also be made of accidents and danger incidents (section 16c). In a matter concerning contained use, the Board may decide to hear the public on certain items, taking the secrecy provided in section 32 (below) into account (section 36a).

862. Deliberate release of GMOs and combinations thereof into the environment for other purpose than marketing is stipulated in sections 16d–19a. For such a release in Finland a permit of the Board for Gene Technology is required, as provided in section 17 of the Gene Technology Act. The release may only be commenced by virtue of a written permit of the Board, and observing the provisions laid down in the permit (section 18b). The procedure within the EU is provided in section 18. A permit shall be granted, if, according to the outcome of the risk assessment pursuant to section 8, there is no risk to the health of man or animals or the environment, and the technical documents meet the requirements in section 17. If these requirements are not met, the application shall be rejected (section 18). The decision shall be made within ninety days of the application, the time for waiting for the required additional information from the operator and the time for public hearing excluded. Provisions on monitoring and risk management may be imposed in the permit (sections 11 and 18). The public shall be heard on a planned deliberate release (for purposes other than marketing) and publish a notice on the filed application and the procedural information specified in section 36b. The provisions on secrecy in section 32 (*see* paragraph 866) shall be taken into account.

863. Provided that there is sufficient experience on the release of certain modified organisms in certain ecosystems and that the organisms meet the requirements of EU law, exceptions to the permit procedure regarding deliberate release may be made (section 18a). The outcomes of the release shall be reported to the Board pursuant to section 19. The obligations of the operator (i.e., the applicant or the permit holder) in case of amendment in the release, that being deliberate or not, or in case of new information, are provided in section 19a. On the basis of new information that is significant in relation to the risks or to the conditions of release, the Board shall assess such information and make it public. The Board may also impose the operator new obligations, if necessary in order to prevent or reduce significant risks to health or the environment.

864. The placing on the market of products containing a GMO or a combination of them is stipulated in sections 19b–21f. A permit of the Board for Gene Technology is required.

865. The Board for Gene Technology and the supervisory authorities are vested in the enforcement powers specified in sections 22–24a, 28–31 and 38. Section 23 provides order for the prevention and remediation of significant environmental damage under the Environmental Liability Directive and the Act on the Remediation of Certain Damages Caused to the Environment (383/2009). If proceedings are not initiated ex officio, they may be initiated (section 36c of the Gene Technology Act) by: (1) one whose right or interest may be concerned, and (2) a registered association or foundation the aim of which is protection of nature or the environment, provided that the relevant impacts appear in its geographical area of activities.

866. The National Supervisory Authority for Welfare and Health maintains the Gene Technology Register (sections 26–27), which only can be used be the relevant authorities (*see* section 26b). The Board for Gene Technology decides on providing data from the register.

The operator is empowered to check the registered information regarding him. The Act on the Openness of Government Activities (621/1999, amendments) is applicable on the documents to and by authorities pursuant to the Gene Technology Act. Pursuant to a specific list in section 32 of the Gene Technology Act, secrecy does not, irrespective of the Act on the Publicity of Administration, cover the date of the document, the name and address of the operator, general description of the modified organisms, the site, purpose, extent and intended use and monitoring of modified organisms, class of contained use and the isolation measures thereof, methods and plans for emergency incidents, risk assessment or permit documents. Classified documents may in addition be used for certain authority purposes (section 33).

867. As a deviation from general provisions, the Gene Technology Board may at the request of the operator decide that the information regarding applications for deliberate release of GMO, as specified and provided in section 32a (481/2021), is classified.

868. The decisions of the Board for Gene Technology are appealed against before the Regional Administrative Court. Regarding a decision of a supervisory authority, administrative review by the Board shall in the first place be requested, and only the decision of the Board may be appealed against in the Regional Administrative Court.

869. Compensations for damage arising as a consequence of GMO operations are mainly decided upon pursuant to either the Product Liability Act (694/1990, amendments) or the Environmental Damages Act (*see* Part IV, Chapter 2, §2 below), depending on the nature of the damage and the option of the claimant, and in cases out of the scope of any of the two, pursuant to the Damages Act.

870. The Act on Restrictions on the Cultivation of Transgenic Organisms (445/2019) sets forth provisions on national arrangements pursuant to Directive (EU) 2015/412 of 11 March 2015 amending Directive 2001/18/EC as regards the possibility for the Member States to restrict or prohibit the cultivation of GMOs in their territory. The provisions, being applicable from 1 January 2020, include restrictions and supervision rules. Pursuant to sections 6 and 7 of the Act, new cultivation of transgenic organism may be restricted or prohibited by Government Decree, regarding whole Finland or part of it. Such measures shall be in conformity with EU law, reasoned, proportional and non-discriminatory as well as based on compelling grounds such as those related to environmental policy objectives, land use planning, land use, socioeconomic impacts, avoidance of GMO presence in other products, agricultural policy objectives, or forest policy objectives. The administrative tasks and powers are vested in the Ministry of Agriculture and Forestry, the Gene Technology Board and the Finnish Food Authority.

§3. Rational Use of Energy

871. There is no coherent legislation on the various duties and incentives to promote rational use of energy and energy efficiency. Such aspects have nevertheless in various manifestations been included in the legislation. For example, in activities under the Environmental Protection Act the use of energy shall be effective (section 8 of the Environmental Protection Act).

872. According to the Land Use and Building Act (up to 2025), a constructor shall see to that the building is planned and constructed in such a way that energy and natural resources are used sparingly. Calculations shall show that the minimum requirements of energy efficiency are fulfilled, as in detail provided in section 117g of the Act. A new building consisting of a covered construction with walls and where energy is used in order to maintain appropriate climate conditions inside, shall be planned as 'nearly zero-energy buildings' (section 117g(2)). Such a building is defined in section 115a, according to Annex I to Directive 2010/31/EU (below). The heating mechanism of a building shall be assessed as provided in section 117h. From December 2021 it is required in the new section 117l that at least 38% of the calculated purchasing energy used in the energy calculation of a new or large-scale renovation building is renewable energy, if technically, operationally and economically feasible. As of 1 January 2025, the corresponding provisions on energy efficiency are included in section 37, provisions on nearly zero-energy buildings in section 11 and provisions on minimum share of energy from renewable sources in section 14 of the Building Act. Anyone undertaking a construction project shall assess the technical, environmental and economic feasibility of an alternative heating system if it is planned to instal a building-specific fossil fuel-based heating system as the heating system for a new building (section 13).

873. Directive 2010/31/EU of 19 May 2010 on the energy performance of buildings was implemented, largely, through the Act on Energy Performance Certificates for Buildings (50/2013). The purpose of the Act is to improve the energy performance of buildings and use of renewable energy in them, particularly by promoting possibilities to comparative methods for assessing energy efficiency. The owner of a building, a few buildings such as buildings for non-commercial leisure dwelling purposes intended for annual use of less than four months, as specified in section 117g of the Land Use and Building Act up to end of 2024 and as of 1 January 2025 in section 37 of the Building Act, is in the first place responsible for obtaining a certificate and for using it. A certificate is also required for Building Permit applications, and in connection of sale or hiring out, as specified in sections 5 and 6.

In addition to the directive-based provisions on certificates, the Act also includes provisions on supervision, coercive measures and registers. The amending Directive 2012/27/EU has caused some amendments in the original Act.

874. Directive (EU) 2018/844 of 30 May 2018 amending Directive 2010/31/EU on the energy performance of buildings and Directive 2012/27/EU on energy efficiency has been implemented, in addition to Ministry of the Environment Decree 718/2020, by the Act on the deployment of recharging points and recharging infrastructure and of automation and monitoring (733/2020). The Act is as such applicable to buildings where energy is used for maintaining indoor climate condition. In addition, it is partly applicable to detached car park buildings for the use one of more dwelling buildings irrespective of the lack of heating. Buildings of the Defence Forces are excluded. The requirements for public recharging points are set forth in the Act on the delivery or alternative fuels used in traffic (478/2017).[54] Recharging points and recharging infrastructure are, as based on the Directive (EU) 2018/844, are regulated in Chapter 2, automation and steering systems in Chapter 3 and the powers of authorities, and supervision, in Chapter 4.

General steering, surveillance and development under the Act is vested in the Ministry of the Environment. In the supervision, the provisions of the Land Use and Building Act up to end of 2024 and as of 1 January 2025 the Building Act are also here applicable, as partly modified in section 17, and the municipal Building Supervision Authorities are the competent authorities. Section 7 on the geographical location of and access to public fuelling and recharging points is supervised by the Transport and Communications Agency.

875. The Act on Biofuels, Bioliquids and Biomass fuels (393/2013), as updated, *inter alia*, due to Directive (EU) 2018/2001 of 11 December 2018 on the promotion of the use of energy from renewable sources (RED II), contains the implementing provisions on requirements of biofuels, bioliquids and biomass fuels and verification of compliancy. The Act, the provisions of which are largely equivalent to those of the Directive, is applicable as provided in the Act on the Promotion of Biofuels in Traffic (446/2007), the Act on Excise Duty on Liquid Fuels (1472/1994), the Emissions Trading Act (1270/2023), the Act on the Reduction of Greenhouse Gas Emissions Caused by Certain Fuels during their Life Cycle (170/2018) and the Act on the Promotion of Biofuel Oil (418/2019).

876. The Act on the Promotion of Biofuels in Traffic (446/2007, as amended, largely to meet Directive (EU) 2018/2001 of 11 December 2018 on the promotion of the use of energy from renewable sources, and in part temporarily, by 657/2022, 1134/2022 and 1279/2023) aims to enhance the use of biofuels in traffic instead of gasoline and diesel oil. The distributors of traffic fuel are obliged to supply biofuels according to minimum quotas of all traffic fuels distributed, as specified in the Act. The obligations under this Act have been a bone of daily political content, larger than its economic size and separate from climatic objectives.

54. Directive 2014/94/EU of the European Parliament and of the Council of 22 Oct. 2014 on the deployment of alternative fuels infrastructure has been implemented by this Act.

877. On the Act on the Requirements for Ecodesign and Energy Label of Products, *see* paragraph 87.

878. Pursuant to section 57a (1129/2008) of the then Land Use and Building Act, it was possible to include in a Detailed Plan an order to connect new buildings to a district heating network, if necessary in respect to effective and sustainable use of energy, targeted air quality or other targets of the plan. It was presupposed that the network is accessible in practice. Based on deregulation aims, section 57a was repealed in 2018.

879. The Act on temporary state budget support for the purchase of alternatively propelled vehicles and for conversion of vehicles with alternative propulsion (89/2021) provides for state budget support for the purchase of an alternatively propelled vehicle, i.e., purchase and long-term rental, and for the conversion of the vehicle with alternative propulsion. Procurement aid may be granted for the purchase of an all-electric passenger car (support for the purchase of an all-electric car) and for the purchase of an electric lorry or electric trailer or a gas-powered lorry (lorry purchase aid) in 2022 and 2023, and for the purchase of an electric or gas-powered van (van purchase aid) in 2022. Conversion aid may be granted for the conversion of the vehicle into alternative propulsion (conversion aid) in 2022 and 2023.

880. The Act on the Promotion of Biofuel Oil (418/2019; amendments) aims at the use of biofuel oil to replace light fuel oil in heating, machinery and fixed engines. A distributor whose light fuel oil delivered for consumption during a calendar year exceeds 1 million litres shall supply biofuel oil for consumption as provided in the Act.

Part II. Nature Conservation and Management

Chapter 1. Main Enactments, Monuments and Landscapes

§1. General Provisions on Conservation and Protection of Nature

881. The Nature Conservation Act of 1996 included a comprehensive system of measures for the protection and conservation of nature. One of the main subsystems was that for establishing preserves of various kinds, both in State-owned and private areas. One modification is the mechanism for preserving individual trees, stones and other natural formations, called natural monuments. There were also mechanisms for the protection of endangered species, which, as those for preserves and monuments, basically originate from the previous Nature Conservation Act from 1923. This Act, of course, had been amended several times during the years, but it still remained unsatisfactory. A more general reform was long politically controversial, but the Finnish membership in the EU changed the situation, as the two EC conservation directives (the Birds Directive, then 79/409/EEC, and the Natural Habitats Directive, then 91/244/EEC) had to be implemented from the beginning of 1995. All the same, the entering into force of the 1996 Act was delayed to January 1997. As a whole, the range of measures available for nature conservation was considerably extended by the reform. An additional extension took place in 2009 due to the entering into force of the legislation implementing the Environmental Liability Directive (2004/35/EC). The provisions were partly included in the then Nature Conservation Act, as far as damage to nature is concerned, and otherwise in several other acts.

882. In force from 1 June 2023 onwards, a new Act (9/2023) replaced the 1996 one. For several parts its regulation is almost direct continuation to those of the predecessor, but there are also new instruments and the general structure is more consequent. The title of the new Act is in Finnish and Swedish identical to its predecessors (*luonnonsuojelulaki/naturvårdslagen*), but because the Act increasingly extends beyond traditional conservation, the translation Nature Protection Act is chosen here.

Åland has nature conservation regulations of its own.

883. The Nature Protection Act applies to the protection and management of nature and landscape. The aim of the Act is: (1) to safeguard biodiversity; (2) fostering natural beauty and landscape values; (3) promoting adaptation to climate change; (4) supporting the sustainable use of natural resources and the natural environment; (5) raising citizens' knowledge of nature and environmental awareness; and (6) promotion of natural research. In order to achieve these objectives, a favourable conservation status for Finnish habitats and wild species shall be aimed to achieve and maintain. Certain provisions do not apply to the management and use of forests insofar as these are stipulated in the Forestry Act (1093/1996). In addition to the provisions of the Nature Protection Act, international agreements binding on Finland laying down provisions on the protection of nature and wild species are applicable. Like its predecessor, the Act implements the Natural Habitats Directive and the Birds Directive, except for the animal species under section 5 of the Hunting Act, and, for its part, the Environmental Liability Directive (Directive 2004/35/EC on environmental liability with regard to the prevention and remedying of environmental damage).

884. A decision issued under the Nature Protection Act may not, alone or in combination with other activities, cause a more than minor deterioration in the conditions for practising traditional Saami livelihoods in the Saami homeland or otherwise maintaining and developing Saami culture, or a minor deterioration in the living conditions of the Skolt people or their opportunities to engage in natural livelihoods in the Skolt region. In decision-making under the Act or a decree issued pursuant to it, attention shall be paid to the threat of significant loss or loss of biodiversity, even in the absence of verified scientific data (*precautionary principle*). In their activities, the authorities implementing the Act shall promote environmental education and the environmental awareness of citizens, private and public actors in order to safeguard biodiversity.

885. The Ministry of the Environment is responsible for the general steering, monitoring and development of nature and landscape protection. In addition, the Finnish Environment Institute is the general management authority under the Convention on International Trade in Endangered Species of Wild Fauna and Flora (CITES) Regulation (Regulation (EC) No. 338/97 on the protection of species of wild fauna and flora by regulating trade therein). The task of each Centre for Economic Development, Transport and the Environment is to promote the protection and sustainable use of biodiversity and the protection of the landscape in its area, to be responsible for the official duties laid down in the Act, to supervise compliance with the provisions of the Act and to represent the public interest of nature conservation and protection in various proceedings. In addition, the Centre acts as the State aid authority under Chapter 4 of the Act and steers, supervises and promotes the implementation of the grants, and, where possible, supports the related activities of municipalities. The Metsähallitus is responsible for tasks related to the management, use and management of the state-owned network of nature conservation areas and other official tasks assigned to it in the Act. The Border Guard participates in monitoring compliance with the Act in conservation areas. Customs supervises compliance with the Act and the CITES Regulation in import, export, re-export and transit. The expert authorities in nature conservation are the Finnish Environment Institute and the Finnish Museum of Natural History. The Finnish Environment Institute produces information on biodiversity and carries out tasks related to monitoring. The Institute is also the competent authority for issuing permits and certificates under the CITES Regulation. The Finnish Museum of Natural History is responsible for tasks related to the protection, monitoring and data management of species and acts as the scientific authority under in the CITES Regulation. Municipalities have to promote the protection of biodiversity and landscape protection in their areas.

886. One of the novelties introduced by the current law is the Finnish Nature Panel appointed by the Cabinet. The Panel is an independent scientific expert body, for a fixed term of four years at a time. Its composition shall include representatives from different fields of science. The task of the Panel is to produce, compile and analyse scientific information for the planning, implementation, monitoring and decision-making of biodiversity policy measures. For these tasks, the Panel may also issue statements on plans and other documents affecting biodiversity and produce other reports and materials, which it communicates to the public and decision-makers as needed.

887. There are several types of planning instruments in the Act (Chapter 3 of the Act), partly derived from the previous Act and partly new.

888. The Ministry of the Environment prepares the National Biodiversity Strategy and the Action Plan implementing the strategy in cooperation with other ministries and key parties (section 13). The Biodiversity Strategy sets national operational, quantitative and temporal targets for halting the loss of biodiversity and improving its condition. The Diversity Strategy is approved by the Cabinet. The Action Plan shall identify the measures needed to implement the Strategy and designate responsible bodies for their implementation and for monitoring the effectiveness of the measures. The Ministry of the Environment is responsible for monitoring the Strategy and Action Plan and reports on the implementation of the strategy to the Cabinet. A Centre for Economic Development, Transport and the Environment may draw up a Biodiversity Implementation Plan for its area in respect to the national Strategy and Action Plan. When drawing up the Implementation Plan, sufficient interaction with the key actors in the region must be ensured. The preparation and monitoring of the Strategy and Action Plan as well as the Regional Implementation Plan shall be based on the best available scientific knowledge. The plans pursuant to sections 9–12 of the Climate Act shall be taken into account in the preparation.

889. Action plans for the protection and improvement of natural habitats, habitats of species, and species may be drawn up to promote biodiversity through voluntary means (section 14). An action plan is drawn up by the competent ministry and approved by the Cabinet. These plans must define multi-year quantitative and qualitative targets for measures to promote biodiversity, the responsibilities of ministries and other State authorities, and the monitoring of implementation and effectiveness. An action plan is drawn up to promote and safeguard nationally significant natural values, but a plan can also be drawn up regionally. The implementation of action plans of this kind has hitherto been based on budgetary decisions and various implementing guidelines and practices. A good example is the METSO programme for the protection of old-growth natural forests.

890. National nature conservation programmes have long been a key steering tool for areally targeted protection under the previous Acts. These include: (1) the National Parks and Natural Parks development programme (1978, as subsequently amended); (2) basic programme for peatland protection (1979 and 1981); (3) bird waters protection programme; (4) grove protection programme (1989); (5) decision on the protection of the Mikkelinsaaret archipelago (1989); (6) shore area protection programme (1990); and (7) programme for the protection of old-growth forests (1996). The legal effects relating to the implementation of these programmes shall continue even under the Act in force, insofar as there are still unimplemented parts of the programmes. According to the current Act as well, national nature conservation programmes may be drawn up to safeguard nationally significant natural values by reserving areas for nature conservation purposes (section 15). A nature conservation programme shall also indicate which measures are to be considered to undermine the purpose of the programme. A programme is drawn up by the Ministry of the Environment. When drawing up a nature conservation programme, concerned parties shall be given an opportunity to be heard. A nature conservation programme shall be approved by the Cabinet. No measure may be carried out in an area covered by an approved nature conservation programme that jeopardizes the conservation purpose of the area. This restriction on measures is valid even before the implementation of the programme, for example, the creation of a nature reserve, and must be complied with regardless of any appeal, unless the Court of Appeal decides otherwise. The Centre for Economic Development, Transport and the Environment of the region may grant permission to deviate from the restriction if the purpose of protection is not significantly jeopardized. When planning their measures and deciding on their implementation, state authorities and institutions have to ensure that the measures do not hinder the implementation of the programme.

891. The provisions on national nature conservation programmes are also applicable in the preparation of a proposal for areas to be included in the network of marine protection areas based on the (Helsinki) Convention for the Protection of the Marine Environment of the Baltic Sea Area (section 63).

892. In all categories of planning, economic, social, and cultural aspects as well as regional and local specificities must be taken into account. When preparing plans and programmes, sufficient public communication as well as cooperation and interaction with various authorities and other parties shall be ensured. In addition, the public shall be given the opportunity to examine the draft plans and programmes and to express their views on them. When the preparation of a national conservation programme begins, the Ministry of the Environment must provide information in such a way as to create the conditions for public debate on the matter.

893. In all categories of planning under Chapter 3, economic, social, and cultural aspects as well as regional and local specificities must be taken into account. When preparing plans and programmes, sufficient public communication as well as cooperation and interaction with various authorities and other parties shall be ensured. In addition, the public shall be given the opportunity to examine the draft plans and programmes and to express their views on them. When the preparation of a national conservation programme begins, the Ministry of the Environment must provide information in such a way as to create the conditions for public debate on the matter.

894. The Ministry of the Environment shall, in cooperation with other competent authorities, organize the monitoring of the distribution, occurrence and abundance of habitat types and wild species, and assess the conservation status of species and habitat types and changes therein. In doing so, particular account shall be taken of endangered species and habitat types and the monitoring of their endangerment, habitat types and species of EU importance pursuant to the Natural Habitats Directive and wild bird species pursuant to the Birds Directive. If, on the basis of monitoring, it can be assessed that the conservation status of a species or habitat is not favourable, the Ministry of the Environment shall, in cooperation with other competent authorities, take measures to achieve the favourable conservation status. The Metsähallitus and the Centres for Economic Development, Transport and the Environment are responsible for monitoring the number and area of nature conservation areas and natural monuments as well as their ecological status. The Finnish Environment Institute is responsible for compiling the information required for the reports referred to in Article 12 of the Birds Directive and Article 17 of the Natural Habitats Directive.

895. The Centres for Economic Development, Transport and the Environment and Metsähallitus must notify most of their decisions by means of a public announcement (also on the Internet), and information about the public notice must be published in the municipality concerned. The Ministry of the Environment, the Centre for Economic Development, Transport and the Environment and Metsähallitus must publish their decisions on their websites. Notwithstanding section 16(3) of the Act on the Openness of Government Activities, a decision published on the Internet may contain location data.

896. The Nature Protection Information System (sections 117–120) consists of information on biodiversity and the activities affecting it. The information system is used for the management and processing of data related to the application and implementation of the Act, nature conservation planning and the implementation of supervision, as well as for monitoring, assessment and research related to biodiversity. The nature conservation information system consists of data that is or has been stored in information systems, registers and case management systems maintained by the Ministry of the Environment; the Centres for Economic Development, Transport and the Environment; the Metsähallitus; the Finnish Environment Institute and the Finnish Museum of Natural History. The Ministry of the Environment; the Centres for Economic Development, Transport and the Environment; the Metsähallitus; the Finnish Environment Institute and the Finnish Museum of Natural History are each controllers of the System with regard to the data they store in the system. The Ministry of the Environment is responsible for the content and functional development of the nature conservation information system in cooperation with administrators. Section 118 of the Act lays down provisions on the data to be stored in the system and section 119 on the quality of data. The information stored in the Nature Protection Information System is public environmental information within the meaning of Directive 2003/4/EC on public access to environmental information and repealing Council Directive 90/313/EEC, unless otherwise provided by other law (section 120). Documents containing information on endangered animal or plant species or the protection of valuable natural areas, if disclosure of such information would endanger the protection of the animal or plant species or area in question, are confidential under section 24 of the Act on the Openness of Government Activities.

897. The Centres for Economic Development, Transport and the Environment supervise compliance with the Nature Protection Act and the provisions and decisions issued under it, as well as with EU regulations. The Metsähallitus supervises compliance with the Act in state-owned nature reserves (section 122). Section 123 lays down provisions on a supervisory authority's right of access to information and inspection. Provisions on administrative enforcement are laid down in section 126 and on the prevention and remedying of damage to nature in section 127. A person suffering harm has the right to bring a matter of administrative enforcement (against someone else) to the Centre for Economic Development, Transport and the Environment if the purpose of the initiation is to prevent the destruction of nature or the deterioration of natural values that is not insignificant, or to initiate the remediation of natural damage. A registered association referred to in section 134 (below) in its area of operation and a municipality have the same right. A case under such initiative must be decided as a matter of urgency (section 28). Appeals against decisions made under the Nature Protection Act may be lodged with the Regional Administrative Court. However, the Cabinet‘s decision on the National Biodiversity Strategy pursuant to section 13 of the Act may not be appealed. The right of appeal (section 134) lies with those whose rights, obligations or interests may be affected. In the case of decisions other than compensation, aid, assistance or assimilation of voluntary compensation, the municipality concerned and a registered local or regional association, the purpose of which is to promote the protection of nature or the environment, in the area in which it operates are also entitled to appeal. Regarding a Cabinet decision approving a nature conservation programme also national associations that look after the interests of landowners or promote nature or environmental protection have the right to appeal. In addition, the Saami Parliament has the right to appeal if the decision weakens the right of the Saami as an indigenous people to maintain and develop their own language and culture.

898. A Centre for Economic Development, Transport and the Environment (environmental division) of the region may appeal against any permit or plan decision pursuant to any enactment on the ground that the decision contradicts the Nature Protection Act or any provisions under it (section 135 of the Nature Protection Act).

§2. LANDSCAPES

899. Before 1997, there was no specific landscape protection legislation, in spite of the committee proposals presented in the 1980s. Of course, many areas protected under the previous Nature Conservation Acts also include, like those under the present Nature Protection Act include, valuable views and landscapes, but outside nature reserves, landscape protection and management either was voluntary or depended on the provisions of various fields of legislation.

900. The previous Nature Conservation Act introduced Landscape Protection Areas as a novelty. They were not exactly preserves. Rather, it was a matter of specific, general and rather vague restrictions on the use of the 'protected' area. In the present Nature Protection Act, the same category is called Landscape Management Area. Such an area may be established, in principle irrespective of the ownership, in order to preserve and manage the beauty of a natural or cultural landscape, historical characteristics or other special values inherent to the area. The mechanism is intended to protect areas of valuable landscapes in areas where human activity has greatly shaped the landscape for centuries. These areas are mainly to be selected for their aesthetic value, and any development which would change the characteristic features of their landscape will not be permitted. The decision on a Landscape Management Area is made by the Ministry of the Environment where the area is nationally important, and otherwise by the Centre for Economic Development, Transport and the Environment (environmental division), on a proposal by the inter-municipal Regional Council.

901. The real importance of such a decision depends wholly on the provisions imposed on it. The provisions have to be necessary to preserve the 'essential features of the landscape', the expression of which may refer, e.g., to the outlines of visually central buildings or of the terrain, or to the tops of visually important trees. The provisions may not, however, cause any immovable property owner disadvantage 'of significance' (on the notion, *see* above). The Centre for Economic Development, Transport and the Environment may also grant exceptions, and the protection may be abolished later on, where the value of the landscape has been lost or a project or plan important to the public interest would be prevented. Moreover, the whole mechanism is not applicable at all in areas with a Detailed Plan or with a Local Master Plan (with full legal effects). In order to protect and manage the beauty, historical features or other special values of a natural or cultural landscape, a National Landscape Management Area or a Regional Landscape Management area may be established (sections 91–93). The Ministry of the Environment decides on the establishment and purpose of a National Landscape Management Area on the proposal of the Regional Council or the Centre for Economic Development, Transport and the Environment of the Region. The Centre for Economic Development, Transport and the Environment decides on the establishment and purpose of a Provincial Landscape Management Area on the proposal of a registered local or regional association, municipality or the Regional Council. The Centre for Economic Development, Transport and the Environment may draw up a management and use plan for a Landscape Management Area. A statement from the Ministry of the Environment must be requested on the management and use plan for a National Landscape Management Area when it is being prepared. The preparation of a management and use plan shall be organized in interaction with the owners of the areas covered by the Landscape Management area and other relevant local actors. In the Saami homeland, a management and use plan must be drawn up in interaction with the relevant Saami communities and in cooperation with the Saami Parliament so that traditional Saami knowledge is part of the planning dataset. A decision to establish a Landscape Management Area may be appealed to a Regional Administrative Court, but a decision approving a management and use plan may not be appealed. The interactive procedure to be followed in establishing Landscape Management Areas and drawing up a management and use plan may be laid down in a decree.

902. The decision to establish a Landscape Management Area may include provisions and recommendations necessary for the protection of essential features of the landscape. However, the provisions must not cause significant inconvenience to any property owner. The provisions are binding, but Centre for Economic Development, Transport and the Environment of the region may grant permission to deviate from them. Where the provisions fall within the scope of application of the Land Use and Building Act (as of 1 January 2025, the Land Use Act), they are not applied in areas where a Detailed Plan or a Municipal Master Plan with legal effect is in force. A Landscape Management Area may be closed down or its protection provisions relaxed if the landscape value of the area has been substantially reduced or if the protection prevents the implementation of a project or plan important to the public interest. The Ministry of the Environment may discontinue a National Landscape Management area or change the decision concerning it. The Centre for Economic Development, Transport and the Environment may, on the proposal of a municipality or Regional Council, close down a Regional Landscape Management Area or amend a decision concerning it.

903. One of the most important enactments with respect to landscape is still the Land Use and Building Act (as of 1 January 2025, the Land Use Act and the Building Act). Especially as regards land use planning, there are provisions for the protection of valuable landscapes. These norms do not, however, guarantee any fixed amount of protection. In glaring situations, however, it may be possible for an appellant citizen to have a plan repealed by an administrative court (but *see also* paragraph 1434). Values of landscape may also be grounds for establishing a National Urban Park (*see* paragraph 1403).

904. Much the same holds true also for the various permits and construction projects under the Water Act (*see* Chapter 8 below). In addition, the protection of landscape is one of the goals of the Rapids Protection Act (*see* Chapter 8, §3, I below).

905. Since eskers, moraines and ridges are important ingredients of typical Finnish landscapes, the protection of eskers has become an important part of landscape protection. This is also the case for visible bedrock formations. This field of protection is mainly based on the Soil Excavation Act (*see* below Chapter 7, §1), which was enacted in 1981 after a heated political debate. The main structures of the Act are still valid.

906. The erection of billboards and other outdoor advertising facilities was prohibited under the original Nature Conservation Act of 1996, except for areas with a Detailed Plan under the Land Use and Building Act. From 2006, the respective provisions were placed in the (then new) Highways Act. In 2018 the ban was revoked. Instead, it is provided in section 52 (572/2018) of the Highways Act that an outdoor advertisement billboard outside of areas with a Detailed Plan shall be made and placed in such a way that traffic safety is not endangered or road maintenance hampered and the billboard suits the environment as well as possible. As a main rule, a notification to the Centre for Economic Development, Transport and the Environment of the region is required. If the requirements above are not met, the centre shall within thirty days from the notification make a decision by which the erection of the billboard is prohibited, or necessary provisions are laid down. As a main rule, the billboard shall not be erected within this period. If not prohibited, the billboard may stand ten years, if a shorter period has not been ordered by the centre. The provisions above do not apply to temporary announcements of various meetings, etc.

As for areas with a Detailed Plan, section 52 of the Highways Act is applicable only to traffic areas. Otherwise, outdoor advertising there is up to 2025 regulated by the Land Use and Building Act, in the first place by requiring a Construction Permit (*see* paragraph 1475). As of 1 January 2025, illuminated advertising devices of at least 2 m^2 shall in all areas have a Building Permit pursuant to the Building Act (section 42).

907. Certain restrictions on billboards are issued to guarantee public access to nature. Pursuant to section 97 of the Nature Protection Act, no sign prohibiting trespassing, mooring or landing or otherwise restricting everyman's rights shall be erected on land or water insofar as there are no legal grounds for doing so.

§3. Natural Monuments

908. A parallel to the establishment of private preserves (*see* Chapter 2, §3 below) is the mechanism for preserving 'natural monuments', i.e., remarkable individual natural objects such as trees, stone formations and other natural (biological or geological) formations.

909. Pursuant to the present Nature Protection Act, a tree, group of trees, post-glacial boulder or other similar natural formation which, because of its beauty, rarity, landscape significance, scientific value or other similar reason, deserves special protection may be designated as a protected natural monument. The decision to protect a natural monument in a state-owned area is made by the authority administering the area. A natural monument must be marked in a clearly visible way. The municipality decides on the conservation of a natural monument in privately owned area at the request or with the consent of the owner of the area. The municipality shall ensure that a natural monument on privately owned land is marked in a clearly visible manner. A protected natural monument must not be damaged or defaced (section 95 of the Nature Protection Act).

910. If there are no longer grounds for protection in a state-owned area or if the protection prevents the implementation of a project or plan of public interest, the authority managing the site may partially or completely terminate the protection of the natural monument. In privately owned areas, a municipality may, at the request of the owner or at the proposal of the Centre for Economic Development, Transport and the Environment, partially or completely terminate the protection of a natural monument if there are no longer grounds for such protection or if the protection prevents the implementation of a project or plan that is significant in the public interest. A statement from the Centre for Economic Development, Transport and the Environment must be obtained on application by the owner of a private area (section 96).

§4. Cultural Monuments

911. The protection of buildings and other monuments of special architectural or historic interest is regulated primarily in a special enactment, today in the Act on the Protection of the Built-up Heritage (498/2010, several parts amended by 1085/2020). Like its predecessor from 1985 (the Buildings Conservation Act), and also the Nature Protection Act, it is based on the principle that a valuable object can be brought under protection through an individual decision of a competent administrative authority. The scope of the Act includes buildings, other constructions, groups of buildings and even built-up areas having significance from the viewpoint of building history, architecture, construction technique, particular environmental values, use of a building, or historical events related to it (section 3). Possible objects of protection also include parts of buildings and permanent interior fittings as well as areas created by building or planting.

The aim of the Act is to safeguard the temporal and spatial diversity of built-up cultural environments, cherish its unique character and specific features, as well as to promote its culturally sustainable care and use. Built-up cultural environment is in the act called built-up heritage (section 1). In a matter regarding protection, the interested parties shall be offered a possibility to take part in the preparatory process.

912. The Act on the Protection of the Built-up Heritage is applicable to all properties, except those owned by the Lutheran Church or the Greek Orthodox Church, for which there are special regulations. The Act covers the whole country, except areas with a Detailed Plan, or a temporary building prohibition (valid until a Detailed Plan will have been adopted), where the plan pursuant to the Land Use and Building Act (as of 1 January 2025, the Land Use Act) is the primary tool of protection. The Act on the Protection of the Built-up Heritage, however, remains applicable here if: (1) the object has national significance; (2) preservation and protection pursuant to the Land Use and Building Act (Land Use Act) cannot be guaranteed under that Act; or (3) for particular reasons due to the actual situation in municipal decision-making regarding Detailed Plan.

913. General development and guidance of the preservation of built-up heritage belongs to the Ministry of the Environment. Preservation of built-up heritage under the Act is promoted and supervised by the Centres for Economic Development, Transport and the Environment (environmental divisions) and the Finnish Heritage Agency. The latter has also been vested in the role of official expert.

914. Today, more than 320 items are protected in pursuance with the previous Buildings Conservation Act and the present Act. Moreover, more than 200 buildings owned by the State about 570 churches (or chapels, etc.) are protected under special regulations and, based on a special agreement, more than 110 railway buildings. As for the Land Use and Building Act (as of 2025, the Land Use Act), it is roughly estimated that at least 10,000 buildings are protected through plan decisions.

915. The power to make a decision on the protection of a building or other applicable object (*see* section 3 above) is vested in the Centres for Economic Development, Transport and the Environment, as provided in section 9. The same procedure applies to amendment and repealing of existing protection. The procedure can be initiated in two ways, either at the centre's own initiative or on the proposal of someone else (section 5). Competence to make a proposal is vested in the owner of the building, a state authority, the inter-municipal Regional Council, certain regional museums, the municipality, such registered associations that are devoted to the cherishing of built-up heritage or quality of built-up environment, and, concerning Saami heritage, the Saami Parliament and the Skolt village assembly. In any case the owner and the neighbours must be heard before the decision, and the municipality, the Finnish Heritage Agency and certain other institutions have to be consulted. Also a public hearing may be arranged (section 7).

916. In order to protect a building (or other corresponding object), it shall be nationally, regionally or locally significant (section 8). The significance is assessed on the following grounds: (1) rarity or uniqueness, (2) being historically typical of the area, (3) typical (representative) features describing the area or a certain period of time, (4) continuity of original or comparable use, manner of construction, architecture or expression of style, (5) importance as evidence of a historical event or as an example giving expression to the event or contributing to the information on it, or (6) the visible constructions, materials and stylistic features from various periods of time, indicating the history and continuity of constructing, care and use.

917. The protection decision by the Centre for Economic Development, Transport and the Environment shall specify the area at stake. The main effect of the decision is that the protected building (or construction) may not be demolished. The decision shall moreover include provisions that are necessary to preserve the cultural and historical values. Such provisions shall, if possible, be drafted in mutual understanding with the owner and the possessor. The provisions may regard: (1) preservation in a condition required by the protection, (2) use in such a manner that the cultural and historical value is not endangered, (3) restoration and related repair works in such a manner that the purpose of the protection is not endangered, and (4) communication with supervisory State authorities (section 10).

There is no direct obligation on the centre or the confirming ministry to make a protection decision, even when the preconditions are met.

918. The final decision of the Centre for Economic Development, Transport and the Environment (irrespective of whether it means protection or non-protection) can be appealed to the Regional Administrative Court (and finally, subject to leave of appeal, to the SAC). From 1 January 2021, confirmation by the Ministry of the Environment is not needed, and the Ministry is not any more the first appellate instance, either. Those directly concerned, the initiator of protection procedure, the municipality, the Finnish Heritage Agency, an authority representing certain public interest, and, where Saami heritage is concerned, the Saami Parliament and the Skolt village meeting have the right to appeal.

919. During the administrative procedure, the Centres for Economic Development, Transport and the Environment have the power to temporarily forbid all activities which would endanger the cultural value of the building (section 6). Such a decision is obligatory always when necessarily needed for the safeguarding of protection. Additionally, the owner or possessor may be ordered to take necessary (temporary) measures. Appeals against the prohibition can be made to the Regional Administrative Court (and finally, subject to leave of appeal, to the SAC), pursuant to the provisions concerning proper protection (above).

After such a prohibition, the final matter shall be decided by the Centre for Economic Development, Transport and the Environment within two years.

920. The Act on the Protection of the Built-up Heritage (unlike its predecessor) also includes provisions on State-owned buildings (and other comparable items). If a building owned by the State that has been protected pursuant to previous regulations is assigned to someone else, the Centre for Economic Development, Transport and the Environment shall initiate the ordinary decision-making procedure under the Act (section 11).

921. The possibilities of conservation under the Act on the Protection of the Built-up Heritage and the Land Use and Building Act (as of 1 January 2025, the

Land Use Act) are indirectly safeguarded by the Demolition Permit or notification system in the Land Use and Building Act (as of 1 January 2025, the Building Act) (*see* paragraph 1478).

922. Protection pursuant to the Act on the Protection of the Built-up Heritage does not mean that the ownership will pass to the State or to the municipality, but that the owner will be obliged to comply with the restrictions specified by protection clauses included in the protection decision.

923. From 1 January 2021, the Centre for Economic Development, Transport and the Environment may grant a right, subject to conditions set forth, to deviate from a valid protection decision, if (1) part of the building or other protected object is damaged and that part endangers appropriate use of the building or preservation of the values at stake, (2) the use of the building for its purpose as well as the transformation to a new purpose is prevented by the protection, or (3) there is other, particularly significant reason that promotes use or care of cultural heritage (section 10a). A deviation is not allowed, however, is the preconditions for protection would not be met any more. A deadline not exceeding two years at a time for the measures or other possible permits shall be set. The content of a deviation application and the procedures, party and expert hearing included, are provided in section 10b. Appellate rights and procedures are the same as for protection decisions.

924. The owner is entitled to full compensation for all damage or impairment with significance caused by the protection or a temporary prohibition (section 13). In assessing the significance, the contents and duration of the protection or prohibition shall be paid attention to. Ordinary upkeep costs or costs incurred due to a reparation order under the Land Use and Building Act (as of 1 January 2025, the Building Act) are not taken into account, but an obligation to take particular measures to maintain the cultural value of the building is compensated. All compensations are paid by the State (represented by the Ministry of the Environment). Possessors specified in the Act are treated like owners. A municipality, the State, or State enterprises are not entitled to compensation.

In the first place, the Ministry of the Environment shall endeavour to agree on the compensation amount. Otherwise, the procedure under the Expropriation Act is applicable (section 15).

925. The owner of a protected item may be granted State subsidies for upkeep and maintenance. Such subsidies are possible also when no protection decision under the Act has been made. The owner shall in any case observe the conditions in the decision on granting (section 16).

926. The supervisory authorities are vested in inspection powers in the items, as specified in section 18. An owner who has failed to comply with his or her obligations regarding care and repair, may by a decision of the Centre for Economic Development, Transport and the Environment be imposed a conditional fine or a threat of taking the neglected action at his or her expense (section 17). The provisions of the Administrative Injunctions (Conditional Fines) Act (1113/1990) are applicable. The same provisions also apply illegal changing, altering or removal of an item.

§5. Ancient Monuments and Stationary Remains

927. All archaeologically valuable objects are protected directly by law. In other words, the system of the Ancient Remains Act (295/1963), unlike the Act on the Protection of the Built-up Heritage, is not based on individual protection decisions. The Ancient Remains Act covers, besides movable relics, various stationary items like ancient graves with buried objects, remainders of ancient dwelling places, sacrificial sites (fountains, stones, etc.) and fortified hills. Especially the latter are often significant components of the landscape and enjoy wider protection under the Ancient Remains Act than under the Soil Excavation Act.

928. Although the protection itself is statutory, it is possible to confirm the boundaries of a stationary relic in a specific procedure, resulting in an appealable administrative decision. A surrounding protection zone may be established, but the disadvantage caused to the owner, if significant, must be compensated.

929. Under certain conditions, the Centre for Economic Development, Transport and the Environment is empowered to give a permit for activities contrary to the Act. As regards previously unknown 'hidden' relics, the owner may be entitled to compensation for inconvenience if such a permit is refused. If the protection affects a public construction project, an eventual disagreement between the project authority and the Finnish Heritage Agency will be settled by the Cabinet. This means that the final decision may be based on arguments contrary to protection. However, the project authority will as a rule be obliged to pay the costs of necessary archaeological investigations and preventive measures. In certain cases, also a private developer may be in the same position as the project authority.

Chapter 2. Parks and Preserves

§1. General Structure of the Preserve Rules

930. The establishment of nature parks and preserves is regulated in the Nature Protection Act, in a rather similar manner to that in the previous Acts. The system in Chapter 6 of the Act is divided into two subsystems depending on the ownership of the relevant area. In privately owned areas it is generally upon the owner to initiate an administrative conservation procedure, whereas areas owned by the State are preserved in a different procedure, by enacting a special parliamentary act or, for minor areas, a decree. However, the contrast is not so sharp in practice, because the Nature Protection Act gives the environmental authorities the possibility to expropriate private areas for conservation purposes. If a private area is transferred to the State either by expropriation or through voluntary sale, typically in order to implement a national nature conservation programme or Natura 2000, it will be treated just like other State-owned areas.

§2. Preserves in State-Owned Areas

I. Preserve Categories

931. The preserved State-owned areas are of three categories, namely the National Parks, the Natural Parks and the other preserves. Despite the resemblance in the notions, the National Parks and Natural Parks are not necessarily to be identified with the national parks or natural parks in other countries. Both are rather strictly protected against damaging measures, but the National Parks are in general open to visitors, whereas in Natural Parks there are restrictions on access. In practice, the expression 'strict nature reserve' can be used to cover both Natural Parks and other preserves, the latter always being strict.

932. A basic precondition for conservation in the sense of establishing a protection area, either a National Park, Natural Park or other preserve, is that the area in question shows at least one of the following characteristics: (1) an endangered, rare or raring species, biological community, natural habitat or ecosystem lives or exists in the area; (2) there are breeding or resting places in the area of an animal species under strict protection as pursuant to section 78; (3) there is a peculiar or rare natural formation in the area; (4) the area is of particular landscape value; (5) this is necessary to maintain or achieve a favourable conservation status for a natural habitat or species; (6) the site is of particular importance for the potential of natural habitats or species to adapt to the effects of climate change; or (7) the site is so representative, typical or valuable, other than above (1) to (6), that its conservation can be considered necessary for the conservation of biodiversity or beauty (section 43).

933. The minimum area of a new National Park is 1,000 hectares, and it is required that the area has importance as a public natural attraction or otherwise contributes to the knowledge of nature or interest in nature (section 44). A National Park is always established through a legislative act of Parliament, where also its purpose is specified. A Natural Park in turn has to be significant to the safeguarding of 'natural development', scientific research or education (section 45). A Natural Park is established through a parliamentary act, if its area is at least 1,000 hectares, and otherwise by Government decree. The establishment of other nature reserves in state-owned areas and the purpose of the reserves are decided upon by Government decree or, if the area does not exceed 100 hectares, by decree of the Ministry of the Environment (section 46). Previously, the Metsähallitus, formerly the National Board of Forests (being the main possessor of State land and water properties, vested with business and conservation duties at the same time; see the Act on the Metsähallitus, 234/2016) was up to 1 February 2005 empowered to establish reserves not exceeding the area of 100 hectares in the areas possessed by it. Provisions on establishing a nature reserve in Finland's economic zone are also decided by Government decree. In doing so, account shall be taken of the limitations on the competence of the coastal State laid down in Parts V and XII of the United Nations Convention on the Law of the Sea.

934. Under the 1923 Nature Conservation Act, the general conservation areas and the special conservation areas were the main legal categories. The former were areas preserved in an entirely natural condition, whereas the latter category was designated to preserve for the future an area of outstanding natural beauty or otherwise significant natural properties, or to protect a particular animal or plant species. These definitions also specified the legal preconditions for the establishment of a preserve. In some particular establishing acts, also other aims than nature conservation had influenced (e.g., protection of local culture or man-made landscapes), which might cause problems insofar as, e.g., the expropriation rules are applied to them.

In practice, terms other than 'general' and 'special' were usually used and even the duality itself was somewhat vague and has had to be interpreted more or less freely. Originally, the category of the special areas was designated for preserves covering only smaller areas and some aspects of protection, but in practice the distinction has been forgotten. But in practice and in the specific establishing enactments general conservation areas were called Natural Parks. The special conservation areas in turn had different official names. The most important of them were called National Parks. Another major group consisted of the Peatland (or Mire, i.e., marsh, bog, wetland, etc.) Reserves. From 1992, the remaining natural groves (i.e., herb-rich forests) have largely been protected as Grove Reserves. There were also Old Forest Reserves consisting of old-growth natural forest areas, which are nowadays rare especially in the south and west.

935. In 1996, there were not many legal differences left between the then two basic categories, general and special, a distinction, which in fact was also rather misleading. The main difference then was that the restrictions for the management and use of general areas were listed in the then Nature Conservation Act, whereas the measures for the preservation of a special area were specified case by case in a decree. In addition to the restrictions mentioned, rules for visitors were specified by administrative regulations for each area. By such regulations, among other things trespassing could be prohibited or limited.

936. From 1997, there was a basic distinction to be made between National Parks and the various strict preserves, Natural Parks included, instead. The previous National Parks, Natural Parks, as well as the Peatland Reserves, Grove Reserves and other strict preserves established under the 1923 Act remained in general as they were, and the new provisions of the respective preserve category are applied to them. Three new National Parks and a group of new types of areas (Seal Protection Areas in the outer Baltic Sea archipelago, the aim of which is to be a refuge for the Baltic Sea seals, *see also* paragraph 944) had been established under the previous Act. In the 2023 reform, the previously established National Parks, Natural Parks and other State natural reserves remained in force.

937. Pursuant to the present Nature Protection Act (section 49), activities that alter the nature are prohibited in National Parks and Natural Parks. It is not permitted to: (1) construct buildings, structures or roads in these areas; (2) take soil or mining minerals or damage soil or bedrock; (3) ditch; (4) take or damage mushrooms, trees, shrubs or other plants or parts thereof; (5) catch, kill or alarm wild vertebrate animals or destroy their nests, or catch or collect invertebrate animals; or (6) take any other action that adversely affects natural conditions of the area, landscape, survival of species or the purpose for which the Park was established. However, in National Parks and Natural Parks, measures that are required for the proper management or use of the area and that do not jeopardize the purpose of establishing the area are permitted (section 50). In these areas, it is permitted to: (1) construct, restore and renovate buildings, structures and paths necessary for the management, supervision, research, public guidance and visitor safety of the area, as well as for hiking and exploring the area; (2) manage and restore natural, cultural, natural and architectural environments and restore the natural development of degraded habitats through restoration; (3) construct such road as is necessary for guidance activities in the area; (4) pick berries and useful mushrooms; (5) fish in accordance with the general fishing rights laid down in the Fisheries Act; (6) engage in reindeer husbandry in accordance with the Reindeer Husbandry Act; (7) operate and rehabilitate roads, infrastructure and related equipment in the area; (8) refurbish navigational safety equipment and waterways and carry out minor clearances required by safety equipment; (9) survey and perform related activities; (10) drive elk and white-tailed deer in accordance with the provisions of the Hunting Act; and (11) kill wounded animals and seize dead game animals in the area in a situation related to hunting outside the area in accordance with the provisions of the Hunting Act. National Parks and Natural Parks may prevent or remove invasive alien plant species pursuant to the Act on the Management of Risks Caused by Invasive Alien Species. It is also permitted to catch and kill mink and raccoon dogs in accordance with the provisions of the Hunting Act. The Metsähallitus may, for reasons related to nature research or other special reasons, restrict the grazing of reindeer in a Natural Park in spite of (6) above. National Parks and Natural Parks may, if the situation so requires, take the necessary measures required by national defence, the tasks of the Border Guard, rescue operations, the prevention of diseases communicable to humans or animals and plant pests, or animal welfare, and cut down a tree that poses an obvious danger to a neighbouring property. The measures must be carried out in such a way that they do not cause greater harm to the purpose of establishing the area than is necessary.

938. In addition, the Metsähallitus may in a National Park or a Natural Park, without jeopardizing the purpose of its establishment, allow an applicant to: (1) capture or kill animals, collect mushrooms and plants or parts thereof, animal nests and mineral samples for research or other scientific purposes or teaching; (2) reduce the number of specimens of plant and animal species if they are too numerous or otherwise harmful; (3) remove specimens of game species that pose an obvious threat to human safety or threaten to cause significant economic damage to property; (4) fish otherwise than under the general fishing right laid down in the Fisheries Act; (5) erect buildings and structures for reindeer husbandry; (6) land on an aircraft; and (7) restore and renovate buildings and structures. The Metsähallitus may also grant a permit for geological research if the activities do not jeopardize the purpose of establishing the area. In such cases, geological surveys shall be organized in such a way that they do not cause more than minor harm to the species, habitats, water management or landscape of the area. Permission to derogate from the protection provisions shall be granted for a fixed period and may be valid for a maximum of ten years at a time. It may be subject to conditions, which may include time or spatial constraints or measures to be followed in order to avoid or limit the harm to conservation values (section 51).

939. As a rule, restrictions concerning National Parks and Nature Parks are also applied to other State nature reserves. There are exceptions either directly in section 51 of the Act or in a manner laid down by Government decree for hunting and fishing. In addition, the Metsähallitus may, under certain conditions, grant a permit for ore exploration in the area. Provisions concerning certain official activities or the rights of the Saami people may also be laid down by government decree.

940. In a Natural Park, you may move outside the designated roads, paths or areas only with the permission of the Metsähallitus, with the exception of moving in tasks that are necessary for reindeer husbandry or the performance of official duties permitted in the conservation regulations concerning the area, or for exercising the special rights of local residents. Moving around the National Park is free due to the purpose of establishing the area. However, in National Parks and other State nature reserves, movement, camping, coming ashore and keeping a boat, ship or other means of transport may be prohibited or restricted either by the decree establishing the area or by an order included in the rules pursuant to section 58 of the Act. A precondition for prohibiting or restricting movement and coming ashore is that it is necessary for the preservation of species or natural habitats in the area. The Metsähallitus may grant permission to deviate from such prohibition or restriction.

941. State nature reserves located in the Saami homeland must secure the prerequisites for maintaining and developing Saami culture. When establishing a State reserve, due account shall be taken of the specific objectives of its conservation and, in the case of National Parks, of the interests of visitors (section 55(1)).

942. A management plan must be drawn up for the organization of the management and use of the National Park, which defines the measures to be taken to achieve the objectives of establishing the area. A management plan can also be drawn up for a Natural Park and other State nature reserves (section 57). The Metsähallitus must draw up rules for the national park for its users, which lay down the necessary restrictions on the use of the area based on section 56(2). If necessary, the Metsähallitus may also draw up user rules for Natural Parks and other State nature reserves (section 58).

943. A State nature reserve established by decree may be completely or partially closed down, or the provisions on the protection of the area may be relaxed only if the conservation of the area prevents the implementation of a project or plan of extremely high public interest and there is no technically and economically feasible alternative to that project or plan (section 63).

944. Natural Parks (nineteen) and National Parks (forty-one) have been established in various parts of the country, the most significant ones, however, in the north. This is largely due to the fact that the State, as a result of the history of land law, here was the main owner of remote areas. The newest ones are nevertheless mainly in the South. The newest national park is Salla National Park in the north, though, established on 1 January 2022. Both Natural Parks and National Parks are possessed and managed by the Metsähallitus (*see* above 933).

There is also a practical modification of the concept of National Parks for archipelagic areas in the Baltic Sea. For example, in the south-western archipelago (excluding the Åland islands) a large 'dotted' park has been established which in principle includes all State-owned islands or parts of them (as well as State-owned water areas) within a determined borderline, whereas private areas do not belong to it.

Presently (2023) the total area of the National Parks is 1,014,600 hectares and that of the Natural Parks 154,200 hectares.

945. In all 163 (Wet) Peatland Reserves have been established – and first acquired by the State either voluntarily or by compulsory purchase – in different parts of the country since 1982 (2023). These reserves are mostly small, but there are also a few with an area of thousands of hectares. Presently, the total protected area is 487,600 hectares. The need to save the last untouched (wet) peatlands containing various biotopes from ditching activities and peat extraction had become acute in the 1970s. Certain wetlands are listed as bird waters, but the implementation of the 1982 Bird Waters Protection Programme is mainly based on other means than establishing formal preserves, mainly by the permit system of the Water Act (*see* below). Several of the areas in this programme have been included in the Natura 2000 network as sites pursuant to the Birds Directive.

The total area of implemented (State) Grove Reserves (forty-five in number) is 1,100 hectares and that of (State) Old Forest Reserves (seventy-four in number) is

8,000 hectares (2023). In addition, there are seven Seal Protection Areas with 18,800 hectares. The various other State reserves in addition to the categories mentioned (736 in number) cover in all 398,400 hectares.

It should moreover be kept in mind that within most of the special conservation categories there are also (to a minor extent, though) privately owned preserves (section 3 below) the areas of which are not included in the figures above. Many of the originally private natural preserves (156 in number, 10,100 hectares) are today parts of State properties. From the viewpoint of the implementation of conservation programmes (*see* below), the strict preserves in privately owned areas are equally relevant.

946. In practice, the development of the network of conservation areas has been based on several national nature conservation programmes approved by the Cabinet from the 1970s (*see also* Part III, Chapter 2). Each programme identifies a target conservation network of areas of certain ecological type, irrespective of the ownership. Because the potential preserve areas are often privately owned, the programmes have indirect impacts on the owners. Before 1997, the programmes had no formal legal effects. All the existing programmes are from the time before the present Nature Protection Act and its predecessor. Hence, the proper legal consequences have been enacted afterwards and are, due to this, partly incomplete in comparison to the ordinary new provisions, those being fully applicable only on possible new programmes. According to the Nature Protection Act, also the older programmes are, however, still a sufficient basis for expropriation (*see* II, below).

Some of the programmes (such as those for the conservation of rapids, eskers, bird wetlands and shore areas) are mainly implemented by means other than the acquisition of land by the State. For example, rapids with valuable natural characteristics and landscapes have not been made preserves under the Nature Protection Act, although this method would in principle be available. Instead, a major share of the remaining undeveloped rapids have been protected directly by the Rapids Protection Act, which prohibits the granting of permits according to the Water Act for the construction of new hydroelectric plants in the fixed watercourses (*see* below Chapter 8, §3, I). The ownership status of the rapids has not changed, although significant compensations are paid to the shareholders of the waterpower. The programme for protecting glaciofluvial eskers and ridges is for its part implemented through the Soil Excavation Permit system in the Soil Excavation Act (*see* Part II, Chapter 7, §1 below), the Bird Waters Protection Programme mainly through the permit system of the Water Act and the programme for shore areas (1990) has been implemented through several different means, of which the establishing of preserves is only one and secondary to the various measures based on the Land Use and Building Act.

947. The implementation of those programmes, which aim at establishing natural reserves, has from time to time been criticized by the landowners because the programmes, although normally creating no direct restrictions on use, may affect the expectations of future use and hence decrease the value of the property. Section 16 of the present Nature Protection Act does not apply to pre-2023 (or in fact pre-1997) programmes – and no newer programmes exist.

The time for implementation for privately owned areas – either voluntary purchase or expropriation – may be several years after the programme has been approved. The time limits in the Nature Protection Act do not cover the pre-1997 programmes. However, the natural values of the programme areas may be endangered in the meantime, although other means based on the Nature Protection Act may be used when necessary. These include the temporary measures prohibition imposed by the Centre for Economic Development, Transport and the Environment of the region by virtue of section 124 of the Nature Protection Act, based on the actual natural values of the site, but not directly on the programme at stake.

Of the various programmes, the programme concerning Natural Parks and National Parks has been fully implemented, whereas the percentage for the rest still varies. However, the relevant programme areas may also be State-owned already, but for the time being without the formal status of a preserve. This is essentially the present state of affairs for old forests.

948. To a large extent, the programme areas were also included in the 1998 Government Proposal to the EU Commission on the inclusion of a total of 1,458 sites into the Natura 2000 network (*see* paragraphs 972–975 and 1407). There is, however, no legal connection between the two systems, and according to the SAC, the inclusion of an area in a conservation programme as such was no reason to include the same area as a site to the Natura network. Nevertheless, the biological and ecological evidence contained by the programme documents, may be taken into account in the governmental decision-making on the Natura.

II. Property Acquisition and Expropriation

949. Properties may be acquired by the State in order to implement the conservation due to national nature conservation programmes, programmes for voluntary promotion of biodiversity (section 14) or the Natura 2000 network, or to complement the existing conservation networks, or otherwise for the purposes of nature conservation (section 108). The Centres for Economic Development, Transport and the Environment and the Metsähallitus are the responsible bodies here.

950. The Ministry of the Environment shall immediately start implementing a national nature conservation programme (other than a pre-2023 one) once the Cabinet's approval decision has become final (section 109). When considering the order of implementation, the significance of the values to be protected and the factors threatening them shall be taken into account. The method of implementation of protection must be adapted to the purpose of the protection, and protection must primarily be carried out by voluntary means. The Ministry of the Environment may decide to abandon the implementation of some part of a nature conservation programme if the natural values of the area have been substantially reduced, if the purpose of conservation is not significantly jeopardized or if the programme prevents the implementation of a project that is essential for the public interest.

951. The Nature Protection Act contains special provisions for compulsory transfer of property in order to make the establishment of preserves possible or to put protection into effect in other respects, even where the owner is not willing to sell the area to the State (the voluntary approach, where possible, always has priority). The two-stage procedure of the Expropriation Act is applicable. First, an Expropriation Permit by the Cabinet (against which appeals to the SAC can be submitted on a legal basis) is needed (section 114 of the Nature Protection Act). It is required that the compulsory purchase takes place for the establishment of a nature reserve or otherwise for the implementation of protection pursuant to the Nature Protection Act. However, if the area in question is included in a conservation programme approved by the Cabinet (either before or after 1 January 1997), or in the Natura 2000 network as a site aimed to be implemented pursuant to the Nature Protection Act (or its predecessor), the Ministry of the Environment may initiate the expropriation procedure without the decision of the full Cabinet. The Ministry of the Environment may decide on an Expropriation Permit even if the area at stake includes a small amount of land outside the nature conservation programme site or a Natura 2000 network site. The provisions also include the rights to use areas. It has nevertheless been ruled by the SAC on several occasions that a programme including a certain private area only creates the formal competence to the ministry. Irrespective of this, the need to expropriate the area at stake has to be based on individual biological evidence on the appropriateness of creating a preserve (or inserting new areas into it).

The permit stage is followed by a second procedure by an ad hoc committee presided by a surveyor. In this second procedure the compensations are determined and new property boundaries established. 'Full' compensation to the owners and holders of right of use is guaranteed here, and the Nature Protection Act does not deviate from the general provisions on expropriatory compensation. The Land Court and the SC are here the appellate bodies. After both procedures have been completed, the private area in question becomes State property, and the establishing of a State preserve will be possible under the rules described before.

952. If a particular area fulfils the general conditions for establishing a nature reserve laid down in Article 43(2) of the Act, the Centre for Economic Development, Transport and the Environment of the Region may, for a maximum period of two years, prohibit the use of such an area that may jeopardize the purpose of protecting the area. The decision may be appealed to the Regional Administrative Court. The Centre's decision shall be complied with regardless of an appeal, unless otherwise ordered by the court. If the protection lapses or the implementation of the nature conservation programme is abandoned (section 109(3)) and the owner of the area has suffered significant harm as a result of the prohibition of action, he or she is entitled to full compensation from the State. The compensation shall be determined in accordance with section 113 (section 124 of the Act).

953. According to the Nature Protection Act, it is also possible that the expropriation procedure is demanded and initiated by the owner himself. This is the case where a nature conservation programme, as far as his particular areas are concerned, has not been implemented or agreed upon within four years from the approval of the programme. The interest of the owner in so doing may be motivated by practical inconvenience or by loss of property value, although no legally binding restrictions are imposed. However, this clause does not cover the pre-2023 programmes, and because new programmes are less probable in the future, it is not very likely to be applied in practice. The owner of the area has the same right if, according to a final Cabinet decision concerning the Natura 2000 network, the protection of the area must be implemented under the Nature Protection Act and four years have passed since the Cabinet decision-in-principle was issued.

III. Protection of Existing Rights of Use

954. When a conservation area has been established, previously acquired private rights may need to be settled. This may refer to, e.g., leaseholds or private roads. By way of derogation from the provisions of the Nature Protection Act, a right that concerns a nature conservation area as an easement, leasehold right or other similar right established before the entry into force of the conservation may still be exercised (section 55(3)). However, such a right may be expropriated to the State in accordance with section 114.

955. Significant problems from the viewpoint of principle have evolved in connection with gold washing, a tradition particularly in certain river areas of the *Lemmenjoki* National Park in Lapland. The old manual methods of washing have been largely replaced by the use of motor excavators, often with far-reaching impacts on nature, landscape and watercourses. The operations as such are regulated in the Mining Act, and mining licences were formerly given rather freely to the operators, in spite of the protection. The SAC had several times dealt with appeals by gold miners against decisions of conservation authorities. In 1991 the Parliament rejected a proposed amendment to the then Nature Conservation Act, under which all mining activities could clearly be prohibited in conservation areas. In the Nature Conservation Act of 1996, no retroactive effect could be included, either, and hence the activities could be continued on the basis of former mining decisions. However, presently the Mining Act is after a transition period resulting in the extinction of existing rights to motorized gold panning in protected areas (*see* below Part II, Chapter 7, §4, IV).

§3. Preserves in Private Areas

956. In private areas, the system of preserves is different from that for State areas. As stated before, it is normally upon the owner to initiate a preserve establishment procedure. A consent of the owner is an alternative to a formal application. The decision of a preserve is made by the Centre for Economic Development, Transport and the Environment of the region (section 47 of the Nature Protection Act). It is required that the preconditions concerning the natural values of the area in section 43(2), i.e., the same preconditions as for State preserves, are fulfilled (*see* above paragraph 932), and also other viewpoints of public interest shall be taken into account. The decision to establish a private nature reserve shall include necessary conservation provisions for the protection of nature in the area and, if needed, its management. The decision may include a prohibition or restriction on movement, camping, landing ashore and the keeping of boats, ships or other means of transport, provided that this is necessary for the conservation of species or habitats in the area (section 53). If the real reason for an application is an attempt to prevent public access to a certain private area, the legal prerequisite will hence not be met. No decision can be made without a prior agreement on the provisions and on the compensations to the owner.

957. There is, however, one exception from the rule that agreement between the State and the owner is required for conservation without expropriation. From 1997 the State has a possibility, albeit a rather limited one, to compulsorily establish a preserve in a privately owned area, without expropriating the area itself (section 47(2) of the Nature Protection Act). It is required that the area in question is included in a national conservation programme or in the Natura 2000 network as a site aimed to be implemented pursuant to the Nature Protection Act. The protection provisions imposed by the Centre for Economic Development, Transport and the Environment may not restrict land use more than needed to implement the programme or Natura 2000, if not agreed otherwise (section 53). The owner is also entitled to compensation for disadvantage 'of significance' (section 111).

958. The Centre for Economic Development, Transport and the Environment may in a particular case grant a deviation from the protection provisions concerning a preserve in a private area if the deviation does not jeopardize the purpose of the site and is necessary for the management, use, maintaining of existing infrastructure or related equipment, or scientific research (section 54 of the Act).

959. It is also possible that the owner and the Centre for Economic Development, Transport and the Environment agree upon a temporary conservation of an area, either totally or with respect to prescribed works or measures (section 48). The maximum time of validity for such an agreement is twenty years. An agreement also binds possible new owners of the property.

960. Of course, the authorities may initiate expropriation procedures in order to transfer the ownership to the State and thereafter use the rules in sections 43–46 of the Act, but then it would no longer be a matter of preserving private areas.

Before 1997, there was actually no intermediate mechanism for compulsory restrictions on the use of private property, except for the possibility to expropriate rights of use to immovable property. The previous Nature Conservation Act widened the range of possibilities to impose partial restrictions (which in turn may result in compensations). This is especially the case with respect to section 47(2), and to protected natural habitats and to certain other measures discussed below.

961. There are at present about 7,800 protected areas established on privately owned land (or, occasionally, in water areas). Quite naturally, they are in general much smaller than the parks and other preserves established in State areas. The practical content of each conservation decision varies, as it is dependent on the detailed provisions drawn up by the Centre for Economic Development, Transport and the Environment on the basis of the application. The starting point is always strict protection, however. The municipality in which the area lies has to be consulted before the centre decides upon the application. Appeals against the decision can be submitted to the Regional Administrative Court. Appeals have at times been made also by neighbours or authorities who oppose the conservation for various reasons (e.g., to safeguard a future road, hydroelectric plant or drainage project, for which the use of the area in question would be necessary). All preserves admittedly bind also third parties in regard to their land use projects, even in cases where they could normally claim access to another's land (ditching, power lines, private roads, etc.) The Act does not, however, particularly provide for damage to third-party interests caused by the conservation, but the regard to public interest may at times be relevant also to such projects.

962. The existence of a private area preserve is not affected by eventual changes of ownership later on. The conservation of an area has no effect on previously acquired private rights of use or easements (section 55(3)), but also such right may be expropriated separately.

If the conservation values of the preserve have significantly decreased or prevent the implementation of a project or plan of extremely high public interest and there is no technically and economically feasible alternative to that project or plan, the Centre for Economic Development, Transport and the Environment of the region may annul the conservation totally or in part, or alleviate the restrictions (section 61). An application by the owner or by a third interested party, or a proposal by the Ministry of the Environment, is needed. A statement of the Ministry is needed in any case. The decision, positive or negative, may be appealed to the Regional Administrative Court and further to the SAC. If the annulling or alleviating has been applied for by the owner who has received compensation for the protection, he may be obliged to pay it back totally or in part.

963. A special form of preserves is constituted by protected natural habitats. This subsystem, being in force from January 1997, is one of the novelties in the previous Nature Conservation Act. It is mainly intended for minor sites with important regard to biodiversity. It was then estimated that there are altogether only a few thousands of these habitats. The original idea was that their protection would follow directly from the Act, and an administrative decision would only be needed to delineate the habitat. This was not fully realized in the 1996 Act, and in the present Nature Protection Act, this starting point has been further weakened. In the Act, natural habitats refer to demarcable land or water areas with similar environmental conditions and characteristic flora and fauna. There is a list in section 64 of the Act specifying thirteen categories of valuable habitat types. The Centre for Economic Development, Transport and the Environment of the region may decide to protect a natural or comparable occurrence of the following habitat types (*protected habitat type*), provided that the occurrence is important for the preservation of the habitat type. The habitat types are:

(1) sandy beaches;
(2) hardwood stands;
(3) hazel scrubs;
(4) alder forests;
(5) seaside meadows;
(6) leaf meadows;
(7) dry meadows;
(8) coastal wooded dunes;
(9) inland alluvial forests;
10) light slopes of ridge forests;
(11) seaweed (Zostera) beds;
(12) sheltered stonewort (Charophytes) bottoms; and
(13) lime cliffs.

Section 4 of the Nature Protection Decree (1066/2023) lays down more detailed provisions on the criteria for defining habitat types.

964. The protection decision shall define the boundaries of the occurrence of the habitat type. The occurrence of a protected natural habitat shall not be destroyed or degraded. The prohibition will enter into force once the decision has been notified to the owners and occupants of the area. The decision shall remain in force notwithstanding an appeal to the Regional Administrative Court, unless the court decides otherwise. If an occurrence of a protected habitat type defined by a decision has lost its significance for achieving or maintaining a favourable conservation status for the habitat, the Centre for Economic Development, Transport and the Environment may terminate the protection of the occurrence. In practice, problems have sometimes emerged on the question whether the area in question is in a natural condition or not. By a ruling of the SAC (SAC 2001:47) a sandy beach (dune) habitat, located in Hanko, the south-western most corner of Finland, was, as defined by the then Regional Environmental Centre, partly degraded due to missing natural condition.

965. Additionally, occurrences of certain rare and endangered natural habitat types are strictly protected, directly by virtue of the Act (section 65). The following shall hence not be destroyed or degraded: (1) serpentine cliffs, rocks and gravels which are the above-ground parts of deposits of cliff, rocks or gravels of serpentinite or other ultra-alkaline rock species on which serpentine plant species are present; and (2) open coastal dunes, which are dunes on the coast or archipelago of the Baltic Sea formed from sand as a result of wind consumption and piling work, and wetlands created in their depressions or seasonal wetlands where species characteristic of sand dunes are present. Section 5 of the Nature Protection Decree lays down more detailed provisions on the criteria for defining habitat types.

966. In individual cases, the Centre for Economic Development, Transport and the Environment of the region may grant an exemption from the protection of an occurrence (with respect to both sections 64 and 65) if the protection objectives of the habitat type in question are not significantly jeopardized or if the protection prevents the implementation of a project or plan of extremely high public interest and there is no technically and economically feasible alternative to the project or plan (section 66). The permit is granted for a fixed period and may be valid for a maximum of ten years at a time. It may be accompanied by provisions to avoid or limit the harm caused by the activities to conservation values. The regulations may contain temporal or territorial restrictions or other obligations. If the project or measure for which the permit has been granted is transferred to another subject, the transfer of the permit must be applied for from the Centre. The authorized person is responsible for all obligations under the permit decision until another person has been approved to replace him. All the decisions of the Centre are appealable to the Regional Administrative Court.

967. If the protection of a habitat causes a disadvantage to the owner or to the holder of a right of use, there exists a right to compensation provided that the disadvantage is of 'significance'. This expression, being derived from the previous Act, was a compromise after a prolonged political dispute. A prerequisite for the obligation to pay compensation is that the owner has applied for permission to derogate from the prohibition and the application has been rejected (section 111).

968. A very similar system of protection has been created for the habitats of specially protected species. These species are listed by decree (*see* Chapter 3, §3 below).

969. Some additional natural habitat types are (from January 1997) protected immediately by the (then and also the present) Water Act. These include natural water springs and fountains, smallest brooks, small ponds up to one hectare (with the exception of the Region of Lapland), and the *flada* lagoons and *glo* lakes, being specific to the coasts of the Baltic Sea. The system is very similar to that of the Nature Protection Act, but the protection is in force directly by virtue of the Act, without any specifying decisions (section 11 of Chapter 2 of the Water Act). The exception power is vested in the ordinary Water Act permit authorities (Regional State Administrative Agencies), but the preconditions for an exception are the rather similar to those in the Nature Protection Act.

970. When finally approving the present Nature Protection Act in December 2022, the Parliament adopted (*inter alia*) the following statement: 'Parliament requires the Government to start preparing a legislative amendment as soon as possible to expand the scope of protected threatened aquatic habitats to cover habitats required by the conservation objectives of aquatic biodiversity, also assessing the need for derogations in individual cases and making possible delimitation decisions with compensation mechanisms and securing the resources required for this.' The idea of delineation decisions mentioned here regarding small brooks, etc., is hardly feasible in practice, and the present mechanism of the Water Act habitats would probably be undermined.

971. Additionally, several small-scale forest biotopes were (also from January 1997) protected by the Forestry Act (*see* Chapter 5, §1 below), in a similar direct way, but with only weak legal effects.

972. The conservation network project Natura 2000 of the EU has influenced the conservation law and its application in many respects. As regards the status of private proprietors, the national proposal has been in several respects equated with the national conservation programmes, although not identical. The drafting of the proposal has to be made public, and all interested parties shall have the possibility to be heard. In practice the drafting, which mainly took place in late 1990s, was a task of the then Regional Environment Centres which submitted their proposals to the Ministry of the Environment. The final national proposal to the Commission was decided upon by the Cabinet and it was, pursuant to an explicit provision in the previous Nature Conservation Act, appealable to the SAC. The drafting during 1990s had been a target of an extremely heated public debate. There was also to be plenty of uncertainty with respect to the legal effects of Natura 2000. Only a minor part of all proposed Natura sites were privately owned, but the problems have concentrated on them. The same procedure still applies to possible new Natura sites and amendments of the network (the latest Cabinet decision on complementation in 2018).

The SAC gave in the Summer of 2000 its rulings on the appeals against the 1998 Cabinet decision on the Finnish Natura 2000 proposal. In all 1,241 appeals (counted by the number of separate appeal documents; the counting of individual appellants or the Natura sites in question results in different numbers) had been lodged, concerning about 750 proposed Natura sites. The number of individual appellants was over 5,000. Part of the appeals focused on the Cabinet proposal as a whole (like those by the associations of landowners) or aimed at the adding of missing sites (like many appeals made by conservationist associations). The SAC issued altogether 694 separate decisions, most of which are extremely extensive. The total amount of text was about 40,000 pages. In about 7% of all, the decision of the Cabinet was repealed totally or in part. The approved appeals had in part been lodged by landowners or other private subjects, in part by conservationist associations.

973. In the present Nature Protection Act there is a specific chapter (Chapter 5) for Natura 2000, and certain other provisions outside that chapter additionally refer to Natura 2000.

974. In Finland, the EU Natura 2000 network, as provided in section 33(1) of the Nature Protection Act, consists (1) of the Special (Bird) Protection Areas (SPA) notified to the Commission (according to the Birds Directive 79/409/EEC, as codified by 2009/147/EC) and (2) of the special areas of conservation designated by Ministry of the Environment Decree, after the Commission or the Council has approved the areas as Sites of Community Importance ((SCI); according to the Natural Habitats Directive 92/43/EEC). Changes in the original scientific information pertaining to a Natura 2000 site may be made only by the Cabinet (section 33(3)). The provisions of section 15 on the preparation and approval of a nature conservation programme shall be followed when drawing up a proposal for sites to be included in the Natura 2000 network. The Ministry of the Environment must notify the proposal for a Natura 2000 network site by public announcement (the Internet included), and the announcement must also be published in the municipality concerned. The list and maps of areas included in Finland's Natura 2000 network are published by decree of the Ministry of the Environment. The list of sites includes the identification number, name, coordinates of the centre point, the grounds for the site being protected and whether it hosts a priority natural habitat type within the meaning of Annex I or a priority species within the meaning of Annex II to the Habitats Directive.

975. The main legal effect of Natura 2000 is that the values of nature which belong to the basis on which a site has been included in the network shall not be significantly weakened (section 34).

An assessment of impacts has to be made where a plan or project is likely to have a significant effect on the relevant natural values of a site. Pursuant to section 35(1), the developer or operator of any project or plan which either individually or in combination with other projects and plans is likely to significantly weaken the nature values of a site included in or proposed for inclusion in the Natura 2000 network, is required to conduct an appropriate impact assessment in respect to these values. The same applies to projects and plans outside the site, if its significant adverse impacts probably reach the site.

A permit authority or a plan approval authority shall see to that such an assessment is performed. The authority shall ask the Centre for Economic Development, Transport and the Environment of the region for a statement on the assessment (section 35(2)). A statement is similarly needed from an authority managing a conservation area pursuant to the Nature Protection Act, if the site contains such. If the Centre for Economic Development, Transport and the Environment itself is the planner or developer, the Ministry of the Environment opts another centre for the task. The statement shall be issued without delay and at the latest in six months from the request (or the decision of the ministry). If also EIA pursuant to the Environmental Impacts Assessment Act is needed, the Natura impact assessment may, depending on the case, be connected to the EIA. In this case, the statements above shall be included in the reasoned conclusion pursuant to the Environmental Impacts Assessment Act.

976. A permit or plan according to any act is necessarily not needed for a project provided in section 35 of the Act, but the legislation may anyway set a notification duty. If such a notification on a project or plan has been submitted to an authority and the impacts provided above may be caused, the authority shall immediately take measures within its ordinary competence to stop the project or plan until the assessment has been made, and inform the Centre for Economic Development, Transport and the Environment (section 36).

If the legislation does not provide any permit, plan or notification requirement for a project provided in section 35 or 36, the subject in charge of the project shall, as a last resort, notify the Centre for Economic Development, Transport and the Environment on the measures to be taken, if significant impacts on the relevant natural values of the site are or may be caused. The notification shall contain information on the measure and its impacts (section 37).

Due to a notification pursuant to section 36 or 37, the Centre for Economic Development, Transport and the Environment shall within thirty days forbid the measure or reduce its extent, if such impacts are or may be caused. The subject in charge shall be consulted.

977. If the assessment procedure pursuant to section 35, the finalizing opinion of the centre included, shows that the project or plan significantly weakens the nature values for the protection of which the site is included in or intended for inclusion in the Natura 2000 network, no authority shall issue a permit or approve a plan with such impacts (section 39(1)). Nevertheless, a permit can be granted and a plan can be approved if the Cabinet decides that the said project or plan must, in the absence of alternative solutions, be carried out for imperative reasons of overriding public interest (section 39(2)).

Where a site hosts a priority natural habitat type referred to in Annex 1, or a priority species referred to in Annex II, of Directive 92/43/EEC, a further precondition for granting a permit or approving a plan is that of a reason relating to human health or public safety, or to beneficial consequences of primary importance for the environment, or any other imperative reason of overriding public interest so demands. In the latter case, an opinion shall be requested from the Commission (section 39(3)).

In an approval decision pursuant to section 39(2) or 39(3) the Cabinet shall also decide on the measures necessary to compensate the negative impacts on the overall coherence of Natura 2000 or the values of nature (section 39(4)). The Cabinet decision may be appealed against in the SAC. The operator or developer shall pay the costs, but the liability may be moderated, taking the overriding public interest at stake into account.

978. The deadline for carrying out Natura 2000 is six years from the final decision of the Commission or the Council. The protection of the SPA shall nevertheless be decided upon immediately after the site has been notified to the Commission (section 41). Various additional duties of authorities in order to promote the goals of Natura 2000 are provided in section 41(2).

979. The protection based on Natura 2000 may be revoked or weakened only on the grounds provided in sections 35(1), 35(2), 39(2) and 39(3). The compensatory measures are provided in section 39(4) (section 42).

980. The network may be implemented according to various legal mechanisms. A preserve according to the Nature Protection Act is not the only alternative. Also the plan or permit systems of the Land Use and Building Act (as of 1 January 2025, the Building Act), the Environmental Protection Act, the Water Act, the Rapids Protection Act and the Soil Excavation Act may be used. This of course results in various types of legal effects. In all cases the provisions of the Nature Protection Act above are applicable.

981. The legal position of the owners and holders of rights is interesting. If a permit according to any act is not granted due to the significant adverse effects on a Natura 2000 site, or if a notification according to sections 36–38 has the same result, and this creates a restriction in the use of property, causing a significant disadvantage, the right to have compensation (from the State) depends on the enactment under which the decision has been made. The legislative Acts the permit denials under which never result in compensations are listed in section 112. In these acts there is no provision on compensation for cases where a permit has been disallowed on an ordinary basis, either. (It would also be difficult to be consistent where a permit also could have to be disallowed also without Natura 2000.) This holds true for the permits under the Water Act and the Environmental Protection Act, which is quite natural already on the basis of the polluter pays principle, and the Mining Act. Similarly, the denial of an Expropriation Permit (of, e.g., a power line) never creates the State an obligation to compensate the 'loss' to the applicant, but if this takes place on Natura 2000 grounds, the same result has been explicitly stated in the law. For the Soil Excavation Act, *see* Part II, Chapter 7, §1, III below.

982. The Environmental Liability Directive (2004/35/EC) has from 2009 been implemented through several acts, besides the act on the Remediation of Certain Damages Caused to the Environment (383/2009), *see* paragraphs 1507–1521. One of these acts was the previous Nature Conservation Act. In the present Nature Protection Act the respective provisions are included in sections 3(7) and 127. In the Act, 'nature damage' refers to damage to protected species and natural habitats refers to a significant, measurable, direct or indirect adverse effect on reaching or maintaining a favourable conservation status: (1) with respect to the ecological values of the areas selected for inclusion in the Natura 2000 network; (2) with respect to the species referred to in Article 4(2) of the Birds Directive and the species listed in Annex I of the Directive, as well as the species listed in Annex II of the Natural Habitats Directive; (3) with respect to the sites providing habitats for species referred to in (2) above that are protected against deterioration and destruction pursuant to section 79 of the Act; and (4) with respect to the species listed in Annex IV of the Natural Habitats Directive or the breeding sites and resting places of individual animal species provided in Annex IV(a) of the Directive, as provided in section 78 (section 3). The significance of the adverse effect shall be assessed in relation to the conservation status of the natural habitat or species in question at the time of the damage and to the services they provide and their natural ability to recover (section 127(3)). Further provisions on factors determining the significance of the adverse effect are provided by Government decree. The enforcement is procedurally linked to ordinary administrative enforcement provisions, also regarding the right to initiate proceedings (section 128).

983. If a natural or legal person operating an occupational activity or de facto controlling such an activity (operator) deliberately or through negligence causes nature damage, or imminent threat of nature damage, to protected species and natural habitats through action in violation of the Nature Protection Act or provisions under it, or by failure to observe such provisions, the operator shall notify the Centre for Economic Development, Transport and the Environment of the damage or the imminent threat thereof without delay and take the necessary measures to prevent or minimize any adverse effects (section 127(1)).

Being notified of damage to protected species and natural habitats or the imminent threat thereof, the Centre for Economic Development, Transport and the Environment shall, in addition to section 126 on regular administrative enforcement, order the operator who has caused the damage take measures to prevent any adverse effects or limit them to the minimum and, if necessary, order the operator to take remedial measures provided in the Act on the Remediation of Certain Environmental Damages, as well as to impose a conditional fine or a threat of taking the neglected action at the defaulting party's expense or of interrupting the activity, applying the provisions of the Administrative Injunctions (Conditional Fines) Act (1113/1990).

984. The provisions above are not applicable if the prevention and remediation at stake is provided in the Environmental Protection Act, the Water Act or the Gene Technology Act.

Notwithstanding the general secrecy provisions, the Centre for Economic Development, Transport and the Environment is entitled to obtain from the operator the information necessary for the prevention of damage to protected species and natural habitats or the imminent risk thereof or for the remediation of damage to the species and habitats.

985. A new chapter on state subsidies for the aiding of protection and management of biodiversity was inserted in the previous Nature Conservation Act. Also the present Nature Protection Act contains a chapter on financial support from the State (Chapter 4). The protection and management of biodiversity can be supported financially (grants) and by goods or services (subsidies).

986. The grants are discretionary within a total maximum laid down in the current state budget and may concern projects and measures to promote the protection and management of biodiversity and the natural and cultural landscape. Grants may also be awarded for research and development. Discretionary support may be granted for measures promoting the restoration and management of species' habitats, habitat types and natural or cultural landscapes within the maximum amount set in the State budget. Support consists of goods and services. The Chapter is administered by the Centres for Economic Development, Transport, and the Environment.

§4. Wildernesses

987. A specific type of protected area has been created for (many of the) wildernesses in northern Lapland by the Wilderness Act (62/1991). Simultaneously twelve Wilderness Areas were established, complementary to the Natural Parks and National Parks existing in the same region. The Wilderness Areas include only areas which are State property, or, to be exact, which have been regarded as being State property but which are also claimed to be traditional Saami property. Private areas not covered by the Act, near or even inside the Wilderness Areas, continue to exist. Such an area will be automatically annexed to the Wilderness Area if it is transferred to the State. Otherwise than under the Nature Protection Act, expropriation is allowed to the State only for private roads or other easements, not for private areas as such. The total area of lands and waters included in the twelve Wilderness Areas is 1,489,100 hectares.

988. The extent of protection is relatively narrow, and the counting of wildernesses – the total area of which is about the same as the area of all preserves according to the Nature Protection Act – in the total protected area of the country is hence misleading. (In public discussion it may be used either to lament the 'excesses of protection' or on the contrary to boast of the progress of conservation, but both are mainly wrong.) The principal goals of the Act are the preserving of the wilderness nature, the safeguarding of the Saami culture and the Saami ways of livelihood (especially reindeer husbandry), as well as the development of the multiple use of nature and its prerequisites. The restrictions on use, which are binding on both authorities and private individuals, include bans on the construction of roads and on mining activities, both with a few exceptions. Where the restrictions in Nature Protection Act or decisions under it concern a wilderness, they are binding as such. For silvicultural purposes, these northernmost regions, near to the Protection Forest Zone (*see* Chapter 5, §1 below), are very sensitive, due to climatic conditions causing a very slow reproduction and, in part, due to the risk of transboundary air pollution. In private forests inside and outside the Wilderness Areas, forestry activities are nevertheless allowed, though within the bounds of the general restrictions in the Forestry Act (*see* Chapter 5 below). Intensive logging activities have here been started at times, giving rise to public criticism. Forestry within the Wilderness Areas themselves is however either forbidden or only allowed when based on methods of 'natural reproduction-like' management.

989. The Metsähallitus, being responsible for the management of the Wilderness Areas, shall draft a plan for the care and use of each Wilderness Area and submit it to the Ministry of the Environment for approval. The plan will be based on specific guidelines for any (eventually allowed) silviculture, also drafted by the Metsähallitus.

§5. Recreation Areas and Trails and Terrain Traffic

990. One further type of special area, also having parallels to nature preserves, is the State Outdoor Recreation Area. These areas are based on the Outdoor Recreation Act (606/1973). This Act, which notwithstanding its title contains no provisions for the (mostly unwritten) public rights of access, contains regulations on specific outdoor recreation arrangements, including the State Outdoor Recreation Areas which can be established by the Cabinet on State properties with importance for outdoor activities. The access to such an area is open to all hikers. Possible activities of forestry, hunting and fishing, as well as other uses of the area, shall be arranged so that the needs of outdoor recreation are sufficiently met. The decision of the Cabinet also specifies the land use restrictions and entitles the State to expropriate private areas inside the State Outdoor Recreation Area or adjacent to it. There are presently five State Outdoor Recreation Areas, with a total area of 242 km^2. All of them belong also to Natura 2000.

991. The Outdoor Recreation Act also contains regulations on Recreational Trails, which can be established also in private areas. These trails are based on specific plans drafted by the respective municipalities and submitted for approval to the Centre for Economic Development, Transport and the Environment (environmental division) of the region. All interested parties are heard. As a specific substantive precondition for approval, the living conditions of game animals shall be taken into account. In a separate procedure thereafter, the exact route is specified and marked in the terrain. Simultaneously a decision on compensation for losses and damages suffered by the owners is made. The procedure gives the trail a permanent status which is independent of ownership changes. In practice, a major proportion of the trails have been created under agreements between municipalities and landowners. In this case the procedure for marking, etc., is possible without a confirmed plan.

Finally, the Act further includes the regulation of the supervision of (commercial) camping sites, today in practice caravan sites.

992. A specific Terrain Traffic Act (1710/1995) contains the rules on motor vehicle traffic in the terrain, i.e., in land areas off roads and in ice-covered water areas. Its purpose is to prevent harm to nature or the environment, reindeer husbandry and similar activities, common recreational use and other public interests, caused by motor vehicles, motor sledges included, and to promote traffic safety. As a starting point, traffic in land terrain is allowed only with the permission of the owner of the area (*see also* General Introduction, Chapter 2, §1). Emergency traffic, certain duties of authorities, reindeer husbandry, professional fisheries and a few other specific situations are exempted, however. The Cabinet has the power to forbid the terrain use of specific vehicle types on environmental or other grounds.

In any case damage and harm to nature and the environment shall be avoided. For additional prevention of such damage or harm Centre for Economic Development, Transport and the Environment (environmental division) of the region is empowered to forbid motor vehicle traffic, with a few exceptions, within a fixed terrain area, ice-covered water areas included (sections 8–12). The procedure may be initiated by the municipality, any member of the municipality, a statutory reindeer husbandry association, another association, or the landowner. The procedure is rather similar to that for motor boating restrictions (*see* Part II, Chapter 8, §3, II below). The decision of the centre can be appealed to the Regional Administrative Court.

993. The Terrain Traffic Act also includes provisions on assigned Motor Sledge Trails (Chapter 3), which can be established in land and water areas by a two-stage procedure similar to that for Recreational Trails (*see* above), except for trails in State conservation areas, where the competence is vested in the Metsähallitus. A Motor Sledge Trail shall not be established, if the use thereof would cause significant harm to nature or other environment, natural sources of livelihood, agriculture and forestry, common recreational use or other public or private interest. Agreement with landowners is not needed, if the trail is needed for public connections or common recreational use and significant harm is not caused to properties or reindeer husbandry. Damage to property, reindeer husbandry or professional fisheries shall be compensated by the trail keeper. Use of Motor Sledge Trails is free for all.

The trail keeper is responsible for environmental damage caused by the trail, in accordance with the Environmental Damages Act. Terrain traffic of motor vehicles is supervised by the police, customs, Border Guard and also the forest authorities on State-owned land.

Chapter 3. Wildlife Protection

§1. General Structure of the Rules

994. Legal regulation of wildlife protection is divided into two main regimes, one today based on the Nature Protection Act, sections 6–9 and Chapter 8, complemented by the Nature Protection Decree (1066/2023), and another contained in the Hunting Act (615/1993). The (more or less) protected animal species are divided into three legal categories: those protected on conservation grounds by the Nature Protection Act, those (partly) protected on game management grounds by the Hunting Act (i.e., game animals) and those without any legal protection (in principle; *see* below) but still regulated in the Hunting Act as non-protected (non-game) animals. In favour of the Fisheries Act, fishes were partly covered by the previous Nature Conservation Act but only insofar as non-economic species were concerned. The thirty-seven non-economic species were listed in Annex 1 to the previous Nature Conservation Decree. As an exception, the protection provisions concerning the few fish species of Community interest in need of strict protection, as specified in Annex IV of the Natural Habitats Directive (92/43/EEC), and the provisions concerning endangered species under the CITES Convention and EC Regulation 338/97/EC, were included in the previous Nature Conservation Act also concerning fishes. In the present Nature Protection Act in turn, all provisions of fish have been removed. The general provisions of the Fisheries Act are applicable instead, and the previously protected fish species have no special status any more.

995. Åland has wildlife regulations of its own.

996. In addition to these main regimes, an important basic norm is given by the Animal Welfare Act (247/1996, from 1 January 2024 onwards, a new Act 693/2023). Pursuant to section 29 of the new Animal Welfare Act, an injured or otherwise helpless wild animal may be taken into short-term custody for first aid or delivery. After first aid, the animal must be released back into the wild, if its condition permits, or taken to a care facility for treatment. If the animal cannot be released and its care cannot be arranged, it must be killed. There is a related provision in the Nature Protection Act regarding protected species (section 70) and partly also in the Hunting Act. Pursuant to section 71 of the Nature Protection Act, an ill, wounded or otherwise helpless animal of a protected species may, however, be helped in accordance with the Animal Welfare Act (from 1 January 2024 onwards). A protected animal found dead must not be caught. However, it may be submitted to a State research institute for examination in order to establish the cause of death and infectious animal diseases. If such an animal has scientific or educational value if properly handled, it may be recovered and handed over without undue delay to a museum, institution or higher education institution, which must apply for a permit from the Centre for Economic Development, Transport and the Environment pursuant to section 89 (section 72).

997. The species protection regulation in (Chapter 8) or under the Nature Protection Act concerns both animal and plant species (*see* §2 below).

998. Import and introducing in the nature of specimens of alien animal or bird species is provided in the Hunting Act (section 42), in addition to provisions on veterinary medicine and animal welfare. Import of specimen, spawn or milt of alien fish species is respectively regulated in the Fisheries Act (section 3(4)). On invasive alien species *see* §12 below.

999. The compliance of provisions of the Nature Protection Act and by virtue of it (covering also the various preserves) is supervised mainly by the Centres for Economic Development, Transport and the Environment. The centres are vested in administrative injunction powers (section 126 of the Nature Protection Act; *see also* paragraph 983 and Part V, Chapter 1). The Centre for Economic Development, Transport and the Environment may also appeal against a permit or plan decision by any authority according to any act on the ground that the permit or plan is not in compliance with the Nature Protection Act or provisions under it (section 135 of the Nature Conservation Act).

§2. Protected Species of Animals and Plants

1000. The provisions of Chapter 8 apply to animal and plant species occurring naturally in their natural range in Finland and the economic zone of Finland, with the exception of game animals and unprotected animals as well as fish and crab species referred to in section 5 of the Hunting Act. However, by way of derogation, the provisions of sections 78, 79 and 83 of the Nature Protection Act shall also apply to bears, lynxes, otters and wolves outside the reindeer husbandry area. The provisions of Chapter 8 regarding species also apply to subspecies, race, strain and form, and the provisions of Chapter 8 regarding plants and plant species also apply to fungi and fungal species, in practice to mushrooms and shelf fungi (section 68).

1001. Vertebrates, i.e., mammals, birds, reptiles and amphibians, falling within the scope of Chapter 8 of the Act, are directly protected by law. If the survival of an invertebrate animal or plant species becomes threatened, or if protection proves necessary for some other reason, such species may be declared protected in the whole country or in a part of the country by Government decree (section 69).

1002. If a plant species is protected by decree, it is not allowed to pick, collect, cut, uproot or dispose of a plant, part thereof or seeds (section 74).

1003. The following are forbidden in respect to protected animal species: (1) deliberate killing or capture of individuals of protected species; (2) taking possession of, moving or otherwise deliberately damaging nests, eggs and other stages of development of individuals; and (3) deliberate disturbance of individuals, in particular during the breeding season of animals, in important resting areas during migration or other places important for their life cycle. However, a viper in a yard or otherwise posing a danger to humans or domestic animals may be apprehended and moved if necessary, and, if this is not possible, killed. Damage to a nest outside the breeding season is prohibited, but only if it is a nest made by an animal and used repeatedly by it. Government decree identifies such animal species. Any method of catching an invertebrate animal that is harmful to nature conservation is prohibited. More detailed provisions on prohibited methods are issued by Government decree (section 70).

1004. A nesting tree of the golden eagle, white-tailed eagle, spotted eagle, lesser spotted eagle or osprey with a nest that is repeatedly in use and clearly visible is always protected (section 74). The location data of such nesting trees is maintained in the Nature Protection Information System, the disclosure of data of which is provided for in section 122 of the Act.

1005. As for the non-game mammals and birds, the protection is hence comprehensive, their nests and eggs included. Before 1993, there were some exceptions concerning birds (the rough-legged buzzard in Lapland, raven, hooded crow, jackdaw, magpie, jay, house sparrow, domestic pigeon, fieldfare, blackbird, eagle owl, goshawk, sparrow hawk and gulls except the common gull). The 'outlaw' birds list had long been criticized in public by conservationists, not without result. Already since 1983 the eagle owl, sparrow hawk and rough-legged buzzard (in Lapland) as well as all gulls excepting the great black-backed gull, herring gull and black-headed gull were protected by decree. The goshawk was finally protected by decree in 1989. Though there is no longer an outlaw list in the Nature Protection Act, some species under the former list are from 1993 under the Hunting Act in the category non-protected (non-game) species. The whole list (section 5(2)(1) of the Hunting Act) now consists of common red-backed vole, water vole, common vole, short-tailed vole, Siberian vole, yellow-necked field mouse, brown rat and house mouse, as well as raven (in the reindeer husbandry area in the north), crow, magpie, herring gull, great black-backed gull, domestic pigeon and fieldfare.

1006. The non-protection of this category is not total, however, as closed seasons are applied to the birds at stake (section 25a of the Hunting Decree). Among the mammals totally protected by the Nature Protection Act are, e.g., arctic fox, weasel, bats, hedgehog and flying squirrel. Also the ringed seal of Lake *Saimaa*, perhaps the most well-known of the endangered animals and a symbol of the conservationist interest groups, is protected under the Nature Protection Act, being hence not a game species under the Hunting Act, unlike the seals of the Baltic Sea. It is also included in Annex IV of the Natural Habitats Directive (92/43/EEC).

It shall also be taken into account that the Birds Directive 2009/147/EC impacts the interpretation of the Hunting Act, also when it (previously) had no such explicit effect on its provisions as on those of the then Nature Conservation Act (e.g., SAC 2004:76). Today the provisions on exceptions to the protection pursuant to the Hunting Act (sections 40–41e) are aligned to those of the two directives, where relevant (*see also* below).

1007. Pursuant to Annex 1 to the Nature Protection Decree, five mollusc species are protected in the whole country. These include the pearly freshwater mussel *Margaritifera*, and *Unio*, a freshwater mussel, as well as three gastropod species of the genus *Vertigo*. Furthermore, among the insects, twenty-two butterfly species are protected in the whole country, as well as seventeen beetle species, six dragonfly species and one flat bug species. Moreover, one butterfly species is protected in the southern half of the country (Annex II).

1008. The game animals and birds and the non-protected mammals and birds are listed in section 5 of the Hunting Act (twenty-nine mammal species and twenty-six bird species).

As for game animals and birds, the detailed regulations in the Hunting Act and the Hunting Decree, such as closed game seasons, exceptionally even total bans, allowed hunting and trapping methods, use of hounds, etc., depend on the species. But already the fact that a species is covered by the Hunting Act and not by the Nature Protection Act implies the basic assumption that the species is in a way 'outlawed', because the possible and admittedly often very effective restrictions are based on the interest of game management, not of conservational values. As game animals are regarded, e.g., European rabbit, mountain hare, European hare, squirrel, European beaver, Canadian beaver, most seals, badger, otter, lynx, farmed arctic fox, wild boar, elk, several deer species and various ducks and fowl. The same holds true for the bear, wolf and wolverine, which could before 1993 be hunted also by others than landowners and other hunting right owners, although the right to hunt these three beasts of prey was strongly restricted by a decree. Today, all three are in principle game animals, but pursuant to section 37 of the Hunting Act, wolf, bear, otter, wolverine, lynx and harbour seal are excluded from hunting all year round. This is largely due to the annexes of the Natural Habitats Directive (92/43/EEC). A possibility for certain restricted exceptions is provided, today by sections 40–41e of the Hunting Act (*see* paragraphs 1032 and 1033).

The Act on the Management of Risks Caused by Invasive Alien Species (1709/2015, *see* §12 below) has transferred some previous game animal species to the invasive alien species category, such as raccoon, muskrat, nutria and mink.

1009. As for the Hunting Act in general, the title could, due to the contents, quite well also be the Game Management Act. The regulation is based on the principle of sustainable use. On game management (*see* §8 below).

1010. The arranger of a carcass feeding site (for wild carnivores, e.g., white-tailed eagle) shall make a notification for registration pursuant to section 33a (1070/2021) of the Act on Animal by-Products (517/2015), containing the information specified in the provision.

1011. There are presently 128 vascular plant species (or in some cases subspecies) totally protected by the Nature Conservation Decree, Annex 3. Additionally, nine species are protected in the southern half of the country and eight in the northern half. Moreover, thirteen moss species are protected.

Plants protected nationwide under the Nature Conservation Decree include, among many others:

- Red forms of water-lilies (*Nymphea*).
- Pale pasque flower (*Pulsatilla vernalis*).

– Another species of pasque flower (*Pulsatilla patens*).
– Lesser butterfly orchid (*Platanthera bifolia*).
– Glacier buttercup (*Ranunculus glacialis*).
– Greater meadow-rue (*Thalictrum aquilegiifolium*).
– Another species of meadow-rue (*Thalictrum minus subsp. kemense*).
– Common rock rose (*Helianthemum nummularium*).
– A northern species of rhododendron (*Rhododendron lapponicum*).
– Lady's slipper (Cypripedium calceolus).
– Marsh helleborine (*Epipactis palustris*).
– Dark-red helleborine (*Epipactis atrorubens*).
– Red helleborine (*Cephalanthera rubra*).
– False musk-orchid (*Chamorchis alpina*).
– A species of marsh orchid (*Dactylorhiza sambucina*).
– Calypso (*Calypso bulbosa*).
– One-leaved bog orchid (*Microstylis monophyllos*).
– A subspecies of early marsh orchid (*Dactylorhiza incarnata subsp. cruenta*).

Plants protected in the southern half of the country under the Nature Conservation Decree, Annex 4, include, among others:

– A subspecies of early marsh orchid (*Dactylorhiza incarnata subsp. incarnata*).
– Narrow-leaved marsh orchid (*Dactylorhiza traunsteineri*).

Plants protected in the northern half of the country under the Nature Conservation Decree, Annex 5, include, among others:

– Wood anemone (*Anemone nemorosa*).
– A species of corydalis (*Corydalis intermedia*).
– Yellow iris (*Iris pseudacorus*).

1012. Up to 2005, certain protected plants were only protected as far as sale or marketing, or collecting for these purposes is concerned. These provisions have been repealed.

1013. The Centres for Economic Development, Transport and the Environment (environmental divisions) are empowered to grant exceptional permits in derogation from the species protection rules in the Nature Protection Act or in the Decree, provided that it does not adversely affect the maintenance or achievement of a favourable conservation status for the species. A permit is granted for a fixed period and may be valid for a maximum of ten years at a time. The permit decision may be accompanied by provisions in order to avoid or limit the harm to conservation values. The provisions may include temporal or territorial restrictions or other obligations (section 83). (There are specific additional provisions with respect to Annex IV of the Natural Habitats Directive and to the Birds Directive, where additionally applicable, *see* paragraph 1024.) In practice, exceptions are mainly possible on scientific or educational grounds or when an animal species has locally multiplied to a harmful extent or caused damages otherwise.

1014. By way of derogation from sections 70 and 74, an area may be used for agriculture, forestry or construction activities, and buildings and equipment may be used in accordance with their purpose. In such cases, however, damage or disturbance to protected animals and plants shall be avoided where this is possible without significant additional costs. The possibility of derogation does not apply to bird species or species requiring strict protection referred to in section 78 (section 82). These exceptions may in practice make the protection, though absolute as such, ineffective, as they give land use for agricultural, forestry and building purposes a general priority over species protection rules. A deficiency in principle is also constituted by the fact that the rules protecting species offer no protection against pollution or destruction of the habitats. Protection in the latter respect may, however, be based on the provisions concerning endangered species and species requiring strict protection (*see* §3 below).

1015. Protected animals may cause damage to agriculture (in the recent years particularly barnacle geese), forestry, fisheries (cormorants, ospreys) or buildings. A decree-based system of State compensations has been applicable here from 1991, but in 2022 it has been replaced by the wider Act on the prevention and compensation of damages caused by protected animals (15/2022). The entering into force of the Act had been left depending on a Government decree aimed to be issued after the European Commission has approved the provided State aid arrangements. Pursuant to such a decree, the Act is in force from 1 February 2023. Pursuant to section 1, the Act aims at preventing damages by protected species, compensating the same, promoting species protection and enhancing the acceptability of nature protection. The Act contains pursuant to section 2 the grounds and procedures for granting, within the allowances in the State budget, funds for preventing and compensating damages by protected species, aiding of reindeer husbandry due to damages by eagles and aiding of fisheries due to nesting ospreys. Detailed provisions on grounds for reindeer husbandry compensations are set forth in Decree 8/2002, as amended. Arrangements regarding EU law State aid, where applicable, are provided as specified in section 3 of the Act. The competences of authorities are provided in Chapter 2, aids for prevention in Chapter 3, compensations for damages in Chapter 4, aids due to the nesting of golden eagle or osprey in Chapter 5 and application procedures in Chapter 6. The decisions are, after rejected rectification claim, appealable to the Regional Administrative Court.

1016. As for game animals under the Hunting Act, such as wolf and most of the seals, there are specific compensation mechanisms in the Game Animal Damages Act (105/2009), *see* §11 below.

1017. Protecting a species from harm to individual members of that species is not necessarily sufficient to maintain the population. The protection of habitats is one means of achieving a more effective protection of species, though also not always sufficient in itself. The legal systems for the general protection of natural habitats, dealt with in Chapter 2 above, may of course be important also to single protected species. But only within the categories of endangered species and strictly protected species has an approach been made to protect the particular environment of each species.

§3. Endangered Species

1018. Prior to the 1996 Nature Conservation Act, there were far more endangered plant and animal species in Finland than those having gained legal protection of any kind. An ad hoc committee had listed a total of 1,011 endangered species of various taxonomic groups. In any case, some of the species protected by the Act or the respective Decree had, and some also presently have, also the status of 'endangered species' or 'specially protected species'. These notions are however not connected to the concept of protected species in the Act. Hence a species may be endangered without being protected under the Act.

1019. A Government decree may designate as an endangered species a wild species whose risk of disappearing from nature is at least high, based on the national assessment of the endangered status of species occurring in Finland. The risk of extinction shall be assessed on the basis of the best available information on the size, changes, fragmentation and continuing decline of the population or range and range of the species, or on the basis of a quantitative analysis of the risk of extinction (section 75). The Ministry of the Environment must prepare a proposal for revising the Decree on the basis of a national assessment of the endangered status of species occurring in Finland within two years of the completion of the assessment.

1020. In the Nature Protection Decree, Annex 6, there is a positive list of endangered species, 2,124 in all. It includes 179 vascular plant species, 183 moss species, 5 algae, about 300 mushroom or fungi species, about 250 lichen species, 5 mammals, 55 birds, one amphibian, and about 700 invertebrates. The primary effect of the endangered species status is not a strictly legal one; the list as such has no direct effects on citizens. The authorities shall nevertheless take endangered species into account in permit considerations and in land use Plan decisions, in accordance with the provisions on safeguarding natural values in the relevant Act (section 76). The status of endangered species also makes it possible to declare a species specially protected (*see* below).

1021. The category specially protected species has existed since 1987. According to the present Nature Protection Act, a Government decree may designate as a specially protected species an endangered species pursuant to section 75 whose risk of disappearing from the wild is at least very high. An endangered species with very few sites of occurrence and their survival may also be designated as a specially protected species (section 77 of the Act). According to the Nature Protection Decree (Annex 6, these species are marked with an asterisk), the category contains species of various taxonomic groups, 680 in all. The Ministry of the Environment is obliged to make a plan to revive the population or populations of a specially protected species where this is necessary.

For this purpose, the law provides a special habitat protection system very similar to that for protected natural habitats described above in Chapter 2, §3. This of course also creates legal obligations for private proprietors. A place of occurrence important for the conservation of a specially protected species can be protected by the decision of the Centre for Economic Development, Transport and the Environment of the region. The protection decision must define the boundaries of the place. The place must not be destroyed or impaired. This prohibition will enter into force once the decision has been notified to the owners and occupants of the area. If the permanence of the location of a specially protected animal species cannot be reliably predicted in advance, the decision may be made for a maximum period of ten years. If the place of occurrence has lost its significance for achieving or maintaining a favourable conservation status for a species, the Centre for Economic Development, Transport and the Environment may terminate the protection of the place (section 78). Derogations from the prohibition are possible pursuant to section 83 (*see* paragraph 1024 respectively).

1022. A related habitat protection mechanism is provided directly by the Act (section 78) regarding animal species requiring strict protection pursuant to the Natural Habitats Directive (Annex IV(a) of the Directive). Of such animals, those occurring in Finland (and the plant species listed in Annex IVb of the Directive) are listed in Annex 7 to the Nature Protection Decree. They are twenty-one mammals (including Saimaa ringed seal and flying squirrel and some game animals mainly under the Hunting Act, such as bear and wolf), one reptile, two amphibians, one mollusc, seven butterflies, six beetles and seven dragonflies (and thirty-one plant species). This category often overlaps with the protected, endangered and specially protected species, e.g., the Saimaa ringed seal belongs to all these. It is prohibited to deteriorate or destroy the breeding sites or resting places of the strictly protected animals.

1023. In contrast, the protection of the places of occurrence of species considered important to the EU requires a decision by the Centre for Economic Development, Transport and the Environment of the region (section 79). Hence, the Centre may decide to protect a site of occurrence of a bird species provided in Article 4(2) of the Birds Directive or listed in Annex I thereto, or of a species listed in Annex II to the Natural Habitats Directive, which is important for achieving or maintaining a favourable conservation status. The protection decision shall define the boundaries of the place of occurrence. The place shall not be destroyed or impaired. The decision is appealable to the Regional Administrative Court, but the prohibition will enter into force once the decision has been notified to the owners and occupants of the area. This protection category goes beyond the Natura 2000 sites, similarly based on the Birds Directive.

1024. The Centre for Economic Development, Transport and the Environment of the region may grant permission to deviate from the protection referred to in sections 78 and 79 if it does not adversely affect the maintenance or achievement of a favourable conservation status of the species (section 83). In addition, the preconditions based on the Natural Habitats Directive or the Birds Directive, the corresponding provisions of which are laid down in section 83, must be complied with. The permit is granted for a fixed period and may be valid for a maximum of ten years at a time. The permit decision may be accompanied by provisions to avoid or limit the harm caused by the operations to conservation values. The provisions may include temporal or territorial restrictions and other obligations. A derogation from the prohibition on disturbing a protected bird species may also be granted to the area of one or more municipalities if, due to the abundance of the species, it is likely that individuals of the species will cause unpredictably targeted, particularly significant damage to farms, fish farming or professional fishing. A prerequisite for the decision is that sufficient areas can be designated for feeding, resting or similar needs during migration (section 84).

1025. The practical protection procedures regarding flying squirrel habitats in forestry contexts were in 2004–2015 provided specifically by section 72a (553/2004) of the then Nature Conservation Act. The Centre for Economic Development, Transport and the Environment had to take measures to define the breeding sites or resting places of flying squirrel and the allowed treatment of forest, after having received from the (local branch of the) Finnish Forest Centre notice on a loggings notification submitted to it (section 14b of the Forestry Act, still in force). The decision of the Centre for Economic Development, Transport and the Environment had been made without delay. The provisions appeared to be far from clear in practice, but they still were significant. For deregulation reasons, section 72a was revoked in 2015. The general mechanism remained applicable regarding also flying squirrel.

1026. The location of a species discovered new in Finland or previously unknown to science may be protected by the decision of the Centre for Economic Development, Transport and the Environment of the region if this is necessary for the study and preservation of the species. The protection decision must define the boundaries of the place of occurrence. The place shall not be destroyed or impaired. The prohibition will enter into force once the decision has been notified to the owners and occupants of the area. The ban is valid for a maximum of ten years. The decision remains in force notwithstanding the appeal to the Regional Administrative Court, unless otherwise decided by the court (section 81).

1027. By way of derogation from section 83, the Centre may also authorize the transfer of specimens or parts thereof of a specially protected species outside the natural range of the species only if this is necessary for the conservation or achievement of a favourable conservation status and for the adaptation of the species to climate change. In other than state-owned areas, the decision can only be made with the consent of the property owner. The prerequisite is that the landowner and the Centre have agreed on the details of the implementation of the measures (section 85).

1028. Chapter 9 of the Act applies to the possession of specimens of species falling within the scope of Chapter 8, *see* §5 below.

§4. Protection of Game Animals

1029. Game animals under the Hunting Act are of course not protected as such, but there are still many protection-type provisions, although the ultimate aim thereof is mainly game management. For example, game animals shall not be disturbed in an area for which the person concerned does not have a hunting right or hunting permit for hunting the game animal in question (section 36 of the Hunting Act).

1030. If required due to the preservation of a game animal population or securing undisturbed reproduction of a game animal species, the game animal species shall be declared protected for a specified period or until further notice. Provisions on game animal species to be protected and on closed seasons are issued by decree. During a closed season a game animal may neither be hunted or damaged nor may its mating, nesting, or the young be disturbed. Wolf, bear, otter, wolverine, lynx and harbour seal are in this context protected at all times (section 37).

The protection of the nests of and adjoining constructions by European beaver and Canadian beaver, and exemptions from the protection, are specified in detail by decree (section 37a).

1031. If the population of a game animal species is deteriorated permanently or temporarily in the area of occurring of the species, or in a part of that area, the hunting of that species may by Ministry of Agriculture and Forestry decree be restricted or wholly forbidden. Hunting may be restricted or forbidden also, if required by the aimed spreading of the species or expedient arrangements of hunting. A restriction may refer to (1) an area, (2) a period of time, (3) sex of the prey animal, (4) prey quota for a hunter, or (5) hunting device or method. A restriction may also refer to a duty to fix identification marking to the quarry. A restriction or prohibition may be in force three years or a shorter term at a time. If the population recovers to viable status during the term, the restriction or prohibition shall be revoked before its expiration (section 38). A prey notification shall be submitted to the Finnish Wildlife Agency, if required to safeguard sustainability of the hunting of a certain game animal or expedient arrangements of hunting, as provided in section 38a. A prey register is provided in section 38b.

1032. The Finnish Wildlife Agency may grant a derogation from protection, prohibition or restriction under sections 37 and 38 and 50(2) subject to preconditions laid down in section 41a–41d of the Hunting Act. The Finnish Wildlife Agency may grant a derogation allowing to kill or capture a game animal or non-protected animal subject to conditions laid down in section 41a(1), 41b(1) and 41c also at a time other than during the closed season laid down under section 37. The annual numbers of the quarry to be hunted by virtue of derogations and the regional quota referred to in section 41a(4) may be restricted. Further provisions on the game animal species to which the restriction applies, maximum allowable quarry numbers, sex and age of the individual quarry animals and the area concerned by the restriction may be issued by Decree.

1033. Section 41a of the Hunting Act, following the Natural Habitats Directive, stipulates the preconditions for a derogation concerning certain game animals. Provided that there is no satisfactory alternative and the decision is not detrimental to the maintenance or achievement of the species at a favourable conservation status in its natural range, a derogation referred to in section 41 may be granted for the capturing or killing of wolverine, wolf, bear, otter, lynx, European beaver, grey seal, harbour seal, Baltic ringed seal, polecat, pine marten and mountain hare: (1) in the interest of protecting wild fauna or flora; (2) to prevent serious damage, in particular to crops, livestock, forestry, fisheries, reindeer husbandry, water body or property otherwise; (3) in the interest of public health and public safety, or for other imperative reasons of overriding public interest, including those of a social or economic nature and beneficial consequences of primary importance for the environment; or (4) for the purpose of research and education, repopulating and reintroducing of these species or preventing animal diseases. A wolf, bear, otter, lynx and wolverine bagged as quarry belongs to the State and must be delivered to a research institute. The research institute must destroy the game animal, hand it over for a purpose of public good or sell it on the State's account.

A derogation concerning a wolf, bear, otter and lynx may also be granted for the selective and restricted capturing or killing of certain individuals in closely controlled circumstances. In the reindeer herding area the derogation from protection may also be arranged by virtue of a regional quota established by decree.

1034. According to the Ministry of Agriculture and Forestry Decree 826/2023, the total number of bears caught on the basis of the derogation and the regional quota provided in section 41a of the Hunting Act may not exceed 180 individuals in the hunting year 2023–2024. A certain part of this may be in the reindeer husbandry area. According to the corresponding Decree 917/2023, the maximum number of lynx derogations south of the reindeer husbandry area in the hunting year 2023–2024 is 320, whereas there is no limit in the reindeer husbandry area, and according to the corresponding Decree 1071/2023 the maximum number of wolf derogations south of the reindeer husbandry area in the same hunting year is 28.

1035. In a ruling of 12 April 2022, SAC 2022:48, the SAC, on appeal by a conservation association, held that the mere existence of a lynx population management plan was not to be regarded as a sufficient ground for a granted lynx shooting derogation. Neither was hunting for population management purposes as such an acceptable objective pursued by derogations. In a previous Finnish preliminary ruling C-674/17 (*Luonnonsuojeluyhdistys Tapiola Pohjois-Savo – Kainuu ry v. Risto Mustonen and Others*) of ECJ in 2019, wolf hunting for population management purposes had not been excluded as such, and not even the then objective of derogation (to combat poaching), but strict directive-based conditions had been listed. Accordingly, the preconditions had not been met in the corresponding rulings SAC 2020:27 and 2020:28 (but had been fulfilled in the safety-based wolf derogation case SAC 2020:29). In SAC 2022:48, the combatting of poaching was not at stake, nor any other specified objective.

1036. In the rulings SAC 2023:99 and 100, the SAC stated that it was clear that an overly dense bear population caused problems that could in practice only be solved in ways that caused at least some harm to the bear population. In that regard, it could not be ruled out that mitigating the social problems caused by the increase in the density of the bear population in a controlled manner by reducing the number of bears and ensuring the maintenance of a favourable conservation status could be regarded as a legitimate objective of derogation under Article 16(1)(e) of the Natural Habitats Directive. However, a derogation could only be applied concretely and on a case-by-case basis and only if there was a specific problem or situation that needed to be addressed. In addition, the derogation had to be based on a sufficient explanation of the above-mentioned effects specifically in the area covered by the application for derogation. Under the Habitats Directive, population management hunting of a strictly protected species or the preservation of hunting culture could not in itself constitute a legitimate objective for derogating from strict protection as a prerequisite for the application of section 41a(3) of the Hunting Act, as interpreted in the light of Article 16(1) of the Habitats Directive. The decision of the Finnish Wildlife Agency did not clearly and precisely indicate what acceptable objective under the Directive the decision on a derogation for hunting bears for population management had pursued in the application area in question. The decision to grant a derogation was therefore unlawful.

1037. Section 41b of the Hunting Act again stipulates the preconditions for a derogation concerning game birds and non-protected birds – anyway covered by the Birds Directive. Provided that there is no satisfactory solution and the decision is not detrimental to the maintenance of the species at a favourable conservation status, a derogation referred to in section 41 may be granted for the capturing or killing of such birds: (1) in the interest of public health and safety; (2) in the interest of air safety; (3) to prevent serious damage to crops, livestock, forests, fisheries and water; (4) for the protection of flora and fauna; or (5) for the purposes of research and teaching, of repopulating and reintroducing and for the breeding necessary for these purposes. Derogation may also be granted to kill, capture, keep or to allow the otherwise appropriate utilization of small number of birds other than the unprotected ones selectively and in closely controlled circumstances. In addition a derogation may, concerning participants to a scheme, also be based on a notification to the Finnish Wildlife Agency, as provided in section 41b(3–6), regarding airports, food premises, waste management installations, berry and vegetable farms with an area over 100 hectares, fur farms, fish farms and production animal facilities

1038. Preconditions for a derogation concerning other game mammals are provided in section 41c. A derogation under section 41 concerning game mammals other than those referred to in section 41a may be granted, provided that there is no satisfactory alternative: (1) in the interest of protecting wild fauna or flora; (2) to prevent serious damage, in particular to crops, livestock, forestry, fisheries, reindeer husbandry, water body or property otherwise; (3) in the interest of public health and public safety, or for other imperative reasons of overriding public interest, including those of a social or economic nature and beneficial consequences of primary importance for the environment; or (4) for the purpose of research and education, repopulating and reintroducing of these species or preventing animal diseases.

1039. Derogations for the destroying of the nest of a game animal or non-protected bird, or eggs thereof, are provided in section 41d.

1040. A derogation may be annulled at the request of the police of the Border Guard, as provided in section 41e.

1041. Chapter 5 of the Hunting Act contains several different provisions, partly specified further in the Hunting Decree, on prohibited or restricted ways of hunting, trapping, etc. included, such as use of motor vehicles, aircraft, boat explosives, poisons, certain weapons, living animals as decoys, carcasses, etc. Some of the provisions are environmentally relevant more broadly, such as the ban on lead pellets in waterfowl hunting. In practice, hunting of wolf from helicopter in the reindeer husbandry area has taken place in spite of the ban in section 32.

1042. For the preservation of a game population, the trade of a certain game animal species hunted in Finland or in the economic zone of Finland may be restricted or prohibited in the whole country or in some part of the country or in the economic zone of Finland or some part of this by Government decree (section 43).

Trade in seal products regarding the seal species under the Hunting Act (grey seal, harbour seal, Baltic ringed seal) is provided in Regulation (EC) No. 1007/2009 of the European Parliament and of the Council of 16 September 2009 on trade in seal products, Commission Implementing Regulation (EU) 2015/1850 of 13 October 2015 laying down detailed rules for the implementation of Regulation (EC) No. 1007/2009 of the European Parliament and of the Council on trade in seal products, and the implementing Act on trade in seal products (355/2020).

1043. The owner or holder of an area is entitled to capture or kill a non-protected animal within the area. This right also applies when the hunting right for the area has been conveyed to another person by virtue of a hunting lease contract (section 48 of the Act). The owner or holder of a building, if the non-protected animal is encountered in a building or its yard, as well as the holder of a hunting lease right or a hunting permit is also entitled to capture or kill a non-protected animal, unless otherwise provided in a lease contract or permit. Additionally, the Ministry of Agriculture and Forestry may decide that, for the prevention of animal diseases, other health reasons, securing of public safety, or prevention of significant damage to property, a certain unprotected animal may be captured or killed in a certain area at a specified time without the permission of the owner or holder of the area or a building.

1044. The capturing or killing of a non-protected animal shall take place in such a way that no danger to humans, farmed or pet animals, game animals or protected animals is caused. Concerning non-protected birds and wild cats, the methods of are limited. Also regarding mammals, the allowed methods and use of motor vehicles are provided in section 49 and certain derogations in section 50.

§5. Possession, Sales, Export and Import

1045. Chapter 9 of the Nature Protection Act applies to the holding, exchange, import, export and transit of species falling within the scope of Chapter 8, bird species found in the wild in the Member States of the EU, species listed in Annex IV to the Habitats Directive requiring strict protection by the EU and specimens of species referred to in the CITES Regulation.

1046. A specimen of a protected animal or plant species may not be held, transported, sold or exchanged or offered for sale or exchange. The same applies to species requiring strict protection in the EU and to specimens of bird species found in the wild in the European territory of the Member States of the EU, with the exception of game animals and unprotected animals pursuant to section 5 of the Hunting Act and species listed in Annex III to the Birds Directive. Such provisions concerning individual specimens also apply to parts, derivatives and eggs of an individual of a species. In addition, the CITES Regulation provides for the purchase, sale, offer to purchase, offer for sale, possession and transport for sale, acquisition for commercial purposes or display for that purpose, use for commercial gain and movement of specimens of animal and plant species covered by the Regulation, parts thereof or derivatives thereof, and the movement of live specimens (section 87).

1047. Finland became early a contracting party to the CITES Convention, i.e., the CITES (1973, as amended in 1979). Due to the EU membership, Regulation 338/97/EC[55] is applicable to the international trade, etc. of individuals of protected animal or plant species and parts or derivatives thereof. The Ministry of the Environment is the administrative authority referred to in the Regulation. However, the licences and certificates according to the Regulation are dealt with by the Finnish Environment Institute. (This is one of the situations where the institute acts as an administrative authority.) The Finnish Museum of Natural History acts as the scientific authority provided in the Regulation. The Ministry of the Environment is empowered to enact by decree detailed provisions on the enforcement of the Regulation. Supervision of import and export is the responsibility of customs (sections 9, 10 and 99 of the Nature Protection Act).

1048. Specimens, parts or derivatives of protected animal or plant species may not be imported or exported. This does not apply to the exchange of scientific collections carried out by the Finnish Museum of Natural History or universities. Live

55. Council Regulation (EC) No. 338/97 of 9 Dec. 1996 on the protection of species of wild fauna and flora by regulating trade therein.

birds of prey, owls and hawks shall not be imported. In addition, the CITES Regulation regulates the importation from countries outside the EU, export and re-export to countries and transit of specimens, parts or derivatives of the animal and plant species referred to therein. Specimens or parts thereof of the African elephant, argal, rhinoceros, polar bear, lion and hippopotamus, which are globally endangered due to international trade and of species listed in Annex B to CITES, may not be imported as trophies from outside the EU (section 88).

The prohibitions have practical importance for transit traffic and especially for export from northern Finland, from where egg robbers have at times attempted to smuggle prohibited items abroad. The provisions on penalties and confiscation (below) in the Protection Act and the Penal Code apply to these crimes, too.

The approved transit points for import from and export to non-EU countries, provided by the Regulation, are specified by section 90 of the Act. There are at present eight points.

The Centre for Economic Development, Transport and the Environment of the region may grant an exemption from the prohibitions laid down in sections 87 and 88 for the purposes of research, protection or training of species (section 89).

1049. Whales and arctic seals are stipulated separately, *see* §8 below.

1050. The catching and possession from nature of specimens of protected animal species, the seizure of eggs and other stages of development of individuals and the seizure of protected plants and parts or seeds thereof are prohibited by sections 70 and 74 of the Act and the exceptions, the additional preconditions following the Natural Habitats and Birds Directives included, by section 83 of the Act (*see* above paragraph 1024).

1051. In regard to game species under the Hunting Act, it is prohibited to import or release to the wild bird or mammal species of foreign origin (European rabbit, Canadian beaver, farmed arctic fox, fallow deer, red deer, sika deer, white-tailed deer,[56] European mouflon, Canada goose and common pheasant) as well as game animal strains of foreign origin without the permit of the Finnish Wildlife Agency (section 42 of the Hunting Act). The permit must be refused if significant harm may be caused by the measure to the natural environment or fauna. Provisions on how the import and release to the wild are to be carried out may be included in the permit. These provisions also apply to bringing an animal from Åland to another part of Finland and to the release of the animal to the wild there. In practice, efforts to import hybrids between wolf and dog for farming have previously been prevented by virtue of section 42. However, these and several other species, etc., have been transferred from being regulated by the Hunting Act to the category of invasive alien species, *see* §12 below.

56. Due to old import and the release, the originally American white-tailed deer is today very abundant in southern Finland, being a main interest of hunters there, and a reason for a great number of traffic accidents. The game value of white-tailed deer has also been one of the counter-arguments against the protection of lynx.

§6. Voluntary Ecological Compensation

1052. As a legislative novelty, the current Nature Protection Act contains provisions on voluntary ecological compensation (Chapter 11). Ecological compensation means here compensation for deterioration caused to species and habitats by improving the status of species and habitats outside the deterioration area, where deterioration has primarily been avoided, secondarily minimized and, where possible, the status of degraded species and habitats has been restored in the degraded area.

1053. An actor that weakens natural values in its operations (*the subject causing the deterioration*) may compensate for the deterioration caused by its operations with natural values produced by compensating measures provided in section 99 or, if the conditions laid down in section 100 are met, with a conservation credit. Substitutability can be either equivalent to or above impairment (section 98). Compensatory measures refer to measures that compensate at least in full for any deterioration caused to a natural habitat or habitat of a species (section 99). These include measures that are not required by law or other obligation, and which: (1) restore an area that has deteriorated its natural values or condition to a natural state or a desired state in terms of biodiversity; (2) increasing the surface area of the habitat of a natural habitat or species; or (3) improving the ecological quality of the habitat of a habitat or species. *Conservation credit* (section 100) in turn refers to the permanent protection of a representative occurrence of an endangered habitat type which: (1) maintains or improves the natural state or the desired state in terms of biodiversity by preventing activities causing deterioration of the natural state; and (2) produces a better ecological outcome than the compensatory measures referred to in section 99.

1054. Compensatory measures shall be taken (section 101): (1) in the same or adjacent sub-area of a forest vegetation zone, in the same marine area and within the same or adjacent main river basin in the same water body type or water nature type where the deterioration occurs; and (2) in the area of the Saami community in whose territory the deterioration occurs. Any deterioration affecting an endangered habitat type or the habitat of an endangered species shall be compensated for by measures targeting the habitat of the same species or the same habitat type. If, for reasons of natural science, the deterioration cannot be compensated for by measures targeting the same natural value, it shall be compensated for by measures targeting an equally endangered or more endangered natural value corresponding to the deterioration. A decree of the Ministry of the Environment may lay down more detailed provisions on the natural value and regional equivalence of compensatory measures (*see* Decree of the Ministry of the Environment on Voluntary Ecological Compensation (933/2023)). Measures to create the conditions for achieving the desired state (*basic measures*) must be taken before deteriorating measures are initiated. If necessary, repeated management measures necessary to achieve the desired state shall be taken. Protection credits must always be implemented before impairment (section 102).

1055. Property owners can by use of credit measures produce natural values to be used for ecological compensation (section 103). A credit plan shall be drawn up for the production of natural values, which shall specify: (1) information on the area used for credit measures (*credit area*), its natural values and their status prior to offsetting measures; (2) information on the natural values to be improved, the status to be achieved and the credit measures to be taken to achieve the improvement of natural values; (3) the timetable for the measures; (4) information on the monitoring of the implementation of measures; (5) an assessment of the risks of the implementation of credit measures and a plan for preparing for them and alternative ways of implementing them; and (6) information on the person who carried out the basic measures in practice and his qualifications. The Centre for Economic Development, Transport and the Environment of the region shall issue a statement on the credit plan on the landowner's application. The statement must be submitted for information to the municipality and Regional Council at stake. After the implementation of the basic measures in accordance with the plan, the Centre issues a statement on the quality and quantity of the natural values produced by the measures upon application by the landowner. At the owner's request, information on the quality and quantity of natural values produced by the measures is stored in a register belonging to the Nature Protection Information System. The provisions of section 64 on protected habitat types and section 77 on the protection of the sites of specially protected species are not applied to natural values produced in the credit area without the owner's consent. A decree of the Ministry of the Environment may lay down more detailed provisions on the content of the credit plan.

1056. The subject causing the deterioration may apply to the Centre for Economic Development, Transport and the Environment of the region for a decision on the compensation (section 104). The application shall include: (1) information on the area to be degraded, its natural values and their status prior to the deterioration and an assessment of the deterioration to natural values; and (2) information on the natural value produced in accordance with section 103 or the conservation credit pursuant to section 100 to compensate for the deterioration caused to the habitat type or habitat of the species. If the compensation presented by the applicant meets the requirements laid down in sections 99–101, the Centre for Economic Development, Transport and the Environment shall approve the application. In its decision, the Centre shall prohibit the destruction and deterioration of the natural values of the compensating area and define the boundaries of it. The prohibition will enter into force once the decision has been notified to the owners and occupants of the area. The decision is appealable to the Regional Administrative Court, but is enforceable regardless of the appeal, unless the Court decides otherwise. The decision must be entered in the Land Register, and the Centre stores information on compensation in a register belonging to the Nature Protection Information System. The Centre may grant an exception to the prohibition laid down in section 104(2) if the prohibition prevents the implementation of a project or plan that is of extremely high public interest and there is no technically and economically feasible alternative to the project or plan (section 105). The decision shall oblige the subject causing the deterioration to take compensatory measures to compensate for the natural values present in the compensation area and intended by the compensatory measures. Everyone has the right to receive information on the natural values produced and their use as advance compensation from the register included in the Nature Protection Information System (section 106). The subject causing the deterioration and the producer of natural values shall bear the costs (section 107) of: (1) the design and implementation of compensatory measures; (2) approval of the compensation plan and entry in the register to the authority. In addition, the subject causing the deterioration shall bear the costs of: (1) assessing the impairment; (2) monitoring the implementation of compensation measures; (3) monitoring the effectiveness of compensation measures.

1057. So far, the use and significance of the compensation mechanism remain to be seen, as well as the possible counterproductive effects. The expression voluntary is not quite exhaustive, as it may amend the preconditions for deviation from the protection of natural habitats and habitats of species. In this sense, the mechanism is more optional than purely voluntary. However, the scope of application of the allowed uses of compensation seems somewhat vague because the meaning of natural habitats and habitats of species has not been defined here exactly, particularly in respect to EU law (e.g., sections 78 and 79).

§7. Confiscation of the Value of a Species

1058. The criminal law regulations for offences against the Nature Protection Act are divided between that Act and the Penal Code, as explained in Part V, Chapter 1. The provisions include various penalties for different crimes. For the most serious crimes, the maximum penalty is a prison sentence of two years. The criminal court may also oblige any offender to surrender the object of the criminal act to the State. Since 1991, the confiscation also includes in any applicable case the value of a protected animal or plant as a representative of the respective species (section 132 of the present Nature Protection Act). With respect to general criminal law, this is a rather special modification of the ordinary confiscation provisions. The guiding values for each protected animal or plant species have been laid down in the Ministry of the Environment Decree 9/2002 (as amended by 837/2010).

§8. Protection of Whales and Arctic Seals

1059. A separate Whales and Arctic Seals Protection Act (1112/1982; title amended by 1107/1996) prohibits the use of Finnish vessels for whaling as well as the import of whale products to Finland. The direct relevance of the Act mainly concerns Finland's participation in international whale protection activities. Whales (dolphins and porpoises included) are only occasionally found in Finnish sea waters. Nevertheless, they are totally protected in Finnish areas and in the economic zone of Finland, and the Nature Protection Act is here respectively applicable. The taking into possession of whales found dead is also prohibited, except for scientific purposes. A living but injured whale may be transported to temporary care. The penalties concerning offences against the Nature Protection Act apply to offences against the Whales Protection Act correspondingly. From January 1997, the Act, insofar as the ban on import is concerned, was extended also to arctic seals and effectively to seal products, in order to give effect to EC Regulation 89/370/EEC.

The protection (where applicable) of the natural seal species in Finland is based on the Nature Protection Act. This applies to the Saimaa ringed seal. The Baltic ringed seal and the common seal are instead game animals pursuant to the Hunting Act, but enjoy rather effective protection in practice. On the trade thereon, *see* paragraph 1042.

As to seal or porpoise that has remained among fish catch, *see* paragraph 1123.

§9. Game Management

1060. Besides the very hunting activities, trapping included, (other) game management is regulated in the Hunting Act. This is related to the fact that the right to hunt, where any, belongs to the owner of a property, with some exceptions, such as those limited common hunting rights of local people in State-owned areas of northern Finland (section 8) and the hunting right of everyone with a habitual residence in Finland regarding Public Water Areas in the sea and the economic zone (section 7). All hunting (other killing than by shooting and using of traps, etc. included) shall be carried out according to the principles of sustainable use and in such a way that the game stocks are not endangered, the natural environment is not unnecessarily damaged and unnecessary suffering is not caused to animals (section 20). It is the target of appropriate game management to safeguard sustainable reproduction of game populations. No danger or damage shall be caused to humans or property. On the contrary, game animals shall not be disturbed by persons who lack right to hunt in the area at stake (section 36). Chapter 5 of the Hunting Act contains several measures and duties aiming at rational game management. *See also* §4 above.

1061. A licence (cervid hunting licence) must be obtained for the hunting of fallow deer, red deer, sika deer, moose, white-tailed deer and forest reindeer (section 26 of the Hunting Act). The licence is granted by the Finnish Wildlife Agency. In granting hunting licences, it must be ensured on the one hand that the cervid population is not endangered by hunting and on the contrary that damage caused by cervids is kept at a reasonable level. In order to take damages to traffic, agriculture and forests into account, the Finnish Wildlife Agency must hear the relevant regional stakeholders on an annual basis, but there is no judicial possibility for controlling the outcomes in this respect. In granting hunting licences for State areas referred to in section 8, consideration must also be given to equitable distribution of hunting opportunities and to appropriate arrangements in general. Granting of a cervid hunting licence is subject to the condition that the licence applicant has access to an unbroken area suitable for hunting (section 27). The minimum land area is, as a rule, 1,000 hectares for moose hunting and 500 hectares for hunting other cervids. A cervid hunting licence is granted to an applicant or applicants who have the right to hunt the cervid at stake in the area in question. In areas other than those referred to in section 8, a hunting licence may be granted for on the basis of no more than one application. The holder of a cervid hunting licence must name a hunting master. A person participating in a hunt must observe orders given by the hunting master. The hunting master may prohibit a person who fails to observe such orders from participating in the hunt.

1062. As to other game than cervids, a licence by the Finnish Wildlife Agency must be obtained for hunting or a regional quota established by the Ministry of Agriculture and Forestry must be complied with in hunting if a game animal population is endangered by hunting or if this is required for the appropriate arranging of the hunting of the game animal species (section 10).

1063. Detailed provisions on the game animal species to be hunted by virtue of a hunting licence or regional quota, conditions for granting a hunting licence and regional quota and the procedures to be followed in granting these and other matters relating to a hunting licence and reporting of the quarry bagged by virtue of the hunting licence or regional quota are included in the Hunting Decree. The annual quarry numbers of the hunt to be allowed by virtue of hunting licences and a regional quota may be restricted. Further provisions on the game animal species to which the restriction applies, maximum allowable quarry numbers, sex and age of the individual quarry animals, and the area to which the restriction applies may be issued by Decree of the Ministry of Agriculture and Forestry. The Finnish Wildlife Agency is responsible for monitoring hunting which is allowed by virtue of a regional quota.

The Cervid Hunting Fee, provided in section 4, shall be paid due to a cervid hunting licence pursuant to section 26 of the Hunting Act (section 4 of the Act on Game Management Fee and Hunting Licence Fee). It is based on the realized prey afterwards. The funds from this fee are channelled to prevention and compensation of damages caused by cervids, and to related data systems. The funds may also be used for the monitoring of and scientific work on elk populations (section 6).

1064. The game management activities are mainly carried out by the statutory hunters' organizations, which are of three levels, as reformed in 2011 by the Wildlife and Game Administration Act (158/2011), *see* §10 right below.

1065. Pursuant to the Act on Game Management Fee and Hunting Licence Fee (616/1993 with later amendments), a hunter or a cervid hunting master must pay a Game Management Fee (today EUR 43 regarding adults and EUR 10 regarding youth under 18 years) to the State for each hunting year. A person assisting a hunter as a dog handler or, in cervid hunting, as a driver, or assisting in hunting in a comparable manner is not obliged to pay. A person who has paid the fee will receive a hunting card. Before paying the game management fee the person concerned must, by taking a hunting examination, demonstrate his/her knowledge of hunting and game management and of the hunting provisions to an examiner appointed by the Finnish Wildlife Agency (*see* below). Besides the examination, a shooting test may be required depending on the weapon and species at stake (section 21 of the Hunting Act; on the mutual recognition of test certificates *see* section 21a).

§10. Game Management Organizations

1066. The Finnish Wildlife Agency, created by the Act on Game Management Administration (158/2011; amendments) is an independent public law institution, the task of which is to promote sustainable game husbandry, support the activity of Game Management Associations, see to the implementation of wildlife and game policy and manage the public administration tasks laid down for it. The Finnish Wildlife Agency is guided and supervised by the Ministry of Agriculture and Forestry. The Agency and the ministry shall annually agree on the strategic and performance objectives to be set for the activity.

The public administration tasks of the Finnish Wildlife Agency are in particular those laid down in the Hunting Act (*see* paragraphs 1031–1037 and 1051–1055) and in the Act on the Game Management Fee and Hunting Licence Fee. Moreover, the tasks encompass appointment, steering and supervision of the hunting wardens of Game Management Associations, appointment, steering and supervision of the examiners of the hunter's examinations and shooting tests, appointment, steering and supervision of the representatives of Game Management Associations working in field inspections under the Game Animal Damages Act (105/2009).

Outside these law enforcement tasks, the Agency shall promote sustainable game husbandry and supervise the public interest relating to game husbandry; monitor the status, development, sustainability and viability of game animal populations and development of activities relating to these together with research, promote game management and management of game habitats, prepare, draw up and update management plans concerning game animal species and the management of their habitats; promote the prevention of damages caused by game animals; promote sustainable, safe and ethically acceptable hunting; promoting the activity of game management associations and training of the staff of Game Management Associations; produce expert, training and advisory services relating to hunting, game husbandry and game animals; take care of information and communication; maintain and develop joint information systems, information resources and information services of the Agency and Game Management Associations and participate in the development of joint information systems, information resources and information services of the sector; participate in international cooperation; and perform other tasks assigned to it which do not involve the use of public power.

1067. The supreme decision-making body of the Finnish Wildlife Agency is the Board thereof. The Ministry of Agriculture and Forestry appoints ten members, of which the National Wildlife Council proposes six members to represent persons who have paid the Game Management Fee from among the persons proposed by the regional meetings. In addition, the Board has one representative from the Ministry of Agriculture and Forestry, one from the Natural Resources Institute Finland and one from an association with national significance as regards agriculture and forestry, as well as one representative of the staff of the Agency. The Ministry of Agriculture and Forestry appoints the chair and vice-chair from among the members proposed by the National Wildlife Council. Provisions on public liability under criminal law apply to the Board members when they manage public administration tasks or deal with matters relating to the use of funds.

The Finnish Wildlife Agency has a Director-General and a Director for Public Administration Tasks, both appointed by the Cabinet. Provisions on public liability under criminal law apply to the Director for Public Administration Tasks. Provisions on public liability under criminal law also apply to the other staff of the Finnish Wildlife Agency when they manage public administration tasks or deal with matters relating to the use of funds. The Director for Public Administration Tasks is independent when managing a public administration task. He or she may order in writing a staff member of the Finnish Wildlife Agency to use public power in certain matters provided that he or she can be considered to have sufficient training and experience in dealing with and resolving such matters. A person ordered to use public power is independent when managing a public administration task. A decision on a licence under the Hunting Act may be signed electronically.

1068. The task of the National Wildlife Council, operating in connection with the Finnish Wildlife Agency, is to deal with matters relating to game husbandry. The members of the Council are appointed by the Ministry of Agriculture and Forestry. The National Wildlife Council has fifteen representatives proposed by the regional meetings. In addition, the Council has representatives from the Ministry of Agriculture and Forestry, the Ministry of the Environment and several other bodies and associations. Matters to be dealt with at a meeting of the Council are prepared and presented by the Director-General of the Finnish Wildlife Agency or a person designated by him/her.

The task of the Regional Wildlife Councils operating in connection with the Finnish Wildlife Agency is to deal with matters relating to game husbandry as well as support, steer and assist the activity of the regional office of the Agency in tasks other than the public administration tasks and personnel administration. The Councils are appointed by the Ministry of Agriculture and Forestry. The Regional Wildlife Council has up to ten members representing various stakeholder organizations within each region. Matters to be dealt with at a meeting of the Regional Wildlife Council are prepared and presented by a staff member of the Finnish Wildlife Agency. The required qualifications of the Director-General include a higher university degree, good knowledge of game husbandry and managerial skills proven in practice. The required qualifications of the Director for Public Administration Tasks include a higher university degree, good knowledge of game husbandry and experience in administration.

1069. The Central Organization of Hunters is based on the Game Management Districts. The latter in turn are based on Local Game Management Associations, which are made up and financed by those who have paid the Game Management Fee compulsory to all hunters. (However, the membership is not compulsory, although the fee is.) The organizations are, although largely organized in the same way as voluntary associations, in fact public law bodies with several statutory official tasks and authority-like competence. This holds true especially for the Game Management Districts, which are competent among other things in various hunting permit matters. On appeals against their decisions *see* below.

1070. Game Management Associations are independent actors with a geographical area of operation based on the self-initiative of hunters who have paid the Game Management Fee. The Finnish Wildlife Agency steers and supervises the activity of Game Management Associations. Each Game Management Association is responsible for promoting sustainable game husbandry in its area of operation, sees to the promotion and organization of voluntary action by hunters as well as manages the public administration tasks laid down for it. The geographical area of operation of an Association consists of one or several municipalities, as confirmed by the Finnish Wildlife Agency. Regional meetings are meetings composed of representatives appointed by Game Management Associations for each area of operation of the Finnish Wildlife Agency. A regional meeting is held at least once a year.

1071. The public administration tasks of a Game Management Association are: organization of shooting tests and hunter's examinations; participation in field inspections under the Game Animal Damages Act; assisting authorities responsible for the supervision of the compliance with the Hunting Act in the supervision of hunting; and other public administration tasks that fall within the scope of the activities of an association. The other tasks encompass promoting of sustainable game husbandry, promoting of sustainable, safe and ethically acceptable hunting and promoting of game management, sustainability and viability of game animal populations and management of game habitats and prevention of damages caused by game animals. Moreover, the associations produce expert, training and advisory services relating to hunting, game husbandry and game animals and related information and communication, and perform other tasks laid down by the Ministry of Agriculture and Forestry or assigned by the Finnish Wildlife Agency.

1072. Any person who has paid the Game Management Fee is, after having taken the hunter's examination, entitled to belong as a member to the game management association in whose area of operation he or she mainly hunts or has his or her permanent place of residence. A person may not be a member of more than one game management association at a time. If a person is not a member, he or she is entered to the Register of Hunters on the basis of the home municipality.

The ultimate decision-making power of a Game Management Association is vested in the annual meeting of the Game Management Association. Each Association has a Board and a Coordinator of Activities, and it may also have hunting wardens, examiners of hunter's examinations and shooting tests as well as other staff. The specific training requirements and the tasks, rights and liabilities of the wardens and examiners are stipulated in sections 21–24 of the Wildlife and Game Administration Act.

1073. The Finnish Wildlife Agency and Game Management Associations may engage in business activities that support the realization of their function and does not compromise their impartiality in the public administration tasks.

1074. Administrative Rectification of most decisions by the Finnish Wildlife Agency and of a decision of a Game Management Association concerning the passing of a hunter's examination or shooting test may be claimed from the Agency as provided in the Administrative Procedure Act. A decision by the Finnish Wildlife Agency issued on a claim for rectification is appealed to the Regional Administrative Court. The decisions pursuant to the Hunting Act and in the Act on the Game Management Fee and Hunting Licence Fee, to which the rectification stage does not apply, are directly appealable to the Regional Administrative Court.

§11. Game Animal Damages

1075. The Game Animal Damages Act (105/2009 with later amendments) provides the grounds and procedures to be followed when granting funds for compensating damages caused by game animals and advance prevention of damages caused by game animals from appropriations included in the State budget.

1076. Damage by cervids is compensable, if caused: (1) to arable land, horticulture land, nursery plantation and harvested crop; (2) to livestock; or (3) to forest and forest reproductive material. When caused by a large carnivore, damage is compensable when caused: (1) to arable land, horticulture land, nursery plantation and harvested crop; (2) to a domestic animal, farmed animal, honey crop and fences, buildings and other similar structures used for the keeping of animals; (3) damage caused to inanimate movable property other than that above; or (4) damage caused to reindeer in the reindeer husbandry area pursuant to the Reindeer Husbandry Act (848/1990). A very significant damage caused by a game animal other than a cervid or large carnivore may also be compensated for within the appropriation included annually in the State budget, if damage caused by a certain game animal is directed to the same livelihood in an extensive area and the damage could not have been prevented in advance and the damage cannot be sufficiently prevented or reduced by hunting the game animal concerned.

Damage caused by a cervid to crops, animals and forest may be compensated only for the part of damage caused to a private farmer or private landowner or certain comparable beneficiaries. Nevertheless, all types of beneficiaries or their assignees may be compensated for personal injury or damage to crops, animals and movable property caused by a large carnivore. A reindeer owner and cooperative may be compensated for damage to reindeer caused by a large carnivore.

1077. The Ministry of Agriculture and Forestry may grant a subsidy for preventing within the limits of the State budget. A subsidy may be granted for the acquisition of materials, research and development work as far as their purpose is to prevent damage. A subsidy does not remove the obligation of the beneficiaries to take action on their own initiative to prevent the damage or its spreading.

A precondition for receiving the compensation is that the party suffering the damage has by reasonable means available made efforts to prevent the damage or its spreading. The compensation may be denied or reduced if the party suffering the damage has contributed to the damage or its spreading or without acceptable grounds prohibited a measure which could have prevented the damage or its spreading.

1078. Sections 9–22 contain detailed provisions on compensation in various damage situations, sections 23–29 on notification and assessment of damage, and sections 30–50 on applications, payment, rectification of decisions, appellate procedures, etc.

1079. On the compensations for damages by animals protected by virtue of the Nature Conservation Act, *see* paragraph 1015.

§12. INVASIVE ALIEN SPECIES

1080. The prevention and management of the introduction and spread of invasive alien species is regulated by the Act on the Management of Risks Caused by Invasive Alien Species (1709/2015). The Act on the one hand contains the necessary complementary provisions regarding the Invasive Alien Species Regulation[57] and on the other hand provides certain other measures in order to prevent and reduce the harmful impacts of invasive alien species. The species covered by the Act are first those listed on the basis of Article 4(1) of the Regulation (section 2) and second the nationally significant harmful invasive alien species not included in the EU list which on the basis of available scientific evidence may cause damage to the diversity of nature, other damage to wild organisms or danger to health or safety (section 11). The species and groups of species are specified by Government decree on the Management of Risks Caused by Invasive Alien Species (704/2019, amended by 912/2023), Annexes A (animals) and B (plants). Among other species and species groups, Annex A refers to hybrids in generations F1–F4 of domestic dog and wolf (*Canis lupus*) or other canid, and crosses between these and other canid than domestic dog, and crosses between (the endangered) lesser white-fronted goose (*Anser erythropus*) and other goose species, Spanish chip snail (*Arion vulgaris*) and blackhead snail (*Krynickillus melanocephalus*). Annex B in turn contains, *inter alia*, Canadian waterweed (*Elodea canadensis*), large-leaved lupine (*Lupinus polyphyllus*), rugosa rose (*Rosa rugosa*) and common jewelweed (*Impatiens capensis*). Far from all species that, e.g., due to climate change are new to Finnish nature have been regarded harmful and listed in the provisions, especially if role of human being in the spreading or possible harm is unclear. One recent example is mistletoe (*Viscum album*), now spreading in the southwest.

1081. The nationally significant listed species shall not be released to the environment or intentionally imported, placed on the market, transferred or sold. Subject to certain exceptions, the EU-based rules are applicable also to the national list.

An alien invasive species shall not be kept, farmed, planted, sowed or treated in such a way that it may be released into the environment (section 3 of the Act, where also certain exceptions are provided). An owner or possessor of property is obliged

57. Regulation (EU) No. 1143/2014 of the European Parliament and of the Council of 22 Oct. 2014 on the prevention and management of the introduction and spread of invasive alien species.

to take care of reasonable measures to destroy the specie other than bird or mammal, or reduce its spreading, if the occurrence or the spreading may cause significant damage to diversity of nature or danger to health or safety (section 4 of the Act).

A person who professionally produces, stores, places on the market, transfers, forwards, sells, or otherwise hands over product or material with which an invasive alien species may spread into the environment, is responsible for making sure that the product or material does not contain such species (section 5).

An animal or a bird belonging to an invasive alien species may be trapped and killed, observing the provisions on non-protected (non-game) species in sections 48 and 49 of the Hunting Act (section 16 of the Act). The prohibition on causing unnecessary pain or suffering to an animal is governed by section 6(1) of the Animal Welfare Act and the killing of animals by section 64 of that Act (section 16 of the Act). If a nest of muskrat is destroyed, also the cubs shall be killed, as far as possible (section 5 of the Decree).

1082. Several authorities are involved in the administration. The Centres for Economic Development, Transport and the Environment as a rule have the supervisory authority. Administrative enforcement measures by them are provided in section 17 of the Act and criminal sanctions in section 21. The centres also decide on rapid eradication at an early stage of invasion pursuant to Articles 17 and 18 of the Regulation. The customs supervise imports, and the Regional State Administrative Agency decides upon the permits and authorizations pursuant to Articles 8 and 9 of the Regulation and supervises the permitted activities. Also the Natural Resources Institute Finland and Finnish Environment Institute contribute. The Ministry of Agriculture and Forestry approves the plans pursuant to Articles 13 and 19 of the Regulation. In exceptional cases, the ministry may also submit the Commission an application for authorization pursuant to Article 9 of the Regulation. Section 88 of the Hunting Act applies to the monitoring of compliance with the provisions on the capture and killing of bird or mammal species that has entered the environment. Provisions on monitoring compliance with animal welfare provisions are laid down in the Animal Welfare Act.

§13. Genetic Resources

1083. The Nagoya Protocol on Access to Genetic Resources and the Fair and Equitable Sharing of Benefits Arising from Their Utilization to the Convention on Biological Diversity, and, where necessary, Regulation (EU) No. 511/2014 of 16 April 2014 on compliance measures for users from the Nagoya Protocol on Access to Genetic Resources and the Fair and Equitable Sharing of Benefits Arising from their Utilization in the Union have been implemented by the Act on the enforcement of the Nagoya Protocol connected to the Convention on Biological Diversity (394/2016), being applicable from 1 September 2016 (Decree 590/2016). The Act applies to such imported genetic resources and associated traditional knowledge of indigenous peoples to which such provisions or regulatory requirements of a party to the Nagoya Protocol by which the provisions of the Protocol on the access to genetic resources and associated traditional knowledge of indigenous peoples and on sharing of the benefits have been implemented. The Act is not applicable to genetic resources the access to which and the sharing of benefits of which has been stipulated in other international agreement binding Finland, or to genetic resources to which the multilateral system of access and benefit-sharing pursuant to the International Treaty on Plant Genetic Resources for Food and Agriculture is applicable. Neither is the Act applicable to human genetic resources. Genetic resources imported before 1 September 2016 and associated traditional knowledge are excluded from the scope of application. Transgenic organisms are stipulated in the Gene Technology Act.

1084. A user who imports to Finland genetic resources or traditional knowledge referred to in the Protocol shall notify the competent authority (Finnish Environment Institute or the Natural Resources Institute Finland, depending on the substance at stake) within one month from the import, as provided in Article 4(3) of the Regulation.

1085. The Saami Parliament shall administrate a database into which the traditional knowledge associated with the genetic resources of the Saami can be saved. The Saami Parliament shall inform the competent authority on the genetic resources the database concerns. A right to utilize knowledge included in the database may be granted by the competent authority, as provided in the Act. For handing over information, it is required that the competent authority accepts the conditions agreed upon by the Saami parliament and the applicant. The Saami parliament may require that the benefits are fairly and equitably shared to the Saami in such a manner that their own language, culture and status as indigenous people are promoted. The competent authority shall, if necessary, negotiate with the Saami parliament on the agreed conditions. Any use of the traditional knowledge included in the database shall not decrease the possibilities of the Saami to utilize their rights as indigenous people to maintain and develop their culture and practice their traditional ways of livelihood, unless insignificant.

1086. The Ministry of the Environment is responsible for general guidance and supervision. The Finnish Environment Institute has been designated as the national focal point on access and benefit-sharing pursuant to Article 13 of the Protocol. The various tasks of the competent authorities (Finnish Environment Institute and Natural Resources Institute Finland) in supervision, cooperation and reporting, as well the rights thereof on access to information and on inspections are stipulated in sections 12–13 of the Act. Administrative enforcement is provided in section 15, appellate procedures before administrative courts in section 16 and criminal offences in section 17.

Chapter 4. Agricultural Resources

1087. There is no specific legislation for the protection of agricultural resources, i.e., of arable land, in Finland. It has not been considered necessary to protect cultivated land from being brought into use of a different kind. Due to agricultural overproduction, a decrease in the quantity of cultivated land has long been a central objective of the official agricultural policy and agricultural legislation. Afforestation of fields has for years been one officially recognized and recommended alternative.

1088. Parts of the best arable lands are yearly altered to settled areas. This is mainly based on detailed land use Plans regulated in the Land Use and Building Act, as of 1 January 2025, the Land Use Act (*see* Part III, Chapter 3 below). In connection with planning, the need to preserve arable land has not emerged as a problem or a relevant item so far. Of course, the flexible plan drafting rules may make arable land protection judicially relevant in the future. Another point connected to agriculture has already gained occasional relevance in planning decisions: the cultural values of traditional countryside settlements. Specific rules for the protection of agricultural landscapes are, however, lacking (*see* nevertheless Part II, Chapter 2, §4).

1089. From 1998, no permit is needed for purchase of agricultural land.

1090. The legal system still contains remainders of the expansive agriculture policies which were dominant long ago. The rather conservative drainage rules in the previous Water Act were up to 1998 partly based on the assumption that a right to acquire new arable land (and even compel others to take part) belongs to every landowner willing to realize (often with State subsidy) a ditching plan resulting in new arable land (or amelioration of existing land; *see* below Part II, Chapter 8, §3, IV).

1091. To some extent, mould is extracted from fields, even as a commercial commodity. Here the Soil Excavation Act is applied (*see* Part II, Chapter 7 below), and a permit is needed as for any other substances under the Act. A permit is hence not admissible, if the impacts on landscape and environment would be those specified in the Act. There are not many precedents on mould extracting situations.

1092. As for erosion abatement, there are particular provisions only concerning vulnerable shoreland forests or precipice forests (in Chapter 4 of the Forestry Act, *see* Part II, Chapter 5, §1 below). The practical effect of these provisions – which in fact merely constitute the power of the Ministry of Agriculture and Forestry to issue detailed provisions – has remained insignificant, and the erosion problem in forests is as a rule not very great. However, the clay erosion of cultivated land in southwestern Finland is a real problem, at least as regards the quality of river and estuary water. Damages to roads and buildings may also occur in these areas.

1093. The rules concerning soil pollution are, of course, applicable to cultivated land. In addition, the rules concerning fertilizers as well as the spreading of sludge from sewage water treatment plants (*see* Part I, Chapter 5, §15) are here of special interest.

1094. Climate change has raised the issue of greenhouse gases from cultivated peatland fields, of which there is an amount in some parts of the country. No specific legislation has been enacted.

Chapter 5. Forests

§1. Restrictions on the Use of Forests

1095. The Finnish forest legislation has traditionally been quite substantive and versatile, due to the importance of silviculture. Public law restrictions on property use are of comparatively early origin. Protection of the environment has, however, not been among the purposes of the forest utilization restrictions. Instead, forest law has been a matter of national economics. The present Forestry Act (1093/1996), however, marked a significant change and strongly reduced the dualism between economy and conservation, as environmental aspects were combined with the rules of reproduction. The Forestry Act, being applicable to the management and use of forests in areas classified as forestry land, entered into force in January 1997. Several amendments have taken place since then.

1096. Traditionally, the legislator has aimed at preventing wasteful utilization of forests and securing proper regeneration (or avoiding of deforestation). This has been important to secure by regulations, because reproduction is a matter of utmost value to the national economy, and at the same time requires investments which normally profit only the following generations. Hence the market economy as such has not offered the necessary tools. In practice, the result is a reproduction rate of nearly 100%. The main tool here is today the reproduction system of the Forestry Act. Unlike its predecessor, the Act is applicable to private and State forests alike.

The implementation of the previous legislation often resulted in a situation where the only viable possibility for the owner was clear felling with subsequent tree planting. This was, of course, problematic to those owners who regarded the natural and recreational values of their forests as more important than the economical profits. Those who would have preferred other, 'smoother' methods, like partial cutting combined with natural reproduction, had run the risk of getting into trouble with the authorities. Courts had in certain well-known cases had to decide upon delicate nuances of forest management science, affected by conflicts between opposite schools. The disputes had been exacerbated by a paradoxical controversy in the former legal structure: the sanctions were not at all applicable to those who left their forests wholly uncared for and unused, but had in practice been applied to those who have a personal opinion on forest management methods. The previous law was partially revised in 1990, aiming at some deregulation. A profound change in the duties was constituted by the present Forestry Act, and changes have been made also later on.

1097. The Forestry Act is supervised by the Finnish Forest Centre, a specific public law creation based on the Act on the Finnish Forest Centre (418/2011). The Centre, as a nationwide independent public law body with regional units, is a development and enforcement organization for sustainable forestry, preserving of forest diversity and promotion of forest-based businesses (section 1 of the Act). Its task is (somewhat tautologically) to promote such businesses, enforcement of forest legislation and management of forest data (section 1). The centre is under the strategic and performance-based guidance and supervision of the Ministry of Agriculture and Forestry. Unless otherwise provided, business activities are excluded.

1098. According to the Forestry Act, there are two equally legal options (section 8) for cuttings (which in practice today overwhelmingly take place using hi-tech one-man run machinery). First, the cutting may aim at raising the remaining tree stand (improvement felling, section 5). This is to many people the smoother method. Second, the cutting may be (almost) total clear-cutting and aim at regenerating a new tree stand (regeneration felling, section 5a). Both options bring about a reproduction duty. The latter for its part may be of two kinds, based either on planting or natural reproduction. Of these two the latter may be regarded as the smoother. Each method is bound to specific preconditions, because there are several risks and various circumstances in each. The regeneration procedure is controlled by the regional units of the Finnish Forest Centre. There are detailed provisions on the responsibility of the various parties (landowner, possible cutting right holder, possible later landowner, cutter).

1099. As for environmental aspects, the Forestry Act includes various provisions to safeguard the diversity of forest nature. In all forestry, general preconditions for the preserving of natural habitats important for forest biodiversity shall be safeguarded (section 1(1)). This is nevertheless merely a rather vague general clause, and the contents of the Forestry Act is continuously a bone of content in public debate. Newly accentuated arguments here are threat to general biodiversity especially in clearcutting, the role of forests in regard to climate change and sustainability in forestry in general. The last mentioned has is now especially topical due to the stop of imports of Russian wood. There is no legal mechanism for safeguarding overall sustainability of forests. For example, in considering Environmental Permits of wood industry, the impacts of raw material supply are legally irrelevant, as in cases like the one described in paragraph 230.

1100. More important in practice, albeit small-scale, are the specified provisions on the (normally small-sized) natural or natural-like forest habitats (biotopes) which are especially important to the biodiversity of forests. They are supposed to be clearly discernible in the forest and either small or economically less important. There are seven listed main categories thereof (section 10(2)). In these habitats only such caring forestry measures are allowed by which their characteristics are preserved or even improved. In the measures, water conditions specific to the biotope, wood structure, old high trees and dead and rotten trees shall be preserved and the flora, variability of terrain, and soil have to be taken into account. No regeneration felling, forest roads, treatment of soil detrimental to plants, ditching, clearing of brooks or use of chemical pesticides is allowed (section 10a). Within some of the biotopes, caring picking-type felling with limited impacts may be allowed, as provided in section 10b. Exceptional permits are in certain circumstances possible on economic grounds, but they shall in no case be approved if the owner or the cutting right holder is granted a sufficient State subsidy (section 11).

The provisions of habitats are in a way parallel to the habitat system of the Nature Protection Act. During the legislative procedure, the division of various forest habitats between the two acts was much discussed. There are indeed some differences. The exceptions according to the Forestry Act are more flexible and they are ultimately decided upon by forestry authorities, not by environmental authorities. Appeal can be made to the Regional Administrative Court. The level of protection and the preconditions for exceptions differ to some extent. The legislative result was that most forest biotopes were brought under the Forestry Act, but not all. One major reason was that the Nature Conservation Act is applicable against all threatening activities, but the Forestry Act only in case of forestry (cuttings, forest ditching, forest roads).

1101. In general, no permit from any authority is needed for cuttings. However, notification shall be made to the Finnish Forest Centre on intended cuttings, etc. (section 14), a state of affairs that may make, e.g., the control of an EIA or Natura 2000 assessment impossible. The Centres for Economic Development, Transport and the Environment have been vested in temporary ban and administrative injunction powers in respect to various situations of non-compliance.

1102. In general, the Nature Protection Act is applicable in forest areas almost as usual (*see* section 2(2) of the Forestry Act). The same holds good for the Ancient Remains Act. The Water Act is, e.g., applicable to forest ditching and the Environmental Protection Act (at least in principle) to forest fertilizing. According to the Private Roads Act, section 4, also when applied to forest roads, the impacts on nature and environment are relevant (*see* Chapter 9, §1 below). There are also areas where the Forestry Act is not at all applicable. These include, among others, nature conservation areas established under the Nature Protection Act, areas acquired by the State for nature conservation purposes and other state-owned areas managed in accordance with a conservation decision by the Metsähallitus or an authority managing State property, areas assigned to a conservation preserve in a land use plan under the Land Use and Building Act (from 1 January 2025, the Land Use Act), as well as areas with a Detailed Plan (except those assigned for forestry) and areas where the right to various measures is temporarily restricted due to the ongoing procedure for a Detailed Plan (section 2 of the Forestry Act). Here (and in some of the additional areas), a Landscape Measures Permit of municipal Building Supervision Authorities pursuant to section 128 (from 1 January 2035, sections 53 and 54 of the Building Act) of the Land Use and Building Act is needed for all tree cutting (*see* Part III, Chapter 4, §1).

The Forestry Act does not prevent the use of forest areas for other purposes, such as building (section 3). Problems with forestry obligations may arise in areas where the future use is not finally decided upon yet. The projects in question may also be environmentally sensitive (man-made lakes, etc.). The main rule is that the relevant permit (e.g., according to the Water Act or the Land Use and Building Act, as of 1 January 2025, the Building Act) has to be final and valid in order that the forestry obligations may be annulled.

1103. There are other forestry provisions of environmental importance. A specific Protection Forestry Act was enacted already in 1922 in order to prevent the decline of forests in the fell areas of northern Finland, where the growth of trees is slow. Now the respective provisions are included in Chapter 4 of the Forestry Act. This means substantive regional restrictions on forest use in areas located within the Protection Forest Zone boundary. However, these northern areas are mainly owned by the State, but there are some entitlements of the local population. Also the Wilderness Act (Chapter 2, §4 above), overlapping the Protection Forest Zones, may impose restrictions on forestry in the northernmost part of the country.

1104. Due to a historical legislative connection, Chapter 4 of the Forestry Act also includes protection rules on vulnerable shoreland forests or precipice forests (*see* Chapter 4 above).

1105. The fixed-term Financing Act for Sustainable Forestry on State Support for Private Forestry expired on 31 December 2023. The Act has often been criticized from nature and environmental perspectives, for example, in relation to forest ditching, forest roads and fertilization. In the case of forest drainage, it has been a question of both loading onto rivers and lakes and very often a failed forestry outcome. The Act will be replaced at the beginning of 2024 by the Act on the Fixed-Term Incentive Scheme for Forestry (71/2023), in which the measures targeted for support have been reduced and new objectives have been included. The purpose of the new Act is to promote and coordinate economically, ecologically and socially sustainable forest management and use. The Act is valid for seven years. Under the Act, measures may be financed aimed at: (1) increasing forest growth; (2) safeguarding and enhancing forest biodiversity; (3) contributing to water protection in forestry; (4) mitigating climate change and promoting the adaptation of forests to climate change; and (5) maintaining the forestry road network. Within the limits of the annual appropriation allocated in the state budget, funding can mainly be allocated only to forests that fall within the scope of application of the Forestry Act and to those private nature reserves based on a Cabinet decision-in-principle for which activities financed under conservation regulations are permitted. This includes ecological aid and aid that promotes forest growth, such as the management of sapling stands and young forests, sanitary fertilization, which, under certain preconditions, refers to ash fertilization of peatlands and fertilization in sites where boron deficiency occurs in the soil, as well as limited peatland forest management measures (Chapter 2), construction of a forest road or renovation of the existing road network under specified conditions (Chapter 3), and maintenance of forest biodiversity and management of forest nature (Chapter 4).

§2. Abatement of Forest Damage Caused by Insects or Fungi

1106. Under the Act on the Abatement of Forest Damage (1087/2013), the owners of forests or timber are obliged to prevent the reproduction and spreading of forest pest insects (e.g., *Tomicus, Ips*) or fungi hazardous to forests. In particular, timber of coniferous wood has to be removed from forests at fixed times. Based on the occurrence of damaging insects and accumulated thermal units, the country is divided in areas A, B and C, where the obligations differ (section 3 of the Act, as amended by 1168/2021). Where removing is not possible, one of the secondary measures listed in section 4 (1168/2021) shall be taken. The trunk parts and stumps of pine and spruce shall be removed as provided in section 5 and damaged trees as in detail provided in section 6. As a deviation, in biotopes pursuant to section 10 of the Forestry Act (above) and Natura 2000 sites, where promoting of rotten wood may be appropriate, damaged trees may be left on site more than ordinarily allowed, as in detail provided in section 6(6). This is due to the fact the windfalls, etc. are parts of variable natural ecosystems with importance to endangered species.

1107. Deviations from the duties above are possible in exceptional or unreasonable situations (section 7).

1108. There are specific obligations for loggers regarding the abatement of the 'root rot', i.e., bracket fungus *Heterobasidion* (section 8a, 1168/2021). One of the allowed exceptions is the case where the cutting object is especially valuable for the preserving of forest biodiversity, as specified in section 5b(1) of the Forestry Act. The logger is neither obliged to combat the fungus if it is not possible to do so due to force majeure or particularly exceptional circumstances (section 8b, 198/2023).

1109. In case of exceptionally extensive damages, the Ministry of Agriculture and Forestry may, on the reasoned proposal of the Finnish Forest Centre, issue orders on emergency cuttings (section 9), due to which compensations for costs incurred by owners, as far above the ordinary level of required caretaking, may be paid (section 10, subject to restrictions due to EU law, section 10a). As an alternative to emergency cuttings may the owners be entitled to perform aircraft-based spraying of biological pesticides, notwithstanding section 20 of the Act on Plant Protection Products (section 11), *see also* paragraph 856. Monitoring and supervision are provided in sections 12–19, administrative enforcement in section 24 and criminal sanctions in section 25 of the Act on the Abatement of Forest Damage.

1110. Where the insects or fungi have spread from an area or other object protected under the Nature Protection Act or acquired to the State for conservation purposes, and caused forest damage, the State may be liable (section 21, 21/2023). When assessing probable causality, attention shall be paid on the type of damage and other possible causes. If the victim has contributed to the spreading or forbidden necessary protection measures, the compensation may be refused or reduced.

1111. In addition to the provisions of Act on the Abatement of Forest Damage, the provisions of the Plant Health Act (1110/2019) apply to the prevention of quarantine pests in forest trees and to preventing their spread. The Plant Health Act aims to issue the national provisions due to the Plant Health Regulation[58] and the respective Official

58. Regulation (EU) 2016/2031 of the European Parliament of the Council of 26 Oct. 2016 on protective measures against pests of plants, amending Regulation (EU) No. 228/2013, (EU) No. 652/2014

Controls Regulation.[59] The Act also otherwise regulates management of risks to plant health and abating of plant pests. Not only farmed plants are covered. The Finnish Food Authority is in charge of enforcement and supervision, to which the Centres for Economic Development, Transport and the Environment contribute. Plant health in the Act, as far as trees are concerned, refers to both forest trees and garden, etc. trees. Also trees may be subject to compulsory measures in order to abate any of the plant pests under the Act. In practice, the Act on the Abatement of Forest Damage may have a role in the same situations. If quarantine pests under the Plant Health Act or provisions issued by virtue of it are found in connection with monitoring or other activities under the Act on the Abatement of Forest Damage, the Natural Resources Institute Finland (Luke) must notify the Finnish Food Authority without delay.

and (EU) No. 1143/2014 of the European Parliament and of the Council and repealing Council Directives 69/464/EEC, 74/647/EEC, 93/85/EEC, 98/57/EC, 2000/29/EC, 2006/91/EC and 2007/33/EC.

59 Regulation (EU) 2017/625 of the European Parliament and of the Council of 15 Mar. 2017 on official controls and other official activities performed to ensure the application of food and feed law, rules on animal health and welfare, plant health and plant protection products, amending Regulation (EC) No. 999/2001, (EC) No. 396/2005, (EC) No. 1069/2009, (EC) No. 1107/2009, (EU) No. 1151/2012, (EU) No. 652/2014, (EU) 2016/429 and (EU) 2016/2031 of the European Parliament and of the Council, Council Regulation (EC) No. 1/2005 and (EC) No. 1099/2009 and Council Directives 98/58/EC, 1999/74/EC, 2007/43/EC, 2008/119/EC and 2008/120/EC, and repealing Regulation (EC) No. 854/2004 and (EC) No. 882/2004 of the European Parliament and of the Council, Council Directives 89/608/EEC, 89/662/EEC, 90/425/EEC, 91/496/EEC, 96/23/EC, 96/93/EC and 97/78/EC and Council Decision 92/438/EEC (Official Controls Regulation).

Chapter 6. Fish Resources

§1. General Remarks

1112. The regulation of fish resources management is based on the fact that the (inland and sea) water areas in Finland are privately owned, the owner being in most cases a statutory shareholders' association for a registered village's common areas (perceived in a historical meaning of property surveying and parcelling law, *see* General Introduction, Chapter 2, §1). Today this association also functions as the statutory fishery association for the respective village. There are also separate, parcelled water areas of individual estates as well as State-owned waters. The ownership and the boundaries of the water areas are, for historical reasons, often very complicated. In addition, there are common rights to fish. All this has contributed to make the Fisheries Act, the previous as the present (379/2015) rather detailed and complicated, especially concerning the administration of the fisheries of private water areas. This field of legislation crosses the borderline between public law and private law.

Åland has fishing regulations of its own. The fishing rights and decision-making there differ from those in the rest of the country.

1113. In outer territorial sea areas (as Public Water Areas), the entire ownership by the State makes the overall picture different, and the fisheries are independent of property law preconditions. Regarding the professional fisheries in the waters of the Baltic Sea, the quota under the Common Fisheries Policy (CFP) provisions of the EU are of essential importance; *see* the present Act on the Implementation of CFP (1048/2016). The Fisheries Act is applicable without prejudice to those provisions or agreements with another country. Regarding inland waters, the regulations in the Fisheries Act have, due to their nature, very little to do with EU CFP legislation.

§2. Organizations

1114. The shareholders' associations (above) are made up of all the property owners in a registered village who have a share in the respective village's common water areas. It represents all owners collectively in matters of fishery rights. It does, however, have duties linked to public fisheries management, like planting of fish, and even regulative powers towards its shareholders. In practice, one of its main concerns is the safeguarding of interests in connection with the permit procedures (pollution or construction) under the Environmental Protection Act and the Water Act. Often the shareholders' associations in the capacity of statutory fishery association, having also the right to appeal, are among the primary opponents to projects claimed to be ecologically detrimental. They can also ask for the project plans to be amended and for conditions, like fish planting, to be included. Finally, damages to the water areas can be compensated to them collectively.

1115. Above the village level, there are special public law bodies for the waters of larger areas, the Fishery Management Areas (in somewhat various forms from

1982), including State-owned water areas except the Public Water Areas in the sea. As organizations, the areas consist of the fishery right holders and the various national associations in the field of fisheries and fishing, recreational fishing included. The fishery right holders in turn consist of statutory fishery associations and owners of parcelled private water areas. In practice, the membership means the right to be represented in the general meetings of the Area. The Fishery Management Area has many features of a voluntary association, but also of a public authority, and one of its main duties is the preparing and approving of a Fish Stock Management Plan for its area. The public law nature of the Areas is characterized by the fact that their decisions may be appealed to the Regional Administrative Court. The officials are in certain respects regarded as civil servants. On the contrary, a shareholders' association or the owner of a separate water area may transfer its/his fishery-related tasks to a Fishery Management Area.

On the regional level, the fisheries units of the Centres for Economic Development, Transport and the Environment, which are in substantive matters subordinate to the Ministry of Agriculture and Forestry, have the responsibility for fisheries administration.

§3. Fishing Rights

1116. The right to fish belongs basically to the owner(s), whose permission is therefore necessary, as well as payment of the yearly fisheries management fee (sections 79–86) to the State (fee receipt = the Fishing Card). Nevertheless, there are important public (common) fishing rights, too.

1117. The Fisheries Act grants citizens several common fishing rights, such as fishing in Public Water Areas in general, although fishery in specified parts thereof may be leased to individual professional fishermen. In both public and private (inland or sea) waters, everyone is likewise allowed to freely angle or jig (fishing through a hole in the ice in the wintertime, a very popular form of ice fishing), and fish for Baltic herring with one rod and a vertically movable hooks on the line (section 7(1)). In these cases, not even the Fishing Card is needed. Also lure fishing is free to all, but those over 18 years and under 65 years of age need for that a Fishing Card. Rapids in rivers hosting migratory fish and separately prohibited areas are excluded, however. Reel fishing and trolling with lure were added to the public right category (subject to a public law fee, though, the income of which was mainly channelled to the shareholders' associations) only from January 1997, after a heated political and also constitutional debate. It was very much like the previous extension of everyman's rights, i.e., the creation of the former jigging rights system in 1982, which also meant that these fishing rights no longer depended on the owners.

1118. More extensive public fishing rights are provided for the Public Water Areas in the sea and Finland's economic zone. In these areas everyone with a Fishing Card and every citizen of an EU or EEA country, being under 18 years and over 65 years of age, is entitled to recreational fishing. In the same areas, commercial fishermen registered in Finland are entitled to commercial fishing. Fishing vessels registered in an EU Member State have the right to fishing in the territorial waters and economic zone pursuant to the CFP legislation. Where the needs of commercial fishing require, the Metsähallitus may concerning Public Water Areas in the sea or the economic zone let out sites for fishing for salmon or trout, excluding the otherwise current common rights. As for fishing in Public Water Areas (besides the sea, also in the middle of certain large lakes) in general, the Metsähallitus may decide upon rights and permits, taking the National Fisheries Management Plan into account.

The regulation of fishing in the sea has long been a controversial issue and the object of legislative efforts in which many conflicting interests are involved, such as the need to protect the stocks of migratory salmon in the last wild rivers, the regional interests of fishermen and fisheries rights owners in various parts of the Baltic Sea and river areas (conflicting with each other), the need for sustainable management of fish stocks in the sea (also linked to international agreements, *see* below), and, finally, a desire to favour professional fishing above others. The state of the Baltic Sea and river waters and certain salmon diseases also impact.

1119. A real problem with fish resources particularly in many inland lakes is in practice often the wrong composition of fish stocks. The 'junk species' like roach may prevail, especially in eutrophic waters, and removing them effectively could improve the ecological status of water bodies. However, even the fishing of these species is not totally free, due to the protection of water area ownership rights. There are on the other hand some recent efforts within food industries to make use of these species, but lack of organized fishing and lack of necessary catch in delivery chains often remains a problem.

§4. Safeguarding of Fish Resources

1120. The aim of the Fisheries Act is, based on best available knowledge, arrange the ecologically, economically and socially sustainable use of fish resources in such a way that a sustainable and diverse productivity, the natural life cycle of fish stocks and the diversity and protection of water nature (section 1 of the Act).

1121. In 2002 the SAC ruled (SAC 2002:12) that angling based on an everyman's right or lure fishing based on the then Lure Cards (above) in a natural lake (with dozens of shoreline owners not involved in the project) where rainbow trout had been planted for commercial purposes could not be restricted by the competent authority (where it had been requested by the relevant businesses, based on rainbow trout plantings by them). The court held that a maximum permanent productivity referred to in the then Fisheries Act could not be at stake, as rainbow trout cannot reproduce in Finnish natural waters. Soon afterwards, the Fisheries Act was amended so that commercial purposes such as those in the ruling are sufficient for imposing a fishing restriction. A similar reason is, in section 54 of the present Fisheries Act, included in the grounds on which common fishing rights may be restricted.

1122. One of the main novelties in the present Fisheries Act is the National Fish Resources Management Plan for the safeguarding of sustainable management of fish resources (section 34). The plan is prepared by the Ministry of Agriculture and Forestry in cooperation with the Ministry of the Environment and approved by the former. The National Fish Resources Management Plan shall be taken into account in the Fish Stock Management Plans of the Fisheries Management Areas, as well as in the arranging of fishing in the Public Water Areas. The Fish Stock Management Plans of the Fisheries Management Areas (sections 34–40) shall safeguard the sustainable and diverse productivity and use of fish resources, and biodiversity, and promote the preconditions of recreational and commercial fishing.

1123. The rules on safeguarding the productivity of fish stocks and other goals of the Act are rather detailed. For individual water bodies, for larger areas and for specified species or stocks, there are several alternatives of decision-making on restrictions in Chapter 6 of the Fisheries Act, and in detail in the Government decree on fisheries (1360/2015). For example, many of the economically significant species of fish are protected for part of the year in order to safeguard their reproduction. Moreover, a minimum size of catch is specified for many species. The same chapter also contains the provisions on fishing restrictions due endangered animal species (or subspecies, etc.) protected under the Nature Protection Act. The restrictions are issued by time-limited decrees (section 59), and the significant harm to the owner or holder shall be fully compensated by the State (section 61). A specific tool here is made up of the agreements between water area owners (or other fishing right holders) and the Centres for Economic Development, Transport and the Environment aiming at the protection of the ringed seal of Lake Saimaa. If a ringed seal has remained in the catch, the Metsähallitus shall immediately be informed, and if another seal or a whale (probably: porpoise, if any) has been remained among the catch, the Natural Resources Institute Finland (Luke) shall immediately be informed (section 62). Fish caught or used as bait must as a main rule be killed as quickly and painlessly as possible by a method and technique suitable for killing (section 58a).

1124. Chapter 7 consists of provisions on migratory fish, e.g., on fishing in estuaries and channels. Chapter 8 in turn planting of fish. Planting of fish or crayfish is forbidden, if it would evidently reduce biodiversity by endangering a natural fish or crayfish species or other species or its stock (section 73). Otherwise, planting is allowed only if provided in the Fish Stock Management Plan of the Fisheries Management Area at stake, without prejudice to the planting obligations in a Water Act or Environmental Protection Act permit. For planting of a new species or stock into a water body a permit by the Centre for Economic Development, Transport and the Environment of the region is required (section 74).

§5. The Impacts of Water Management Projects

1125. In practice, the fate of fish resources is often primarily dependent on the regimes of the Water Act and the Environmental Protection Act. This is also the case for various construction and management projects (*see* Chapter 8 below) as well as for pollution-related permits (*see* Part I, Chapter 4). A water level regulation project, a drainage project, a hydroelectric plant or the discharges of an industrial establishment may have dramatic impacts on fish stocks and fisheries. In such cases, private and public interests involved in fish resources are among the main factors affecting the permit decision. Various legal persons may at the same time, for different reasons, claim the *locus standi* to safeguard fish resources, e.g., the fisheries units of the Centres for Economic Development, Transport and the Environment, the Fishery Management Areas, statutory fishery associations, private water area owners and professional fishermen.

1126. It may even be said that the fishery interests, being as such traditionally recognized, have a value beyond mere economic aspects. In a way they represent ecological and environmental values in general. There are cases where entire construction projects have been rejected by the courts, largely because of the impacts on fish resources (combined with, e.g., natural values and landscapes). One well-known example is a permit application for a hydroelectric plant in Central Finland (the *Huopanankoski* case in the SAC in 1978). Here also cultural values, such as memories of trout fishing by a famous author, were considered relevant.

1127. If a permit under the Water Act or the Environmental Protection Act is granted with the result that fish resources are affected, very detailed fish management provisions are as a rule included therein by the Regional State Administrative Agencies (*see* Part I, Chapter 1, §13 and Part II, Chapter 8, §2). In certain situations and areas the implementation of such a permit condition may be the most important factor affecting fish resources and fish management.

Chapter 7. Subsoil and Minerals

§1. Soil Excavation

I. General Objectives of the Legislation

1128. Soil excavation activities except mining are regulated in the Soil Excavation Act (555/1981 with later amendments) and, containing mainly detailed provisions of procedural character, the Government decree on the Excavation of Soil (926/2005). The most important object is esker gravel, but the Act is also applicable to all kinds of soil except peat, and also to mould, cliffs and bedrock. The Act mainly functions through permits. It has two main goals, namely protection of landscapes and protection of nature (and partly also abatement of other environmental impacts) in connection with soil extraction projects. It had originally in principle no other purposes, such as rational use of soil resources or economical goals. That is why the Act as a whole could very well be classified as a part of landscape and nature conservation legislation. However, in the 1997 reform some elements of resource economy were inserted, but the main focus remained unchanged. Moreover, the relevance of groundwater impacts was clarified and stressed. In practice, nuisance to neighbours may also be taken into account among the negative environmental impacts.

II. The Grounds of the Permit System

1129. The Soil Excavation Act is based on a general permit system, mainly for the protection of landscape and nature. A permit from a competent municipal body (presently always the Municipal Environmental Protection Authority) is always necessary for extraction, conventional private household use (building or private road maintenance for dwelling or agriculture) excepted (section 4). There are also a few further exceptions for situations where the activities are regulated by other fields of legislation. For example, for mining activities regulated by the Mining Act no Soil Excavation Permit is necessary, though the objectives of the two acts are very different and the boundary between the two regimes are not seldom far from clear. The Mining Act contains practically no binding environmental provisions. However, unlike the Mining Act, the Soil Excavation Act makes no expropriation-like extraction licences in someone else's area possible. Extraction for the construction of roads in accordance with the appropriate (Highways) Engineering Plan decisions (*see* Part II, Chapter 9, §1 below) is allowed without a permit in the road areas, but if the expropriatory rights of the State, available under the Highways Act (*ibid.*), concern areas outside the proper road area, a permit under the Soil Excavation Act is also needed. Extraction of sand from the seabed or lake bottom is in principle covered by the Soil Excavation Act. However, to avoid double work, no Soil Excavation Permit is necessary if a permit under the Water Act is needed (as is usually the case for underwater extraction, because of the altering of water bodies combined with the impacts on fisheries). The seabed sand formations are mostly located in Public Water Areas owned by the State, whose consent is then needed in addition to the permits mentioned above. As for groundwater protection, both acts are applied, resulting at times in two parallel permits (or denials).

1130. The permit procedure is initiated by a permit application which must normally be followed by a detailed extraction plan, focusing the very extraction, caretaking of the environment and, if possible, the later use of the area, except for small-scale extraction with minor impacts (section 5 of the Soil Excavation Act). In the plan, local natural conditions and impacts on them and on the environment must be examined. The quantity and quality of the substances shall also be explained. Where EIA is required, the EIS and the reasoned conclusion shall be attached.

1131. For the permit procedure in the Municipal Environmental Protection Authority, the opinion of the Centre for Economic Development, Transport and the Environment of the region is necessary, if: (1) the area at stake has nationwide or other significance for the protection of nature; (2) the area has importance for the protection of waters; or (3) the extraction impacts immediately the area of another municipality (section 7(2) of the Act).

1132. An Extractive Waste Management Plan (*see also* Government decree on Extractive Waste, 190/2013), shall be worked out by the permit applicant as a part of the extraction plan if extractive waste referred to in section 112(1)(2) of the Environmental Protection Act will be generated in the activities and an Environmental Permit is not needed (section 5a of the Soil Excavation Act). In cases where no extraction plan or Environmental Permit is needed, section 114 of the Environmental Protection Act is applicable. These provisions are intended to (partly) implement Directive 2006/21/EC on the management of waste from extractive industries and amending Directive 2004/35/EC. *See also* paragraphs 588–590, 593, 605, 1172 and 1181.

1133. In the permit consideration by the permit authority there is, at least in principle, no room for discretion, because a permit in each case must be either given or denied, depending on the environmental impacts. The provisions of the Act do, however, require interpretation. The forbidden impacts are expressed in section 3(1) of the Act as follows:

- damaging of a beautiful landscape; or
- destruction of significant aesthetic values of nature or destroying natural formations of special character; or
- significant or far-reaching detrimental impacts on natural conditions; or
- risk to the quality or quantity of water 'in an important groundwater area or in a groundwater area which is suitable for water supply' (the notions of which refer to the groundwater inventories of environmental administration, *see* paragraph 1228), if there is no permit decision according to the Water Act (this provision and the Water Act partly overlap each other and are juridically intermingled).

1134. Section 3(2) is applicable also to such household extraction that takes place in an area common to several properties, without need of Excavation Permit.

As of 1 January 2025, a Permit is explicitly not required for excavation in preparation for construction related to the implementation of a Detailed Plan, but section 3(1) must nevertheless be complied with.

1135. If one of these impacts would result, the permit must be denied, provided that the impacts cannot be abated by means of permit conditions. In the opposite case, the permit authority is obliged to give consent (with conditions, *see* below). In practice, it has not always been easy for the competent municipal bodies to cope with the lack of discretionary powers. For example, the effects on the local economy or the supply of building materials may not be taken into account, but may nevertheless be of importance in reality.

1136. If the provisions of the Nature Protection Act or decisions under it concern the aimed excavation area, they are binding in the permit consideration as such (section 1(2) of the Soil Excavation Act).

1137. In the 1999 a separate extraction permit system for certain plan or planning areas in the Land Use and Building Act was revoked and the applicability of the Soil Excavation Act was also extended to these areas. An additional precondition for a permit was inserted, however. In an area where either a Detailed Plan or a fully valid Local Master Plan is in force, care shall, in addition to the ordinary preconditions, be taken so that the extraction measures do not hinder the use of the area for its assigned purpose and that townscape or landscape will not be destroyed (section 3(2)). Section 3(2) is applicable also to such household extraction that takes place in an area common to several properties. In areas where a Landscape Measures Permit under section 128 of the Land Use and Building Act (as of 1 January 2025 the Land Use Act) is temporarily needed (for measures other than soil extraction), due to the ongoing procedure for a Local Master Plan or a Detailed Plan, the planning procedure shall not be hindered and townscape or landscape shall not be destroyed and the obstacles in section 3 shall be observed, but the permit may be also denied on other acceptable grounds (section 6(2)).

1138. It is totally prohibited to extract substances of soil in any shore belt (of sea or inland water body), except for a particular assignment in a Detailed Plan or a fully valid Local Master Plan (section 3(3) of the Soil Excavation Act).

1139. Post-glacial eskers with national conservation values are specified in a National Esker and Ridge Protection Programme from 1984, i.e., on actual list based on scientific landscape analysis and approved by the Cabinet. The programme as such is not binding in a permit decision, but in legal practice it has gained a strong guiding effect. Similar regional analyses have subsequently been prepared by the environmental authorities on valuable bedrock cliffs.

1140. A Soil Excavation Permit is not a mere consent, but it is normally a complex of various permit provisions. This means at the same time that there may be several alternatives between a total rejection and a total approval of a permit application. Some of the provisions are obligatory, like those regulating the boundaries, shape and depth of the extraction area. The same is the case for preventive and restoration measures, including those for landscape management after the extraction activities have been completed. In general (section 3(4) of the Act), the sites of extraction shall be placed and the excavation arranged in such a way that the detrimental impacts on nature and landscape remain as small as possible and that there will be no danger to the surrounding population or to the environment, or any disadvantage that could be avoided at reasonable cost. From 1997, an additional requirement takes into account the need to exploit the substances sparingly and economically. All these requirements may lead to specific permit provisions, where the applicant's plan is considered insufficient. The practice of the appellate courts has a guiding role in drawing up the contents of permit decisions. As to conventional household use extraction for which a Permit is not needed, section 3(4) is anyway applicable.

1141. As for groundwater protection, a permit may be restricted to the soil layers at a level high enough above the groundwater surface; but also the restrictions in and the separate permit system of the Water Act bans is applicable. This may result in that the extraction is ultimately not allowed at all, even though there is a valid permit decision pursuant to the Soil Excavation Act.

Permits are normally issued for a fixed period, normally up to ten years. In certain circumstances the maximum is twenty years (section 10 of the Soil Excavation Act).

1142. Up to 1997, a permit decision under the Soil Excavation Act had in certain cases to be submitted to the then Regional Environment Centre for approval. This obligation aimed to guarantee national values of landscape and nature protected by the law and to safeguard the independence of the decision-making authority in cases where the municipality itself is the applicant or where another municipality's area is affected. Today the submission system exists no more. Instead, the Regional Environment Centres, replaced later on by the Centres for Economic Development, Transport and the Environment (environmental divisions), were given the right to be heard in certain situations (section 7(2) of the Act) and the right to appeal against the permit decisions. The latter was feasible, because the task of the centre itself as the first appellate body was changed to the ordinary, i.e., Regional Administrative Court (*see* below). At the outset, the appellate system of the Municipality Act was (untypically) applied, which meant that any member of the municipality had the right to appeal. Today the appeal type is the normal administrative judicial appeal, but the right of appeal of the members of municipalities has been (untypically) inserted. There are procedural specialties, however. For example, an appeal by the permit applicant shall by the Regional Administrative Court be made public, as provided in section 20b.

1143. In 2015, a combined permit procedure was created for cases where both a Soil Excavation Permit and an Environmental Permit for the same project are needed (section 4a of the Soil Excavation Act). If not unnecessary for particular reasons, both permit applications have to be dealt with together and decided upon by one common decision (section 4a). The procedural provisions in sections 42–45,

84–86 and 96 of the Environmental Protection Act are applicable, as well as section 7(2) of the Soil Excavation Act (above). The competent permit authority is determined pursuant to sections 34–37 of the Environmental Protection Act (section 7(1)).

1144. Also the combined procedure pursuant to the Act on the Adjusting of Certain Permit Procedures Pertaining to the Environment (*see* paragraph 67) is possible also regarding the Soil Excavation Act (section 4c). In certain respects, the provisions of that Act replace the procedure pursuant to the Soil Excavation Act, but, e.g., the right to appeal is determined in the ordinary way.

1145. Appeals are anyway important, also in substantive matters. Presently, the following have the right to appeal to the Regional Administrative Court: (1) concerned parties (including the applicant); (2) members of the municipality; (3) a registered association or foundation the aim of which is protection of environment, health or nature or promotion of amenity of an inhabited area, provided that the relevant impacts of the project appear in its geographical area of activities; (4) the municipality where the project is performed, and any municipality in the geographical area of which the environmental impacts of the project appear; (5) the Centre for Economic Development, Transport and the Environment of the region and Municipal Environmental Protection Authorities of the impact are; and (6) other authority representing public interests (section 20a).

1146. If the combined procedure for extraction permit and Environmental Permit (above) is applied, the appellate procedure is determined pursuant to the Environmental Protection Act (section 20(2)). This also means that a member of the municipality has no standing, although the projects in the combined procedure may be very significant. A concerned party is determined pursuant to section 43(1) of the Environmental Protection Act. It is unclear for the time being, what this will mean regarding the Soil Excavation Act, due to the difference between pollution and impacts on landscape.

1147. As examples of rulings of the SAC the following few excerpts from the yearbooks are rather characteristic and still representative of the Soil Excavation Permit practice:

- The ridge was the last remaining esker in the region, and it was regarded as a natural formation of special character, which would have been destroyed by the gravel extraction. No permit was issued (1983).
- The planned gravel extraction would have cut through a narrow but long esker between two small lakes. Moreover, the natural shore would have been affected. Hence a beautiful landscape would have been damaged, and the permit application was rejected (1983).
- The gravel extraction area was sited 80–100 m from the shore of a lake with pleasant scenery. No damaging of a beautiful landscape was caused, and the permit was granted (1985).

- A gravel extraction permit was disallowed, because a natural shore stone wall of the ancient Baltic Sea, regarded as a natural formation of special character, would have been destroyed (1986).
- The permit application dealt with extraction of rock. The rock, or a small mountain, being very visible in the landscape, was regarded as a natural formation of special character. Attention was paid to the fact that rocks were rare in the province, the topography of which was dominated by large plains. The application was rejected (1986).
- The rock was situated on the sea coast, but not specially visible. From the top there was no special view over the sea or land areas. No legal obstacles to a permit existed, and the permit was granted. The court voted on the matter (1988).
- From the top of a rock area there was an open view to a large sea area. Taken that the similar rock formations in this archipelagic region were common, no damaging of a beautiful landscape was expected. The permit was to be granted (1998).
- The application dealt with gravel extraction as deep as 5 metres below the groundwater level. A municipal water intake was endangered. No permit lower than 1 metre above the groundwater surface could be granted (1985).

III. The Rights of the Owner

1148. If a permit is denied, the applicant (as a rule the owner) is not entitled to any compensation. In exceptional situations he may, however, have the right demand that the area be expropriated by the municipality, or in certain cases by the State, but this claim is only available if he cannot use the area for agricultural or silvicultural purposes, or for other comparable purposes resulting in a reasonable benefit. In practice the possibility of silvicultural use most often excludes the duty to expropriate. It might be applicable in cases where a permit to crush surface bedrock has been disallowed. Quite another thing is that compensations have been paid by the State during a transitional period in the 1980s to those who were prohibited to continue extraction begun before the Soil Excavation Act came into force.

1149. The Soil Excavation Act also contains compensation regulation of quite another kind (section 9). The excavator is obliged to pay for damage caused to the neighbours, irrespective of negligence or conformity to law and permit conditions. Even mere loss of value of neighbouring properties has to be compensated (e.g., loss of a beautiful view). This is quite exceptional, as is also the applicable procedure. Compensation claims are not dealt with by courts, as is the case for civil law damages in general, but by an ad hoc surveying body constituted in accordance with the Expropriation Act (although the case is one of civil liability). The Land Court and the SC, subject to leave of appeal, are the appellate bodies. The substantive relationship between this regulation and the Environmental Damages Act is somewhat problematic, however.

§2. QUARRYING AND STONE CRUSHING

1150. Quarrying and stone crushing to produce a substitute for natural gravel has significantly increased during the last few decades. This is a result of the fact that esker gravel is not any more available in several densely populated areas and their surrounding areas. Crushing may be done of various waste stones, of natural boulders gained as by-products of gravel extraction and of natural bedrock. The two last-mentioned categories fall, as does the extraction (quarrying) itself, within the permit system of the Soil Excavation Act. In practice, the specific environmental impacts of the quarrying and crushing are often combined, and the crushing itself can also be taken into account in the permit (permit conditions included) consideration.

1151. Nuisance aspects (noise, vibrations, dust) caused by the crushing are mainly dealt with in the permit procedure according to the Environmental Protection Act (*see* Part I, Chapter 1). An Environmental Permit is in practice needed for all independent non-temporary stone quarrying, as well as for all non-temporary crushing. Pursuant to Table 2(7c) and (7e) of Annex 1 to the Environmental Protection Act an Environmental Permit is always required for stone quarries or stone quarrying for purposes other than civil engineering work, where stone is processed for at least fifty days, and for stationary crushing plant or limestone grinding mill, or a mobile crushing plant or limestone grinding mill located in a certain area and in operation for at least fifty days in total. In addition, an Environmental Permit may be needed due to nuisances on a case-by-case basis as provided in section 27 (2)(3) of the Act.

For example, sufficient buffer zones may be required in an Environmental Permit, or, for least suitable sites, no permit is granted.

1152. Government decree on the environmental protection of quarrying plants, other quarrying and stone crushing plants (2010/800), issued under the 2000 Environmental Protection Act, but remained into force also under the present Act and amended in 2017, is applicable as minimum requirements in Environmental Permit considerations. The requirements, e.g., set minimum distances between the activity and various items sensitive to noise or dust (400 metres concerning hospitals, day-care centres, care institutions and schools, and, as a main rule 300 metres concerning dwelling areas), technical means to reduce dust or noise and siting of noise sources.

Where both an Environmental Permit and a Soil Excavation Permit are needed, the combined procedure (*see* paragraphs 67, 81 and 1143–1146) is applicable.

1153. The Waste Act has been applied to the surplus stone, which has been regarded as waste. Depending on the notion of waste, the scope of application of the provisions of the Waste Act, the Environmental Protection Act and the Soil Excavation Act was, however, somewhat unclear here. On the older preliminary rulings by the ECJ *see* paragraphs 516 and 517, and on compulsory plans regarding extractive waste *see* paragraph 1132 with references.

§3. PEAT PRODUCTION

1154. Peat cutting (extraction) may have considerable ecological effects, particularly at the drainage stage of peat cuttings (*see also* paragraph 145). There are no detailed regulations focused on peat cutting, due to the largely individual character of the impacts and the measures to be taken.

1155. The provisions of the Environmental Protection Act are applicable to discharges caused by peat production. An Environmental Permit is needed for peat production projects (Table 2 of Annex 1 to the Environmental Protection Act). The practical water pollution prevention problems relate, among other things, to various methods of prevention and the application of the BAT approach on an activity of this kind. The Environmental Protection Act also applies to the harmful dust caused by peat extraction. Due to the air pollution risk through small particles, a peat cutting project has once been rejected (SAC 2005:70).

1156. It has also been ruled by the SAC that the Environmental Permit considerations do not include impacts on nature, landscape or game, if affected physically by the project but not through pollution and if not protected directly by the Nature Protection Act or provisions by virtue of it (SAC 2005:27). The reasoning is system based: the Environmental Protection Act as a whole is (almost merely) a pollution prevention act.

On the other hand, e.g., a permit for a peat extraction project was annulled by the SAC due to the probable adverse impacts of the discharges on river trout, partly based on the impacts on freshwater pearly mussel (*Margaritifera*), that being essential to the reproduction of natural trout stocks (SAC 2014:176). Several other precedents deal with the allowed level of discharges otherwise.

There are several cases where an EIA has been required for peat cutting in practice. Also the assessment of impacts on a Natura 2000 site may have been needed before a permit can be decided upon (SAC 2008:72).

1157. The cutting of peat is of course prohibited if the area has been made a (Peatland) Reserve under the Nature Conservation Act (*see* Chapter 2, §2 above). On the nature-related provisions on the location of peat production in the Environmental Protection Act, *see* paragraph 145.

§4. MINING

I. The Role and Scope of the Mining Act

1158. The Mining Act (621/2011) replaced from 1 July 2011 on the former Mining Act (503/1965). The former Act contained an overall system for prospecting of minerals and treating mining claims and licences (patented claims) and for settling the relationship between the claimant/licensee and the landowner. The same holds in principle good also regarding the new Act, although the scope of the latter is larger more integrating, and new aspects have been included. Anyway, there is still a significant difference between the Mining Act and the Soil Excavation Act. In the 2023 reform (505/2023), several amendments to the Mining Act have been made.

1159. Unlike the licences pursuant to the Mining Act, the Soil Excavation Act never allows exploitation of resources within another's property. The legislative character of the substance is here decisive: e.g., soapstone (*vuolukivi* marble) is regarded as a mineral and hence falls within the Mining Act, whereas granite extracted for gravestones, etc. is not and hence is treated as a soil substance under the Soil Excavation Act.

1160. Prospecting pursuant to the previous Mining Act was as such free to anyone. There were some restrictions aiming at the protection of certain public interests, but in general the Act contained no proper environmental provisions. In fact, it is highly dubious whether a claim or licence could be rejected on environmental grounds, if there is no obvious obstacle pursuant to the Mining Act (e.g., vicinity of dwellings, etc.). Even the relationship between the Mining Act and environmental legislation had at times been interpreted so that the Mining Act would have preference over any other laws. This was not, however, the whole truth. The Nature Conservation Act and the decisions based on it were relevant almost in the normal way (on the relation to nature conservation, *see also* paragraph 955). Moreover, the Environmental Protection Act and the Water Act were and still are applicable as usual. Hence the rights based on the Mining Act were not necessarily enough for implementing a mining project, but, e.g., an Environmental Permit may also be needed, irrespective of the rights based on the Mining Act. EIA could also be required (*see* Part I, Chapter 1, §21). In these respects, the relation between environmental legislation and the present Mining Act is in principle similar, although the present act itself includes also provisions that more or less aim to protect the environment. Nevertheless, the preconditions for an Environmental Permit or a Water Act permit may be more crucial than those set forth in the Mining Act (e.g., SAC 2022:38). Also the general mechanism of land use planning under the Land Use and Building Act (from 1 January 2025, the Land Use Act) had traditionally been irrelevant to the claims and licences under the old Mining Act, but in 2000 the effects of valid plans and the aspects of ongoing planning were inserted into the then Mining Act. In the 2023 reform, the role of land use planning and of the municipalities in general was developed further.

1161. The present Mining Act includes a large number of provisions concerning the rights and obligations of parties engaged in ore prospecting, mining and gold panning, both during their operations and as termination measures are taken, including aftercare. The Mining Act is supplemented by the Government decree on Mining (391/2012).

1162. The old Mining Act was largely administered directly by the Ministry of Economic Affairs and Employment, also in everyday practice. Presently the various decision-making and supervisory tasks are mainly vested in the newly defined Mining Authority, whereas the ministry has remained in charge of general guidance. The

Mining Authority is not a new organization, however. The pre-existing Finnish Safety and Chemicals Agency (Tukes) functions as the Mining Authority instead.

1163. Aiming to secure the preconditions for mining and ore prospecting effectively, the present Act at the same time takes account of environmental issues, the rights of people and landowners, and the opportunities for municipalities to have an influence on decision-making. Based on an integrating overall approach, the Act aims at reconciling various public and private interests and thereby, as a whole and insofar as possible, takes due account of the various competing interests. The task has been challenging, as may be seen in section 1 of the Act:

> The objective of the Mining Act (section 1(1)) is to promote socially, economically and ecologically sustainable exploration and mining and to organise the use of areas required by them. In order to fulfil the purpose of the Act, the securing of public and private interests is required, with particular attention to: (1) the preconditions for engaging in mining activities; (2) the legal status of landowners and private parties sustaining damage; and (3) impacts on the environment, land use and biodiversity, as well as the conserving and sustainable use of natural resources. A further objective of the Act (section 1(2)) is to ensure the municipalities' opportunities to have an influence on decision-making, and the opportunities of individuals to influence decision-making involving them and their living environment. Furthermore (section 1(3)), an objective of the Act is to promote the safety of mines and to prevent, decrease, and avert any harm and damage incurred in the activities provided in the Act, and to ensure liability for damages for the party causing the harm or damage. Moreover, there is a specific clause in section 1(4) that, where applicable, aims to pay special attention to the impacts on the indigenous Saami people.

1164. The scope of application of the Mining Act (section 2(1)) is defined by proclaiming that the Act lays down provisions for the exploration and exploitation of a deposit containing mining minerals, gold panning in an area owned by the State, the termination of related operations and the proceedings for establishment of a mining area.

In spite of the ambitious overall legislative approach, the preconditions of and requirements for mining industries still largely depend on other legislation, such as the Environmental Protection Act, the Water Act and the Land Use and Building Act (as of 1 January 2025, the Land Use Act). Pursuant to section 3, both the decisions by authorities under the Mining Act and other (i.e., private) activities under it shall comply with several other acts, in addition to the three mentioned above also the Nature Protection Act, the Wilderness Act, the Reindeer Husbandry Act, the Radiation Act, the Nuclear Energy Act, the Ancient Remains Act, the Terrain Traffic Act and the Dam Safety Act.

1165. In the Mining Act, the expression 'mining mineral' refers to (section 2(2)):

(1) concerning chemical elements: actinium, aluminium, antimony, arsenic, barium, beryllium, boron, caesium, mercury, fluorine, phosphorus, gallium,

germanium, hafnium, silver, indium, iridium, cadmium, potassium, calcium, cobalt, chromium, gold, copper, lanthanoids, lithium, lead, magnesium, manganese, molybdenum, sodium, nickel, niobium, osmium, palladium, platinum, radium, iron, rhenium, sulphur, rhodium, rubidium, ruthenium, selenium, zinc, scandium, strontium, thallium, tantalum, tellurium, tin, titanium, thorium, uranium, vanadium, bismuth, tungsten, yttrium, and zirconium, as well as minerals containing these chemical elements;

(2) concerning minerals: andalusite, apatite, asbestos minerals, barite, bauxite, bentonite, beryllium, dolomite, phlogopite, fluorite, graphite, garnet, ilmenite, calcite, kaolin, corundum, quartz, kyanite, leucite, feldspar, magnesite, muscovite, nepheline, olivine, pyrophyllite, rutile, sillimanite, scapolite, talc, diamond, vermiculite, wollastonite and other precious stones;

(3) concerning rock types: marble and soapstone.

In addition to the mining minerals, the Act is applicable to the exploitation of materials in the bedrock and soil in the mining area (section 2(3)).

1166. Section 6 of the Mining Act contains the general principles for all activities and measures under the Act. They are: (1) that the necessary expertise concerning the quality and extent of the activity, and sufficient resources for all other preconditions, are available; (2) that sufficient clarity prevails concerning the impacts of the activity and the possibilities for preventing and reducing damage and detrimental impact; (3) that necessary measures are taken to ensure the safety of activities and that technological development is taken into account in this context; (4) that, as far as possible: (a) damage and detrimental impacts caused by the activity are prevented; (b) operations that cause detrimental impacts are eliminated, or, if this is not possible, they are replaced with less detrimental ones; (c) disturbances and dangerous situations are prepared for; (d) ensure that all mining minerals found in the area that are techno-economically exploitable are exploited at all stages of mining operations; (e) avoid adverse effects on the environment; (5) that any inconvenience or damage caused by the activity is compensated for; and (6) that the management of mining minerals is properly organized.

II. Exploration

1167. The possibilities of exploration are of two stages. First, there is the right of everyone to prospecting work even in another's area (section 7), and then there are the more extensive rights based on an individual Exploration Permit (sections 9–11).

1168. In order to find mining minerals, everyone has the right, also on another's land, to prospecting work, i.e., to perform geological measurements, make observations and take minor samples, provided that this does not cause any damage or more than minor inconvenience or disturbance (section 7). The following are nevertheless excluded (section 7(2)):

(1) a cemetery referred to in the Funerary Services Act (457/2003), and an area belonging to a private grave, and within 50 metres of these;
(2) an area used by the defence forces, and any area controlled by the Border Guard where movement is restricted or prohibited, and within 100 metres of such an area;
(3) an area where movement is restricted or access denied to outsiders;
(4) a traffic route or passage in public use;
(5) within 150 metres of a building intended for residential or work use, or comparable space, and any adjoining private yard, and the site for such a building, if a permit required for building under the Land Use and Building Act (as of 1 January 2025, the Building Act) has been granted for it and construction has been commenced;
(6) an area in horticultural use;
(7) within 50 metres of a public building or utility, a power line with a voltage of over 35,000 volts or a transformer station; and
(8) any other area, corresponding to those under 1–7, designated for special use. However, prospecting work is allowed in an area under 2–8 with the consent of the competent authority or institution or the holder of rights at stake.

Regarding (2)–(8) above, the body or entitled subject at stake may grant exceptions (section 7(3)).

1169. Before any sampling measures are begun, the owner and possessor of any property in the area where prospecting work is to take place (prospecting area), whose right or advantage the matter may involve, shall be notified (section 8). The notification must include the contact information of the party in charge, information on the prospecting area, and a plan regarding the sampling. Information on the equipment and methods to be used, the sampling schedule and the targeted mining mineral shall be included decree.

1170. But where exploration cannot be carried out as prospecting work in accordance with section 7, or the property owner has not consented to it, an Exploration Permit by the mining authority is needed (section 9). Such a permit is also required if: (1) exploration could cause any harm to health or general safety, damage to another industrial and commercial activity, or deterioration in values of landscape or nature protection values; (2) the exploration is targeted at locating and exploring a deposit containing uranium or thorium; or (3) the permit is necessary for gaining a privilege under the Mining Act, for exploiting the deposit. Regarding restrictions on possible exploration areas for exploration, sections 7(2) and 7(3) are applied. In addition, the consent of the competent authority or institution or the holder is required where one of the following is at stake: a street area or market place, a road area of a highway, an airport or another area in aviation, a railway area, a canal used for public traffic or another such traffic area, or an area within thirty metres of any of the traffic areas above, unless provisions concerning a larger exclusion area are laid down in or under the relevant Act.

1171. By virtue of an Exploration Permit, the holder thereof has the right, be his own area or that owned by another at stake, in the exploration area specified in the permit, to explore the structures and composition of geological formations and to conduct other exploration for preparation of mining activity and other exploration in order to locate a deposit and to investigate its quality, extent and degree of exploitation, as provided for in detail in each Exploration Permit. The permit holder is allowed to build, or transfer from elsewhere, temporary constructions and equipment necessary for exploration, as specified in detail in the permit. An Exploration Permit neither entitles to exploitation of the deposit nor does the permit limit the property owner's right to use the area or to govern it in other respects than above (section 10). In any case, the permit holder shall limit exploration and other use of the exploration area to measures that are necessary for exploration purposes. The measures shall be planned so as not to cause an infringement of public or private interests that is avoidable by reasonable means (section 11). Exploration and other use of the exploration area shall not cause: (1) harm to health or a danger to public safety; (2) essential damage to another industrial or commercial activity; (3) significant changes in natural conditions; (4) essential damage to rare or valuable natural occurrences; (5) significant damage to the landscape, or (6) any other significant adverse effect on the environment.

The holder of the Exploration Permit shall notify the property owners and holders in the exploration area in advance of all field work that could cause any damage or harm, and of any temporary constructions to be erected (section 12). There are additional notification obligations regarding the Saami area and reindeer husbandry. Also the supervisory authorities shall be informed, as provided in the permit.

1172. An Exploration Permit holder is moreover obliged to attend to prevention of the generation of soil and rock waste, decreasing its harmfulness, alongside its reclamation or processing (section 13). Hereby also an Extractive Waste Management Plan shall be prepared, including information about the environment of the area, soil and rock waste, waste areas, environmental impact, measures taken to prevent contamination of the environment, monitoring of activities and measures concerning termination of activities. However, a Waste Management Plan is not needed if the holder is obliged to prepare one under the Environmental Protection Act. The permit holder shall also submit an annual report to the Mining Authority of the activities carried out and the results thereof (section 14). In addition (as of 1 June 2023), the holder of an Exploration Permit is obliged to organize an annual event open to the public, in which an account shall be given of: (1) the research work carried out and its results; (2) the environmental and other effects of the research work carried out; (3) future research work; and (4) the estimated environmental and other impacts of future research work.

1173. Aftercare measures in an exploration area are provided in section 15. Once an Exploration Permit has expired or been cancelled, the holder shall: (1) immediately restore the exploration area to the condition required by public safety, remove temporary constructions and equipment, attend to restoration and tidying of the area and render the area to natural status as far as possible; (2) within six months, submit to the Mining Authority an account on the exploration work, the exploration data and a representative set of core samples. The Mining Authority, the property owners and holders in the exploration area shall, among others, be notified on the completion of the measures.

The provisions of section 15 above are not applicable to an area for which the permit holder applies for an extension to the validity of the existing Exploration Permit, or for a Mining Permit. For cases where such an application is rejected in part or in full, the aftercare obligations shall be complied with within six months of the entering into legal force of the decision on the rejection of the application.

1174. An Exploration Permit is valid for a maximum of four years after the decision on it has gained legal force (section 60). When considering the period of validity, the Mining Authority shall pay special attention to the time necessary for implementing the exploration plan and to the limitation and alleviation of any damage and harm to public or private interests. Additionally, under preconditions set forth in section 61, the validity of an Exploration Permit may be extended for a maximum of three years at a time. In total, the permit may remain valid for a maximum of fifteen years.

III. Mining Permit

1175. For the establishment of a mine, as well as for undertaking of (proper) mining activity, a Mining Permit is required (section 16). A Mining Permit entitles the holder to exploit: (1) the mining minerals found in the mining area; (2) the organic and inorganic surface materials, excess rock and tailings generated as a by-product of mining activities; and (3) other materials of the bedrock and soil of the mining area, insofar as their use is necessary for the purposes of mining in the area. In addition, a Mining Permit entitles its holder to perform exploration within the mining area in accordance with section 11 and the detailed provisions in the Mining Permit (section 17).

1176. The holder of a Mining Permit is obliged to ensure that: (1) the mining activities do not cause damage to health or danger to public safety; (2) mining activities neither cause significant harm to public or private interests, nor, in relation to the overall costs of the mining operations, reasonably avoidable infringement of public or private interests; (3) the excavation and exploitation do not result in obvious wasting of minerals; (4) the future use of the mining area or the future exploitation of the deposit is not jeopardized or impeded; (5) the planning of mining operations takes into account, as far as possible, the possibility of phasing out the mine; (6) measures relating to the closure of a mine are carried out in such a way that the closed mine does not cause significant adverse effects on human health or the environment; (7) the compliance with the Permit is monitored and any deviations are reported to the Mining Authority without delay; and (8) adverse environmental impacts are prevented and reduced (section 18). The permit holder is moreover obliged to submit an annual report to the Mining Authority on the extent and results of the exploitation of the deposit and to inform of any essential changes in the information on mineral resources. In addition, the holder of a Mining Permit is obliged to organize an annual event open to the public, unless it is considered manifestly unnecessary. The event shall include information on: (1) the schedule, extent and results of the exploitation of the deposit and any significant changes in information on mineral resources; and (2) the effects of mining.

1177. A mining area shall be continuous in size and shape so that compliance with requirements concerning safety, location of activities and technology, is facilitated. The area may not be larger than necessary for the purposes of mining, in view of the quality and extent of the deposit at stake (section 19).

In addition to the proper mining area, an area located in the vicinity thereof, being indispensable regarding mining activity and necessary for the purposes of road access, transport equipment, power lines or water pipes, sewers, treatment of waters, or a transport route to be excavated to a sufficient distance from the surface, can be designated as an auxiliary area to the mine (section 19).

The location of the mining area and any auxiliary area shall be planned so as not to cause infringement of public or private interests that is reasonably avoidable in respect to the overall costs.

1178. The Cabinet can grant the right to utilize another's property as a mining area (expropriation permit for a mining area, section 20). The real impacts of granting such a compulsory right are often near to an assignment of ownership. Provisions on granting a limited right of use and other rights to another's area as an auxiliary area depend on the permit and are laid down in section 49(2). A mining area and an auxiliary area to a mine may only be used for the purpose for which the right has been granted.

IV. Gold Panning

1179. Gold panning, which has traditionally been performed in small-scale in parts of northern Finland (Lapland), practically within one municipality (Inari), has decades ago changed to a non-traditional, motor-driven activity with impacts on landscape and river environment, particularly in the area of *Lemmenjoki* National Park. The same areas mainly belong to the Saami homeland, special reindeer area and wilderness areas. Gold panning is strongly restricted by the Nature Conservation Act in protected areas, but some older and continued rights were still in force when the present Mining Act entered into force in July 2011. Such rights lapsed in July 2020 (*see* paragraph 1221 below).

There is still a whole chapter (Chapter 4) for gold panning in the Mining Act. The provisions are essentially different from those in the previous Mining Act, and in practice allow only traditional panning.

In addition, a permit pursuant to the Water Act may be needed depending on the impacts, and where not, registration pursuant to the Environmental Protection Act (Annex 4(3)) is required when the amount of excavated earth masses is under 500 cubic metres per year surface layers included and the working time does not exceed fifty days per year.

1180. Gold panning in an area owned by the State is subject to a Gold Panning Permit by the Mining Authority (section 22 of the Mining Act), whereas the consent of the owner is sufficient in private areas (but such consents hardly occur in practice). In the permit not only an obligation is at stake, but by virtue of a Gold Panning Permit, the permit holder (an applicant prior to others, where any) gains the exclusive right within the area specified in the Permit (gold panning area), as provided in the permit in detail, to: (1) prospect for and survey gold deposited in the soil; (2) recover and exploit gold deposited in the soil by means of panning; and (3) recover and exploit nuggets of platinum and gemstones and precious stones found in loose soil as by-products of panning (section 23). A Gold Panning Permit does not limit the property owner's (i.e., the State's) right to use the area or to govern it otherwise. A gold panning area shall be a continuous area of a maximum of seven hectares. Gold panning shall be limited to necessary measures (section 24). Operations based on a Gold Panning Permit and other use of the gold panning area may not cause a consequence as referred to in section 11(2), or harm or damage to other needs for the use of nearby areas. No damage may be caused to culturally and historically valuable buildings and their yards or other similar objects, or to reindeer husbandry structures or reindeer transport routes. The gold panner shall keep the gold panning area in such a condition that it meets safety requirements on a continuous basis and does not cause any detrimental environmental impact. A Permit may be valid no more than four years at a time (section 65).

1181. The panner has to take care of the prevention of the generation of soil and rock waste, decreasing its harmfulness, alongside its reclamation or processing. He shall also prepare an Extractive Waste Management Plan (section 25). Building is prohibited in a gold panning area. Nevertheless, a building or other construction is allowed if the gold panner proves it to be necessary for his temporary stay and for the storage of equipment, and if the authority or institution responsible for the management of the area does not oppose the construction for a justified reason. The building or other construction must be minor in terms of its size, lightweight and easily movable. If no such impediment to construction exists, the Mining Authority decides on the necessity of the building or construction, and the location, in connection with the Gold Panning Permit (section 26).

1182. The gold panner shall in advance notify the authority or institution responsible for the area of all field work that could cause damage or inconvenience (section 27). There are additional notification duties in respect to the Saami people and reindeer husbandry.

The panner is obliged to submit a report to the Mining Authority annually on the quantity of gold recovered and loose soil treated, and on construction in the panning area and other use thereof. The Mining Authority shall annually organize an event open to the public, at which a report shall be given: (1) on gold panning based on Permits; and (2) on the effects of gold panning on reindeer husbandry, other livelihoods, the status of the Saami rights of the Skolt people (section 28). After a Permit has expired or been cancelled, the panner shall immediately restore the gold panning area to the condition required by public safety, remove any buildings, other constructions and equipment, see to restoration and cleaning of the area and return the area to as close to natural as possible and to a satisfactory condition regarding the landscape. The Mining Authority shall be notified as provided in section 29.

Having received the notification, the Mining Authority shall arrange a final inspection unless this can be considered evidently unnecessary (section 30). Should the notification be neglected, the Mining Authority may initiate a final inspection on its own initiative. The final inspection shall establish whether the measures pursuant to section 29 have been accomplished. An inspection report shall be compiled.

V. Permit Consideration

1183. An Exploration Permit, a Mining Permit and a Gold Panning Permit shall be granted if the applicant proves that the respective preconditions are met and there is no impediment stipulated in the Mining Act to the granting of the permit (section 45). However, despite an impediment, a permit may be granted if it is possible to remove the impediment stake through provisions laid down in the permit or by decreasing the size of the area.

1184. Neither an Exploration Permit nor a Gold Panning Permit shall be granted for the following (section 46(1)): (1) an area in section 7(2) (above); (2) an area in section 9(4) (above); (3) an area that has previously been an exploration area unless two years have elapsed since the expiry or cancellation of the Exploration Permit; (4) an area that has previously been a mining area unless two years have elapsed since the decision concerning termination of mining activities gained legal force; (5) an area belonging to an exploration area, mining area, or gold panning area, or for which reservation notification has been made; (6) an area where activities in accordance with the application would impede the implementation of a legally binding land use Plan under the Land Use and Building Act (as of 1 January 2025, the Land Use Act); (7) an area for which the municipality opposes the granting of the Permit for a weighty reason related to land use planning or other use of the areas, unless an important public interest requires the granting of the Permit; (8) an area where the activities applied for cause significant harm to other business activities; as well as (9) if there are serious grounds to suspect that, due to the extent of the area applied for or other reasons revealed in connection with the processing of the application, the applicant does not have the prerequisites or apparently even the intention to engage in activities in accordance with the Permit, or if the applicant has previously essentially neglected the obligations based on the legislation applicable to the activities (from 2023 also other than those based on the Mining Act); when assessing the essentiality of negligence, particular account shall be paid to the planned nature of the negligence, its duration and repetition, and the amount of damage caused by the negligence; or (10) if the operations are assessed to endanger national defence, security of supply, the operation of infrastructure essential to society or other comparable national security interests. However, an Exploration Permit and a Gold Panning Permit may as a rule be granted for an area provided in section 1(1–4) by the consent of the competent authority or institution or the holder of property rights (section 46(2)). A building or facility intended for residential purposes or work use in a mining area or gold panning area shall not prevent granting of a permit. Moreover, in order to prevent chicane attempts, an Exploration Permit may not be granted unless there are grounds for concluding that there are mining minerals in the area.

1185. A basic prerequisite for granting a Mining Permit is that the deposit shall be exploitable in terms of size, ore content and technical characteristics (section 47). The applicant must have the necessary expertise and sufficient financial capacity for the activities. Moreover, the mining area and the auxiliary area to a mine shall not be located in an area for which an Exploration Permit or a Gold Panning permit cannot be granted due to section 46(1)(1–5) (above). However, a Mining Permit may be granted also here regarding (1)–(4) if the preconditions in section 46(2) are met, or if the mining area cannot be otherwise implemented in pursuance with section 19 and the area in question is not one provided in section 7(2)(1) or (2) or 9(4). The relationship of the mining area and any auxiliary area to other usage of land has to be accounted. Mining activity must also (from 2023 in all cases) be based on a legally binding land use Plan under the Land Use and Building Act (as of 1 January 2025, the Land Use Act), where the location of the mining area and the auxiliary area of the mine and its relationship to other uses of the areas have been determined.

1186. A Mining Permit may not be granted if there are serious grounds to suspect that, for reasons revealed in connection with the processing of the application, the applicant does not have the necessary expertise or sufficient financial prerequisites for the operations, or apparently even the intention to ensure the commencement of mining operations, or if the applicant has previously essentially neglected the obligations based on the legislation applicable to the operations (from 2023 also other than those based in the Mining Act). When assessing the essentiality of negligence, particular attention shall be paid to the planned nature of the negligence, their duration and repetition, and the amount of damage caused by the negligence. And irrespective of other preconditions and impediments, a permit shall not be granted at all if the mining activity creates danger to public safety, causes highly significant detrimental environmental impacts, or substantially weakens the living conditions or industrial conditions of the locality, and the said danger or impacts cannot be remedied by imposing permit provisions (section 48).

1187. Expropriation for a mining area may be granted if the mining project is based on public need and the mining area meets the requirements in section 19. Public need shall be assessed particularly on the basis of the impact on the local and regional economy and employment, and the social need for raw material supply (section 49). In a Mining Permit a right to use the auxiliary area to the mine may be granted, if the auxiliary area meets the requirements in section 19, and only insofar as the placement of functions planned for the area cannot be otherwise arranged satisfactorily and at moderate cost.

1188. Additional provisions on permit consideration apply in the Saami area and the reindeer husbandry area An Exploration Permit, a Mining Permit, or a Gold Panning Permit may not be granted (section 50) if activities under the permit: (1) alone, or together with other permits and other land use would substantially undermine the preconditions for traditional Saami sources of livelihood or for other maintenance and development of the Saami culture; (2) would substantially impair the living conditions of Skolt Saami and the possibilities for pursuing a livelihood in the Skolt area; or (3) in the special reindeer husbandry area, would cause considerable harm to reindeer farming. However, a permit may be granted if it is possible to remove such an impediment through provisions in the permit.

VI. Provisions Laid Down in Mining Act Permits

1189. An Exploration Permit shall first include provisions for the location and borders of the exploration area (section 51). In addition it shall include necessary provisions for securing public and private interests concerning the following: (1) the times and methods of exploration surveys and the equipment and constructions related to exploration; (2) measures to reduce the harm caused to reindeer husbandry in the special reindeer husbandry area and to other traditional Saami livelihoods in the Saami homeland; (3) measures to ensure that the activities do not jeopardize the right of the Saami to maintain and develop their language, culture and traditional livelihoods or the rights of the Skolt people; (4) obligation to report about exploration activities and results; (5) termination measures and the deadline for notification concerning such measures; (6) the Extractive Waste Management Plan and compliance therewith; (7) the obligation to report on the exploration work to authorities representing public interests; (8) the schedule for decreasing the size of the exploration area; (9) collateral according to Chapter 10; (9a) measures to ensure that exploration and other use of the exploration area do not cause harm to human health or danger to public safety, substantial harm to other business activities, significant changes in natural conditions, material damage to rare or valuable natural occurrences, significant disturbance to the landscape or other significant adverse environmental impact; and (10) other items concerning exploration and use of the exploration area in order to ensure that no prohibited consequence would result; and (11) other items necessary in view of public and private interests and pertaining to the fulfilment of the preconditions of the permit. When issuing permit provisions on the dates and methods of exploration and on equipment and structures related to exploration, good practices shall be taken into account in order to reduce the environmental impacts caused by exploration.

1190. Similarly, a Mining Permit shall contain provisions for the location and borders of the becoming mining area, and for the auxiliary area to the mine, taking the provisions in sections 19 and 47, and the content of the rights of use to the auxiliary area into consideration. The permit authority may here make certain changes to the location and borders presented by the applicant. A Mining Permit shall specify a term, up to ten years, within which the permit holder shall engage in mining or other such preparatory activity that indicates that he is seriously aiming to initiate actual mining operations (section 52). Each Mining Permit shall include the necessary provisions for securing public and private interests in respect to the following: (1) avoidance or limiting of detrimental impacts of mining activity, and ensuring people's health and public safety; (2) measures for ensuring that mining activities do not entail obvious wasting of minerals or endanger or hamper potential future use of the mine and excavation work there; (3) obligation to report on the extent of exploitation of the deposit and results; (4) to reduce the harm caused to reindeer husbandry in the special reindeer husbandry area and to reduce the harm caused to other traditional livelihoods of the Saami people in the Saami homeland; (5) to ensure that the activities do not jeopardize the right of the Saami people to maintain and develop their language, culture and traditional livelihoods or the rights of the Skolt people; (6) collateral (Chapter 10) for termination of activity and other obligations regarding termination and time after termination; (7) the deadline to be set for submission of accounts needed for review of provisions in the permit afterwards; (8) other items in order to ensure that the activity does not result in any prohibited consequence; (8a) the preservation and renewal of trees and other vegetation and new plantings during mining operations; (8b) the location of activities in the mining area, taking into account impacts on biodiversity and other environmental impacts; (8c) measures to prevent significant adverse effects on the environment; (8d) measures to prevent any significant deterioration in the living or economic conditions of the locality; (8e) the gradual closure of a mine; and (9) other items that are necessary from the viewpoint of public and private interests and pertaining to the fulfilment of the preconditions of the permit.

1191. A Gold Panning Permit shall define the location and borders of the panning area (section 54). The permit shall moreover include the necessary provisions for securing public and private interests in respect to the following: (1) the times and methods of panning; (2) maintenance of the panning area; (3) to reduce the harm caused to reindeer husbandry in the special reindeer husbandry area and to other traditional Saami livelihoods in the Saami homeland; (4) to ensure that the activities do not jeopardize the right of the a people to maintain and develop their language, culture and traditional livelihoods or the rights of the Skolt people in the Skolt area; (5) obligation to account on the panning; (6) aftercare measures; (7) the Extractive Waste Management Plan and compliance therewith; (8) collateral (Chapter 10); (9) other items regarding gold panning and use of the panning area in order to ensure that no prohibited impact would result; (10) other items that are necessary from the viewpoint of public and private interests and pertaining to the fulfilment of the preconditions of the permit.

VII. Procedural Provisions

1192. An Exploration Permit, a Mining Permit and a Gold Panning Permit may be applied for by a natural person of age who is not declared bankrupt and whose competency has not been restricted under the Guardianship Services Act, and by a legal person (section 31). Hence there are no requirements regarding domicile or nationality. Moreover, subject to the conditions laid down in the Act, a governmental institution may apply for an Exploration Permit. The applicant for a Mining Permit may also apply for an expropriation permit for a respective area (section 31).

1193. The right of priority to an Exploration Permit can be obtained by submitting a reservation notification or by submitting the Exploration Permit application first. The right of priority to a Mining Permit and a Gold Panning Permit can be obtained by first submitting an application for a Mining Permit or an application for a Gold Panning Permit. For the preparation of an Exploration Permit Application, the applicant may reserve an area by notifying the Mining Authority (reservation notification). The right of priority based on a reservation notification is valid when the reservation notification has been made in the manner prescribed in section 44 of the Act, and there is no statutory obstacle to accepting the reservation. Among other areas, National Parks and Natural Parks in accordance with the Nature Protection Act (but not other nature reserves) must be demarcated from the reservation area. The right of priority expires when a decision made by the Mining Authority on the basis of a reservation notification (reservation decision) lapses or is revoked. As a rule, the reservation decision is valid for a maximum of twelve months from the date of the reservation notification. The right of priority to Exploration Permit, Mining Permit and Gold Panning Permit is vested in the person who first applied for a Permit in the manner prescribed by the Act. However, the Natura 2000 assessment pursuant to section 35 of the Nature Protection Act as well as the assessment report pursuant to the Act on Environmental Impact Assessment Procedure and the liaison authority's reasoned conclusion may also be submitted to the Mining Authority without losing priority after the permit application has been submitted, but before the statement procedure pursuant to section 37 and the notification of the permit application pursuant to section 40. However, if a Mining Permit is applied for a deposit in an Exploration Area, the holder of the Exploration Permit has the right of priority if the holder submits an application for a Mining Permit in the manner prescribed by the Act before the Exploration Permit expires or is cancelled. The holder of the Exploration Permit retains the right of priority to the Mining Permit also if the Natura 2000 assessment, the EIA report and the reasoned conclusion are submitted to the Mining Authority only after the Exploration Permit has lapsed or been cancelled (sections 32 and 44). A reservation or priority has relevance only in the relations between different actors within the mining industry and hence does not in any way entitle to exploration or mining activities.

1194. The Mining Authority makes the decisions on reservation notifications, Exploration Permits, Mining Permits and Gold Panning Permits (section 33). However, the Cabinet decides on expropriation and on ordinary Mining Permits for mining activities containing the production of uranium or thorium. This is a very exceptional task for the Cabinet; *see* also paragraph 1199.

1195. The contents of the different permit applications are stipulated in detail in section 34 (and regarding expropriation, in section 35). A permit application shall include a necessary and reliable account, as regards permit consideration, on several items. Opinion statements on a permit application shall be requested (section 37) from the impacted municipalities, the Centre(s) for Economic development, Transport and the Environment, the authority or institution responsible for management of the area, and, where appropriate, from other authorities representing public interests, and the Regional Council. Moreover, the permit authority shall acquire the other statements and reports that are necessary in view of permit consideration.

1196. Section 38 contains provisions on the investigation of the matter and the cooperation procedure in the Saami homeland, the Skolt region and the special reindeer husbandry area. An event may be arranged, to which the representatives of the Saami Parliament, the Skolt (saami) village assembly, the Skolt Council, the statutory local reindeer owners' associations, the applicant, the authority or an institution responsible for management of the area, the municipal authority, the Fishing Area and forests in joint ownership are invited for consultation.

1197. Before making a decision on a permit, the permit authority shall reserve an opportunity for the parties involved to lodge remarks and express opinions in a sufficient time. Also those who are involved otherwise shall be provided with an opportunity to express their opinions (section 39). In addition, the Mining Authority shall organize an event open to the public to support objections and opinions in the case of an application concerning a Mining Permit, an amendment to a Mining Permit or an extension of the validity of a Mining Permit, unless the organization of the event is considered manifestly unnecessary. An account on the content of the permit application shall be provided at the event.

1198. The permit applications shall be made public in several ways provided for in sections 40 and 41. The applicant and other parties concerned shall be provided with an opportunity to provide an explanation concerning such requirements and reports presented in the statements and remarks by public and private impacted parties that may influence the decision on the matter (section 42). In consequence of the explanation again, those concerned shall be provided with an opportunity to provide a responsive explanation if such an explanation could influence the decision to be made.

1199. Where production of uranium or thorium are at stake, the permit application for the same activity under the Nuclear Energy Act shall be dealt with at the same time and decided upon by the Cabinet in the same decision as the Mining Permit, pursuant to section 23 of the Nuclear Energy Act (section 43 of the Mining Act). *See also* paragraph 1088.

1200. The decision on a permit shall explain the purpose of the application and comment on the individual claims, objections and opinions presented in statements and remarks (section 56). If the Environmental Impact Assessment Procedures Act is applicable to the project, the reasoned conclusion shall be included in the permit, and the decision must indicate how permit consideration has taken account of the EIS, the reasoned conclusion and, where applicable, the documents due to transboundary impacts, as provided in section 29 of the Environmental Impacts Assessment Act. A permit shall be issued after public notice, and those entitled to appeal shall be considered to have been given notice at the time of issuing (section 57). The decision shall be available on the date of issue mentioned in the notification, an electronic format included. The applicant shall be informed, the permit authority shall submit a copy of the decision to parties having specifically requested this, as well as the municipality, the Centres of Economic development, Transport and the Environment and other authorities who have been informed about the matter during handling, or who have been invited to comment (section 58). A copy of a decision on a Mining Permit shall be delivered to the Radiation and Nuclear Safety Authority. Depending on the area and the impacts, a copy of the decision shall also be submitted to the Saami Parliament, the Skolt village assembly and the statutory local reindeer owners' association(s). The permit authority shall additionally inform any parties that have filed a remark or asked to be informed. The permit authority shall ensure that the municipalities at stake publish the decision without delay. Moreover, the decision shall as a rule be publicized at least in one newspaper.

VIII. Validity Terms

1201. A final Mining Permit is normally valid without any time limit, but it can also be granted for a fixed term, if this is justified in view of the quality and extent of the deposit, the applicant's ability to be in charge of the commencement of mining activities, and other factors that have emerged during the application procedure. A permit with a fixed term may remain valid for a maximum of ten years after the decision has gained legal force (section 62(1) of the Mining Act).

1202. The provisions in a non-term-limited permit shall be reviewed later on by the permit authority, at the maximum interval of ten years, as specified in the permit (section 62(2)). In certain circumstances also a fixed-term Mining Permit may be designated to be revisited. The review of shall not in any significant way decrease the benefit gained from the mining project. The validity of an Exploration Permit may under certain prerequisites be extended as provided in section 61. As an additional condition for the extension, when the permit has been valid for at least ten years, the applicant must as a main rule demonstrate that the public bodies responsible for the management of the area or property owners whose properties cover at least half of the exploration area have given their consent to the extension, as provided in section 61a. Section 61b lays down provisions on extending the validity of an Exploration Permit in exceptional situations.

1203. The validity of a fixed-term Mining Permit may under certain prerequisites be extended for a further period (section 63). One of the prerequisites is that the permit holder has not materially neglected the obligations in the applicable legislation (as of 2023, also other than those based on the Mining Act) or the permit provisions, when assessing the essentiality of negligence. Particular attention shall be paid to the planned nature of the negligence, their duration and repetition, and the amount of damage caused by the negligence. A Gold Panning Permit is valid for a maximum of four years after the decision has gained legal force (section 64). The period of validity depends on the criteria provided in section 64. Extension for a maximum of ten years at a time is possible under the prerequisites in section 65. Reports and accounts required for an application for extending are provided in section 66.

1204. Normally an Exploration Permit and a Gold Panning Permit expire at the end of the fixed period. The Mining Authority can nevertheless decide that such a permit shall expire if operations have been interrupted for a reason dependent on the permit holder continuously for at least one year. This process may be initiated by the Mining Authority on its own initiative, the municipality, or those suffering harm (section 67). The Mining Authority shall decide that an Exploration Permit and a Gold Panning Permit expire upon the request of the permit holder. The holder is obliged to submit such an application if he no longer intends to engage in activity based on the permit. A Mining Permit in turn expires at the end of the fixed term (section 68). The permit authority shall nevertheless decide that the permit will expire if the permit holder has not, within the time specified in the permit, initiated mining activity or such preparatory work as indicates that the he is seriously aiming at actual mining operations. The permit authority shall also decide that a Mining Permit expires if mining activities have been interrupted due to a factor dependent on the permit holder continuously for at least five years, or mining activities are considered to have actually ended. The matter may be initiated by the permit authority, the municipality, or those suffering harm. In certain circumstances the expiry of a Mining Permit can be postponed.

1205. The Mining Authority shall, at its own initiative, or upon application by an authority representing public interest in its field, or a party suffering harm, reshape an Exploration Permit, a Mining Permit, or a Gold Panning Permit (section 69), if: (1) a consequence prohibited by the Mining Act is caused; or (2) the detrimental impacts deviate substantially from the assessments made during permit consideration.

The permit authority may cancel an Exploration Permit, a Mining Permit, or a Gold Panning Permit (section 70), if: (1) the applicant has given incorrect or incomplete information that has essentially affected the preconditions for granting a permit, or the permit consideration otherwise; (2) the permit holder no longer meets the preconditions for granting of a permit; or (3) the permit holder has essentially neglected or violated the applicable obligations and restrictions, or provisions in a permit. Where the deficiencies, etc. can be corrected or are less significant, the permit authority shall set a time limit for the permit holder to rectify the situation.

1206. An Exploration Permit, a Mining Permit and a Gold Panning Permit may be assigned to another subject. The assignee shall meet the same requirements that apply to a permit holder (section 73). In addition, the assignee of a Mining Permit concerning the production of uranium or thorium shall hold an appropriate permit under the Nuclear Energy Act. Sections 73 and 74 contain provisions on applications to the Mining Authority for assignment, and on the respective decisions. The assignee is responsible for different obligations as his predecessor.

IX. Expropriation, Compensations and Fees

1207. The Expropriation Act is applicable to compulsory establishing of property rights to alien property under the Mining Act, with a number of procedural and substantive modifications (sections 77–98). All this means competence of the land surveyor (being a public authority) as regards to compensations (both expropriation compensations and certain compensations for harm and damage), and also, as regarding the establishing of the mining areas and performing the related property formation. Also arrangements concerning private roads, as well as necessary land consolidation may be included. Proceedings establishing a Mining Area may not be terminated before the Expropriation Permit for a mining area and the Mining Permit have gained legal force.

1208. The reservation holder is obliged to pay a reservation fee, which is laid down in Chapter 8 of the Mining Act (505/2023). The amount of the fee depends on the size of the reservation area and is EUR 1 per hectare. The size of the reservation area is the area of the reservation area stated in the reservation decision. The fee shall be paid to the Mining Authority.

1209. Compensations for the very mining activities, i.e., exploration, mining activity and gold panning are contained in Chapter 9. These refer mainly to the property owners at stake.

1210. An annual compensation (Exploration Fee) to the owners of land included in the Exploration Area shall be paid by each holder of a valid Exploration Permit (section 99). The annual amount of the is EUR 20, EUR 30, EUR 40 or EUR 50 per hectare depending on the amount of preceding years of validity. Correspondingly, an annual Excavation Fee (section 100) shall be paid by each Mining Permit holder. The basic amount is EUR 50 per hectare. In addition, the following shall be paid as an Excavation Fee: 0.15% of the calculated value of metallic minerals, excavated and exploited during the year; considering the average price of the exploited metals included in the ore during the year, and the average value of other products exploited from the ore during the year. The grounds for assessment an Excavation Fee are specified further in section 100. An elevated compensation of EUR 100 is required in certain situations.

A Mining Permit holder shall moreover pay annual property-specific compensation (By-product Fee) to each landowner in the mining area for the benefit gained from by-products of mining activities that are used for purposes other than mining activity (section 101).

Each gold panner shall pay the authority or institution responsible for management of the area an annual compensation (Gold Panning Fee) of EUR 50 (section 102).

1211. The holder of an Exploration Permit holder shall, as a main rule, compensate for any harm and damage caused in the Exploration Area by his activities (section 103). Within a prospecting area, the same applies to the subject in charge for prospecting work, and to the gold panner in a panning area. If not agreed upon (section 104), the claim for compensation can be presented in the proceedings before a land surveyor (*see* above 1207).

As concerns damage or harm caused by pollution of water, air, or soil, or by nuisance (i.e., noise, vibration, radiation, light, heat or smell), the section 12 of the

Environmental Damages Act is applicable (section 105); making the procedure before the competent land surveyor competent also here (but substantively the Environmental Damages Act is applicable).

1212. Separate from the provisions of the Mining Act, the Mining Minerals Tax Act (314/2023) has been enacted, entering into force as of 1 January 2024. The tax must be paid on mining minerals pursuant to section 2 of the Mining Act. The taxpayer is an operator who has extracted a mining mineral and who is required to have a Mining Permit.

X. Other Provisions

1213. Collaterals are stipulated in Chapter 10. As a main rule, the holder of an Exploration Permit and a gold panner shall provide sufficient collateral for compensating for any damage and inconvenience and for carrying out follow-up measures, taking into account the nature and extent of the operations and the special characteristics of the area of operation (section 107), the termination and follow-up measures specified in the mining permit (partly for a period of at least thirty years) and safety measures in abnormal situations for a period of one year, as well as for an amount corresponding to the annual amount of the one-year mining compensation, unless the holder of the mining permit owns part or all of the properties belonging to the mining area. The collateral must be sufficient, taking into account the nature and extent of mining operations, the permit provisions and the collaterals required under other legislation (in particular, the Environmental Protection Act). It shall also be taken into account that the operations to be carried out by means of a collateral are assessed or carried out by a party other than the operator or public authority (section 108). The permit authority determines the type and quantity of collateral (section 109). The mining authority shall, on its own initiative, adjust the amount of the collateral if the nature and extent of the operations or the effects of the operations on public safety, human health or the environment have changed since the Permit was granted in such a way that the type or amount of the collateral needs to be adjusted as a result. Costs to be paid from the collateral are stipulated in section 110.

1214. Mining safety is stipulated in Chapter 11. The provisions on prevention of accidents are relevant also on the environmental viewpoint. A specific, separate Mining Safety Permit (sections 121–132) is required for the construction of a mine, and its productive operations.

1215. The planning and construction of a mine, as well as the mining itself, must take into account the gradual closure of the mine, the use of the area after the end of mining operations, and the fact that mining operations can be stopped and the mine safely closed (section 120). Chapter 15 of the Mining Act deals with termination of mining activity. Mining activity ends when the mining permit expires or is cancelled (section 142). The provisions concerning termination of mining activity apply correspondingly if the Mining Permit is altered in such a way that the area or rights of use are reduced.

The mining operator shall within two years of the termination of activity restore the mining area and the auxiliary area to a condition complying with public safety, ensure their restoration, cleaning and landscaping and perform the measures already specified in the Mining Permit and Mining Safety Permit, in such a way that the closed mine does not cause significant adverse effects on human health or the environment (section 143). The operator may leave in place the excavated minerals, mining facilities and equipment and the buildings and other constructions on the ground for up to two years after termination of activity (section 144). Thereafter they are transferred, free of charge, to the landowner, who may nevertheless demand the removal thereof at the operator's cost. However, the Mining Authority can temporarily prohibit the removal of buildings and other constructions. Notification of mine-closure measures by the operator is provided in section 145. After that, final inspection is arranged by the Mining Authority (section 146). The operator, the interested parties, the municipalities the Centre for Economic Development shall, *inter alia*, be informed. The Mining Authority shall thereafter make a decision on terminating mining activity once the fundamental bulk of required measures have been completed in a way that protects public and private interests (section 147). However, if the mining activity in question has been carried out for producing uranium or thorium, the decision cannot be made before the Radiation and Nuclear Safety Authority has found the termination measures appropriately completed in respect of radiation and nuclear safety and approved them. Provisions can be included in the decision similarly as in a permit. Necessary provisions are stipulated in section 148.

After the decision to terminate mining has become legally valid, the operator's right of use and possession to the mining area and the auxiliary area are terminated and the areas are returned to the possession of the landowner, free of charge (section 149). After the end of mining operations, the operator is still responsible for monitoring the mining area and the auxiliary area, as well as for the necessary corrective measures and their costs, in accordance with the provisions issued in the Mining Permit or in the decision to cease mining operations. The Mining Authority shall be informed of any significant adverse effects on public safety, the environment or human health revealed during monitoring and the necessary corrective measures shall be taken without delay. The mining authority may issue orders on the measures (section 150).

1216. Chapter 16 of the Mining Act contains provisions on supervision, administrative enforcement and sanctions. The Mining Authority shall ensure appropriate and sufficient supervision and monitoring of operations falling within the scope of the Mining Act by obtaining information and carrying out inspections (section 151a). The other provisions relate to authorities' rights of access to information (section 152), the Mining Authority's right of inspection, take samples, and engage in other supervisory measures (section 153), periodic supervision of mining safety (section 154), executive assistance by the police, etc. (section 155), administrative enforcement by the Mining Authority to rectify an offence or neglect (section 156), temporary prohibition of operations (section 157) and conditional fine or threat of taking the neglected action at the defaulting party's expense or of interrupting the activity pursuant to the Administrative Injunctions (Conditional Fines) Act (section 158). The administrative enforcement proceedings may be commenced at the Mining Authority's own initiative or initiated (section 159) by: (1) a person concerned suffering harm; (2) a registered association or foundation whose purpose is to promote protection of the environment or health, nature conservation, or the pleasantness of the living environment, and in whose operating area, in compliance with the regulations thereof, the environmental an impact appears; (3) the municipality where the activity is located, or another municipality in the area of which the detrimental impacts appear; (4) the Centre for Economic Development, Transport and the Environment and another authority protecting the public interest in its field; (5) the Saami Parliament, when the detrimental impacts appear in the Saami homeland; and 6) the Skolt Saami village meeting, if the detrimental impacts appear in the Skolt area.

1217. Criminal law penalties are provided in section 160 of the Act.

1218. Appeals against decisions by the Mining Authority or the Ministry of Economic Affairs and Employment are submitted to the Regional Administrative Court, pursuant to the Administrative Judicial Procedures Act (section 162). Appeals against Cabinet decisions on an Expropriation Permit or, where any (*see* paragraphs 1178 and 1192), on a Mining Permit are appealed against directly to the SAC. The right to appeal against a decision including or concerning an Exploration Permit, a Mining Permit, or a Gold Panning Permit belongs to (practically) the six groups who are entitled to initiate administrative enforcement proceedings (paragraph 1216 above). Moreover, the Mining Authority has the right to appeal against a decision by which the Regional Administrative Court has altered its decision or overruled the decision.

1219. As a main rule, operations based on a permit may only be commenced when the administrative decision is final, i.e., gained legal force. Certain further requirements and exceptions are provided in sections 168–170, e.g., situations where a decision may exceptionally and under specified requirements be declared executable (often a permit being exploitable to the operator) regardless of appeal (or appealability). The administrative court can nullify such an order or amend it. A decision on enforcement is usually in force instantly.

1220. The operator shall inform the Mining Authority, without delay, of any serious accident, dangerous situation, or incident that has occurred in the mine, as provided further in section 171 of the Act. An accident investigation pursuant to section 172 may appear to be necessary.

1221. According to the numerous transitional provisions of the Mining Act, the main rule is that the old Mining Act is applied to the existing operations. However, there are a number of detailed exceptions that require the application of the new Act. Previously granted mining rights for gold panning will be terminated after a transitional period of nine years. Under the present Act, holders of rights have the prerogative to apply for a gold panning permit for the corresponding area. Starting in July 2020, new gold panning is permitted in the *Lemmenjoki* National Park based on traditional methods only.

Chapter 8. Water Management and Construction Projects

§1. Legal Grounds of Water Management

1222. Water areas of various kinds and sizes are an essential part of the environment throughout the country. Consequently, there are many ways of using water areas and water resources – and in turn also many ways of influencing them. These circumstances, where rights and interests of many kinds are involved, have made the legal regulation in this field rather sophisticated. Up to March 2000, the then Water Act of 1961 consisted of twenty-two large chapters and of almost 500 sections, and had the longest text of all parliamentary acts enacted in Finland.

In the extensive environmental law reform of 2000, the regulation on discharges and pollution was mainly removed to the integrated Environmental Protection Act. The previous Water Courts were replaced by the then new, similarly rather independent Environmental Permit Offices. Along with the permit and enforcement tasks under the Environmental Protection Act, the Environmental Permit Offices had a similar role in water management and watercourse construction under the 1961 Water Act. In January 2010, the Environmental Permit Offices were abolished and their tasks transferred to the newly established Regional State Administrative Agencies, or more exactly. to the Environmental Permit Divisions of four of the new agencies.

1223. A totally new Water Act (587/2011) replaced the Water Act of 1961 from 1 January 2011. In many respects, the previous structures were preserved, aiming at more coherence, clarity and modern language, however. The number of sections was strongly reduced, especially regarding such activities that have lost more or less of their importance, such as timber floating. One novelty consisted of particular rules on restoration of water bodies, especially elevation of formerly lowered water level. The relevant EU directives have been taken into account. The (Environmental Permit Divisions of the) Regional State Administrative Agencies continued in the capacity of permit authority. Like the previous Regional Environmental Centres, the divisions for the environment and natural resources of the Centres for Economic Development, Transport and the Environment, are the State-level supervisory authorities practically without any formal decision-making competence. The Municipal Environmental Protection Authorities are, as previously, vested in supervisory powers, and in some decision-making competence.

Complementary technical and procedural provisions are included in the Government decree on Water Management Matters (1560/2011).

As its predecessor, the current Water Act encompasses both surface water bodies and groundwater bodies. As surface water body are also regarded the Finnish territorial waters in the Baltic Sea, and, as inserted to the previous Act from February 2005, also the then established economic zone of Finland.

1224. The role of private ownership of water areas is not as dominant as one would expect. In part, this is due to the general restrictions on use (the bans on altering and closing off water bodies without a permit and the corresponding restrictions on polluting water bodies in the Environmental Protection Act), which apply to owners, outsiders and authorities alike. Further, the rules on the various forms of common use (*see* General Introduction, Chapter 2, §1) make that the owners cannot forbid normal boat traffic, recreational boating, traffic on ice, swimming, minor water intake, minor dredging, or some forms of fishing (for the latter *see* above Part II, Chapter 6, §3), etc. Finally, the permit system, under certain circumstances, makes it possible to acquire water and even land areas necessary for the project. This resembles expropriation for public purposes, but also private permit applicants may extend their rights of use to other subjects' property. These rights are granted by the Environmental Permit Division of the competent Regional State Administrative Agency under specific regulations in connection with the proper constructing permit.

1225. The exceptionally wide notion of building or constructing of or in water areas as a basic concept of the 1961 Water Act has in the present Water Act been replaced mainly by the notion of water management project, but almost the same is targeted at. As water management measure[60] is hence regarded any measure or use of a construction that takes place in water area or land area and that may affect surface water, groundwater, water-related environment, water management or use of a water area (section 3(1)(9) of Chapter 1). The main function of the notion is to define the scope of application of the Water Act.

1226. A Water Management Matter in turn, being a concept of procedural nature, is defined as implementation of a water management measure and other use or care for water-related environment (section 3(1)(1) of Chapter 1). The Water Act is applicable to Water Management Matters (section 2(1) of Chapter 1). However, if a permit pursuant to the Water Act is not needed, but the water management project at stake poses a risk of pollution of a water body, the Environmental Protection Act is applied instead. Many other acts, such as the Nature Protection Act and the Land Use and Building Act (as of 1 January 2025, the Land Use Act and the Building Act), are, where appropriate, applied to water management projects alongside the Water Act.

As previously, the regulation in the Water Act covers measures and construction projects of various kinds and sizes, such as the construction of hydroelectric plants, dams, quays, piers, jetties, waterways, timber floating facilities, cables, water abstraction pipes, sewage outlets, embankments, bridges, road banks, reservoirs and fish farms, as well as damming up or impounding water, lowering of the surface of water, drainage and ditching, filling of water areas with earth, extraction of sand from the seabed, dredging and clearing of rapids. Also continuous and permanent activities like water intake from surface water or from groundwater, and regulation of the water level for various purposes are encompassed.

1227. As for the substantive rules, some of the projects listed above are regulated merely by the general water management and permitting rules in the Water

60. Water management *project* would be a formally exact translation, but the main focus is on single measures and their impacts.

Act. For some others, more or less modified forms of the basic regulation are additionally provided for. The latter category includes water intake (Chapter 4 of the Act), drainage and ditching (Chapter 5), permanent altering of mean water level in a water body (Chapter 6), water level regulation (Chapter 7), use of hydroelectric power (Chapter 8), timber floating (Chapter 9) and waterways and other water traffic areas (Chapter 10).

1228. Groundwater and groundwater areas are in several ways provided and protected by the Water Act and also by other legislation such as the Environmental Protection Act. For these purposes, the areas have in an established way been invented and classified by the Centres for Economic Development, Transport, and the Environment (and their predecessors). There was long no legislation on this, and the inventories had no direct effects, although they have been, as a kind of presumption, been taken into account in various decisions. In 2015 Chapter 2a on the determining and classification of groundwater areas was inserted in the Act on the Arranging of Water Management and Marine Waters Management. Pursuant to section 10b of the Act, the Centres for Economic Development, Transport, and the Environment determine the boundaries for areas where groundwater is accumulated (accumulation areas) and outer boundaries for areas which affect the accumulation or quality of groundwater (groundwater area). A mere point marking is allowed, if those boundaries for a groundwater area in water supply use or suitable for use cannot be determined. The areas are classified on the basis of suitability for water supply use and protection needs as follows (section 10b):

- Class 1: for water supply important groundwater area the water in which is used or is intended to be used for the water supply of a community, or as household water more than 10 cubic metres per day on average or for the purposes of more than fifty persons.
- Class 2: other for water supply suitable groundwater area the water in which is, due to the availability and other properties of the groundwater is suitable for use as above.
- Class 3: groundwater area on the groundwater in which a surface ecosystem or a terrestrial ecosystem directly depends.

The previous classes I, II and III are parallelly applicable in a transition period.

Chapter 2a also contains provisions on the procedure for the determining and classifying, as well as participation by concerned subjects and bodies. A municipality may draw up a protection plan for a groundwater area if required by the environmental objectives in the Act.

No direct legal effects have in the Act been attached to the determined areas or the classes. However, 'important or other, for water supply suitable groundwater areas' have been protected in other legislation, particularly in the Water Act and the Environmental Protection Act.

§2. PERMIT SYSTEM

1229. Water and watercourse management regulation is largely based on a permit system, based on individual approach and application of law case by case. The permit procedure (hearings, participation, etc.) provisions remind of the respective provisions of the Environmental Protection Act (*see* Part I, Chapter 1, §11), as well as the appellate procedure (Part I, Chapter 1, §15). A permit application to the Regional State Administrative Agency often consists of a large amount of various legal, technical and ecological documents on the project, and also detailed assessments on the impacts, those on individuals included, are to be submitted. The contents of a permit application, hearings and opinions and the procedures in the permit authority, as well as the contents and issuing of a permit decision, are stipulated in Chapter 11 of the Water Act.

1230. As a main rule, the various hearings and all other measures of the permit authority are the responsibility of the Regional State Administrative Agency. But if the impacts of the project, and especially the probable economic losses to individuals (in practice: a multiplicity of individual property owners), have to be examined in detail, the permit authority had under the previous Act the possibility to set a special ad hoc Inspection Procedure (in Finnish: *katselmustoimitus*, in Swedish: *syneförrättning*), chaired by an expert on water management technology or water ecology, in motion. The purpose was to examine the project or an aspect of it thoroughly and to prepare the final decision in the matter. During the procedure, the parties involved and also others who have their home or place of work in the area were given the opportunity to make themselves familiar with the application and to comment upon it. Consequently, the inspection may also be characterized as a kind of public enquiry. Because of the ex officio handling of compensations, the possible damages were also investigated during the procedure. It was also possible for the permit authority to focus the inspection merely on damages and compensations. In the recent years, unlike in the 1960s–1990s, an Inspection Procedure has been used only in a small minority of all permit matters, and most often it has been confined only to compensations, not necessarily to the permit-requiring project as a whole.

1231. In new cases initiated pursuant to the current Water Act, no new Inspection Procedures are possible from January 2011. However, a plainer and less formal procedure called specific account (section 16 of Chapter 11) is still available regarding such particular needs for information that cannot be acquired otherwise. This means that the Regional State Administrative Agency, after having made the ordinary public and individual notifications on the application, appoints either one of its own civil servant or an official from other environmental administration (in practice, from the division for the environment and natural resources of a Centre for Economic Development, Transport and the Environment), as an independent reporter to focus the item in question and, where necessary, after having heard the parties, to submit his reasoned opinion to the Regional State Administrative Agency within three months.

1232. In complicated cases the permit procedure can under certain conditions take place in two stages (section 18 of Chapter 11) so that the compensations are mainly separated from the proper permit, to be dealt with in a later-stage.

1233. Concerning the res judicata and permanence of various management permits, water level regulation and water intake included, the legal position of the permit holder has traditionally been very strong, also in changed circumstances and regarding competing interests of all kinds. The permits are as a rule not time-limited. The possibility of fixed time permits has been developed in practice, however, and it has been explicitly stated in the current Water Act, section 8 of Chapter 3, pursuant to which a permit is granted either without time limit, or, for particular reasons, for a fixed period of time. However, some amendments already in the 1961 Water Act had been made in 1991 and 1994 in order to make it possible to moderately check the individual water level provisions in existing permits without time limitation, and to require such checking in new permits.

1234. In the 2011 Water Act, such arrangements have been developed further. In all project categories it is now possible to attach to new permits provisions on future review of permit provisions related to water environment and its use, if this is appropriate for preventing significant harm (section 20 of Chapter 3). If so, the permit shall contain provision for a fixed time within which the permit holder shall make an application for review consideration and the accounts to be submitted. But if such an application is neglected, the Regional State Administrative Agency may at the application by (the division for the environment and natural resources) of a Centre for Economic Development, Transport and the Environment or by a subject suffering harm or damage order the permit be void, and issue related provisions. Also otherwise, i.e., without a pre-existing order in the permit, the Regional State Administrative Agency may, at the application of an harmfully impacted holder of property rights, a municipality (the division for the environment and natural resources) of a Centre for Economic Development, Transport and the Environment, or other authority representing public interests review the provisions in a permit and issue new provisions (section 21 of Chapter 3), but only in one of three situations. These are: (1) the performing of the permitted project causes adverse effects which were not anticipated when the permit provisions were issued and which cannot be sufficiently reduced otherwise, (2) due to changed circumstances, the observing of the existing provisions causes adverse impacts that cannot be sufficiently reduced otherwise, and (3) required by safety reasons. In addition, should the review cause losses that are not insignificant, the applicant of review is liable. The previous special stipulation on existing water level regulation permits have been preserved in sections 7 and 8 of Chapter 19. Additionally, the review of fisheries management obligations is regulated separately in a more flexible way (section 22 of Chapter 3). A permit may also be reshaped at the application of the permit holder (section 23 of Chapter 3), and declared void, if: (1) the permit holder does not exist any longer or cannot be identified in practice, (2) the project has lost its original meaning, or (3) requested by the permit holder, as provided in detail in sections 24 and 25 of Chapter 3.

1235. Substantively, the permit system had before 2011 essentially been based on the bans on closing off and altering water bodies (*see also* Part I, Chapter 4, §1). In the 2011 the Water Act, largely the same substantive contents have been preserved, but the ban-based wordings have been replaced by formulations that are based on a mere necessity to have a permit for such violations. A measure taken without a necessary permit is anyway still forbidden.

The previous ban on closing off (sections 12–14 of Chapter 1 of the 1961 Water Act), originating from medieval Swedish-Finnish law, applied to rivers, major straits and waterways, where there is automatically an 'artery.' Permits were under certain conditions possible, but even in this case water-borne traffic, eventual timber floating and migration of fish ought to be guaranteed. During last century, most of the biggest rivers have been closed off by hydroelectric plant dams, preventing the natural reproduction of, e.g., migratory Baltic salmon in the river rapids. Many of the old permit decisions have included (and partly still include) an obligation to construct and maintain fish ladders, but often without any positive results. There are also permit provisions requiring fish planting, often in a large scale.

In the 2011 Water Act, the actually corresponding provisions on arteries are contained in section 3(2)(1) of Chapter 3. The very notion of artery is defined in section 6 of Chapter 1.

1236. The ban on altering water bodies (section 15 of Chapter 1 of the 1961 Water Act), sea areas included, had previously been the most common legal reason for the necessity of a Water Act permit. The structure of this ban can be divided in three consecutive stages, and the same elements now make up the main parts of the corresponding section 2 of Chapter 3 of the 2011 Water Act. The latter, called generally applicable necessity of a permit, also covers altering of groundwater, unlike its predecessor, where the groundwater rules were separate.

1237. First, to be covered by this new general rule, a water management measure must be going to be taken somewhere, pursuant to the definition of such measure either in a land area or in a water area. This measure in turn has to be going to cause a physical change (concerning the position, depth, water level or water discharge of a water body, the shore or water-related environment, or the quality or quantity of groundwater). And this physical change again has to be going to violate either public interests or private rights or interests. If so for all parts, a prior permit is needed for the measure at stake.

Examples of relevant violations regarding public interests are listed in section 2(1) of Chapter 3 of the 2011 Water Act. They are: (1) threat of flooding or of general lack of water, (2) deterioration of nature and its functions or of the status of the water body or of groundwater, (3) significant deterioration of the natural beauty or of the amenities or cultural values of the environment, or the environment's suitability for recreational purposes, (4) danger to health, (5) essential reduction of the abundance of an important groundwater area or of other groundwater area suitable for water supply, or other impairment of the usefulness thereof, or other damage or harm to water supply or to use of water for household use, (6) damage or harm to fisheries or fish stocks, (7) hindrance to the use of a waterway or a timber floating route, and (8) endangers the natural status of a brook. But because these examples do not make up an exhaustive list, also (9) other comparable violation of public interest constitutes the same effect.

1238. Violations of private rights and interests are equally relevant, regarding alien water area, fisheries, water supply, land, immovable property or other property (section 2(2) of Chapter 3 of the 2011 Water Act). A permit is nevertheless not needed, if merely private interest are going to be violated and the measure at stake has been agreed to by the owner of the private good (or, in fact, all the owners of the private goods) going to be violated is a good example of the intermingling of features of both public and private law aspects in Finnish Water Law. If a permit is given, it means that the activities are no longer forbidden, not even concerning the relation between the applicant and the eventual victim, who will be compensated at the same time. Damages are assessed and decided upon ex officio by the Regional State Administrative Agency. A decision on compensations is a part of the permit procedure in the same way as in water-related Environmental Permits pursuant to the Environmental Protection Act. However, compensations for latent damages can be claimed later on.

1239. Consequently, a permit may turn out to be necessary for many different reasons. The environmental aspects in the wording of the (1961) Act were strengthened already in 1987. However, merely the violation of only one neighbour's interests has the same effect as the violation of vital public interests. In both cases the result is that a basically similar permit is needed.

1240. A permit is also needed for certain alterations of natural or man-made ditches, causing harm to another. The same holds good for the use of constructions in water areas, that causing nuisance to another's property (section 2(3) of Chapter 3 of the 2011 Water Act). In both cases the necessity of a permit may be replaced by agreement with those who are going to be violated.

1241. A permit is additionally needed for amendments of a water management measure, whereby public or private interest is going to be violated in a way provided in section 2(1–3) of Chapter 3 of the 2011 Water Act (section 2(4) of Chapter 3 of the same Act).

1242. And in addition to the various situations of generally applicable necessity of a permit dealt with above, there are measures for which a permit is always required, without having to assess on a case-by-case basis the probable impacts and the consequent violations of interests. Such measures are exhaustively listed in section 3(1) of Chapter 3 of the 2011 Water Act.

These are the following:

(1) closing off of an artery, a public waterway or a public timber floating route, or reducing the width thereof, or setting of hindrance therein;
(2) water intake to a water supply system operated under the Water Supply and Sewerage Act, or to a subject that supplies such a system with water, and

intake of water to be used elsewhere and other intake of groundwater where intake quantity is 250 cubic metres per day or more as well as a measure other than water intake if an amount of at least 250 cubic metres per day groundwater is due to it going to be removed from the groundwater area;
(3) processing of artificial groundwater, and re-infiltration of groundwater in order to improve the quality of water;
(4) constructing of a bridge or a transportation device over a public waterway or an artery, and the construction of a tunnel, water pipe, sewerage pipe, power cable or other such line under the same;
(5) permanent transformation of a land area into a water area by permanent raising of the water level in a water body;
(6) construction of a hydroelectric power plant;
(7) dredging of the bottom of a water body, if the amount mass to be dredged exceeds 500 cubic metres, except for the maintenance of public waterways;
(8) dumping of dredged masses in Finnish territorial waters in the Baltic Sea, except for insignificantly small amounts;
(9) extracting of soil from the bottom of a water body, except for usual household purposes; and
(10) establishing of a permanent site for timber floating activities.

A permit is additionally needed for amendments of already permitted establishments or measures within the list, and for amendments in the use thereof, if public or private interest is going to be violated (section 3(2) of Chapter 3 of the Water Act).

1243. In certain situations, one single project may need permits both under the Water Act and under the Environmental Protection Act. In such cases, called mixed projects, the two are procedurally, but not substantively, integrated (*see also* paragraphs 180, 235 and 1297).

1244. For example, water intake for cooling purposes and its immediate discharge to the water body may create such combination. Fish farming is the most common example in practice, and also, e.g., a harbour may be a mixed project, as well as (parts of) a mine project. In mixed projects the procedural and appellate provisions of the Water Act are applied to the whole, but the two substantive regimes are applied independently.

1245. The permit judgment rules are somewhat complicated. In the 2011 Water Act, the basic structures for this in the 1961 Act have largely been preserved. Basically, a permit has to be granted, equipped with various provisions, however, if no obstacle is present. The preconditions are nevertheless several and of several levels. Pursuant to a provision of an *ultima ratio* nature, a permit has always to be disallowed if a threat to public health or safety, significant negative impacts on nature, or essential deterioration in the conditions of local people and economic life would result (section 4(2) of Chapter 3 of the 2011 Water Act; very similarly already in section 5 of Chapter 2 of the 1961 Water Act).

This absolute provision has, however, practically never become an obstacle to granting a permit. However, the long debated *Vuotos* reservoir project in Lapland, being the most significant single water project for decades, was at the end of 2002 eventually rejected by the SAC, by virtue of the said provision (SAC 2002:82).

1246. Normally, the least harmful projects excepted, the permit consideration has traditionally depended on a weighing of interests. The relevant legal framework is now included in sections 4(1), 6 and 7 of Chapter 3 of the Water Act. These include the following: a permit is granted, if the benefit from the project to public or private interests is significant in comparison to the losses from the project to public and private interests. The public interest benefits and losses are assessed from the general point of view. A monetary value may here be used, if the quantity of the benefit or loss can be assessed in terms of money. What has in a Water Management Plan or a Marine Waters Management Plan pursuant to the Act on the Arranging of Water Management and Marine Waters Management (1299/2004) been presented on items related to the status and use of waters shall be taken into account. The same applies to Flood Risk Management Plans according to the Flood Risk Management Act (620/2010). As private benefit in the weighing is regarded the increased use value of property and other immediate benefit, and as private loss are regarded: (1) rights of use of alien property, or of compulsory purchase, that are granted to the applicant; (2) costs for damages, rights of use and land acquisition that already have been agreed upon; and (3) other losses suffered by outsiders or passive shareholders of certain projects.

All this means that the benefits from the project have to be significant compared to the various damages, inconveniences and losses of benefits caused by it. Otherwise the permit application shall be rejected. At the outset, the comparison is of an economical nature, being based on evaluation in money terms. The costs of the project or agreed damages were not included, which also means that it is not a matter of economic cost-benefit analysis, and that many negative impacts were left without relevance. This was regarded as a legislative defect by a parliamentary committee. As a result – but only as a compromise – the 1961 Water Act was in 1996 amended in a way that some of the costs, namely those caused by agreed damages or private rights acquired in advance, are taken into account (of course in addition to those rights that are established by the very permit). This holds good also pursuant to the present Water Act.

1247. However, the weighing or comparison shall not be confined to monetary values, if the project would have impacts relevant to priceless or difficult to evaluate public interests. In this case the comparison is based on a freer evaluation, even between various public interests, the result being a kind of value judgment of the Regional State Administrative Agency (or of an appellate body). An example: are the values of nature and water landscape more important than the benefits from a drainage project, or not? Or is it important to maintain the possibilities for public boating on a water body, as compared to the hydroelectric benefits from proposed water level regulation?

1248. As an alternative to the weighing of interests, and irrespective of it, a permit was up to 1994 also granted when the project was considered necessary for a public purpose. This prerequisite originated from expropriation law, although the permit in general is something else than expropriation (but may also include aspects of expropriation, which are regulated separately within the Act). In practice this alternative could only be claimed by the authorities of the State or of the municipalities, and even for them it was a matter decided on a case-by-case basis. A problem was caused by the fact that in the weighing of interests also competing public interests would be weighed against each other (and against private interests), while the requisite 'necessary for a public purpose' only meant assessing the interest of the applicant. In other words, to take an example, public water supply interests, road planning interests, waterway interests, public energy supply interests, interests of public recreation, fisheries management interests and the need to protect valuable wetlands could all constitute a 'public purpose', but if a permit application was in fact intended to serve only one of the interests mentioned, the others would be ignored. The practice of the SAC was to bring the two alternative prerequisites closer to each other by applying a general rule according to which a water project had in any case to be carried out in a way as harmless to competing interests as possible. Due to the evident disadvantages, the alternative precondition 'necessary for a public purpose' was finally removed from the previous Water Act in 1994.

1249. A Detailed Plan under the Land Use and Building Act (as of 1 January 2025, the Land Use Act), where any, shall be taken into account. Moreover, the legal effects of a Regional Plan and a Master Plan pursuant to the said Act apply also here. A Water Act permit shall not cause significant hindrance to the drafting of a future plan, either (section 5 of Chapter 3).

1250. Like the permits under the Environmental Protection Act, permits for water management and construction projects are far more than mere consents. Normally they include quite a number of various provisions by which the harmful impacts on public and private interests are reduced or eliminated. Fish management obligations are a good example. A fish ladder obligation is historically a typical version thereof, although it is now very uncommon and juridically only an alternative to the detailed fish planting obligations, which can be carried out either by the permit holder himself or by fisheries authorities. If carried out by authorities, the permit holder is obliged to pay a sufficient yearly Fish Management Fee. Fish management of another kind or a combination of obligations can also be imposed. Of course, a fish ladder obligation is not even thinkable for impacts of projects such as water level regulation. Various types of conditions may further be included to protect the interests of timber floating, waterway connections, agriculture and forestry, water supply and recreational use of water areas and shores. In cases of damming, lowering of the water level and regulation of the water level, the conditions for allowed water levels may be very detailed, often being compromises between contradictory interests such as agriculture, conservation, power production and recreational needs (especially those of summer home owners).

1251. An obligation to monitor and survey the implementation of the project and its impacts (e.g., on hydrology, water quality and fish stocks) is included, where necessary; in the permit, *see* Chapter 3, section 11 of the Water Act. Also joint obligations for several permit holders together are possible. The monitoring and surveillance are carried out under the auspices of the Centres for Economic Development, Transport and the Environment, both the environmental divisions and the fisheries units thereof. The contents of an obligation of this kind may, when disputed, give rise to daughter procedures before the Regional State Administrative Agency. The same is also the case for certain fisheries management obligations the details of which have not been specified in the permit decision. In spite of the various conditions included in the permits, damages may result. Insofar as these may be conceived as private economical losses, they are compensated to the victims in advance, if possible, pursuant to the provisions of Chapter 13 of the Water Act.

1252. The appellate courts are the Regional Administrative Court in Vaasa and (now subject to leave of appeal) the SAC. The appellate courts are free to alter also the technical provisions, where necessary. Appeals against a permit decision (and other decision concerning a permit) can be lodged by the same kind of persons, associations and authorities as in appellate procedures pursuant to the then Environmental Protection Act. The applicable provision of the 1961 Water Act had in the reform of 2000 been made identical to that on right of appeal in the then Environmental Protection Act (section 191 in the present Environmental Protection Act, *see* Part I, Chapter 1, §15). Also the corresponding section 2 of Chapter 15 of the present Water Act is rather similar. Under it, the following are entitled to appeal: (1) parties to the proceedings, by which anyone whose right, interest or obligation may be concerned is meant (section 7 of Chapter 11); (2) a registered association or foundation the aim of which is protection of environment, health or nature or promotion of amenity of an inhabited area, provided that the relevant impacts of the project appear in its geographical area of activities; (3) the municipality where the project is performed, and any municipality in the geographical area of which the environmental impacts of the project appear; (4) the supervisory State authority under the Water Act, i.e., (the environmental division of) the Centre for Economic Development, Transport and the Environment at stake, and the Municipal Environmental Protection Authorities of the municipality of the performing site and of the impacted municipalities; (5) other authority representing public interests, such as (the fisheries unit of) the Centre for Economic Development, Transport and the Environment; and (6) the Saami Parliament, if the project is located in or the impacts thereof appear in the Saami homeland and the project may have adverse impacts on the rights of the Saami as indigenous people.

1253. In practice, especially the right of appeal of the Centre for Economic Development, Transport and the Environment (environmental division) is important from the viewpoint of public interests, although a certain contradiction is created by the fact that the same division is at times also a permit holder regarding major water level regulation projects.

1254. Also the supervisory system for water management is very similar to that of the Environmental Protection Act (*see* Part I, Chapter 1, §20). However, power to make enforcement decisions (administrative injunctions, etc.) is here only vested in the Regional State Administrative Agency.

§3. PROJECT CATEGORIES

I. Hydroelectric Plants

1255. Specific permit consideration rules are provided for certain project categories such as hydroelectric plants (Chapter 8). By such plants, the ecological conditions have already been totally changed in most of the country's largest rivers. A plant not only closes the artery, but the damming up of water and the clearing of the rapid below the plant together (called 'stepping' of a river if there are several subsequent plants) make that the water levels are manipulated in a way similar to that for canals. For the sake of clarity, a permit from the Regional State Administrative Agency is always necessary (section 3(1)(6) of Chapter 3), irrespective of the impacts and the ban rules. The regulation is somewhat complicated, due to the fact that the ownership of a rapid is often split into small shares for historical reasons. But even a minority share owner, in practice a power company, can get a permit, an expropriatory right to use other shares included, in principle together with voluntary shareholders. The proper Construction Permit is juridically independent of the arrangement of shares, although these two intertwine procedurally.

The preconditions for a permit and the contents thereof are considered pursuant to the general provisions in Chapter 3, which normally means weighing of interests (paragraphs 1246 and 1247). But a specific provision defines how the benefit to power production is taken into account as a positive factor (section 2(2) of Chapter 8). The minimum value shall be twenty times the value of the yearly produced electricity, but also possible benefit from regulation of water and other particular power-related benefits may be noticed.

1256. On man-made lakes, *see* VII below.

1257. The rivers which have been remained in a natural state are mostly small, but nevertheless often represent valuable landscapes and ecosystems, being at the same time unfit for a relevant contribution to national power production. Many of them have been protected against the construction of new hydroelectric plants by the Rapids Protection Act (35/1987), in which case no permit for a hydroelectric plant can be given. But proposals to rescind parts of it have been made recently, until now without success. Already the enacting of the Act was influenced by conflicting interests. The owners of potential hydroelectric power capacity were guaranteed compensation for their losses, the amount of which is determined by the Act. The result has been regarded as somewhat contradictory by several legal scholars, because the granting of a power plant permit under the Water Act would have been unlikely for many of the rapids protected by the Rapids Protection Act, as natural values are relevant also to the Water Act. If a permit under the Water Act is not granted, the applicant is entitled to no compensation. However, the protection under the Rapids Protection Act is absolute and of a more permanent nature than the protection following from the rejection of a permit application under the Water Act.

In practice, one of the main interpretation problems has been the notion of 'constructing a new hydroelectric plant', especially in cases where there already exists a smaller old plant.

II. Waterways

1258. Another specific group of projects under the Water Act is that of establishing and construction of waterways (Chapter 10). The general rules in Chapters 2 and 3 on water management projects and permits are applicable also to the establishing of public waterways, and to the constructing (dredging, blasting of bottom bedrock, dumping of dredged bottom masses, etc.) and maintenance thereof. The regulation on dredging and bedrock blasting is in principle common to the sea and to the inland water bodies. In addition to the impact-based generally applicable necessity of a permit, permit is always and irrespective of the impacts needed for dredging of the bottom of a water body, if the amount of mass to be dredged exceeds 500 cubic metres, except for the maintenance of public waterways, and for dumping of dredged masses in Finnish territorial waters in the Baltic Sea, except for insignificantly small amounts.

1259. As for dumping of dredged bottom masses in inland waters, a permit of the Regional State Administrative Agency is needed only depending on the assessed impacts. This may sound illogical, as the need of control may be at least similar also in inland waters, but the provision (already inserted in the previous Water Act) is ultimately based on the 1992 Convention for the Protection of the Marine Environment of the Baltic Sea Area (the Helsinki Convention). The polluting constituents of the mass are specifically taken into account in the permit consideration. In the current Water Act, the possibilities for this are nevertheless smaller than pursuant to the previous Water Act. When a permit for dredging or dumping is decided upon by the Regional State Administrative Agency in accordance with the Water Act and there is a risk of pollution, also the substantive provisions of the Environmental Protection Act on provisions to be laid down in a permit are applied in addition to the provisions of the Water Act (section 10(3) of Chapter 3 of the Water Act). In the previous water act, the scope of partial application of the Environmental Protection Act was larger than this, because also the provisions thereof on legal preconditions for a permit were covered. In practice, the provisions of the Environmental Protection Act have been applied especially on permits to dredge and dump masses containing TBT compounds.

In practice, the Finnish Transport Infrastructure Agency is the main permit holder for major projects.

1260. If no permit of the Regional State Administrative Agency is needed, the (probably very small-scale) dredging may anyhow be allowed also to others than the owner, by force of a general right, but only if harm to the owners or pollution pursuant to the Environmental Protection Act is caused (section 6 of Chapter 2). A prior notification to the authorities and to the owner(s) and to the Centre for Economic Development, Transport and the Environment (environmental division, as supervisory authority) has to be submitted anyway (sections 6(3) and 15 of Chapter 2). And if no permit of the Regional State Administrative Agency is needed, also the dumping (depositing) in a water area is allowed also to others than the owner, by force of a general right (section 6 of Chapter 2). *See also* paragraphs 468, 469, 593, 1242, 1258 and 1259.

1261. Also the use of existing waterways may be environmentally controversial because of swelling. In some cases, speed limits have been set for ferryboats (which today takes place according to the Water Traffic Act), and compensation claims have been dealt with by the Regional State Administrative Agencies.

1262. Concerning motor boating and other water traffic, specific regulations on the laying down of local prohibitions or restrictions are contained in the Water Traffic Act (782/2019). If necessary for the protecting of traffic, environment, fisheries, or other business, or to safeguard common recreational use or other public interest, the Transport and Communications Agency is empowered to forbid motor boating or other traffic by watercraft in a specified water area, with or without a time limitation (section 101(1) of the Water Traffic Act). The Agency may also forbid or restrict the use of certain motor-driven watercraft in a specified water area, if the use would cause particularly significant disadvantage to nature or other environment, fisheries, or other business, or to safeguard common recreational use or other public interest (section 101(2)). A prohibition or restriction, other than speed limit, does not cover use of watercraft which is necessary for work or location of dwelling or by severely disabled person, unless differently in the decision for weighty reasons ordered (section 101(3)).

The procedure (section 102) may be initiated by the municipality, any member of the municipality, or a concerned authority, association or water area owner, or the Finnish Transport Infrastructure Agency, a Centre for Economic Development, Transport and the Environment, or the Transport and Communications Agency itself. The decisions may, after compulsory request for administrative rectification, be applied to the Regional Administrative Court (section 133).

1263. A permit by the Municipal Environmental Protection Authority is required for repeated or permanent motor boat races, training or other similar event in a fixed area, except for areas assigned in a Detailed Pan or for which an Environmental Permit pursuant to the Environmental Protection Act has been granted. If the event is extended to more than one municipality, the Centre for Economic Development, Transport and the Environment of the region is the permit authority. The issuing of a permit requires that sufficient safety requirements are met and unreasonable disadvantage to nature or other environment, fisheries, other business, common recreational use or other public interest is not caused. The consent of the owner of the water area is needed (section 106).

Even for a single event a permit is needed, if significant harm to the environment is to be expected.

1264. The Act on the Safety of and Emission Requirements for Certain Recreational Craft (1712/2015), implementing the Recreational Craft Directive[61] is aimed to safeguard compliance with the applicable requirements of products under the Act in order to protect the health and safety of persons, property and the environment against the hazardous properties of recreational watercraft, personal watercraft and equipment and against exhaust and noise emissions from recreational watercraft and personal watercraft. In addition, the provisions of the Act on the Market Surveillance of Certain Products (1137/2016, as amended) are applicable.

III. Timber Floating

1265. The floating of timber took up an extensive subsection of the previous Water Act, including both the floating activities themselves and construction projects. Floating has for a long time constituted an important means of timber transport, the right to which has been guaranteed by the rules on public use of water bodies. Nevertheless, the traditional form of floating, loose driving, has practically ceased to exist. In brooks and small rivers it was stopped for the most part already during the 1960s. Before that, thousands of kilometres of natural brooks with valuable fish stocks were mechanically cleared for floating purposes, though many of them were never actually used. The restoration of these brooks for recreational and fishing purposes after the cancelling of old floating routes has been a task of the authorities since the 1970s. In this regard the SAC has held that even the restoration of brooks is a duty of the floating authorities. As for the large river systems, the *Kemi* river in Lapland was the last floating river (until 1992).

1266. Floating as such has no polluting impacts (eventual bark litter, or noise from operating sites, excepted), but it may be environmentally rather problematic otherwise from the viewpoints of fisheries, waterway connections and recreational use. The traditional conflict between timber floating and water power plants in turn has mainly become history.

1267. Another form of floating is the towing of timber bundles. It is still economically important – and significant also from the environmental viewpoint – in certain water systems and some coastal sea areas. The current Water Act merely envisages towing of bundles, related measures included and the provisions thereon are contained in section 9 of the Water Act. Where floating (i.e., bundle operations) are allowed, the operator has, in addition to the very floating in water, certain general rights to perform measures in alien water areas, and some more powers may be granted by the Regional State Administrative Agency.

1268. The environmental impacts of bundle floating are concentrated in the few areas where the timber is dropped into the water from motor vehicles and where it is again taken out of the water. The nuisance such as swells and noise caused to

61. Directive 2013/53/EU of the European Parliament and of the Council of 20 Nov. 2013 on recreational craft and personal watercraft and repealing Directive 94/25/EC.

neighbouring properties – often summer homes – and to fish stocks makes that these operating sites are not always welcomed. A permit of the Regional State Administrative Agency is always necessary (section 3(1)(10) of Chapter 3). The regular permitting provisions of the Water Act are applicable, weighing of interests included. When permits are granted, they normally include provisions, including, e.g., fish planting obligations. The damage for nuisance to neighbours is compensated ex officio at the same time.

The bundle operating sites may be problematic also from the viewpoint of land use planning. The floating networks are normally much larger than a municipality. This is one reason why floating is partly taken into account in regional planning. However, the legal effects of a Regional Plan on the implementation of the Water Act imply a difficult complex of judicial problems (compare Part III, Chapter 3, §2).

IV. Drainage Projects

1269. Drainage projects are traditionally an important group of projects under Water Law, often with environmental problems. There was a time when they were encouraged by all legislative means and subsidies. In many parts of the country, plenty of wetlands and even lakes have been changed by draining into cultivated land or forests. However, many projects totally failed, the destroying of a lake being the only result of the drainage efforts. Consequently, the provisions for drainage were repeatedly tightened from the nineteenth century onwards. The next stages of the process were the 1987 and 1991 amendments of the then Water Act, by which certain forms of draining were prohibited or controlled on environmental grounds, and the 1996 amendment, which made the smallest ponds (northern Finland excluded) and streams protected natural habitats (*see* paragraphs 969 and 1270). But even after that the rules in a way favoured the active party at the expense of other interests. The initiator of a drainage project may oblige others whose areas would be drained not only to allow the infringement but also to take share in the expenses. This has been the case even if the aim is to acquire new land for cultivation; a result which was simultaneously counteracted by agricultural policy legislation and which was finally amended in 1997. In the current Water Act, the provisions have been balanced further, but the main elements still exist.

1270. The drainage projects are divided into two legal categories. In the current Water Act, the smaller projects are called ditching (Chapter 5) and the larger lowering of mean water level (subcategory of alteration of mean water level in Chapter 6). Ditching as a category includes normal draining of especially cultivated land and forests on various scales, but also the clearing of natural brooks and even total draining of small ponds (of which some are from 1997 automatically protected as natural habitats). Additionally, the rules on lowering partly also apply to embankments and major river clearings. The legal difference between the two categories is important, because ditching is basically free of proper permit control, whereas a permit from the Regional State Administrative Agency is normally needed for projects for the alteration of the water level. The same dualism in the previous Water Act, as it originally stood, was the basic reason for one the most famous environmental conflicts with civil disobedience in Finland's history, the lake *Koijärvi* case in the 1970s and 1980s. From 1987, largely as a result of the *Koijärvi* debate, no lake with natural values and in the present Water Act no lake, large or small, can be lowered any more pursuant to the ditching provisions.

1271. An administrative procedure may however be necessary also for a ditching project on various grounds, e.g., in order to realize the right to make a ditch on another's property or to settle the relationships between the landowners who would gain an advantage from the project, the advantage being understood in the traditional sense of drainage. Basically, the Municipal Environmental Protection Authorities are competent in the former cases (sections 5, 7 and 9–14 of Chapter 5), whereas a specific ad hoc procedure (sections 15 and 31–39 of Chapter 5) is to be held for the latter, the Vaasa Regional Administrative Court being the first appellate body concerning both of them. But neither the Municipal Environmental Protection Authority nor the ad hoc procedure makes a real consideration of the permit possible. In principle it is only a matter of realizing a pre-existing right to ditch in a proper manner. Of course the possible necessity of a permit by the Regional State Administrative Agency is controlled at the same time. In addition, according to the current Water Act (section 6 of Chapter 5), a prior notification to the State supervisory authority under the Water Act (Centre for Economic Development, Transport and the Environment) has to be submitted on planned ditching, unless insignificant.

However, in certain cases a permit of the Regional State Administrative Agency is necessary for ditching (section 3 of Chapter 5). This is today the case always when pollution or harmful alteration in a water body, as specified in the said section, would result. The permit consideration is based on the normal weighing of interests.

1272. In projects regarded as aiming to lower the water level, a permit of the Regional State Administrative Agency is practically always needed, because at least alteration of water body and also some harm by it is evident. The general provisions on permit considerations in Chapter 3 are applied. In addition, there are specific prerequisites connected to the relationships between those who would gain drainage advantage and those having shares in the lake in question. From the environmental viewpoint, the most important additional precondition is that no permit can be granted for such lowering (unless required by public necessity) that results in: (1) such essential impairment of possibilities to use a property in shore area that causes unreasonable harm or damage to the owner or possessor who has not consented, or (2) significant impairment of specific value for the conservation of the nature (section 4 of Chapter 6)

1273. A total draining of a lake, which from 1987 under the previous Water Act was absolutely forbidden, unless the lake was insignificant and had no specific value for the conservation of nature, is not at all covered by the scope of Chapter 6 of the present Water Act, at least not pursuant to the wording.

From 1997, all ponds with an area up to one hectare south of Lapland are protected as natural habitats (*see* Chapter 2, §3 above), irrespective of other provisions of the Water Act.

1274. Otherwise, the permit decision rules are the same as for water management measures in general, which in practice means weighing of interests. Here the environmental interests may have a great significance despite the specific protection rules described above.

1275. Chapter 6 of the Water Act also encompasses embankments and agricultural river clearings. As for these, the general permit consideration rules in Chapter 3 are the only (but also practically relevant) possibility for environmental aspects to be taken into account.

1276. Regarding both ditching (forest ditching included) and drainage-aimed embankments, among others, a permit of the Regional State Administrative Authority under the Water Act is needed where the channelled or pumped waters would imply a polluting discharge. In this case, the substantive provisions of the Environmental Protection Act on provisions to be laid down in a permit (but not anymore those on preconditions for a permit) are additionally applied (*see* correspondingly paragraph 1259).

V. Water Level Regulation

1277. The alteration of the mean water level may in practice also include regulation of water discharge and water level, in which case the projects are highly complex. But as such, the water level regulation makes up a separate legal category, now regulated in Chapter 7 of the Water Act. In Finland water level regulation has been traditionally connected with hydroelectric plants. Regulating a major lake (or a man-made lake) makes it possible to adjust the supply of energy to the annual, weekly or daily fluctuation of energy demand. However, the environmental impacts of a regulation project may be significant. In practice, many of the major lakes have been regulated for decades. In certain cases this means that normal use of shorelands is impossible. The interests of the environment, recreation, agriculture and fisheries are often opposed to the projects. Moreover, large dams require special care and attention in both construction and maintenance, in order to avoid the significant risks caused by accidental floods.

1278. Besides the Water Act, a special Dam Safety Act (494/2009) is applied to major and medium-sized dams (irrespective of the purpose thereof). *See* paragraphs 1379–1394 below. For the most significant dams under the Dam Safety Act and the Water Act, an EIA is always required by the Environmental Impact Procedures Decree.

1279. Because regulation has traditionally been legally regarded as comparable with construction measures, the permit holder has been very strongly protected, and it has been difficult to alter the permit decisions later on. This has largely been regarded as unsatisfactory. A periodical permit reviewing system was enacted in 1991, but it only refers to new regulation permits. A mechanism for the existing permits was finally created by the amendments of the previous Water Act in 1994, but that was in many respects a moderate compromise as for the substantive provisions, and the procedure is rather complex. The effectiveness of the system is reduced by the fact that the Centres for Economic Development, Transport and the Environment have a kind of monopoly to initiate the procedure in the Water Act, and due to certain history-related administrative changes, the centres themselves are today also the most common permit holders concerning water level regulation.

1280. The traditional water level regulation projects were designed only for the purposes of power production. Later on, more multipurpose solutions have been developed. The State, represented by the Centre for Economic Development, Transport and the Environment (environmental division) of the region, is often the formal permit holder, even if someone else would profit most. Water level regulation is also possible, e.g., water supply purposes.

1281. The permit decision rules as well as the provisions which may be imposed in the permit are, with a few exceptions, the same as those for water management permits in general. In the weighing of interests, however, the advanced possibility to use hydroelectric power is taken into account in the same way as in water power plant permits (*see* paragraph 1255). One typical category of provisions consists of obligations concerning fisheries management (planting, etc.).

1282. Those outsiders who would gain benefit through a regulation project in permit proceedings have the right to participate by making a notification to the permit authority (Regional State Administrative Agency). A participant shall contribute to the costs, and a statutory Regulation Company pursuant to section 6 of Chapter 7 and Chapter 12 of the Water Act will be established to jointly manage the project and hold the permit.

VI. Rising of Water Level

1283. Permanent rising of water level in a water body (in practice in a lake) is provided as a subcategory of alteration of mean water level in Chapter 6. Permit by the Regional State Administrative Agency is always required for permanent transformation of a land area into a water area by permanent rising of the mean water level in a water body (section 3 of Chapter 3 of the Water Act). The purpose of rising may vary, but the present rules were particularly drafted for restoration of previously (often for agricultural purposes) lowered lakes, now for purposes of recreation, fisheries, environment, water supply, etc. Application for a rising permit may be made by: (1) owner of a property that would gain benefit from the rising, (2) an association under the Water Act (*see* section 9 of Chapter 6 and Chapter 12 of the Water Act) made up of those who gain private benefit from the rising, (3) a shareholders' association for a registered village's common areas or a single shareholder, (4) a State authority and (5) the municipality (municipalities) at stake (section 3 of Chapter 6 of the Water Act).

1284. The general provisions in Chapter 3 on permit considerations are applicable. In addition, no permit for rising may be granted for such rising (unless required by public necessity) that results in (1) such essential impairment of possibilities to use a property in shore area that causes unreasonable harm or damage to the owner or possessor who has not consented, or (2) significant impairment of specific value for the conservation of the nature (section 4 of Chapter 6 of the Water Act)

1285. Before the present Water Act it was not possible to oblige those (e.g., shore land owners) who gain benefit from the rising to participate in the costs of the project (unlike in lowering for drainage purposes). Pursuant to section 6 of Chapter 6 of the Water Act, the permit authority (Regional State Administrative Agency) may now oblige those who gain private benefit to participate in the performance costs in proportion of his share of benefits.

VII. Man-Made Lakes

1286. Man-made lakes (reservoirs) constructed for hydroelectric, water supply or recreational purposes are not a legal project category as such, although provisions of Chapter 6 on water level rising may be applicable. The proper water level regulation rules (Chapter 7) are in a man-made lake the same as for natural lakes, whereas the actual creation of the lake is regarded as an ordinary water management project (Chapter 3 as such). In the permit decision the applicant may be granted the right to expropriate third parties' land areas which would be flooded by the future reservoir, which may in practice be very large. A proposed hydroelectric project in Lapland (the *Vuotos* reservoir, 220,000 hectares) has been a controversial issue through the 1990s. The standpoint of the government was finally positive, but the permit application (of a major energy company) still depended on the Water Court and also on the Vaasa Regional Administrative Court. In December 2002, the permit application was finally rejected by the SAC, on environmental grounds (*see* paragraphs 31 and 1245). No new application has been submitted.

VIII. Water Intake

1287. Water supply projects in the previous Water Act were of two categories, one for the abstraction of surface water and one for that of groundwater. In the current Water Act, the provisions are mainly uniform instead (Chapter 4 of the Act).

1288. Small-scale intake from a water body or from groundwater is allowed to the owner of the area without a permit, as specified in section 2 of Chapter 3 of the Water Act. Also intake from alien area may be allowed (sections 3 and 4 of Chapter 4), and even general rights to temporary minor intake by anyone are provided (section 4 of Chapter 2). Otherwise, the need to have a permit of the Regional State Administrative Agency depends, regarding owners and others alike, on the in advance assessed harmful impacts pursuant to section 2 of Chapter 3, but irrespective of this, a permit is needed always for water intake to a water supply system under the Water Supply and Sewerage Act, or to one who supplies such a system with water, and to intake of water to be used elsewhere, and to other intake of groundwater of at least 250 cubic metres per day or more (section 3 of Chapter 3).

1289. In addition to the general provisions on permit considerations, section 5 of Chapter 4 contains rules on adjusting different water supply needs in a permit. If there is not enough water for all actual needs, the following priority order is applied: (1) intake of water to be used in the nearby area for ordinary use by single properties, (2) intake of water for municipal water supply in the local area (3) intake of water for local industries or otherwise for local use, as well as intake for municipal water supply outside the local area and (4) intake of water to be channelled or conveyed for use elsewhere for other purpose than municipal water supply.

1290. A permit is always needed also for the processing of artificial groundwater, and for re-infiltration of groundwater in order to improve the quality of water (section 3 of Chapter 3). In such projects, the bans on polluting groundwater and soil in sections 16 and 17 of the Environmental Protection Act shall be observed, as well as section 28 of the same Act on the need to have an Environmental Permit for certain reasons (section 1(2) of Chapter 4). Intake of artificial groundwater is regarded as intake of groundwater under Chapter 4.

1291. Dealing with a water intake project is largely a matter of regulation between conflicting and competing water supply interests, although the interests of environmental protection can be relevant, too. A good example is the 1980s water supply project of the coastal city of Turku in south-western Finland, to which water would be conducted from the inland lake *Pyhäjärvi*. This lake is famous for its clean water and exceptional natural conditions, reflected by the unusually high levels of fish (mainly vendace) production. The permit then granted was actually a compromise between water supply interests and environmental interests. Later on, a different water supply project, based on artificial groundwater processed from river water at *Alastaro* has been commenced, with several environmental and nature-related implicated, *see* SAC 2008:58.

1292. Concerning the intake of groundwater, all natural water springs and fountains are (from January 1997) protected by the Water Act as natural habitats (*see* paragraph 969). There is an exemption power vested in the Regional State Administrative Agencies, but the preconditions for an exception are the same as in the Nature Conservation Act. According to judicial practice, the protection of the Water Act habitats is taken into account also in the permit procedures pursuant to the Environmental Protection Act or the Soil Excavation Act.

1293. As for the protection of groundwater, there are special rules safeguarding individual water intakes and aquifers from dangerous activities (*see* paragraph 445). Irrespective of these rules, a permit from the Regional State Administrative Agency is needed, e.g., for the extraction of soil substances, if the harmful altering of groundwater provided in section 2 of Chapter 3 of the Water Act would be caused. For reasons of clarity and security, permit is unconditionally needed for a measure other than water intake if an amount of at least 250 cubic meters groundwater per day would due to such a measure be removed from the groundwater occurrence (section 3 of Chapter 3 of the Act).

1294. On the regulation on water supply and sewerage services, *see* paragraphs 424, 425, 428–435, 438, 445 and 1242.

IX. Other Forms of Water Management Projects

1295. There are many additional types of construction projects without a specific formal category. The normal construction rules are hence applied. For example, construction of quays, piers and jetties, often linked with water area filling and shoreline transforming, is a very common problem affecting the shores in front of summer dwellings. If harmful altering of bodies of water would be caused, even based on the interests of one single neighbour, a permit from the permit authority, i.e., the Regional State Administrative Agency is required. Public interests of landscape protection are also involved, especially if there are many such projects in the area. It is not always easy to determine whether permit application is required. It is in any case not a matter of pure equality: a project may even be denied even if a neighbour was once allowed to make a similar construction without a permit.

1296. Sand extraction from the seabed is not a legal category of its own, but it is treated under the normal rules on water management. Impacts on fish regeneration are here one of the main concerns relevant to permit decisions and permit conditions.

1297. One more project type is worth mentioning: the fish farms in the sea. Here the two main regimes of the original Water Act were united; a permit may have been needed both because of the ban on altering water bodies (the construction) and because of the ban on polluting water bodies (the farming). Both permit matters were normally dealt with at the same time by the then Water Court and included in one decision. Also today, only one permit procedure is needed, but substantively the Environmental Protection Act is applied instead of the Water Act, as far as polluting impacts are concerned (on the mixed projects, *see* paragraphs 180, 235 and 1243). On the basis of harmful altering, the general permit rules of the Water Act on water management projects are also applied. In practice the impacts on the landscape may also be relevant.

§4. Supervision and Enforcement According to the Water Act

1298. The supervision of activities covered by the Water Act is vested in the Centres for Economic Development, Transport and the Environment and the

Municipal Environmental Protection Authorities in a very similar way than that pursuant to the Environmental Protection Act (*see* Part I, Chapter 1, §20). Nevertheless, the competence regarding administrative orders or prohibitions is almost entirely vested in the Regional State Administrative Agency. The powers of the supervisory authorities concerning access to information and right to inspections are provided in section 3 of Chapter 14 of the Water Act.

1299. If illegal activities come to light, the supervisory State authority, i.e., the Centre for Economic Development, Transport and the Environment (environmental division) and the Municipal Environmental Protection Authority, have, taking the nature of the case into account, a duty (section 2 of Chapter 14) to:

(a) advise the person in question to put an end to the illegal activity;
(b) make an application for administrative injunction (enforcement order on prohibition or reinstatement, *see* Part V, Chapter 1) to the Regional State Administrative Agency, pursuant to section 4 of Chapter 14 of the Water Act; or
(c) inform the police of the offence, in order to initiate a criminal law pretrial, where the act is not insignificant.

Regarding (b), a coercive prohibition or order may also be addressed to a new owner or possessor of a property, although he himself would not be the originator of the illegal situation. – section 5 of Chapter 14 contains procedural provisions (hearing, etc.) as a rule, a conditional fine or a threat of taking the neglected action at the responsible party's expense is imposed at the same time ad in the same administrative decision (section 8 of Chapter 14). The provisions of the Administrative Injunctions (Conditional Fines) Act (1113/1990) are here applicable.

1300. If no enforcement procedure before the Regional State Administrative Authority has been initiated by a supervisory authority (the Centre for Economic Development, Transport and the Environment or the Municipal Environmental Protection Authority), it may be initiated (section 14 of Chapter 14) by: (1) a party, by which anyone whose right, interest or obligation may be concerned is meant (section 7 of Chapter 11); (2) a registered association or foundation the aim of which is protection of environment, health or nature or promotion of amenity of an inhabited area, provided that the relevant impacts of the project appear in its geographical area of activities; (3) the municipality where the project is performed, and any municipality in the geographical area of which the environmental impacts of the project appear; or (4) other authority representing public interests, such as (the fisheries unit of) the Centre for Economic Development, Transport and the Environment,

1301. The forum of the criminal proceedings is an ordinary District Court. Also here the supervisory authority has the procedural powers of a party.

1302. In practice, administrative enforcement is far more important. If necessary, a supervisory authority may (as may also the offender and an interested person who has the required supervisory measures) appeal the decision of the Regional

State Administrative Agency to the Regional Administrative Court (in Vaasa) and further, subject to leave of appeal, to the SAC.

1303. Instant coercive measures by a supervisory authority are possible, if immediate harm or danger to safety, health or other important public interest or significant danger to alien property is caused by operations that are taken in violation of the Water Act or provisions under it (section 10 of Chapter 14).

1304. The provisions and procedures on administrative enforcement in Chapter 14 of the Water Act, right to initiate the proceedings included, are also used for decision-making on environmental liability and remediation under the Act on the Remediation of Certain Damages Caused to the Environment (383/2009), as far as measures or omissions related to water impounding or intake, performed in violation of the Water Act or provisions under it, are at stake. If such a measure or such an omission causes significant adverse altering of a water body or groundwater, or damage to the nature as provided in section 5a of the Nature Conservation Act, or immediately imposes a risk of one of these, the Regional State Administrative Agency shall, in addition to a possible ordinary administrative injunction based on section 4 of Chapter 14 (section 6 of Chapter 14), order the one who has caused the harm to take necessary measures to prevent or keep the adverse effects as minimal as possible, or to take remediation measures pursuant to the Act on the Remediation of Certain Damages Caused to the Environment. The same provisions of Chapter 14 also apply to damage to nature that has been intentionally or by neglect caused through other measure or omission than those mentioned above. What has been presented on items related to the status and use of waters in a Water Management Plan pursuant to the Act on the Arranging of Water Management and Marine Waters Management (1299/2004) shall be taken into account when the significance of a detrimental impact on water body or groundwater is assessed. The responsible party has a duty to immediately notify the Centre for Economic Development, Transport and the Environment, and to take measures necessary to prevent or confine the damage (section 7 of Chapter 14).

§5. DIRECTIVE-BASED WATER MANAGEMENT

I. Implementation of the Water Management Framework Directive

1305. The Directive of the European Parliament and of the Council establishing a framework for Community action in the field of water policy (2000/60/EC, the Water policy framework directive) is mainly implemented through the Act on the Arranging of Water Management and Marine Waters Management (1299/2004, in force from 31 December 2004, with later amendments) and the Government decree on the Arranging of Water Management (1040/2006, in force from 1 December 2006). Certain (partly amended) provisions of the Water Supply and Sewerage Act, the Water Act and the Environmental Protection Act as well as of the Public Health

Act are likewise relevant. Also Directive 2006/118/EC on the Protection of groundwater against pollution and deterioration was (in part) implemented through the original Act and Decree on the Arranging of Water Management.

1306. After the entering into force of original Act on the Arranging of Water Management (1299/2004), its scope of application has been extended to cover also the implementation of Directive 2008/56/EC establishing a framework for community action in the field of marine environmental policy (Marine Strategy Framework Directive). Hence, from April 2011, the title of the Act has been the current Act on the Arranging of Water Management and Marine Waters Management.

II. Arranging of Water Management

1307. In the Act on the Arranging of Water Management and Marine Waters Management, surface water refers to water-covered areas, coastal waters, transitional waters and territorial waters. Groundwater means water which is below the surface of the ground in the saturation zone and in direct contact with the bedrock or subsoil. Coastal water again is defined as means surface water on the landward side of a line, every point of which is at a distance of one nautical mile on the seaward side from the nearest point of the baseline from which the breadth of territorial waters is measured, and which at some point is bounded by a river. Body of surface water means a discrete and significant element of surface waters such as a lake, reservoir, brook, river or canal, a part of a brook, river or canal, a transitional water or a stretch of coastal water, whereas body of groundwater means a distinct volume of groundwater within a porous and permeable subsurface layer or bedrock formation that allows either a significant flow of groundwater or the abstraction of significant quantities of groundwater. River basin (literally: area of a water system, such systems in Finland are very complex and largely made up of other bodies than rivers only) means an area from which all surface run-off flows through a brook, lake, river or estuary (in practice, it is always question of a river and its estuary) into the sea, and part of basin the area (of land) from which all surface run-off flows through a brook, lake or river into a particular body of water. Transitional waters are bodies of surface water in the vicinity of river mouths which are partly saline in character as a result of their proximity to coastal waters but which are substantially influenced by freshwater flows. Marine waters consist of: (a) waters, the seabed and subsoil on the seaward side of the baseline from which the extent of territorial waters is measured extending to the outer border of the Finnish economic zone, and (b) coastal waters, their seabed and their subsoil, insofar as particular aspects of the environmental status of the marine environment are not already addressed through the provisions on water management. A marine ecosystem is a complex of organisms and the environment in which they live, and status of marine environment the overall state of the environment in marine waters, taking into account the structure, function and processes of the constituent marine ecosystems together with natural physiographic, geographic, biological, geological and climatic factors, as well as physical, acoustic and chemical conditions, including those resulting from human activities inside or outside the area concerned.

1308. The Act on the Arranging of Water Management and Marine Waters Management includes provisions on the arrangement of water management, covering the relevant inventory work, cooperation and participatory measures in the Water Management Areas, as well as on the pertinent transboundary cooperation, where applicable. As a general aim is specified that waters are protected, improved and reinstated in such a manner that the status of surface water and groundwater is not deteriorated and that the status thereof is at least good. In addition to water quality, also the sufficiency of waters, sustainable use of waters, water services and the economic analysis thereof, flood control, recreation, diseases spread by waters, protection of aquatic ecosystems and terrestrial ecosystems and wetlands directly depending on them are taken into account. The environmental objectives provided in the Act are in detail specified in the Decree 1040/2006.

1309. From 2015, the Act additionally contains a mechanism for the determining of groundwater areas and classification thereof (Chapter 2a). This Chapter is of a domestic nature only. *See* paragraph 1228.

1310. The area of Finland, sea areas included, is divided into Water Management Areas, as specified in the Government decree on Water Management Areas (1303/2004; amended by 754/2020). According to the Act on the Arranging of Water Management and Marine Waters Management, a Water Management Area consists of one river basin district or of several river basins. Bodies of coastal water and bodies of groundwater shall be included in the most appropriate Water Management Area bounding them. In cases of transboundary river basins, the parts within Finland belong to the Water Management Area. An international Water Management Area shall be formed where river basins extend into the territory of another country, as separately provided.

The Management Areas specified in the Decree are: (1) The *Vuoksi* Area, (2) the *Kymi* River and Gulf of Finland Area, (3) the *Kokemäenjoki* River, Archipelagic Sea and Bothnian Sea Area, (4) the *Oulujoki* river and *Iijoki* River Area and (5) the *Kemijoki* River area. Moreover, there is a common Area with Sweden for the *Tornionjoki* River catchment area and adjoining sea area, as well as a common Area with Norway for the catchment areas of the rivers *Teno*, *Näätämöjoki* and *Paatsjoki*.

1311. The general guidance of the enforcement of the water management regulations is vested in the Ministry of the Environment and the Ministry of Agriculture and Forestry. The Finnish Environment Institute and Finnish Game and Fisheries Research Institute participate as expert bodies in the implementation. The Ministry of the Environment is responsible for cooperation with other Baltic Sea States regarding planning of marine water management. At regional level, the Centres for Economic Development, Transport and the Environment are in a key position. Because the boundaries of the Water Management Areas are mainly nature-based and hence do not coincide with the administrative areas of the Centres for Economic Development, Transport and the Environment, one of the Centres is designed as the Adjusting Centre for Economic Development, Transport and the Environment for each Management Area.

Several other authorities take part in the enforcement. It is the task of the Ministry of the Environment and the Ministry of Agriculture and Forestry to perform general guidance on the enforcement. The Finnish Environment Institute, the Natural Resources Institute Finland (Luke), the Finnish Meteorological Institute and, regarding State properties such as the Public Water Areas, the Metsähallitus.

1312. For the purposes of collecting environmental information under the Act, the authorities and civil servants at stake have access to alien land and water areas. They are entitled to make checks and investigations, palace measuring devices, make measurements and take samples and save sounds and pictures, areas used by permanent dwelling excluded (section 28a). Unnecessary harm and damage shall be avoided. Possible damages are compensated pursuant to the Expropriation Act. Such tasks may also be assigned to private actors, having the criminal law responsibility of a civil servant in the task.

1313. For water resources management purposes, surface waters shall be divided into different categories according to their geographical and scientific characteristics (section 7 of the Act). Regarding groundwater, the characteristics to be determined are the location and boundaries of important groundwater areas and other groundwater areas suitable for water supply, and the general bedrock and soil characteristics. In determining these characteristics, waters may be examined as entire entities. It is hence allowed here to envisage waters as (large) entities. This provision is related to the extremely complicated and diverse morphological detailed structure of many Finnish surface water body conglomerates, as well to the fact that Finnish groundwater areas are often not definable as separate bodies.

1314. The surface waters and groundwater bodies shall be further classified according to the strength of the impact of (or the extent of modification caused by) human activity (section 8). The surface water bodies and groundwater bodies (or, in fact, the status thereof) shall be further classified according to strength of the impact of human activity. The status of a surface water body is determined by the poorer of its ecological status and its chemical status. The ecological status of surface water shall be classified as high, good, moderate, poor or bad. The classification shall be established in proportion to reference conditions. As to heavily modified and artificial surface water bodies, reference condition is made up of the best achievable ecological status, in proportion to which the status of each such body is classified as high, good, moderate, poor or bad. The status of a surface water body is good, if it meets the environmental quality standards for the hazardous substances designated by EU legislation and defined by Decree. The status of groundwater bodies shall be classified as good or bad, according to the chemical and quantitative characteristics thereof. Detailed provisions on the classification are set forth in the Decree 1040/2006.

1315. Monitoring of surface waters and groundwaters (section 9) in a Water Management Area shall be organized in such a way that a consistent and comprehensive overview is gained for the status of the waters. The water monitoring programmes drawn up by the Centres for Economic Development, Transport and the

Environment shall be coordinated within each Water Management Area and appended to the Water Management Plan. Monitoring by individual permit holders as provided by the Water Act or the Environmental Protection Act shall be taken into account, as appropriate, in drawing up the monitoring programmes.

1316. More detailed provisions on the following are issued by Government decree (section 10):

(1) the division of surface water categories according to geographical and scientific characteristics, the examination of artificial and heavily modified surface waters, determination of the comparison State peculiar to each surface water category and selection of areas for comparison;
(2) examination of groundwater characteristics;
(3) detailed content of the accounts drawn up on the status and use of waters and of the economic analysis of water services, and the drawing up of this information;
(4) monitoring of waters and the monitoring programme; and
(5) the criteria for classifying surface waters and groundwaters. Detailed provisions on other similar items may additionally be issued by Government decree where necessary to implement the Framework Directive 2000/60/EC.

1317. Regarding each Water Management Area, it is the task of the Centre(s) for Economic development, Transport and the Environment to work out an analysis of the characteristics of the waters, a review of the impact of human activity on the status of surface waters and on groundwater and the economic analyses of water use. Moreover, the centre shall collect the information on areas that are under protection pursuant to the EU legislation and specified by Decree, collect the necessary information on areas assigned for the abstraction of water intended for human consumption, prepare the classification of the status of waters, prepare the monitoring of waters and draft a monitoring programme.

1318. There is at least one Collaboration Group for each Water Management Area, being organized by the Adjusting the Centre for Economic Development, Transport and the Environment. Representatives of central State and municipal bodies, businesses, associations, water area owners and water users are invited to participate. For adjusting purposes, there is also a Steering Group composed of representatives of the Centres for Economic Development, Transport and the Environment at stake and of representatives of fisheries administration.

1319. A Water Management Plan for the Area shall summarize:

- data on the Water Management Area;
- data on the characteristics of the water bodies of the Area;
- amendments to a previous programme, where any;
- implemented measures, implemented temporary supplementary measures and on assessment of the effects of exceptional conditions;

- assessment of the achievement of the environmental objectives and account on the choice between options; and
- account on the standpoints put forward during the preparation and on the negotiations between State parties, and account on how the standpoints and negotiations have impacted the Programme and the choices.

A Marine Waters Management Plan under Chapter 4 of the Act shall be taken into account.

A Water Management Plan shall also include an environmental report as provided in the SEA Directive (2001/42/EC).

1320. A Programme of Measures shall be worked out for each Area to implement the applicable environmental objectives, taking the analysis on the characteristics of the waters and on the impacts of human activity thereon, as well as the economic analyses of water use into account. A Programme of Measures is dealt with as a part of the respective Water Management Plan. A Programme of Measures shall include:

- the basic measures, such as the general requirements provided by the legislation on waters and environmental protection (in detail specified in section 24 of and Annex 6 to the Decree 1040/2006; amended by 753/2020); and
- the supplementary measures, such as other administrative and economic means, agreements, reinstatement of water bodies and education and research projects (in detail specified in section 25 and Annex 6b of the Decree 1040/2006).

1321. Each Water Management Plan and Programme of Measures shall aim at preventing the deterioration of the status of surface and groundwater bodies and achieving at least a good status thereof. However, concerning artificial or heavily modified water bodies the status thereof shall not be deteriorated and they shall have at least good achievable ecological status and a good chemical status. Surface water bodies shall be protected, improved and reinstated in such a way that the status just mentioned is achievable at the latest in 2015. Respectively, groundwater bodies shall be protected, improved and reinstated in such a way that the good status is achievable at the latest in 2015. Moreover, the persistent and significant growth of the concentration of substances causing pollution of groundwater shall be prevented. The status of waters of areas aimed to be protected shall be at the level appropriate to the protection at the latest in 2015 (section 21).

The deadlines above may in the Water Management Plan be extended for the purposes of phased achievement of the objectives for water bodies, provided that this is the only option and no further deterioration appears in the status of the affected water body when the following conditions are met: improvement in the status of the water body within the plan validity period is technically or economically unreasonable, or natural conditions do not allow it; and the status of the water body is not deteriorated further. Extension is not allowed in more than two plan periods (=2016–2021 and 2022–2027), unless the natural conditions do not make possible improvements in time (section 25, as amended in 2020).

The status of waters is not regarded to be in breach of the environmental objectives, if the environmental objectives cannot be met due to an exceptional natural condition or accident, provided that the objectives cannot be met by available means.

1322. A surface water body which as a result of constructions or other physical alterations by human activity is changed in character, may in a Water Management Plan be designated as artificial or heavily modified, if the changes to the hydro morphological characteristics of that body which would be necessary for achieving good ecological status would have significant adverse effects on:

- navigation, including port facilities;
- recreation;
- water supply or production of hydroelectric power;
- water level regulation, flood risk management or land drainage; or
- other equally important sustainable human development activities.

It is moreover required that the beneficial objectives served by the artificial or modified characteristics of the water body cannot, for technical or economic reasons, reasonably be achieved by other means, which are a significantly better for the environment. The specific environmental objectives for artificial or heavily modified water bodies shall be presented in the Water Management Plan.

1323. Less stringent environmental objectives than generally required may be provided in a Water Management Plan when the body of water is so affected by human activity or its natural conditions are such that the achievement of the objectives would be infeasible or disproportionately expensive, and all the following conditions (section 24) are met:

- the benefits from uses of waters or loading of waters cannot be achieved by other means, which are significantly better to the environment;
- the disadvantages of the activities cannot be reduced without disproportionate costs;
- for surface waters, the best possible status is achieved, given the impacts that could not reasonably have been avoided due to the nature of the human activity or pollution;
- for groundwater, the least possible changes to good groundwater status, given impacts that could not reasonably have been avoided due to the nature of the human activity or pollution; and
- no further deterioration appears in the status of the affected body of water.

1324. During the preparation of a Water Management Plan (including the related Programme of Measures), publicity, information and participation by interested parties are arranged as provided in section 15 of the Arranging of Water Management and Marine Waters Management. The proposal to a plan, after being dealt with and adjusted by the Collaboration Group, is submitted to the Ministry of the Environment by the Adjusting Centre for Economic Development, Transport and the Environment. It is the task of the Cabinet to approve the Water Management Plans. A decision of the Cabinet can be appealed against on judicial grounds before the SAC by those affected, by municipalities, by authorities representing public interests and by such registered local or regional associations and foundations whose purpose is to promote protection of environment or nature and the geographical area of which the Water Management Plan concerns.

1325. The goals of water management set forth in a Water Management Plan and the combinations of measures set forth in a Programme of Measures shall be reviewed and updated every six years. The procedure here is the same as that for the approval of the first Water Management Plan, where appropriate.

1326. Due to the fact that many important obligations related to water management and water pollution prevention are set forth by general nationwide legislation, it has been assessed appropriate to avoid assessing the same requirements in the Water Management Plans or the Programmes of Measures. Hence a large group of general regulations (eighteen different parliamentary acts or Government decrees) are by the Decree 1040/2006 (section 26 and Annex 6) listed and as such declared to be part of the basic measures of each Water Management Area (but not updated later on).

1327. As groundwater quality standard pursuant to the said Decree 1040/2006 is regarded both a common EU standard expressed as the concentration of a particular pollutant group of pollutants or indicator of pollution in groundwater, which should not be exceeded in order to protect human health and the environment and a nationally stipulated threshold value provided in Article 2(2) of Directive 2006/118/EC on the protection of groundwater against pollution and deterioration.

1328. Where a new significant project is going to alter a water body physically, causing a failure to achieve good ecological status of surface water or good status of groundwater, a deviation from the environmental objective in section 21 is available (section 23 of the Act), provided that:

- the project is particularly important to public interest and significantly promotes sustainable development, public health or maintenance of human safety;
- all practicable steps are taken to mitigate the adverse impact on the status of the body of water; and
- the aimed benefits cannot be achieved by technically and economically reasonable and to the environment significantly better means other than by the modification of the water body.

1329. The deterioration of the status of a surface water body from high to good is not regarded as a breach of the environmental objectives (above), if the deterioration is caused by a new, significant, sustainable project and if the preconditions corresponding to those listed above are met. The Water Management Plan shall include an account on the preconditions and an account on the modifications in the water body and its status that are caused by the project.

1330. There is a general provision in section 28 of the Act on the Arranging of Water Management and Marine Waters Management providing generally that all State and municipal authorities shall in their activities, where applicable, take into account the Water Management Plans, the Marine Waters Management Plan and in a specific action plan, where in force.

1331. In the consideration regarding an Environmental Permit or decision due to a notification attention shall be paid to what in the Water Management Plan and the Marine Waters Management Plan has been presented on items pertaining to the State and use of the waters and marine environment of the area to be impacted (section 51 of the Environmental Protection Act). In the permit shall come out how the Water Management Plan and the Marine Waters Management Plan have been taken into account (section 43 of the Environmental Protection Act).

In the previous ordinary review of a valid Environmental Permit according to the previous Environmental Protection Act (*see* paragraphs 230–231) a Water Management Plan, a Marine Waters Management Plan and a Programme of Measures had to be taken into account. Because the present Environmental Protection Act has renounced such review (IED installations partly excepted), the influence of the Plans and Programmes has diminished respectively.

Regarding permit considerations according to the Water Act, in the weighing of interests (*see* paragraphs 1246 and 1247) attention has, among many other things, to be paid to what has been presented in a Water Management Plan concerning status of waters and use of waters. A permit decision shall include a comment on how the Water Management Plan has been taken into account.

1332. Government decree on Substances Dangerous and Harmful to the Aquatic Environment (1022/2006, amendments), aiming to implement in detail Directive 2000/60/EC concerning priority hazardous substances and Directive 2006/11/EC of the European parliament and of the council on pollution caused by certain dangerous substances discharged into the aquatic environment of the Community, has been issued on the basis of authorizations in the Environmental Protection Act, the Act on the Arranging of Water Management and Marine Waters Management, and the Water Supply and Sewerage Act. In practice, the Decree mainly functions within the permit and surveillance mechanisms of the Environmental Protection Act.

III. Marine Waters Management

1333. The provisions on marine waters management are also included in Chapter 4a of the Act on the Arranging of Water Management and Marine Waters Management. The Act is here complemented by Government decree on the Arranging of Marine Waters Management (980/2011).

1334. A Marine Waters Management Plan shall be prepared for Finnish territorial waters and the economic zone, by the Ministry of the environment, in cooperation with the Ministry of Agriculture and Forestry and the Ministry of Transport and Communications. The scientific characteristics of marine waters, the water management areas and the Water Management Plans shall be taken into account. The Centres for Economic Development, Transport and the Environment are responsible for coordination of planning. One of them is assigned the task of adjusting. In the Marine Waters Management Plan measures shall be presented by which the marine environment is protected and preserved, the deterioration of its status is prevented and marine ecosystems are restored in such a way that its good status can be maintained or achieved by 2020.

Measures shall be presented to reduce inputs in the marine environment and prevent and reduce other adverse impacts on the sea so that marine biodiversity can be safeguarded, and marine ecosystems, human health or legitimate uses of the sea are not significantly endangered.

1335. The plan shall include an environmental account and an initial assessment of the status of the marine environment, comprising (section 26c, as amended by 908/2020): (1) the essential features and impacts of marine waters and an analysis on the current status; (2) anthropogenic pressures on the status of marine environment, covering the qualitative and quantitative mix of the various pressures and discernible trends, as well as impacts on marine environment, covering the main cumulative and synergetic effects; (3) an economic and social analysis of the use of those waters and of the cost of degradation of the marine environment; and (4) assessments made in the Water Management Plans and within international marine protection cooperation. On the basis of the initial assessment, a good status of marine environment and its characteristics shall be determined by using descriptors separately laid down, taking pressures and impacts by human activity into account. The environmental status is regarded good, when the sea is ecologically diverse and balanced, dynamic, within its intrinsic conditions clean, healthy and productive, and its use is sustainable and safeguards the potential for uses and activities by current and future generations.

The plan shall also include, on the basis of the initial assessment, a comprehensive set of environmental targets for the marine waters in order to achieve their good environmental status. In the laying down of environmental targets and in the determination of the characteristics, pressures and impacts that describe them, and significant transboundary impacts and compatibility with national, union and international targets shall also be taken into account.

1336. The environmental targets, or the achieving of good environmental status of marine environment in every aspect, can be exempted in individual cases, if caused by: (1) action or inaction that is not caused by national measures, (2) natural cause, (3) force majeure and (4) modifications or alterations to the physical characteristics of marine waters brought about by actions taken for overriding public interest which outweigh the negative impact on the environment, including any transboundary impact, provided that it is safeguarded that the modifications or alterations to the physical characteristics of marine waters do not permanently prevent or endanger the achieving of good status of marine environment in the sea waters of Finland or another Baltic Sea coastal State. Additionally, individual exemption is allowed where natural conditions which do not allow timely improvement. The exemptions shall be specified in the Programme of Measures (below), and their impacts on other Baltic Sea coastal States shall be taken into account.

1337. In spite of any exemptions, necessary measures shall be taken aiming to continue pursuing the environmental targets, to prevent further deterioration in the status of the marine waters and to mitigate the adverse impact on the sea waters of Finland or another Baltic Sea coastal State. If possible, the exemptions shall be included in the Programme of Measures.

1338. Cooperation and cooperation with other States in planning is provided in section 26i. Participation by interested parties and dissemination of and access to information is provided in section 26j.

1339. The final Marine Waters Management Plan is adopted by the Cabinet, and the decision may be appealed against before the SAC. The procedure is similar to that concerning a Water Management Plan.

The plan shall be reviewed every six years.

1340. A Programme of Measures is prepared by each coastal Centre for Economic Development, Transport and the Environment in order to achieve the environmental targets of the Marine Waters Management Plan, taking the cost-effectiveness and technical feasibility of the measures intro account. The programme may cover one part or several parts of the sea waters, and also the impacts on the sea outside the economic zone shall be envisaged. The measures necessary for achieving and maintaining a good status of marine environment shall be specified. Also protection measures contributing to coherent and representative networks of marine protected areas shall be included.

Should the status of the Baltic Sea be critical to the extent that urgent action is needed, the Ministry of the Environment shall, for its part, take measures in order to initiate cooperation with other EU Member States in the Baltic Sea area or to participate in cooperation initiated by another Baltic Sea State, aiming at devising a plan of action. Such a plan, decided upon by the Cabinet, includes an earlier entry into operation of Programmes of Measures, and, where necessary, stricter protective measures to improve the status of the sea. A plan of action shall not prevent the achieving or maintaining a god status of marine environment in another sea area or part of it.

1341. For the ongoing assessment of the status of marine environment, monitoring programmes shall be prepared and implemented. The monitoring programmes shall be appropriately coordinated with the monitoring by other States and with monitoring programmes of the coastal Water Management Areas.

IV. Flood Risk Management

1342. The Flood Risk Management Act (620/2010) stipulates the organization of flood risk management, aiming to reduce flood risks, prevent and mitigate the adverse consequences caused by floods and promote the preparedness for floods. Additionally, the Act coordinates flood risk management and other management of river basins, taking account for the needs relating to sustainable use and protection of water resources. The objective of flood risk management (section 11) is to reduce the adverse consequences provided in section 8(1). In addition, efforts must be made to minimize the adverse consequences caused by floods in the river basin as a whole.

1343. Section 2 of the Act includes the relevant definitions. Flood is defined as the temporary covering by water of land caused by rise in the water level, rise in the sea level or accumulation of storm water and meltwater; and flood risk as the combination of the probability of a flood event and the potential adverse consequences of the flood event for human health, safety, the environment, economic activity and cultural heritage. Storm water and meltwater again mean such water accumulated on the land surface or other similar surfaces in densely built-up areas. The meanings of river basin, sub-basin and Water Management Area are the same as in the Act on the Arranging of Water Management and Marine Waters Management. The coordinating Centre for Economic Development, Transport and the Environment means the coordinating Centre for Economic Development, Transport and the Environment of the river basin referred to in section 6 of the Act on the Arranging of Water Management and Marine Waters Management.

1344. The Ministry of Agriculture and Forestry steers and follows the implementation of the Act together with the Ministry of the Interior, Ministry of Transport and Communications and Ministry of the Environment. The State and municipal authorities participate in the planning of flood risk management in their respective fields of activity.

1345. It is the task of the Centre for Economic Development, Transport and the Environment (section 4) to: (1) perform a preliminary assessment of flood risks in river basins and coastal areas; (2) prepare a proposal for designating significant flood risk areas in a river basin or coastal area; (3) prepare flood hazard and flood risk maps for river basins and coastal areas; (4) prepare proposals for Flood Risk Management Plans for river basins and coastal areas; and (5) assist municipalities in preliminary assessment of storm water and meltwater flood risks, designation of significant flood risk areas and preparation of Flood Risk Management Plans. Otherwise, the task of the centre is, in particular, to:

(1) see to planning which serves flood risk management in areas other than those with significant flood risk;
(2) in case of flood threat and during a flood event, see to the organization of the cooperation between authorities and steer the measures in the water body;

(3) issue recommendations on the coordination of the regulation and discharge of a water body;
(4) promote flood protection and other measures which improve flood risk management;
(5) see to the hydrological monitoring and water situation and flood warning service together with the Finnish Environment Institute and Finnish Meteorological Institute;
(6) see to other tasks necessary for flood risk management assigned by the Ministry of Agriculture and Forestry.

1346. Municipalities, Regional Council and Regional Rescue Services participate in the planning of flood risk management in a river basin and in coastal areas. Each municipality sees to the planning of run-off (storm water and meltwater) flood risk management. The Finnish Environment Institute and Finnish Meteorological Institute produce expert services needed in flood risk management in their respective fields of activity.

1347. Preliminary flood risk assessment (section 7 of the Flood Risk Management Act) is performed on the basis of data available on the occurred flood events and the on trends in water conditions with due account for the climate change in the long term. An area where a potential significant flood risk is detected on preliminary assessment or where such a risk might otherwise be considered likely to occur shall by a decision by the Ministry of Agriculture and Forestry be designated as a significant flood risk area (section 8). When assessing the significance of flood risk account shall be given to the likelihood of the flood event and the following adverse consequences from the general viewpoint which may be caused by the flood: (1) adverse impact on human health or safety; (2) long-time interruption of indispensable services, such as water and wastewater services, energy supply, communications, road transport or other similar activities; (3) interruption of economic activity which ensures the functions vital to society; (4) long-term or extensive adverse impacts on the environment; or (5) irreparable adverse impact on cultural heritage. The regional and local conditions shall also be taken into account. Flood maps (section 9) are prepared for the significant flood risk areas indicating the areas which may be flooded at different probabilities (flood hazard map) and showing the potential adverse consequences of such floods (flood risk map).

1348. A Flood Risk Management Plan (section 10 of the Flood Risk Management Act) is prepared (by a flood management group; *see* sections 15 and 16 of the Act) for river basins with one or several designated significant flood risk areas and a significant flood risk area in the coastal area. Participation and communication before decision-making are provided in section 17. Power of final approval is vested in the Ministry of Agriculture and Forestry, the decision of which is communicated and publicly notified as provided in section 18. If the flood risks caused by flooding in a water body and rise in the sea level relate to the same area, the flood risk management plans concerning the river basin and coastal area can be combined. Storm water and meltwater flood risk management plans are prepared separately for certain areas by municipal authorities (section 19).

1349. The planning activities shall be coordinated with the Act on the Arranging of Water Management and Marine Waters Management (section 12 of the Flood Risk Management Act). It must be ensured, in particular, that the measures are coordinated with the environmental objectives of a Programme of Measures pursuant to that Act. The participation and communication under both the acts is coordinated as necessary. Flood risk management in transboundary river basins is regulated in section 14. A Water Management Area constitutes a flood risk management unit and an international Water Management Area constitutes an international flood risk management unit (section 28 of the Flood Risk Management Act).

1350. An environmental report is presented as part of the Flood Risk Management Plan (section 13 of the Flood Risk Management Act), as provided in the Act on Environmental Impact Assessment of Plans and Programmes of Public Authorities (200/2005).

The preliminary flood risk assessment, designation of significant flood risk areas, flood hazard maps and flood risk maps and Flood Risk Management Plans are reviewed, where necessary, every six years (section 20).

1351. A decision of the Ministry of Agriculture and Forestry concerning the approval of a Flood Risk Management Plan may be appealed against to the Regional Administrative Court. The ministry's decision may be temporarily implemented in spite of the appeal (section 22). The right to appeal belongs to: (1) a party who's right, obligation or interest may be impacted by the decision; (2) relevant municipality, Regional Council or Regional Rescue Service; (3) an authority representing public interest; and (4) a registered local or regional association or foundation whose purpose is to promote environmental or nature protection or use of water resources and in whose territory the flood risk management plan is applicable. Regarding municipal plan decisions (flood risk management plans for run-off water flood risks), certain provisions in the Land Use and Building Act (as of 1 January 2025, the Land Use Act) are additionally applicable.

1352. In their activities, all State and municipal authorities and regional development authorities must take account of the approved Flood Risk Management Plans, as appropriate (section 23 of the Flood Risk Management Act). In addition, the Flood Risk Management Plans must be observed as laid down in other Act; regarding the Water Act *see* paragraph 1246.

The Centres for Economic Development, Transport and the Environment and the Finnish Environment Institute create and maintain an information system in which the relevant maps and plans are recorded (section 26). Information on significant areas, maps and plans shall be are available to the public in the information network (section 27).

Chapter 9. Other Sectors

§1. Planning and Construction of Roads

1353. The rules on road construction include certain environmentally relevant provisions. In Finland there are two basic kinds of roads (public), highways and private roads. A highway is defined as a road assigned for general traffic and maintained by the State. Today, the Highways Act (503/2005), from 2018 officially titled the Act on the Traffic System and Highways, provides, *inter alia*, a system for the planning, construction and maintenance of highways and for traffic management. Highways (maantie/landsväg) are classified as main roads Class I (valtatie/riksväg) and Class II (kantatie/stamväg), regional roads (seututie/regional väg) or connecting roads (yhdystie/förbindelseväg) depending on their transportational significance. Main roads Class I serve long-haul traffic on the national level and between provinces. Main roads Class II complement the network of main roads Class I and serve traffic in provinces. Regional roads serve transport needs in subregions and provide links to main roads Class I and Class II. Other highways are connecting roads. Highways may be motorways or semi-motorways or otherwise intended only for certain types of traffic. Highways may be used free of charge, except for ferry vessels in certain situations.

The explicit purpose of the Highways Act is to arrange the traffic system planning in a way that coordinates the national and regional goals and creates preconditions for a functioning traffic system and its development. The Act also aims to maintain and develop functional and safe highway connections promoting sustainable development as part of the transport system and to safeguard opportunities for participation in planning relating to road decisions by delivering and promoting good governance and judicial relief in matters pertaining to highways. The Act lays down provisions on a nationwide traffic system planning that covers all forms of traffic and transportational means (in 2018 inserted Chapter 1a), and provisions on highways, highway management and the rights and obligations of the party responsible for road management as well as the legal status of real estate owners and other concerned parties. A basic instrument is the road planning procedure, where all relevant facts and impacts are examined and where the landowners and other concerned private parties as well as various authorities have the opportunity to be heard. Expropriation procedures are integrated into the planning mechanism.

1354. According to the Environmental Impact Assessment Procedures Act, EIA is today automatically necessary for construction of motorways and semi-motorways, construction of a new road of four or more lanes, where such new road would be 10 kilometres or more in a continuous length, and realignment and/or widening of an existing road as to provide four or more lanes, where such realigned and/or widened section of road would be 10 kilometres or more in a continuous length. On a case-by-case basis also other public roads have been made subject to EIA (*see* Part I, Chapter 1, §21).

1355. The road planning mechanism, after having gained a concrete stage, is made up of the Preliminary Engineering Plan (sections 18–20 of the Highways Act) and the Final Engineering Plan (sections 21–26 of the Highways Act). A Preliminary Engineering Plan shall be worked out, if the impacts of the highway undertaking are not insignificant or if the location of the highway and the impacts thereof have not been determined to an adequate degree in a Detailed Plan or in a Local Master Plan with legal consequences. Moreover, a Preliminary Engineering Plan is automatically required if an EIA pursuant to the Act on Environmental Impact Assessment Procedures Act is applied. As for amendment of highways, the planning mechanism is respectively applicable.

A Preliminary Engineering plan shall contain a report on the necessity of the highway and alternatives studied, on the transportational and technical fundamental decisions, the approximate location of the road and its estimated impacts such as impacts on road and transport environment, road safety, land use, real estate structure and the environment as well as the health, living conditions and environment of human beings. The plan shall also present the opportunities for eliminating or reducing adverse impacts and a preliminary budget.

The preliminary Engineering Plan serves as a guideline in drafting the respective Final Engineering Plan(s). Once the decision to approve a preliminary engineering plan has been announced and has gained legal force, the granting of Building Permits according to the Land Use and Building Act (as of 1 January 2025, the Building Act) is restricted as provided in section 20 of the Highways Act.

1356. A Final Engineering Plan shall be drafted and adopted prior to any highway construction, except for certain situations of highway upgrading with minor effects. A Final Engineering Plan concerning the construction of a highway shall indicate the location and elevation of the road as well as a cross-section so that the road area can be marked in the terrain. An assessment of the impacts of the road shall be appended to the plan and the measures necessary to eliminate or reduce the adverse impacts shall be presented. Ownership conditions shall be taken into account in the plan inasmuch as possible. The plan shall indicate the buffer zones and lateral clearance areas of the road and also indicate whether any areas shall be reserved for subsequent widening of the road.

1357. In the drafting of Preliminary and Final Engineering Plans, real estate owners and other parties individually concerned, as well as those upon whose housing, employment or other conditions the plan may impact shall by the Centre for Economic Development, Transport and the Environment (the traffic division) of the region be served an opportunity to participate in the preparation of the plan, to assess the impacts of the plan and to comment on the matter. Before the adoption of the plan, the parties concerned shall be reserved an opportunity to submit their objections to the plan. To this end, the municipality shall keep the plan available for public viewing for a period of thirty days. Objections to the plan shall be submitted to the municipality before the end of the viewing period. The centre shall moreover send a written notification of the plan being made available for viewing to such owners or holders of real estate in the area impacted by the plan that reside in another municipality and that have been mentioned in the documents or otherwise identified. Parties submitting an objection who have so requested shall be notified of the comments, inclusive of grounds, of the road management authority to their objection. The road management authority shall request comments on the plan from the concerned authorities, Regional Councils and municipalities, and where appropriate, from other authorities.

1358. An EIS and a reasoned conclusion pursuant to the Environmental Impact Assessment Procedures Act, where any, shall be appended to any Engineering Plan, as provided in section 25 of the said Act. Also section 26 of the said Act is applied. However, if EIA has in accordance to the Environmental Assessment Procedures Act been applied to the Preliminary Engineering Plan, it is not any more required for the Final Engineering Plan, provided that the latter is aligned with the former. Preliminary and Final Engineering Plans shall indicate how the assessment has been taken into account in the plan. When an EIA has been applied to the Preliminary Engineering Plan, it shall no longer be applied to the respective Final Engineering Plan, given that it is in accordance with the Preliminary Engineering Plan. If the road project is subject to an EIA, the decision approving an Engineering Plan must also indicate what opinions, comments and opinions have been made on the matter and how they have influenced the decision. The decision shall also describe the measures proposed to prevent or reduce significant adverse effects on the environment. The provisions in section 29a of the Environmental Impact Assessment Procedures Act on the submission of permit applications and permit decisions to the Finnish Environment Institute shall also apply to the public display phase of the Engineering Plans and to the approval decision pursuant to section 99 (section 29).

1359. For minor changes of Engineering Plans, simplified procedures may be used (section 30).

1360. The drafting of a Final Engineering Plan shall as a main rule be initiated within eight years from the day the Preliminary Engineering Plan gained legal force (section 31).

1361. The Centre for Economic Development, Transport and the Environment at stake makes a proposal on approving an Engineering Plan to the Finnish Transport and Communications Agency Traficom, as provided in section 27c.

1362. Through the road planning procedure, the State (the road administration, mainly represented by the Finnish Transport Infrastructure Agency, assisted by the Centre for Economic Development, Transport and the Environment) is empowered to expropriate the necessary areas and to carry out the project in private areas. Compulsory purchase is an ordinary legal effect of an Engineering Plan after having gained legal force (section 26). It is also possible to include the expropriation of soil extraction rights in the plan (section 23; regarding other rights than ownership, section 59). Compensations and issues connected with the changes in the real estate system are treated in a separate expropriation and land consolidation procedure by surveying authorities after finishing the proper plan procedure (sections 53–87).

1363. There are specific provisions, e.g., on rest areas and adjacent parking areas with equipment. The placement of equipment, constructs and buildings serving the purposes of café and restaurant services, fuel distribution, motor vehicle servicing and other services to road users may be placed in rest areas subject to the provisions of the Land Use and Building Act (as of 1 January 2025, the Building Act) and with the consent of the road management authority.

1364. Preliminary and Final Engineering Plans are approved by the Finnish Transport and Communications Agency Traficom. For particular reasons, the task may be transferred to the Ministry of Transport and Communications (section 99 of the Highways Act).

1365. Appeals against the plan approval decisions can be submitted to the Regional Administrative Court. In addition to those individually concerned, the right of appeal has been extended to municipalities, Centres for Economic Development, Transport and the Environment and Regional Councils at stake. Also registered local or regional associations and foundations are entitled to appeal. Appeals concerning decisions to adopt preliminary and final engineering plans that shall be considered socially significant shall be dealt with as urgent (section 105).

However, a decision on a Preliminary Engineering Plan may not be appealed against as far as the location of the highway and technical solutions have already been approved with legal force in a land use plan pursuant to the Land Use and Building Act (as of 1 January 2025, the Land Use Act) with legal consequences (section 106 of the Highways Act). The same restriction applies to a decision on a Final Engineering Plan. In addition, a Final Engineering Plan may not be appealed inasmuch as the location of the highway and its technical solutions have already been approved in a Preliminary Engineering Plan having gained legal force. Decisions on Engineering Plans may be enforced despite appeal unless otherwise ordered by the appellate court (section 107).

1366. The substantive rules on public road planning are also environmentally relevant. Many different and in part contradictory interests and viewpoints are to be taken into account in the consideration (section 13 of the Highways Act). In the development of the road network, among other things, reducing of emissions shall be promoted. It is required that highways shall be constructed so that the detriments caused by the network and traffic are minimized as far as possible and natural resources are used as sparingly as possible. No one shall be caused more damage or inconvenience than necessary. Issues of road safety, the transportational and technical functioning of the road and environmental aspects shall be taken into particular consideration in construction. Highways may not be constructed in breach of land use plans with legal consequences pursuant to the Land Use and Building Act (from 1 January 2025 onwards, the Land Use Act).

This means a kind of relative legal protection of environmental interests. The norm itself is in the first place interpreted by the traffic administration authority (i.e., the Finnish Transport and Communications Agency Traficom and the Centre for Economic Development, Transport and the Environment at stake) Environment. As to traffic noise, the general traffic noise level guidelines are largely observed. The Regional Administrative Court and finally, subject to leave of appeal, the SAC have the ultimate power to make an individual decision concerning the minimum acceptable requirements for a road project. In practice, there are not many cases where an Engineering Plan (or a previous Public Road Plan) has been rejected by the court on such grounds, but amendments may have been required anyway, *see*, e.g., SAC 2003:99.

1367. In all cases, the provisions of the Nature Protection Act and issued pursuant thereto shall be observed in Preliminary and Final Engineering Plans (section 17.4 of the Act). Hence the Nature Protection Act and decisions under it are hence directly applicable.

1368. It is required by section 17 of the Highways Act that Preliminary and Final Engineering Plans shall be based on land use Plans with legal consequences as provided in the Land Use and Building Act, from 1 January onwards, the Land Use Act (*see* Part III, Chapter 3) wherein the location of the highway and its relationship to other land use has been determined, except for the case that the location and the relation to another use may, in cooperation with the municipality and the region, be assessed properly taking the nature of the planned road into account. In areas where a land use Plan with legal consequences is being drafted or amended, measures may be taken to draft Preliminary or Final Engineering Plans based on the goals of the land use Plan.

Preliminary Engineering Plans shall not be adopted contrary to a Regional Plan or a Local Master Plan with legal consequences. Preliminary Engineering Plans may nevertheless be adopted contrary to a valid Detailed Plan with the support of the municipality. Final Engineering Plans may be adopted contrary to any land use plan with legal consequences, with the exception of a deviation with minor impacts, provided the municipality and immediately concerned property owners support it. Additionally, attention shall be paid to National Land Use Goals (*see* paragraph 1408), a Regional Plan and a Local Master Plan, as provided concerning authorities in general pursuant to the Land Use and Building Act (as of 1 January 2025, the Land Use Act).

1369. If a nature preserve established under the Nature Protection Act happens to be in the area of a planned road, it has to be observed as long as it is in force. (That is why the road authorities have in some cases been granted *locus standi* in preserve establishing procedures concerning private areas.) The legal effects of Natura 2000 sites are of course relevant (*see* Part II, Chapter 2, §3 above) as well as the prohibition to deteriorate or destroy the habitats of animals listed in the Natural Habitats Directive Annex IV(a) (*see* Part II, Chapter 3, §3 above). Among the latter, certain conflicts between road planning and flying squirrel have emerged (*see,* e.g., SAC 2003:98 and SAC 2003:99).

A valid Engineering Plan does not make the possibly required permits under other legislation unnecessary. For example, a permit under the Soil Excavation Act is necessary for soil extraction outside the proper road area, even though a Final Engineering Plan may permit expropriation also for that purpose. For a bridge or a road bank across a watercourse, a permit under the Water Act is often necessary.

1370. The Finnish Transport Infrastructure Agency has a general obligation to systematically monitor the impacts of realized highway projects (section 32).

1371. The Private Roads Act (560/2018) is applicable to all private roads to the use of which also others than the owner are entitled. Such rights can be attained without any agreement, by force of a decision of the surveying authority in a process stipulated in section 6 of the Act. It is presupposed that every real property shall have a road connection. The owner of the property which has to be crossed is of course compensated. A property owner may also be obliged to participate in the administration and costs of a private road with several entitled properties. From the environmental viewpoint, cases where the right mentioned above also implies the construction of a new road and not only the power to use an existing road are most relevant. The preconditions are legally twofold; first those which regard the establishment of the necessary entitlement itself (section 4) and second those which regard road construction (section 19). An entitlement always requires importance for the appropriate use of the property at stake, and significant harm to no one shall be caused. The final option shall be as appropriate as possible, the purpose of the road shall be gained as economically as possible, and either the road itself or the use thereof shall cause no unnecessary harm to the environment or anyone more damage or harm than necessary. An entitlement shall not be established at all, if the road construction or use would be against other act, or if the entitlement would be inappropriate from the viewpoint of existing road network, or if significant endangerment of traffic safety, significant deterioration of nature or decreasing of the cultural values of the environment, or other comparable violation of public interest would be caused. The viability of a Detailed Plan shall not be hampered, either (section 4 of the Private Roads Act). Regarding specifically road construction only, it is among other things required in section 19 that a new road or the use thereof will not cause unnecessary harm to anyone or to the environment, or cause other violation of public interests. Also traffic safety has to be taken into account. The restrictions based on the Nature Protection Act have to be observed ordinarily in the construction, as well as the provisions of the Water Act, the Ancient Remains Act, Chapter 3 of the Forestry Act, the Environmental Protection Act, or other act. If permit pursuant to any act is required, the construction shall not be initiated before such a permit. In or near Natura 2000 sites, the authorities shall strive to find such a road option where the impact to the site would remain minimal. If it is not possible for reasonable extra costs to construct the road for serving the users in a satisfactory way, the State is obliged to compensate the disadvantage or purchase the area for which the entitlement has been applied (section 21). Section 113 of the Nature Protection Act is applicable in such cases. If a road is aimed to be led to the vicinity of a Natura 2000 site or another area with special natural values, the Centre for Economic Development, Transport and the Environment has standing in the proceedings under the Private Roads Act (section 74).

1372. However, the rules in the Private Roads Act are not at all applicable to the 'most private' roads, i.e., cases where the owner of a property constructs roads in his own area and solely for his own purposes, or if a property owner allows somebody else to make a road on his property. The law may be regarded as insufficient, because the environmental values are independent of ownership. In Finland large networks of forestry roads have been constructed during the last few decades, partly within the regime of the Private Roads Act and partly outside it (roads within large forest estates or State forests).

§2. Planning and Construction of Railways

1373. The planning and construction of railways is regulated by the Railways Act (110/2007). Before that, no corresponding regulation existed. The general structure of the Railways Act is rather similar to that of the Highways Act (*see* §1 above).

The explicit main purpose of the Railways Act is to maintain and develop functional and safe railway connections promoting sustainable development as part of the transport system. A basic instrument is the railway planning procedure, where all relevant facts and impacts are examined and where the landowners and other concerned private parties as well as various authorities have the opportunity to be heard. Expropriation procedures are integrated into the planning mechanism.

1374. In the developing of the railway network, attention shall among other things be paid to economical use of natural resources and minimizing the environmental disadvantages caused by the network and its traffic. No one shall be caused any more damage or inconvenience than necessary. Railways may be constructed where a public need of traffic or safety requires or in order to eliminate or reduce disadvantages caused by traffic, or where called for by land use. Railway may not be constructed contrary to a land use plan with legal consequences. Issues of railway safety, the transportational and technical functioning of the railway, the present and planned land use and environmental aspects shall be taken into particular consideration in construction. The Nature Protection Act has to be observed as such.

The planning and decision-making mechanism, based on a Preliminary Engineering Plan and a Final Engineering Plan, EIA included, is very similar to that provided in the Highways Act. In practice, however, a parallel planning and investment mechanism has emerged under private corporate law, as three project companies for certain important railway connections have been established after 2020, mainly with the State and certain municipalities as the shareholders. In some cases, the companies have proceeded to concrete land use planning and kind of assessment of impacts, of course without any legal guarantees of openness or participation by landowners or environmental groups, or by Regional Councils. No procedures under the Railways Act have been initiated so far. This has caused confusion in public and in local communities. On the other hand, due to the changed will of the State, the projects of two companies have already been changed and reduced significantly.

A railway is managed either by the Finnish Transport Infrastructure Agency (by now practically always) or by a private subject. Rail traffic is regulated by the Rail Traffic Act (1302/2018).

§3. CONSTRUCTION OF POWER LINES AND TRANSMISSION PIPELINES

1375. The construction of power lines may have significant impacts on the environment and land use. Nevertheless, there is no planning or permit procedure where the environmental effects would be juridically taken into account. Pursuant to section 14 of the Electricity Market Act (588/2013), a permit of the Electricity Market Authority is needed for the constructing of a power line with an electric potential of at least 110 kilovolts. The preconditions entirely refer to market aspects. The taking into account of environmental aspects would all the same be difficult, as the exact location of the line is not decided upon in the permit decision. EIA is not any more linked to this permit, but the Act on the Expropriation Permit of Certain Projects with Impacts on the Environment (768/2004) in 2017 been extended to cover all power lines with an electric potential of at least 110 kilovolts, and EIA is due to the reference to the Expropriation Act required at the Expropriation Permit stage, irrespective of whether real expropriation takes places or not.

In addition, the Electricity Market Act requires the approval of the municipality, if the line is going to be sited in an area which has not been reserved for the purpose in a land use Plan according to the Land Use and Building Act (as of 1 January 2025, the Land Use Act) and the Expropriation Act is not applied. The approval may not be disallowed, or made conditional, without acceptable reasons of land use planning or of environmental aspects, if unreasonable disadvantage would be caused to energy transmission in general or to the applicant (section 17). The possessor of the power network is generally obliged to be in cooperation with the municipalities, in order to take general land use aspects into account. However, this is far from a legally relevant link to the mechanism of the Land Use and Building Act (as of 1 January 2025, the Land Use Act), and problems have not been avoided in all cases.

1376. Often, the constructor has not reached agreement with the owners of the property on which the power line or pipeline for transmission of oil, gas or chemicals is going to be sited. In this case – but in principle only then (*see*, however, the Act on the Expropriation Permit of Certain Projects with Impacts on the Environment (768/2004)) – he needs an Expropriation Permit (pursuant to the Expropriation Act (603/1977)), normally from the Cabinet, and also in connection with this permit an EIS is, where necessary, required (section 5(4) of the Expropriation Act). However, the Cabinet is up to 1 February 2024 practically free to decide on the locating of power lines, provided that the ordinary preconditions in the Expropriation Act are followed and provided that the expropriation decision may not be against the provisions in the Nature Protection Act or provisions or decisions based on it (section 5(5) of the Expropriation Act), the provisions on the Natura 2000 network and on habitats of specially protected species included. The Centre for Economic Development, Transport and the Environment is entitled to appeal the expropriation permit on such grounds (section 135 of the Nature Protection Act). An environmental association has not been given a similar standing, although such organizations are entitled to appeal against decisions based (immediately) on the Nature Protection Act.

Due to the *Århus* Convention, the Act on the Expropriation Permit of Certain Projects with Impacts on the Environment (768/2004) has, however, changed as of 30 November 2004 the state of affairs in that for construction of: (1) overhead electrical power lines with a voltage of 220 kilovolts or more and a length of more than 15 kilometres an Expropriation Permit pursuant to the Expropriation Act became necessary irrespective of whether compulsory purchase is needed for the project or not. And such a permit may be appealed against by environmental associations and foundations (*see* paragraph 1578). The applicability limit of 110 kilovolts was in 2017 adopted regarding all such lines for which EIA is needed, overhead or not. In 2023, the Act has been developed further (1238/2023), mainly due to the EIA Directive (*see also* paragraph 1578). Hence, as of 1 February 2024, the Act is applicable to: (1) an above-ground power line with a voltage of at least 220 kilovolts and a length of more than 15 kilometres; (2) a transmission line for transporting gas, oil or chemicals with a length of more than 40 kilometres and a diameter of DN 800 mm; and (3) an above-ground power line or transmission pipeline other than in (1) or (2), if EIA is applied to the project. Also, as of 1 February 2024, if an ordinary Expropriation Permit application concerns a power transmission line or a gas, oil or chemical transmission pipeline to which the EIA Act applies, the Act on the Expropriation Permit of Certain Projects with Impacts on the Environment shall also be complied with. This reference makes the new substantive and procedural provisions of the latter applicable also in ordinary expropriation for (1), (2) or (3) above. Hence, the Permit decision shall include the necessary provisions on the route of the power line and transmission line, the method and timing of implementation of the project, and the monitoring of the impacts in order to limit its significant adverse effects. The line shall be constructed in a technically and economically feasible manner to minimize adverse effects on the environment and the use of the areas. Construction must not cause more damage or inconvenience to anyone than is necessary. A project located in or having an impact in the Saami homeland or Skolt area may not substantially impair the right of the Saami to maintain and develop their own culture and to engage in their traditional livelihoods and the living conditions of the Skolt people or their natural livelihoods.[62] When constructing the power line

62. The final wordings were drafted in the parliamentary select committee at stake (the Commerce Committee, not the Environmental Committee), on the following grounds: 'The Commerce Committee proposes that the proposed regulation be clarified as set out in the detailed explanatory memorandum. The aim of the proposed amendments is to ensure that the regulation would not run counter to the – objectives of streamlining permit procedures. At the same time, it would ensure that the proposed implementation of the EIA Directive does not create a national regulatory burden exceeding the requirements set by EU provisions. The Committee also considers it essential to promote a well-functioning investment environment and equal competition conditions at EU level in order to secure the investments needed for a clean transition. The committee's amendments relate in particular to limiting permit provisions to significant adverse environmental impacts in accordance with the EIA Directive, limiting permit provisions to the necessary ones in accordance with the grounds for the provision, and specifying the provision on the rights of the Saami to apply to projects that could substantially weaken the rights of the Saami and Skolt people, so that the wording of the provision would better correspond to the regulatory approach followed in the Mining Act, for example.' This might imply a remarkable policy change in general, because previously EU environmental legislation (other than internal market) has not been regarded as indication of maximum level of environmental requirements to be included in Finnish substantive law. It seems surprisingly also that the EIA Directive has by the Committee been regarded as one of substantive environmental law.

and transmission pipeline, a Detailed Plan (where any) must be taken into account. Where a Regional Plan or a Local Master Plan with legal effect is in force, the construction of a line may not impede the use of the area for the purpose indicated in the current Plan. Additionally, the new provisions on appeals (*see* paragraph 1578), supervision and administrative enforcement are applicable.

1377. As for minor electricity lines (in practice below 110 kilovolts), the municipal Building Supervision Authority is pursuant to section 161 of Land Use and Building Act (as of 1 January 2025, section 131 of the Building Act) competent to decide upon the siting thereof on another's property. Due to the nature of the decision, the environmental aspects are not necessarily taken into account. But as of 1 February 2024, where EIA is needed, need of Expropriation Permit will follow also here.

1378. The rights to site telecommunications cables, base stations and radio masts in alien areas are provided in section 229 of the Information Society Code (917/2014).

§4. Dam Safety

1379. The Dam Safety Act (494/2009) applies to dams and the structures and equipment belonging to them. Here the material of which the dam is constructed or how the dam has been constructed, is irrelevant, as well as the substance impounded. Pursuant to the definitions in the Act, dam means a structure such as a wall or embankment the purpose of which is to permanently or temporarily prevent the spread of a liquid or substance that behaves like a liquid impounded by the dam or to regulate the surface level of the impounded substance.

The objective of the Dam Safety Act is to ensure safety in the construction, maintenance and operation of dams, as well as to reduce the hazard that may be caused by a dam. The provisions concerning a dam also apply to flood embankments, but not to sluice gate structures of canals. In addition, the provisions of the Water Act and under it are applicable, where relevant. Moreover, the environmentally relevant provisions of the Environmental Protection Act and the Waste Act apply to waste dams. Regarding mine safety, the provisions of the Mining Act and under it also apply (to mine dams). Additionally, the provisions of the Land Use and Building Act (as of 1 January 2025, the Building Act) on the permits required for building activities, structures and other measures apply to dams. Rescue service arrangements are stipulated in the Rescue Act. The provisions of the Dam Safety Act shall be taken into account in the decision-making pursuant to the Water Act, the Environmental Protection Act and the Land Use and Building Act (as of 1 January 2025, the Land Use Act and the Building Act).

1380. The Ministry of Agriculture and Forestry is responsible for the general guidance, follow-up and development of activities under the Act. The Centre for Economic Development, Transport and the Environment which is competent in dam safety matters (one centre may be assigned to be competent also in another's area) functions as the Dam Safety Authority pursuant to the Act.

1381. Any person who prepares the plan on the construction of a dam and a person who is responsible for the operation, monitoring and inspections of the dam must possess sufficient expertise in dam safety matters, taking account of the type of the dam and the hazard it may cause (section 6). All dams must be designed and constructed in such a manner that their use does not cause any danger to safety (section 7). The plan and design prepared for constructing a dam must show how the safety requirements pursuant to or under the Act have been taken into account (section 8).

1382. In a permit application concerning the construction of a dam under another Act – which in practice most often means the Water Act, but also the Environmental Protection Act or the Mining Act – the owner of the dam must describe sufficiently the dam hazard and its impact on the dam dimensioning and design criteria (section 9). When an authority is under the obligation to take into account the provisions of the Dam Safety Act in its decision-making pursuant to the Water Act, the Environmental Protection Act and the Land Use and Building Act (as of 1 January 2025 the Building Act) concerning the construction of a dam, the authority at stake shall request a statement from the Dam Safety Authority concerning the dam safety requirements. In the statement, where necessary, an estimation of the design criteria from the dam safety perspective shall be presented.

1383. Before bringing into operation the dam must be classified and a dam break hazard analysis and monitoring programme must be approved for it (section 10). Depending on the risk, each dam is placed in one of the following classes, as decided upon by the Dam Safety Authority:

(1) Class 1 dam, which in the event of an accident will cause danger to human life and health or considerable danger to the environment or property;
(2) Class 2 dam, which in the event of an accident may cause danger to health or greater than minor danger to the environment or property; or
(3) Class 3 dam, which in the event of an accident may cause only a minor danger.

1384. Pursuant to section 2 of the Dam Safety Decree, a dam in a water body (or a water body system) is designed for a water flow which causes the maximum need for discharge. The dimensioning is presented as the annual probability or frequency of flooding which corresponds to such a water flow, this being called design flood. As for dams in water bodies, the design flood is based on a flood which occurs: (1) in case of class 1 dam, with a probability of 0.02%–0.01%, i.e., once in 5,000–10,000 years on average; (2) in case of class 2 dam, with a probability of 0.2–0.1%, i.e., once in 500–1,000 years on average; and (3) in case of class 3 dam with a probability of 1%–0.2%, i.e., once in 100%–500% years on average. The flood the water level in the dam basin may not rise above the safe water level when the discharge capacity of the dam excluding the flow through the turbines of a possible hydropower plant is in operation.

Classification is unnecessary if the dam safety authority considers that the dam does not cause any danger (section 11 of the Dam Safety Act). However, the provisions on the maintenance or the operation of a dam, on preventing accidents and on the control of these provisions apply also to such a dam.

1385. The owner of a class 1 dam must prepare a more detailed analysis than that stipulated in section 9 to establish the risk to humans, property and the environment (dam break hazard analysis). The dam safety authority may moreover decide that the dam break hazard analysis must also be prepared on a dam other than *class* 1 if this is necessary for the classification of the dam or assessment of the need to change the class (section 12).

1386. The owner of any dam has to prepare and regularly update an emergency action plan of a dam. This plan contains measures in case of accidents and disturbances concerning a class 1 dam (section 13).

1387. The owner of a dam is moreover obliged to prepare a monitoring programme concerning a classified dam, and organize the monitoring. The monitoring at stake refers to factors which may impact on safety both when the dam is brought into operation and during operation. Such a programme is, however, not needed if similar factors are being monitored under other Act, as approved by the Dam Safety Authority.

1388. The owner of a dam shall inspect the condition and safety of class 1 and 2 dams at least once a year. The owner of a dam must notify the written report prepared on the inspection of a class 1 dam to the dam safety authority (section 18). Moreover, the owner of must organize a periodic inspection of class 1–3 dams at least every five years and, where necessary, more frequently (section 19). The Dam Safety Authority and the rescue authority have the right to participate. In the periodic inspection, changes in the conditions of the dam and factors impacting on safety are studied, with due account for changes in land use, weather and hydrological conditions. If in the periodic inspection it cannot be established with sufficient certainty that the dam fulfils the safety requirements set for it, the owner of the dam must prepare a thorough study of the condition of the dam or its part. On the basis of a periodic inspection, the dam safety authority may order the owner to update a dam break hazard analysis under section 9 (section 20).

The class of a dam may be changed by the Dam Safety Authority if the dam hazard can be considered to have changed in an essential way due to a change in circumstances (section 21).

1389. The provisions of on the planning, design and construction of a dam and on classification and dam safety documents apply, where appropriate, to alteration and repair works which significantly impact on dam structures or are otherwise significant in regard of dam safety (section 22).

A dam is recorded as removed from service to the information system of the Dam Safety Authority when the dam structure has been pulled down or the dam has been decommissioned in such a way that it can no longer cause hazard (section 23). The obligations under the Dam Safety Act cease to be applicable when the dam has been recorded as removed from service.

1390. The owner of a dam must, considering properly the hazard, take the necessary actions to prevent accidents and to limit the possible damages (section 24). Provisions on rescue activity are laid down in the Rescue Act (section 26). The owner of a dam and the Dam Safety Authority must assist in performing rescue activity. The Dam Safety Authority shall communicate and keep available information on the dam hazard (section 28). The Dam Safety Authority has the right to perform the necessary inspections at the dam to control the compliance with the Dam Safety Act and provisions issued under it (section 29).

1391. The Dam Safety Authority may prohibit one who violates the Dam Safety Act or provisions under it from continuing or repeating an action which violates the provision or order that the obligation shall be fulfilled, as far as the infringement does not concern other Act (such as the Water Act) as well (section 30). Moreover, the dam safety authority may order that rectifying, remedial or communication measures are to be implemented within the time and in a manner determined by the Dam Safety Authority if an immediate danger related to the dam can be efficiently prevented or the magnitude of the danger essentially reduced through such a measure (section 31). The Dam Safety Authority may additionally impose a conditional fine or a threat of taking the neglected action at the defaulting party's expense or of interrupting the activity (section 32). The provisions of the Administrative Injunctions (Conditional Fines) Act (1113/1990) apply here.

1392. The Finnish Environment Institute maintains an information system for control of dams (section 33). The Dam Safety Authority and owner of the dam must keep up-to-date printouts from the information system for each dam as well as other important documents as regards dam safety so that these are readily available in case of disturbances (dam safety file). The owner of a dam must notify essential changes in information to the Dam Safety Authority. When the owner of the dam changes the owner who gives up the ownership must deliver the safety file to the new owner and notify the Dam Safety Authority of the change.

1393. Pursuant to section 34, the penalty for impairment of the environment, aggravated impairment of the environment, environmental infraction and negligent impairment of the environment committed in violation of the Dam Safety Act or provisions or orders issued under it is stipulated in Chapter 48 of the Penal Code. The penalty for criminal mischief, aggravated criminal mischief, negligent endangerment or gross negligent endangerment committed by creating a water flood is again set forth in Chapter 34 of the Penal Code.

1394. Section 35 on a fine for a dam safety offence in turn applies, unless a more severe penalty is provided for, to one who intentionally or negligently (1) neglects the preparation of a dam break hazard analysis, emergency action plan of a dam referred monitoring programme or the delivery of these documents or an explanatory note to the dam safety authority; (2) brings a dam into operation contrary to section 10 before the classification of the dam or approval of dam safety documents; (3) operates the dam in violation of section 16(1) or neglects the technical safety arrangement pursuant to section 16(2); (4) neglects the maintenance of a dam, monitoring annual inspection, organization of a periodic inspection or the updating of a dam break hazard analysis and its delivery to the dam safety authority; (5) neglects the obligation to take the necessary action to prevent a dam accident and to limit the damage caused by an accident; (6) neglects giving a notice or the delivery of information to the Dam Safety Authority, or (7) undertakes repair or alteration works of a dam contrary to section 22.

Part III. Zoning and Land Use Planning

Chapter 1. The General Structure of the System

1395. Finland is one of those countries where administrative land use planning, or spatial planning, including zoning and town planning, plays an essential role also in environmental protection. Both land use planning and building are presently (until 31 December 2024, *see* paragraph 1398 below) regulated by the Land Use and Building Act (132/1999, several amendments) complemented by the Land Use and Building Decree (895/1999, several amendments) and certain additional decrees. The Act contains the whole system of physical (spatial) planning and zoning (together called planning), including both substantive and procedural rules. It also contains a complex of various permits and consents regarding building and constructing, and a system of official supervision. A Municipal Building Bylaw may lay down certain additional provisions and reliefs within one municipality.

1396. The previous Building Act (370/1958) was amended many times, and the reformed act also served as a model to the Land Use and Building Act in several respects, although the latter makes up a coherent legal regime with many wholly new aspects. One of the major reforms (1990) was aimed at transferring certain powers from central governmental authorities to municipal bodies. The latter had a key position in applying and enforcing the act. Also the principles of public participation were stressed. A substantive novelty was the introduction of the principle of sustainable development as a general starting point. The procedural reform of 1990 was continued in 1996, and, in connection with the then new Nature Conservation Act, a totally new system of regulating and restricting building in shore areas was inserted from January 1997. During many years, a total reform of the Act was under elaboration, and a bill including a proposal for a new Land Use and Building Act was introduced in the Parliament in 1999. The Land Use and Building Act entered into force on 1 January 2000. Several, mostly minor amendments have taken place since then, until the reform enacted in 2023.

1397. An all-round reform on land use and building has been in preparation for several years. Due to political difficulties, a new approach was adopted in March 2022. Pursuant to this, in the first place the parts concerning building and permits would be separated as a new Building Act, and subsequently a new Land Use Act would be enacted. The legislative task was nevertheless more complicated technically and systematically than perhaps alleged.

1398. As a result, no new Land Use Act was enacted, however, but the Land Use and Building Act was split into two parts, first the formally new Building Act (751/2023) repealing the building-related provisions in the Land Use and Building Act, which, in turn, or in fact its land-use related provisions after the cut-out, remains in force under a new title, the Land Use Act. All these changes will enter into force as of 1 January 2025. Only a few minor substantive amendments were made in this context. The difference in section 2 of the Land Use Act (changing to the Land Use Act) defining the scope of application before and after the reform is seemingly small but essential. The original Act regulates the planning, construction and use of areas and buildings, whereas the new stripped-down version declares to regulate the planning of areas and the construction and use of areas. The Building Act (section 1) in turn regulates the planning/design, construction and operation of buildings and construction items. 'Construction item' in the Act refers to any building or construction which may have an impact on the surrounding spatial use, the implementation of which must take account of essential technical requirements and any area constructed for a specific activity which has implications for the use of surrounding areas.

1399. The general aim of the Land Use and Building Act, as of 1 January, the Land Use Act, as expressed in section 1 of the Act, is to arrange land use and building in a way that they create preconditions to a good living environment and to promote an ecologically, economically, socially and culturally sustainable development. A parallel aim is to safeguard for everyone a possibility to take part in the preparatory stages of decision-making and to safeguard quality and interactive nature of planning, all-round expertise and openly active dissemination of information. These general wordings are primarily aimed at making up the value basis for more detailed provisions in the same act and in decrees. Sometimes these general wordings are also taken as a part of legal reasoning of decisions of courts.

1400. The general aim of land use planning has been specified in section 5 of the Land Use and Building Act (as of 1 January 2023, the Land Use Act). The aim is to, on a basis of interactive planning and adequate impact assessment, promote:

(1) creation of a safe, healthy, pleasant and socially well-functioning living and working environment that meets the needs of various population groups, such as children, old people and the disabled;
(2) economic community structures and land use;
(3) preconditions for a sufficient production of dwellings;
(4) beauty of a built up environment and fostering of cultural values;
(5) preservation of biodiversity and other natural values;
(6) environmental protection and the prevention of environmental harms;
(7) economic use of natural resources;
(8) well-functioning of communities and good construction;
(9) economy in building for dense population;
(10) proper preconditions for business and industry;
(11) accessibility of services; and

(12) practical traffic arrangements, in particular good preconditions for public transport and non-vehicular traffic.

1401. In the preparation of any land use plan, interactive consultation with all interested persons, authorities and organizations is required. The general provision in section 6, being complemented by several other provisions, refers not only to landowners, but also to all those whose living or working conditions or other circumstances the plan is likely to affect. The preparing authority is also obliged to provide information on planning in such a way that all interested parties may follow the different stages and their impact. Each municipality is also obliged to publish a Land Use Planning Review at least once in a year and deliver it to all households (section 7). The review shall include information on planning items that are either already pending or coming soon into preparation.

1402. The main contents of the Land Use and Building Act deal with (spatial, physical, land use) planning on the one hand and (up to 2015) with permit mechanisms for building and various constructions on the other. There are also some related sectors. Sectors that are not dealt with in detail here include compulsory land acquirement, construction of streets and squares, compensations and the requirements for products used in building. Compared to the 1958 Building Act, there are also some new related elements in the Land Use and Building Act, such as the provisions on National Land Use Goals (*see* Chapter 2 below), the provisions on National Urban Parks, not to mention the chapter on urban run-off, inserted in 2014 (Part I, Chapter 4, §5). All these remain in the Land Use Act as of 1 January 2025.

1403. A National Urban Park (sections 68–71 of the Act) can be established primarily on land owned by the State or the municipalities or other public body, provided that the area has been allotted by a land use plan as park, recreational or protected area, valuable landscape area or other appropriate use. The aim is to create and maintain extensive parks, recreation areas and green belts in urban conglomerations so as to provide a good living environment and protect the natural and cultural heritage. Private areas can be included if the owner agrees. A National Urban Park is established by a decision of the relevant ministry (primarily the Ministry of the Environment), but proposal or consent by the municipality is required. The decision may, in agreement with the municipality, include necessary provisions in order to preserve essential values of the area. The provisions for management in practice are issued by a plan for management and use, prepared by the municipality in cooperation with the Centre for Economic Development, Transport and the Environment of the region and approved by the Ministry of the Environment.

1404. Another novelty in 1999 was the notion of Development Area (sections 110–112, amendments 1441/2006). The municipality may assign a certain area to a Development Area, where some exceptional arrangements are available and the role of private organizations may be somewhat increased. In practice this option has so far been used only a few times.

1405. The conceptual distinction between the zoning and planning cannot be maintained in the system of the Land Use and Building Act (and the Land Use Act). Assigning (or zoning) of areas for different categories of land use purposes is one of the functions of the various plan decisions. All forms of planning and zoning are therefore hereinafter, pursuant to the terminology of the Act, referred to as planning. Planning is always (one specific plan category partly excepted) a task of the authorities. It is primarily performed by municipal authorities, but the State environmental authorities have a role, too. The system is based on a hierarchy of various land use plans with different areal scopes and precision.

1406. The activities under the Land Use and Building Act (and the Land Use Act as well) are guided by the Ministry of the Environment and the Centres for Economic Development, Transport and the Environment. However, the municipalities have a key position, as the power of land use planning basically belongs to them. However, the role of the municipalities is juridically twofold, as the municipal Building Supervision Authorities (section 21) are independent supervisors of all building and constructing activities (encompassing those of the municipality itself), and normally also separate from the decision-making on planning. A municipality may, however, decide that the powers belonging to a Building Supervision Authority are vested in another municipal body, however not in the Municipal Executive. As of 1 January 2025, most of the tasks of the Authority refer to the Building Act, not the Land Use Act.

Chapter 2. Planning at the National Level

1407. At the national level, there is no general land use planning. This means that the Cabinet or the Ministry of the Environment has no general power to decide directly upon nationally vital land use matters, e.g., concerning areas to be protected because of their important natural value or the location of locally unpopular items like hazardous waste disposal plants or large dumping areas.

There are, instead, many types of sectoral plans at the national level, some of which are statutory and some of which are not. In the field of nature conservation many national Conservation (Protection) Programmes, also called Conservation Plans, have been elaborated and approved by the government, though until the previous Nature Conservation Act without a statutory basis and with no direct legal effects. Normally they consist of lists of nationally valuable areas or other objects (e.g., peatlands, eskers, rivers, groves, shore areas). They have served primarily as a policy basis for the activities of State authorities (e.g., purchasing or expropriation of land), but gained some legal relevance afterwards, also pursuant to the present Nature Protection Act (*see* paragraph 890). In certain cases they, however, have had some legal effects also in other legal systems, e.g., the esker protection plan in connection with the Soil Excavation Permits (*see* Part II, Chapter 7, §1). Pursuant to the Land Use and Building Act, the programmes, old and new alike, have had a guiding effect regarding the drawing up of Regional Plans (*see* below). The Natura 2000 network consists largely of areas included in existing conservation programmes.

1408. Although the Land Use and Building Act (or the Land Use Act) provides for no formal nationwide plan, the entering into force of the Land Use and Building Act created a new administrative (or political) instrument for nationally significant objectives. Pursuant to section 22 of the Act, the Cabinet is entitled to set National Land Use Goals. These goals (or guidelines, as they have been officially translated) may comprise:

(1) issues with an international or more extensive than regional importance for regional structure, use of areas, traffic networks or energy networks;
(2) issues with a significant impact on national cultural or natural heritage; or
(3) issues with a nationally significant impact on ecological sustainability, economy of areal regional structure or abatement of significant environmental harms.

1409. A decision of the Cabinet on laying down National Land Use Goals can be appealed against the SAC, but, due to lacking special provisions, the scope of persons or organizations with appellate standing has been regarded as narrow. On the restrictive standing approach regarding appeals against National Land Use Goal decisions, *see* SAC 2001:59.

The first ever Cabinet Decision on National Land Use Goals was made in November 2000. This decision was textually reviewed in 2008, and no appeals were submitted against it. A wholly new decision was made in December 2017.

1410. In this decision, the following categories of goals (headings of chapters) are included:

- well-functioning communities and sustainable movement;
- an effective traffic system;
- a wholesome and safe living environment;
- a viable natural and cultural environment and natural resources; and
- an energy supply with ability to renew.

1411. Since the 2010s, in addition to statutory Land Use Planning, an unregulated steering and cooperation instrument, land use, housing and transport agreements (MAL agreements), has developed in addition to statutory planning, which state representatives have concluded with municipalities in the largest urban areas. The agreements define objectives and concrete measures for housing production in the coming years and for the development of a sustainable community structure and transport system. Land use, housing and transport are planned as a whole, with an eye to far-sighted plans for the development of the community structure and the implementation of major transport investments. The aim is to build climate-smart urban regions, increase housing production in easily accessible areas and increase the share of sustainable modes of transport, such as public transport. The agreements are intended to support the vitality of urban regions and the building of smooth everyday life. The parties to the agreements on behalf of the State are the Ministry of the Environment, the Ministry of Transport and Communications, the Ministry of Economic Affairs and Employment, the Ministry of Finance, the Housing Finance and Development Centre of Finland (ARA), the Finnish Transport Infrastructure Agency, the Finnish Transport and Communications Agency Traficom and the relevant Regional Centre for Economic Development, Transport and the Environment. The final confirmation is a matter of the Cabinet and the Municipal Councils. The judicial nature and validity of the agreements are unclear, to say the least, and their implementation depends in practice on the confidence of the parties.

Chapter 3. The System of Land Use Plans

§1. Plan Hierarchy

1412. The hierarchy of the three types of (proper) land use plans is based on the size of the area concerned: the drafting of a detailed physical plan for a small area is guided by another plan concerning a larger area and with less detailed contents, if there is one. However, the more detailed the plan, after becoming valid and as long as it is valid, displaces the plan higher in the hierarchy in terms of legal consequences. The higher plan remains in a way latent, until alteration of the more detailed plan is considered. No higher plan is however necessary for the drafting and approval of a plan lower in the hierarchy. The hierarchy is often described by calling the two highest plan types, Regional Plan and (municipal) Local Master Plan, general (or master-type) land use plans, while the third level is called detailed (municipal) plan level. As from 1 January 2000, there is only one type of this level, because the three previous types were merged into one detailed plan with flexible contents. The traditional English translation for one of the old types has been Town Plan but because the current plan is not applicable only in towns, the expression Detailed Plan is more proper and consequently used also in this monograph.

1413. However, the previous Shore Area Plan is in a way preserved, as the Detailed Plan for Shore Area is a specific version of the Detailed Plan, for which certain special provisions are applied in addition to those generally applied to a Detailed Plan. A Detailed Plan always concerns an area of one municipality and is decided upon by the same. The same holds normally true for Local Master Plans, but also joint Local Master Plans for several municipalities, regulating, e.g., road planning, and the locating of retail trade, workplaces and residential areas, are possible.

1414. Any plan shall meet the various substantive requirements expressed in the Land Use and Building Act (in the Land Use Act respectively) and other enactments. A plan shall be based on planning where the significant impacts thereof are assessed, and on the investigations and accounts required for this. The function and purpose are taken into account. The environmental impacts of the plan and its options shall be studied, including the impacts relating to municipality economy and social, cultural and other impacts. The accounts shall cover the whole area on which the plan may be assessed to have impacts (section 9).

1415. If a plan is drawn up for a project provided in section 3 of the Environmental Impacts Assessment Act, it is possible to assess the impacts jointly in the planning procedure instead of applying Chapter 3 of the said Act. In this case, the developer shall submit the information provided in sections 16 and 19 of the said Act to the planning authority (section 9(3)). The liaison authority is still responsible for checking the sufficiency of the impact and the reasoned conclusion (section 9(3)). This possibility of joint assessment is, however, excluded if the planning authority at the same time is also the developer (section 9(4)). But, in any case, the public hearings in accordance to both the acts may be combined pursuant to section 22 of the Environmental Impacts Assessment Act (section 62a).

1416. If the implementation of a Plan to be drawn up is likely to have significant effects on the environment in the territory of another Member State of the EU, the Finnish Environment Institute or another responsible authority assigned by decree shall ensure the notification procedure provided for in Article 7 of Directive 2001/42/EC of the assessment of the effects of certain plans and programmes on the environment and the negotiation of significant environmental effects with another Member State. If significant environmental impacts are likely to occur on the territory of a State party to an international agreement binding on Finland, or if a State subject to significant environmental impacts so requests, the Finnish Environment Institute shall correspondingly take care of the notification and negotiation task with the State in question. Chapter 26a contains more detailed procedural provisions.

1417. Participation and hearings are organized separately plan by plan, in consultation with all interested parties. A scheme on participation and hearings (section 63 of the Land Use and Building Act, as of 1 January 2023, the Land Use Act) has to be drawn up at the initial stage of preparation of each land use plan, focusing on participation and interactive procedures and assessment of the impacts of the coming plan. For this purpose, consultations between the municipality and the Centre for Economic Development, Transport and the Environment were originally required at an early stage, but this provision has been revoked in 2017. It is in all cases required that the very planning procedure is arranged and information on the starting points, goals and possible alternatives are provided in such a way that the landowners and those whose living or working conditions or other circumstances the plan is likely to affect, and the relevant authorities and organizations, are provided with a possibility to participate, assess the impacts of planning and give an oral or written opinion (section 62). The initiation of a planning procedure shall be notified in such a way that all interested persons and organizations defined above are able to have information on the starting points of the planning. A proposal to plan shall be publicly notified. All citizens and all relevant parties shall be provided with an opportunity to state their view. A reasoned answer shall be given to all who have done so. The final plan decision, which is normally made by the Municipal Council, shall be notified separately to all those who have stated their view and to any citizen of the relevant municipality (relevant municipalities) who has beforehand asked for notification.

1418. Appeals against plan decisions at all levels are lodged with the Regional Administrative Courts. Both procedural and substantive illegality may be pleaded. This means that also the application of the substantive plan requirements may be challenged.

Appeals (municipal appeal, *see* paragraphs 102, 1482 and 1565) against a plan decision can be made by all citizens and organizations with a domicile in the municipality (municipalities) in question, all concerned land owners and holders and other parties, and, due to the special clause in section 191 of the Land Use and Building Act (as of 1 January 2025, the Land Use Act), by registered local or regional associations, or, regarding Regional Plans, also nationwide associations as far as National Land Use Goals are pleaded. Also the concerned State authorities are entitled to appeal, as well as the inter-municipal Regional Council and, if impacted by the plan, another municipality. As an exception, Detailed Plan amendments with only insignificant impacts may, as far as private subjects are concerned, only be appealed against by the immediately concerned. As insignificant impacts are not regarded as amending the main purpose of an area, reducing parks or other areas for local recreation, raising rights to build or allowed building heights in an environmentally relevant way, or deterioration of values of built-up or natural environment.

1419. Prior to 2017, the traditional right of appeal of the Centres for Economic Development, Transport and the Environment encompassed all plan decisions, and it was commonly regarded as a procedural safeguard for legality and maintenance of plan hierarchy in municipal decision-making. In 2017 the explicit provision on the item in section 191 was revoked. The remaining provision on the standing of authorities in general (above) is far from the same, because the remaining supervision task of the centres in planning, building and other land use, pursuant to the present section 18, only encompasses items with nationwide impacts or significant regional impacts.

Without prejudice to the right of appeal of the Centre for Economic Development, Transport and the Environment, the centre is still entitled to suggest to the Municipal Council that a plan decision be reconsidered. In this case the Municipal Council shall make a new decision within six months; otherwise the Plan will be void (section 195).

1420. Whereas only legal grounds (which are, however, rather wide) may be pleaded by the appellants, the appeal has (regarding all plan categories) a twofold function: both general control of legality by citizens, and legal protection of individual rights and protected interests. Often these two intertwine in practice. If a plan as such is disapproved by the court but could be acceptable after certain amendments, the decision cannot, due to the principles of Municipal Appeal, be directly amended, but the plan decision is repealed and returned by the court to the municipal authority in question for new consideration.

If the EIA regarding a project has been combined with the planning procedure (section 9(3)), an appeal may not be based on a lacking or allegedly insufficient EIA, but section 34 of the Environmental Impacts Assessment is applied instead (section 188(4)).

§2. Regional Plans

1421. The most general and widest-ranging of all the plans under the Land Use and Building Act (as of 1 January 2025, the Land Use Act) is the Regional (Land Use) Plan, which is drafted and approved by each of the nineteen inter-municipal Regional Councils, for each region. In principle regional planning, like the other forms of spatial planning, though common to several municipalities, belongs to the category of municipal decision-making. In the original system of the Act, the decision of the Regional Council had to be submitted for final approval (confirmation) to the Ministry of the Environment. This obligation was in 2016 repealed. A plan decision is now appealable to the Regional Administrative Court in the ordinary way (of municipal appeal).

The law determines minimum standards for regional plans in many respects, e.g., concerning several public interests and the circumstances of the landowners.

1422. According to the Land Use and Planning Act (as of 1 January 2025, the Land Use Act), the purpose of a Regional Plan is to steer other land use planning. In a Regional Plan, National Land Use Goals are taken into account and adjusted with regional and local goals. The principles of land use and urban structures are presented and areas important to the development of the region are allocated. Proper allocation decisions are made only insofar and only with such preciseness that is necessary from the viewpoint of National Land Use Goals or regional goals or necessary to coordinate the use of areas in two or more municipalities (section 25). The substantive plan requirements (section 28) include, in addition to taking into account the National Land Use Goals that special attention is given to the specific needs of the region. Adjusting with the neighbouring regions is needed as far as possible. Nature conservation programmes and founding decisions of Landscape Management Areas under the Nature Protection Act shall have a guiding effect. Special attention shall be paid to:

(1) an appropriate regional and community structure;
(2) ecological sustainability in the use of areas;
(3) environmentally and economically sustainable arrangements in traffic and technical infrastructure;
(4) sustainable use of water and soil resources;
(5) operating conditions for regional business and industry;
(6) care of the values of landscape, nature and cultural heritage; and
(7) sufficient amount of areas suitable for recreation.

Attention shall moreover be paid to economic use of areas and avoiding unreasonable disadvantage to a landowner or other holder of rights. It shall be made clear in the plan who will be responsible for implementing the plan and the necessary measures. All requirements apply only insofar as the function of the Regional Plan as a non-detailed plan requires.

1423. Pursuant to the amended wording of sections 29, 29a and 30 of the Act (432/2023) a Regional Plan shall be drawn up in a nationally interoperable data model format, instead of traditional maps. A Regional Plan consists of sites and provisions. The sites and provisions shall be presented in nationally common standard form on a map and, if necessary, as a separate document. The Regional Plan is accompanied by an explanatory memorandum that, without being an actual part of the Plan, presents the information necessary for assessing the objectives of the Plan, the different alternatives and their impacts, as well as the grounds for the opted solutions. Such provisions are laid down that, taking into account the purpose of the

Plan and the requirements set for its content, are required in future planning or construction. Special provisions may, where necessary, relate to protection of values of landscape, built-up environment or cultural heritage.

1424. The original idea of regional planning was to achieve an overall plan for all kinds of land use and related activities in the whole region concerned. In practice, plans of this kind long remained drafts. At the outset, most of the approved plans had a limited purpose and a limited or scattered areal scope. The continuation of this state of affairs is also made possible by the Land Use and Planning Act (and as of 1 January 2025 by the Land Use Act), pursuant to which a Regional Plan can also be drawn up stage by stage or area by area (section 27). Among the purposes of the plans, protection of nature and the safeguarding of recreational needs have been central objectives in practice. The plans have, e.g., set valuable esker areas aside for protection and sustainable use and reserved forest areas for recreation purposes. Matters of national importance have often been dominating. This has been a consequence of the lack of national level planning.

1425. The legal effects of a Regional Plan (section 32) are mostly of a guiding nature. The most important effect is that of guiding other, more detailed land use planning and land use related activities of other public authorities. This may be important in practice and, e.g., prevent the execution of projects by which, e.g., environmental values would be endangered. However, pursuant to the idea of plan hierarchy, a Regional Plan is not valid in areas where a Local Master Plan with full legal effects or a Detailed Plan is in force, except for guiding the possible amending of such a plan. Against private citizens the plan has no direct legal effect, however, except in certain situations a restriction of the right to build (section 33 of the Land Use and Building Act, as of 1 January 2025 section 49 of the Building Act). These situations encompass, e.g., plan reserves for recreation or conservation, in which building is prohibited, if the implementation of the plan would be hampered. Depending on the nature of the building, the restriction may create an obligation for the municipality or the State to compensate the loss to the owner or to purchase the area. Between these two situations (authorities are bound by the plan, property owners are not) there are juridically interesting and difficult intermediate situations when permits or plans of various kinds are needed for private land use. This may lead to legal effects of a relative character. Moreover, an area set aside for nature protection in the Regional Plan may, or is in fact supposed to, get stronger protection status afterwards, by applying the protection and purchasing means in the Nature Protection Act. This means of course as a rule that the State or the municipality shall pay for the final protection.

§3. Local Master Plans

1426. The other plans concern only a single municipality or part of its area (except for possible joint Local Master Plans). The power of initiative and decision-making in planning belongs primarily to municipal authorities, however not entirely. The most general of the local level plans is the Local Master Plan, which is in many respects similar to the Regional Plan and has mainly similar legal effects (*see* above). The Regional Plan (if there is one) serves as a legal guideline in the drafting work. In addition, the Local Master Plan has to meet certain general requirements specified by law. These requirements refer to various public interests and the rights of the landowners. A Local Master Plan is, like all plans under the Land Use (and Building) Act, in a way a compromise between various public and private needs and points of view.

The purpose of a Local Master Plan is to generally steer community building and land use planning in the area of a municipality or part thereof, and adjust various activities with each other. It is also possible to draw up a Local Master Plan to steer land use and building in a certain area. A Local Master Plan shall include a presentation on the principles of the development pursued and on the various areas that make up the necessary basis for detailed planning and for building and other land use (section 35). Like a Regional Plan, a Local Master Plan can also be drawn up stage by stage or area by area. The guiding effects of the Local Master Plan are rather similar to those of the Regional Plan.

1427. The substantive plan requirements (section 39) include, in addition to taking the Regional Plan into account, that attention is paid to:

(1) functionality, economy and ecological sustainability of community structure;
(2) utilization of existing buildings;
(3) residential need and access to services;
(4) possibilities for appropriate arrangements concerning traffic, in particular public transport and non-vehicular traffic, and concerning infrastructure regarding energy, water and waste, in a sustainable way from the viewpoints of environment, natural resources and economy;
(5) possibilities to have a safe, healthy and, considering the various population groups, balanced living environment;
(6) operating conditions for local business and industries;
(7) abatement of environmental harms;
(8) care of the values of a built-up environment, landscape and nature; and
(9) sufficient amount of areas suitable for recreation.

The requirements above apply only insofar as the guiding function and level of accuracy of the Local Master Plan require. It is required that landowners or other holders of right are not caused unreasonable disadvantage.

1428. Pursuant to the present section 40 and 40a of the Act (432/2023), a Municipal Master Plan shall, like a Regional Plan, be drawn up in a nationally interoperable data model format, instead of traditional maps. A Municipal Master Plan consists of sites and provisions. The sites and provisions shall be presented in nationally common standard form on a map and, if necessary, as a separate document. The regional plan is accompanied by an explanatory memorandum that, without being actual part of the Plan, presents the information necessary for assessing the objectives of the Plan, the different alternatives and their impacts, as well as the grounds for the opted solutions. Such provisions (section 41) are laid down that, taking into account the purpose of the Plan and the requirements set for its content, are required in future planning or construction. They may be made up of various contents, considering the purpose and substantive requirements of the plan. They may also focus on particular steering of planning and building in a certain area, or the prevention or restriction of harmful environmental impacts. Special provisions may, where necessary, relate to protection of values of landscape, built-up environment or cultural heritage.

1429. Due to the plan hierarchy, a Local Master Plan is not valid in areas where a Detailed Plan is in force, except for steering the possible amending of a Detailed Plan. A Local Master Plan has a guiding effect in detailed planning and other land use. All authorities are obliged to avoid hindering the implementation of a Local Master Plan by their various decisions and activities (section 42(1–2)). This may be pleaded in appeals to administrative courts. However, if the valid Local Master Plan is evidently outdated, a Detailed Plan may, for particular reasons and under certain conditions, be approved or amended without having to observe the guiding effect of the Local Master Plan (section 42(4)).

Against private citizens a Local Master Plan, like a Regional Plan, has no direct legal effect, except in certain situations a restriction of the right to build (section 42 of the Land Use and Building Act). Depending on the nature of the building, the restriction may create an obligation for the municipality or the State to compensate the loss to the owner or to purchase the area.

1430. Like Regional Plans, the Local Master Plans in practice often focus on scattered areas and activities sharing a specific characteristic (component plans). An example is a Local Master (use and conservation) Plan for shore areas. This type has evolved owing to the pre-1997 lack of general shore area protection (*see* §6 below). In the system of the Land Use and Building Act (as of 1 January 2025, the Land Use Act), a Local Master Plan for shore areas (section 73 of the Act) may have specific legal effects (*see* §6 below). Also regarding other areas, a Local Master Plan may, under certain conditions, serve directly as a legal basis for building in such a way that no Detailed Plan is needed at all (section 44).

However, it is also possible for a municipality to draw up a 'lesser' Local Master Plan (section 45 of the Land Use and Building Act). A Local Master Plan of this kind will, however, only exceptionally have legal effects. The 'normal' Local Master Plan (a Local Master Plan with full legal effects) has all the regular legal effects mentioned above, but until recent years it has not been very common, and when there is any, it often includes only certain areas or land use purposes. A clear shift towards fully effective Local Master Plans has nevertheless taken place in municipal practice.

1431. A Local Master Plan is drawn up by the municipality, observing the provisions of the Land Use and Building Act (as of 1 January 2025, the Land Use Act) on procedures and participation (*see* Part III, Chapter 3, §1 above), and approved by the Municipal Council. A joint Local Master Plan for several municipalities (section 46) is possible. Approval by each municipality is required for such a plan, but the municipalities may also assign the task to the Regional Council or another joint body (section 47). As for the metropolitan area (the municipalities Helsinki, Espoo, Vantaa and Kauniainen), the joint Local Master Plan is provided by law (section 46a).

The procedures and the minimum substantive requirements of a Local Master Plan are legally controlled through the appeal system, in the first place by the Regional Administrative Court (*see* paragraph 1418).

§4. Detailed Plans

1432. As is the case with master planning, detailed planning with legal effects is (Detailed Plans for Shore Areas excepted) entirely the responsibility of the municipalities. The term 'planning monopoly' is often used to describe this situation. However, each municipality is obliged to draw up and keep up-to-date Detailed Plans where required by the development of the municipality or a need to steer land use, paying attention in particular to the need to produce dwellings and promote the functioning competition in business (section 51 of the Land Use and Building Act, as of 1 January 2025, the Land Use Act). The purpose of a Detailed Plan is to arrange in detail land use and building through designating necessary areas for different purposes and steering building and other land use depending on local conditions, townscape and landscape, good building practice, promoting the use of existing buildings and other goals (section 50). In a typical Detailed Plan, areas are designated for dwelling houses or blocks of various kinds, industrial establishments, roads, squares, parks, recreational areas, etc.

1433. The substantive plan requirements (section 54) include, in addition to taking the Regional Plan and a fully valid Local Master Plan into account, that preconditions are created for a healthy, safe and pleasant living environment, local access to services and traffic arrangements. Built-up environment and natural environment shall be cherished and values attached to them shall not be left destroyed. The plan area or its very neighbourhood shall include a sufficient amount of parks or other areas suitable for local recreational needs. A Detailed Plan may not cause anyone such deterioration of the quality of the environment that, unless insignificant, is not appropriate considering the purpose of the plan. Moreover, a Detailed Plan may not impose on a landowner or other holder of right such unreasonable disadvantage that can be avoided without displacing the goals or requirements of the plan.

Due to the nature of land use planning, conflicts between diverging interests may arise, which are to be solved by the planning authority. The ultimate power of decision belongs to the appellate administrative courts, but only as far as the legal requirements are concerned. This means that a plan is rejected by the court only if it is clear that it does not meet the minimum requirements. The choice between the alternatives that do meet these requirements – even if one would be better than another – belongs to the municipality itself. Due to the general nature of the substantive provisions, it is not always easy to draw the borderline between these two regimes. But there are anyway several cases where a plan has been rejected by the

SAC, e.g., because of disregard for cultural or natural values, or due to unjustified inequality between landowners. An example from 1990: The Municipal Council of an originally medieval town had decided to change the existing Detailed Plan for certain, mainly privately owned parts of the town centre, in order to make possible a total renewal of the existing buildings, with the exception of a few buildings which would be protected. After submission according to the then Building Act, the then Provincial Office (here as the predecessor of the Centre for Economic Development, Transport and the Environment) annulled the decision. The Municipal Executive appealed against the latter to the SAC. The appeal was rejected by the court, which, voting four to one, declared that certain parts of the area were valuable from the viewpoints of architecture and townscape. The present buildings here were of Empire or Neo-Renaissance style from the late 1800s and early 1900s, making up a rather integrated and well-balanced whole. Parts of the buildings were well conditioned or able to be repaired. The area was considered characteristic for the whole town. According to the court, the planning rules concerning cultural and landscape values had not been taken into account in a proper way.

1434. The Building Act of 1958 (in force up to end of 1999) was quite efficient in respect to the preservation of parks and natural environments within areas under municipal detailed planning. Pursuant to it, special attention had to be paid to arranging parks and other recreational areas in the various urban areas and in a sufficient quantity and to that the areas previously reserved for these purposes are not reduced without a particular reason (section 34 of the 1958 Act). This clause was relevant also in judicial practice. In the present Act of 1999, it is enough that there are sufficiently parks and other areas suitable for refreshment within the plan area or surrounding areas (section 54 discussed above). In addition, particular values of nature, where any, shall be preserved. In practice, the present, more vague provision has had only a very slight greenness preservation impact in judicial practice, in contradiction to its predecessor. This regulative background may be relevant, e.g., in the future implementation of the proposed Regulation of the European Parliament and of the Council on nature restoration (COM(2022) 304 final).

1435. There are some special categories of Detailed Plan, such as Detailed Plan for (perhaps merely) underground premises (section 56), and Detailed Plan for shore areas (section 73 of the Act, *see* §6 below).

1436. Pursuant to the present sections 55 and 56 (432/2023) of the Land Use Act (as of 1 January 2025, the Land Use Act), a Detailed Plan shall, like a Regional Plan and a Municipal Master Plan, be drawn up in a nationally interoperable data model format, instead of traditional maps. A Detailed Plan consists of sites and provisions. The sites and provisions shall be presented in nationally common standard form on a map and, if necessary, as a separate document. The Plan is accompanied by an explanatory memorandum that, without being actual part of the Plan, presents the information necessary for assessing the objectives of the Plan, the different alternatives and their impacts, as well as the grounds for the opted solutions. An appropriate, detailed, accurate and up-to-date base map, showing the terrains shall be used (section 54a). In the Plan shall, according to the needs of steering, be shown (section 55):

(1) the borders of the plan area and different sub-areas;
(2) the public and private purposes for which the land or water areas are intended;
(3) the quantity of buildings; and
(4) the principles on locating buildings and, where necessary, on the building practice.

1437. Plan provisions (section 57), aimed to be applied in future planning and building are part of the legally binding plan. They may be made up of various contents, considering the purpose and substantive requirements of the plan. Among other things, the plan provisions may be focused on the prevention or abatement of harmful environmental impacts, or, if necessary to safeguard commercial services, the character or quantity of commercial premises.

Special protection provisions may, where necessary and reasonable to the owner, be issued to protect an area or a building because of its landscape, natural values, built-up environment or cultural heritage. However, also such provisions that are unreasonable to the owner are possible, if an item under the Act on the Protection of the Built-up Heritage (*see* Part II, Chapter 1, §4) is at stake. In this case the owner, being other than a public body, is, however, entitled to pecuniary compensation by the municipality, or regarding nationally significant items, the State. The compensation is defined according to the rules in the Act on the Protection of the Built-up Heritage.

1438. The legal effects of a Detailed Plan are direct and essential. On the one hand, a Detailed Plan creates the necessary legal basis for building in an area where there is a planning need (*see* §5 below). On the other hand, no building may be erected against a Detailed Plan. As for other physical measures and works other than building, a Detailed Plan shall be observed as more closely provided for different purposes. No such activities shall be located in an area of a Detailed Plan that causes harm to such other land use than has been allocated by the plan. Also activities that are contrary to plan provisions on the prevention or restriction of harmful environmental impacts are forbidden (section 57 of the Land Use and Building Act, as of 1 January 2025 the Land Use Act).

1439. New premises for retail business larger than 4,000 square metres may be permitted in an area outside of areas assigned in a Regional Plan or a Local Master Plan for centre activity purposes only when the site is specially designated for that purpose in a Detailed Plan (section 71d). Section 9a contains provisions on large commercial premises, also regarding Regional Plans and Local Master Plans.

1440. There is a secondary plan within areas of a Detailed Plan, called Site Layout Plan (sections 78–82 of the Land Use and Building Act, as of 1 January 2025, the Land Use Act). Through a Site Layout Plan the building quarters are, where necessary, as either included in a Detailed Plan or separately, divided into future real properties observing the Detailed Plan. The Site Layout Plan may be of either binding or guiding nature. This Plan may also be three-dimensional, partly or totally. No building may be erected in contradiction to a binding Site Layout Plan.

1441. In addition to the provisions on planning need (below), building may be temporarily forbidden by the municipality in a certain area where local master planning or detailed planning is going on (sections 38 and 53 of the Act). In certain situations, a building prohibition follows directly from the Act. An Exceptional Permit as an exemption from the prohibitions may, due to the circumstances, be available, however.

§5. A Permit as a Substitute for a Plan

1442. The legal significance of a Detailed Plan lies in the fact that building in certain areas is only possible if either a Detailed Plan is in force there or, alternatively, certain extra preconditions are met in addition to those of an ordinary Building Permit (that as of 1 January 2025 provided for in the Building Act instead of the Land Use and Building Act). These areas are called areas with planning need (section 16 of the Land Use and Building Act, as of 1 January 2025, the Land Use Act). Planning need prevails if there is reason to take particular measures to meet the topical land use needs, such as the construction of roads, water conduits or sewerage, or the locating of areas free from buildings. Also significant environmental impacts of planned building make extra consideration necessary resulting in planning need. Moreover, the municipality may in a (fully valid) Local Master Plan or in Municipal Building Bylaw (as of 1 January 2025 provided for in the Building Act instead of the Land Use and Building Act) designate as an area with planning need an area where, due to its location, community development requires land use planning, or where planning is needed due to particular environmental values or environmental harm. Such designation will be valid for not more than ten years at a time. For shore areas there is a different legal framework, however (below §6). In particular regarding buildings and constructions of new kind, assessing of planning need may be more or less inconsistent in practice. With regard to solar panel fields (e.g., 100 ha), which have become more common in recent years, interpretations of planning need are not coherent in the administration so far. There are no specific land-use or protection regulations for them.

1443. If planning need is in force, the ordinary way to make building possible is to draw up and approve a Detailed Plan. The owners of the area have no direct right to demand this from the municipality. However, the Ministry of the Environment may, under certain conditions, use administrative enforcement measures against a passive municipality. This does not take place often, however. But there is also an important alternative to a plan. In connection with an ordinary Building Permit, or separately, a permit to build without a Detailed Plan may, in spite of the actual planning need, be granted, if the additional preconditions set forth in section 137 of the

Land Use and Building Act (as of 1 January 2025 the Land Use Act) are met. The competence for deciding on the matter is vested on a municipal authority (either the Building Supervision Authority or, when decided separately, another municipal authority appointed for the task). For this, it is in any case required that no buildings with significant impacts or otherwise significant environmental or other negative impacts result (section 137(4)). It is also required (section 1371(1)) that the planned building:

(1) does not cause disadvantage to detailed planning, master planning or other arranging of use of areas;
(2) is appropriate from the viewpoint of putting into practice civil engineering networks or traffic routes, as well as from the viewpoint of traffic safety and access to services; and
(3) is appropriate from the viewpoint of landscape and does not make difficult the preserving of particular values of nature or cultural heritage or the safeguarding of recreation possibilities.

1444. However, these preconditions in section 137(1) do not apply to the setting up of an outbuilding that is connected to an existing dwelling or farm, or certain other rural buildings, or to repair of a building or to minor expansion to a dwelling building (section 137(2)).

1445. As of 1 January 2025, pursuant to section 46 of the Building Act, prerequisite for placement in an area with planning need pursuant to section 16 of the Land Use Act is that the construction: (1) does not significantly impede the preparation of a municipal Master Plan or Detailed Plan in accordance with the municipality's Land Use Planning Review; (2) does not lead to construction with significant effects or cause such significant adverse environmental or other effects that require the preparation of a town plan; (3) is appropriate for the implementation of infrastructure networks and transport paths, as well as for road safety and accessibility of services. However, notwithstanding these conditions, a construction licence shall be granted in an area with planning needs: (1) for the construction of a commercial building belonging to an existing dwelling or agricultural holding; (2) the construction of a building necessary for the pursuit of agriculture, forestry or ancillary activities belonging to an existing rural enterprise; (3) renovation and alteration of the building; and (4) minor expansion of a residential building.

1446. In rural villages or other rural areas assigned particularly in a valid Local Master Plan with legal effects, a decision on the additional preconditions pursuant to section 137(1) may refer to several properties to be built. Such a decision may be valid no more than ten years (section 137a of the Land Use and Building Act, as of 1 January 2025, section 47 of the Building Act). Such a joint decision may not lead to construction with significant impacts or cause significant adverse environmental or other effects.

1447. For shore areas, the provisions on planning need are different and independent (*see* section 6 below). For wind power purposes a special type of Local Master Plan (section 77a–c of the Act) may create a direct legal basis for a Building Permit (*see* below).

1448. When dealing with the preconditions in section 137, either in connection with a Building Permit application or by virtue of a separate application, the procedural provisions for Exceptional Permits (section 173 of the Act, *see* below Chapter 4, §2) shall be observed by the competent municipal authority. Also the appellate procedure is common to both (*see* Chapter 4, §2).

§6. Shore Areas

1449. As for shore areas, the legal framework for detailed planning is different, however. According to the pre-1999 legislation, there was a specific category of detailed plans, namely the Shore Area Plan. This plan was not among the original plans when the 1958 Building Act came into force. In the 1960s, a proposed protection of shore areas gave rise to a lively public debate between the owners (and eventual purchasers) of shorelands and those concerned with the environmental and recreational values thereof. A bill based on general restrictions was drafted by the Cabinet in order to protect the shore areas against excessive summer home construction, like, e.g., in neighbouring Sweden. However, when it seemed that the bill would not be passed by Parliament, it was cancelled and a new bill was introduced including a quite different system with significantly slighter restrictions on land use. This bill was passed by Parliament and a new chapter was added to the Building Act of 1958 in 1969. The system was based on a new type of plan, the Shore Area Plan.

Pursuant to the previous Building Act in its various manifestations, a Shore Area Plan, hundreds of which are presently in force, was rather often needed for holiday-type dwellings in shore areas, but the need for planning was assessed case by case according to certain rules and established practice. From January 1997, the new juridical concept of shore belt expanded the areas where a plan – here optionally a Detailed Plan or a (certain type of) Local Master Plan – was needed for all kinds of building, with some exceptions.

1450. Also pursuant to the Land Use and Building Act, and as of 1 January 2026, the Land Use Act (section 72) there is a shore belt on the shorelands of all lakes and rivers and the sea. Within any shore belt, no building is allowed without a Detailed Plan or such a Local Master Plan in which specific provisions on shore area building, applicable directly as a basis for a Building Permit have been included. (Alternatively, an Exceptional Permit is possible, *see* below Chapter 4, §2.) The depth of a shore belt depends on local morphologic, etc. conditions. Normally it is about 100 metres and not more than 200 metres. The municipality has a limited power to temporarily nullify the belt rule in specified areas. To that end, it is required that spatial planning in the area is not needed and that the area shows no special values of nature or landscape, and that it is not needed for general recreational purposes (which in turn relates to the rules on public access). The Centre for Economic Development, Transport and the Environment (environmental division) may appeal against such a decision of the municipality. There are also certain exceptions for outbuildings to houses built before 1997.

1451. Irrespective of the shore belt rule, a Detailed Plan or a (specific type of) Local Master Plan (or an Exceptional Permit pursuant to the Land Use and Building Act, as of 1 January 2025 to the Building Act) is needed for a shore area where land use planning is regarded necessary in order to arrange holiday-type dwelling.

The provisions on planning need in shore areas above (section 72) do not, however, apply to:

(1) building for the purposes of agriculture, forestry or fisheries;
(2) building for the purposes of the Finnish Defence Forces or the Border Guard;
(3) building for navigational purposes;
(4) setting up of an outbuilding that belongs to the courtyard of an existing residential house; or
(5) repairing or insignificant enlarging of an existing residential house.

1452. A Detailed Plan or a Local Master Plan for shore areas is subject to certain additional substantive requirements. It is required that:

(1) the planned building and other land use is adjusted to shore landscape and the environment in general;
(2) nature, landscape, recreational needs, water protection and water supply are taken into account, as well as the characteristics of the water body, of the terrain and of the nature; and
(3) a sufficient amount of shoreline will remain not built.

1453. However, the primary purpose of the Detailed Plan for a shore area is not to protect the environment or to guarantee public recreation and free admission to lakes, rivers or the seashore. Rather its purpose is to be an instrument of controlled area development and, where appropriate, to guarantee a right to build – equally divided between all shore owners (or, more properly, between the areas of 'original' real estates with shoreline, i.e., those of (about) the year 1969, when the first shore area planning regime was introduced in legislation). However, certain environmental requirements such as a sufficient proportion of free shore areas, prevention of too dense building in areas, and, indirectly, water pollution prevention, have been traditionally included, and these aspects had been strengthened by the Land Use and Building Act. The Detailed Plan for shore areas is different from all the other plans in one important respect: the landowner (or the landowners together) has the power to take care of the drafting of the plan proposal, observing rules on procedure, hearing and participation that are normally applied by the municipality. This option does not imply any exception to the substantive requirements, either. The municipality has an obligation to deal with a plan proposal laid down by the landowner (or, in practice, by his expert) without delay. The appellate provisions are the same as for other detailed plans.

1454. An additional factor may in practice affect the Local Master Plans and Detailed Plans for shore areas. In 1990, the public discussion on eventual shore area protection resurfaced. Because it was evident that the political preconditions for general legislation on the matter were still lacking, the government tried to find other solutions. The Cabinet in December 1990 approved a national Shore Area Protection Programme drafted by the Ministry of the Environment. This plan was based on the then existing legislation and implementation measures: voluntary purchasing of land in order to establish preserves under the then Nature Conservation Act (where appropriate), expropriation where necessary, land use agreements with owners, Local Master Plans, etc. Actually it is a kind of policy paper for State authorities, without any (direct) legal effects. In 1992, however, the SAC held that the programme is a decision which can be appealed against. The actual appeals (of the owners of two properties within the programme) where rejected, though. From January 1997, the legal framework was strongly changed. The relevance of the existing legal measures in regard to protection was reduced, because all shore areas now were made subject to the planning obligation (*see* above). However, the programme may still affect planning in practice. For example, building may not at all be allotted to important programme areas, but this in turn may result in compensations by the State to landowners.

§7. Updating of Detailed Plans

1455. The accuracy and update of a Detailed Plan shall be assessed by the municipality. When necessary, measures to review the plan have to be taken (section 60 of the Land Use and Building Act, as of 1 January 2025, the Land Use Act). Where a Detailed Plan has been in force more than thirteen years but is still to a large extent unrealized, no Building Permit may be granted for any new building with significance to land use or land/townscape unless the accuracy and update has been assessed. The period of thirteen years may be beforehand altered by a Detailed Plan (between five and twenty years). Amendment of a Detailed Plan does not mean that the possible losses to owners, e.g., due to reduced scope of permitted building, should be compensated, but the losses are one of the factors affecting the legality of the plan amendment. However, if a plan is approved or amended in a way that a certain area may not be used for building purposes at all and this state of affairs is regarded unreasonable, the municipality (or in certain cases the State) is obliged to purchase the area or compensate the losses (section 101).

§8. Maritime Spatial Planning

1456. Chapter 8a on maritime spatial planning was inserted in the Land Use and Building Act in 2016, in order to implement Directive 2014/89/EU of the European

Parliament and of the Council of 23 July 2014 establishing a framework for maritime spatial planning. The purpose of maritime spatial planning is to promote sustainable development and growth of different maritime uses, sustainable use of marine natural resources and achieving good environmental status in the marine environment (section 67a of the Land Use and Building Act, as of 1 January 2025, the Land Use Act). Maritime spatial planning shall consider the needs of different uses and aim to coexistence thereof. The uses focused are in particular energy sectors, maritime transport, fisheries and aquaculture, tourism, recreation and preservation of environment and nature. Attention shall also be paid to maritime characteristics and land-sea interactions, as well as to defence needs (section 67a).

1457. A Maritime Spatial Plan shall be drawn up and approved for the territorial waters and for the economic zone by those of the Regional Councils the geographical areas of which contain territorial waters. Pursuant to the respective decree (816/2016), there are three planning areas, and the planning had to be finished by the end of 2016. The Regional Councils shall cooperate in the planning and coordinate the plans of each (section 67b). The concerned authorities and other concerned subjects shall have an opportunity to participate in the preparation and they shall be provided with an opportunity to state their opinions. The public shall be provided with an opportunity to get acquaintance with the preparation material and give opinions on it, by publishing a notification on the Internet. The term for opinions shall be at least thirty days (section 67c). Information on the plans shall be available on the Internet, and the Ministry of the Environment shall immediately be informed on an approved plan or amendment to it.

1458. As described above, the inserted provisions on spatial maritime planning are technically part of the Land Use and Building Act (as of 1 January 2025, the Land Use Act), but conspicuously without any integration or adjusting provisions on the relations to the pre-existing planning systems in the same Act. On the possible legal effects or other relevance of the plans nothing has been provided, unlike on the various land use plans under the Act – which likewise aim to adjust various uses to each other and may encompass water areas, also in the sea. Also the legal position of owners and various private rights has raised questions. The inner boundary of territorial waters is the coastline, and the inner parts are privately owned in the same way as inland lake areas (*see* paragraph 37). Due to this, overlapping and contradictory solutions in respect to same areas may be laid down, e.g., by a Local Master Plan and a spatial maritime plan (or a Water Management Plan or a Marine Waters Management Plan pursuant to the Act on the Arranging of Water Management and Marine Waters Management). And, again, unlike the Regional Plans, Local Master Plans and Detailed Plans, or the Water Management Plans or a Marine Waters Management Plans, nothing has been provided on the opportunity to appeal against a decision of a Regional Council by which a spatial maritime plan has been approved. The possible relevance of spatial maritime plans, e.g., in permit decisions under the Environmental Protection Act or the Water Act remains to be seen. In all, Chapter 8a is an example of law drafting where a directive has been implemented by minimal legislative effort without adjusting it properly to the legal system. In practice, the significance of the plans will be seen in the allocation of possible sites for wind power stations, at ministry level (economic zone) or by the Metsähallitus (Public Water Areas in territorial waters).

Chapter 4. The Permit System

§1. Regular Permits

1459. Plans are largely implemented through the different permit systems under the Land Use and Building Act (as of 1 January 2025 the Building Act). No plan implies an immediate right to build. A Building Permit (section 125) from the municipal Building Supervision Authority is needed for any new building (all kinds of residential houses, industrial buildings, other major constructions, etc.), irrespective of whether there is a plan for the area or not, unless the item is of such a nature that a 'lighter' Construction Permit may be used instead (*see* below). A building is defined (section 113 of the Land Use and Building Act) as 'a new stationary or otherwise standing construction, structure or facility that is intended for dwelling, working, storing or other use and, due to its properties, requires official supervision for reasons of safety, health, landscape, amenities, environmental aspects or other reasons connected to the goals of the Act'. Enlargement to an existing building is regarded as building, as provided in section 113. However, a construction with a small size and light structures is not regarded as a building, unless it has particular impacts from the viewpoints of land use or environment. However, these constructions shall also meet reasonable requirements regarding health, safety, appearance and adjustment to the environment (section 168). This is supervised by the Building Supervision Authorities, as well as the storing of various items in open air (section 169). Irrespective of this category, various constructions that are not regarded as buildings may require Construction Permit. A Building Permit is also needed for repair and amending works comparable to building. Also the change of purpose of an existing building may require a Building Permit (section 125(3)), as is the case of changing a holiday dwelling to a permanent dwelling (section 125(6)). So all this until 1 January 2025.

1460. From 1 January 2025 the permit mechanism based on the new Building Act is different. The Building Permit and Construction Permit have been combined as a single permit category called Building Permit. The construction of a new construction item requires a Building Permit if the object is: (1) a residential building; (2) a building of at least 30 square metres or 120 cubic metres in size; (3) a canopy of at least 50 square metres; (4) a public structure that can be used simultaneously by at least five natural persons; (5) a mast or chimney at least 30 metres high; (6) illuminated advertising equipment of at least 2 square metres; (7) energy well; or (8) an area to be built for a specific activity that has implications for the use of surrounding areas. A new construction item also requires a Building Permit if the construction has a more than minor impact on the use of areas, the cityscape, landscape, cultural heritage or environmental aspects, the construction requires regulatory supervision to ensure that the essential technical requirements are met, or it is necessary for supervising the construction from the point of view of the public interest. However, a Building Permit is not necessary if the measure is based on a detailed municipal Street Plan in accordance with the Land Use Act, an approved Final Engineering Plan in accordance with the Highways Act, or an approved Final Engineering Plan in accordance with the Railways Act. However, a municipality may

stipulate in the Building Bylaw that a Building Permit is not required due to the impacts in the municipality or part thereof if the project can be considered minor (section 42 of the Building Act).

1461. 'Construction item' in the Building Act refers to any building or construction which may have an effect on the use of surrounding areas and the implementation of which must take account of essential technical requirements, and any area constructed for a specific activity which has implications for the use of surrounding areas. 'Building' in turn refers to a separate, fixed object, intended to be stationary, with its own entrance, containing covered space separated by walls (sections 2(4) and 25)).

1462. A Building Permit is also required for repair and alteration work comparable to the construction of a building, as well as for expanding the building or increasing its floor area. When renovating a construction item, a Building Permit is required if the repair is aimed at removing a health hazard found in the intervention area to a more significant extent, the load-bearing structure of the intervention area has been damaged, or the repair measures may endanger the health or safety of the construction site, or if the repair has a significant impact on the cityscape, landscape or cultural heritage. A Building Permit is also required for repairs that target the essential characteristics of the construction item. A Building Permit is always required for repairs if: (1) a building protected by a Plan under the Land Use Act or by the Act on the Protection of the Built-up Heritage is repaired or altered in a manner that has a significant impact on the protected or architectural value of the building; (2) renovation or modification of the building envelope or technical systems can have a significant impact on the energy performance or energy and environmental impacts of the building throughout its life cycle; or (3) substantially change the use of the building or part thereof (section 42 of the Building Act).

1463. Building Permit consideration by a municipal Building Supervision Authority is pursuant to the Building Act (as of 1 January 2025) twofold. It consists of an examination of the preconditions for the use of areas (*conditions for location*) and an examination of the essential technical requirements (*conditions for implementation*). If the applicant so requests, the municipality may decide on the existence of the conditions for placement in a separate decision (*Location Permit*) (section 43 of the Building Act).

1464. All the legal prerequisites for the building project are examined by the permit authority (municipal Building Supervision Authority), such as the existence of a plan or Exceptional Permit, if needed, and the environmental effects of the building insofar as they are relevant to the Land Use and Building Act, as of 1 January 2025 the Building Act.

1465. As of 1 January 2025, in advising, steering and supervising under its responsibility, an authority, as well as those responsible for planning and implementation in their own activities, shall take into account the starting points of guidance: (1) a construction item must be suitable for their intended use and contribute to the creation of a healthy, safe and comfortable, high-quality, socially functional and aesthetically balanced living environment; (2) a building must be suitable for the built-up environment and landscape and be beautiful, of high architectural quality or proportionate; (3) construction must mitigate climate change by basing on sustainable and economical, energy-efficient, socially and ecologically functional solutions and solutions that promote the circular economy; (4) construction shall be based on solutions that create and preserve cultural values in such a way that buildings or cultural environments of historical or architectural value are not defaced and the construction also enables the creation of new valuable buildings and new cultural environments; and (5) the building stock and the surrounding built-up environment shall be systematically managed and maintained (section 5 of the Building Act).

1466. The requirements for an appropriate building site are decided upon by a valid Detailed Plan, where any. In areas without a valid Detailed Plan, it is required that the site is appropriate for its purpose, suitable for building and large enough, at least 2,000 square metres. In assessing the suitability, the risks for flood, fall of earth or landslide are taken into account. It shall also be possible to locate the building at a sufficient distance from property border, public road and another's land (section 116 of the Land Use and Building Act up to 1 January 2025). The Land Use and Building Decree (section 57) includes additional requirements for the site of a building. Among other things, the risk for industrial hazards is taken into account. No building creating a fire risk shall be located at a distance closer than fifteen metres from another's land or at a distance closer than twenty metres from a building on another's land. In an area without a Detailed Plan, no building shall without an acceptable reason be located at a distance closer than five metres from another's land or at a distance closer than ten metres from a building in another's land, unless agreed upon between the parties.

1467. All buildings shall be suitable to the existing built-up environment and to the landscape (section 117 of the Land Use and Building Act). A building shall also meet the requirements of beauty and harmony, be appropriate for its purpose, repairable and capable for service measures, and, depending on the planned use, also be suitable for persons with a limited ability to move or function (section 117). Any building shall, taken the planned purpose into account, meet the essential technical requirements regarding strength and stability of constructions, fire resistance, health, maintenance safety, energy efficiency, accessibility, noise abatement and acoustics and assembly uses, and all building plans shall meet the requirements of good construction practice (sections 117, 117a–117k and 120 of the Land Use and Building Act). As of 1 January 2025, the corresponding requirements are set for construction, building repair, strength and stability of structures, fire safety, healthiness, operational safety, accessibility, noise abatement and sound conditions, energy efficiency, low-carbon building, life-cycle characteristics of buildings, living, accommodation and workspaces, and meeting spaces (sections 29–41 of the Building Act). The special procedure pursuant to section 116 of the Act is required, among other grounds, if the site involves a special risk that the requirements for structural safety, fire safety, healthiness or the physical functionality of the building will not be met or that cultural-historical values will be lost. In all construction, renovation and alteration of a building and the demolition of a building or part thereof, care must be taken to ensure that buildings of historical or architectural value or the cityscape are not defaced (section 12).

1468. Within an area where a Detailed Plan is in force, it is required (section 135) for granting a Building Permit that:

(1) the building project complies with the Detailed Plan;
(2) the building meets the requirements laid down in section 117 or elsewhere;
(3) the building is suitable for its site;
(4) there is usable access by road or a possibility to arrange it;
(5) water supply and sewer may be arranged in a satisfactory way and without harm to the environment; and
(6) the building is not built or located in such a manner that it unnecessarily harms the neighbour or hinders the possibilities to appropriate building in the neighbour's area.

1469. As of 1 January 2025, a prerequisite for placement within a Detailed Plan area is that: (1) the project complies with the current Detailed Plan; (2) the works are suitable for the built-up environment and landscape and meet the requirements of beauty, high-quality architecture or harmony; (3) there is a useful access road to the site or the possibility of arranging one; (4) the supply of water and wastewater can be managed without harming the environment; (5) the construction does not cause inconvenience to neighbours and does not complicate the construction of neighbouring properties; (6) the granting of the permit does not impede the use of the rest of the block for the purpose indicated in the plan; and (7) the applicant is holder of the entire construction site. The Building Supervision Authority may grant a Building Permit without an assessment of the conditions for placement solely on the basis of the conditions for implementation if the work in question is repair and modification work that has no effect on the fulfilment of the conditions for placement. If construction in accordance with the Building Permit requires the demolition of a building, the conditions for granting a Demolition Permit are also subject to the provisions on the granting of a Demolition Permit (section 44 of the Building Act).

1470. Where no Detailed Plan is in force, it is required (section 136) that:

(1) the building site meets the requirements laid down in section 116;
(2) the building meets the requirements laid down in section 117 or elsewhere;
(3) the requirements laid down in subsections 3–6 of section 135 (above);
(4) the constructing of access roads or the arrangements for water supply or sewer do not cause the municipality extra costs; and
(5) the restrictions caused by a Regional Plan or Local Master Plan in pursuance of sections 33 and 43, where any, are taken into account.

If there is planning need according to section 16, and no Detailed Plan is in force, the additional provisions laid down in section 137 (above Chapter 3, §5) may be examined in the Building Permit procedure, or separately.

1471. As of 1 January 2025, placement outside a Detailed Plan area requires that (1) the building site is at least 1,000 square metres in size; (2) there is no risk of flooding, collapse or landslide at the construction site; (3) buildings may be located at a distance of at least four metres from the boundary of the property, taking into account also the protected area and field of vision pursuant to the Highways Act, the protected area and field of vision pursuant to the Railways Act, and the need for a flight obstacle permit pursuant to the Aviation Act; (4) the construction works are suitable for the built environment and landscape and meet the requirements of beauty, high-quality architecture or harmony; (5) there is a useful access road to the construction site or the possibility of providing one; (6) the supply of water, waste-water and storm water can be managed without harm to the environment; (7) the provision of roads, water supply or sewerage does not entail any special costs for the municipality or the State; (8) the construction does not cause inconvenience to neighbours and does not complicate the construction of neighbouring properties; (9) the construction is appropriate from a landscape point of view and does not impede the maintenance of specific natural or cultural environmental values or the safe-guarding of recreational needs; and (10) the construction will not interfere with the implementation of the provisions laid down in the Regional Plan, Local Master Plan or Building Bylaw (section 45 of the Building Act).

1472. Where the use of the building in question would need an Environmental Permit according to the Environmental Protection Act, the Building Permit procedure may be suspended by the Building Supervision Authority, if this is regarded reasoned, considering the possibilities to use the building and the environmental impacts of the planned use (section 134(5) of the Land Use and Building Act, as of 1 January 2025 section 68(3) of the Building Act).

1473. Up to 1 January 2025, a Construction Permit may, instead of a Building Permit, be used for setting up constructions and establishments, such as masts, cisterns and chimneys, for which overall building supervision is unnecessary (section 126 of the Land Use and Building Act). Moreover, a Construction Permit is required for the setting up of such constructions and establishments not regarded as buildings that have impacts on natural conditions, land use of surrounding area or landscape or townscape, as defined more closely by decree (section 126). Additionally, a Construction Permit is needed for certain façade changes and structural rearrangements inside residential houses. In the new Building Act, no separate Construction permit is provided.

1474. Up to 2025, Construction Permit is also necessary for the changing of a part of a building or its technical system, if significant impacts on energy efficiency may result. A permit is not needed, however, for buildings the energy efficiency of which need not be enhanced due to section 117g(2) of the Land Use and Building Act, except for the construction of such automation and steering system which is provided in sections 11–13 of the Act on Deployment of Recharging Points and Recharging Infrastructure and of Automation and Monitoring (733/2020).

1475. Regular items of a Construction Permit up to 2025 are listed in section 126a of the Land Use and Building Act. These are: (1) canopy, shed, kiosk, detached lavatory and similar construction, as well as constructing or amending of a property's wastewater system; (2) sports centre, assembly place, caravan areas and corresponding area other than those provided in the Outdoor Recreation Act, and establishing or constructing of audience stand, audience tent or similar construction; (3) keeping a caravan or houseboat or similar item on a place for use not pertaining to customary camping or boating; (4) mast, chimney or stack, cistern, ski lift, monument, major antenna, wind power plant, major lamppost or similar item; (5) major quay, bridge or other construction amending shoreline or impacting it significantly, channel, breakwater or similar item; (6) arranging of separated major storage area or parking area or similar area; (7) amendment of façade, roof shape, covering or colouring of building, or installing canvas awing impacting street view or change of window dividing; (8) installing of other construction than that provided in section 52 of the Highways Act, text or picture outdoors in advertising or other commercial purpose, or permanent or long-time covering of window by advertisement; (9) stationary fence in a built-up environment or edge wall of a street; (10) other arrangement impacting townscape or environment view significantly and long; (11) combining or dividing flats; (12) drilling a heat well for geothermal heating or installing a heat collecting pipe system when a building's heating system is changed or renewed, or for use as additional heat source; and (13) installing or constructing sun panel with significant impacts on townscape or environment.

A municipality may in Municipal Building Bylaw free insignificant measures other than that under (11) above from the permit requirement.

1476. No Construction Permit is (up to 2025) needed where the construction is based on a Street Plan under the Land Use and Building Act or an Engineering Plan according to the Highways Act or to the Railways Act. However, a Construction Permit is not an alternative to other possible permit systems. For example, a permit according to the Water Act may be necessary for a quay or bridge in addition to the Construction Permit.

1477. Municipal Building Bylaws may include certain reliefs to the Construction Permit system. It is also possible that a notification to the Building Supervision Authority is made sufficient instead of a permit (section 129 of the Land Use and Building Act up to 2025), but the scope of this option is somewhat unclear, because a permit shall still be required, if this is necessary for reasons of public interest or legal protection of neighbours. If such decision is not made in fourteen days after the notification, the measure may be taken.

The provisions regarding a Building Permit are also applicable on Construction Permits, but only insofar that it is necessary to assess the impacts of the construction from the viewpoints of land use and environment (section 138 of the Land Use and Building Act up to 2025).

1478. A Demolition Permit (section 127 of the Land Use and Building Act, as of 1 January 2025, the Building Act) is needed for the demolition of buildings in areas with a Detailed Plan and certain other areas. If a permit is not needed, a written notification of a planned demolition shall be lodged with the Building Supervision Authority at least thirty days before. Within this period, the Building Supervision Authority may, for justified reasons, require an application for a permit. The granting of a Demolition Permit requires that the values of cultural heritage or beauty are not destroyed (section 139 of the Land Use and Building Act), but in practice, the preconditions for demolition may in practice depend on whether the building has been protected or is at least going to be protected by a Detailed Plan or according to the Act on the Protection of the Built-up Heritage. As of 1 January 2025, the preconditions (section 56 of the Building Act) are somewhat different. Then it is required that: (1) the demolition does not adversely affect land use planning, the implementation of a plan or other arrangements for the use of the areas; and (2) demolition does not impede the achievement of the objectives of protecting the built-up environment. (1) above shall not apply where the items to be demolished are located in an area where the buildings have lost most of their value. In such cases, demolition requires that the demolition leads to significant reuse or recycling of demolition materials. The applicant shall investigate the arranging of the demolition work and the prerequisites for ensuring the treatment of the generated construction waste and the reuse of usable building elements.

1479. A Landscape Measures Permit (section 128 of the Land Use and Building Act, as of 1 January 2025, section 53 of the Building Act) is required for all earthworks by which landscape is altered, for cutting of trees and for similar measures, but only within:

(1) areas with a valid Detailed Plan;
(2) areas with a valid Detailed Plan for Shore Area, if so ordered in the Plan;
(3) in areas with a Local Master Plan, if provided by the said plan, excluding cutting of trees in areas assigned in the Plan as mainly agricultural and forestry-based; and
(4) in areas under planning where building is temporarily forbidden.

Measures with insignificant impacts are excluded, as well as measures necessary to implement a Local Master Plan or a Detailed Plan and measures based on a Building Permit or a Construction Permit. The same is true for measures based on a Final Engineering Plan according to the Highways Act or to the Railways Act. The Landscape Measures Permit is not applicable to extraction of soil substances, for which a permit according to the Soil Excavation Act is needed (*see* Part II, Chapter 7, §1).

1480. In areas with a valid Detailed Plan or a Local Master Plan, a Landscape Measures Permit has to be granted, if the measures do not impede the use of the area for the purpose defined by the plan or destroy townscape or landscape. In areas where building is temporarily prohibited, a Landscape Measures Permit may be granted, provided that the measures concerned do not significantly impede land use planning or destroy townscape or landscape. In specific situations the landowner may be entitled to compensation for denying a permit (section 140 of the Land Use and Building Act, as of 1 January 2025, section 54 of the Building Act).

1481. According to general opinion and established practice, a Building Permit *has to be granted* if the legal preconditions exist. This is why there is, in principle, no scope for free discretion. However, the vague legal clauses admit certain interpretation, ultimately by the appellate courts. The same principles hold true for the rest of the permit categories above, except for the Landscape Measures Permit in areas where the building is temporarily forbidden. Here, at least in principle, a permit may also be denied on reasons of expediency.

1482. A decision on a permit application can be appealed to the Regional Administrative Court. The legal preconditions are regarded as a matter of law only. Hence the courts decide upon permit matters to the same extent as the Building Supervision Authority. Unlike in the case of land use plans, the ordinary appellate rules are applied to permit decisions, not those for municipal appeals. The right to appeal against a decision on a Building Permit (or on a Construction Permit up to 2025) belongs (in addition to the applicant), to the owners or possessors of neighbouring properties, to the owners or possessors of properties the building within or other use of which may be essentially affected, to those on who's right, duty or interest the decision has an immediate impact and to the municipality (section 192(1) of the Land Use and Building Act). Hence a relevant individual interest is required and a member of the municipality in merely that capacity has no standing (compare the planning procedure). The right to appeal against a decision on a Landscape Measures Permit decision or on a Demolition Permit decision in turn belongs (in addition to the applicant) to those on whose right, duty or interest the decision has an immediate impact, to any member of the municipality, to the municipality and to such a neighbouring municipality the land use planning of which is impacted. From 2021, associations which promote environmental, health or nature protection are also entitled to appeal in their geographical domain, but only if the permit regards a building within a project to which the Environmental Impact Assessment Procedures Act is applied. From 2017, the Centre for Economic Development, Transport and the Environment of the region is no more entitled to appeal against a Landscape Measures Permit decision, but a Demolition Permit may still be appealed against by the centre, if the building is nationally or regionally significant (section 192(3)). The same applies to a Building Permit, if it means demolition of such a building. So, all this until 2025.

1483. The right to appeal against a Building Permit in a Detailed Plan area, a Building Permit for a building site outside Detailed Plan areas to which the provisions on planning need are not applied, and a separate Location Permit in these areas is vested in: (1) the owner and possessor of adjacent or opposite property or other area; (2) the owner and possessor of property or other area, the construction or other use of which may be materially affected by the decision; (3) a person whose rights, obligations or interests are directly affected by the decision; (4) the municipality;

(5) a neighbouring municipality whose land use planning is affected by the decision; (6) a museum authority, if the decision concerns a building site protected under a Plan or law. In addition, the Centre for Economic Development, Transport and the Environment, a museum authority and a registered association whose field of activity includes safeguarding cultural heritage or influencing the quality of the built-up environment in its area of activities have the right to appeal if the construction involves the demolition of a building that requires a Demolition Permit and is protected under a Plan or law, or other historically or architecturally valuable building. Moreover, a registered association whose purpose is to promote environmental, health or nature protection has in its area of activities the right to appeal if the Building Permit concerns a building in a project to which the Environmental Impact Assessment Procedures Act applies (section 179).

1484. The right to appeal against a Demolition Permit is vested in: (1) the owner and possessor of adjacent or opposite real estate or other areas; (2) the owner and possessor of property or other areas, the construction or other use of which may be materially affected by the decision; (3) the person whose rights, obligations or interests are directly affected by the decision; and (4) the municipality. In addition, the Centre for Economic Development, Transport and the Environment, a museum authority and a registered association whose field of activity includes safeguarding cultural heritage or influencing the quality of the built environment in its area of activities have the right to appeal if the decision concerns the demolition of a building protected by law or another building of historical or architectural value (section 182).

1485. The right to appeal against a Landscape Measures Permit is vested in: (1) the person whose rights, obligations or interests are directly affected by the decision; (2) a member of the municipality; (3) the municipality; (4) a neighbouring municipality whose spatial planning is affected by the decision; and (5) other authorities in matters falling within their operational field (section 183).

1486. For some reason, the appeal rights in the new Building Act apply to 'permit', not 'permit decision', as in the previous law. Nevertheless, it is clear that, at least as far as the applicant is concerned, the right of appeal also applies where the application has been rejected.

1487. There are also some special cases. For example, where an Exceptional Permit (§2 right below) or, within a planning need area, a permit to build without a Detailed Plan should have been acquired but has been omitted, the more extensive rules on standing regarding these permits (below paragraphs 1494–1498) are in administrative judicial practice applicable. If the decision happened to be contrary to the Nature Protection Act or provisions based on the same, the Centre for Economic Development, Transport and the Environment of the region (the environmental division thereof) would have right of appeal by virtue of section 135 of the Nature Protection Act. Also the specific rules on standing based on omitted EIA (*see* Part I, Chapter 1, §21) are applicable where necessary.

§2. EXCEPTIONAL PERMITS

1488. In addition to the in a way exceptional permits authorizing the building within a planning need area without a Detailed Plan (*see* Chapter 3, §5 above), proper Exceptional Permits are also possible, in principle, regarding any provision in the Land Use and Building Act, in the Land Use and Building Decree, in the regulations based on them, or in any land use Plan (section 171 of the Land Use and Building Act). However, the provisions on Landscape Measures Permits and on the preconditions for building within a planning need area (section 137) are excluded (section 171(4)). The planning need in shore areas (section 72) is nevertheless included. Also an exception for a larger area than one property is for particular reasons possible, as provided in section 172 of the Land Use And Building Act. So all this up to 1 January 2025.

1489. In the system of the 1958 Building Act, the permit competence was basically vested in the then Regional Environment Centres, or, with respect to some of the largest cities, in the Ministry of the Environment. From 1994, the Municipal Executives had also a general competence regarding exceptional permits, except for a list of qualified situations where the State authorities were exclusively competent. So the rule turned the opposite: the competence was vested in the municipality (section 171 of the Land Use and Building Act). The Centre for Economic Development, Transport and the Environment (environmental division) of the region was until 2016 the competent authority regarding certain exceptions. In 2016, that being one part of a larger reform to weaken the influence of the centres, the competence of the municipality was made exclusive.

1490. Up to 1 January 2025, an Exceptional Permit is only possible (section 172 of the Land Use and Building Act) when:

(1) no harm to land use planning, enforcement of a plan or other arrangements of land use is caused;
(2) the achieving of the goals of nature protection is not hampered;
(3) the achieving of the goals of the protection of a built-up environment is not hampered; and
(4) building with significant impacts does not result, and significant adverse environmental impacts are not caused; as such is not regarded constructing of wind power plant in an already built-up industrial or harbour area assigned in a Detailed Plan.

1491. Pursuant to section 57 of the Building Act, the general preconditions are as of 1 January 2025 the same as in (1)–(4) above. Particular reason is always required. Location in an area with planning need may be allowed by Exceptional Permit only provided that the location does not lead to such construction with significant impacts or cause such significant adverse environmental or other effects that require a Detailed Plan (*see* paragraphs 1470–1471). A Site Layout Plan or the need or preconditions of Landscape Measures Permit may not be exempted. Changing the purpose of use of a building or part of it in deviation from a Detailed Plan for housing or other use that does not cause environmental disturbance is not considered to cause harm to detailed planning, the implementation of Plan or other arrangement of land use, and it is not considered significant construction in terms of its effects. Changing the purpose of use of a building or part of it can be considered a particular reason if the change can support the circular economy and low-carbon nature of the built-up environment. An exception for several properties within a certain area is possible if the premises of an existing residential, commercial or office building in a Detailed Plan area are converted for residential use or other use that does not cause environmental disturbance and the preconditions in section 57 are met. A further condition is that it promotes the use, development and maintenance of existing buildings (section 58). A municipality may, as provided in section 18 of the Building Act, indicate in the Municipal Building Bylaw the areas and conditions under which the conversion of a holiday home into permanent residential use does not require an Exceptional Permit or an examination of the preconditions for placement in a planning need area before granting a Building Permit.

1492. Before a decision on an application for an Exceptional Permit is made by the municipal authority, the neighbours and others whose living or working conditions or other circumstances the planned measure is likely to affect shall be reserved the right to state their comments in writing. The application shall, at the expense of the applicant, be notified to the relevant parties (section 173 of the Land Use and Planning Act until 2025, as of 1 January 2025, section 64 of the Building Act correspondingly). Opinion of the Centre for Economic Development, Transport and the Environment of the region, another State authority or the Regional Council shall be obtained if the exception concerns them significantly. The opinion of a neighbouring municipality shall be obtained if land use there would be significantly impacted. However, the municipality is unconditionally obliged to obtain the opinion of the Centre for Economic Development, Transport and the Environment of the region, if the application relates to:

(1) an area that is significant to nature conservation;
(2) an area that is significant for the conservation of buildings valuable from the viewpoint of cultural heritage; or
(3) an area assigned for recreation, protection or traffic in a Regional Plan.

1493. As of 1 January 2025, the municipality must request a statement from the Centre for Economic Development, Transport and the Environment on an application for an Exception Permit (or a Building or Location Permit application, to which the provisions on planning need apply) if the application is likely to concern: (1) an area significant for the environmental or nature conservation; (2) an area or site of importance for the protection of cultural heritage or for recreational needs; or (3) the State transport network. A statement from the museum authority must be requested if a permit is applied for a site or area: (1) that is subject to building protection by virtue of a Plan or law; (2) is included in the World Heritage List as a cultural heritage site or may contribute to the preservation of universally specific values of such a site; (3) is subject to protection pursuant to section 1 of the Ancient

Remains Act; or (4) that belongs to a landscape area of national value, a built cultural environment of national significance or an archaeological site of national significance. Municipalities must request a statement from other State authorities and Regional Councils if the application significantly concerns their field of activity. The opinion must be issued within one month of receipt of the request for an opinion (section 67 of the Building Act).

1494. Up to 2025, the decision on an Exceptional Permit is made public and notified to the relevant parties as specified in section 174 of the Land Use and Building Act. Pursuant to section 193, appeals to the Regional Administrative Court can be lodged, in addition to the applicant, by:

(1) owners or possessors of properties next or opposite;
(2) owners or possessors of properties the building in which or other use of which may be essentially affected;
(3) those whose living, working or other conditions the project may significantly affect;
(4) those on whose right, duty or interest the decision has an immediate impact;
(5) the municipality and such a neighbouring municipality, the land use planning of which is impacted by the decision;
(6) registered associations, the aim of which is the protection of nature, environment or cultural heritage or otherwise influencing the quality of living environment; and
(7) an authority concerning items within its scope of activities.

1495. The procedural and appellate rules for Exceptional Permits also apply to the decisions on the additional preconditions (section 137) for building in planning need areas.

1496. The provisions on right of appeal referred to in paragraphs 1494 and 1495 above also apply when an ordinary Permit has been granted without the necessary Exceptional Permit or without considering the additional preconditions in areas of planning need.

1497. As of 1 January 2025, the right to appeal against Exceptional Permits and such Building Permits, which are subject to planning need, is vested in: (1) the owner and occupant of adjacent or opposite real estate or other area; (2) the owner and occupant of real estate or other area, the construction or other use of which may be materially affected by the decision; (3) the person whose housing, work or other conditions may be significantly affected by the project; (4) the person whose rights, obligations or interests are directly affected by the decision; (5) the municipality; (6) a neighbouring municipality whose land use planning is affected by the decision; (7) in its area of activities a registered association whose field of activity includes the promotion of natural or environmental protection or the preservation of cultural heritage or otherwise influencing the quality of the living environment; and (8) other authorities in matters within their operational field (section 180 of the Building Act).

1498. An Exceptional Permit may, depending on the circumstances, be a *conditio sine qua non* to a regular permit, e.g., to a Building Permit or a Construction Permit. If so, no ordinary permit is possible without a valid exception.

1499. There are additionally two specific categories of exceptions. Pursuant to section 175 of the Land Use and Building Act (up to 2025), the municipal Building Supervision Authorities are competent for minor, mostly technical exemptions as side decisions of ordinary Building Permits (section 175). Here the substantive provisions of section 171 are applied, but the procedure is simpler. As of 1 January 2025, a minor exception may be granted pursuant to section 59 of the Building Act. Such an exception may not jeopardize the fulfilment of the essential requirements set for construction. And pursuant to section 176 of the Land Use and Building Act (as of 1 January 2025, section 10 of the Building Act), a Building Permit for temporary buildings is under certain preconditions possible (up to five years, as of 1 January 2025 up to ten years).

§3. Wind Power Stations

1500. Wind power stations are today a project category with particular arrangements and provisions in the Land Use and Building Act, as of 1 January 2025 in the Land Use Act (Chapter 10a). A Building Permit for a wind power station may be granted without a Detailed Plan, if particularly provided in a Local Master Plan with legal effects, for specified areas (section 77a of the Land Use and Building Act, as of 1 January 2025, the Land Use Act, and section 52 of the Building Act). In drafting and approving such a Local Master Plan care shall, in addition to the general substantive requirements of a Local Master Plan, be taken of that (1) the plan sufficiently steers building and other land use in the area at stake; (2) the planned wind power constructing and other land use suits the landscape and the environment; and (3) it is possible to arrange technical maintenance of the plant and transfer of electricity (section 77b). If the drafting of the Local Master Plan mainly serves private interest and is initiated by a private operator or landowner, the municipality may decide that the private party shall pay the costs of drafting (section 77c).

In addition to a Building Permit or a Construction Permit up to 2025, or a Building Permit as of 1 January 2025, an Environmental Permit may on a case-by-case basis be needed for a wind power plant, due to possible unreasonable nuisance pursuant to section 27(2)(3) of the Environmental Protection Act.

1501. Government decree on the guideline values for outdoor noise by wind power plants (1107/2015), issued by virtue of section 142 of the Environmental Protection Act, is applicable in the land use planning, permit procedures and supervision according to the Land Use and Building Act (as of 1 January 2025, the Land Use Act and the Building Act) and in the Environmental Permit procedures and supervision according to the Environmental Protection Act.

§4. OTHER LEGISLATION

1502. The Act on the Information System for the Built Environment (431/2023) lays down provisions on the Built Environment Information System, which serves the information needs related to land use and construction. The purpose of collecting data is to use it for essential official purposes laid down by law. The System consists of the spatial use information pool and the building information pool. The Finnish Environment Institute is responsible for establishing, maintaining and developing the System. The task of the Finnish Environment Institute is to compile and share information on the built environment and to compile and maintain the necessary statistics on the data stored in the built environment information system.

1503. Construction may be forbidden or restricted also by virtue of other legislation, such as the Highways Act.

1504. Obstacles to air navigation caused by outside construction activities are provided in the Aviation Act (864/2014). A mast, wind turbine, crane, lighting, radio equipment or other device, building, structure or sign shall not be set up, arranged or aligned in such a way that it may be mistakenly regarded as a device or sign serving aviation. In addition, the structure or component must not interfere with equipment serving aviation or air traffic or otherwise pose a danger to aviation safety. The placing of a device, building, structure or sign liable to cause such confusion, disturbance or danger shall require a flight obstacle permit (section 158–158d). Activities that endanger aviation or impede a smooth traffic are forbidden (section 159). The Transport and Communications Agency may issue detailed decisions. In the previous Act, shooting, fireworks or blasting activities and the use of airborne or ground devices or a laser beam, were mentioned as examples on the activities at stake.

Chapter 5. Supervision

1505. Supervision of all activities within the regime of the Land Use and Building Act, and as of 1 January 1 2025 both the Land Use Act and the Building Act, is carried out by the municipal Building Supervision Authority (*see* Part III, Chapter 1 above). In most respects, the provisions of the Building Act also apply to the supervision situations within the Land Use Act (section 176a of the latter). As is the case for other statutory tasks of the Authority, the supervision is independent of the general management of the municipality. In cases of illegal constructions or other activities prohibited under the Act, the Authority has the duty to react. It (or in certain situations one of its officials) is empowered to decide upon injunctions and prohibitions, under a conditional fine or at the risk that the measures needed will be taken by the Authority at the expense of the offender (section 182 of the Land Use and Building Act; as of 1 January 2025, section 147 of the Building Act); *see also* Part V. The Authority is also entitled to order ongoing building activities be interrupted (section 180 of the Land Use and Building Act; as of 1 January 2025, section 146 of the Building Act). The decisions of the Authority can be appealed to the Regional Administrative Court. Such illegal acts or omissions as a rule constitute a criminal offence under the Act (sections 185 and 152 respectively). Hence the Authority is also obliged to inform the public prosecutor, except where the act or omission, in respect to the circumstances, is regarded insignificant and no public interest requires criminal charge (sections 186 and 153 respectively). In practice, criminal procedure, if there is any, is secondary to administrative coercive measures.

Part IV. Liability Questions

Chapter 1. Liability Notions

1506. The notion of environmental damage is not always unambiguous. The word is most typically used to imply civil liability in the regime of the law of torts, but the same word is at times – especially in public discussions – also used to describe detrimental impacts to the environment in general. Here the concept is significantly wider, because also impacts on public interests and nature itself are taken into account, irrespective of whether there are any personal or property losses traditionally dealt with under private law. In this part environmental damage only refers to civil liability. Another source of confusion is that environmental damage, even as a civil liability concept, may or may not be restricted to pollution damage, noise pollution as a rule included. Outside this core area, the word may refer to damages such as loss of a beautiful view from a property, property damage caused by man-made inundation of a lake, or damage caused to migratory fish stocks and hence to fishermen by damming.

In Finnish and Swedish law texts, also the expressions for accident (spill) and damage are partly overlapping in a confusing way (*see* for 'oil damages' paragraph 716).

Chapter 2. Legislation

§1. Directive-Based Remediation of Environmental Damage

1507. The Environmental Liability Directive (Directive 2004/35/EC on environmental liability with regard to the prevention and remedying of environmental damage) deals mainly with liability issues outside the sphere of traditional tort liability and is in Finland mainly regarded as a matter of public environmental law. The implementation legislation entered into force on 1 July 2009.

1508. The directive has been implemented largely by using the pre-existent administrative enforcement mechanisms. There is, true, a separate new Act on the Remediation of Certain Damages Caused to the Environment (383/2009), complemented by Government decree 713/2009 on the same. The immediate scope of application of this Act is nevertheless small and secondary to the Nature Protection Act, the Environmental Protection Act, the Water Act and the Gene Technology Act. In these four acts, the general frameworks for administrative enforcement are essentially used as a procedural basis, with necessary complements and extensions. The Act on the Remediation of Certain Damages Caused to the Environment mainly serves as a list of definitions and general rules and as a key to the application of the relevant provisions in the four acts. In present legislation, the provisions at stake are in sections 127 and 128 of the Nature Protection Act, sections 137, 176–178 and 186 of the Environmental Protection Act, sections 6–7 and 14 of Chapter 14 of the Water Act and section 23 of the Gene Technology Act,

In addition to the pieces of legislation above, also section 147 of the Act on the Transport of Dangerous Substances deals with remediation of environmental damage.

1509. The scope of application of the Act on the Remediation of Certain Damages Caused to the Environment encompasses: (1) damage to the environment defined in section 3(7) of the Nature Protection Act, (2) considerable pollution in a water body provided in section 177 of the Environmental Protection Act and (3) a substantially harmful change in a water body or groundwater, referred to in Chapter 14, section 6 of the Water Act. The Act on Remediation, etc. is nevertheless not applicable in cases where the damage has been caused by: (1) an exceptional natural phenomenon, (2) a measure whose sole purpose is to protect against natural disasters, (3) a measure whose primary purpose is national defence or international security, (4) an occurrence to which Chapter 10 and 10a of the Maritime Act apply, or (5) an activity regulated under the Nuclear Liability Act.

1510. The very remediation, as well as the competent authority and its functions, are nevertheless in the first place regulated pursuant to the Nature Protection Act, the Environmental Protection Act, the Water Act and the Gene Technology Act. The obligation to prevent the causation of damage and the obligation to limit damage incurred are regulated under these four acts and in the Act on the Transport of Dangerous Substances.

1511. Regarding remediation, 'natural resource' is defined as the natural habitats and living environments of the species referred to in section 3(7) of the Nature Protection Act, as well as the species and their localities and the places where they reproduce and rest. 'Natural resource service' again means the useful effect of a natural resource on another natural resource or on humans, and baseline condition the status prior to damage to natural resources and natural resource services.

1512. Pursuant to section 5 of the Act on the Remediation of Certain Damages Caused to the Environment, natural resources and natural resource services must be restored to baseline condition by eliminating the harmful change caused by the damage (*primary remediation*). If the baseline condition cannot be fully restored, the impairment that the damage has caused to the natural resource and natural resource service should be replaced by measures undertaken in the damaged area or elsewhere (*complementary remediation*). The temporary losses caused to a natural resource or natural resource service shall be replaced by taking measures in the damaged area or elsewhere until primary and complementary remediation have exerted their full effect (*compensatory remediation*).

1513. Pursuant to section 6 of the same Act, the competent authority (specified by the Nature Protection Act, the Environmental Protection Act, the Water Act or the Gene Technology Act) shall, when considering the measures to be undertaken, take into account: (1) the nature, scope and severity of the damage; (2) the possibility for natural restoration; (3) health risks; (4) expenses incurred in remedying the damage; and (5) other damages that may have occurred in the area. Here the proposal of the operator who caused the damage, as well as the comments of the parties entitled to institute proceedings at stake under the four acts, shall be taken into consideration.

1514. Pursuant to section 7 of the Act on the Remediation of Certain Damages Caused to the Environment, the operator who caused the damage may be granted the right to perform the measures of complementary or compensatory remediation outside the damaged area. The measures must not cause any inconvenience that could be avoided. The authority shall hear the owner or holder before decision-making. If the remedial measures cause considerable inconvenience to the owner or the holder, the owner or holder has the right to receive full compensation for any damage. Compensation for considerable inconveniences incurred in undertaking the measures shall be paid. If the operator who caused the damage is unable to pay, the government shall be liable.

1515. Ending of remediation is decided upon in the proceedings under the Nature Protection Act, the Environmental Protection Act, the Water Act or the Gene Technology Act (section 8). Ending may take place, if: (1) the remedial measures implemented guarantee that the risk to human health and natural resources has been eliminated; and (2) the costs of continuing remediation would be disproportionate compared to the environmental benefits going to be gained.

1516. Under certain conditions, the authorities (the Centres for Economic Development, Transport and the Environment) are entitled to undertake the necessary measures relating to prevention or limitation, or perform remedial measures in the damaged area, or assign someone else to perform these measures, at the government's expense (section 9). It is required that: (1) the matter is urgent and the procedure prescribed in the applicable Act cannot be delayed without substantial exacerbation of the damage; or (2) the operator who caused the damage cannot be determined without difficulty.

1517. The provisions on liability (sections 10–15) are, as the whole act, secondary or complementary to the pre-existing provisions on administrative enforcement and reinstatement, those being largely based on a more extensive liability, where applicable. In such cases sections 10–15 do not limit the obligations of the responsible party. In any case, matters concerning the allocation and limitation of liability and making the costs equitable are decided upon by means of the administrative procedures stipulated in the Nature Protection Act, the Environmental Protection Act, the Water Act or the Gene Technology Act concerning the requirement to undertake remedial measures (section 13). Also the appellate procedures are stipulated in those acts (section 17).

1518. Pursuant to section 10, the operator who caused the damage shall be liable for any costs arising from the remedial measures and that the authority incurs in assessing the damage and the immediate threat posed by it, and in deciding upon remedial measures and supervising them. If the damage was *caused* by more than one activity, the responsibility for the costs shall be allocated among the operators according to their share of the total damage, or, if this cannot be done, the responsibility shall be divided per capita. According to the rule on limitation of liability (section 11), the operator is not liable for the costs if he can prove that the damage: (1) was caused by a third party and incurred despite appropriate safety measures taken by the operator; or (2) it was caused as a result of complying with such a requirement or instruction issued by an authority that was not based on an emission or other occurrence resulting from the operator's own activity. Pursuant to the equity rule in section 12, an operator who proves that he has acted carefully, shall not be responsible for the full amount of the costs. For making the costs equitable it is required that: (1) the damage is due to an emission or an occurrence that complies with the provisions included in the permit issued for the operation or other decision of an authority; or (2) the obligations prescribed in the legislation concerning the operation were complied with in carrying out the operation.

1519. The costs incurred by the government in performing the measures referred to in section 9 shall be collected from the operator who caused the damage within five years from the conclusion of the measures, or within five years from the date of determination of the identity of the operator who caused the damage (section 14). If the expenses of the claim for recovery exceed the amount to be recovered, the costs may be left uncollected.

1520. If the operator is not responsible for the costs due to section 11, or the liability of the operator has been made more equitable by virtue of section 12, the Centre for Economic Development, Transport and the Environment may perform the remedial measures, or have them performed, as measures benefiting the environment.

1521. The Act on the Remediation of Certain Damages Caused to the Environment does not apply to remedying damage caused by activities that concluded before the Act entered into force, even though the damage may have become apparent only after the Act took effect.

§2. Legislation on Civil Liability

I. The Present Situation

1522. In Finland, civil liability for environmental damage has been based on different legal rules. A comprehensive legislation on the subject did not exist until 1994, when the Environmental Damages Act (737/1994) was enacted. The Act entered into force on 1 June 1995. The reform reduced the amount of legal mechanisms applicable to environmental damages, but the Environmental Damages Act, being confined to damage caused by stationary activities, is nevertheless not the entire legal basis for treating all kinds of non-contractual environmental damage. The other compensation systems applicable to certain situations or types of environmental damage are based partly on typical civil liability, partly on sui generis liability.

Apart from civil (or related) liability, there are a few public law systems according to which the State is responsible for damage caused by someone else. The main example is the Oil Pollution Prevention Fund (until 31 December 2014), or instead from 1 January 2025, the Environmental Damage Fund (*see* Part I, Chapter 4, §8, IX). If compensation from the fund is paid to a victim, the right to claim damages from an eventual liable person in court passes to the State, i.e., to the fund.

No obligation exists to maintain liability insurance policies to cover liability for environmental damage (*see* however §3 below on secondary liability).

II. General Law

1523. An important starting point is the general law of torts, which is largely codified in the Damages Compensation Act of 1974 (412/1974). Under this Act, it must normally be shown that the damage has been caused intentionally or negligently. However, strict liability has been provided for in certain special acts or has evolved through legal practice concerning certain activities (such as the use of explosives). In addition, international agreements have resulted in a strict (but quantitatively limited) liability for oil damage (*see* paragraph 488) and nuclear damage (*see* Part I, Chapter 8, §3).

1524. Generally, however, the victim of environmental damage has earlier had to prove the negligence (and the causal link) in the 'normal' way. The task is often far from easy. This was one of the main reasons to enact the Environmental Damages Act which imposes an overall strict liability in regard to the damage covered by it. The Act did not, however, constitute any abrupt change. The SC had several times already come very near to strict liability in ruling that the industrial operator causing (temporary) pollution was liable unless he was able to prove that he had acted carefully. There is also an important ruling (SC 1995:108) by the SC, according to which damage caused by the oil pollution of soil and groundwater, which in turn was caused by a leakage in the facilities of a petrol station, was to be compensated by the operator on the basis of strict liability, although the Environmental Damages Act was not applicable yet. Moreover, the permit-compensation systems in the Water Act and the compensation provisions in the Neighbourhood Relations Act were also previously strict, as well as the liability for damage caused by faulty sewer pipes, etc.

III. Compensations for Property Nuisance

1525. There are also other possibilities in alternative regimes. One of them is the Neighbourhood Relations Act. Under this Act, permanent and unreasonable nuisance to a neighbour, when caused on the property of another, is in principle prohibited. The risk of such nuisance at new establishments is as a rule controlled by a permit system, from March 2000 the environmental permit under the Environmental Protection Act. A permit gives a certain protection to the operator but does not eliminate the risk of being obliged to pay damages for, e.g., noise or polluted air. The damages which may be compensated include property damage and hindrance to property use, and evidently also certain types of personal inconvenience. If a neighbour sues the operator for damages, there is no need for him to prove the negligence of the latter. This means strict liability. In practice, lawsuits based on the Neighbourhood Relations Act have not been very common, however (and are not at all available for claims on prohibiting the nuisance, where administrative enforcement under the Environmental Protection Act would apply).

The Environmental Damages Act has strongly reduced the importance of the Neighbourhood Relations Act in its core area, as far as compensations are concerned. When applicable, the Environmental Damages Act always displaces the compensation provisions of the Neighbourhood Relations Act, the latter being now in practice merely applicable to nuisance caused and suffered within one single building (e.g., in separate apartments).

IV. Water Pollution Damage

1526. In Finland one significant category of environmental damage consists of the various forms of water pollution damage. These have largely been regulated on the basis of a permit-related compensation system contained in the previous Water

Act, Chapter 11, and in the present Water Act, Chapter 13. Typical to these provisions is the immediate connection with the permit procedure, a feature common to all Water Act damages also out of the pollution regime. From March 2000, this traditional feature has been attached to the environmental permits under the Environmental Protection Act, but, as previously, only insofar as pollution of surface waters (territorial waters included) is concerned. No such permit-connected arrangement exists concerning pollution of groundwater, soil or air, noise, etc. The Environmental Damages Act is applied substantively (section 124 of the Environmental Protection Act), but not procedurally, as no civil lawsuit is concerned.

1527. Pursuant to the provisions of Chapter 13 of the Environmental Protection Act, the compensations for all kinds of surface water pollution damage are determined ex officio in the Environmental Permit decision, often as yearly fees, if they can be anticipated and assessed in advance. The compensations are, if needed, an integral part of permit procedure (before the Regional State Administrative Agency). The victim does not have to claim compensation himself. He may be, e.g., a shore owner, a water area owner (which normally also means fisheries rights owner) or a water supply operator.

If damage appears which had not been anticipated in the permit decision or if a permit had beforehand objectively seemed unnecessary, the victim may submit an application for compensation by the permit holder to the permit authority, i.e., the Regional State Administrative Agency. Even here negligence does not have to be proved. All this means a special kind of strict liability for damage, although the term is not very illustrative here, because no proper civil suit is at issue. The system is in a way analogous to decisions on compensations in an expropriation procedure. This analogy may also be seen in the objective determination of certain property damages, partly irrespective of subjective losses.

However, compensations of water pollution damage are at times determined in a lawsuit procedure on the basis of normal negligence liability. Such situations arise when damage is caused 'illegally', either without a necessary permit or against its conditions. One typical situation is pollution of groundwater, because no permits will be granted allowing, this and consequently the damage is always illegal or perhaps accidental. Here the ordinary District Court may be competent. To make it even more complicated, a claim for compensation for illegal damage, where occurring in surface waters, can also be joined to an application (either a permit application or a compensation application) procedure before the Regional State Administrative Agency, if the damage has at least partly been caused 'legally'.

1528. As for the permit system of the Water Act, the specific provisions of Chapter 13 of the said act are applicable instead of the Environmental Damages Act, to other activities than wastewater or effluent discharges and to other kinds of damage than pollution. Typical examples are harmful impacts on shores or fish stocks caused by water level regulation or water power plants, as well as draining of wells for various reasons. The applicability of a specific compensation regulation is mainly due to the fact that it is not a question of pollution damages and because it is partly a question of compensating expropriatory rights. But if one of these damages has been caused in contradiction to the provisions of the Water Act, the permit-connected compensation system of the Water Act is not applicable at all. The general Damages Compensation Act applies instead.

V. The Environmental Damages Act

1529. The Environmental Damages Act aims to promote the judicial protection of the victims of pollution and nuisance. This takes place on the basis of a model in many respects similar to that adopted in Swedish and Norwegian law. The Act covers in principle all non-contractual damages caused by a stationary (literally: 'performed in a certain area') activity, provided that they result from either pollution of water, air or soil, or nuisances like noise, vibration, radiation, heat or smell. It is additionally presupposed that the damage takes place 'in the environment', the notion of which has not been legally defined, but, e.g., noise from an apartment to another within the same building clearly is not encompassed. No positive list of fixed activities or chemical substances limits the scope of application of the Act. Consequently, strict liability is general and comprehensive. Pursuant to section 36 of the Gene Technology Act, the Environmental Damages Act is applicable to damage caused in the environment by an activity provided in the Gene Technology Act (*see also* paragraph 869).

By the expression 'performed in a certain area', damage caused by the use of vehicles, ships or aircraft, e.g., normal oil damage at sea, has been excluded from the scope of application of the Act. The notion of 'activity' is to be understood in a broad sense, covering any industrial, commercial, agricultural, silvicultural and municipal activities, except traffic and carriage. But also regarding the latter, the possessor of a 'traffic area' (trade port, airport, road, etc.) may be liable according to the Act for the total damage (e.g., noise) caused in it. Even private housing is included in that, e.g., the possession of a single oil tank is regarded as an activity. The relevant damage or the pollution resulting in damage may be either temporary or continuous. The consequences of undesirable incidents and accidents are covered by the Act as well as those of regular activities. This also means that the Act has combined different legal traditions, especially that of tort law and that of neighbourhood relations.

1530. The scope of application in relation to other legislation is not always easy to determine. In principle, damage stipulated by another act is excluded, but the nature and contents of the various external compensation-related provisions vary strongly. It is clear that, e.g., nuclear damage is not covered. As for those obviously uncommon situations where product liability seemed to be a competing approach, the Product Liability Act (694/1990) and the Environmental Damages Act are optional to the victim. The rather complicated relationship between the Water Act and the Environmental Damages Act has been explained above. Of special systematic importance is the general Damages Compensation Act, the provisions of which supplement the Environmental Damages Act.

1531. 'Damage' in the Environmental Damages Act means loss of life and personal injury, loss of or damage to property and loss of profit. The last-mentioned is recoverable irrespective of the special qualifications otherwise provided by the general Damages Compensation Act. Also the costs of the measures of prevention and reinstatement by authorities or individual victims are recoverable under the Environmental Damages Act. In continuation of the old practice under the Neighbourhood Relations Act on nuisance, even personal inconvenience of the neighbour may be compensable, depending on considerations of equity, although this possibility is alleged to be clearly exceptional.

There are no pecuniary limitations of liability. The liability is always strict. This outcome was not politically controversial to any significant extent, largely because of the gradual development explained above in §2, I and II above.

1532. A *probable causal link* between the activity and the damage (in fact: activity pollution/nuisance damage) is sufficient instead of the traditional 'full' evidence. This rule of course favours the victim who only has to prove that the link between the activity of the defendant and the occurred damage is 'probable'. The wording itself is perhaps not very informative. In the preparatory documents of the Act this expression has been explained to refer to a probability of clearly more than 50%. In practice the rule obviously often refers to excluding the less probable causal explanations of the individual damage.

The existence or non-existence of any permit, or compliance with the environmental regulations in other respects, has in general no effect on the liability. But as a kind of counterbalance to the rights of the injured party, he may be obliged to tolerate the nuisance (or pollution) without compensation, up to a level based on the consideration of reasonableness. Local circumstances and the nature of the activity are here taken into account, case by case. The old-time priority rule of the Neighbourhood Relations Act is not applicable as such here, but the chronology may be among other things taken into account in the total consideration. It is important to note that the toleration test is not at all applicable to every category of damage. Personal injury and significant damage to property are always compensable, as well as all damage that has been caused punishably or intentionally. The toleration test always results in either full compensation or no compensation at all, without a possibility to adjust the amount of compensation. But, at least in principle, the general rules on equity (reasonableness) in the Damages Compensation Act are applicable to the amounts of compensation, although it is less likely that the regular 'full' compensation for environmental damage would be reduced on this ground in practice.

1533. As a clear starting point, the formal operator is held liable. Nevertheless, also other subjects may in certain circumstances be considered liable according to the equating provisions of section 7 of the Environmental Damages Act. This possibility applies to corporate arrangements and the use of dummies, and in qualified situations obviously also to such lenders that are de facto in charge of the activity. A parent company cannot become liable for damages caused by a formally independent subsidiary (the proper operator) merely due to the ownership relation, but it is required, based on an individual consideration by the court, that the parent company may be equated to the operator, taking into account the actual command by the parent company, the mutual economic relations and the economic interests pursued. Moreover, there is another equating rule in section 7 which extends the liability to the transferees of such activities that have already caused pollution or at least risk of pollution of the environment in a certain area. It is required that the new operator, perhaps a mere receiver of an area where chemical or oil tanks are being stored, at the time of acquisition knew or should have known of the pollution or the risk thereof.

There is a parallel to the last-mentioned equating rule in the Environmental Protection Act, section 133(2), which similarly may pose the new owner or other holder of the area – often being identical to the new operator – an obligation to clean up polluted soils or groundwater (*see* Part I, Chapter 6, §1). Of course the obligation in the Environmental Protection Act is one of public law, and the provision is in the first place applied by administrative authorities in the enforcement procedure (and of course by administrative courts at the appellate stage). But in practice the two come very near to each other. Due to the similarities, there are cases where both the Environmental Protection Act, section 137, and the Environmental Damages Act, section 7, when applied to costs of reinstatement, could be used as a basis of responsibility.

1534. The Environmental Damages Act belongs, of course, as a whole to the regime of civil liability and private law. This characterization is not, however, true in all respects. The Act includes, as stated above, provisions on the costs of prevention and reinstatement measures, which make a separate category of recoverable damage. These costs may be claimed by both private victims and authorities, e.g., by the Centre for Economic Development, Transport and the Environment, or by the municipalities, depending on the actual expenditure. As for private claimants, an individually protected interest is required, and hence a mere popular action is out of the question. Regarding the costs incurred by authorities, no damage to any individual or the authority itself is required, but it is sufficient that the measures taken by the competent authority have been reasonable for the sake of the environment itself. Hence it may be said that the basis of liability here is of a public law character, although it is exceptionally implemented by means of normal civil law procedure.

Only pecuniary compensations may be based on the Environmental Damages Act, but not, e.g., orders of reinstatement, for which the administrative enforcement mechanisms (*see* Part V, Chapter 1) have to be used. However, the liability based on the Act, where applicable, is the only means for the authority to have the expenses reimbursed from the liable person in cases where there has been no time or possibility for the authority to impose a schedule for compliance.

1535. The provisions on prescription in the Act on Prescription of Debt (728/2003; in force from 1 January 2004) are applicable also to damages under the Environmental Damages Act. Hence the normal prescription period is three years from the day specified in section 7 of the Act on Prescription of Debt, i.e., regarding tort liability, from the day when the injured party has learned or should have learned the damage and the liable person. Regarding ordinary tort liability, prescriptive time limits shall anyway be interrupted before ten years have elapsed from the incident from which the damage has resulted. However, this time limit does not restrict the right to claim (personal or) environmental damages. Hence it has been taken explicitly into account that the appearance of the individually suffered environmental damage may occur years after the original incident and also a long time after the pollution of the environment (which then takes place in the middle of the causal link), e.g., the pollution of groundwater in relation to subsequent personal damage or loss of profit.

1536. In practice the situations vary. In the case SC 2013:9 (also below) a land property was situated in the aviation noise area of an airport that was established 1952. A Local Master Plan, where the area of the property was assigned to an outdoor activity and recreation area, had been approved 1992. At least from 1992 it had been clear that the property cannot be used to building purposes. Hence the prescription period began 1992.

1537. Damages caused by a combination of several individual activities are also covered. Here all the respective operators are jointly and severally liable.

1538. It is moreover possible to claim compensation in advance, before any damage has occurred. This is an effort to minimize the differences to the joint permit-compensation system of the previous Water Act (and the present Environmental Protection Act insofar as surface water pollution is concerned). In comparison to these permit-connected systems, compensation (e.g., the nuisance caused by a future noise) has to be claimed individually, though. It is not probable that this clause would be applied often in practice.

1539. The Environmental Damages Act entered into force in June 1995 without any retroactive effects. In regard to 'historical pollution', it is sufficient for applying the Act that the activity contributing to the damage has continued after 1 June 1995. If not, older provisions are applied even though the damage would have appeared after that date. This rule may be problematic in practice, e.g., in regard to road traffic noise.

1540. Only a few proceedings based on the Environmental Damages Act have occurred so far (so also up to 2022), and no boom is expected in the future, either. However, the mere existence of the Act has evidently facilitated compensation agreements in some cases. Because the text of the Act contains several wordings of a general nature which could perhaps be interpreted in more or less differing ways, there is certain interest in having some guiding rulings of the SC. Today, a couple of such rulings exist, albeit perhaps in atypical situations:

- In SC 1999:124 construction repair company using sand blowing apparatus was, irrespective of negligence, held liable for damage caused by dust emitted by the repair works to the environment, that was regarded as nuisance pursuant to section 1 of the Environmental Damages Act.

- In SC 2001:61 damage to house ceilings, resulting from vibration caused by nearby street construction works, was assessed according to the Environmental Damages Act. The municipality as the proper client was held liable, not the contractor.
- SC 2011:62 dealt with the question of liable operator in respect to a franchise gasoline station operated by a bankrupt subject.
- SC 2012:29 dealt with the same question regarding damages to alien buildings, caused by dam emitted from the soil operations by an undertaker performing enlargement of a cemetery owned by a parish.
- SC 2013:9 dealt with noise in the vicinity of a major airport, losses of property value, impact of a Local Master Plan and prescription.

§3. Secondary Liability for Environmental Damage

1541. Regular civil liability for environmental damage is of no use to the victim if the polluter remains unidentified or if he appears to be insolvent. Due to these problems, and also to meet the requirements of Article 12 the *Lugano Convention*, a specific secondary liability mechanism – i.e., secondary in relation to the regular civil liability and, where any, to a regular liability insurance – has been introduced by law. Among different legislative alternatives, a compulsory insurance system of a totally new kind was chosen. As a result, the Environmental Insurance Act (81/1998) entered into force on 1 January 1999. The Environmental Insurance was different to any existing domestic or foreign insurance. It was (and is up to 2025) required from all major industrial and commercial activities involving a risk of environmental damage, as specified by decree. The main rule here is that all permit holders according to the Environmental Protection Act (or its predecessors) or to the Chemicals Act were under the insurance obligation. Compliance is controlled by the Centres for Economic Development, Transport and the Environment.

1542. Unlike a traditional liability insurance, Environmental Insurance under the Act did not cover environmental damages under regular circumstances. It was applicable only when the individual polluter, being liable according to the Environmental Damages Act, is insolvent. Additionally, the insurance covered damage which would fall within the Environmental Damages Act in case the unknown polluter could be detected. Hence the Environmental Insurance was, though having some resemblance to public funds or fund-like collective insurances (such as the Swedish Environmental Insurance), always based on individual insurance policies. The public Oil Pollution Prevention Fund (Part I, Chapter 4, §8, IX), from which among other things compensations may be paid to individual victims of oil damage, this also being a secondary liability mechanism, was then preserved.

1543. The participating domestic or foreign insurance companies have no right to refuse an individual insurance policy. In addition, a special Environmental Insurance Centre, being mandatorily created by the participating companies, is responsible for the damages caused by unidentified polluters or by those who have neglected their insurance duty. In general, all damages defined by the Environmental Damages Act as environmental damage, prevention and reinstatement costs included, are covered. There is a pecuniary upper compensation limit for one event. In practice, real compensation situations have hardly occurred so far.

1544. Entering into force on 1 January 2025, both the Environmental Insurance and the Oil Pollution Prevention Fund have been replaced by a new State fund operating outside State budgets, called Environmental Damage Fund (Environmental Damage Fund Act, 1262/2022). The Fund is primarily not for the covering of individual damages, but to safeguard good environmental status. The Fund shall compensate for the costs of pollution prevention and restoration of polluted environment, as well as for damage caused in certain secondary liability situations. In addition, discretionary grants may be awarded for procurement to prevent environmental damage. The Act lays down provisions on the Environmental Damage Fund and its operations, the Environmental Damage Fee and the Fund's assets, as well as the compensation and subsidies paid from the Fund. The Environmental Damage Fund is an off-budget fund under the Ministry of the Environment. The Ministry has the right to issue general orders concerning the organization of the administration of the Fund and the financial management of it. The Ministry has the right to obtain the necessary information and reports from the Fund. The Ministry also approves the Fund's performance targets on the proposal of the Fund's Management Board. The highest decision-making power in the Fund is exercised by the Board. The Fund's assets consist of Environmental Damage Fees, which are recognized as income to the Fund. In addition, the assets consist of surpluses from previous financial years and repayments of claims paid from the Fund, together with interest and other items. The Fund does not have an independent right to borrow or invest the Fund's assets. An operator (other than public law body) engaged in activities causing a risk of environmental pollution listed in Annex 1 to the Act shall pay an annual Environmental Damage Fee in accordance with the Annex. For the purposes of this context, activities involving a risk of environmental pollution refer to the establishment or operation of an installation and activities closely linked to it technically and functionally, or the use of an area or the arranging of activities in such a way that it may cause environmental pollution. If the funds collected as Environmental Damage Fees are not sufficient to pay compensation, the necessary funds can be transferred from the State budget to the Fund. When sufficient funds have been accumulated from the Fees, the funds received from the State are returned to the state budget.

1545. The Environmental Damage Fees must be paid from the beginning of the calendar year in which the operations begin. The party liable to pay the Fee is the body or person who was entered in the Environmental Protection Information System at the beginning of the year as the operator responsible for the activities subject to the obligation to pay. Annex 1 to the Act contains five payment categories, where the annual payment varies between EUR 200 and EUR 30,000. An operator carrying out an activity in accordance with Annex 2 shall pay a one-off Environmental Damage Fee. This fee is EUR 400. The annual and one-off environmental damage fee is determined by the Centre for Economic Development, Transport and the Environment of the region of Etelä-Pohjanmaa.

1546. Payment of compensation for damage or prevention and restoration costs requires that: (1) compensation cannot be fully recovered from the party liable to pay compensation for the damage under another law or from the person responsible for the costs of prevention and restoration; or (2) the party liable under another law or the party responsible for the prevention and restoration costs cannot be identified. The payment of compensation is also subject to the condition that compensation for the damage or prevention and restoration costs is not paid in full from a security collateral, statutory or voluntary insurance or other compensation system provided for by law provided by the party liable for compensation or the party responsible for the costs. The injured party shall be compensated for: (1) environmental damage caused by activities carried out in Finland as referred to in the Environmental Damages Act as well as the costs of damage prevention and restoration and necessary accounts pursuant to the said Act; (2) damage caused outside a vehicle in Finland as a result of an oil or other chemical spill caused by the vehicle or its use in Finland; (3) damage caused outside a railway vehicle in Finland as a result of an oil or other chemical spill caused by a railway vehicle or its use in Finland; and (4) damage caused outside a ship in Finland as a result of an oil or other chemical spill caused by the ship or its use. No advance compensation pursuant to the Environmental Damages Act is paid to the injured party, and the Fund has no obligation to compulsory purchase pursuant to the said Act.

1547. Compensation shall not be paid to a person liable for damage or to a person in possession of the oil, other chemical or source of disturbance that caused the damage or its danger at the time of the damage or on whose behalf it was transported at the time of the damage. If the injured party has contributed to the damage, compensation shall be paid only to the extent that other causes contributed to the damage. However, if the injured party is a natural person, his or her contribution may only be taken into account as a factor reducing compensation if the contribution was intentional or grossly negligent. An authority shall be compensated for: (1) the costs of responding to oil and ship chemical spills pursuant to the Rescue Act; (2) the costs of recovery pursuant to the Rescue Act; and (3) the costs of measures necessary to prevent and control environmental pollution referred to in section 182a of the Environmental Protection Act. The costs of studies necessary to carry out such activities shall also be reimbursed. An authority shall also be compensated for other prevention and restoration costs, as provided in the Environmental Damages Act.

1548. Compensation for damage caused by a single pollution incident or other similar disturbance and for prevention and restoration costs shall not exceed EUR 30 million. Compensation from the Fund shall be applied for in writing within three years of the date on which the injured party or the authority which carried out the prevention and restoration measures became aware that compensation or the costs of prevention and restoration cannot be recovered from the person liable for compensation or from the party responsible for the costs, or that the person liable or responsible for the costs has not been identified. For special reasons, an application submitted after the deadline may be admissible. However, the application must always be made within ten years of the occurrence of the damage or pollution or other disturbance. However, if a compensation case concerning the same damage or costs is pending before a court or other authority, compensation may be applied for within one year of the judgment or other decision in the matter becoming final. Advance compensation may be granted to an authority due to the lack of clarity regarding liability, the level of costs or the urgency of the action.

1549. The right of a recipient of compensation from the Fund to receive compensation from the person liable for compensation or from the party responsible for the costs shall be transferred to the Fund to the extent that compensation has been paid. For special reasons, the Fund may waive the collection of compensation in whole or in part.

1550. A decision by an authority concerning an Environmental Damage Fee and a decision of the Fund on compensation can in the first place be reviewed following request of rectification, and appeal against the decision regarding the request can be lodged to the Regional Administrative Court.

Part V. Juridical Actions

Chapter 1. Administrative and Judicial Remedies

1551. In Finnish environmental law the differentiation between administrative and judicial remedies needs some clarification. Some, although a minority, of the relevant permit-type procedures were juridical in the sense that they were dealt with by courts of justice from the very beginning. However, after the Water Courts were abolished in 2000, this is not any more a relevant alternative. Various permit-type or coercive decisions of administrative authorities (of the State or the municipalities) in turn may be very judicial in essence and directly serve the legal protection of private affected parties as well. Such administrative decisions cannot be reviewed by courts of general jurisdiction but *only by administrative courts*. Moreover, when administrative authorities (and, consequently, administrative courts) have powers in the field of environmental law, a 'horizontal' dispute between an operator and one or more victims may very well be at issue in the same administrative procedure where the relations between the public power and the operator are decided upon. The important appellate system, operated by independent administrative courts, makes this procedure even more 'judicial'.

Before Finnish administrative court no lawyer is necessary, though often useful. The proceedings are not very expensive, given also the provisions on the division of the costs incurred by the parties.

All administrative decisions, permit decisions by the administrative authorities of the State and the municipalities included, can be appealed against in administrative courts. This is always the legal presumption based on the Administrative Judicial Procedures Act, even if the appealability had not been provided in the specific sectoral provisions at hand, though it most often is. Normally, the appeal in environmental matters is 'reformatory', i.e., the court also has the power to amend the decision. In Finland, even the individual provisions in the permits are at times directly amended by the Regional Administrative Court or the SAC. This does not, however, generally apply to those few environmental decisions against which the 'municipal appeal' is used.

1552. In the Finnish system, a permit is valid and enforceable only after having gained legal force. This means that the applicant, i.e., the operator, has to wait until the time for appeals has elapsed or, where any appeals have been lodged, until the time for appeals against the final decision of the Regional Administrative Court has elapsed. Regarding appeals against that decision, leave of appeal to the SAC is today needed due to a very comprehensive rule. At this stage, the decision of the

Regional Administrative Court is in principle enforceable, but not, if the appeal would turn useless. Hence the operations may normally not be started already after the decision of the Regional Administrative Court, and, in addition, this may be explicitly forbidden by the SAC. On the contrary, the permit applicant has, if there are particular reasons, the possibility to request the administrative permit authority to grant a right to start the activities immediately after the permit decision. In this case a financial security is required. A basic precondition here is that the appeals do not become useless due to the start. Section 199 of the Environmental Protection Act is a good example, but there are quite similar provisions, e.g., in the Land Use and Building Act (as of 1 January 2025 in the Building Act), the Water Act and the Soil Excavation Act. Such orders by permit authority are valid also during the appellate stage, but the court forbid the enforcing.

1553. In any case, large areas of environmental law are in Finland regulated by legal systems dominated by public law characteristics. This means that a victim of environmental damage often does not need (or even may, *see* below) to bring actions against the operators in order to stop the activities and restore the environment; his interests are parallel to those of the active authorities. This is especially true for the disturbing activities as such. Compensations for damages are, except in the regime of the Water Act and partly that of the Environmental Protection Act, of course solely a matter between the operator and the victim. In general, the formal requirements for lodging an administrative appeal are not very high, and the procedure before administrative courts is in general inexpensive, compared to that before the courts of general jurisdiction. All this has also made it possible that administrative authorities are competent to decide upon matters which are crucial from the viewpoint of private rights and duties.

1554. As for new impacts on the environment, their lawfulness is normally tested in advance in the administrative permit procedures and subsequent appellate procedures. When remedies apart from criminal actions are needed for unlawful activities, there are in principle two alternative procedures available, namely an administrative procedure and an action in a court of general jurisdiction. In practice, the former is in many cases the only real alternative. This is due to the fact that most environmental provisions are referred to as public law, which means that lawsuits for prohibition or injunction are not available in courts of general jurisdiction, the civil procedure of which is designed for substantive private law issues only.

For example, a valid permit decision according to the Environmental Protection Act, or even the mere necessity of such a permit, or a notification registration duty, makes it impossible to bring an action in a court of general jurisdiction in order to prohibit the nuisance caused by the activities (section 19(1) of the Neighbourhood Relations Act). The priority of administrative enforcement also holds true where the nuisance at the same time implies threat to public health and the Public Health Act is applicable (section 19(2) of the Neighbourhood Relations Act). And the competence to issue injunctions and reinstatement orders is according to many enactments vested solely in administrative authorities, especially in environmental law, but the procedures may be initiated also by the impacted subjects. There is, of course, always the possibility to appeal to the Regional Administrative Court, if the reaction of the authority does not satisfy the initiating party (or the opposite party). Legal actions for environmental damage in turn belong to a District Court, where the Environmental Damages Act is then applied (sections 18, 19 and 20 of the Neighbourhood Relations Act).

1555. The most manifestation of the coercive injunction procedure is based on the administrative powers of supervisory authorities. The result may be either mandatory or prohibitory. This means that the authority (often a municipal one) may order an individual offender, e.g., to restore the environment to the state it was in before the unlawful activity, or that the illegal activity has to be ceased, under a conditional fine or at the risk that the measures necessary will be taken by the authorities at the expense of the offender. There are rules for this procedure in various laws, such as the significant Environmental Protection Act, the Water Act, the Waste Act, the Chemicals Act, the Public Health Act, the Nature Protection Act, the Land Use and Building Act (from 1 January 2025 onwards, the Land Use Act and the Building Act) and the Soil Excavation Act. If the relevant supervision authority itself does not have the powers of administrative enforcement, like the Centres for Economic Development, Transport and the Environment or the Municipal Environmental Protection Authority in cases under the Water Act where only the Regional State Administrative Agency is competent, then it is the responsibility of the supervision authority to apply for administrative enforcement. Such an application can be submitted directly by private interested parties as well. In most cases the injunction procedure can be initiated either by the authority itself or by a (private or public) applicant. The decision, positive or, in some cases, negative, can be appealed (in most cases) to the Regional Administrative Court (concerning the Environmental Protection Act and the Water Act, to the Regional Administrative Court in Vaasa) and thereafter, subject to leave of appeal, to the SAC.

1556. The procedure and the preconditions for injunction or other enforcement vary, depending on the substantive rules of the respective enactment, although common parts of the procedures are regulated in the Administrative Injunctions (Conditional Fines) Act (1113/1990). As for the substantive prerequisites, it is most often required that an 'offence' against the respective rules exists. The deed or the omission is neither supposed to be punishable under criminal law, nor are the preconditions, at least directly, linked to negligence or other notions of the law of torts. In practice, injunctions have been available, e.g., against measures taken long, say more than ten years, ago, or in order to correct offences against permit conditions irrespective of eventual negligence. Acute problems of legal interpretation exist in cases where a chemical has been discharged into the environment before its hazardous properties were known, as in the case of the old sawmills where chlorinated phenols were for years released into the soil.

1557. The role of criminal law and procedure in the field of environmental protection is in general rather small. It is a matter of penalties only, without a possibility of injunction. (In certain cases damages which otherwise should be treated by the same court of general jurisdiction in connection with a separate lawsuit can be joined.) Criminal law is neither among the primary tools for the implementation of environmental legislation and environmental policies nor for the legal protection of pollution victims; other means than those of criminal law are as a rule more effective. To the operator, the risk to be obliged to, e.g., reinstatement measures in an administrative procedure is often far more essential. And, however, the various environmental provisions are observed to a large extent, which probably depends on the legalistic culture and partly also on the effectiveness of the supervisory authorities. Moreover, the overall picture of Finnish criminal law in regard to the environment has been split, because criminal regulations were sometimes by-products of legislative efforts in various fields of environmental legislation. The maximum penalties have in most cases been fines or short prison sentences, the latter having been used only exceptionally.

1558. The 1995 partial reform of the Penal Code was aimed at making the environmental penalty regulations more homogeneous and coherent. In the reform, all penalty regulations in which prison sentences were considered appropriate, at least as an alternative, were removed from the various environmental enactments and replaced by a specific Chapter 48 on Environmental Offences in the Penal Code, with a clearly more unified content than in the previous separate provisions. In the various environmental enactments, solely crimes which may be sanctioned only by fines remained. The latter mainly apply to minor formal offences from which pollution, etc. has not resulted. At the same time coherent penalty levels were pursued.

Nevertheless, Chapter 48 could not be drafted as an array of 'traditional' type provisions on penal sanctions, because provisions of this kind are, for obvious reasons, in several respects clearly connected to proper environmental law and its administrative or judicial (non-penal) applications. Hence it has not been possible to make it punishable to cause undesirable environmental impacts of any kind, if the deed or omission leading to it has been, e.g., directly based on a valid permit decision and the provisions in it. This problem of *Verwaltungsakzessorität* is also well-known in many other legal systems. Similarly, the punishability may have been more or less linked directly to the proper environmental (and waste) legislation, EC or national. Consequently, the provisions include detailed technical references to non-penal environmental legislation. Due to this, the relevant sections in Chapter 48 of the Penal Code have to be amended any time the environmental enactment titles or sections referred to by it, not to mention the directly applicable EU Regulations (presently nineteen references to different EU Regulations), are in whole or in part replaced by new provisions or new such enactments enacted. And the various sectoral acts still additionally contain dozens of criminal provisions on (usually) less serious crimes not covered by the Penal Code.

Moreover, many of the criminal offences are acts or omissions against the provisions in an Environmental Permit or other environmental law permit. The project plan of the permit applicant has here the same status as the explicit permit provisions, e.g., as the basis for administrative coercive measures. This has also been confirmed by the SC regarding criminal responsibility (SC 2019:102).

1559. According to the present sections 1–6 of Chapter 48, Penal Code, the offence type applicable to, e.g., unlawful pollution and other impairment of the environment is either aggravated impairment of the environment (imprisonment for minimum four months, maximum six years) impairment of the environment – presently containing twenty-six references to domestic or EU legislation – (fines, or imprisonment for maximum two years), environmental infringement (fines, or imprisonment for maximum six months), or negligent impairment of the environment (fines, or imprisonment for maximum one year). The crime type for offences in the field of nature conservation is aggravated natural protection offence (imprisonment for minimum four months, maximum four years) and natural protection offence (fines, or imprisonment for maximum two years). There is today also the built-up environment offence in the chapter (fines, or imprisonment for maximum two years).

Compared to most of the pre-1995 provisions in various sectoral enactments, the maximum imprisonment terms were in 1995 raised to some extent. However, imprisonment has remained a rather unusual penalty for environmental offences, *see* SC 2002:39 and 2006:88, while also criminal proceedings for environmental offences in general have also remained unusual. The general principles of criminal law, often favouring the defendant in the grey interpretation zone, make that criminal law cannot be a primary effective tool of the protection of the environment.

A sentence for conduct penalized in Chapter 48 shall be passed on the person of whose duties the act or omission is to be deemed a breach. In assessing the same, due regard shall be given to the status of the person, to the nature and extent of his assignment and competence, and also to his participation in the creation or sustenance of an unlawful state of affairs (section 7). The minimum statute of limitations for an environmental offence other than environmental infraction is ten years (section 8).

1560. Similarly, Chapter 48a on Natural resources offences was in 2002 inserted in the Penal Code. The offence types presently consist of aggravated hunting offence, hunting offence, fishing offence, forestry offence and concealing pouched game. Also a hunting prohibition may be imposed in criminal proceedings.

Also some of the offences pursuant to Chapter 34 (400/2002) on Endangerment relate to environmental law. The offence types here include health endangerment (with, i.e., direct references to the Radiation Act, the Nuclear Energy Act and the Gene Technology Act), aggravated health endangerment, nuclear device offence, negligent endangerment, gross negligent endangerment and preparation of endangerment.

1561. Simultaneously with the 1995 reform on environmental penal law, also another reform in the field of criminal law entered into force. Previously criminal penalties only could be inflicted on natural persons, but from 1995 also legal personalities, governmental and municipal bodies included, may be imposed a corporate fine (from 2001 and still today EUR 850 to 850,000). This punishment is applicable to a specified group of crimes, environmental crimes included. There have been, however, not many environmental cases so far, except for the SC case SC 2008:33 (negligent discharge of oil from oil industry), where a corporate fine has been imposed, and SC 2011:17 (non-compliance by a company of an administrative order under the Environmental Protection Act regarding ban of use of certain type of fuel in combustion). The possible applying of a corporate fine to a pollution crime was also considered in SC 2002:39.

The general penal law provisions of confiscation (of, e.g., illegal profit, which has been applicable for some unlawful pollution cases in practice) are often applicable at least in principle. On the special confiscation rules for the defined value of endangered species, *see* Part II, Chapter 3, §7.

1562. A recent trend has been to vest in administrative authorities the power to impose fines due to certain environmental offences, *see* on oil discharge fee Part I, Chapter 4, §8, VII.

Chapter 2. The Locus Standi of Different Subjects

1563. In spite of the powers of the environmental authorities, there are, of course, situations where citizens need individual legal protection in matters concerning not only compensations but also the disturbing activities themselves. It is moreover possible that the authorities are not willing to use the powers they have or that they are, for various reasons, incapable of using them. In such situations it is upon private citizens to make the legal provisions function in a proper way. Here the rules concerning a citizen's right to bring various actions (*locus standi*, standing) are of primary importance.

1564. In criminal procedures, it is up to each violated subject to prosecute the offender, irrespective of what the public prosecutor does. It is, however, required that the victim's individual rights are involved.

1565. In most cases the legal environmental boundaries to an operator's activities are decided upon in an administrative procedure (permits, etc.). The same is largely true for various administrative injunction decisions. The rule is that those whose own interests are at stake in a juridically relevant manner have *locus standi*. This means that, e.g., all those whose property has been or probably will be affected may be a party and possess the individual right to appeal. The main exception is the municipal appeal (pursuant to the Municipal Act) to which also every member of the municipality is entitled irrespective of his individual rights and interests. In the field of environmental law, however, the municipal appeal is applicable only in a few procedures (land use planning in the first place). As a starting point, the applicable definition of *locus standi* is the 'normal' one, where all whose relevant rights or interests may be affected are entitled to use the procedural powers of a party.

1566. Besides private concerned parties, also environmental authorities of municipalities and of the State have in many cases the right to appeal. For example, a Centre for Economic Development, Transport and the Environment, in its capacity of environmental authority, has normally the power to appeal against a permit decision of a Municipal Permit Authority and a permit decision of a Regional State Administrative Agency and the Municipal Environmental Protection Authority against an Environmental Permit decision of a Regional State Administrative Agency (or properly its quite autonomous division for environmental permits). If the Regional Administrative Court has upset the administrative decision pursuant to the Environmental Protection Act, also the authority that had made that decision is today as a rule entitled to appeal before the SAC (subject to ordinary leave of appeal). It is also common that the Municipal Executive has right of appeal, irrespective of the bodies discussed above. The sectoral details on *locus standi* vary somewhat. Under the Soil Excavation Act the then Regional Environment Centres had in 1997 been granted the right of appeal against the permit decisions by the municipal permit authorities, as a kind of compensation for no longer being the first appellate stage (now the Regional Administrative Court) and, in important cases, the body vested with the power to approve permit decisions submitted to it.

In the regime of the Nature Protection Act, the Centres for Economic Development, Transport and the Environment and other competent authorities are empowered to appeal against a court decision by which its decision has been annulled or amended. Moreover, the Centre for Economic Development, Transport and the Environment, in its capacity of environmental authority, may appeal against a permit decision or plan approval by any authority pursuant to any piece of legislation whatever on the ground that the permit or plan is in contradiction of the Nature Protection Act or provisions by virtue of it (section 135 of the Nature Protection Act).

1567. In particular under the Water Act and, where pollution of waters is concerned, also under the Environmental Protection Act, the possible appellants make up a heterogeneous group: private parties such as various property owners and holders, statutory fishery associations, professional fishermen, State authorities which have the duty to take care of public interests (especially the Centres for Economic Development, Transport and the Environment, in their environmental capacity, and, where fisheries are concerned, the fisheries units of the same centres), and also Municipal Environmental Protection Authorities. An appeal by an environmental authority may of course in fact also be of influence in favour of possible victims. Pecuniary compensations, however, if not included ex officio in the permit or if unsatisfactory, can be claimed before the appellate body only by the victim (normally: the potential victim) himself.

1568. The environment, of course, concerns more than just the sum of the private interests of those who have *locus standi* on grounds of property rights. It is well-known in Finland that, for example, the law of torts or procedural remedies based on individual interests are not necessarily the best available or even relevant means of protecting the environment. This has caused a tendency to widen the grounds of standing, in the first place to authorities (other than the one by whom the decision in question has been made), as described above.

1569. Another possibility, at least in principle, consists of *the actions of voluntary organizations*. Previously there were no explicit rules on the matter, and the present general code for administrative judicial appeals, the Administrative Judicial Procedures Act, does not recognize the standing, at least not explicitly, whereas many relevant sectoral acts presently do. The courts had already in the 1980s voted on it (e.g., in cases concerning pollution of waters), but the result then often was that the association or society in question lacked individual interest with sufficient legal relevance to the matter. A well-known and publicly debated example is from 1991. Here the National Nature Conservation Association appealed to the SAC for the cancelling of a valid Highway Engineering Plan, because the road in question was going to be constructed in a National Park. The court refused the standing of the association, however not unanimously, because of the lack of an individual interest. But soon afterwards a similar application was made by the Young Women's Christian Association (YWCA), to which standing was granted (this decision was given the status of *Yearbook* precedent, SAC 1991:A 83). This was due to the fact that part of the same road would be outside the National Park and the YWCA happened to possess a holiday dwelling in the neighbourhood. Hence the traditional, formal grounds of standing seemed to prevail, even though the result was detrimental to the real substance of the matter. But today the 1991 precedent is not any more representative of the totality of enactments, because major steps in explicit provisions on the standing of associations and foundations have taken place in sectoral environmental and natural resource legislation and the outcome is today quite comprehensive.

1570. The predominantly negative position towards the standing of citizens' organizations still exists in some permit and injunction procedures, but however important changes towards a less restrictive approach have been made in sectoral legislation. Even traditionally, there is one important exception of principle: in the regime of municipal appeals, every member of the municipality has traditionally the right to appeal to the Regional Administrative Court. If a subject happens to have domicile in the municipality, it also has the right to appeal. This is today the case for (most of the) land use plan decisions under the Land Use and Building Act (as of 1 January 2025, the Land Use Act), but the Act also contains explicit provisions on, e.g., associations' right to appeal, partly also regarding certain permit decisions (as of 1 January 2025 in the Building Act) for which the appeal category is the ordinary administrative judicial appeal. The latter holds good also regarding permits under the Soil Excavation Act.

Regarding municipal appeal in general, the extensive right to appeal is traditionally considered important for safeguarding legality in municipal decision-making at large. Indirectly, this is crucial also in respect to the prevention of corruption, e.g., in municipal land and property policies, with indirect impacts also to the environment. The Cabinet 2015–2019 nevertheless initiated a preliminary deregulatory law drafting project in order to get rid of the whole municipal appeal category, generally and also regarding the land use plans, by adopting instead the prototype of ordinary administrative judicial appeal with a right of appeal only by those directly concerned. This project did not proceed to the stage of governmental bill, however.

1571. In the regime of administrative injunctions, a new trend of widening the standing, in this case in order to widen the right to initiate administrative enforcement procedures, had been initiated in 1993 by the then Waste Act. This was influenced by certain proposals then topical in the EC and Article 18 on requests by organizations in the 1993 Council of Europe *(Lugano)* Convention on environmental liability (a basically private law Convention signed by but not ratified by Finland). Section 59 of the previous Waste Act included a rule on the *locus standi* of registered environmental associations (and private injured parties), insofar as administrative injunctions are concerned. The section was applicable to situations where an act or omission has allegedly violated the provisions of the Waste Act. A similar provision was inserted in the then Air Pollution Prevention Act in 1995. Finally, in the general reform of 2000, the Environmental Protection Act came to include a general clause covering the whole regime of pollution and nuisance prevention (*see also* below).

Pursuant to section 186 of the Environmental Protection Act, the power to initiate administrative enforcement (injunction) procedures includes, in addition to private affected parties and several authorities, also registered associations and foundations whose purpose is to promote protection of environment, health or nature, or the amenities of living environs, and within the geographical area of which the relevant environmental impacts emerge. The present wording of section 134 of the current Waste Act is similar.

1572. The Nature Protection Act includes provisions on standing of a similar character. Registered local or regional associations the aim of which is to promote the protection of environment or nature, are entitled to initiate an administrative injunction procedure according to section 126 of the Act before the Centres for Economic Development, Transport and the Environment, if the request aims at preventing the destroying of nature or the impairment of values of nature, if not insignificant (section 128). The same right is given to (the here less probable) private injured parties, and to the municipality. As a later insert, the same powers also apply to proceedings on environmental liability for damage to nature under the Environmental Liability Directive (sections 127 and 128 of the Act), and similar standing provisions also cover the initiation of the corresponding proceedings regarding environmental liability (and traditional administrative injunctions) in the Environmental Protection Act, the Water Act and the Gene Technology Act.

1573. Pursuant to the Nature Protection Act, the associations referred to in section 126 of the Act (above) are, according to section 134(4) of the Act, also empowered to appeal against most of the various administrative decisions pursuant to the Act. This possibility does not extend to decisions on pecuniary compensations to proprietors, which is understandable. But the right does not apply to certain exceptional permits accorded by the Centres for Economic Development, Transport and the Environment, either, which is less consistent. If, e.g., a permit to deviate from the rules on the protection of natural habitats has been granted in contradiction with the relevant provisions, there is practically no mechanism for review. The restriction does not, however, apply to municipalities which in general have the same appellate standing, but the importance of this possibility probably remains small. As for the decisions by the Cabinet on national conservation plans or on the amendments of the scientific information in respect to the Natura 2000 network, also national level environmental associations and landowners' associations may appeal (in this case directly to the SAC).

1574. As a whole, the rules on standing in the then Nature Conservation Act were in 1996 the most generous of that time in regard to environmental associations. But rather soon, in the Land Use and Building Act of 1999, similar provisions were included. Regarding Land Use Plans and Municipal Building Bylaws (against both of which the organizations with domicile in the municipality in question already before had the right to appeal) *locus standi* was explicitly extended to any registered local or regional association in matters within the geographical area of its activities. As for Regional Plans, a similar right was also given national organizations insofar as alleged breach of National Land Use Goals were concerned (section 191 of the Land Use and Building Act, from 1 January 2025 onwards of the Land Use Act). Concerning an Exceptional Permit or, within a planning need area, a permit to build without a Detailed Plan, right to appeal has been given, among others, to such a registered association within its geographical area the purpose of which is natural or environmental protection or the preservation of cultural heritage or otherwise influencing the quality of the living environment (section 193 of the Land Use and Building Act). As of 1 January 2025, a similar provision is in the Building Act (section 180(7)).

1575. In the 2000 reform of pollution prevention law, a similar reform was made. Pursuant to the then Environmental Protection Act (section 181 of the present Environmental Protection Act) and the then Water Act (section 2 of Chapter 15 of the present Water Act), right of appeal covering all permit decisions has been assigned to any registered association and foundation whose purpose is to promote protection of environment, health or nature, or the amenities of living environs and within the geographical area of which the relevant environmental impacts emerge.
Quite similarly, the Highways Act (503/2005, section 105(5)) and the Railways Act (110/2007, section 92(3)) contain a provision where right of appeal is granted to registered local or regional associations and foundations (not necessarily environmental, etc.).

1576. Also in the few cases where there still are no explicit provisions on standing, the SAC has often heard the appeals of environmental organizations. For example, the Hunting Act long lacked such a provision, but the right of appeal had been granted to environmental associations in respect to the protection of wolf (SAC 2007:74) and the protection of 'outlaw birds' (SAC 2004:76). Here the provisions of the Birds Directive and the Natural Habitats Directive impacted, among other arguments, the consideration. Now there is an explicit provision on standing of associations in section 90 (159/2011) of the Hunting Act, regarding, however, merely exemptions pursuant to sections 41 and 41b by the Finnish Wildlife Agency.

1577. Most of the projects listed in Annex I to the *Århus Convention* (Convention on access to information, public participation in decision-making and access to justice in environmental matters; *see also* paragraphs 57 and 1376) require a prior permit against which appeals can be lodged as required by the provisions on access to court of the Convention (and later on, also in the EIA Directive). However, there were three exceptions in the national legislation. Construction of overhead electrical power lines with a voltage of 220 kilovolts or more and a length of more than fifteen kilometres, pipelines for the transport of gas, oil or chemicals with a diameter of more than 800 millimetres and a length of more than forty kilometres, and construction of lines for long-distance railway traffic required a permit, in this case an expropriation permit, only if compulsory purchase was necessary. And the provisions on right to appeal in the Expropriation Act did not meet the requirements of the Convention (or, correspondingly, the EIA Directive). For these reasons, a separate piece of legislation was enacted in order to safeguard the right of appeal to those concerned and to certain registered associations, as provided in Article 9 of the Convention.

1578. The said Act, the Act on the Expropriation Permit of Certain Projects with Impacts on the Environment (768/2004), in force as of 30 November 2004, originally concerned merely the three project groups above (section 1), and only when the implementation of the project is not in all respects based on a land use Plan with legal consequences pursuant to the Land Use and Building Act, in which the location of the project and its relation to other use of areas has been accounted. The main contents of the Act are made up by section 4, where it is provided that a prior Expropriation Permit pursuant to the Expropriation Act is needed irrespective of whether compulsory purchase is necessary for the project or not, and section 5, where the right of appeal has been granted such associations and foundations the task of which is protection of environment, health or nature or promotion of amenity of an inhabited area, provided that the project impacts their geographical area of activities.

The Act was amended as of 2008 (111/2007) by dropping off the construction of lines for long-distance railway traffic. This was due to the enacting of the Railways Act (110/2007) with a sufficient appeal mechanism, *see* Part II, Chapter 9, §2.

In 2017, as connected to the new Environmental Impacts Assessment Procedures Act, construction of all electrical power lines with a voltage of 110 kilovolts or more and transboundary pipelines for the transport of gas, provided that EIA was needed, were added to section 1. At the same time, section 4a was inserted providing the right to be heard also for others than those concerned pursuant to section 8 of the Expropriation Act. As of 1 February 2024, the Act has been complemented with a widened EIA-based scope of application and new substantive and procedural provisions, and the Act has been made applicable also in proper expropriation of corresponding projects (*see* paragraph 1376). The right of appeal here, in addition to the ordinary administrative procedure provisions, lies now with a registered association or foundation operating in the area where the project is located or where its effects extend, the purpose of which is to promote the environment, health or nature conservation or to promote the comfort of the living environment. In addition, the Saami Parliament and the Skolt village assembly have the same right on the grounds specified in the Act (in the same manner as presently common in various enactments).

1579. Group actions or class actions have traditionally not been available in the Finnish legal system. The topic has been discussed repeatedly, though, and finally the Group Actions Act (444/2007) was enacted. Nevertheless, it is applicable only on litigation between consumers and enterprises. The application on environmental damages was deliberately rejected after a long debate, although environmental damage proceedings were one of the intended targets during the preparation. As such, the idea might be worthy of consideration concerning compensation claims for environmental damages, but it is not without problems. For example, the intensity of forest damage caused by one operator would probably vary from area to area, i.e., from victim to victim, even in nearby forests. As for administrative enforcement procedure, many significant issues like prohibition of illegal activities, or permit issues, function largely irrespective of the number of appellants. Here a group action would probably not be of any benefit.

Selected Bibliography

Juridical literature is, in a way, a virtual source of law. This is also true for Environmental Law. The progress of legislative work in this field has, however, been so rapid that there have been evident vacuums. In some sectors (like Water Law) the basic literature is more or less obsolete, due to the subsequent reforms. The printed material is (for foreign readers unfortunately) largely written in Finnish and partly also in Swedish. The following books and articles on environmental law (and partly also on related legal areas) may be mentioned here:

Johanna Ahonen. *Yhdyskuntien jätevesien typenpoiston oikeudelliset perusteet ympäristöluvituksessa.* Joensuu 2016, 465 pages (The legal basis of nitrogen removal from urban wastewater in environmental permitting, English abstract).

Antti Belinskij. *Oikeus veteen: talousveden saatavuus Suomen ja Etelä-Afrikan oikeudessa.* Helsinki 2010, XXXVI, 386 pages (Right to water: Access to household water in Finnish and South African law).

Jan Darpö. *Nordic Environmental Permitting Processes. Results from a Comparative Study of Environmental Law and Processes in Denmark, Norway, Iceland, Sweden and Finland.* TemaNord 2023:522. Nordic Council of Ministers 2023. http://dx.doi.org/10.6027/temanord2023-522.

Jan Darpö, Kari Kuusiniemi & Pekka Vihervuori. 'Miljöprövningen i vågskålen: landskampen mellan Finland och Sverige'. *Förvaltningsrättslig tidskrift* 72 (2009): 3, 323–361. (Comparison between Swedish and Finnish environmental law with a focus on procedural aspects, in Swedish).

Ari Ekroos. *Kauneus ja rumuus ympäristöoikeudessa.* Helsinki 1995, XXX, 427 pages (A Monograph on Beauty and Ugliness in Environmental Law, with an English Summary).

Ari Ekroos & Vesa Majamaa. *Maankäyttö- ja rakennuslaki.* Helsinki 2018, XLI, 1158 pages. (A thorough commentary in Finnish on the Land Use and Building Act).

Auvo Haapanala, et al. *Maankäyttö- ja rakennuslaki.* Helsinki 2020, e-book (A Thorough Commentary in Finnish on the 1999 Land Use and Building Act).

Lea Halonen. *Metsäojitukset ja vesiensuojelusääntely.* Joensuu 2016. 77 pages + attached articles (A monograph on forest ditching and the functionality of water protection regulation, in Finnish).

Casper Herler. *Markföroreningsansvaret.* Helsinki 2008, L, 374 pages (A monograph on liabilities and responsibilities arising from soil pollution, in particular on retroactivity and reasonableness in respect to reinstatement, with a German summary, in Swedish).

Selected Bibliography

Mikael Hildén, et al. 'Evaluation of Environmental Policy Instruments – A Case Study of the Finnish Pulp & Paper and Chemical Industries'. *Monographs of the Boreal Environment Research* No. 21, 2002, 134 pages.

Erkki J. Hollo, *Introduction to Environmental Law*. Helsinki 2009, 570 pages.

Erkki J. Hollo, 'Le développement du droit de l'environnement en Finlande de 1999 a 2001'. *Revue européenne de droit de l'environnement* 1/2002, 49–73.

Erkki J. Hollo. *Maankäyttö- ja vesioikeus*. Helsinki 2006, XVI, 579 pages (A rather detailed overview on the Finnish legislation on land use, surveying, use of waters and mining).

Erkki J. Hollo. *Pilaamiskiellon sisältö vesilain mukaan*. Helsinki 1976, XL, 561 pages. (A monograph on water pollution law, in Finnish, with a German summary).

Erkki J. Hollo. *Vesioikeus*. 2nd edition. XXVII, 658 pages. Helsinki 2021 (A substantial overview on Finnish water law).

Erkki J. Hollo. *Ympäristönsuojelu- ja luonnonsuojeluoikeus*. Helsinki 2004, XXIII, 499 pages (An overview on Finnish legislation on environmental and nature protection, in Finnish).

Erkki J. Hollo, Tuomas Kuokkanen & Robert Utter. *Ilmasto-oikeus*. Helsinki 2011, 494 pages (A thorough overview on Finnish climate law).

Erkki J. Hollo, Pekka Vihervuori & Robert Utter. *Ympäristövahinkolaki*. Helsinki 2018, XV, 402 pages (Updated Commentary on the Environmental Damages Act, in Finnish).

Lauri Jääskeläinen, et al. *Maankäyttö- ja rakennuslaki selityksineen*. Helsinki 2018, 1053 pages (A thorough commentary in Finnish on the 1999 Land Use and Building Act).

Kai Kokko. *Biodiversiteettia turvaavat oikeudelliset periaatteet ja mekanismit*. Helsinki 2003, XXXII, 306 pages (A monograph on the legal principles and mechanisms safeguarding biodiversity, in Finnish, with an English summary).

Kai T. Kokko. *Ympäristöarviointi SOVA oikeudellisesta näkökulmasta*. Helsinki 2007, XIX, 188 pages (An analysis of strategic environmental assessment, in Finnish).

Tarja Koskela & Leila Suvantola (eds). *Ympäristörikokset*. Helsinki 2023 (A digital book on environmental crimes in Finnish law, in Finnish) ISBN 978-951-37-8656-4.

Anne Kumpula. 'Environmental Law'. In *An Introduction to Finnish Law*, edited by Juha Pöyhönen. Helsinki 2002, 499–555.

Anne Kumpula. *Ympäristö oikeutena*. Helsinki 2004, XXXI, 397 pages (Environment as a right, English abstract).

Kari Kuusiniemi. 'Environmental Law and Administrative Courts in Finland'. In *The Role of the Judiciary in the Implementation and Enforcement of Environmental Law*, ICEF – International Court of the Environment Foundation, Bruxelles 2008, 291–307.

Kari Kuusiniemi. 'Finland'. In *Access to Justice in Environmental Matters in the EU – Accés à la justice en matiére d'environnement dans l'UE*, edited by Jonas Ebbesson. The Hague 2002, 177–202.

Kari Kuusiniemi. 'The Principle of Proportionality and the Protection of Biological Diversity'. In *Afmælisrit til heidurs Gunnari G. Schram sjötugum 20. February 2001*, Reykjavik 2002, 287–304.

Kari Kuusiniemi. *Ympäristönsuojelu ja immissioajattelu*. Helsinki 1992, LXXII, 895 pages (A monograph on nuisance law and related pollution control systems, in Finnish, with a German summary).

Kari Kuusiniemi (ed.), Ari Ekroos, Anne Kumpula & Pekka Vihervuori. *Ympäristöoikeus*. Helsinki 2013, 1865 pages (An overview on Finnish environmental law. Also on the Internet).

Kari Kuusiniemi (ed.), Jukka Leinonen, Kari Marttinen, Jari Salila, Mika Seppälä & Eija Siitari-Vanne. *Ympäristönsuojelulainsäädäntö*. Helsinki 2017, 448 pages (A general presentation on the Environmental Protection Act), Also digital.

Niina Mäntylä. *Luonnon edustajien puhevalta*. Vaasa 2010, XVI, 363 pages (Acting on behalf of nature. English abstract).

Tapio Määttä. *Maanomistusoikeus*. Helsinki 1999, LI, 538 pages (A theoretically based monograph on land ownership and use of properties from the viewpoint of environmental law, in Finnish, with an English summary).

Hanna Nieminen-Finne. *Asiantuntija tuomarina. Tekniikan ja luonnontieteiden alan hallinto-oikeustuomarit ympäristönsuojeluasioissa.* Helsinki 2020, X, 288 pages (A monograph on expert judges of technical and natural sciences in environmental protection cases at the administrative court. English abstract).

Elina Nyholm. *Jälkivalvonta ympäristönsuojelulaissa: Tutkimus ympäristönsuojelulain jälkivalvontasäännösten soveltamisalojen rajautumisesta.* Turku 2015, XXXVIII+132 pages + attached articles (A monograph on ex post supervision under the Finnish Environmental Protection Act, in particular on the delineation of the ex post supervision provisions scopes of application under the Finnish Environmental Protection Act, in Finnish, with an English abstract).

Eero Henrik Nordberg. 'Biotechnology, Property Rights and the Environment: Towards a New Legal Order Especially Considering GMOs and the Finnish Agriculture'. In *Aspects of Finnish Contemporary Law*. Finnish national Reports to the XVIth Congress of the International Academy of Comparative Law in Brisbane, 2002, edited by Tore Modeen. Helsinki 2002, 59–90.

North European Environmental Law, Publications of the Finnish Society for Environmental Law 25 (1995), includes articles by several authors on Finnish environmental law in English.

Tiina Paloniitty & Sinikka Kangasmaa. 'Securing Scientific Understanding: Expert Judges in Finnish Environmental Administrative Judicial Review'. European Energy and Environmental Law Review 27(4) (2018): 125–139.

Sinikka Pärnänen. *Vesistöjen ennallistaminen uiton jälkeen.* Helsinki 2012, XXVI+293 pages (A monograph on the restoration of water bodies after finished timber floating, in Finnish).

Ismo Pölönen & Juha Perho. *YVA-oikeus: uudistunut ympäristövaikutusten arviointimenettely.* Helsinki 2018, X, 2003 pages (An overview on the renewed of Environmental Impact Assessment, in Finnish).

Juha Pöyhönen (ed.). *An Introduction to Finnish Law*. 2nd edn. Helsinki 2002, 582 pages (An introduction to the Finnish legal system, the then environmental law included, in English).

Selected Bibliography

Jouni Ranta. *Varautumisperiaate ympäristöoikeudessa*. Helsinki 2001, XXXIX, 261 pages (A monograph on the precautionary principle, in Finnish).

Jari Salila. *Metsäalueen oikeudellisesta asemasta*. Helsinki 2005, XXXVI, 306 pages (A monograph on the public law status of the owner of a forest area, largely consisting of legislative comparison between Finland, [Canadian] British Columbia, Sweden and [German] Bavaria, in Finnish, with a German summary).

Björn Sandvik. *Miljöskadeansvar. En skadeståndsrättslig studie med särskild hänsyn till ansvarsmotiv, miljöskadebegreppet och ersättning för skada på miljön*. Åbo 2002, 496 pages (A study in tort law with particular reference to motives for liability, the notion of environmental damage, and compensation for damage to the environment, in Swedish, with an English summary).

Jukka Similä & Leila Suvantola. *Luonnonsuojeluoikeus*. Helsinki 2011, 386 pages (Updated commentary on the Nature Conservation Act, in Finnish).

Jukka Similä. 'Pollution Regulation and Its Effects on Technological Innovations'. *Journal of Environmental Law* 14, No. 2 (2002): 143–160.

Jukka Similä. *Regulating Industrial Pollution. The Case of Finland*. Helsinki 2007, 222 pages (An empirical study on regulatory policies, in English). Available on the Internet.

Niko Soininen. *Vesioikeudellinen perusteluvelvollisuus. Tutkimus vesilain intressivertailuperustelujen oikeudellisista edellytyksistä*. Helsinki 2016, XXV, 335 pages (Transparencies in Legality: A Legal Analysis of the Reason-Giving Requirement in Water Management Permitting in Finland).

Pauli Ståhlberg. *Ydinvastuusta*. Helsinki 1993, XXXVII, 408 pages (A monograph on nuclear liability, in Finnish, with an English summary).

Markku Suksi. 'Finland. Developments in Zoning Law Against the Background of the Constitution'. *European Public Law* 8, No. 1 (2002): 1–15.

Suomalais-saksalais-ranskalainen vertailevan vesioikeuden kollokvio – Colloque fenno-franco-allemand sur le droit comparé de l'eau – Finnisch-Deutsch-Französisches Kolloquium zum Vergleich des Wasserrechts. Helsinki 31.5.–1.6.2001. Maa- ja metsätalousministeriö (Ministry of Agriculture and Forestry). Helsinki 2001, 161 pages.

Markku Suksi. 'Finland. The Constitution 2000'. *European Public Law* 5, No. 3 (1999): 338–349.

Leila Suvantola. *Huominen ei koskaan kuole. Luonnonsuojelulain ja ympäristönkäytön kilpailutilanteen ratkaisemisesta*. Helsinki 2006, XVI, 294 pages (A monograph on conflicts between nature conservation and proposed new land and resources use, with English summary).

Jukka Pekka Tolvanen. *Maankäytön luonnonsuojelullinen sääntely*. Helsinki 1998, LXII, 461 pages (A monograph on nature protection in land use contexts. In Finnish).

Jouko Tuomainen. *Vastuu pilaantuneen ympäristön puhdistamisesta*. Helsinki 2006, 260 pages (An analysis of responsibility for clean up of polluted soil, in Finnish).

Jouko Tuomainen. *Vastuu saastuneesta ympäristöstä*. Helsinki 2001, XXII, 513 pages (An overview on environmental liability in public law, private law and criminal law, in Finnish).

Robert Utter. 'A Short Introduction to Climate Law in Finland'. In *Ympäristöjuridiikka* 33 (2012): 1, 61–81.

Robert Utter. *Normativ miljökvalitet: Funktionen av en rättsligt institutionaliserad måttstock beträffande kvaliteten av miljön*. Helsinki 2007, 316 pages (A monographic study on normative environmental quality, in Swedish, with an English abstract). Available on the Internet.

Vertaileva vesioikeus. Publications of the Finnish Society for Environmental Law 35 (2003), includes surveys on the future implementation of the EC Water Framework Directive, in Finnish.

Pekka Vihervuori. 'Environmental Law in Finland, A. The Environmental Law System'. In *Environmental Law in Europe*, edited by N.S.J. Koeman. The Hague-London-Boston 1999, 177–194.

Pekka Vihervuori. 'Finland'. In *The Yearbook of European Environmental Law*, Vol. 1, edited by H. Somsen et al. New York 2000, 477–481.

Pekka Vihervuori. 'Finland'. In *The Yearbook of European Environmental Law*, Vol. 2, edited by H. Somsen et al. New York 2002, 469–480.

Pekka Vihervuori. 'Finland'. In *The Yearbook of European Environmental Law*, Vol. 3, edited by H. Somsen et al. New York 2004, 591–600.

Pekka Vihervuori. 'Finland'. In *The Yearbook of European Environmental Law*, Vol. 4, edited by H. Somsen et al. New York 2004, 563–570.

Pekka Vihervuori. 'Legal Aspects of Emission Control in Finland'. In *A World Survey on Environmental Law*. Rivista Giuridica dell'Ambiente 1986–1996, 141–157.

Pekka Vihervuori. *Maa-ainesten ottaminen ja suojelu*. Helsinki 1989, XLIV, 649 pages (A monograph on soil excavation and its environmental aspects, in Finnish).

Pekka Vihervuori. 'Miljörättsreformen 2000'. In *Tidskrift*, utgiven av Juridiska Föreningen i Finland 1–2/2000, 105–147 (A general review on the 2002 legislative reform, in Swedish).

Pekka Vihervuori. 'Private and Public Ownership of Water Areas – Structures and Implications of the Finnish Model'. In *Water Resource Management and the Law*, edited by Erkki J. Hollo, Cheltenham, UK, Northampton, MA, USA 2017, 98–117.

Pekka Vihervuori. *Viranomaisen asianosaispuhevallasta vesiasioissa*. Helsinki 1981, XL, 444 pages (A monograph on the *locus standi* of administrative authorities in the permit, etc. procedures at the Water Courts, in Finnish, with a German summary).

Pekka Vihervuori. 'Public Environmental Law in Finland'. In *Public Environmental Law in the European Union and the United States. A Comparative Analysis*, edited by René J.G.H. Seerden, Michiel A. Heldeweg & Kurt R. Deketelaere, The Hague/London New York 2002, 127–170.

Peter Wetterstein. 'The Finnish Environmental Damage Compensation Act – and some Comparisons with Norwegian and Swedish Law'. *Environmental Liability* (1995): 41–48.

Additionally, a few English-language publications, although mainly non-juridical, may be interesting from the viewpoint of environmental law.

Implementation of Agenda 21 in Finland, Finnish National Commission on Sustainable Development. Helsinki 1994.

Selected Bibliography

There is a legal periodical specialized in environmental law, the *Ympäristöjuridiikka-Miljöjuridik*, published since 1981 by the Finnish Society for Environmental Law (SYS). The topical articles are mainly in Finnish and, to a lesser degree, in Swedish or English.

The *Publications of the Finnish Society for Environmental Law* contain more comprehensive studies on environmental law. Here too the main language is Finnish, but English and/or German summaries are often included. In the recent years not many issues of this series have come out, however. Instead, the *Ympäristöpolitiikan ja -oikeuden vuosikirja* (Yearbook of environmental policy and law, by the University of Eastern Finland) includes many interesting studies on environmental law, mainly in Finnish.

Also the major general law periodicals, the *Lakimies* and the *Defensor Legis* (both mainly in Finnish), as well as the Tidskrift, utgiven av Juridiska Föreningen i Finland, *JFT* (mainly in Swedish) publish at times articles on environmental law. Such articles are also included in the anniversary books published in honour of distinguished legal scholars.

The publications (in the series *The Finnish Environment*, *Environmental Administration Guidelines*, *Environment Guides*, and *Reports*) of the Ministry of the Environment and the Finnish Environment Institute contain several surveys, studies and statistical publications with more or less direct relevance to environmental law.

Unofficial English translations of several of the most important enactments, though unevenly and more or less updated, are freely accessible on the governmental site FINLEX, www.finlex.fi/en/.

Index

The numbers here refer to paragraph numbers.

Index

Index

Index

www.ingramcontent.com/pod-product-compliance
Lightning Source LLC
LaVergne TN
LVHW011100300926
849160LV00008B/238